THE AMERICAN STATE
CONSTITUTIONAL TRADITION

John J. Dinan

The American State Constitutional Tradition

University Press of Kansas

Publication made possible, in part, by a grant from Wake Forest University.
Published by the University Press of Kansas (Lawrence, Kansas 66045),
which was organized by the Kansas Board of Regents and is operated and
funded by Emporia State University, Fort Hays State University, Kansas
State University, Pittsburg State University, the University of Kansas, and
Wichita State University

Library of Congress Cataloging-in-Publication Data

Dinan, John J.
    The American state constitutional tradition / John J. Dinan.
      p.   cm.
    Includes bibliographical references and index.
    ISBN 0-7006-1435-4 (cloth : alk. paper)
      1. Constitutional conventions—United States—States—History.
  2.Constitutional history—United States—States—History.   I. Title.
    KF4541.D56 2006
    342.7302′92—dc22   2005032375

British Library Cataloguing-in-Publication Data is available.

Printed in the United States of America

10 9 8 7 6 5 4 3 2 1

The paper used in this publication meets the minimum requirements of
the American National Standard for Permanence of Paper for Printed
Library Materials Z39.48-1984.

FOR MY TEACHERS

Contents

Acknowledgments

In the course of my research into the state constitutional tradition, I have received assistance from many individuals and institutions. I was fortunate to have access to extensive collections of state convention debates at the Duke University Law Library and University of Virginia Law Library; and the Wake Forest University Interlibrary Loan Department helped in securing additional sources. Financial support for the research and publication of this book came from Wake Forest in the form of a Reynolds Leave, a Zachary T. Smith professorship, and grants from the Archie Fund and the Publication and Research Fund, as well as from the Earhart Foundation in the form of a research grant. I am also grateful for permission to include in Chapter 2 a substantially revised version of "'The Earth Belongs Always to the Living Generation': The Development of State Constitutional Amendment and Revision Procedures," *Review of Politics* 62 (Fall 2000): 645–674, and for permission to include in Chapter 7 a substantially revised version of "The State Constitutional Tradition and the Formation of Virtuous Citizens," *Temple Law Review* 72 (Fall 1999): 619–672 (reproduced with the permission of Temple Law Review, Volume 72 © 1999, Temple University of the Commonwealth System of Higher Education). Finally, I thank my professors at the University of Virginia, especially Martha Derthick, James Ceaser, and Henry Abraham, for guiding my study of federalism, American political development, and constitutionalism and thereby preparing me to carry out this project.

Introduction

All polities must provide some means of deliberating about and revising their governing principles and institutions, but there are various ways in which this deliberation and revision can take place. The framers of the U.S. Constitution placed significant barriers in the way of constitutional revision and amendment, such that no additional conventions have been held and only twenty-seven amendments have been ratified. As a result, changes in governing principles and institutions at the national level have taken place primarily outside of formal processes, whether through presidential or congressional actions or through decisions of the U.S. Supreme Court, a body that has been described as a continuing constitutional convention. The situation is quite different in the American states, however, where amendment and revision procedures are generally more flexible, and where constitutional change has frequently proceeded through these formal processes. All told, the fifty states have held 233 constitutional conventions, adopted 146 constitutions, and ratified over 6,000 amendments to their current constitutions.

Although extensive studies have been conducted of the debates surrounding adoption of the federal constitution—*Madison's Notes of Debates in the Federal Convention, Elliot's Debates,* and *The Federalist* have attracted significant attention from political scientists and introductory American politics students alike— scholars have generally not taken the opportunity to analyze the debates that have taken place in state constitutional conventions, which have been held either to draft inaugural constitutions or to amend or revise existing constitutions.

The lack of a comprehensive study of these state convention debates can be attributed in part to the sheer amount of material to be examined, given that the debate records have been retained for a total of 114 state conventions. Thus, the studies that have been undertaken have generally focused on procedural aspects of state conventions, such as their powers and limits or the manner in which they are called and their work approved.[1] To the extent that scholars have examined the substance of state convention proceedings, they have generally focused on developments in specific conventions,[2] states,[3] or regions,[4] or during particular eras[5] or regarding particular issues.[6]

In addition, the predominant scholarly view is that state conventions have rarely debated the sorts of fundamental issues that preoccupied delegates to the federal convention, and moreover that these proceedings have not been characterized by the kind of deliberation that was seen in the federal convention. On this view, then, there is little to gain from studying state convention debates, because few issues of importance were taken up in these proceedings and because delegates have not engaged these issues in a theoretically sophisticated fashion.[7] This understanding of state conventions was perhaps best expressed by James Willard Hurst, who concluded that "on the whole there is little evidence that most state constitution makers deliberated their choice of government structure."[8] This view was recently expressed in particularly stark form by James Gardner, who argued, "Typically, state constitutions do not seem to have resulted from reasoned deliberation on issues of self-governance, or to express the fundamental values or unique character of distinct polities. Lacking these qualities, state constitutions, to put it bluntly, are not 'constitutions' as we understand the term."[9] As Morton Keller has concluded, although on occasion "state constitutional conventions have seen important confrontations on significant issues of governance and public policy[,] . . . what emerges far more clearly from the record is their inadequacy as innovative instruments of government." In his view,

> the length and detail of state constitutions, the structure of federalism, and most of all the realities of public life have made these gatherings arenas (and by no means ideally representative or responsible ones) for the clash of particular interests, and not devices whereby lasting principles and large socioeconomic developments can be enshrined in the commonwealths' basic laws. John Marshall's adjuration to his colleagues to remember that it was a *Constitution* that they were construing has little relevance to the history of state conventions.[10]

In light of this prevailing view of state constitutional development, it is not surprising, as Christian G. Fritz has observed, that "little attention has been devoted by constitutional historians to the evolving constitutional thought of delegates to state constitutional conventions as revealed in the debates of their proceedings."[11]

Moreover, to the extent that scholars have examined state convention debates as part of a recent resurgence of interest in state constitutionalism, these investigations have been conducted primarily by legal scholars with an eye toward assessing and influencing the work of state judges. At a time when the Burger and Rehnquist Courts generally proved less eager than the Warren Court to issue expansive interpretations of the U.S. Bill of Rights, lawyers, law professors, and even U.S. Supreme Court justices came to appreciate the way that state courts might make use of state bills of rights to provide increased protection for individual rights. Consequently, lawyers and law professors have become quite interested in mining the historical record for evidence of distinctive state understandings of various rights. For the most part, though, these studies have not been concerned with examining the wide range of issues other than individual rights or with considering the broader purposes that might be served by such analyses other than guiding state court decision making.[12]

My purpose in this book is to undertake a comprehensive analysis of the extant state convention debates and to study the extent to which state conventions have addressed fundamental questions of the kind that were treated in the federal convention; to explain how and why state convention delegates resolved these questions; and to consider the ways that scholars and constitution makers might benefit from studying these deliberations.

In fact, as I will argue, state conventions have been a forum for reconsidering, and ultimately revising or rejecting, a number of governing principles and institutions that were adopted by the federal convention of 1787 and that have remained relatively unchanged at the national level. In particular, whereas the drafters of the federal Constitution established a rigid amendment and revision process, state convention delegates have almost uniformly rejected this approach and adopted relatively flexible procedures for constitutional change. In addition, whereas federal convention delegates understood the principle of representation to confine citizens to an indirect role in governance, state constitution makers have adopted a number of mechanisms that allow citizens to participate directly in the lawmaking process. Moreover, the separation of powers system, which has not been amended at the national level, has been the subject of extensive discussions in state conventions. Although state constitution makers have not deviated from the tripartite division of powers, they have made several important changes to the executive and judicial veto powers. Similarly, although bicameralism has not been the subject of any serious scrutiny at the national level, state convention delegates have engaged in extensive debate about the wisdom and purpose of retaining a bicameral system; and the structure and composition of state bicameral legislatures have undergone important changes through the years as a result. With respect to individual rights, federal convention delegates generally adhered to a negative conception of liberty in that they placed a premium on protecting individuals from governmental action. By contrast, a number of state constitution makers have adopted a positive conception of liberty, insofar as they have recognized various rights that depend for their enforcement on governmental action. Finally, whereas delegates to the federal convention declined to provide for an explicit governmental role in the formation of citizen character, state constitution makers have frequently concluded that a polity should take active steps to form the character of the citizenry and that this commitment should be expressed through constitutional provisions.

Once we examine the state convention debates regarding each of these issues, it becomes possible to explain why state constitution makers have departed in various respects from the federal model. The adoption of distinctive principles and institutions in state constitutions is best understood not as the product of an immature understanding of constitutionalism, but rather as a result of the greater ease and frequency with which state constitution makers have been able to revisit issues of institutional design during the course of the American regime. At various times in American history, especially during the Jacksonian Era and the Progressive Era and in the aftermath of the Reapportionment Revolution, state constitution makers have identified deficiencies in the operation of certain institutional structures and have responded by devising alternative institutional mechanisms. State convention delegates during each of these periods were fully aware of the reasons why federal convention delegates had chosen to design national institutions in a particular fashion. However, state delegates ultimately decided to reject the federal approach, primarily because they benefited from institutional knowledge and experience that was unavailable to the eighteenth-century federal founders, and occasionally because of a desire to supplement aspects of the federal constitution that were seen as incomplete, or in order to take account of the different circumstances in which state constitution makers found themselves.

The principal benefit of examining these state convention debates is that they provide a better expression of the American constitutional tradition than is yielded by a study of the origin and development of the federal constitution alone. In several instances, differences in the state and federal constitutional traditions are attributable to the incomplete nature of the federal constitution or to the different circumstances in which state constitution makers found themselves. State convention debates on these issues therefore serve to complement the federal convention debates, and the state convention arguments in favor of these distinctive state institutions are at least entitled to be placed alongside the arguments in *Madison's Notes*, *Elliot's Debates*, and *The Federalist*. In most instances, though, differences in the state and federal constitutional traditions are best viewed as a product of the greater flexibility of state amendment processes. Parallel reform proposals in these areas have been introduced at both the state and federal levels throughout American history, only to be repeatedly stymied at the federal level by the rigidity of the federal amendment process. In these cases, state convention debates throughout the course of the American regime deserve to be treated as a better representation of the accumulated wisdom and experience of the American constitutional tradition than is found in the standard eighteenth-century federal sources.

To summarize my principal conclusions, therefore, I show that a number of federal governing principles and institutions have been revised or rejected in the course of state conventions; I demonstrate that state constitution makers' departures from the federal model are primarily attributable to the flexibility of state amendment processes and the resulting opportunities to benefit from institutional knowledge and experience throughout American history; and I argue that the state convention debates are in many ways a better expression of the considered judgment of the American constitutional tradition than can be found in the eighteenth-century federal sources.

These conclusions should be of interest not only to scholars of American political development who seek a better understanding of the logic underlying the distinctive state constitutional tradition, but also to constitution makers in other countries who want to draw lessons from the American constitutional tradition. A complete evaluation of these distinctive state institutions would, of course, require an analysis of their consequences, as well as a comparison of the operation of the respective state and federal institutions. Nevertheless, an analysis of the reasons why state constitution makers adopted these distinctive institutions can be valuable insofar as it can contribute to an ultimate judgment on their merits. At the least, individuals who are struggling with various questions of institutional design in drafting constitutions for emerging democracies would benefit from taking account of the arguments advanced by delegates who encountered these same issues in state conventions throughout the course of the American regime.[13]

There are, to be sure, other aspects of the state constitutional tradition that are not addressed in this study but that may be of interest to students of American constitutionalism. Questions concerning the extent of the franchise, particularly regarding restrictions based on property, race, and sex, were debated at great length in state conventions, and these convention debates have been the subject of several comprehensive books and articles.[14] Meanwhile, other scholarly studies have drawn on state convention debates in tracing the development of various civil rights and liberties, such as guarantees of equal protection, due process, free speech, religious exercise, and a fair trial.[15] Still other studies have made use of state convention debates in examining the relationship between state and local governments, particularly in regard to municipal home rule.[16] Scholars who are intrigued by these aspects of the state constitutional tradition will benefit from the careful studies that have been conducted in these various areas.

Other scholars may be interested in explaining differences in the ways that convention delegates in various states and regions addressed the topics examined in this study. In certain respects, states have been nearly universal in their rejection of the federal model, such as in regard to devising more flexible amendment and revision procedures. In other respects, though, states have differed in the degree to which they have rejected the federal model. Thus, in these areas, scholars may want to go further in explaining, for instance, why certain states have surpassed others in departing from the federal model of indirect representation, or adopting restrictions on the exercise of judicial review, or providing for social, economic, and environmental rights.[17]

Still other scholars may be interested in explaining differences in the ways that groups of delegates within particular state conventions addressed the topics examined in this study. In much the same way as delegates to the federal convention of 1787 disagreed about and engaged in spirited debates concerning various institutions that eventually became part of the U.S. Constitution, state convention delegates have engaged in equally spirited debates about various aspects of state constitutional design that were heavily contested in particular conventions but were generally resolved in a uniform fashion around the country. Just as scholars have examined the voting records of delegates to the federal convention in order to identify and explain patterns of support for particular aspects of the federal constitutional design, students of the state constitutional tradition may benefit from conducting similar studies of the voting behavior of delegates to the various state conventions throughout American history.[18]

It has not been my intent here to pursue each of these additional questions, whether in regard to examining other aspects of the state constitutional tradition or investigating particular differences within the state constitutional tradition. My principal purpose has been to identify, explain, and draw lessons from the ways in which the dominant trends of state constitutional development have departed from the federal constitutional model. To the extent, however, that this study calls attention to the general benefits of examining state constitutional convention debates and stimulates additional investigations along these and other avenues, it will have succeeded in one of its additional purposes.

STATE CONSTITUTIONAL CONVENTIONS

State constitutional change has taken place in a variety of ways, including through legislative amendments, popular initiatives, and revision commissions, and during the twentieth century, each of these mechanisms assumed increasing prominence. For much of American history, though, the constitutional convention was the primary forum for debating and revising state foundational documents. To set the stage for an analysis of the debates in these conventions in Chapters 2 through 7, it will be helpful to discuss the common features of these conventions, and at the same time take note of important differences, in regard to their number and frequency, their manner of proceeding, and the recording of their debates.[1]

Number and Frequency

A total of 233 conventions have been held between 1776 and 2005, but these conventions have not been distributed equally throughout this 229-year period

Table 1-1. State Constitutional Conventions

Alabama (6)—1819, 1861, 1865, 1867, 1875, 1901
Alaska (1)—1955–1956
Arizona (1)—1910
Arkansas (8)—1836, 1861, 1864, 1868, 1874, 1917–1918, 1969–1970, 1978–1980
California (2)—1849, 1878–1879
Colorado (1)—1875–1876
Connecticut (3)—1818, 1902, 1965
Delaware (5)—1776, 1792, 1831, 1852–1853, 1896–1897
Florida (5)—1838–1839, 1861–1862, 1865, 1868, 1885
Georgia (12)—1776–1777, 1788, 1789 (2), 1795, 1798, 1833, 1839, 1861, 1865, 1867–
    1868, 1877
Hawaii (3)—1950, 1968, 1978
Idaho (1)—1889
Illinois (6)—1818, 1847, 1862, 1869–1870, 1920–1922, 1969–1970
Indiana (2)—1816, 1850–1851
Iowa (3)—1844, 1846, 1857
Kansas (4)—1855, 1857, 1858, 1859
Kentucky (4)—1792, 1794, 1849–1850, 1890–1891
Louisiana (12)—1812, 1845, 1852, 1861, 1864, 1867–1868, 1879, 1898, 1913, 1921,
    1973–1974, 1992
Maine (1)—1819
Maryland (5)—1776, 1850–1851, 1864, 1867, 1967–1968
Massachusetts (4)—1779–1780, 1820–1821, 1853, 1917–1919
Michigan (5)—1835, 1850, 1867, 1907–1908, 1961–1962
Minnesota (1)—1857
Mississippi (7)—1817, 1832, 1851, 1861, 1865, 1868, 1890
Missouri (7)—1820, 1845–1846, 1861–1863, 1865, 1875, 1922–1923, 1943–1944
Montana (4)—1866, 1884, 1889, 1971–1972
Nebraska (3)—1871, 1875, 1919–1920
Nevada (2)—1863, 1864
New Hampshire (17)—1776, 1778–1779, 1781–1783, 1791–1792, 1850–1851, 1876, 1889,
    1902, 1912, 1918–1923, 1930, 1938–1941, 1948, 1956–1959, 1964, 1974, 1984
New Jersey (3)—1844, 1947, 1966
New Mexico (8)—1848, 1849, 1850, 1872, 1889–1890, 1907, 1910, 1969
New York (9)—1776–1777, 1801, 1821, 1846, 1867–1868, 1894, 1915, 1938, 1967
North Carolina (6)—1776, 1835, 1861–1862, 1865–1866, 1868, 1875
North Dakota (2)—1889, 1971–1972
Ohio (4)—1802, 1850–1851, 1873–1874, 1912
Oklahoma (1)—1906–1907
Oregon (1)—1857
Pennsylvania (5)—1776, 1789–1790, 1837–1838, 1872–1873, 1967–1968
Rhode Island (8)—1842, 1944, 1951, 1955, 1958, 1964–1969, 1973, 1986
South Carolina (5)—1790, 1861, 1865, 1868, 1895
South Dakota (3)—1883, 1885, 1889
Tennessee (8)—1796, 1834, 1870, 1953, 1959, 1965, 1971, 1977

Table 1-1. (continued)

Texas (7)—1836, 1845, 1861, 1866, 1868–1869, 1875, 1974
Utah (1)—1895
Vermont (11)—1777, 1786, 1793, 1814, 1822, 1828, 1836, 1843, 1850, 1857, 1870
Virginia (9)—1776, 1829–1830, 1850–1851, 1861, 1864, 1867–1868, 1901–1902, 1945, 1956
Washington (2)—1878, 1889
West Virginia (2)—1861–1863, 1872
Wisconsin (2)—1846, 1847–1848
Wyoming (1)—1889

Source: Updated from Albert L. Sturm, "The Development of American State Constitutions," *Publius* 12 (Winter 1982): 82. By permission of Oxford University Press.

or among the fifty states (Table 1-1). An initial round of state conventions was held in the late eighteenth century to draft and revise the first batch of state constitutions.[2] Inaugural constitutions were drafted in all of the original thirteen states except Connecticut and Rhode Island, whether by legislators acting as constitution makers or by delegates selected primarily for this purpose. As the century drew to a close and several more states joined the union, additional conventions were held for the purpose of framing inaugural constitutions, and several states also held conventions in order to refine, or occasionally make dramatic changes in, their initial documents.

Although the first few decades of the nineteenth century were somewhat quieter on the constitution-making front, the Jacksonian Era brought another round of conventions as new states drafted inaugural constitutions and as other states heavily revised their original documents.[3] These revision conventions were frequently called in reaction to particular events, such as when many states responded to increasing levels of public debt in the late 1830s and early 1840s by adopting limits on state participation in internal improvements. In part, these conventions were also called in reaction to developments in the realm of political thought, especially the growing movement for a democratization of state governing institutions.

The Civil War was responsible for another burst of state convention activity, and more conventions were held during the 1860s than in any other decade in American history.[4] All but one of the southern states held conventions in order to secede from the union, as well as for the secondary purpose of making changes to their constitutions in order to join the Confederacy. Most of these states also held conventions near the end of the war to organize provisional governments and, again, for the additional purpose of making appropriate constitutional changes. These states then held still other conventions to make constitutional changes in preparation for rejoining the union, particularly by securing the rights of freedmen and recognizing federal supremacy.

The Progressive Era provided the next occasion for widespread state constitution making.[5] Several western states held conventions in the late nineteenth and early twentieth centuries in order to draft inaugural constitutions. Conventions were also called in many southern states for the purpose of eliminating provisions that had been adopted by Reconstruction Era conventions populated in part by African Americans and nonsoutherners. Other states held conventions in order to make general revisions to their existing documents and, in particular, to permit the people to play a more direct role in governance and to regulate railroads and other corporate interests.

After several decades in the mid-twentieth century when few conventions were called, the 1960s marked the start of another period of intense state constitutional activity.[6] The key event, which eliminated the reason why many state legislatures had for so long declined to call conventions, was the U.S. Supreme Court's 1962 ruling in *Baker v. Carr* declaring that legislative malapportionment claims were no longer nonjusticiable and thereby ushering in the Reapportionment Revolution. For several decades before the Court's decision, rural legislators had sought to continue to reap the benefits of inequitable legislative apportionment plans and therefore had prevented the calling of conventions that they feared would produce more equitable apportionment plans. Once the Court made it clear that legislative malapportionment would no longer be tolerated, rural legislators were no longer able to prevent the calling of conventions, and many long-standing constitutional reform proposals were finally taken up.

The final decades of the twentieth century and first few years of the twenty-first century have seen no shortage of state constitutional activity, but constitutional changes during this period have generally taken place in forums other than conventions.[7] Legislative amendments and constitutional initiatives have been frequent vehicles for constitutional change during this period. However, legislators have been hesitant to call conventions, and the people have routinely voted down convention questions that have appeared on the ballot. Moreover, a number of the conventions that were held in the latter part of the twentieth century were limited in the topics that they were permitted to address.[8]

Not only have there been differences in the number of conventions held during various periods of American history, but there have been significant differences in the number of conventions called by particular states. On one hand, ten states have held a single convention.[9] At the other end of the spectrum, four states have held ten or more conventions—New Hampshire (17), Georgia (12), Louisiana (12), and Vermont (11)—and another eighteen states have held between five and nine conventions: New York (9), Virginia (9), Arkansas (8), New Mexico (8), Rhode Island (8), Tennessee (8), Mississippi (7), Missouri (7), Texas (7), Alabama (6), Illinois (6), North Carolina (6), Delaware (5), Florida (5), Maryland (5), Michigan (5), Pennsylvania (5), and South Carolina (5).

These differences in the frequency of conventions, and particularly the large number of conventions in certain states, are partly due to the significant amount of constitutional activity in the original thirteen states during the Revolutionary Era and in the southern states before, during, and after the Civil War. Thus, the list of twenty-two states that have held five or more conventions includes ten of the original thirteen states, as well as all eleven states that made up the Confederacy.

The large number of conventions in several states can also be attributed to distinctive amendment and revision mechanisms. For instance, fourteen states currently require the question of whether to call a convention to be submitted to the people at regular intervals. It is no surprise that seven of these states appear on the list of frequent-convention states: Illinois, Maryland, Missouri, and New York (all of which provide that voters shall pass judgment on a convention question every twenty years), Michigan (every sixteen years), Rhode Island (every ten years), and New Hampshire (which submitted such a question every seven years up to 1964 and every ten years after that). Another frequent-convention state, Vermont, provided before 1870 for an unusual mode of constitutional revision whereby a council of censors assembled every seven years and was empowered to call a convention to consider amendments.[10]

In several states, the large number of conventions is also a product of the relative difficulty of achieving constitutional change through the legislative amendment process. Thus, in some states, it has been practically impossible for legislative-initiated amendments to be ratified because they must receive a majority of all votes cast in the entire election rather than on the particular question. The only realistic opportunity to secure constitutional change in these states—Tennessee is a leading example—has been through constitutional conventions, and in fact five limited conventions were called in Tennessee in the second half of the twentieth century alone in order to enact constitutional changes.[11] Moreover, in some states it has sometimes been literally impossible to enact legislative amendments, as in New Hampshire, which did not permit such amendments before 1964. As a result, conventions were called at regular intervals in New Hampshire throughout the nineteenth and twentieth centuries, and New Hampshire clearly outpaces all other states in the number of conventions.[12]

It is also important to take account of the distinctive political culture of various states. Louisiana, which is different from other states in many respects, is no less distinct in its approach to constitution making. In large part because of the civil law system it inherited from France, Louisiana has drafted constitutions that are much longer and more malleable than most other states.[13] In fact, commentators have noted that constitutional revision in Louisiana "has been sufficiently continuous to justify including it with Mardi Gras, football, and corruption as one of the premier components of state culture."[14] It is no surprise that Louisiana is tied for second in the number of conventions.

Organization and Proceeding

The 233 state conventions have much in common in the way their delegates have been selected, their business conducted, and their work submitted. At the same time, important decisions have been made in regard to each of these matters, and particular conventions have resolved these issues in different ways.

Most conventions have been composed of delegates chosen in elections held for the express purpose of selecting convention participants, but this has not been a universal practice. In some cases, conventions have been made up solely of legislators. Thus several eighteenth-century constitutions were drafted by legislatures that resolved into conventions for the purpose of making constitutions. This also happened on a pair of occasions in the twentieth century, when the Texas Convention of 1974 and Louisiana Convention of 1992 were both made up of legislators, with Texas voters approving such an arrangement in a preceding convention call[15] and Louisiana legislators making such a decision on their own.[16] As for the conventions that have been made up of elected delegates, these elections have in some cases been organized on a nonpartisan basis but have in other cases been partisan affairs. In fact, in one extraordinary case, delegates to the Minnesota Convention of 1857 were so riven by partisan divisions that they assembled in separate Republican and Democratic conventions, each with its own record of proceedings and with their disputes ultimately resolved by a conference committee.[17]

Most conventions were populated by delegates who had served or were currently serving in federal, state, or local offices. The Massachusetts Convention
of 1820–1821, New York Convention of 1821, and Virginia Convention of 1829–
1830 were particularly notable in this regard: each included a number of distinguished public officials. In attendance at the Massachusetts Convention of
1820–1821 were John Adams, Lemuel Shaw, Joseph Story, and Daniel Webster.
Meanwhile, James Kent and Martin Van Buren played lead roles at the New York
Convention of 1821. The Virginia Convention of 1829–1830 counted among its
delegates James Madison, John Marshall, James Monroe, John Randolph, and
John Tyler, among others, and was described by the reporters of the convention
debates as "an assembly of men . . . which has scarcely ever been surpassed in
the United States."[18]

Although these 1820s conventions were composed of particularly distinguished assemblages, subsequent conventions also included a number of individuals of note, whether from the political world or other pursuits. For instance,
Morrison Waite was in the midst of serving as president of the Ohio Convention
of 1873–1874 when word came down that he had been nominated to serve as
chief justice of the United States, at which time he resigned his post.[19] Other
convention participants whose names would be familiar to students of American politics or arts and letters include Melville W. Fuller, delegate to the Illinois Convention of 1862; Richard M. Daley, delegate to the Illinois Convention
of 1969–1970; Charles Sumner, delegate to the Massachusetts Convention of
1853; Brooks Adams, delegate to the Massachusetts Convention of 1917–1919;
George Romney, vice president of the Michigan Convention of 1961–1962; Joseph Pulitzer, delegate to the Missouri Convention of 1875; Franklin Pierce,
president of the New Hampshire Convention of 1850–1851; Samuel Tilden,
delegate to the New York Convention of 1846; Horace Greeley, delegate to the
New York Convention of 1867–1868; Francis Lieber, delegate to the New York
Convention of 1867–1868; Elihu Root, delegate to the New York Convention
of 1894 and president of the New York Convention of 1915; Henry L. Stimson,
delegate to the New York Convention of 1915; Robert F. Wagner and Alfred E.
Smith, both delegates to the New York Conventions of 1915 and 1938; Robert
Moses, delegate to the New York Convention of 1938; Thaddeus Stevens, delegate to the Pennsylvania Convention of 1837–1838; James Michener, secretary
to the Pennsylvania Convention of 1967–1968; and Carter Glass, delegate to the
Virginia Convention of 1901–1902. As is clear from this list, it was not unusual
for individuals to serve in several conventions. Robert McClelland, for instance,

served in three Michigan conventions (1835, 1850, and 1867), and Daniel Chipman served in five Vermont conventions (1793, 1814, 1836, 1843, and 1850). In fact, it was not unheard of for individuals to serve in conventions in more than one state, as in the case of Benjamin Platt Carpenter, a delegate to the New York Convention of 1867–1868 and the Montana Convention of 1889.[20]

Once delegates were seated at these conventions, they then faced the question of how to proceed, which raised the particular questions of what should serve as the basis for their work and what lessons to draw from other states' experiences. These questions were especially important for states drafting inaugural constitutions, because delegates had to decide whether to take the federal constitution as a model, to rely on one or more existing state constitutions, or to start from scratch. States holding revision conventions also encountered these questions when deciding whether to purchase for the delegates one of the many available compilations of state constitutions, and also whether to invite officials and scholars from other states to share their insights.

Delegates were occasionally inclined to view the federal constitution as an appropriate model, and to suggest that their convention proceed by taking up each article of the federal constitution and making modifications as necessary for their state's circumstances. Thus when this issue surfaced in the California Convention of 1849, L. W. Hastings argued that convention delegates

> were not without a guide; there was one book to which they had access, containing the Constitution adopted by the wisdom of the age in which the framers lived—sanctioned by long experience—pronounced superior to any ever adopted in the known world. If the lawyer appears at the bar to argue his cause, he knows well where to find the best book extant on human rights and human government—the Constitution of the United States. . . . The best plan would be to take up that great instrument as a guide, and proceed to form a Constitution for the State of California.[21]

Although nearly every post-1787 state convention drew to some extent on the federal constitution, delegates were far more likely to contend that the best model—to the extent they were seeking a particular model—was the constitution of another state. Several states borrowed liberally from the constitution of one particular state, especially when a neighboring state shared a similar political culture or when a particular state constitution was seen as particularly well crafted, such as the Virginia Constitution (in the eyes of many southern constitution makers) and the New York Constitution (in the view of many northern constitution makers). Over time, new state constitutions also came to serve as models for succeeding generations of constitution makers. Thus, delegates to the Nevada Convention of 1864 urged, with mixed success, that attention be given to the California Constitution. As Charles DeLong argued,

> Now in following the line of the California Constitution, we are only follow-ing in that of the Constitution of a still greater State; a Constitution which received the indorsement of many wise men. I speak of the Constitution of the State of New York; a State which has given her Constitution to very many of the western States of this Union. The Constitution of California was derived from that of New York, and from California it comes to us, and then we have a Constitution which all may understand and upon which there need be no disagreement.[22]

Still other delegates, relatively few in number, disdained any reliance on other state constitutions on the grounds that constitutions could not be easily transplanted from one polity to another and therefore it made little sense to draw heavily on other states' experiences. This position, which attracted some support in various conventions but was generally rejected as being excessively parochial, was best articulated by Robert Crouse in the Michigan Convention of 1850. He argued,

> It is of little importance to us what constitutions the States of Kentucky or Mississippi, or California may have; they may be adapted to their wants, or the habits and character of their people, but would probably be unsuitable to the habits and character of our people. We are not sent here to telegraph from one end of the Union to the other, from Maine to California, for constitutions upon which to model our own, but to make those few amendments to our excellent constitution which the people require.[23]

For the most part, convention delegates chose not to take the federal con-stitution as a model, or to rely solely on a particular state constitution, or to entirely reject the lessons of other state constitutions, but rather to draw on a variety of other state constitutions and experiences as appropriate.[24] To this end, a number of conventions chose to obtain and make use of the many compila-tions of state constitutions that were in circulation.[25] In some cases, delegates purchased copies of these compilations on their own initiative in preparation for the convention proceedings. In other cases, conventions purchased copies and then either made them available for the use of delegates on the convention floor or distributed a copy to every delegate.[26] As Anson Pease argued in the Ohio Convention of 1873–1874, when the question was raised as to whether the convention could afford to purchase copies of one such compilation, *Hough's Constitutions:*

> I regret, of course, that it cannot be obtained for less money. But it consists of two large volumes; it contains a large amount of matter, and it is arranged in such manner that you can refer to any special subject in any of the Constitutions of the States without examining the whole constitution of each State. Therefore, in connection with any proposition that may come before us, by reference to this work you can readily see what other states have done in regard to it. It seems to me such a work as this must be valuable to us. I do not believe we have the experience among ourselves that will justify our shutting out the light that can be obtained by reference to what has been done in other States, or that if we do we will succeed in making a Constitution that will be acceptable to our people. I believe this is an age of progress, and I believe it will be to our advantage to look at the steps which have been taken by other States, to see the advances they have made, and to see if we can profit by them.[27]

A number of conventions also drew on other states' experiences by inviting public officials and scholars to offer advice on general or specific points of constitution making. In several cases, conventions extended invitations to national officials, with the expectation that they would discuss federal-state relations in a way that would be of interest to the delegates. The most notable of these convention appearances was a speech delivered by former president and current presidential candidate Theodore Roosevelt to the Ohio Convention of 1912, where he expressed his support for the recall of judicial decisions, among other Progressive reforms.[28] Three-time presidential candidate William Jennings Bryan was a particularly frequent convention speaker who made a case for the democratization of state institutions at a number of Progressive Era conventions.[29] Meanwhile, former presidents Herbert Hoover, Harry Truman, and Dwight Eisenhower were all invited to speak to the Michigan Convention of 1961–1962, and although Hoover and Truman declined, Eisenhower accepted and expressed his hope that state constitution makers would assume responsibility for a number of governing functions and thereby ensure that power would remain in the states rather than in the federal government.[30] Chief Justice Earl Warren chose a similar theme for his address to the New York Convention of 1967, wherein he urged delegates to modernize state governmental institutions as one way of stemming the flow of power from the states to the federal government.[31]

State officials from around the country were particularly frequent convention speakers, and they were often invited to assess the operation of institutional devices that had been adopted in their states. Thus Thomas Cooley, former Michigan supreme court justice and author of the leading state constitutional treatise, gave the benefit of his expertise to delegates at the North Dakota Convention of 1889.[32] Meanwhile, officials from Oregon and California were in particular demand when delegates debated adoption of the initiative and referendum process throughout the twentieth century, given that these states were seen as having the most experience with these institutions.[33] In similar fashion, because Nebraska was the only state to have adopted unicameralism in the twentieth century, officials from that state were much sought after by the many conventions that considered eliminating one of their legislative houses in the aftermath of the U.S. Supreme Court's reapportionment rulings.[34]

State constitutional scholars were also invited to speak at a number of conventions, particularly during the twentieth century. For instance, the Illinois Convention of 1920–1922 heard from Ernst Freund on the advantages of municipal home rule and from Charles Merriam on the benefits of the initiative and referendum.[35] The Alaska Convention of 1955–1956 requested the assistance of Vincent Ostrom, Weldon Cooper, and Ernest Bartley on various issues.[36] Meanwhile, the Rhode Island Convention of 1964–1969 invited Frank Grad to offer general advice on constitution making,[37] and the Tennessee Convention of 1965 invited Avery Leiserson to discuss the benefits of unicameralism.[38]

These state constitutional compilations and invited speakers were all means to an end of amending or revising constitutions, and each convention had to face an additional question of whether and how to submit its work to the people. Although it is now understood that conventions should submit constitutional changes for popular ratification before they can take effect, this was not always the case. A number of late eighteenth- and early nineteenth-century conventions did not submit their work to the people because this had not yet become a universally accepted practice. It is not that popular ratification was unheard of during this period; in fact, the Massachusetts Convention of 1779–1780 was the first convention whose work was approved by the people. However, popular ratification was not understood to be necessary to legitimate the work of a convention. Even after this understanding had taken hold by the mid-nineteenth century, several conventions still opted against submitting their work to the people, whether because delegates were not persuaded that popular ratification was essential to ensuring the legitimacy of their work, or because delegates were only making minor revisions, or as a result of uncertainty about whether voters would approve of their work. This was particularly the case with several southern and border-state conventions in the late nineteenth and early twentieth centuries.[39]

Conventions that chose to submit their work for ratification then faced an additional question of how to do so. Several conventions opted to submit their proposed changes as a series of amendments, whether because delegates were limited in the topics they were permitted to address,[40] or because they simply chose to submit their work in piecemeal fashion rather than as a wholesale revision.[41] Other conventions chose to make a wholesale revision and to submit a new constitution in its entirety, subject to an up-or-down vote by the people. Still other conventions undertook a wholesale revision but then submitted several of the more controversial changes separately from the general constitutional revision.[42]

Finally, there was the question of whether the work of the conventions would actually be approved by the people. Although the work of conventions has been approved more often than not, a number of conventions have seen large portions of their work rejected at the polls. In fact, it was not uncommon for new states to hold several conventions before the people finally approved of an initial constitution, particularly during the nineteenth century.[43] Popular rejection also greeted the work of a number of revision conventions in both the nineteenth and twentieth centuries.[44]

Recording the Debates

An additional question faced by these state conventions was whether and how to report their debates, which, it should be noted, was distinct from the question of whether to publish a journal of the proceedings, a nearly universal practice. Once again, this question was answered in various ways, with slightly under half of the conventions ultimately making some provision for reporting the debates. Even among the conventions whose debates have been retained, however, delegates varied in how they provided for the reporting and publication of the debates.

Delegates who opposed reporting the debates advanced a number of arguments against the practice, but their primary concern was that the expense of hiring a stenographer and publishing the proceedings would be prohibitive. Augustus Landis asked in the Pennsylvania Convention of 1872–1873, "Is it necessary that we should perpetuate, at so great a cost, all that is said upon this floor, all that is here read, all that is here done, all that men here choose to give utterance to in the proceedings of this Convention? I submit, sir, it is not equal to the cost."[45] The answer to this question might well be different, several of these delegates argued, if there were unlimited funds available or if there were no other worthy purposes to which existing funds could be applied; but, they felt, such was not the case. Thus Charles Underhill pleaded with delegates to the Massachusetts Convention of 1917–1919 not to squander valuable resources on reporting the debates. He explained,

> I hold the position in my city of president of one of the great charitable organizations of that city of 100,000 people, and sir, the things that I have seen during this last hard, cold winter make me appreciate, if nothing else would, the value of a dollar. I ask you of what value to the unborn generations this volume or these several volumes of the proceedings of this Convention will be if, when born, the mothers hold to their dying or drying breasts the mouths of the babes they are unable to satisfy.[46]

These delegates argued, moreover, that previous volumes of convention debates contained little of value; the failure to produce another such volume would thus hardly be regretted. Thomas Laine therefore argued in the California Convention of 1878–1879, "Now, it has been my fortune to wade through a number of constitutional debates, and I have found them, in the main, trashy and worthless. . . . In my judgment, there is not one man, woman, or child out of every ten thousand that would ever read it."[47] In fact, several delegates noted, only partly in jest, that a decision against publishing the debates might actually be welcomed. Thus, when the question of reporting the debates arose in the Ohio Convention of 1873–1874, Seneca Griswold drew on his experience with the reported debates of that state's most recent convention:

> Now, as to the use of this report to be read; you will find this book, and all such books in the old book stores, and they cannot be sold for enough to pay for storage. I have been told that there are but two men in the whole of the State of Ohio who have read this book. One was the proof-reader, and he died shortly afterwards; the other was our worthy friend from Franklin; but he being sick at the time, it acted upon him somewhat according to the principles of the ho-

meopaths *similia similibus curantur,* or upon the principle that the hair of the dog will cure its bite; and he got well [Laughter]. He was thus saved from the fate of the proof-reader, and his valuable services preserved to the State.[48]

In the view of delegates such as Messrs. Laine and Griswold, citizens were interested in the constitution that ultimately emerged from the convention proceedings, and to some extent in the convention journal that would indicate how their representatives voted on particular questions; but they had no desire to trace every twist and turn of the arguments on the convention floor. As Stanley Bowdle argued in the Ohio Convention of 1912,

> I am interested in the standing timber of the state of Ohio. I never pass a tree without feeling ashamed to reflect that at any moment that tree may be cut down so that some articles of literature may be printed. And we are requested here to mow down a quarter section of good timber for the purpose of saying what we have to say as a necessary preliminary to the real work, the only work in which the people are interested. And I cannot bear to think that every word I am uttering may be drawing on the standing timber of the good old state of Ohio. I am therefore, Mr. President, opposed to this thing.[49]

An additional benefit of foregoing publication of the debates, in the view of several of these delegates, was that this would encourage shorter and more focused conventions. When the New Jersey Convention of 1844 considered (and went on to reject by a single vote) a proposal to report the debates, Robert Kennedy objected that the reporting of the debates would lead to a longer convention, and he adduced as an example the fourteen-volume debates of the Pennsylvania Convention of 1837–1838. He argued, "In Pennsylvania the Convention was in session nine months—and he thought that was three months longer than it would have been in session, if there had been no reporter present."[50] The logic of this position was particularly well expressed by Milton Gregg, who contended in the Indiana Convention of 1850–1851 that the presence of a stenographer "would necessarily tend to protract the session," because it would encourage what he took to be "a wonderful proclivity in the human mind for immortality; an innate grasping after fame and notoriety; an insatiable longing for a name to live when we are dead." He explained,

> Now here are at least 150 of us, all deeply imbued with the same perhaps laudable, ambition to do something to immortalize our names, and transmit them to posterity; and it is quite natural that we should seek to avail ourselves of this

golden opportunity, now offered us to do so. And how is this desirable end to be attained? Why sir, each of us have got to set our wits to work, to concoct a speech—no matter on what subject, nor how irrelevant it may be to the subject matter under consideration, so it be of sufficient length, and full of sound and fury, signifying nothing.

He concluded: "Why sir, I am told that in the Kentucky Convention where they employed a Stenographer to report, one member alone made 199 speeches, and would have made the even 200 if the previous question had not been sprung upon him."[51]

Several specific objections to reporting the debates were also voiced in particular conventions. Among the more notable arguments was one advanced in the Alabama Convention of 1901 to the effect that the delegates' task would be best accomplished if accompanied by as little publicity as possible. This convention, like other turn-of-the-century southern conventions, had as one of its primary purposes the disenfranchisement of African Americans, and although delegates were committed to meeting this goal, they wanted to attract as little attention as possible from their critics. To be sure, some delegates in this convention welcomed the publicity. Thomas Espy proclaimed,

What are we here for, Mr. President? Why it has been proclaimed by the press, from the platform, from the mountains to the seaboard, that the prime purpose of this convention was to disfranchise the negro. If it is morally wrong, and it is not for the best interest of the State of Alabama to do that then we ought not to do it. If it is morally right, and it is to the benefit of the people of the State of Alabama, we ought to do it, and we ought to make a record of our actions, and file it in the archives of our State, so that future generations will not only see what we did, but they may know the reasons why we did it.[52]

For the most part, though, delegates in this particular convention took a different view. Thus John Long argued,

I believe we should have a record of what we do but I do not believe we should have a record of what we say. I do not think it is right and just to any of the members on this floor to have these speeches recorded so that the Colored Cooks Union can go searching through them in the years to come and get up a labor strike and refuse to allow any of its members to take employment in any house, the head of which voted in favor of disfranchising the negro. . . . I am not afraid to speak my sentiments at any time but I do not think we should have a political record there in black and white that some of the delegates will have to be dodging for twenty years to come.[53]

His colleague J. Thomas Heflin was particularly concerned about the effect that these reported debates would have on the North, and particularly on the U.S. Supreme Court:

> There will be things done and said in this convention that we do not want the Northern papers to have. There will be, Mr. President, when the battle comes between the Anglo-Saxon and the African, things said here that we do not want to go before the court of the United States in determining the plank in our constitution of the suffrage question. We will say things down here in our Southern way, and in the great old commonwealth of Alabama, that we do not want read and criticised day after day as we deliberate in this body.[54]

These arguments against publishing the debates—or, more precisely, against appropriating funds to report and publish the debates—were advanced in a number of conventions and often carried the day. However, these arguments were also frequently met and overcome by other delegates who saw significant benefits in recording the debates.

Delegates who supported publication of the debates acknowledged the financial costs of such an undertaking, but they argued that these costs were far outweighed by the benefits, whether for the citizenry or public officials, and whether in the short or long term. As William Ramsdell argued in the Montana Convention of 1889, "There are occasions in the life of nations and individuals, when, it occurs to me, that many considerations which would otherwise have unusual weight, are unworthy of being entertained; and it strikes me that the present moment is one. . . . As a question of economy, it seems to me, we might set it aside, this being the birthday, you might say, of the nation."[55] On such an important occasion, a number of delegates argued, it was only appropriate for the citizenry, when it came time to pass judgment on the work of the convention, to be fully informed about the deliberations conducted in that body. Along these lines, Thompson Campbell argued in the Illinois Convention of 1847,

> The constitution that we are to adopt, will be presented to the people for their ratification or rejection, and it is due to them, that the motives and influences that have entered into its adoption by us, should go forth with it, to aid the people in forming an opinion in regard to its merits and value. Let them have the same light and the same means of forming their judgment that we have.[56]

The public would also reap future benefits from these debates, as George Flournoy argued in the Texas Convention of 1875, insofar as the debates "would be a guide to the courts in the future in determining upon doubtful clauses in the Constitution just what the real purpose of the Constitution was. . . . The cost would be something, but there were some things which were not dear at any price."[57]

Although judges were expected to be among the chief beneficiaries of the recorded debates, delegates stressed that the benefits would extend to a wide range of public officials. As Robert Luce argued when the question surfaced as to whether to record the debates of the Massachusetts Convention of 1917–1919, public officials and constitution makers had in the past benefited from the decisions of previous conventions to publish their debates, and future generations of public officials and constitution makers would benefit from a similar decision on the part of the current convention: "Precedents are not alone the province of the lawyer; precedents are the province of mankind. We all look back to the accumulated record of the past in order that we may avoid its errors and profit by its wisdom." He noted that delegates need only read several of the speeches from the state's mid-nineteenth-century convention to "find that there is nothing new under the sun, and that we in our turn are to answer questions our fathers answered. Let us hope we shall answer them more wisely, because we shall have not only the benefit of their wisdom, but also the experience of the years that have gone by since they spoke."[58]

Moreover, delegates who favored the reporting of the debates argued that the benefits extended far beyond the state boundary lines. Many convention delegates took great pride in the task in which they were engaged, and they believed that other states, and even nations, would want to emulate their handiwork. In the view of these delegates, therefore, it would be unwise to rely solely on newspapers to accurately report the daily proceedings; and these newspaper accounts would not necessarily be transmitted around the country and the globe in the way they deserved. In the words of Richard Field in the New Jersey Convention of 1844,

> I confess I have a little State pride in having these debates correctly reported. . . . I cannot agree in the belief, that our labors here will be of little value. I see no reason why we may not form a Constitution which will be a model for other States and other Countries. The institutions and laws under our form of government are destined to exert an influence far beyond the limits of the Union, and I want the Constitution of New Jersey and the debates in this convention

to be looked up to, as well as those of New York and Pennsylvania, as affording a valuable precedent for the consideration of others.[59]

William Barnes in the California Convention of 1878–1879 held a similar view. He was prepared to acknowledge his debt to and reliance on other states' convention debates, and he thought it only appropriate that California constitution makers carry on the state constitutional tradition by reporting their own debates.

> We are about to consider some hitherto untried experiments in government, and some are threatened which have been tried and rejected elsewhere, and their incorporation in the organic law of this State will be urged and earnestly pressed. . . . If there is anything to be done by the gentlemen who proposed to establish these promised radical reforms, I desire that others who may wish to adopt Constitutions, perhaps like this, may have the benefit of these debates, and that they shall remain in the great libraries of every State, and be to them what the proceedings and debates of the States of Massachusetts, New York, Pennsylvania, Ohio, Illinois, and Michigan have been to us in the preparation of our work, and that our record shall stand side by side with theirs.[60]

In fact, several delegates did not shy away from comparing their work to that of other esteemed founders in world history, and they argued that previous state convention delegates who had opted against publishing their debates were now regretting the missed opportunity to place their deliberations alongside those of other great polities. Robert Harman in the Delaware Convention of 1896–1897 criticized such short-sighted decisions as "penny wise and pound foolish":

> In after years, when it has become impossible to replace what has been lost, more enlightened public opinion commonly finds cause to regret a paltry economy which deprives history of its most important data. It should be remembered, that our Conventions lay the foundations of States, many of which are the rival to the greatness and glory of Rome, of England, and of France. In a hundred years from now, what treasures would they not expend, could they purchase therewith complete copies of their early Constitutional records— documents standing to their several organizations in the same relations as would the discussions of those ancient sages who framed the Twelve Tables of the Roman Law, to the Republic of Rome.[61]

Mr. Harman conceded that the speeches in American state conventions were not always as sophisticated as the orations in these classical polities. Nevertheless, when measures are under deliberation, which rest on principles alone, the opinions of commonplace men are frequently of as much value, and are likely to be quite as original, as those of the more gifted debators. At all events, it is eminently useful to a public assembly to listen to the observations upon any subject of many men of various callings, and of unequal attainments. If their thoughts are not generally profound, they are often suggestive.[62]

Additionally, these delegates argued that the presence of a stenographer would have the effect not of encouraging excessive debate, as the critics contended, but rather of contributing to solemnity and excellence in the proceedings. Milton Clark argued in the Ohio Convention of 1873–1874,

I understand that there are some gentlemen who object to the publication of these debates because it will lead members to talk more than they otherwise would do, to prepare speeches to be made here for record. It seems to me that will not be the effect of printing our debates; but rather if gentlemen know that what they say here is to go upon the record, they will be more careful, and more cautious in what they say, and weigh their words more than if such was not the case. . . . I think the publication of our debates will have a good effect; it will, perhaps, have the effect of shortening our debates.[63]

In a similar fashion, Delazon Smith in the Oregon Convention of 1857 thought that recording the debates would help preserve a certain degree of decorum, insofar as "the knowledge that every word that is uttered within these walls will go upon the record may prove, if there be danger of excess, a check upon those who might be disposed to indulge in improprieties here."[64] It was not just that delegates would be prevented from delivering ill-prepared remarks or making ill-tempered comments; it was also the case, as L. W. Moore argued in the Texas Convention of 1875, that in their speechmaking, "gentlemen would be incited to excellence by knowing that the fruits of their investigations would be preserved in some substantial form."[65]

Several specific arguments in favor of reporting the debates were also advanced in particular conventions. Just as several southern conventions at the turn of the twentieth century chose not to report their debates partly to prevent their speeches from reaching the North, at least one southern convention at the close of the Civil War was intent on publishing its debates primarily for the benefit of the North. As William Martin argued in the Mississippi Convention of 1865,

It is also necessary and proper that we should show . . . that it is a mistake to suppose that in surrendering, and as a people giving our paroles, we merely did it to gain time, and that there was still a disposition among the people of the State of Mississippi to carry on the war against the Northern States—against the Federal Government. . . . I think there is no surer and better way of showing the conservatives of the North and the Government of the United States, that we are in earnest and that we are sincere, than by publishing the debates of this Convention.[66]

Ultimately, delegates in a number of state conventions were persuaded by the arguments put forth in favor of reporting the debates. In many of these cases, the complete and official record of the debates was published shortly after the convention adjourned. In several instances, though, the debates were incomplete, whether because a stenographer was not hired until the fourth day of the proceedings, as in the Wyoming Convention of 1889,[67] or because a payment dispute with the printer prevented publication of more than a single volume, as in the Virginia Convention of 1850–1851.[68] In several other instances, the debates were published in their entirety, but sometimes not until years after the convention adjourned, whether as a result of difficulties in securing a legislative appropriation,[69] or the misplacement of the debate records for several decades,[70] or the long and painstaking work of state historical societies or other groups in publishing the transcripts.[71]

In several other cases, convention debates were recorded and published through the enterprise of a particular individual or company. Several nineteenth-century convention debates were made available in this fashion, including the Maine Convention of 1819, whose debates were reported by a private individual[72]; the Virginia Convention of 1829–1830, whose debates were reported by a publishing company[73]; and the Alabama Convention of 1861, whose debates were recorded by one of the delegates.[74] In fact, the debates of the New York Conventions of 1821[75] and 1846[76] were both reported by not one but two printing companies, each acting on its own initiative.

In still another set of cases, stenographic records of the conventions were either not made or not retained, but it has been possible to piece together a narrative of the convention debates from contemporaneous newspaper accounts and delegates' journals.[77] In several of these cases, the debates were assembled on the eve of, or in preparation for, a later convention, in the belief that these records would be of particular benefit for contemporary constitution makers. In other cases, these debates were compiled by enterprising scholars or through the work of state historical societies. Although several of these records are fragmentary and cover only a portion of the proceedings, contemporaneous

Table 1-2. Extant State Constitutional Convention Debates

Alabama (2)—1861, 1901
Alaska (1)—1955–1956
Arizona (1)—1910
Arkansas (1)—1868
California (2)—1849, 1878–1879
Connecticut (2)—1818, 1965
Delaware (3)—1831, 1852–1853, 1896–1897
Georgia (1)—1877
Hawaii (3)—1950, 1968, 1978
Idaho (1)—1889
Illinois (4)—1847, 1869–1870, 1920–1922, 1969–1970
Indiana (1)—1850–1851
Iowa (3)—1844, 1846, 1857
Kansas (1)—1859
Kentucky (2)—1849–1850, 1890–1891
Louisiana (3)—1845, 1864, 1973–1974
Maine (1)—1819
Maryland (4)—1850–1851, 1864, 1867, 1967–1968
Massachusetts (3)—1820–1821, 1853, 1917–1919
Michigan (5)—1835, 1850, 1867, 1907–1908, 1961–1962
Minnesota (1)—1857
Mississippi (1)—1865
Missouri (2)—1861–1863, 1875
Montana (2)—1889, 1971–1972
Nebraska (2)—1871, 1919–1920
Nevada (1)—1864
New Hampshire (12)—1876, 1889, 1902, 1912, 1918–1923, 1930, 1938–1941, 1948,
    1956–1959, 1964, 1974, 1984
New Jersey (2)—1844, 1947
New York (7)—1821, 1846, 1867–1868, 1894, 1915, 1938, 1967
North Carolina (1)—1835
North Dakota (2)—1889, 1971–1972
Ohio (3)—1850–1851, 1873–1874, 1912
Oregon (1)—1857
Pennsylvania (3)—1837–1838, 1872–1873, 1967–1968
Rhode Island (7)—1842, 1944, 1951, 1955, 1958, 1964–1969, 1973
South Carolina (1)—1868
South Dakota (2)—1885, 1889
Tennessee (5)—1953, 1959, 1965, 1971, 1977
Texas (3)—1845, 1875, 1974
Utah (1)—1895
Virginia (7)—1829–1830, 1850–1851, 1861, 1867–1868, 1901–1902, 1945, 1956
West Virginia (1)—1861–1863
Wisconsin (2)—1846, 1847–1848
Wyoming (1)—1889

newspaper accounts have often made it possible to assemble a comprehensive account of the debates.[78]

All told, I have been able to locate the records of the debates for 114 state conventions (Table 1-2). Although it has not been possible to obtain debate records for any conventions held during the first four decades of the American regime, the available records encompass twenty-two conventions held before 1850, forty-four conventions held from 1851 to 1900, twenty conventions held from 1901 to 1950, and twenty-eight conventions held after 1950. In addition, although it has not been possible to obtain any records of convention debates for Colorado, Florida, New Mexico, Oklahoma, Vermont, or Washington, the list does include at least one convention from a total of forty-four states. Moreover, a number of states are particularly well represented, including, not surprisingly, New Hampshire (12), as well as New York (7), Rhode Island (7), Virginia (7), Michigan (5), Tennessee (5), Illinois (4), Maryland (4), Delaware (3), Hawaii (3), Iowa (3), Louisiana (3), Massachusetts (3), Ohio (3), Pennsylvania (3), and Texas (3). The extant records of these 114 debates, which range in length from the thirty-seven-page record of the Rhode Island Limited Convention of 1944 all the way to the fourteen-volume record of the Pennsylvania Convention of 1837–1838, make it possible to trace the development of the American state constitutional tradition.

2

AMENDMENT AND REVISION

There is no denying the significant differences between the amendment and revision procedures in the federal constitution and in most state constitutions. Whereas Article V of the U.S. Constitution places substantial barriers in the way of amendment and revision, state procedures are generally more accessible and provide additional mechanisms for bringing about constitutional change.

When it comes to explaining the divergence in the federal and state approaches, we find that the origin of the rigid federal amendment process is well enough understood. As the debates in the federal convention make clear, delegates were intent on devising a more flexible process than under the Articles of Confederation (where amendments required a unanimous vote of the states), and the convention considered several proposals before approving the procedure that remains in place today. According to Article V, conventions can be called upon the application of two-thirds of the state legislatures to Congress; amendments require approval by two-thirds of both houses of Congress; and ratification requires approval by three-fourths of state legislatures or conventions.[1]

There was some discussion during the ratification debates and in subsequent years about whether the framers should have gone even further in liberalizing the amendment process. Thomas Jefferson, in particular, argued in an exchange with James Madison that "the earth belongs always to the living generation," and therefore each generation (which lasted nineteen or twenty years by his calculation) should rewrite the constitution in the light of its own experience.[2] Madison was fully prepared to defend the work of the federal convention, though. In general, he argued in Federalist No. 43, Article V struck a middle ground between two problematic extremes, in that it "guards equally against that extreme facility, which would render the Constitution too mutable; and that extreme difficulty, which might perpetuate its discovered faults."[3] And in response to Jefferson's specific call for periodic constitutional revision, which was first expressed in his *Notes on the State of Virginia,* Madison argued in Federalist No. 49 that there were "insuperable objections against the proposed recurrence to the people." Not only would "frequent appeals . . . deprive the government of that veneration which time bestows on everything," but they would "[disturb] the public tranquility by interesting too strongly the public passions" and become intertwined with the "spirit of party."[4]

Although various proposals have been introduced to change the federal amendment process through the years, none has come close to passing. An initial proposal from Rhode Island in 1790 sought to make the process even more rigid by requiring amendments to be ratified by eleven of the thirteen states.[5] Virtually all of the remaining proposals, which were first introduced during the Civil War and then advanced with some frequency in the Progressive and New Deal eras, have sought to make the process more flexible. Efforts have been made to permit the calling of conventions upon the application of only three-fifths or a majority of state legislatures. Other proposals would permit the proposal of amendments upon the vote of only three-fifths or a majority of both houses of Congress and would allow for their ratification by something less than three-fourths of the states. Measures have also been introduced to provide additional mechanisms for constitutional change, such as requiring conventions to be held every thirty years or permitting amendments to be initiated by the people directly.[6] As a result of the rigidity of the federal amendment process itself, though, none of these efforts has come to fruition, and, therefore, Article V has remained unchanged since the founding.

Much less is known about the origin and development of state amendment and revision processes, which are now sufficiently similar that it is possible to speak of a general state approach that is more flexible than the federal approach.[7] All states provide for an amendment procedure whereby the legislature may propose amendments—usually by a supermajority vote in one session or a majority vote in consecutive sessions, but in some states by a majority vote in a single session—which are then approved by the people, in nearly all states by a majority of voters. Most states also make explicit provision for the legislature to call conventions, with states rather evenly divided over whether to require a majority or supermajority vote. In most cases, the call for a convention must be approved by the voters before the delegates can convene, and the convention's recommendations must also be approved by voters. In addition, fourteen states give the people an opportunity to periodically vote on whether a convention should be called. Finally, eighteen states permit the people to initiate amendments.[8]

To the extent that efforts have been made to explain the development of these more flexible state procedures, several approaches have been taken. Several scholars have tended to view state amendment procedures as the product of an undeliberative and unreflective process and thus, much like other aspects of state constitutions, as decidedly inferior to the federal approach.[9] Several other scholars, by contrast, have identified a variety of theoretical influences on the development of state amendment procedures, whether in the form of Jefferson's theory of periodic constitutional change or anti-Federalist views of limited government.[10] However, with the exception of several studies of particular amendment procedures or of developments in particular regions or eras, there have been few efforts to undertake a comprehensive analysis of the development of state amendment and revision procedures.[11] Moreover, to the extent that such analyses have been conducted, they have generally not benefited from the records of the state convention debates in which these matters were addressed.[12]

The benefit of examining these convention debates is that it becomes clear that state constitution makers have given extensive consideration to the merits of adhering to a rigid approach to amendment and revision, but were led, on the basis of experiences in the nineteenth century, and then again in the twentieth century, to reject the logic underlying the federal model.[13] First, state constitution makers encountered problems that were not fully anticipated by the eighteenth-century framers of the federal constitution and that could not be overcome through rigid amendment procedures. Thus, in the nineteenth century, state convention delegates determined that a flexible amendment process was necessary to overcome entrenched geographic interests and thereby bring about a more equitable distribution of power. Then, in the twentieth century, an even more flexible amendment process was seen as necessary to overcome obstructionist interests and intransigent judges, and thereby secure the enactment of popular reform legislation. Second, state constitution makers concluded during the course of these debates that the purported disadvantages of a flexible amendment process had been exaggerated, and any disadvantages were seen as being outweighed by several important advantages, such as the opportunity to register political progress, enhance citizen knowledge and participation, and discourage revolutionary change.

Nineteenth-Century Developments

It was not a foregone conclusion in the founding era that states would even draft constitutions, and once they chose to do so, there were many meanings that could have been assigned to these documents. However, after a period of wide-ranging experimentation with various forms of constitution making in the 1770s and early 1780s, the understanding took hold that constitutions were necessary to impose limits on popular majorities, and that these limits should only be altered through a difficult and deliberative process.[14] Still, the amendment and revision procedures that emerged from this initial wave of state constitution making varied greatly. Several states permitted legislatures to enact amendments. Other states permitted conventions to be called, whether at the directive of the legislature or the people. Several states provided for a council of censors to convene periodically to recommend constitutional changes. Still other states provided no formal means of amendment or revision.[15]

It was not until the 1820s and 1830s, when many states revised their foundational documents and other states drafted inaugural constitutions, that state constitution makers began to reflect in a sustained fashion on the merits of various approaches to amendment and revision. The particular concern at this time was that entrenched geographic interests were advantaged by existing legislative malapportionments, and that there was a need not only to secure more equitable apportionment plans but also to liberalize amendment procedures so as to make it easier to fix these problems in the future. At the same time that delegates were seeking to fix these particular problems associated with rigid amendment procedures, developments in the realm of political thought were also leading to a greater appreciation of the merits of a flexible amendment process. At this point the dialogue was joined between supporters and critics of a flexible process, and for the next several decades, delegates on both sides of the question took the opportunity to articulate their respective positions.

The Case for a More Flexible Amendment Process

The proximate cause of the nineteenth-century movement to liberalize state amendment procedures was the desire to overcome entrenched geographic interests in order to secure a more equitable distribution of legislative power. The precise nature of the malapportionment problem varied from state to state, but the common concern was that certain regions enjoyed disproportionate power and there was little hope of remedying this state of affairs, because legislators from advantaged regions were unwilling to cede power, and there was no means of compelling them to do so through the nonexistent or inflexible constitutional amendment procedures. Therefore, when representatives from disadvantaged regions were eventually able to call constitutional conventions during the nineteenth century—and this alone was quite a struggle—they frequently sought to reform the amendment process, whether by instituting such procedures for the first time or liberalizing existing procedures.[16]

In states such as North Carolina and Virginia, the chief problem was that older tidewater regions were unwilling to cede power to the growing piedmont and mountain regions. The population was shifting from the eastern counties to the western counties in these states, but few steps were being taken to bring about corresponding changes in legislative representation of these regions. As a result, when revision conventions were eventually called in these states, western delegates were primarily concerned with securing a more equitable legislative apportionment plan, but they also sought to make it easier to call future conventions. Thus Rowan Fisher in the North Carolina Convention of 1835, although not himself a supporter of a more flexible amendment process, could well understand the motivation of those who desired such changes. In his view, it "was easily accounted for. For 30 or 40 years, the West had been seeking a Convention, and the East had been opposing it. It was natural, that having had so much difficulty in succeeding, the West should provide an easier mode of calling Conventions in future, and that the East, from policy, should want to make it as difficult as possible."[17]

In other states, such as Maryland and Delaware, legislatures were dominated by representatives of sparsely populated rural areas who were unwilling to permit district lines to be redrawn to reflect population growth in the cities. When conventions were called in these states, many urban delegates tried to secure a more equitable apportionment, and they also pressed for more frequent opportunities for future constitutional revision. Thus in the Maryland Convention of 1850–1851, Robert Brent was concerned with the need "to alter the basis of representation" to be more accommodating to the city of Baltimore, and he feared that this could not be achieved through the current "anti-reform majority in the Legislature." When it came to crafting an amendment and revision procedure, he therefore "thought the political waters should be moved periodically by fresh agitations; he would say that whenever old dynasties had become rotten and decayed, he was willing to see them changed."[18]

In still other states, although the lower house of the legislature was apportioned by population, the upper house was apportioned on another basis, whether by county, as in New Jersey, or by taxation, as in Massachusetts. The concern on the part of many delegates in these states was with securing a more population-based apportionment of the senate, and one means toward this end was to liberalize the amendment process. Thus Joseph Hornblower in the New Jersey Convention of 1844 advocated a flexible procedure because "it was possible the time might come when the people would desire a revision of the Constitution as to the basis of representation. The change in the population, and other circumstances, would happen once in 10 or 15 years, which would render it proper that the people should have the power of revising the laws."[19]

While these delegates were highlighting the practical advantages of adopting a more flexible amendment process, they also called attention to several theoretical benefits of such a process. The principal benefit, which Jefferson had emphasized earlier, was that a flexible process would permit succeeding generations to take account of progress in constitution making.[20] Many delegates emphasized the need to take account of moral and scientific progress. Isaac Preston urged delegates to the Louisiana Convention of 1845 to consider the advances that had been made in the last twenty years alone. He argued,

> Let them look at the progress that has been made in the arts and sciences, in mechanics, in agriculture, in morality, and then say if they have reason to expect that those who may survive for that period, or those who are now pursuing their onward course, are likely to retrograde from what we are now? . . . Those who are to come after us, advancing, as the world is, in morality, in peace and tranquility, and in the repudiation of vices which have been too common in our days, will certainly know better how to govern themselves than we can.[21]

Other delegates emphasized the progress that would inevitably take place in the field of political science in particular. In their view, the states were providing increasing opportunities for conducting experiments and obtaining knowledge about governing institutions. William Steele argued in the Indiana Convention of 1850–1851,

> We live in an age of progress. . . . The very purpose for which we were sent here was to make improvements in our system of government, to avail ourselves of all the lights which the experiences of other States and of our own furnishes us, in order to make our organic law as perfect as it is possible to make it, and as consistent with the theory and practice of free government as it is in our power to do. But when we have done all this, shall we say that we have arrived at the farthest point in the progress of improvement—that no further advance can be made—that we have attained perfection—that there will hereafter be no necessity for alteration—that we are to remain stationary and seek no further advance in the science of government?[22]

An additional benefit of a flexible amendment process was that a frequent recurrence to fundamental principles would produce a more educated citizenry. Albert Todd argued in the Missouri Convention of 1875 that this was especially important in a republican government:

> Since we have abandoned the practice of keeping up an active militia service throughout the country, . . . I am of the opinion that we cannot too often call the people out by a supreme duty to consider their laws, their fundamental laws particularly. It brings them, as it were, to a review. Our country is governed by laws; other countries are governed by arms. Hence it is that emperors and monarchs have their grand military reviews three or four times throughout the year. . . . We have given up that altogether. Votes, ballots we say instead of bullets, and therefore the people should be exercised in regard to them until they understand them thoroughly and can manipulate them with facility; and see what is requisite for the good of the whole people.[23]

To be sure, this would likely produce a fair amount of political excitement, given that campaigns for constitutional change could be expected to be mounted on a regular basis, but this was seen as preferable to the alternative of an inert citizenry. George Tuttle argued in the Ohio Convention of 1873–1874 in regard to that state's amendment procedure,

> Great as has been the inconvenience, I believe it has also been the cause of great good. Subjects of political economy, and of general polity have been

agitated, discussed, and considered, and if it were that alone that has been the result, I believe that it has been a matter of much good, and I believe that occasionally such things ought to be. There ought to be something to stir the torpid calm that naturally settles down upon questions that are considered as fixed, and the public regard them as irrevocable, and I believe it will be so in the future. I have much more fear of indifference than of excitement, agitation, and consideration.[24]

Along these lines, Mr. Preston of Louisiana defended a flexible amendment process by arguing,

The great bug-bear which is held out to us is, that it will create too much agitation. . . . To agitate a question that is to result beneficially to our fellow man, cannot be injurious in a free government—on the contrary, it must be beneficial. We should encourage men to study government in every department. The only means of learning any science, either of political government or any other, is by study; and if no question or problem is ever propounded to a man for study, why his intellect would be as a stagnant pool.[25]

Moreover, delegates argued that it was far better that this political agitation be directed into constitutional change than that it find an outlet in extraconstitutional, or even revolutionary, channels. Thomas Earle in the Pennsylvania Convention of 1837–1838 drew lessons in this regard from other countries: "If we examine the history of the republics of Southern America, we may find, among the prominent causes of revolution and disorder, the fact, that their constitutions, while they profess to give the sovereignty to the people, actually withhold it from them, through long terms of office, and through obstacles thrown in the way of quiet changes in the form of government, as the people may desire them."[26] Nor were these consequences confined to other countries. The Dorr Rebellion in Rhode Island in the early 1840s served as an ever-present reminder of the direction that popular movements could take when mechanisms for pursuing constitutional change were unavailable or too cumbersome.[27] As Mr. Hornblower of New Jersey argued in regard to a flexible amendment procedure,

It has been said that it will keep up continual excitement and agitation. He did not fear it. It would only spread intelligence among the people and make them wiser and better—but shut the door against them, and tell them that they cannot make amendments without the consent of two-thirds, and he feared the scenes of Rhode Island would be enacted over again; and he wanted to prevent the possibility of such an occurrence.[28]

In fact, as H. H. Farmer argued in the Kentucky Convention of 1890–1891, although it might seem counterintuitive, the best way to prevent "radical changes in our system of Government" was to devise an amendment process that was flexible rather than "iron-bound." He explained,

> Experience teaches that when Constitutions are too difficult to amend, they will be changed in spite of written restrictions. If the disaffection of restless individuals can find vent in voting, it will be harmless; but if, especially, there is any plausible excuse for it, it will gather strength from restraint, and if the Constitution is not destroyed, great disturbances will occur in the State. . . . Inflexible constitutions are not necessarily the strongest. The willow will stand the storm when the oak will break. The Damascus blade of Saladin, whose point could be bent so as to touch the hilt without injury, was stronger in the end than the heavy sword of Richard Coeur-de-Lion.[29]

The Case against a More Flexible Amendment Process

These arguments in favor of a flexible amendment process, although they generally proved persuasive in nineteenth-century conventions, did not go unanswered. Supporters of the federal model began by responding to the claims that a rigid process served primarily to preserve the disproportionate power wielded by entrenched interests in tidewater regions, rural areas, or less populated counties. Supporters of a rigid process generally acknowledged that this was the case; however, they argued that there were good reasons to deviate from a strict population basis of representation, and therefore it was desirable to place barriers in the way of constitutional amendments that might impose a population-based apportionment.

Thus delegates from tidewater regions in several states opposed a flexible amendment process on the grounds that it would lead to what William Gaston in the North Carolina Convention of 1835 referred to as "an unlimited Government of numbers." At a time when eastern and western representatives disagreed strongly about issues of legislative apportionment, internal improvements, and methods of taxation, Gaston argued,

> It is well known that the difficulties which for some time prevented the late compromise between the East and the West, arose from a jealousy entertained by the East, that the West intended to take some unfair advantage of the East

in the arrangement. He believed this jealousy to be unfounded, and therefore did all in his power to promote the arrangement. But, if he should carry home with him a decision of this Convention, that a majority of two successive Legislatures should have the power of changing or annulling any and every part of the Constitution, he should be obliged to say that he had *been deceived,* and that the West had bound the East *hand and foot.*

With such a flexible amendment procedure in place, he complained, there would be nothing "to prevent [the West], if so disposed, from carrying into effect whatever plans of aggrandisement the wildest demagogues may excite the people of the West to favor."[30] Out of a similar concern with forestalling any apportionment plan that would force him to "live under King Numbers," John Randolph declared in the Virginia Convention of 1829–1830 that he would "not agree to any rule of future apportionment, or to any provision for future changes called amendments to the Constitution."[31]

Meanwhile, delegates from rural areas in several states opposed a flexible amendment process out of a desire to preserve existing malapportionments that worked in their favor. These delegates argued that rural regions were entitled to extra representation as a means of preventing urban representatives from enacting improper legislation. Thus William Saulsbury in the Delaware Convention of 1896–1897 was concerned about the possibility that if "any political party should happen to get in power that would believe that representation according to population throughout this State would be to its advantage," then such a party might take advantage of the constitutional amendment process to achieve this goal. He therefore thought it was "an erroneous principle to make it so easy for the Constitution to be amended."[32] In similar fashion, Augustus Sollers in the Maryland Convention of 1850–1851 responded to proposals for a more flexible amendment process by proclaiming,

> What, he would ask, was to become of us gentlemen from the counties? Was the city of Baltimore never to be satisfied? Were we to be subject to downright vassalage? What had we done? And, he might ask, what had they not done? We had, from the sweat of our brows, contributed to the wealth and prosperity of the city of Baltimore, and now, in the day of her pride and strength, she sought to strip us of the little we had left us.

Not only would Baltimore residents make use of the amendment process to increase their representation in the legislature, but, he feared, they would then make use of this power to advance particular policies. He concluded that Baltimore "was doing all she could in various ways to strip us of our political power. He did not know how rapid were her strides in the cause of abolition, but he knew sufficient to satisfy him and others of the insecurity of their slave property, and were not willing to trust it under such a constitutional provision as that which had been presented for the sanction of this Convention."[33]

In fact, Mr. Sollers's concern that a flexible amendment process would permit nonslaveholders to advance the cause of abolition was echoed in other southern states in the antebellum period. In the course of defending a rigid amendment process, Albert Talbott in the Kentucky Convention of 1849–1850 made an explicit link between proposals for a flexible amendment process and calls for abolition when he argued, "Say what you please sir, in the constitution about slavery, but the very moment you agree and insert in it, this mode of amendment, you have done all the emancipationists now wish or ask, and you yield for ever, the question, the great question, the question I never intend to yield, that they may take our slaves without our consent, or without compensation."[34] Meanwhile, Robert E. B. Baylor in the Texas Convention of 1845 desired a rigid amendment process on the ground that "it will be found in practice better calculated to secure a certain interest concerning which almost every gentleman in this House has manifested such an extreme sensibility; I mean the great slave interest. If we have the population which we expect, two-thirds of the population may be very small slave-holders, and perhaps one-third will not be the owners of a slave at all."[35]

In still other states, delegates from less populated counties feared that a flexible amendment process could lead to the overturning of arrangements that entitled them to disproportionate representation in the state senate. Thus Abraham Browning in the New Jersey Convention of 1844 supported a rigid amendment process "as a protection of the small counties against the avowed wish to deprive them of their representation in Council; an amendment to that effect might be carried at some future time of excitement; the majority ought not always to govern; they might be collected in large cities and might seek to advance some interest peculiar to themselves at the sacrifice of the agricultural or other interests."[36] The situation was somewhat different in Massachusetts, where senate districts were apportioned based on wealth, but the effect of the current arrangement was similar, as John Phillips noted in the Massachusetts Convention of 1820–1821, in that "a larger proportion of power in the senate was given to the seaboard, to balance the undue influence of the inland parts of the Commonwealth in the other branch."[37] If the amendment process was made too accessible, his colleague Josiah Quincy argued, then "if [the senate] should render itself unpopular, the state of political parties may be such as to destroy the organization of the senate."[38]

Critics of a flexible amendment process also rebutted their opponents' theoretical arguments and emphasized the harmful consequences of frequently reopening fundamental political questions. Many of these delegates followed Madison in suggesting that constitutional questions would inevitably become intertwined with partisan divisions, and therefore these questions should be raised infrequently. William Meredith argued in the Pennsylvania Convention of 1837–1838,

> Why, he asked, were we about to place Pennsylvania, hitherto steady in her policy, steady in her republican principles—why place the whole of her laws in the arena of the party politics of the day? . . . Change in the fundamental law ought not to be made on trivial or light grounds. And while the right was renewed to the people to alter their constitution, the attainment of that object ought not to be rendered too easy, and accomplishable by mere party cries.[39]

Andrew Gray in the Delaware Convention of 1852–1853 was of a similar mind; he warned that "a constitution is an instrument which is not to be put on and put off as we would our coats; which is not to be set aside or changed from party prejudice, or party or personal feeling, or from any other motive than a desire to secure the best interests of the community which it is to regulate and govern."[40]

Other delegates shared Madison's concern that frequent revision would threaten governmental stability. To make constitutions more malleable, these delegates argued, would inevitably reduce citizens' reverence for governing institutions. John Clayton in the Delaware Convention of 1831 argued that the federal constitution was particularly instructive in this regard and should serve as a model for state constitution makers: "Nothing was further from the thoughts of the framers of the United States constitution than that the work which the[y] had done, should be altered at every popular election. They said that what they had done should not be changed by popular excitement, and the consequence was that our primary institutions were growing stronger as they became more venerable in the eyes of the people."[41] However, veneration was just what state constitutions were lacking, according to G. Volney Dorsey in the Ohio Convention of 1873–1874:

> If there be anything which this Convention should endeavor to do, and if there be any want which we should endeavor to supply to the people of the State it

is this: that by some means or other, by any means in our power, we provide for something like stability in the institutions of the State. It is the great want of the State, it is the great want of the present day. We need stability; we need an organic law which the people should become used to; which they may learn to like; which they may regard with a certain degree of reverence, and which they are unwilling to have changed, except for very good and very sufficient reasons.[42]

On this view, a flexible amendment process, rather than producing citizens who were knowledgeable and confident about the working of their governing institutions, was more likely to produce doubts in the minds of citizens about the wisdom of constantly shifting governmental arrangements. Francis Phelps in the Maryland Convention of 1850–1851 therefore "desired above all things, a fixed and stable government. The mind required repose. If this amendment prevail, every ten years agitators and demagogues will be seen traversing the whole State, spreading broadcast through the land the doctrines of Conventional Reform, and the people made discontented with their government, however wholesome its provisions may be."[43]

The Adoption of a More Flexible Amendment Process

During the course of the nineteenth century, advocates of a flexible amendment process generally succeeded in overcoming the critics and demonstrating the merits of departing from the rigid federal approach. Still to be resolved, though, were several questions about the specific form that state amendment and revision procedures should take.

The first specific point of contention concerned the wisdom of providing any sort of procedure by which legislatures could initiate amendments. Although in the revolutionary era Maryland, Delaware, and South Carolina took the lead in permitting legislatures to adopt constitutional amendments,[44] many states initially made no allowance for legislative amendments, preferring that constitutional revision take place only through conventions or councils of censors. In fact, when the question surfaced in several mid-nineteenth-century conventions as to whether to permit legislative-initiated amendments, several delegates continued to voice their opposition. The cost of such a procedure was a key concern for several delegates. Christopher Graham in the Indiana Convention of 1850–1851 complained, "Men would come up to the Legislature from different

portions of the State, and bring a favorite proposition for amending the Constitution, and long discussions would ensue, and finally it would cost the State
more to amend and improve the Constitution in that way, than the calling of a
Convention once in ten or fifteen years would cost."[45] Other delegates preferred
that constitutional change be entrusted solely to convention delegates chosen
specifically for such a task, rather than to legislators with no particular expertise
in this area. Thus James Borden in the same convention feared that "if we leave
it in the power of the Legislature, or by a simple majority to propose amendments, this evil will result: there will be frequent changes made in the organic
law, and a necessity will be created for the calling of a Convention in order to
modify the provisions thus made in a hasty manner by the Legislature."[46] Still
other delegates were concerned that the mere presence of an amendment procedure would amount to an imprudent acknowledgment of the imperfection of
the state's foundational document. Mr. Randolph of Virginia complained,

> Gentlemen, as if they were afraid that this besetting sin of Republican Gov-
> ernments, this *rerum novarum lubido*, . . . this *maggot* of innovation, would
> cease to bite, are here gravely making provision, that this Constitution, which
> we should consider as a remedy for all the ills of the body politic, may itself
> be amended or modified at any future time. Sir, I am against any such provi-
> sion. I should as soon think of introducing into a marriage contract a provision
> for divorce; and thus poisoning the greatest blessing of mankind at its very
> source—at its fountainhead.[47]

Despite these objections, every state but New Hampshire adopted a legislative amendment procedure during the nineteenth century. The prevailing view
was that it would actually be less costly to permit legislative amendments than
to rely solely on occasional conventions. Moreover, the benefits of permitting the
correction of errors were seen as outweighing any disadvantages associated with
an admission of imperfection. As James Read argued in the Indiana Convention
of 1850–1851,

> If there should be a change of popular sentiment in relation to the establish-
> ment of a State bank, or in relation to the negro question, or in relation to the
> rights of married women, and a change should be desired in any provision
> that we shall make in reference to any of those subjects, instead of calling a
> Convention at the expense of some eighty thousand dollars, the amendments
> could be made without burthening the people with any expense whatever.[48]

Once legislative amendment procedures were adopted, many states then set about eliminating various impediments to their use. The prevailing practice in the early nineteenth century was to require amendments to be approved by supermajority votes in consecutive legislative sessions, as well as to be ratified by voters. But there were variations on this general theme. Several states required legislative approval by a majority vote in one session and a supermajority vote in another session, thereby following the Connecticut Constitution of 1818, which was also the first to provide for popular ratification of amendments.[49] Other states provided for popular ratification in between supermajority votes in two legislative sessions, thereby following the lead of the Alabama Constitution of 1819.[50] Still others required a supermajority vote in one house and a majority vote in the other house in two sessions before popular ratification, thereby following the approach of the Massachusetts Convention of 1820–1821.[51]

As the nineteenth century progressed, delegates began to reconsider the need for several of these requirements, beginning with the stipulation that amendments be approved in two legislative sessions. At one time, this had permitted the people to register their approval of amendments indirectly, by giving them a chance in an intervening election to unseat legislators who had supported an unpopular amendment. However, once the people were permitted to register their approval of amendments in a direct fashion, through a ratifying referendum, there was less need to require an intervening election and approval at a subsequent legislative session. In addition, once legislatures began to be elected biennially, the traditional arrangement made it quite difficult to amend the constitution in a reasonable period of time. As Jonathan Hall argued in the Iowa Convention of 1857, it made sense to require approval by two legislatures as long as there were "annual sessions of the legislature. But with only biennial sessions of the legislature, it seems to me that it is putting off too long what may be essential amendments."[52] In fact, John Bartow noted in the Michigan Convention of 1850 that delegates at that convention had already "adopted the biennial system," and therefore, "if we pursued the mode pointed out in the original article, six years might elapse—four must—between proposing an amendment to the constitution and carrying it into effect."[53]

To be sure, some delegates were reluctant to dispense with the consecutive-legislatures requirement, because this provision was seen as promoting deliberation in the amending process. Thus George Nourse argued in the Nevada Convention of 1864 that "the arguments are very strong in favor of requiring such a lapse of time," so that amendments would be "adopted upon due reflection, and not subject to the charge of being passed by means of excitement and passion." Thus, even if the advent of popular ratification of amendments had eliminated the original purpose of requiring approval by two legislatures, Nourse maintained that the requirement might still be understood as satisfying another, no less important, purpose of "provid[ing] that no sudden whirlwind of passion, or feeling, or of fancied interest, shall bring about the hasty adoption of an amendment perhaps radical in its character, and changing important features in our Constitution."[54]

Although some states therefore chose to retain their consecutive-legislatures requirements, a greater number chose to follow the lead of the Maine Constitution of 1819 in eliminating them, particularly during the second half of the nineteenth century.[55] The rationale for this change was best expressed by Nathaniel Hammond, who argued in the Georgia Convention of 1877 that "two-thirds of two general assemblies plus a vote of the people amounts to a declaration that this constitution shall be as unchangeable as the laws of the Medes and Persians."[56]

Some states also considered liberalizing their legislative amendment procedures by eliminating the requirement that amendments be approved by a supermajority legislative vote. The advantages and disadvantages of eliminating this requirement were plain enough. On one hand, to retain a two-thirds requirement, which was the most popular of the various supermajority requirements, would be to follow the federal model. As George Chambers argued in the Pennsylvania Convention of 1837–1838: "We who are in favor of it, say that it is a constitutional principle recommended to us by the opinion of those distinguished men who framed the constitution of the United States." An additional benefit was that it would "prevent the people from being unnecessarily harassed to vote upon questions affecting the fundamental law of the land."[57] Henry Tefft argued in the California Convention of 1849 that a supermajority requirement would also ensure that, "in amending the fundamental law of the land, men should return to their sober second thought. . . . There are times, sir, when political excitement makes it absolutely necessary that the people should be restrained, and for the purpose of having this regulating check upon political parties, I shall certainly vote for the two-thirds rule."[58]

On the other hand, a majority requirement would "be more in conformity with republican principles" and would prevent minority obstructionism, as Daniel

Lamb noted in the West Virginia Convention of 1861–1863: "If we say that an amendment cannot be proposed unless by two-thirds of the legislature, that proposition has a converse to it. It is in substance saying that [a] legislature representing one-third of the people and supposed to express the will of one-third of the people may prevent amendments."[59] As John Fuller maintained in the Pennsylvania Convention of 1837–1838, which was the first to dispense completely with legislative supermajority requirements,

> The two-thirds principle, then, is in direct opposition to that fundamental principle of our government to which I allude. It is anti-republican—it is anti-democratic. . . . If it be true, as I have asserted, that our government is based upon the fundamental principle that the majority shall govern, to what end should this convention decide that, for the future time, in making any changes in the fundamental law of the state, the vote of more than a majority of the legislature shall be required?[60]

On the whole, the nineteenth-century trend was in the direction of eliminating the consecutive-legislative-session requirement,[61] as well as, to some extent, the legislative supermajority requirement.[62] By the turn of the twentieth century, all but seven states had dispensed with at least one of these requirements,[63] and four states had eliminated both requirements (thereby permitting amendments upon a majority vote of a single legislature).[64]

Convention delegates also turned to consider the procedures for calling conventions, and this led, in particular, to the question of whether the people should be permitted to vote at regular intervals on calling a convention. The concept of a periodic convention question had its origin in the founding era, when the Massachusetts Constitution of 1780 provided that the people should vote in 1795 on whether to call another convention, and the New Hampshire Constitution of 1784 provided that a convention question should be submitted to the people every seven years.[65] At that time, though, this was the only mechanism by which constitutional change could be achieved in these states. The question in the nineteenth century was whether to provide for periodic convention referendums in addition to other amendment and revision procedures.

Ultimately, ten states chose to experiment with a periodic convention question at some point during the eighteenth and nineteenth centuries, although it is noteworthy that these provisions attracted support for a wide range of reasons.[66] In some cases, delegates supported periodic convention questions out of a belief that this would limit the number of constitutional changes. Thus Thomas Donaldson argued in the Maryland Convention of 1850–1851 that such a measure would help "to avoid agitation":

> The agitation often arose from uncertainty as to the true sentiment of the people; politicians got up a factitious public opinion and by concerted clamor produced an appearance of general excitement, by which many were deceived. If the sense of the people were regularly tested on this point, there could be no misrepresentation in regard to it, and all the agitation which grew out of the doubt concerning the public opinion would be at an end. He did not apprehend that Conventions would be oftener held with than without such a provision in our Constitution. He was inclined to look upon it as conservative in its nature.[67]

But the most common justification for the periodic convention referendum was that it would enable the people to bypass entrenched interests and thereby secure passage of constitutional changes that would otherwise be blocked in the legislature. Thus in the Maine Convention of 1819, Nahum Baldwin wanted to submit a convention question to the people every seven years, as a way of ensuring that legislators could not prevent the adoption of necessary constitutional reforms. He argued, "Suppose, Sir, your Legislature should be made up of men, that from year to year, and for ten years, should deem it unnecessary to revise the constitution, and if for ten, why not for twenty, or even for a hundred years. Suppose this should be the case, when is your constitution to undergo a revision?" He concluded, "Is it more safe to trust the people with the right of revising, or to give their rulers unlimited power? Every man acquainted with history can easily answer."[68] There were several reasons why legislatures might stand in the way of constitutional reform, and therefore why a periodic convention question might be useful. The leading concern was that entrenched interests would not permit a fair and timely reapportionment of legislative power; but it was also possible, as John Clark explained in the Iowa Convention of 1857, that "the legislature may have some outside pressure, and may not represent the wishes of the people; or we may have a governor who will veto a provision of that kind, and defeat the wishes of the people."[69]

The next question, for states that chose to provide for a periodic convention referendum, concerned the length of time between submissions. Delegates used all sorts of reasoning in arriving at an answer. Many delegates followed Jefferson in consulting the actuarial tables to measure the length of a generation. Thus

Rufus Ranney in the Ohio Convention of 1850–1851 "calculate[d] that a generation of men passes away about once in twenty years, and this therefore is the period that has been fixed upon, for the laws of one to pass into the hands of another."[70] Other delegates preferred a shorter time frame, as did Joseph Bagg, who argued in the Michigan Convention of 1850 that a ten-year interval would be necessary to take account of the current rate of political and social progress:

> For, within the last ten years, such has been the rapid improvement in the mechanical arts, the scientific professions, the electric telegraph, together with California coming into the Union, etc., that in my opinion, this period would be the best. And another reason: because these things must necessarily, within the next ten years, revolutionize not only this whole nation, but the entire world. I hold that in the next ten years we are going to have an improvement much greater than we have already had in the science of government and the condition of society.[71]

The most creative approach, however, was taken by Mr. Todd of Missouri, who offered the following defense of a fourteen-year interval:

> Fourteen was in my mind for a physiological reason; according to physiology it is stated to be a fact that we undergo an absolute change in every bone, muscle, tissue, fibre, and nerve matter, in short we undergo a thorough change throughout in every seven years; so that in the period of fourteen years we shall have gone through this process twice, whereby our ideas would thus become tried twice or by two new physical developments which might functionate at one time one way and at another time another.[72]

In the end, twenty years proved to be the most popular interval, although various states also provided for convention questions to be submitted at periods of sixteen, twelve, ten, and seven years.[73]

Twentieth-Century Developments

Whereas the nineteenth century was a period of sustained interest in state constitutions and vigorous debates about amendment procedures, there was less interest in state constitutionalism in general, and amendment processes in particular, during the twentieth century.[74] However, the period 1900–1920, and to a somewhat lesser extent 1960–1980, saw substantial interest in revising state constitutions and reforming amendment procedures. As with nineteenth-century efforts to liberalize amendment procedures, the twentieth-century movement to further liberalize these procedures was rooted in a concern with eliminating certain harmful effects of existing procedures and was also influenced by developments in the realm of political thought. In this case, the principal concern, particularly during the early twentieth century, was with easing the passage of social and economic reforms that were repeatedly blocked in legislatures by special interests or overturned by activist judges. At the same time that state constitution makers sought to rectify this particular problem, in part by further liberalizing amendment procedures, they also took note of several theoretical benefits of a more flexible process, such as the opportunity for citizens to play a more direct role in governance.

The Case for an Even More Flexible Amendment Process

The chief aim of Progressive Era state constitution makers was to increase governmental responsibility for the social and economic welfare of the citizenry. Convention delegates supported more governmental regulation of utilities, railroads, and corporations. They also sought to enact measures to better protect workers, including adoption of maximum-hours, minimum-wage, and workers' compensation legislation, and abolition of the assumed-risk, fellow-servant, and contributory-negligence doctrines. Delegates also sought to win passage of assorted social-insurance measures, such as unemployment insurance and mothers' and old-age pensions.[75]

All too often, though, delegates were frustrated with the pace of efforts to secure enactment of these policies. In many instances, measures were blocked in the legislature, and these defeats were frequently attributed to pressure tactics employed by corporate and railroad interests.[76] As Lawton Hemans argued in the Michigan Convention of 1907–1908, "When the contest comes between our great commercial and industrial interests, and what might be termed the popular interests, then too often the great commercial interests by reason of their great strength, as compared with the numerical strength of the constituency, exercise a preponderating influence upon the minds of the legislators."[77]

Even when reform legislation was adopted, it risked being overturned by judges. Admittedly, state courts differed in the zeal with which they struck down social and economic reforms during this period. Several state courts were relatively inactive; others invalidated many statutes. Across the country, though, state court reversals of social and economic reforms were sufficiently numerous to be a source of much concern.[78] Joseph Walker lamented in the Massachusetts Convention of 1917–1919, "The laws in which we are most interested are commonly known as social welfare legislation,—legislation to protect the health, the safety, the general welfare of the individuals who make up the masses of our community; to protect men and women in industry, to protect children; and it is those laws that are declared unconstitutional frequently in other States and in this State."[79] It was not that judges were necessarily seen as corrupt, although this could not always be ruled out entirely. Rather, judges were thought to be relying on outdated precedents or creating novel interpretations of traditional doctrines in order to overturn popular legislation.[80] Sherman Whipple argued in the same convention:

> Suppose a body of people impressed with the social injustice of some particular institution, or industrial injustice or some other injustice, attempt to correct it by means of legislation. Assume that they get a responsive Legislature, and they get through some bill, as they have so many, many times, which to their mind represents legislation which will be helpful to the general public as well as to themselves. It has gotten so now that that is practically but one step in legislation. Nobody seems to know whether to depend upon any legislation of that sort on public questions until it has been carried before our courts for them to determine whether or not it is constitutional. . . .
>
> Unfortunately, because the Constitution was established something like one hundred and thirty years ago, it is not adapted to dealing with the problems of a modern civilization. It frequently results, therefore, that, on account of its restrictive clauses, and more particularly on account of precedents laid down by courts in earlier decisions, our courts find themselves constrained to say that a measure is unconstitutional.[81]

Given that so many social and economic reforms were being blocked, either in the legislature or judiciary, the challenge for reformers was to overcome the powerful interests and rein in the unresponsive judges. To some degree, relief was secured through existing institutional arrangements. Thus citizens in several states adopted specific amendments to overcome particular instances of judicial intransigence and reinstate invalidated reforms.[82] Citizens in several states also made use of the amendment process to adopt various institutional reforms, such as the initiative, referendum and recall, and in some cases the recall of judges or judicial decisions, with an eye toward increasing popular control over legislators and judges.[83]

At a certain point, however, delegates' inability to secure relief solely through these avenues led them to consider reforming the constitutional amendment procedures themselves.[84] Thus John Lord O'Brian argued in the New York Convention of 1915,

> Three or four years ago when some of us were combating what we thought were heresies, we told the people that the remedy was not recall of decisions, the remedy was not the initiative, referendum, etc. The remedy, we told them, was that, if the method of amending the Constitution was not satisfactory, it should be made easier for the people to amend. That was my position, and it is my position today, that if any changes were needed, the change should be in that direction.[85]

In the view of many Progressive Era delegates, liberalizing the amendment procedure was far preferable to adopting these more radical proposals, especially the recall of judges or judicial decisions, each of which stood a good chance of adoption unless alternative reforms were enacted. As William Ostrander argued in the same convention, "If there is no way to amend the Constitution, why, we will have all sorts of fellows stirring up the mob here to have recalls and have all sorts of short and speedy remedies."[86] His colleague Edward Franchot therefore argued that "our action should be directed towards this end, of forestalling public sentiment of this kind, of making it difficult for demagogues to stir up the populace," and one of the best approaches was to respond to the "real, genuine, earnest, underlying feeling among a great number of our people that the fundamental law of this State was not sufficiently responsive to the public will."[87]

A principal benefit of adopting more flexible amendment procedures, in the view of these Progressive Era delegates, was therefore to permit a more ready reversal of errant judicial rulings. Mr. Walker of Massachusetts explained, "It is said frequently by our courts that these people should have liberty of contract, that they should have liberty to work for such wages as they see fit, and that no law should be passed to prevent it. In the name of liberty they seek to create, or to permit our industries to create, a state of industrial slavery." In the face of these decisions, he argued, "Let us tell the people that they may have what our Constitution says they may have,—a right to amend that Constitution when their liberty and their happiness and their welfare require it."[88]

Delegates also expected that the mere presence of a more flexible amendment procedure would influence judicial behavior by permitting well-intentioned judges to play a reduced role in updating constitutional provisions. The idea was that certain judges had taken an active role in constitutional interpretation in part as a consequence of the rigidity of the constitutional amendment process. These judges believed, understandably, that they alone were in a position to perform the necessary updating of constitutional doctrines. Once the amendment process was made more accessible, though, these judges would be free to relinquish their role as principal guardians of the constitution and could permit other public officials to play more of a role in this regard.[89]

This connection between the need to overcome judicial opposition to social and economic reforms and the adoption of more flexible amendment procedures was made at several Progressive Era conventions, but nowhere more forcefully than by Theodore Roosevelt in an address to the Ohio Convention of 1912. Roosevelt maintained that he was "emphatically a believer in constitutionalism," but that he wanted to "no less emphatically protest against any theory that would make of the constitution a means of thwarting instead of securing the absolute right of the people to rule themselves and to provide for their own social and industrial well-being." He argued,

It is a false constitutionalism, a false statesmanship, to endeavor by the exercise of a perverted ingenuity to seem to give to the people full power and at the same time to trick them out of it. Yet this is precisely what is done in every case where the state permits its representatives, whether on the bench or in the legislature or in executive office, to declare that it has not the power to right grave social wrongs, or that any of the officers created by the people, and rightfully the servants of the people, can set themselves up to be the masters of the people.

He therefore urged the assembled delegates "clearly to provide in this constitution means which will enable the people readily to amend it if at any point it works injustice."[90]

Thus, in the same way that mid-nineteenth-century convention delegates had been immediately concerned with securing more equitable apportionment plans but then set about devising a long-range solution in the form of a more flexible amendment process, early twentieth-century delegates sought not only to address immediate concerns about the passage of social and economic reforms but also to make their constitutions more easily amendable for future generations. Additionally, just as nineteenth-century reformers had articulated various theoretical benefits of a flexible amendment process that had gone unappreciated by federal constitution makers, twentieth-century delegates also took the opportunity to highlight several theoretical advantages of a further liberalization of the process.

For the most part, twentieth-century supporters of a more flexible amendment process advanced theoretical arguments that were similar to those of their nineteenth-century predecessors, albeit with different emphases and evidence due to intervening developments. Thus delegates called attention, as had their predecessors, to the need to take account of rapidly changing political and economic conditions. If anything, these delegates argued, the pace of change had accelerated by the turn of the twentieth century, and so it had become even more important to provide an effective means of registering change through constitutional channels. Noting that "fifty-seven years ago, when the present Constitution of Michigan was enacted, the conditions in the State of Michigan were far different than they are today," Justin Sutherland argued in the Michigan Convention of 1907–1908: "I do not believe that it is a principle of Constitutions or of Constitution making that Constitutions should be made for a people that are rigid and inflexible in character. I believe that the Constitution should be promulgated and enacted in such form that the people may, as conditions change, change that fundamental law."[91]

These delegates also contended that the danger of revolutionary change had become even greater by the early twentieth century, and therefore the case had become even stronger for adopting a more flexible process that would divert radical political activity into constitutional rather than extraconstitutional channels. John Fairlie, an academic authority on state government as well as a delegate to the same Michigan convention, was one of several delegates to refer to a recent essay by James Bryce extolling the benefits of flexible, as opposed to rigid, constitutions.[92] Fairlie was impressed by the comprehensive nature of Bryce's study, which examined constitutions "over the whole sweep of the world and the whole sweep of civilized history," as well as by his conclusions, which were, in essence, that "the flexible constitutions—the constitutions which in legal form are flexible and apparently easy of change—are the constitutions where the fundamental principles are in fact least changed, and that the rigid constitutions are the constitutions which by their very rigidity are most in danger of revolutionary and radical changes because they are not easily subject to changes in smaller matters when those are necessary."[93]

These delegates also stressed, to a much greater degree than their predecessors, that a more flexible amendment process would permit citizens to play a more active role in governance. The concern in the twentieth century, however, was not just with giving citizens an opportunity to discuss constitutional questions but with permitting them to participate directly in the resolution of these questions. Ernest Snow argued in the same Michigan convention,

> This question is a simple one. It involves simply the proposition as to whether or no[t] the people of this commonwealth shall reserve unto themselves the inherent right of amending their constitution, a right which they now possess, or whether, without restrictions it shall be delegated to the legislative branch of the government. No one can dispute but what the making of the Constitution is an inherent right in the people. Nobody denies but that the changing of that Constitution from time to time, amending it from time to time, as conditions shall demand, is a right inherent in the body politic, the people of this state.[94]

The Case against an Even More Flexible Amendment Process

These twentieth-century efforts to further liberalize amendment processes met with a variety of criticisms, both from delegates who opposed the particular goals of social and economic reformers and from delegates who voiced traditional theoretical concerns about adopting a flexible amendment process. Delegates who opposed further liberalization of the amendment process were generally critical of the social and economic reforms that would likely emerge from such a process, and their first response was to highlight the radical nature of these reforms. Wellington Burt in the Michigan Convention of 1907–1908 therefore argued in relation to calls for a more flexible amendment process:

> Look for a minute where this demand is coming from. It is coming from a class. I have no war to make upon the labor organizations, I have no war to make upon the farmers' alliance, but let me tell you that right here is the truth, as shown by the petitions which have come in here, over eighty percent have come from these classes—from the socialist party, and you may as well understand it.[95]

This connection between calls for a more flexible amendment process and the enactment of social and economic reforms was just as apparent, and even more disturbing, to Hugh Stewart, who argued in the same convention that "with this proposal incorporated in the constitution, the socialist party would gain another step in the establishment of its principles. And when that finally happens you may confidently expect the man on horseback to bring order out of disorder, and after the man on horseback, as all history discloses, a monarchy follows."[96]

These delegates also contended that the reformers' complaints about the degree of legislative and judicial obstructionism of social and economic reforms tended to be overstated. In their view, legislatures and courts had been credited with frustrating far more reform measures than the record could actually support. Mr. Burt of Michigan was

> surprised here so many times by the insinuations thrown out against the legislature. Let me say to you that the larger portion of that sentiment comes from men who have gone to the legislature with the one idea that what they proposed was just what the people wanted, but when those men came to present their ideas to their fellow-legislators they could not agree, and such men go away disgruntled, and say they cannot get anything through the legislature.[97]

Nor had most state courts erected barriers to the passage of Progressive reforms, in the view of these delegates. Henry Lummus declared in the Massachusetts Convention of 1917–1919, "It is not a fact that our court has found that our State Constitution interferes with social welfare legislation. The tremendous mass of social welfare legislation that our State has adopted and enforced negatives that statement conclusively."[98]

Even if certain state courts had occasionally invalidated popular reform legislation, these delegates argued, this hardly warranted a change in the amendment process. William Kinney in the Massachusetts Convention of 1917–1919 charged that calls for a more flexible amendment process were primarily advanced by "those who feel a spirit of unrest when the Supreme Judicial Court declares a statute unconstitutional, and therefore they hope to change the Constitution immediately, to override that adverse decision of the Supreme Judicial Court." He cautioned against lending support to such an "attack on the judicial system," which he viewed as an effort to change "the whole structure and fabric of government as we have known and lived under it."[99] On this view, to the extent that any errant judicial decisions were in fact being issued, it would be far better to secure relief through existing institutional mechanisms than to make wholesale revisions to the constitutional amendment process.

These delegates also raised theoretical concerns about adopting an even more flexible amendment process. For the most part, their critiques were a continuation of long-standing arguments from previous eras. For instance, Harold Hinman expressed a Madisonian concern for stability and veneration when he cautioned in the New York Convention of 1915: "Unless the Constitution is something more sacred, more enduring, less susceptible to change, than are laws, constitutional government is a mere vagary, an airy nothingness, to be blown away by every passing breath of public opinion. If the Constitution is to be amended by impulse, it might just as well not exist at all."[100] In addition, Walter Wixson in the Michigan Convention of 1907–1908 gave voice to Madisonian concerns about the dangers of stirring up public passions by a frequent reopening of constitutional questions. After quoting Thomas Cooley to the effect that the best constitutions provided for "*stability, permanence* and *security* against disorder and revolution," Wixson went on to argue, "But some one will say, 'We want to have it so it will be more flexible. It is too rigid.' Pass this proposal, gentlemen, and with the shifting and changing of public opinion you will be in grave danger of making it not to say flexible but absolutely wobbly."[101] He viewed the pending proposals for a more flexible amendment process "as opening the door to a pure and absolute democracy, something as I think, to be greatly deplored."[102]

To the extent that twentieth-century critics of a flexible amendment process supplemented these traditional arguments, this came in the form of a greater concern for protecting the rights of ethnic and religious minorities. These twentieth-century delegates argued that insofar as constitutional provisions and judicial decisions were guarantors of minority rights against majority transgressions, then an easier resort to the amendment process and a greater ability to overturn judicial rulings would necessarily place minority rights at greater risk. Along these lines, Charles Choate complained in the Massachusetts Convention of 1917–1919 that proposed reforms of the amendment process represented a decisive break with the "compact . . . between the majority and every individual citizen, by which certain restraints are voluntarily placed upon their power by the majority in recognition of the feebleness of the minority or the individual."[103]

The Adoption of an Even More Flexible Amendment Process

Ultimately, supporters of a more flexible amendment process generally prevailed, both during the Progressive Era and throughout the twentieth century, although when it came to specific reforms, supporters enjoyed varying degrees of success, depending on the particular issue. When it came to making legislative amendment procedures even more accessible, these delegates enjoyed a great deal of success around the country. In regard to proposals to make it even easier to provide for periodic conventions, delegates made somewhat more headway than in previous years. Meanwhile, efforts to permit popular initiation of amendments were successful in just over a third of the states.

In regard to legislative amendments, the twentieth century saw continuing efforts to remove impediments such as consecutive-session and legislative supermajority requirements. Several states that had not yet eliminated their consecutive-session requirements chose to do so, and several more states eliminated their requirements that amendments be approved by a supermajority legislative vote. In fact, the view that legislative amendment procedures should be readily accessible became so prevalent during the early twentieth century that William Jennings Bryan could report to the Ohio Convention of 1912 that "the state constitutions bear witness to a growing confidence in the people; they are much more easily amended as a rule than the federal constitutions, and the later state constitutions are more easily amended than the earlier ones." In fact, Bryan noted, as a recent example of the trend toward flexible amendment processes, that "when New Mexico's constitutional convention recently attempted to unduly restrict the power of amendment, congress compelled a separate vote on this specific provision and the electors promptly modernized the method of amendment."[104] In particular, the New Mexico Convention of 1910 had decided that amendments must receive a two-thirds legislative vote, but Congress disapproved and required, as a condition for statehood, that New Mexico voters have a chance to approve an alternative procedure that permitted amendments upon a mere majority vote of the legislature.[105]

This trend of removing impediments to the use of the legislative amendment process continued throughout the twentieth century, so that by the twentieth century's end, all but four states had eliminated either the consecutive-session requirement or the legislative supermajority requirement.[106] Most states permitted amendments by a supermajority vote in one legislature or a majority vote in two legislative sessions.[107] Ten states went so far as to eliminate both requirements and permit amendments by a majority vote in a single legislative session.[108]

The one relatively new development in regard to legislative amendment procedures during the twentieth century was a sustained effort to make it easier to secure popular ratification of amendments. The chief concern was that various states during the nineteenth century required legislative amendments to be approved by something other than a majority of popular votes on the question. In fact, at the start of the twentieth century, two states required a supermajority of voters to approve amendments, and another eleven states required approval by a majority of voters participating in the entire election rather than voting on the particular amendment.[109] The problem with the latter requirement, as Michael Cunniff explained when a majority-in-the-election rule was proposed in the Arizona Convention of 1910, was that ballot drop-off rates made it extremely difficult in practice to secure ratification of amendments:

> It is a matter of well known fact that the voters will cast the full strength of their vote for the higher offices on the ballot, going down the ballot, the vote will get smaller and smaller. Matters of legislation and amendments to the constitution practically always have a smaller vote than the vote for the head of the ticket. So a provision of this kind, requiring a majority of all the votes cast at an election, is practically a demand for a two-thirds vote of all those who vote upon the amendment at that election.

He preferred a majority-on-the-question rule and argued that "this proposition is in accord with recent constitutions which have made amendment easy."[110] To be sure, amendments had occasionally been secured even with majority-in-the-election requirements in place; therefore these rules did not render passage of amendments completely impossible.[111] However, as John Norton explained in the Nebraska Convention of 1919–1920, it frequently took all sorts of creative devices to secure the requisite majority in these instances, such as "resort[ing] to party endorsements, and count[ing] all straight party votes for the amendments; that has been the only way by which we have been able to make a majority voting on the question equal or exceed a majority at the election."[112]

Proposals to eliminate majority-in-the-election requirements were successful in a number of states during the twentieth century, but they did not command universal agreement. For instance, Mr. Hinman in the New York Convention of 1915 defended majority-in-the-election rules, arguing that "there is a feeling throughout the country, as I have stated, and very properly so, that too small a body of voters should not be permitted to amend the Constitution."[113] In general, though, twentieth-century convention delegates sided with Herbert Parsons in the same convention, who argued, "It is regrettable that more people do not take interest enough, but those who do take an interest in them are the more thoughtful. Why should the thoughtful have the result of their thought burdened by compelling the thoughtless to vote upon the question? Are we not going to reach a better, more intelligent result if we abide by the majority decision of those who vote upon the proposition?"[114] On the strength of this sort of argument, by the end of the twentieth century only one state required a super-majority of voters to approve amendments, and only five states still required approval by a majority of voters in the election.[115]

Twentieth-century constitution makers also turned their attention to reform-ing the procedures for calling conventions, and they were particularly intent on making it easier for conventions to be called without legislative approval. Several states that had not yet provided for periodic convention questions con-sidered adopting such a procedure, with the resulting debates generally serving as a reprise of the exchange between Jefferson and Madison on the issue.[116] Supporters such as Woody Jenkins in the Louisiana Convention of 1973–1974 sought to "give to each generation an opportunity to decide whether or not they were satisfied with the constitution they had or whether they wanted to hold a convention to offer another one." He asked, "What if for some reason the leg-islature is no longer representative of the people? For example: from the years 1921 until just a couple of years ago the legislature of Louisiana did not meet its constitutional obligation of reapportionment." He therefore sought to provide "some safeguard and check to make sure that the people do have basic control of their government."[117] On the other hand, John Schenk in the New Jersey Con-vention of 1947 was concerned that a periodic convention referendum might lead to a convention being called "at the very worst period to have one, such as during a period of grave political or economic crisis, or while the country was at war." Moreover, "a periodic convention vote might result in a convention whether it was actually needed or not, due to pressure group activity, thereby possibly producing a poor document."[118] As a result of renewed concerns about the malapportionment problems mentioned by Jenkins, as well as a continu-ing appreciation for the Jeffersonian case for generational revision, eight more states adopted periodic convention referendums during the twentieth century, bringing the total number of states with such provisions to fourteen by the twen-tieth century's end.[119]

During the late twentieth century, several states considered going even further in this regard and adopting an automatic convention provision, which would require that a convention be held at periodic intervals. Supporters of an automatic convention provision argued that periodic convention referendums were well intended but were still sometimes ineffective in bypassing interest-dominated legislatures, because powerful interests still wielded too much in-fluence over the people's decision about whether to approve or disapprove a convention call. Yule Kilcher explained in the Alaska Convention of 1955–1956 that "history has shown . . . that when the time approaches that the referendum is due . . . those that hold the actual political power . . . will find ways and means of advising against it." He was prepared to

> trust the electorate, if they are given all the facts, but the choice of making all the facts available always has and always will rest with those that have access to the facts and also have the power to publicize these facts. So, if a case arises where the people interested in the status quo of any sort are against a change, they will find ways and means to advise against and in such a way influence the otherwise free will of the people. The people will not have a true picture. Whereas, with this [automatic convention] provision, here there will be a convention nohow.[120]

Critics, by contrast, were more or less prepared to accept the periodic convention question but had their doubts about the automatic convention provision. Thus when a proposal was introduced in the Maryland Convention of 1967–1968 to require conventions to be held at least once every fifty years, Elroy Boyer argued that this would amount to "defeating the wishes of the people." He was prepared to permit the people to vote periodically on whether to call a convention, but he wanted to respect their wishes if they voted against holding a convention. "To now say nevertheless notwithstanding whatever the people may do at this next general election approving or rejecting [a] constitutional convention, that there shall be automatically a new convention in fifty years, seems to me is putting a term ceiling on the life of what we are doing here today."[121] In the end, arguments such as Mr. Boyer's proved persuasive, and automatic convention provisions were not adopted by any states.

Of all the twentieth-century developments in regard to state amendment and revision procedures, the most important was the movement to add a mechanism that did not appear in the federal constitution or in any nineteenth-century state constitution: the constitutional initiative. This represented the most dramatic challenge to the federal approach, in that it permitted the people to initiate and ratify amendments, generally without any participation of the legislature. As a result, it provoked much debate, primarily during the Progressive Era and then again in the second half of the twentieth century.[122]

Progressive Era supporters argued that the constitutional initiative would be particularly useful in overcoming institutional obstacles to the passage of social and economic reforms. Along these lines, several delegates argued that the constitutional initiative could help to overcome interest-dominated legislatures. Colon Lillie in the Michigan Convention of 1907–1908 argued that the people would be able to make use of the "right to amend their Constitution by the initiative" to overcome "the magnitude of commercialism and corporate interests and their influence upon representative government that we have today."[123] Other delegates stressed the benefits of being able to overturn errant judicial decisions. Mr. Walker of Massachusetts explained that with the adoption of the constitutional initiative,

> if the court declares the law,—passed by the people, if you please,—unconstitutional, or whether passed by the people or by the Legislature, unconstitutional, the people have the remedy in their own hands, and they may change their own Constitution so as to permit the passage of that law. In other words, the people with consciousness of power to get such laws as they see fit would not be so restive as they would when they are conscious that their will may be blocked by the Legislature, and perhaps a Legislature under the undue influence of interests that are opposed to such legislation.[124]

Progressive Era supporters argued that the constitutional initiative would also permit a greater degree of popular control over and participation in constitutional development. William Jennings Bryan claimed in an address to the Ohio Convention of 1912 that "it is the most effective means yet proposed for giving the people absolute control over their government. With the initiative in a constitution, a constitution's defects, either of omission or commission, become comparatively harmless, for the people are in a position to add any provision which they deem necessary and to strike out any part of the constitution which they dislike."[125] It was true that the people already had some opportunity to participate in the amendment process, by ratifying or rejecting measures submitted by the legislature. However, as George Anderson argued in the Massachusetts Convention of 1917–1919, under the current system, "the real discussion upon amendments has been in the Legislature." He thought "that one result of very great practical value in the proposed new method of amending the Constitution will be to increase the popular intelligence about the Constitution and the popular interest in questions of fundamental importance."[126]

An additional argument advanced by supporters of the constitutional initiative, particularly in the 1960s and 1970s, was that it would permit reform in areas where legislators' self-interest often prevented them from acting. In fact, the constitutional initiative procedure that was ultimately adopted by the Illinois

Convention of 1969–1970 only permitted amendments of the legislative article. The virtue of such a provision, Louis Perona explained to the assembled delegates, was that it "introduces the initiative into the area of government where it probably would be most needed because of the vested interest of the legislature in its own makeup."[127] He argued that

> if we are dependent upon an amendment suggested by the legislature to reduce its size or to abolish cumulative voting or possibly to change to a unicameral legislature, I don't think we are going to get it done. I would also feel that it is unlikely that the Constitutional Convention—because of its ties, in many cases, or obligations to members of the legislature [would approve such measures]. . . . And so if we are to leave open the possibility of effective change in the legislative article, I think we have to have something like the initiative.[128]

Royce Hanson, a delegate to the Maryland Convention of 1967–1968 and an academic authority on legislative apportionment, reached a similar conclusion. He was generally confident that "a representative and reapportioned legislature should be able to handle the initiation of amendments to the constitution," but he had no such faith when it came to "the area of reform of the legislative branch itself." It was evident to him that "there is probably no group of people in creation less likely to reform themselves than the members of the legislature when the time for that reform has arrived, and it is for this reason that it seems to me that we should provide in the constitution a means external to the legislature for the revision of that part of the constitution which pertains to the legislature."[129]

Critics of the constitutional initiative were particularly concerned, however, both in the Progressive Era and later in the twentieth century, that such a device would permit a popular majority to amend the constitution with no participation from public officials and little regard for minority rights. Thus Hugh Stewart in the Michigan Convention of 1907–1908 charged that

> it strikes at the foundation of constitutional government, and sweeps away at one stroke every reason for a written constitution, as it places in the hands of a majority the power, without the intervention of any branch of the government to nullify and erase every vestige of the constitution, and thus leaving a minority helpless in the hands of a majority to be despoiled of their goods, and even their lives will be at the mercy of a victorious majority.[130]

Later in the twentieth century, after the constitutional initiative had been in place for some time and been the subject of various studies, delegates argued that these concerns were even more valid. As Anthony Hall argued when the issue was debated in the Texas Convention of 1974,

> I have some concern about some of the experiences of some other states. Has not this technique been used by people in other states, in fact, to controvert what had been the will and judgment of some legislative bodies in some areas that were intended, in my judgment, to implement in fair spirit that protection that government ought to give to minorities? I don't mean necessarily racial minorities; I mean minorities in the sense of those elements in our society who are least able to speak for themselves in statewide elections or in referendums and the questions that are put to them for various reasons.[131]

Despite these concerns, Oregon in 1902 became the first of thirteen states to adopt the constitutional initiative during the Progressive Era. Four more states added the procedure between 1968 and 1972, and another followed in 1992, bringing to eighteen the total number of states where citizens could initiate and ratify amendments at the close of the twentieth century.[132]

Conclusion

The principal benefit of examining state convention debates about amendment and revision procedures is that it becomes possible to appreciate the logic underlying state constitution makers' decisions to depart from the federal model. Madison's defense of the more rigid federal amendment process in *The Federalist* is readily available and widely known—and partly as a result, better appreciated. However, the unavailability, to this point, of a defense by state constitution makers of their more flexible state processes has prevented a full understanding and appreciation of the state approach.

Moreover, this analysis suggests that state amendment and revision procedures are entitled to be considered a better expression of the accumulated wisdom and experience of the American constitutional tradition than the corresponding federal procedures. As we have seen, parallel proposals to liberalize amendment and revision procedures were introduced at both the state and federal level throughout American history, but the federal reform proposals were stymied by the rigidity of the federal amendment process itself. At the state level, however, constitution makers have had more frequent opportunities to reconsider and reject the logic of the Madisonian model.

In the course of reconsidering the persuasiveness of the Madisonian model throughout American history, state convention delegates concluded, first, that a rigid amendment process is incapable of addressing several perennial problems of governance. A main concern, particularly in the nineteenth century, was with overcoming entrenched geographic interests and thereby securing an equitable distribution of power. Another concern, especially in the twentieth century, was with preventing judges from exercising inordinate power over constitutional development. In both cases, state constitution makers concluded that a more flexible amendment process was necessary in order to deal with problems whose existence or extent had not been fully anticipated by the framers of the federal constitution.

Second, state constitution makers concluded that a rigid amendment process deprives the polity of the benefits associated with a frequent consideration of constitutional questions. State convention delegates were well aware of the purported disadvantages of permitting frequent recourse to amendment and revision procedures. However, they determined that any such harms were outweighed by the advantages. A flexible process would permit future generations of constitution makers to take better account of progress, whether in politics, society, or political science. Additionally, citizens would become more knowledgeable about their constitutional provisions and would be able to participate in and exert control over governing institutions. Finally, political agitation would be directed into constitutional channels rather than into extraconstitutional or revolutionary acts.

3

REPRESENTATION

The contrast between the republican character of the federal government and the democratic character of state governing institutions has been the subject of much discussion, especially in recent years as citizens have made increasing use of state initiative processes. Whereas the U.S. Constitution does not permit citizens to play a role in lawmaking other than by voting in representative elections, state constitutions provide several other mechanisms by which citizens can participate in governance. Many state constitutions require certain measures to be submitted to the people before they can take effect. Several state constitutions permit legislatures to condition the enactment of statutes on the outcome of a popular vote. Slightly under half of the state constitutions also provide for the popular initiative and/or referendum.[1]

The reasons why the federal convention delegates chose to exclude "the people, in their collective capacity, from any share" in the administration of government are well known.[2] James Madison explained in Federalist No. 10 that the principal threat to popular government stemmed from majority factions that were "adverse to the rights of other citizens, or to the permanent and aggregate interests of the community."[3] He argued,

> If a faction consists of less than a majority, relief is supplied by the republican principle, which enables the majority to defeat its sinister views by regular vote. It may clog the administration, it may convulse the society; but it will be unable to execute and mask its violence under the forms of the Constitution. When a majority is included in a faction, the form of popular government, on the other hand, enables it to sacrifice to its ruling passion or interest both the public good and the rights of other citizens.[4]

It was evident to Madison that "a pure democracy" would "admit of no cure for the mischiefs of faction," because "a common passion or interest will, in almost every case, be felt by a majority of the whole; a communication and concert results from the form of government itself; and there is nothing to check the inducements to sacrifice the weaker party or an obnoxious individual."[5] The effect of creating a "republic," however, would be "to refine and enlarge the public views, by passing them through the medium of a chosen body of citizens, whose wisdom may best discern the true interest of their country and whose patriotism and love of justice will be least likely to sacrifice it to temporary or partial considerations." According to Madison, "Under such a regulation, it may well happen, that the public voice, pronounced by the representatives of the people, will be more consonant to the public good than if pronounced by the people themselves, convened for the purpose."[6]

We have much less of an understanding of why state constitution makers gradually rejected this federal model and chose to permit various forms of direct popular participation in the lawmaking process. Several scholars, it is true, have analyzed the development of direct democracy at the state level, and as a result we know a great deal about the order and pattern of adoption of these direct-democratic institutions.[7] However, with the exception of several accounts of the political thought underlying the adoption of the initiative and referendum in the Progressive Era, little has been done to identify the logic underlying the distinctive model of representation that has prevailed in many state constitutions.[8]

In fact, these decisions to permit direct popular participation in the lawmaking process have been the subject of extensive debate in state conventions, and these state convention debates provide a largely untapped resource for analyzing the logic of state constitutional development in this area.[9] Certainly many other issues regarding the concept of representation have arisen in state conventions, such as whether to permit instruction of representatives,[10] provide for compulsory voting,[11] adopt proportional representation,[12] or allow for the recall of elected officials.[13] However, in this chapter, I focus solely on the convention debates surrounding popular participation in the legislative process, whether in regard to constitutional provisions requiring legislatures to seek popular approval before enacting certain measures (the mandatory referendum),[14] provisions that permit legislatures to refer acts to the people of the state or in various localities (the optional referendum),[15] or provisions that empower the people to initiate laws or overturn laws that have already been enacted (the popular initiative and referendum).[16]

The principal benefit of examining these convention debates is that it becomes possible to identify the reasons why state constitution makers have perceived that the public voice, as pronounced solely by the people's representatives, will not necessarily be consonant with the public good. Beginning in the mid-nineteenth century, state constitution makers argued that on certain issues particular groups and officeholders were frequently able to secure the passage of measures that advanced their own interests rather than the public interest. Second, and also stemming from mid-nineteenth-century developments, constitution makers determined that certain issues were so controversial and so dependent on citizen compliance that the people's representatives were frequently unable to resolve them in a fashion that would be deemed legitimate. Finally, early twentieth-century constitution makers concluded that particular groups wielded such extraordinary influence in the legislative process that they were frequently able to prevent the passage of legislation in the public interest. In each of these instances, the adoption of direct democratic institutions was viewed as a means of remedying deficiencies in representative government and thereby better securing the public interest, whether by inhibiting the passage of partial legislation, permitting an acceptable resolution of controversial issues, or preventing powerful interests from blocking the passage of popular legislation.

An additional benefit of examining the state convention debates regarding the concept of representation is that they provide a better expression of the accumulated wisdom and experience of the American constitutional tradition than is found in the standard Madisonian arguments in favor of indirect representation. The absence of any direct democratic institutions at the federal level turns out to be attributable less to the continuing persuasiveness of the Madisonian critique of these institutions than to the rigidity of the federal constitutional amendment process. In fact, the problems that state constitution makers encountered throughout American history that have led to the adoption of direct democracy were not limited to the state level. Several of these problems have also given rise to parallel reform proposals at the federal level, only to be stymied by the rigidity of the federal amendment process.[17] At the state level, however, flexible amendment procedures permitted state constitution makers to periodically reconsider the logic and persuasiveness of the Madisonian arguments and to adopt a wide range of institutional mechanisms in response to changing conditions and unforeseen problems.

The Mandatory Referendum

The first state constitutions did not provide any opportunities for direct popular participation in lawmaking. The people were permitted to participate in representative elections by passing frequent judgment on the performance of legislators and in most instances of governors. They were also permitted to play a variety of roles in the constitutional amendment and revision process, such as ratifying constitutions and amendments and determining whether revision conventions should be called. In regard to the lawmaking process, however, the popular role was much more circumscribed, in that "the people could take no authoritative part in acts of government whereby their will might be formulated and given expression in such a manner as to have the sanction of law."[18] The general understanding was that the people could express their views at periodic elections and, in extraordinary cases, through the constitutional amendment process, and this would be sufficient to ensure that representatives did not betray the public trust.

The people were occasionally permitted to vote on certain questions. For instance, when residents in the northern district of Massachusetts wanted to form a separate state of Maine, this was put to a vote in 1819.[19] As another example, the Massachusetts Constitution was amended in 1821 to require decisions about granting municipal charters to towns to be put to a direct vote.[20] However, these were isolated cases, and as Frederick Cleveland later observed, "The subjects of referendal provisions made by the legislatures of the States during the first fifty years of our national life were comparatively few."[21]

It is also true that many states eventually decided to permit the people to regularly vote on questions such as the location of the state capital,[22] the extent of the suffrage,[23] and the basis of apportionment,[24] as well as on local questions such as the site of the county seat[25] and changes in county boundaries.[26] However, permitting referendums on these matters was seen as a relatively uncontroversial step, given that these were viewed as fundamental questions on which the people were entitled to speak directly.

Beginning in the 1840s, however, concerns about state debts, state-aided internal improvements, and state-chartered banks prompted a series of debates around the country about whether to require referendums on these additional issues.[27] On one hand, many state constitution makers argued that steps needed to be taken to prevent legislators from betraying the public trust, and a leading solution was to require popular approval before legislatures could undertake these sorts of projects. On the other hand, critics responded that such a device was inconsistent with the republican character of American institutions and would only encourage certain regrettable tendencies in legislative behavior.

The Case for the Mandatory Referendum

Repeatedly during these mid-nineteenth-century state conventions, delegates took note of instances when legislatures had failed to act in the public interest. These instances could conceivably have been viewed as isolated problems to be remedied through existing institutional channels, such as by unseating legislators who violated their trust and replacing them with representatives who were more committed to securing the public interest. However, state constitution makers increasingly came to conclude that the electoral process was not always capable of securing the public good in certain areas, and that on certain issues, legislative failure was the rule rather than the exception.

The leading instance of legislative failure was public indebtedness, which was brought about by state participation in internal improvements, and which led in turn to increased taxation. Especially after the Panic of 1837, delegates argued that legislatures were routinely incurring debts and then defaulting on them or levying prohibitive taxes to pay them off. Thus Beverly Clarke in the Kentucky Convention of 1849–1850 was convinced that "a wild and reckless system of running into debt, had pervaded the legislature in by-gone times, for a number of years, and that their heedless, head-long practice in this particular, should be restrained."[28] Many factors contributed to the growing state debts during this period, but a leading problem was that legislatures had become caught up in the mania for internal improvements. Thus although Horace T. Sanders in the Wisconsin Convention of 1847–1848 did not oppose all internal improvements, he was more than willing to acknowledge that "many of the states had engaged in wild and impracticable schemes of internal improvement, and had undertaken works which they neither needed nor were able to pay for. In this way enormous state debts had been contracted, and some of them had been reduced to a condition little short of bankruptcy."[29]

When convention delegates considered the extent of these problems and the prospects for remedying them, they often concluded that legislatures were likely to incur debts not merely in exceptional situations but on a routine basis, and that the incurring of future debts could not effectively be prevented through existing institutional arrangements. Charles Faulkner in the Virginia Convention of 1850–1851 went so far as to label these tendencies a "defect in our existing system of government, which places in the power of the agents of the people, in a single department of the government, the power of mortgaging, *ad libitum*, the property and labor of the people of this State."[30] The chief problem, as Lorenzo Shepard explained in the New York Convention of 1846, was that legislators were all too willing to fund projects as a way of advancing their own electoral prospects and responding to the entreaties of special interests. He argued,

> Legislatures have a very slight interest to keep them from a career of reckless extravagance. They desire to secure votes by pleasing particular localities with the grant of an improvement at the public expense and then the members are too often willing to vote an improvement in a remote neighborhood against their judgment and their principles, in order to secure a few votes for an improvement in their own vicinity. And even when they have the most earnest disposition to do right, they are liable to be deceived by the representations of those who fill the lobby, and are deeply interested in the completion of the project.[31]

This capacity of special interests to prevail upon legislators to "secure special privileges and partial legislation" was of particular concern to John Morrison in the Indiana Convention of 1850–1851:

> It is a notorious fact, mortifying as it may be to our pride, that hitherto the agents of corporations have been able, in the capacity of lobby members, to carry through the Legislature almost any measure which their principals deemed of sufficient importance to expend money enough to carry. Corporations and combinations of wealthy men, have this immense advantage over the people; they can act as an unit; they concentrate all their power under the direction of one will; the objects to be accomplished are of such financial

importance and are sure to bring such abundant pecuniary returns, that they can afford to bring all their influences to bear, first in the formation of the Legislature, by the selection and election of their friends, and then to influence and control the Legislature after it assembles here.[32]

Not only did legislators frequently approve projects that increased the public debt, but the people encountered tremendous difficulties in overcoming the effects of these errant decisions. Michael Hoffman explained in the New York Convention of 1846, "In almost any case if a bad law is passed by the legislature, it can be repealed—the legislature have few temptations to pass a bad one. It is not so in relation to the subject of debts and compound interest. It is silent, creeps along, gets into the State, and when the act is once passed, the debt incurred, the obligation is as strong as death for its payment."[33] For these reasons, it soon became clear, as Charles Beard and Birl Schultz later observed, that "legislatures cannot be given a free hand in laying taxes, incurring debts, and making appropriations. This nearly all of our states have learned by bitter experience."[34]

Delegates were equally concerned about legislative performance in regard to the chartering of banks. In fact, the degree of public hostility toward banks reached a point during the mid-nineteenth century that John Cook could report in the Michigan Convention of 1850 that "the people have lost more by banks than would pay the public debt."[35] Some delegates were concerned about the mere existence of banks. For instance, David Gregg in the Illinois Convention of 1847 "was one of those who believed banks, in any shape, manner or form, to be an unmitigated evil, and that their consequences were always disastrous and destructive to the people."[36] Many delegates were also concerned about the procedures by which legislatures chartered banks, and particularly by the influence wielded by banking interests in the chartering process. Thus John Pierce spoke in the Michigan Convention of 1850 about "instances in which the Legislature had refused to pass bank charters, but which had been lobbied through at the close of the session."[37]

When it came to assigning responsibility for the problems associated with legislative chartering of banks, many delegates argued that the difficulties stemmed not from a weakness in legislators' character, but rather from an institutional design that permitted narrow interests to wield excessive influence in the legislative process. Robert McClelland argued in the Michigan Convention of 1850 that it was "a well established fact that most of our bank charters are drafted by those to be interested in them, and that therefore the provisions are favorable to the bankers."[38] Similarly, Mr. Cook of Michigan explained that legislatures are not beyond the influences of those who want those institutions. Sir, the history of this State and of others demonstrates the fact. You never knew a Legislature to come together but they would decide against banks by a three-fourths vote, and before the close they would charter banks by a two-thirds vote. I think no gentleman will say but when the Legislature assembles here directly from the people [that] it expresses the views of the people.[39]

State constitution makers took a variety of steps to increase the likelihood that the public interest would prevail over particular interests in regard to debts, taxes, internal improvements, and banks. If the problem was merely that the people were unaware of upcoming legislative votes and therefore unable to convey their views to their representatives, then one solution was to require the legislature to give adequate public notice before incurring debts, raising taxes, embarking on internal improvements, or chartering banks.[40] If the problem stemmed from the lack of an opportunity for the people to exert adequate pressure on legislators in regard to these measures, then another approach was to require that legislative action in these areas be approved in successive legislative sessions, so that the people could defeat wayward representatives in the intervening election. And if the problem turned out to be so severe that legislatures simply could not be trusted in these areas, there was always the option of requiring a legislative supermajority before action could be taken,[41] or prohibiting legislative action in a particular area altogether.[42] All of these approaches, which were implemented in various states, were consistent with the original conception of indirect representation, in that public opinion would be expressed solely through representative elections.

At a certain point, though, state constitution makers began to reject these approaches as insufficient and to suggest that certain measures be required to be submitted to a popular referendum before taking effect. In several cases, such referendum requirements were proposed by delegates who supported legislative action in a given area but feared that prevailing sentiment among convention delegates might be strong enough to prohibit legislative action altogether. Therefore, as a way of ensuring that legislative support of various projects could continue, these delegates proposed referendum requirements in order to reassure their fellow delegates and the public that the legislature would exercise this power responsibly. For instance, Mr. Sanders of Wisconsin wanted to permit continued legislative support of internal-improvement projects, but he was well aware that "a strong prejudice had been imbibed of late years against the undertaking of such works by the state." He therefore proposed a "substitute" that "guarded against the abuse of the power," in part "by requiring a vote of the people upon any law authorizing any such work."[43] Similarly, Albert Hawley in the Nevada Convention of 1864 favored permitting the state to loan its credit for "the construction of the Pacific Railroad"; he therefore stressed to skeptics that "not one dollar can pass from the pockets of the tax-payers to the State, and thence to this railroad enterprise . . . without the consent of the people of the new State, solemnly recorded at the ballot-box."[44]

For the most part, referendum requirements were proposed by delegates who took a very different view of these projects; these delegates wanted to prohibit legislative action in these areas altogether, but they realized that such an extreme proposal would not be accepted by the convention or by the citizenry. Therefore, these delegates turned to referendum requirements as the most effective and feasible way of limiting legislative power in these areas. For instance, William Foster in the Indiana Convention of 1850–1851 announced that he was "pledged to go against any provision for the contracting of a public debt, unless the law for that purpose shall, before it goes into effect or is binding upon them, be submitted for their adoption or rejection at the next annual election after its passage by the Legislature."[45] Meanwhile, James Blood in the Kansas Convention of 1859 was opposed to all banks but knew "that if we prohibit banking in this Constitution it will be voted down by the people," and therefore he supported as the next best option a proposal "that any general banking law passed by the Legislature shall be submitted to the people."[46]

Regardless of the diverse motivations that generated these referendum proposals, the main purpose of instituting these referendum requirements was to ensure that the public good would prevail over particular interests. Thus if legislators knew that all banking laws would have to be approved by the voters, Mr. McClelland of Michigan argued, then "those who desire a general banking law will make it as perfect as they can before they submit it to the criticisms and scrutiny of the people. Their object will be to obtain their approval; and knowing the extreme sensitiveness that exists, and that the slightest defect exposed may defeat the project, they will act honestly and in good faith."[47] And in the event that particular individuals or groups might try to secure the passage of self-interested measures, the people could be counted on to reject such measures at the ballot box. As Henry Nicoll argued in the New York Convention of 1846, "Management and chicanery may and too often will carry an iniquitous project through the legislature, but who would not see that such a thing was next to impossible with the whole people."[48] In the words of Alvin Hovey in the Indiana Convention of 1850–1851, "You *may* corrupt a few men, but you *cannot* corrupt the masses—you cannot succeed with political log-rolling with the people at large."[49]

Supporters of referendum requirements made it clear that they did not mean to reject the traditional concept of representation altogether. In most cases, the legislature could still be trusted to act in the public interest; therefore, there was no reason to burden the people with the responsibility of passing judgment on ordinary legislation. However, in the limited set of cases in which legislatures had shown themselves to be incapable of acting responsibly, it made sense to require direct popular participation as an additional safeguard. William Chapman in the Iowa Convention of 1844 therefore "came pledged to vote against letting the Legislature create indebtedness, without the people sanction[ing] it. That was the true Democratic principle. Gentlemen had introduced propositions for taking the will of the people in cases in which he could not go for it. But he was not afraid to trust the people with the question of indebtedness. . . . It was a wise provision to let the people decide upon questions of this character."[50] Similarly, Amos Harris in the Iowa Convention of 1857 emphasized the limited nature of this mid-nineteenth-century movement for direct democracy when he argued, "I think if there is any subject which should properly go before the people for them to act upon, to consider like the democracy of olden time, to sit upon as a jury, if you please, it is this very system of entering upon these public improvements."[51] Meanwhile, E. B. Danforth in the Michigan Convention of 1850 differed with these other delegates as to the precise area of legislation that he felt deserved to be submitted to the people, but he was no less committed to limiting the range of issues that would be subjected to mandatory referendums. He thought that "if any one principle should be submitted to the people, it was this one on banking. It was the only thing about which he was ever embarrassed in the Legislature."[52]

The Case against the Mandatory Referendum

These proposals did not go unchallenged in mid-nineteenth-century conventions. Opponents contended that referendums were inconsistent with the traditional concept of representation and deserved to be rejected for that reason alone. Garrett Davis argued in the Kentucky Convention of 1849–1850, "I am opposed to this mode of saying whether any law should become a law of the land or not. I believe it is not congenial with the genius of a representative government, that such proceedings should take place."[53] Many opponents were inclined to side with John Hall in the Iowa Convention of 1844, who contended that public opinion was best expressed in an indirect fashion, and that representative elections would provide an adequate check on faithless legislators. He referred to the proposed mandatory referendum as "a splendid spectacle" that initially "excited his imagination" and "seemed magnificent," but turned out upon further consideration to be "a step that struck at the representative form of our government." He "believed not quite so much in the first thought of the people, as in their sober *second* thought. If the Legislature passed a law that made taxes oppressive, the people would not elect them or any others to do the same thing again. That was the proper remedy."[54] Meanwhile, John Edwards reminded his colleagues a decade and a half later, when a similar proposal surfaced in the Iowa Convention of 1857, that direct democracy had been a feature of classical polities but had been decisively and properly rejected by the founders of the American regime. He was "opposed to going back to the barbarous days of ancient Greece, when the whole people met for the purpose of making laws for their government. Ours is a representative form of government, and we are not compelled to look to ancient, and different forms of government for models upon which to shape our conduct."[55]

On this view, the adoption of the mandatory referendum would not only "be an imputation on the integrity of the Legislature,"[56] as J. R. White argued in the Michigan Convention of 1850, but would "be saying to the world in so many words, that republican governments had proved a failure," according to Alvah Worden in the New York Convention of 1846.[57] And Mr. Worden, for one, was not prepared to "admit in this or any way, that the experiment of a republican, representative, responsible form of government, after a trial of more than 70 years, had proved a failure, and was not to be trusted in the exercise of an essential function—that the people in point of fact, were not capable of judging of the action of their representatives, and of correcting their errors."[58] After all, if a mandatory referendum was adopted on these issues, John Bartow argued in the Michigan Convention of 1850, then "you may as well say that every act of the Legislature shall be sanctioned by the people before it takes effect."[59]

Critics also argued that an institutional innovation of this sort would bring with it regrettable consequences. Although several of these delegates opposed the referendum on the grounds that it would unduly limit legislatures' ability to undertake worthy projects, most critics opposed the referendum for the opposite, and at first glance counterintuitive, reason: because it would increase the likelihood of additional projects being undertaken and debts incurred. Mr. Worden argued that with the adoption of the mandatory referendum, "a member of the legislature might ease his conscience by voting for a tax law, (which he really did not [ap]prove,) merely because it was to be submitted to the people; and that they would have the power to do as they pleased about it."[60] He was concerned that the people might be less likely to scrutinize such measures and unseat legislators who voted for them, because the referendum would "lull the people into a false security, where they will believe that all is going right, when in truth it is not; and you will disarm them of that vigilance in regard to the action of their representatives, that is so highly essential to the preservation of public liberty."[61] It was in part for this reason that George Hillard in the Massachusetts Convention of 1853 condemned "the principle of shifting our responsibility upon the shoulders of the people" as "not manly, not courageous."[62]

Not only would the referendum have the paradoxical effect of reducing popular control over this sort of legislation, but it would also make it easier for corporate interests to secure support for their pet projects. If a referendum were required for the loaning of state credit, Richard Henry Dana argued in the same Massachusetts convention,

> the legislature become the mere doorkeeper, and the corporation comes up and asks admission to go through to the people. It claims the right to do so. I can imagine how they might press upon the legislature a scheme of appropriation and say to the legislature, you are not the people, you are not the law-making power, you are put forth as an advance guard to look at things and see that nothing frivolous or scandalous goes to the public. The people is the tribunal and we wish to go to them. . . . I wish to know whether any legislature can stand between the corporation or section of the country and such arguments as these.[63]

Finally, and along similar lines, several delegates feared that adoption of referendum requirements might actually enable legislators and citizens alike to exceed the limited purposes of constitutional government. Thus Henry Page in the Ohio Convention of 1873–1874 complained that "a tax was not purified from the taint of illegality by being filtered through a ballot box. If the will of the majority is a sufficient reason for taxation, the day may come when those who have property will need protection against those who have none."[64] He predicted that "we shall see under this system, reckless taxation, and reckless expenditure, without any adequate results to the country."[65]

The Adoption of the Mandatory Referendum

Although the opponents' concerns proved persuasive in several mid-nineteenth-century conventions, insofar as some states chose to rely on devices other than the referendum to restrict debts, taxes, internal improvements, and banks, a growing number of states found the arguments in favor of the referendum to be compelling. Rhode Island in 1842 became the first state to provide for a mandatory referendum of this kind when it stipulated that the legislature could not incur a debt in excess of $50,000 without the direct approval of the people.[66] Over the next decade, and throughout the nineteenth century, other states enacted similar requirements.[67] Illinois in its Constitution of 1848 became the first state to require certain tax levies to be approved by a popular vote,[68] and several states went on to enact similar provisions.[69] The Iowa Convention of 1844 was the first to approve a provision that required a popular vote on all banking laws, and the Wisconsin Convention of 1847–1848 was the first to approve such a provision that was then ratified by voters.[70] This precedent was then followed by several other states during the next three decades.[71]

At the same time that state constitution makers adopted these referendum requirements, they occasionally took steps to respond to the critics' concern that the referendum might make it even easier for interested individuals or groups to secure support for their favored projects. In response to concerns that legislators might use the referendum to shirk responsibility for various funding projects, several states stipulated that legislators who voted to refer a measure to the people would be required to express their approval of this measure. Under such a provision, Mr. Hoffman of New York explained, each legislator "must say that he believed the law to be extremely right and proper, and the people ought to sanction it. He therefore cannot avoid the responsibility."[72] Then, to avoid the possibility that referendum measures would pass by securing the votes of an apathetic public at general elections, some states stipulated that these measures must be approved at a special election and/or that they receive a majority of the votes cast in the entire election or a supermajority of those voting on the particular question.[73]

The Optional Referendum

Referendums inspired another set of debates in the mid-nineteenth century, albeit in a different fashion and for a different reason, when legislatures began to submit questions to the people out of a desire to resolve controversial issues in a fashion acceptable to the citizenry. The question of whether to regulate or prohibit the liquor traffic was the most prominent of these issues, but several other matters were also settled by optional referendums, most notably the establishment of public schools.[74] Beginning in the 1840s, legislatures began to submit these sorts of questions for popular approval, whether to residents of particular localities, as when Rhode Island and Pennsylvania enacted several of the first local-option liquor laws in 1845 and 1846, respectively,[75] or to a statewide electorate, as was the case with the New York Free School Law of 1849.[76]

Debates about the propriety of these referendums were frequently carried out in state legislatures that adopted or rejected these devices, or in state courts that heard challenges to the legitimacy of such devices. In fact, beginning in 1847 when the high courts in Delaware[77] and Pennsylvania[78] invalidated their states' local-option liquor laws, and continuing for the rest of the nineteenth century, state courts across the country decided many cases concerning the validity of legislative referendums.[79] As far as statewide referendums were concerned, state courts were nearly unanimous in declaring that they were an illegitimate departure from a republican form of government, with the Vermont Supreme Court offering the main dissenting view.[80] When it came to local referendums, state court judgments were mixed. On one hand, several courts followed the high courts of Delaware and Pennsylvania in declaring local-option laws unconstitutional.[81] The overwhelming majority of courts reached a different conclusion, however, and held that local referendums could be distinguished from statewide referendums and therefore sustained.[82]

On a number of occasions during the mid-nineteenth century, the legitimacy of legislature referendums was also debated in state conventions. For the most part, the issue surfaced when convention delegates who supported optional referendums sought to respond to state court rulings that cast doubt on the constitutionality of the practice. In some of these states, supporters were responding to a decision that had been handed down by their own state court. Thus, in the Delaware Convention of 1896–1897, Edward Bradford took note of the Delaware Court's 1847 decision "in the case of *Rice v. Foster,*" a decision that he did "not believe to be law, and never did believe to be law; but it is nevertheless, a decision which stands until it is reversed." He therefore "proposed to remove any question of the Constitutionality of a Local Option Law," and to "recognize the Constitutional authority of the General Assembly to submit the question to the people in order to ascertain the sense of the people upon the question as to whether there shall be license or no license."[83] In other states, supporters sought to remove any uncertainty that had been brought about by decisions issued by neighboring state courts. Along these lines, John Powell in the West Virginia Convention of 1861–1863 noted that referendums on liquor laws had been held in other states, and that "in some states in which such laws have been passed they have been decided as unconstitutional by the courts. Now, we wish to have this inserted to the end that if the Legislature of West Virginia shall pass such a law, the courts will not be able to decide the law unconstitutional."[84] In similar fashion, James Kelly in the Oregon Convention of 1857 expressed his support for "a clause inserted in the constitution to this effect: that the legislature may submit the question to a vote of the people." He was particularly interested in submitting liquor laws to the people, but he thought "that there may be many cases where the people ought to have the right to express their will; where the law ought not to take effect until the vote of the people establishing it decides the point."[85]

In other cases, debates about the legitimacy of legislative referendums arose when critics tried to halt a practice that had developed without any explicit warrant in the state constitution. Thus Simeon Nash in the Ohio Convention of 1850–1851 supported a constitutional provision to prohibit any laws from being passed "contingent upon the approval or disapproval of any other authority, except as provided in the Constitution." He "agreed with the Supreme Court of Pennsylvania, that all such laws were unconstitutional. He never had but one opinion upon the subject. But a different practice had grown up in this State; and to suppress it, he thought there should be engrafted into the constitution what he understood always to have been the true construction of the law."[86]

The ensuing debates over these constitutional proposals served to illuminate the reasons why supporters such as Messrs. Bradford, Kelly, and Powell viewed the legislative referendum as a necessary device. These debates also gave critics such as Mr. Nash a forum for expressing their concerns about the practice.

The Case for the Optional Referendum

Supporters of the optional referendum argued that certain issues were, by their nature, exceedingly difficult for the legislature to resolve in a legitimate fashion. In part, this was because legislators were occasionally uncertain about the status of public opinion on issues that may not have arisen in the electoral campaign. As a result, legislators were understandably interested in obtaining the sense of the public directly. As John North argued in the Minnesota Convention of 1857, "It very frequently happens that the Legislature is called upon to legislate upon important matters, in reference to which they were not elected. They, in their discretion, refer the matter to the people and ask them to decide upon it."[87] Even when issues had been thoroughly debated in electoral campaigns, it was not always possible for legislators to take a precise reading of public opinion, because it was difficult to untangle the many issue stances that might have contributed to their electoral victory. On uncontroversial issues, this was not such a problem; legislators were fully prepared to hazard a guess as to where public opinion stood on routine matters. But when it came to divisive moral issues, such as liquor, gambling, or schooling, legislators were fearful of proceeding upon an incorrect reading of public opinion, because this could imperil their reelection prospects. Supporters of the optional referendum argued that one might wish that legislators had the courage to address these issues, and one might even implore them to do so; but experience demonstrated that legislators were driven by electoral considerations and were frequently disinclined to accept responsibility for resolving these sorts of questions.[88]

Moreover, to the extent that legislators might try to address these controversial issues, the people would be unlikely, for several reasons, to view a legislative settlement as a legitimate resolution of the matter. As John Bowdle argued in the Utah Convention of 1895 in regard to the liquor question, "Whenever legislators get the idea that they are the people and that in them lies the sovereign power, it is time to step down and out." In his view, "the people have a growing distrust of the legislators," and therefore, in cases involving "all great principles, when it is possible that the people can express directly their will, they ought to have that right and that privilege to do it."[89] To be sure, there was no need for the people to vote directly on routine matters. However, on questions such as liquor regulation, especially, the people would be more likely than the legislature to reach a proper resolution of the issue. As William Spruance made clear in the Delaware Convention of 1896–1897, "Understand . . . I do not want to be taken to be an advocate of the universal application of this principle of referendum. I think carried to an extreme it would be a very dangerous thing," but "this question of the sale of intoxicating liquors . . . is a proper question to be submitted to the vote of the people."[90] Similarly, James Taylor argued in the Ohio Convention of 1850–1851, "The question was not, whether all the laws should be thus submitted. The honest pride of the Legislature would prevent that. It would only be done in extraordinary cases."[91]

Not only would the people's voice on these issues be seen as more legitimate than any pronouncement by their representatives, but the people would also be more likely to comply with policies that they had a direct role in crafting. In part, this was because legislators who tried to resolve these questions ran the risk of misjudging the specific policies that would command the assent of the people.[92] Thus Amos Townsend in the Ohio Convention of 1873–1874 argued that other states' experiences highlighted the difficulties encountered by legislators who adopted sumptuary laws without first obtaining the sense of the people. "In the good old State of Massachusetts, where obedience to law is a part of every man's education, it had been found that acts passed in advance of public opinion, affecting the tastes and habits of the people, have proved inoperative." The lesson from this story, in his view, was that provision ought to be made for "an adjustment of the whole question by the people for themselves, and their action should be final."[93] Permitting a direct popular vote on controversial questions would also increase compliance because citizens would be more likely to obey a law that they had voted on directly, even if they found themselves on the losing side. The idea was that if the legislature handled the issue, then individuals on the losing side might still cling to the belief that the legislature had failed for some reason to reflect the majority will. But if the people were given a chance to resolve the question, these same individuals would be much more likely to accept the outcome. As Richard Bishop argued in the same Ohio convention,

> We learn from the friends of both sides of the question, that the people want to speak out on this liquor question, and that the friends of license will be better satisfied if the people have a right to speak out, and if they reject it, say that they will be satisfied. Those who are in favor of prohibition make the same statement, and, I think, under existing circumstances, it is best to let the people have a voice on this subject.[94]

A final benefit of optional legislative referendums—which was cited by those who supported not only statewide but especially local referendums—was that they permitted a diversity of policy outcomes on issues where such diversity was a virtue. On certain issues, a uniform state policy was possible and desirable; but as Henry Stanbery argued in the Ohio Convention of 1850–1851, "It might be wished that all were uniform; but the thing is impossible. Every town—every city, must, of necessity, have its own peculiar laws enacted by its own lawmakers, to suit its own peculiar circumstances. What would be proper for a small town might not be for a large one—what would suit a city in one location would not suit a city in another." He was prepared to "agree with gentlemen, that it is desirable that there should be uniformity in General Laws, but if that uniformity were enforced in every possible subject of Legislation, it would be intolerable."[95]

Local referendums were thought to be particularly appropriate on school laws. It was true, as Thomas Ewart admitted in the same convention, that "if this power is not given to the people, of course, it must be exercised by the Legislature, and the only practical difference will be, that that body will have a little more to do. It must first create the general law, and then, by a series of local enactments it must apply it to this or that township, county, or school district as the exigencies of the people shall demand." Therefore, it would still be possible to allow for diversity, even in the absence of the optional referendum. It would be far better, though, to permit the people of each locality to vote directly on the matters that directly concerned them. He thought that

> there must be cases in which it will be for the interest of the people to act of themselves, upon questions regarding the school laws of the State, that do now or hereafter may exist. Some portions of the State are waked up upon the subject of schools. They have done much, and want to do more. They may have progressed as far as is possible under one system, and may desire to advance to a higher; and in all such cases, it seems not only necessary, but in the highest degree proper that they should have the privilege to act in their own case, as their view of their own welfare and interest shall demand.[96]

Such an argument was equally applicable to liquor regulations. As Ephraim Hall noted in the West Virginia Convention of 1861–1863, "It may not be the sense or wish of the people of the entire State to exclude all over the State the sale and use of intoxicating liquors, and I desire that if there be a county in the State where people desire that they shall be entitled to have legislation to establish that as a rule for their county, and this proposition would do that, I desire to make that practicable."[97] In fact, the case for the referendum was especially strong in regard to liquor regulation, because of the notorious difficulties in securing compliance with measures in this area. As Alvin Voris explained in the Ohio Convention of 1873–1874,

> Indifference to the obligation of obedience to the laws is exceeding dangerous to the well-being of any people. Better have such laws as will secure obedience, though they fall short of much that is needed, than have rigid laws which are generally disobeyed. What will adapt itself to the cities of the first class, may not be up to the sense of propriety in cities of the second class; and cities of

the second class may be far behind villages and the agricultural districts. That such of these municipalities may have the benefit of as high order of laws as will be backed by public sentiment, it would be sound policy to give to these political subdivisions, within the limits prescribed for the state at large, perfect autonomy over the traffic in these liquors and its concomitant evils.[98]

Better, then, to permit the liquor question to be resolved by a referendum in each locality than to "commit the State to a procrustean rule."[99]

The Case against the Optional Referendum

Critics of the optional referendum responded with the same sort of theoretical objections that were raised against the mandatory referendum. In particular, delegates sought once again to portray the device as a departure from the traditional concept of representation. Charles Reemelin in the Ohio Convention of 1850–1851 understood "public sentiment in Ohio, to be in favor of a representative democracy, voting through the ballot box, for the men who are to exercise the powers conferred by the constitution, we are about to make; and all that I mean to contend for is, that the exercise of the sovereign right of the people in counties, or townships, to legislate through the ballot-box, is inconsistent with the structure of our government."[100] Delegates were also quick to criticize what they took to be the extreme implications of proposals to permit optional referendums. As Delazon Smith argued in the Oregon Convention of 1857, "We might as well abolish the legislature, and appoint a committee to frame laws for submission to the people; if the legislative power was to be exercised by the people en masse, why incur the expense of a legislative assembly."[101]

Critics were also concerned that such an innovation would encourage certain regrettable tendencies that were already present to some degree in the American political system. In response to those who argued that the referendum would permit the resolution of controversial issues that legislators were disinclined to address, critics such as Daniel Read in the Indiana Convention of 1850–1851 argued that, in practice, "it has been resorted to for the mere purpose of evading responsibility."[102] In fact, Benjamin Dean criticized an optional referendum proposal advanced in the New York Convention of 1894 by arguing that "the title of this measure should be 'an act to encourage cowardice on the part of the representatives of the people.' That will be the logical effect of the measure. . . . It is simply an effort to avoid the responsibility of representatives, and is entirely vicious, antagonistic to every proposition of a republican form of government."[103] In similar fashion, Mr. Reemelin of Ohio contended that there was already a tendency for legislators to "shove off responsibility"; therefore, in adopting the optional referendum, "members of the General Assembly are playing into the hands of this tendency."[104]

In response to claims that the referendum would lend more legitimacy to policies adopted on controversial issues, critics responded that there was already too much of a tendency to distrust legislatures, and this problem would only be exacerbated by the referral of the most important policy issues to the people. As Mr. Reemelin explained in response to one supporter, "It was merely the tendency of the principle to which he desired to call the attention of his friend. The idea of the popular sovereignty, as distinct from the power of the Legislature, he did not desire to see adopted into the Constitution."[105]

Additionally, whereas supporters argued that the referendum would permit a diversity of policy outcomes, critics pointed out that there was also a downside associated with diversity. Mr. Nash of Ohio acknowledged that it was often the case "that one portion of the State wanted the enactment of laws, which another portion of the State did not want, and the consequence was a diversity of laws in different counties and even in different townships." In his view, though, this was a development that ought to be discouraged. He noted that "there were at this time some three or four different laws regulating this matter of Temperance in different portions of the State. This whole thing—including the diversity of school laws—was all wrong. There should be but one law for the regulation of any single subject throughout the whole State; and then every man, having his rights in his own county or township, need not feel that he must change or lose his rights by passing from one country or township to another."[106]

Finally, critics of the optional referendum argued, in much the same fashion as critics of the mandatory referendum, that this device would contribute to the recent tendency of legislators to exceed the limited purposes of constitutional government. In this case, critics were concerned that the referendum would be used not so much to legitimize the appropriation of funds for constitutionally questionable purposes, but rather to introduce sumptuary laws that might otherwise be seen as violative of individual liberty. Mr. Reemelin argued,

> Our Senators and our Representatives might, in the legislative halls, argue till doomsday that certain propositions were unconstitutional—the ever ready reply would be, "we will submit it to the people, and their approval shall be the

arbiter between us." However clear and convincing might be the arguments that "the election of tavern keepers by the people," was demoralizing in its character, and that no such power should be granted or exercised by the people at large, still they would be met by the oily tongues of men who prate about the "sovereignty of the people," and the right of the people to decide all questions, while in their hearts they despise the people, expecting only to use them in particular instances for nefarious purposes, and with a view to the exercise of powers which the government itself would not dare to exercise, or from which they were precluded by the terms of the constitution.[107]

The Adoption of the Optional Referendum

These debates over the optional referendum were resolved in different ways in different states. In some cases, convention delegates were sufficiently concerned about the dangers associated with these referendums that they prohibited them in most instances.[108] In other cases, delegates declined to take any action, thereby permitting legislatures to continue issuing referendums, whether binding or advisory, and whether on a statewide or local basis, at least where they were not prohibited by a contrary state court ruling.[109] In still other cases, constitution makers made explicit provision for the legislative submission of certain matters to the residents of various localities,[110] and, with increasing frequency during the late nineteenth and early twentieth centuries, to residents of the state as a whole.[111]

The Popular Initiative and Referendum

In the first two decades of the twentieth century, state constitution makers grew increasingly concerned about still another deficiency in representative government and began to consider additional mechanisms that would permit the popular voice to be expressed even more directly. The chief concern during this period was that particular interests such as railroads and corporations had grown so powerful that they were frequently preventing the passage of legislation favored by a broad majority of the public. Constitution makers who sought to overcome these problems proceeded to draw, in part, on the long-standing Swiss experience with direct democracy, and in part on the states' long-standing experiences with mandatory and optional legislative referendums, and were eventually led to propose the adoption of the popular initiative and referendum.[112]

Debates about the popular initiative and referendum were initially carried out in state legislatures, several of which responded to intense public dissatisfaction with legislative inertia and corruption by proposing constitutional amendments to give these powers to the people. This was the means by which South Dakota in 1898 became the first state to adopt the initiative and referendum, and by which Utah (1900) and Oregon (1902) soon followed suit.

Assorted state legislatures continued to adopt the initiative and referendum during the next two decades, but the issue also surfaced in state conventions. At times (such as in the Oklahoma Convention of 1906–1907 and the Arizona Convention of 1910), delegates debated whether to provide for such institutions in their states' inaugural constitutions. At other times (such as in Michigan in 1907–1908, Ohio in 1912, Massachusetts in 1917–1919, and Illinois in 1920–1922), delegates considered adopting the initiative and referendum as part of wholesale revisions of existing constitutions. At still other times (such as in Nebraska in 1919–1920), delegates debated whether to retain and/or modify initiative and referendum procedures that were already in effect.

The Case for the Initiative and Referendum

Although twentieth-century supporters of the initiative and referendum were concerned to some extent with preventing the enactment of partial legislation, in the same fashion as nineteenth-century supporters of the mandatory referendum, their principal concern—and the distinctive aspect of this Progressive Era movement—was with securing the passage of measures that were favored by the public but blocked in the legislature. Repeatedly during these conventions, delegates pointed to measures that had been bottled up in legislatures for several decades, and were in some cases still pending. Francis Horgan argued in the Massachusetts Convention of 1917–1919:

> The working-men injured in the course of their employment waited sixty-four years for a partial measure of justice in the Workmen's Compensation Act, into which the profit-making insurance companies, through unwise influence on the Legislature, intruded themselves. Working hours for women and children: It has taken over seventy-five years to reduce the hours for women in mills and factories to a point where they work ten hours per day, with Saturday half-holiday. A minimum wage for women and children: Not yet has the Legislature seen fit to protect women and children from exploitation by greedy employers.

One day's rest in seven: Notwithstanding religious sentiment, the demands of humanity and the necessities of health, enormous numbers of men still work seven days per week. The food situation, national and local: With all the agitation, the cost of living has steadily advanced, and it has as yet been impossible to secure any legislation to stop monopoly or speculation. The coal situation: Nine dollars a ton for coal which should sell for $5.50. Forty-nine legislative bodies failed to do anything effective to check the monopolies or the present condition as to consolidations, increase of fares, etc., of street railways. Taxation: A discredited and inequitable system, the Legislature apparently being powerless to remedy it.[113]

In the view of George Horton in the Michigan Convention of 1907–1908, there was no doubt that legislation to remedy these hardships often enjoyed the overwhelming support of the public. Therefore, this was not a case of reformers seeking legislation in advance of public opinion. Rather, legislatures were failing to respond to a demonstrable public desire and support for legislative action. He argued,

The history of legislatures for the recent past decades is prolific with disregard for the prayers of the people. Cases are fresh within the minds of the delegates here, when, notwithstanding the fact that questions pending were so popular with the people that both dominant political parties felt compelled to declare for them in their respective party platforms, yet small combinations of legislators were formed against said reforms, and beyond which and over which the people could not go.[114]

At the root of the problem was the growing influence wielded by corporate interests over representative officials. David Walsh explained in the Massachusetts Convention of 1917–1919:

In the past governments have had to battle against the evil influences of individual selfishness, but we have discovered in the last sixty years the development in our State and Nation of organized human selfishness, great organizations, financial, social and political, more powerful, and even richer than the very State itself. We have found that in our legislative bodies these organized human selfish forces were very powerful and, indeed, at times were able to thwart the will and judgment of the majority.[115]

It was not that early twentieth-century legislators were less trustworthy than their predecessors. Lawton Hemans in the Michigan Convention of 1907–

1908 spoke for many other delegates when he argued that "the average legislator is honest but he yields to the human influences that affect the great
body of the people."[116] Rather, the problem was not with the declining character of public officials but with the increasing capacity of corporate interests
to overpower even the most conscientious representatives. Ex–Illinois governor
Edward Dunne therefore concluded in an address to the Illinois Convention of
1920–1922, "The people have ascertained that at the State Capital in recent
years a third house, not recognized by the laws or Constitution of the State, has
exercised potent and malign influence in the matter of drafting legislation; that
contaminating lobbies, financed by corporate influence, have infested legislative
halls and the hotels where legislators live, and have influenced the legislators by
sinister arguments delivered in closets and bathrooms, behind closed doors."[117]

In the view of many delegates, reports of legislative corruption had become
sufficiently widespread that representative institutions could no longer be viewed
as functioning effectively. Thus Edward Niles in the New Hampshire Convention of 1902 took note of an oft-expressed view at the turn of the twentieth century that "government of the people, by the people, and for the people, *has,* in
fact, to some extent, perished from the earth, so far at least as New Hampshire
is concerned, and that there has been established here, by the apparent consent
of the governed, a government of the people, *by the railroads, and for the railroads.*"[118] Nor had the situation improved appreciably two decades later, when
Justin Wellman observed in the New Hampshire Convention of 1918–1923:
"In our Commonwealth the legislative machinery is entrusted to representative bodies who are nominally under public or popular control. Their output,
however, with the exception of constitutional amendments, are not under public
control. This lack of popular control is a fundamental defect in the machinery
of government, which the growth of modern industrial combinations and their
concomitant influence upon legislation has revealed."[119]

Theoretically, the people retained control over representative institutions
through their ability to replace wayward representatives; in practice, however,
representative elections were too blunt an instrument to give the people any sort
of effective control over the lawmaking process. As James Brennan noted in the
same convention,

An obnoxious law may be passed, or the legislature may refuse to pass a bill
the people desire[,] and the people as a whole have absolutely no power in the
world to get rid of the one or have the benefit of the other. To be sure they can

make it an issue in some future campaign and elect a legislature that may be more responsive to the popular will, but this at best is admittedly a long extended and uncertain process.[120]

Moreover, as Henry Heald pointed out in the Michigan Convention of 1907–1908, there was no guarantee that the new representatives would be any more successful than their predecessors in resisting the insidious influence of corporate interests. In modern representative bodies, "every possible influence is being brought to bear upon these men—and I know it from my own experience—to break their pledges. There is used the specious argument that others may be elected the next time in their places," but it would only be a matter of time before "a sufficient number will be persuaded to go back on their pledges."[121] Nor was there any indication that various efforts on the part of previous reformers to limit corporate influence had proven to be effective. To be sure, steps had been taken to try to prevent lobbyists from influencing representatives during the legislative session or on the chamber floor, but these efforts had met with few apparent results. As Mr. Dunne of Illinois argued, "We attempted by resolutions in the legislature to drive from the anterooms and corridors of the State House the insidious lobbies that were mutilating and sometimes defiling the people's will. . . . It simply resulted in driving the lobbyists into the hotels and apartments, where members of the legislature dwelt during sessions of the legislature."[122]

The remedy to which delegates increasingly turned during this period was the adoption of the popular initiative and referendum, which was seen as increasing the likelihood that legislatures would respond to the public interest rather than particular interests. As George Duncan argued in the New Hampshire Convention of 1912, legislators "are not unworthy of trust, but sometimes they are a little deaf, and the initiative and referendum gives the legislature a hearing trumpet, so they can hear clearly what the people want."[123] In part, the mere presence of these institutions was expected to prevent the legislature from acting against the public interest, by supplementing existing checks such as the gubernatorial veto and judicial review, and thereby providing such additional "checks and balances as will tend to subordinate private interests to public,—to make legislation as far as possible in the general public interest," in the words of George Anderson in the Massachusetts Convention of 1917–1919.[124] Additionally, in case legislators did act in such a way that betrayed the public, these institutions would permit the people to overturn such errant decisions. As Matthew Hale explained in the same convention, the problem was, "How can a principal retain his power over the agent, because of course the people as a whole cannot constantly get together and say they do not like what the agents are doing? There has got to be some mechanism for carrying out that principle." And the solution was to adopt the initiative and referendum, which "provides that a certain proportion of the population of the State,—if it is dissatisfied with the acts of the representatives, and if it thinks that the principals if they had a chance to vote upon this question would reach a different conclusion from what the agents have reached,—shall have a right to take an appeal from the agents to the principals."[125]

Supporters of these devices maintained that the initiative and referendum were best understood as a continuation of long-standing efforts to ensure representation of the public interest. Floyd Post pointed out in the Michigan Convention of 1907–1908 that the referendum had already been used in "numerous laws permitting the people to settle many local questions themselves—such as local option on the liquor question and nomination by primary election, self-government by school districts, etc., and what the people now ask is, that this right be extended by provision in the proposed Constitution so that they may initiate, if need be, and have referred to them, if they do desire, any legislation."[126] In addition, George Latchford in the Illinois Convention of 1920–1922 noted that Illinois had already made use of the referendum on "State bond issues," and on "city charters, on local bond issues, on franchises, and other local questions," and for the last two decades the state had also resorted to "the advisory referendum." Therefore, "the I&R are common institutions in Illinois and have been for years. They were not the result of a theory at all, but of conditions which the people were trying to meet in a practical way. Experience was the guide in the making of the Initiative and Referendum in its dozen different forms in this State. And it is practical experience that has made the plan we present to you necessary and desirable."[127]

In fact, several delegates argued that the initiative and referendum could be understood as a logical outgrowth of not only nineteenth-century institutional developments, but also eighteenth-century founding principles. George Clyde in the New Hampshire Convention of 1902 described these direct democratic devices as "not a breaking away from the old, but the bringing of our whole fabric of government into larger fulness in accord with that great foundation principle that all just governments among men derive their power from the consent of the governed. A carrying out of that principle to meet the changed conditions."[128] He argued that "if the fathers could speak out of their graves they would say . . . 'Apply the principles we used in new forms if necessary to meet your conditions that you may enjoy and secure the blessing God has given you through the inventive genius of men and do not be thwarted in your purposes by the power of corporate wealth.'"[129]

Viewed in this fashion, the initiative and referendum would serve not to replace, but rather to supplement and perfect, representative institutions. It was important to keep in mind, C. Petrus Peterson argued in the Nebraska Convention of 1919–1920, that these devices would not be used very often, because "the failure of a majority to find adequate machinery and a means of expressing through representative institutions, is the exception and not the rule." As a result, "we shall continue in the future as we have in the past, to place our major reliance upon representative government as distinguished from pure democracy for arriving at our legislative decisions."[130] In addition, as Frank Hobbs argued in the New Hampshire Convention of 1912, within a few years' time, the initiative and referendum would likely be used even less frequently, because they would exert "an indirect, as well as a direct, influence, and when the system is fully established and the people thoroughly understand it, it is not likely to be employed often, because those elected to represent the people will be more in sympathy with their constituents."[131]

To be sure, delegates occasionally went beyond these arguments and claimed that the initiative and referendum would have additional benefits other than overcoming special interests, and therefore that these procedures might be used on a routine basis. For instance, Harriet Treadwell, an invited speaker at the Illinois Convention of 1920–1922, took note of the educational benefits of the initiative and referendum. She argued that they offered "a universal opportunity for education. It really is a university of the public where the men and the women will go to school to study the laws; that is, the laws that we present to them, and instead of talking twaddle over the dinner table they will begin to talk about what is worth while. I look upon it as a liberal education for the people to have a chance to discuss the laws."[132] Meanwhile, Mr. Brennan of New Hampshire thought that the initiative and referendum would help to "develop a sense of personal responsibility for governmental action in the heart of every citizen. . . . When we have the privilege, as we propose, of participating directly in every piece of constructive legislation, we would feel that we are really worth something as citizens."[133] To the extent that the case for the initiative and referendum rested on these sorts of arguments, there would be little reason to limit their use to exceptional cases. Rather, it would make sense to maximize the benefits of direct democracy by permitting the people to pass judgment on routine issues of public policy, and perhaps even to decide most—or even all—questions of governance, and thus dispense with legislatures altogether.

For the most part, though, delegates advanced a more modest set of arguments (rooted in the benefits of overcoming the influence of special interests), and they expected that the initiative and referendum would be used in a limited class of cases, primarily when special interests prevailed over the public interest in the legislative process. Delegates were generally inclined to agree with Mr. Duncan of New Hampshire that "no advocate of the initiative and referendum, so far as I know, has ever advocated doing away with representative government. We only ask that representative government shall be representative."[134] Albert Washburn in the Massachusetts Convention of 1917–1919 therefore made it clear that "I, for one, do not want to substitute direct government for representative government. Conceding that representative government has sometimes been misrepresentative, that the Legislature may sometimes misrepresent, I am interested only in the creation of a reserve power which will enable the people in the last resort to express their deliberate will."[135] Along these lines, A. Ross Read concluded in the Ohio Convention of 1912, "The statement that it will destroy representative government is preposterous. Instead of a destroyer of representative government, we offer you its conservator, with power to rescue it from the selfish, crafty schemers who manipulate it to secure special privileges. We propose means to free it from annoyance and danger and make it more representative, more stable, and more reliable."[136]

The Case against the Initiative and Referendum

Opponents of the initiative and referendum took issue with each of these claims, beginning with the claim that these institutions could be viewed as consistent with the traditional concept of representation. Critics were particularly hard-pressed to accept the contention that these devices could be reconciled with the principles adhered to by the eighteenth-century founders of republican government in the United States. Thus Samuel Kingan in the Arizona Convention of 1910 quoted at length from Federalist No. 10 and concluded, "A republican form of government has always been distinguished from a democratic form of government. . . . A republic is a government by representation, a democracy a government by the people acting directly. These distinctions were well understood by the founders of this government."[137] Nearly as difficult for the critics to accept was the contention that the popular initiative and referendum were a logical extension of the legislative referendums of the nineteenth century. In the view of Humphrey Jones in the Ohio Convention of 1912, it was true that nineteenth-century constitution makers had frequently required financial matters to be referred to the people and had occasionally permitted the legislature to submit controversial issues for popular resolution. He was therefore willing to admit that the legislative referendum was "an essential and invaluable feature of representative government." But he was equally convinced that "the direct initiation of laws, passing laws directly by the people, cannot be employed in any form or in any manner without an abandonment of representative government."[138] In the words of Nathan McDonald in the Nebraska Convention of 1919–1920, "It is, and must be admitted to be, an undermining of the fundamental principles upon which our state government is based and established."[139]

One of the critics' main concerns was that citizens were too ill-informed to vote directly on legislation, and that this would lead to the passage of ill-advised measures. Henry Walbridge in the Michigan Convention of 1907–1908 argued that "if mistakes, errors and fraud have been committed by the legislature, it seems to me that there is far greater danger along this line when the law-making power is vested in the people at large." In fact, he was convinced that few people would "leave their business and avocations of life to vote upon questions of this kind and character when submitted to them," and as a result, "we would have laws made and passed by a very small percent or minority of the electorate."[140]

Even if the people could be persuaded to turn out to vote on these measures, the critics argued, one need only look at the various experiences with the initiative and referendum to get a sense of the difficulties that even the most public-spirited citizens would encounter in casting an informed vote. Oregon made more extensive use of these institutions than any other state during the Progressive Era, and critics found fault with several aspects of the Oregon experience.[141] For instance, Charles Choate in the Massachusetts Convention of 1917–1919 sought to draw lessons from the 1908 Oregon election, where voters approved two seemingly conflicting initiatives concerning fishing on the Columbia River. As he explained, "One set of men at one part of the river caught fish, salmon, by one method, the weir I believe, another upon the upper reach of the river caught the salmon in traps or nets. Each wanted to stop the other from exercising the privilege he was enjoying. Each initiated a law. Both went to the people and both were passed." When he considered "the possibilities of absurdity, the possibilities of irrational results" of this sort, he found it difficult to believe that his fellow delegates wanted to entrust such matters to the voters.[142] In similar fashion, John Riley in the Ohio Convention of 1912 called attention to the 1910 Oregon election, when "thirty-two measures were submitted to the people under the initiative and referendum at one election. They covered two hundred pages, law-book size. Please think for a moment of the utter impracticability of the voters of average intelligence and education marking a ballot with any discriminating judgment in the time given at the polls!"[143]

Another danger of permitting the people to initiate legislation was that this would permit fewer opportunities for deliberation or compromise. It was true that the process would be deliberate, in that much time would necessarily elapse between the date that an initiative or referendum petition was first circulated and the day that the vote was actually held. But insofar as deliberation also required opportunities for compromise and amendment, the initiative and referendum process would be inadequate. In the words of Henry Campbell in the Michigan Convention of 1907–1908,

> The initiative method offers no opportunity for consultation or deliberation respecting the matters to be acted upon. Whatever is proposed must be voted upon precisely as presented, without modification or change. The agitator may write his law or amendment, and if he induces a sufficient number of people to sign his petition, it goes directly to a vote, without possibility of change, and with only such discussion as chance may offer or the newspapers may choose to give it.[144]

Still another concern was that popular majorities might trample on minority rights, especially at times when passions were inflamed. Mr. McDonald of Nebraska wondered whether there would be occasions

> when the people were angered or stirred with some emotion that soon would pass away, by which they would be willing to annul that right of religious freedom to you and to me? They would not do it in time of sober judgment with time to deliberate and discuss, they would not do it then, but in the passing hour, when the feelings are stirred, when emotion is high. . . . I have seen the time within the past few years when I fear that a substantial number of the people of our state would be deprived of their liberties under this Constitution if the movement had been started at the critical moment.[145]

To be sure, opponents were unable to cite any particular instances when the initiative process had actually been used in this fashion during the first two decades of its operation, but as Mr. Jones of Ohio argued, anyone familiar with human nature and its "weaknesses," "frailties," and "passions," would "know there is no power that may be so tyrannical on occasion as the power of a mere majority."[146]

Opponents also feared that the initiative and referendum would do little to achieve their intended goal of combating special-interest influence, and they might actually enable special interests to more readily secure enactment of their favored policies. When Felix Streyckmans, an invited speaker at the Illinois Convention of 1920–1922, pondered the question of "who would control legislation under the I and R," he thought it unlikely that it would be "the little member of the little organization." It was far more likely to be "the great interests."[147] In fact, as David Cunningham concluded in the Ohio Convention of 1912, the initiative and referendum would permit "every well organized interest, such as single tax, socialistic measures, corporations and kindred interests, by concentrating upon a single law where a number are submitted to have their pet measures pass, thus putting a dangerous power in the hands of selfish interests, bringing about the very danger its friends are professing to try to avoid."[148] The logic of this position, as John Brackett explained in the Massachusetts Convention of 1917–1919, was that "representatives of 'invisible government'" were likely to "take advantage" of the initiative process by crafting

> a bill which ostensibly will be for the benefit of the public but which is really in the interest of some scheme by which the promoters seek to enrich themselves at the expense of the rest of the people. . . . They then send out their paid agents to secure the requisite twenty thousand or twenty-five thousand signers to the petition. Then it is submitted to the people and the people are induced by the influences referred to to enact it.[149]

The Adoption of the Initiative and Referendum

When the popular initiative and referendum were proposed in early twentieth-century conventions, the resulting debates were generally, although not always, resolved in favor of the supporters. In fact, "in the sixteen years between 1902 and 1918, over two-fifths of the states then in the union adopted the initiative,"[150] and by the end of the twentieth century, the statutory initiative and/or referendum were in place in a total of twenty-four states.[151] In some instances, though, convention delegates took account of the critics' concerns when drafting initiative and referendum procedures. Thus some states set relatively high signature requirements before measures could be placed on the ballot (as much as 15 percent of the voters in the last election, in the case of Wyoming).[152] Several states chose to provide for the indirect initiative, so that measures are first submitted to the legislature, which has the option of approving them or placing them on the ballot, and in some cases amending them.[153] In still other states, the initiative and referendum process cannot be used to adopt particular types of measures (such as the single tax, as in Ohio),[154] or to address issues covered in particular aspects of the constitution (such as the judiciary, religious institutions, declaration of rights, or legislative appropriations, as in Massachusetts).[155]

Conclusion

The principal benefit of analyzing the state convention debates regarding the concept of representation is that it becomes possible to view the adoption of direct democratic institutions as the product of a sustained confrontation with, and rejection of, Madison's argument in favor of relying solely on representative institutions. State constitution makers concluded, in the first place, that Madison was too sanguine about the capacity of representative institutions to combat the problem of minority faction. Madison had written that "if a faction consists of less than a majority, relief is supplied by the republican principle, which enables the majority to defeat its sinister views by regular vote: It may clog the administration, it may convulse the society; but it will be unable to execute and mask its violence under the forms of the Constitution." However, state constitution makers determined that particular groups could occasionally be successful in securing the passage of legislation adverse to the public interest or preventing the passage of public-interest legislation. Second, state constitution makers concluded that Madison was excessively optimistic about the capacity of representative institutions "to refine and enlarge the public views," such that "the public voice, pronounced by the representatives of the people, will be more consonant to the public good, than if pronounced by the people themselves." To be sure, this was one possible effect of creating distance between the people and their representatives. However, state constitution makers argued that another effect of such an institutional design was to enable office holders to advance their own interests at the expense of the public interest. Third, state constitution makers argued that Madison had given insufficient consideration to the possibility that representative institutions might be incapable of resolving certain controversial issues, because the people's representatives would be unwilling or unable to address these issues in a fashion that would be deemed legitimate by the people. In each of these cases, therefore, state constitution makers identified a deficiency in the operation of representative institutions that could not be remedied by relying solely on existing institutional arrangements.

A complete evaluation of the direct democratic devices to which state constitution makers turned in order to remedy these problems would, of course, require an examination of the operation of these institutions and a determination of whether the critics' fears have been realized. One would want to consider the possibility—raised by several convention delegates—that the mandatory referendum has actually contributed to increased appropriations and debt levels, because legislators have become more willing to approve projects that they know will be submitted to the voters. One would also want to determine whether the optional referendum has actually made it easier for legislators to avoid taking responsibility for addressing controversial issues, as several opponents predicted. In addition, it would be important to measure the extent to which the popular initiative and referendum have produced legislation that is poorly drafted, violative of minority rights, or in the service of particular interests.

Although these sorts of empirical studies can ultimately go a long way toward determining the merits of these various direct democratic institutions, a complete evaluation should also take account of the reasons why state constitution makers adopted these institutions. As we have seen, state constitution makers have had frequent opportunities to reconsider the logic of governing institutions and to revise these institutions in light of their accumulated experience and wisdom through the years. Understood in this fashion, the adoption of direct democratic institutions at the state level was not the result of instinctive and undeliberative acts, but rather was the product of long-standing concerns about deficiencies in representative institutions and a belief that existing institutional arrangements were incapable of remedying these problems. Consequently, the arguments from various state conventions in favor of direct democratic institutions are at least entitled to be placed alongside Madison's arguments in *The Federalist* about the superiority of representative institutions, and in many ways they deserve to be considered a more authentic expression of the accumulated wisdom and experience of the American constitutional tradition in this area.

SEPARATION OF POWERS

The separation of powers system at the federal level has been relatively stable and unchallenged throughout American history. Delegates to the
federal convention established a presidential, rather than a parliamentary, system, and no serious challenges have been mounted to this arrangement. It was
determined that the executive would be elected and wield power independently
of the legislature; and although several constitutional changes have been made
to particular aspects of the executive branch, its composition and powers have
not been the subject of important constitutional revision. Also in place from the
founding era is a judiciary whose members are nominated by the president and
confirmed by the Senate, and who did not take long to make good on the widespread expectation that they would exercise the power of judicial review.[1]

When we turn to the states, we find that the broad outlines of the separation of powers systems are similar in most respects to the federal system, but
that state constitution makers have also been willing to challenge and reject
several aspects of the federal model.[2] There are, of course, several oft-noted and
well-studied ways in which states have challenged the federal model, primarily

in regard to the selection of executive and judicial officers. Many states elect assorted executive officials whose federal counterparts are appointed to their posts.[3] And (in a development that has been particularly well explored through studies of state convention debates) most states have departed from the federal model of judicial selection, whether by electing judges, making them stand for retention elections, or selecting them by the legislature.[4]

What has generally received less scholarly attention are the ways that state constitution makers have challenged the federal model in regard to the powers of the executive and judiciary.[5] The executive veto has been the subject of considerable debate in state conventions.[6] In the early nineteenth century, many state constitution makers either delayed adoption of the executive veto or enacted a weaker version than the federal model by permitting legislative overrides upon less than a two-thirds vote. Then, in a move that has attracted much scholarly interest, beginning in the mid-nineteenth century, state constitution makers changed course and adopted an even stronger version of the executive veto than at the federal level, primarily by enacting the item veto. Meanwhile, judicial review came under attack in the early twentieth century, when state constitution makers debated whether to abolish the power or to restrict its exercise, including by requiring a supermajority of judges to invalidate legislation or providing for the recall of judges or judicial decisions.[7]

In each of these cases, state constitution makers were reacting to developments that were present at the state and federal level and that prompted parallel proposals at the federal level. Thus, beginning in the early nineteenth century, proposals were introduced at the federal level to abolish the executive veto or provide for a majority legislative override.[8] Then, from the late nineteenth century onward, Congress has considered item veto amendments and, for a brief period in the late twentieth century, provided for the item veto on a statutory basis.[9] Meanwhile, federal amendments to abolish or restrict judicial review have been proposed on several occasions.[10] However, because of the flexibility of state amendment processes, in contrast with the rigidity of the federal amendment process, these reform proposals were given serious consideration, and in some cases adopted, only at the state level.

The lesson to be drawn from these state convention debates is that the American constitutional tradition encompasses a broader conception of the executive and judicial veto powers than is evident from a study of the federal constitution alone. In fact, constitution makers have concluded that developments since the founding era required changes in the form of the executive veto and judicial review in order to remain faithful to the original purposes that these institutions were intended to serve. Given that state constitution makers have had more frequent opportunities than their federal counterparts to respond to these developments and to implement institutional reforms, a strong case can be made for viewing these distinctive state institutions as a more authentic expression of the accumulated wisdom and experience of the American constitutional tradition.

In the case of efforts to weaken the executive veto, early nineteenth-century constitution makers were responding to developments that appeared to render the veto no longer necessary, whether to prevent legislative encroachments on the executive or to overturn hasty or inadvertent legislation. The first of these goals was no longer seen as a pressing concern because of the enhanced stature of the executive; in any event, this concern could be addressed in other ways, such as through the exercise of judicial review. Meanwhile, to the extent that the second goal was recognized as legitimate (and there was much debate on this point), it could be achieved without requiring a supermajority legislative override.

In the case of later efforts to strengthen the executive veto, late nineteenth- and twentieth-century constitution makers were primarily seeking to restore what they took to be the original balance of power between the legislative and executive branches. In their view, this balance had been upset by several developments, particularly the increasing resort to omnibus bills and the growing use of legislative riders. Accordingly, the item veto was proposed and frequently enacted in order to combat these legislative devices and permit the executive to once again wield the veto power effectively.

In the case of efforts to weaken judicial review, early twentieth-century constitution makers were seeking to restore a proper balance between the legislative and judicial branches. In their view, state and federal judges had begun exercising judicial review in ways that were not intended by the founders, particularly by striking down laws for reasons of policy rather than constitutionality. Proposals to require a supermajority for the exercise of judicial review or to permit the recall of judges or judicial decisions were envisioned as a response to this development and a restoration of the original balance of power between these branches.

The Executive Veto

Delegates to the federal convention generally agreed on the need for an executive veto, although there were disagreements about the specific form that the power should take. For instance, James Madison sought several times to permit the veto to be wielded by the president together with the Supreme Court justices, in a fashion that resembled the veto wielded by the Council of Revision under the New York Constitution of 1777. A majority of delegates preferred, however, to vest the veto power solely in the executive, thereby following the Massachusetts Constitution of 1780. There was also a question of whether to provide for an absolute or qualified veto. Alexander Hamilton preferred an absolute veto, of the kind that had been exercised in South Carolina from 1776 to 1778; but most delegates supported a qualified veto that could be overridden by the legislature. The resolution of this issue in favor of a qualified veto led, in turn, to the question of how many votes would be required for a legislative override. After initially deciding that vetoes could be overridden by a two-thirds vote of both houses, as was the practice in Massachusetts, the federal convention then moved to raise the bar even higher by requiring a three-fourths vote, before reverting to a two-thirds requirement.[11]

The framers of the federal constitution also generally concurred about the purpose of the executive veto. It would primarily be used to overturn legislative acts that encroached on the executive and thereby violated the constitutional division of powers.[12] As Hamilton explained in Federalist No. 73, "The primary inducement to conferring the power in question upon the executive is to enable him to defend himself."[13] Noting that "the propensity of the legislative department to intrude upon the rights, and to absorb the powers, of the other departments has been already more than once suggested," he concluded that few could doubt "the propriety of a negative, either absolute or qualified, in the executive upon the acts of the legislative branches."[14] Although this was the primary purpose of providing for the veto power, Hamilton also took note of a "secondary" purpose, which was "to increase the chances in favor of the community against the passing of bad laws, through haste, inadvertence, or design."[15] As he went on to explain, "The oftener the measure is brought under examination, the greater the diversity in the situations of those who are to examine it, the less must be the danger of those errors which flow from want of due deliberation, or of those missteps which proceed from the contagion of some common passion or interest."[16]

Although little attention was given to the design of the presidential veto power in the ensuing several decades, state constitution makers remained divided over the need for an executive veto and the form it should take. Several states followed the Massachusetts Constitution of 1780 in adopting an executive veto with a two-thirds legislative override. Other states chose to provide for the veto but to follow the Kentucky Constitution of 1799 in permitting a majority over-ride. Still other states did not provide for the veto in any form.[17]

It was not until the 1820s and 1830s that state constitution makers began to engage in extended debates about the veto and its proper form. In part, this reconsideration was a product of long-term developments, such as the increasingly strong position of the executive and the growing use of judicial review at both the federal and state level. Both of these developments suggested that the veto was no longer necessary to prevent the passage of unconstitutional legislation. In part, also, this reconsideration was due to particular events, such as the issuance of several prominent presidential vetoes for policy reasons. These vetoes for reasons of policy—Andrew Jackson's veto of the national bank reauthorization was the most prominent, but far from the only, example—led many state constitution makers to conclude that the veto power was inconsistent with republican government, and at the least, that a majority legislative override would be more consistent with republicanism. However, supporters of the federal model responded to each of these claims, by arguing that the executive veto was still needed to overturn unconstitutional as well as unwise legislation and by showing that these goals could only be met by providing for a two-thirds legislative override.

The Case for Weakening the Executive Veto

Nineteenth-century convention delegates who sought to weaken the executive veto argued that the primary, and—in the eyes of some—the sole, purpose of the veto was to prevent unconstitutional legislative actions. For the most part, delegates expected these unconstitutional actions to come, if at all, in the form of encroachments on the executive branch. As Henry Green noted in the New Jersey Convention of 1844, "This principle was incorporated in that instrument, Hamilton tells us in the Federalist, as a protection of the Executive against the legislature, and that it would never be resorted to but for that purpose, and in the last extremity."[18] Several delegates also took note of the possibility that the legislature might invade the province of the judiciary. As Edward Bradford argued in the Delaware Convention of 1896–1897,

> What is the true nature, what is the legitimate function of the veto power in this Country, and in this age? Various reasons have been assigned in times past for

the existence of the veto power. One, that the prerogatives of the Crown should not be encroached upon. In latter times, and in this Country, that the Legislative Branch of the Government should not encroach upon the Judicial Department on the one hand, on the Executive Department on the other hand.[19]

By the mid-nineteenth century, however, some delegates were prepared to conclude that the governor no longer needed the veto to ward off legislative encroachments. Delegates pointed out that the executive had become stronger by virtue of being directly elected by the people and making extensive use of the patronage power. Several delegates, such as Mr. Green of New Jersey, were not convinced that legislative encroachments had ever posed a threat to the executive, but to the extent that they had, governors were now strong enough to protect themselves without resorting to the veto. As he explained,

> We all know that its object was originally to protect the Executive, and this idea of protecting the people is a modern idea to make the principle more palatable. The object is to protect the Executive. Our Executive has been weak enough. Has he ever needed protection from legislative encroachment? The evil has never been experienced here. I have yet to learn that the people of New Jersey have ever thought the legislature had usurped the powers of the Executive.[20]

Moreover, these delegates concluded that the veto was no longer necessary in light of the growing power of the judiciary and the increasing exercise of judicial review, which offered an alternative means of invalidating unconstitutional acts. As Peter Livingston noted in the New York Convention of 1821, "It had been asked where was the security against an infraction of the rights and liberties of the people? He answered, the shield between the rights of citizens and the encroachments of legislative power, was an independent and upright judiciary."[21] This view was echoed by Daniel Tompkins, who presided over the same convention while also serving as U.S. vice president: "There can be no use for a veto on the passing of laws, but to prevent violations of the constitution; and for this purpose your judicial tribunals are sufficient. If laws, encroaching on the independence of the executive or judicial departments, should be enacted, or such as violated any private rights, they would be void, and it would be in the power of the courts to declare them so."[22]

Not only did judicial review offer an alternative means of invalidating unconstitutional legislation, but the judiciary was actually better positioned than the executive to perform this role. In part, this was because constitutional interpretation was seen as the peculiar province of the judiciary. As Horace Biddle argued in the Indiana Convention of 1850–1851, "Shall the Governor say that a law is unconstitutional? No, sir. That is a judicial question, and we have a department expressly to decide it."[23] In addition, as William West explained in the Ohio Convention of 1873–1874, the executive was markedly ill-suited to make determinations about the constitutionality of legislation:

> It is urged that to clothe the Executive with the power of vetoing or prohibiting the passage of laws will prevent unconstitutional legislation. . . . We must look, however, Mr. President, to the facts and circumstances that surround the gubernatorial election, and the character of the incumbent. As a general rule, he is not selected with a view to his profound learning in constitutional law. He is not intended, designed or supposed to be one that has experience and skill in the mysteries of constitutional interpretation. . . . Is it not sufficient that we have a judicial tribunal, open at all times, to which application shall be made, whose decisions are final, whose interpretations shall be enforced, and shall become a rule of law, and of the Constitution?[24]

At the same time that institutional developments were prompting constitution makers to doubt that the veto was necessary to prevent unconstitutional acts, high-profile presidential vetoes were leading them to question the propriety of vetoes for reasons of policy. For the framers of the federal constitution, this had been seen as, at most, a secondary purpose of the veto, and for the first several decades of the operation of the federal government, this expectation had been generally borne out in that presidential vetoes were rarely issued for policy reasons.[25] President Jackson's veto of the bank bill in 1832, however, focused attention on the legitimacy of vetoes for policy reasons, and subsequent vetoes by presidents John Tyler, James Polk, and Andrew Johnson sparked additional controversy and ensured that the debate would continue for the next several decades.[26] Although a good deal of this debate took place at the national level, with congressional critics decrying these vetoes and calling for reforms of the presidential veto, the effects were also felt at the state level, where state constitution makers argued that these national developments were also pertinent to debates about the gubernatorial veto.

Repeatedly in these nineteenth-century conventions, delegates argued that presidents' issuance of vetoes for policy reasons were a clear departure from the original justification for the power. Thus George Brown in the Texas Convention of 1845 concluded that "if I understood its history correctly, the veto power was engrafted then with the idea, that the legislature having all powers, would be making constant aggressions on the Executive; and that he should have this in order to repel them. But, sir, the power has been extended far beyond this: it has been applied in many cases not appropriate for its exercise."[27] He argued that "the principle perhaps would never have been incorporated into the Constitution of the United States, if it had been foreseen, that so far from the Legislative Department trespassing upon the Executive, the Executive would be eternally intruding upon the Legislature."[28]

There was, to be sure, a good deal of disagreement about which president bore primary responsibility for this departure from the founders' intentions, which had in turn emboldened governors in their issuance of such policy vetoes. Many delegates sided with Andrew McCallen of the Illinois Convention of 1847 in pinpointing President Jackson (1829–1837) as the leading culprit. McCallen was concerned with the policy consequences of Jackson's bank veto, which had led to more "state banks, which had produced an inflation of the currency, and a desire to speculate; out of that desire had grown the internal improvement speculation—and then had come the ruin. All of this he attributed to the veto of the charter of the United States Bank." But he was equally upset about the precedent that had been set in regard to the exercise of the veto power. He "denounced the veto power as one giving the executive an authority to encroach on the legislative department, which he said had been done gradually by every President since the first exercise of it."[29]

Other delegates charged President Tyler (1841–1845) with legitimating the issuance of vetoes for reasons of expediency. Ira Harris in the New York Convention of 1846 argued that even Jackson's vetoes were still grounded to some degree in considerations of constitutionality, but the same could not be said of Tyler's vetoes:

> Before General Washington would resort to it, he required the written opinions of Mr. Jefferson, Mr. Madison, and Mr. Randolph, then Attorney General, that the law, in reference to which it was proposed to exercise this extraordinary power, was clearly unconstitutional. On one other occasion during his eight years administration, and but one, was this power employed by General Washington. Neither the elder Adams nor Mr. Jefferson employed it at all. Mr. Madison vetoed six bills and Mr. Monroe one, during their administrations—always upon the ground that the laws were unconstitutional. Even General Jackson, in his eleven vetoes, had never ventured to place his objections upon other than constitutional grounds.

According to Harris,

> It remained for John Tyler to exercise this prerogative on the ground of *expediency*. It was left for one who had accidentally become President—who had been elevated to that office, without any popular election, by a sad dispensation of Providence, to set up his will against that of the people, and by a series of Executive vetoes to defeat and nullify the whole action of the legislative authority of the Union, with reference to the most important interests of the nation. . . . It is the part of wisdom to profit by experience—and such an abuse of this power in the national Executive admonishes us to beware lest we expose ourselves to the like abuse, by giving too wide a scope for its exercise.[30]

Still other delegates emphasized the way that President Polk (1845–1849) had made increasingly bold use of the veto for policy reasons. As David Woodson argued in the Illinois Convention of 1847, "The veto of Mr. Polk of the western river and harbor bill, has certainly not been approved.—I ask the gentleman to pause and reflect, and tell me whether there has not been one universal voice of condemnation in regard to that veto. Sir, have not men of all parties recently met at Chicago and expressed their disapprobation of the veto of that bill?"[31]

After the Civil War, delegates were particularly apt to focus on the frequent, and just as frequently overridden, vetoes issued by President Johnson (1865–1869). Thus James Bayne proclaimed in the Illinois Convention of 1869–1870, "Veto! If there is any word in the English language that I detest, it is that word, when it is associated with the idea of unlimited power in the hands of one man. It savors too much of despotism for me." He was indignant that "in our boasted republic, an Andrew Johnson could send in his veto messages to congress by the dozen during one session. . . . The consequences might have been very different, for the peace and safety of our country, had there not been two-thirds of the Congress of the United States opposed to the usurpation of power by the President. Let us then learn wisdom by the past, and not put our trust in princes."[32]

Despite their disagreements about which president bore primary responsibility for the prevalence of vetoes for policy reasons, these delegates were generally of one mind about the illegitimacy of the practice. They thought that the founders and the early presidents had, with good reason, eschewed the notion that the executive might substitute its policy views for the deliberate judgment of the people's legislative representatives. Just as one could hardly expect the executive to be better positioned than the judiciary to determine the constitutionality of legislation, they argued, there was little reason to prefer the judgment of the executive to that of the legislature in assessing the wisdom of particular policies. Mr. Green of New Jersey argued, "I know it is a modern doctrine that the Executive is the representative of the people.—But I maintain that for purposes of legislation the Executive is not the representative of the people; but the sovereignty of the people as respects legislation is vested in the legislative branch." He explained, "The governor has been called here the representative of the people. He is so for one purpose—to execute the laws—but he is not the people's representative for making the laws." After all, "at the election of governor the people rarely or never think of selecting him with reference to legislation."[33]

Still to be determined were the specific steps to be taken in response to these various developments. Some delegates so opposed the veto power that they argued against its inclusion in any form in state constitutions. Thus several states that had not yet adopted the veto were urged during the nineteenth century to continue to refrain from doing so. For instance, Henry Farnandis in the Maryland Convention of 1867

> did not think that it was necessary in our case to give the veto power to the Governor. . . . The reasons set forth why the veto power should be possessed are to prevent the Legislature from encroaching on the Executive, and the dangers of hasty legislation. As to the first, no instance could be cited in the history of Maryland where either one or the other department attempted to encroach on the other. As to hasty legislation, guards had already been placed.[34]

In similar fashion, Daniel Corbit in the Delaware Convention of 1852–1853 claimed that "the introduction of a veto power in the State of Delaware, would be one of the most odious features which we could possibly insert in the Constitution. . . . I consider it an anomaly in the government of a republic, that the opinion of one man should put down the united opinions of the direct representatives of the people."[35] Rufus Ranney in the Ohio Convention of 1850–1851 was "unhesitatingly brought to the conclusion, that the veto power ought not to find a place in the constitution, in any case whatever."[36] Meanwhile, in several states where the veto had already been adopted, the call was put forth to abolish the power. For instance, Mr. Biddle of Indiana urged the reconsideration of an earlier decision to provide for the veto, on the grounds that the veto was "an unnatural plant to free soil. It was transplanted to America from a crown, and far better does it become a monarchy; but even there it has died out. It is not indigenous to American soil, and I trust its last root may be extirpated." He thought the power was "an anomaly in a free government, and ought not to find a place in an American State."[37]

Another group of delegates supported reform of the veto, rather than its abolition. In particular, they sought to permit legislative overrides upon the vote of a mere majority (or seven-twelfths or three-fifths, or some other fraction less than two-thirds). The logic of this position, according to Mr. Bradford of Delaware, was that although the veto might not be necessary to prevent unconstitutional legislation or to overturn the deliberate policy judgment of the legislature, it might still serve as a useful check "to be interposed against hasty and improvident legislation." This purpose, in his view, was distinct from any intent to empower the "Governor to defeat the will of the people when that will, through their chosen representatives, is expressed after full opportunity of examination and reconsideration, and a close scrutiny." And this goal could be fully satisfied by permitting "a majority of all the Members elected to each House, after mature consideration and deliberation, to override the veto power of the Governor upon the principle of majority rule, after having had full light thrown upon the subject and ample opportunity to discuss, examine, and reconsider the measure."[38] Jacob Ferris in the Michigan Convention of 1867 reached the same conclusion, explaining, "The only object I can conceive of in preserving the veto power is, that it may be a check upon hasty and inconsiderate legislation, upon legislation under excitement, without that due and proper deliberation which the public interests require. It does not seem to me to be possible that any gentleman can desire to preserve the veto power for the purpose of overruling the deliberate and considerate action of the Legislature."[39] Therefore, he supported a majority, rather than a two-thirds, legislative override.

In the view of these delegates, a majority-override provision not only fulfilled the sole legitimate purpose of the veto (calling attention to hastily enacted legislation), but it also adhered to principles of republicanism. As William Beckner argued in the Kentucky Convention of 1890–1891, "The veto power is given simply for the purpose of calling the attention of the Legislature to inadvertences; to mistakes or to errors it may commit through want of proper consideration, and not to give the Governor more power than the General Assembly has; or, in other words, the people through the representatives have."[40] As William Saulsbury argued in the Delaware Convention of 1896–1897, "What we want in an Executive veto then is, more than anything else, to send the matter back to the Legislature and require them to consider it again. Any other Executive veto, I think, in a State like this, especially with the sentiments of our people and our past history, is utterly unwarranted."[41]

Still a final group of delegates argued that the veto power should be retained but with different override requirements depending on whether laws were invalidated on constitutional grounds or for policy reasons. In the view of some delegates, such as William Dodge in the New York Convention of 1821, vetoes of unconstitutional bills were entitled to more protection than vetoes of hasty or inadvertent bills. Accordingly, he sought "to require two-thirds of the members of both houses, to pass bills that may have been returned by the governor, only in cases when the objections were of a constitutional nature. In cases of bills being returned on grounds of inexpediency, or as being detrimental to the public good, the amendment would require only a bare majority to pass them, notwithstanding."[42] In contrast, his colleague Ezekiel Bacon was willing to establish different override requirements, but he disagreed about which vetoes were in particular need of protection. He would

> prefer to reverse the proposition, and require a majority of two-thirds where the objections related solely to the expediency of a bill, and a bare majority only when they were on constitutional grounds, and for this obvious reason;—constitutional difficulties it was always within the competence of the judiciary power to correct; and should a law clearly unconstitutional, at any time make its way through all branches of the legislature, there was still a redeeming power left by an appeal to the judiciary.[43]

The Case against Weakening the Executive Veto

Critics of the executive veto were met with responses at each of the nineteenth-century conventions in which the issue was raised. Delegates who supported the veto in the same form as at the federal level argued, in the first place, that such a power was still needed in order to prevent unconstitutional legislation. In response to those who considered legislative encroachments on the executive and judicial branches to be a thing of the past, William Minshall in the Illinois Convention of 1847 contended that "the legislative department has constantly encroached upon the province of the executive; and that is almost always the case with State legislatures, they being the active branch and concentrating the sovereignty of the people." He pointed out, "Did not the legislature take from the governor the appointment of prosecuting attorneys, and various other privileges which had been originally conferred upon him? . . . The veto power, then, is necessary to enable the executive by the exercise of this negative power, to protect itself and its co-ordinate department from the encroachments of the legislature."[44] On this view, depriving the executive of a strong veto would leave the officeholder unable to defend himself, just as the founders had feared. As Richard Field contended in the New Jersey Convention of 1844,

> The Executive & the Legislature often come into collision with [each] other.—
> The Legislature may invade the province of the Executive, and encroach upon
> his just rights. And will you give him no means of protection? I would not arm
> him with a sword to bathe in the blood of his enemies, but I would give him a
> foil with which to defend himself against their deadly thrusts. I would not put
> in his hands offensive weapons, but I would cover him with a shield that would
> enable him to repel the darts that were aimed at him.[45]

John Slough warned in similar fashion in the Kansas Convention of 1859, "If we take this power from the hands of the Governor, we leave him the Executive office only, and his chief prerogative will be to pardon criminals."[46]

Defenders of the veto were particularly intent on emphasizing that unconstitutional acts could take the form not only of encroachments against the executive and judiciary but also of violations of various other constitutional principles and provisions. William Spruance argued in the Delaware Convention of 1896–1897:

> True, the Governor is not often called upon, or a President is not often called
> upon to veto a measure which is supposed to encroach upon the Constitutional
> rights of particular departments of the Government. But he does sometimes;
> and instances could be readily found where the President of the United States
> has vetoed legislation upon the ground that he considered it unconstitutional,
> that is, as in conflict with some provision of the Constitution. That is a very
> useful exercise of power, that if he may see any legislation which violates any
> provision of the Constitution to veto it, not to approve of it and let it go into
> operation and leave it to be annulled by the Courts when questions arise under
> it. It is a part of his function to veto any legislation which is unconstitutional;
> and there have been plenty of examples of that kind.[47]

He concluded, "I find when I read the history of the exercise of the veto power, not merely that it is improvident and hasty legislation which has to be checked, and sometimes, unfortunately, corrupt legislation, but sometimes unconstitutional legislation."[48]

Defenders of the veto also warned against relying solely on the judiciary to overturn these sorts of unconstitutional acts. Anson Pease explained in the Ohio Convention of 1873–1874, "There is a vast difference between the Governor exercising his veto upon the constitutionality of an act before it becomes a law, and the Supreme Court doing it *after* it becomes a law. In the first instance, no rights have been acquired under the act; in the second, rights have been acquired under it, and it has become a rule of property."[49] Abraham Van Vechten went on to emphasize in the New York Convention of 1821 that "the judicial power operates correctively, and cannot be called into exercise until a law is in operation—until wrongs have been committed under it, and the sufferer presents his case in due form to a judicial tribunal for decision, and that in the meantime, great mischiefs may result from the operation of unconstitutional laws."[50] Not only was the judiciary incapable of preventing unconstitutional laws from taking effect, but judicial invalidation of legislation was bound to bring about even more interbranch conflict than would result from the issuance of an executive veto. John Sergeant, president of the Pennsylvania Convention of 1837–1838, concluded, "Surely, no man will deny, that it is better to arrest the enactment of unconstitutional laws in their passage, than to be obliged to invoke the aid of the Judiciary to declare them unconstitutional, after they have been passed. This is a conflict to be avoided as far as possible. It lessens the respect due to the Legislature, and it adds little to the strength or stability of the courts."[51]

Defenders of the veto also responded to the critics' second claim: that vetoes for policy reasons were illegitimate (because they overturned the people's deliberate judgment) and therefore that the only legitimate occasion for policy vetoes (to prevent hasty or inadvertent legislation) could be adequately addressed through a majority-override provision. For one thing, defenders of the veto were intent on rebutting the charges that had been leveled against the policy vetoes of various presidents. In fact, delegates argued, although these presidential vetoes were much maligned at the time by members of Congress, they had generally attracted popular support and, with the benefit of hindsight, were now recognized as having furthered the public interest. In addition, Robert Lucas in the Iowa Convention of 1844 emphasized that although one of Washington's two vetoes had been based on constitutional objections, the other had been issued for policy reasons, and therefore policy vetoes enjoyed a distinguished pedigree.[52] He argued, "Gen. Washington vetoed bills, not for constitutional reasons, but for reasons of expediency. . . . The veto power had been exercised most salutarily."[53] Meanwhile, Stoddard Judd in the Wisconsin Convention of 1847–1848 argued that, with the passage of time especially, even Jackson's controversial bank veto had come to be appreciated. He concluded, "But for that power, we should now have had a United States bank; and whatever might have been the opinions of men at the time President Jackson vetoed the bank charter, there were but very few in this convention, who would not admit that that was a most salutary measure."[54]

Defenders of vetoes for policy reasons also sought to show, on a theoretical level, that instances of hasty or inadvertent legislation did not exhaust the legitimate purposes for which such policy vetoes should be exercised. For one thing, cases occasionally arose in which legislators were responding to pressure groups rather than to their constituents, and therefore in these cases the executive was entitled to be viewed as the legitimate representative of public opinion. Thomas Davis defended the veto in this fashion in the Illinois Convention of 1847, when he argued, "It is not a restraint upon the people, but is a restraint upon the public agents of the people. It is not intended to control the people, for the people are not here, as in a pure democracy, in person; they are here by their representatives, and it sometimes turns out that the representatives are not the true exponents of their wishes."[55] David Gregg argued along similar lines in the same convention: "It was a mistaken view of our system of government that the Legislature is the sole representative of the people; the Governor was also their representative."[56]

In addition, these delegates noted that legislators, by virtue of their selection by local constituencies, were occasionally less capable than the governor of representing the general interest. Gideon Bailey in the Iowa Convention of 1844 contended, "The Governor was more the representative of the people, than the Representatives themselves. The Representatives were chosen by sections, and represented local interests, and they might continue to pass bad laws. But the Governor had no local feelings."[57] And James Springer argued in the Delaware Convention of 1852–1853,

> The executive department is the proper locality where the check-power should be lodged, for being an individuality, if influences are brought to bear upon it, both sides of every question will be laid open for consideration by those interested in securing the patronage of the Executive, and thus having all the evidences upon a question that can be adduced, he can deliberately and impartially balance the testimony and shape his actions accordingly. Not so with the Legislature. The cherished schemes of those wishing a particular enactment, have partisans previously elected in view of gaining this darling project—those

again have their opposites, their opponents. All are acted upon by opposite and conflicting influences. . . . Hence the Legislature, although possessing a knowledge of the wishes of the people, are subject to influences which render a reconsideration of questions frequently politic.[58]

These delegates emphasized that in neither of these two prominent cases of justifiable policy vetoes could the executive be charged with setting his views against the deliberate judgment of the people and thus could the exercise of the executive veto be deemed inconsistent with republican principles. More importantly, in the view of defenders of the federal model of the veto power, in neither of these cases could a majority-override provision be counted on to preserve the purposes for which vetoes were legitimately issued. As James Kent argued in the New York Convention of 1821, "It would be better to have no veto, than such as is here proposed. He would rather see laws passed by the votes of the two houses alone without any check whatever, than to adopt one so weak, inefficient, and useless. The veto as it would be constituted by adopting the report of the committee, would be a harmless power in the hands of the executive."[59] He thought it "wise and prudent, that there should be a check lodged somewhere, of sufficient energy to control the legislature when impelled by passion, or influenced and operated upon by improper views; or with a disposition to encroach upon the other departments."[60] George Gill in the Maryland Convention of 1867 was of a similar mind about the virtues of a two-thirds, rather than a majority, override. He

> wanted something practical, and either desired that we should have no veto power, or if we are to have it, that it will answer the purposes for which it only ought to be granted to the Governor. This amendment would destroy its energy, its power and its usefulness. . . . The most efficacious way of preventing unwise, and even corrupt legislation is to place this power in the hands of the Governor, and a majority of two-thirds of all the members should be necessary to overrule it.[61]

The Adoption of Alternative Forms of the Executive Veto

Ultimately, the federal model of the executive veto prevailed in the vast majority of states by the close of the nineteenth century. In terms of whether to adopt the veto power, this was more or less settled by the early nineteenth century, although not in all states and not without dissent. Each state admitted to the union after 1812 provided for the veto at its time of admission, with the exception of West Virginia, which waited another decade to do so.[62] In addition, most states that had joined the union before 1812 went on to adopt the veto by the Civil War, or in the case of Maryland, South Carolina, Tennessee, and Virginia, in the war's aftermath. Excepting the five states (Oklahoma, Arizona, New Mexico, Alaska, and Hawaii) that joined the union in the twentieth century and adopted the veto upon admission, Delaware (1897), Ohio (1902), Rhode Island (1909), and, many years later, North Carolina (1996) were the last states to adopt the veto.[63]

The question of whether to permit a two-thirds or a majority legislative override took longer to resolve and generated even more controversy, but this was also generally settled in favor of the federal model by the Civil War. During the first half of the nineteenth century, states that adopted the veto were slightly more likely to adopt a majority than a two-thirds override provision.[64] By the start of the Civil War, though, the count had tipped in favor of the two-thirds provision: fourteen of the twenty-three veto states provided for a two-thirds override (whether of members elected or present), and only nine provided for a majority override (again, whether of members elected or present).[65] By the early twentieth century, the two-thirds override had been adopted in all but thirteen of the states, eight of which chose to permit majority overrides and five of which required a three-fifths vote.[66] These numbers did not change much during the twentieth century, so that by the end of the twentieth century, a total of twelve states permitted overrides upon less than a two-thirds vote, including six states that permitted majority overrides and six states that required a three-fifths vote.[67]

The Item Veto

After spending much of the nineteenth century debating ways to weaken the executive veto, state constitution makers changed course during the final third of the nineteenth century and considered adopting an even stronger veto power than at the national level. This push for an enhanced veto power, which led to the adoption of the item veto in many states, as well as the reduction veto or amendatory veto in several states, actually had its immediate origin in neither federal or state constitutional developments. Rather, it stemmed from the Confederate Constitution, and in particular a proposal by Robert H. Smith that was adopted by the convention that drafted the provisional constitution and then was carried over in the actual constitution.[68] Although never exercised by CSA president Jefferson Davis, the item veto generated much debate after the Civil War among former Confederate states, as well as states across the country and the federal government.[69] One group of state constitution makers, who were frequently successful in pressing their case in the late nineteenth and twentieth centuries, argued that new forms of legislative behavior had upset the balance of power between the legislative and executive branches and therefore necessitated adoption of a stronger veto power. Another group of state constitution makers, who generally came out on the losing end of these debates, defended the federal model, with its stipulation that the president approve or disapprove bills in their entirety. These delegates countered that the various proposals to strengthen the veto would actually do more to upset than restore a proper balance of power between the branches.

The Case for Enhancing the Executive Veto Power

State convention delegates who supported a stronger veto power than at the federal level argued that legislatures in the postbellum era were engaging in all sorts of behavior that had not been envisioned by the founders and that had reduced the executive to a station beneath what the founders would have desired. The main concern was with the increasing resort to legislative riders and omnibus bills. Thus in the New York Convention of 1867–1868, in the first recorded state convention debates on this topic, Cornelius Allen complained about the practice of creating a "supply bill, which has been not inappropriately denominated a sort of *omnium gatherum* bill, in which everything is inserted, and in which members often have specific clauses included making particular appropriations for independent and improper purposes and objects, which they calculate will be forced through in consequence of the very necessary provisions of other parts of the bill, and which therefore must pass unless the whole bill fail." A principal effect of these sorts of bills, he pointed out, was to force the legislature "to consent to the passage of measures which never could have received a majority of votes had they been presented in different bills." He argued, quoting from a committee report on the subject, "Indeed, it is well known that obnoxious propositions have been artfully inserted in bills, for the purpose of enforcing their enactment under the calculation, not often ill-founded, that honest members of the Legislature would be induced to suffer them to pass into laws, rather than lose the benefit of the unobjectionable features."[70] As S. E. DeHaven explained in the Kentucky Convention of 1890–1891, "Those of us who have had any Legislative experience at all, know that it very often occurs that claims are inserted in an appropriation bill which, if left to their own merits, would not pass either House."[71]

Another problem with legislative riders and omnibus bills, especially when they were submitted to the governor in the closing days of the session, was that they forced the governor to accede to unconstitutional or unwise provisions in bills that could not realistically be vetoed. At times, these additional measures were included in bills due to inadvertence on the part of the legislature. Thomas Jones argued in the Alabama Convention of 1901:

> Every one acquainted with legislation, especially in latter days, knows in the hurry which seems to be a necessity when so much legislation is before the houses, that there are innumerable slips in bills. Sometimes the author says what he does not mean; sometimes he overlooks some good provision in other laws, which he does not wish to destroy, but in fact he repealed; sometimes accidentally he runs counter to some provisions in the Constitution of the State. It is highly proper in these cases that the Executive should have an opportunity to get these matters corrected, without putting the General Assembly in the attitude of passing the bill as it is, or letting it die.[72]

Jones's explanation was a rather generous interpretation of legislators' motives for engaging in these practices. Other delegates pointed out that legislators frequently added improper riders not only out of inadvertence but rather because of a conscious desire to force governors to accept measures that would not be approved if they stood on their own. Edward McCabe argued in the Missouri Convention of 1875,

> We all know, especially those who have had experience in legislation . . . that a vast injury is frequently inflicted on the Commonwealth by sticking in, and injecting into appropriation bills some improper items with those that are necessary and proper in order to carry on the government smoothly and properly. It has come to be a common practice in the Legislature to stop the wheels of government and keep back the pay of members by putting in a bill items which the Governor cannot approve in all respects, but is compelled to approve, thus carrying the good with the bad.[73]

Regardless of the precise nature of the problem, these delegates agreed that there had been a transformation in legislative behavior since the adoption of the veto in the late eighteenth century, and in such a way as to prevent the veto from accomplishing its intended purpose. As long as measures were submitted in separate statutes, as they had been in previous years, the governor could still wield his veto power to uphold the constitution or protect the public against unwise expenditures. But the increasing resort to legislative riders and omnibus bills gave the legislature the upper hand and made it much less likely that the governor could accomplish these goals. Charles Meredith argued in the Virginia Convention of 1901–1902, "An appropriation bill is sometimes composed of twenty absolutely different subjects, just as distinct as they could be if they were in separate bills; and yet, by the method of passing these bills, they are lumped together, and upon the Governor is put the responsibility of vetoing all or none. Is not that tying the hands of the Governor as to the veto power?"[74] These delegates made it clear that in considering various enhancements of the veto power, they were not seeking "to give more power to the governor than he originally had under our Constitution," as Lane Dwinell sought to make clear in the New Hampshire Convention of 1984:

> What we're really saying is, we should attempt to restore some of the authority and power that he had under the original constitution for over a hundred years, and make it possible for him to have the same interchange with the Legislature in the veto process that he had in the original Constitution and had in those days when budgets were not a factor, or later on when appropriations were by separate acts and were not packaged in just one big document so that it was a take it, or leave it proposition.[75]

The challenge for these delegates was to settle on a particular reform that would restore the balance between the legislative and executive branches. The leading proposal, which was defended on varying grounds from the late nineteenth through the late twentieth century, was to permit the governor to disapprove particular items in a bill while approving the remaining provisions.[76] In the late nineteenth century, this item veto power, which was generally, although not exclusively, proposed in regard to appropriations bills, was seen as a way of permitting the executive to check improper legislative acts. Typical of the defenses of the item veto during this period were the comments of William Spruance in the Delaware Convention of 1896–1897. He argued,

> I do not suppose anybody who is at all familiar with the legislation either of the Federal Government, or of the States, would object to now at this day, because

we know so well how different subjects of appropriation are mingled together, some of which are wise, and some of which are dreadfully unwise, and when the President has always been hampered by an inability to do anything except to accept the whole or reject the whole. Provisions in regard to his power to veto separate items over appropriations bills, have been adopted into all the new Constitutions, and the absence of it in the Federal Constitution is a fact greatly to be lamented.[77]

By the early twentieth century, defenders of the item veto were still emphasizing the need to overturn instances of legislative malfeasance, but they were also arguing that the executive ought to take a lead role in budgeting. At a time when state constitution makers were seeking to give the governor a formal role in drafting and submitting state budgets, the item veto came to be seen as an essential component of the overall goal of creating an energetic executive.[78] In a speech exemplifying these aspirations of item-veto supporters during the Progressive Era, John Fairlie, an academic authority on the veto power, argued in the Michigan Convention of 1907–1908 that the executive branch ought to bear responsibility for the budget no less than for other matters: "As has been said here the danger is in the legislature, in that mutual exchange of courtesies among members of the legislature whereby one agrees to support the appropriations desired by the others, if the others will support those in which he is interested. By placing the responsibility upon the Governor there will be a real responsibility fixed for the appropriations of the state."[79] The logic of this position was expressed most bluntly by Henry Elson in the Ohio Convention of 1912 in the midst of a wide-ranging debate not just about whether to adopt the item veto but also about whether to permit the executive veto in any form: "I would trust a governor quicker than I would a legislature every week," he exclaimed.

> The governor is in the lime light. The public gaze is upon him. The public gaze may be in some way upon the legislature, but not on particular members, and one can hide behind another. We know a law-making body is far more apt to make blunders and mistakes and be led into corruption than an executive, and I think the more power you give an executive the better he will do. He is sure to do the best he can if you give him responsibility.[80]

By the mid-twentieth century, delegates were no less concerned about preventing particular cases of unconstitutional or unwise appropriations, but they were also apt to support the item veto as part of a general effort to reduce budget deficits. Thus Frank Prescott, a delegate to the Tennessee Convention of 1953 and an academic authority on the gubernatorial veto, sought to persuade the assembled delegates that the item veto would "[permit] the exercise of selective economy on the appropriation bills without destroying essential services of government" and thereby serve "as an emergency weapon to check irresponsible mass attacks upon the public treasury."[81] Or, as Gardner Turner put the matter in the New Hampshire Convention of 1948, "This is a resolution which might be well termed an anti pork barrel resolution. We don't slice the pork quite as thickly in New Hampshire as in some other places, but it is still pork."[82]

Once the item veto had been established in many states by the end of the nineteenth century, delegates also began to consider adopting the reduction veto, which would permit the governor to reduce the dollar amount of appropriations items. The reduction veto was first exercised in the late nineteenth century by Pennsylvania governors who claimed that this power was implicit in their item veto power. The practice soon spread to other states, and in several of these states, the legitimacy of the reduction veto was discussed not only in courts but also in constitutional conventions, where delegates sought to formally authorize the governor to exercise this power.[83] Supporters of the reduction veto argued that this power was a logical extension of the item veto. As C. Nils Tavares explained in the Hawaii Convention of 1950, "The legislature, by lumping a lot of items together into one big item and then putting a lot of water in it, can force the governor to take it or leave it as a whole. It seems to me it would be a healthy thing to allow the governor to not only veto a whole item but to take some of the water out of an item without eliminating it entirely."[84] Consequently, the reduction veto was seen as an essential means of fulfilling the main purpose of the item veto. The presence of the reduction veto, as Frederic DeYoung argued in the Illinois Convention of 1920–1922, would ensure that "the men that make these appropriations will at least exercise the care which they exercised in the past, if not a greater measure of care."[85] In addition, as J. Edward Hutchinson argued in the Michigan Convention of 1961–1962, the reduction veto would "provide a method for the spotlight of public attention to be turned upon some appropriations which, in the opinion of the governor, might be a little bit more generous than necessary," and therefore it would serve "the interest of economy in government."[86]

The twentieth century also brought calls for still another enhancement of the veto power, in the form of the amendatory veto, which would permit governors to make a formal recommendation that the legislature modify or eliminate particular items in a bill. As William Fitts explained in the Alabama Convention of 1901, which was the first convention to adopt this device, the amendatory veto would essentially give a constitutional imprimatur to a long-standing practice. He argued that "the Governor has the right to veto the measure now," just as he has the option of "sending for members of the legislature to come down to go through tedious machinery of recalling the legislature . . . and reconsidering it, in order to meet suggestions which he makes in a semi-official manner." The amendatory veto would simply provide that "instead of the right of vetoing the legislation that is passed he may simply point out wherein there has been some error, or some technical mishap to the bill, and send it back with the suggestion that with that simple amendment it will meet with his approval." The advantage of formalizing this exercise of the veto power, Fitts argued, was that "it provides the best and simplest means for [the governor] to make known in a public manner, and not in a quasi-private manner, any technical objection which occurs to him in connection with bills that have passed."[87]

The Case against Enhancing the Executive Veto Power

Convention delegates who opposed an enhanced veto power questioned whether the balance of power between the executive and legislature was, in any real sense, in need of restoration. It was true, these critics acknowledged, that legislators were engaging in all sorts of behavior that had not been envisioned, at least to such an extent, by the founders. However, even if one admitted that omnibus bills and appropriations riders were on the increase, one would have to acknowledge that the executive was also exercising newfound powers. Robert Raiche in the New Hampshire Convention of 1974 argued that "at the present time, there is a very delicate balance between the Legislative branch and the Executive branch." He acknowledged the calls for an enhanced veto power, but maintained that there was no need to adopt these reforms because the executive had developed its own tools for responding to improper legislative appropriations. Among other things, "the Executive branch prepares the budget and presents it to the Legislature. . . . The Governor has the right and does, in fact, call members of the Appropriations Committee into his office." Moreover, "the Governor also has the press. If the Governor feels that the Legislature is going in the wrong direction, he has the prerogative of going to the press to express his feelings of dissatisfaction with the direction being taken by the Appropriations Committee and ultimately the House and the Senate." He concluded, "The founding fathers of our Constitution provided within this Constitution, in my estimation, the balance of power which has worked."[88]

Delegates who opposed an enhanced veto power were further fortified in their opposition when they considered the consequences of adopting each of the specific reform proposals, which they saw as doing more to upset, rather than restore, a proper balance of power. The item veto generated much criticism along these lines. In part, delegates feared that the governor would wield the item veto in such a way as to upset delicately crafted legislative compromises. Beverly Hancock argued in the Virginia Convention of 1901–1902, "To allow the Governor to veto any single item, or several items, in an appropriation bill, and not to require him to veto the whole bill, is an invasion of the legislative department. Legislation is nothing in the world but compromise after all." In his view, the governor ought to be permitted "to veto the whole measure or not be allowed to touch it. It is a piece of completed legislation, and he ought not be allowed to destroy it by taking the executive knife and cutting off such portions of it as he may think to be unpopular and thus destroy an appropriation bill passed by the General Assembly."[89] David Lynde made a similar point in the New Hampshire Convention of 1984, when he likened legislating to the knitting of a sweater. He argued that under the current system, the governor

> is given the choice of either returning the sweater to the Legislature because he feels that it doesn't fit properly, or that it wasn't what he desired and asks them to construct a new sweater, or he may keep the sweater if it meets his specifications. But with a line item veto, what we are looking at, is giving the power to the Governor to cut the sweater, to alter the sweater and to pull threads in the sweater. The difference there is that the Governor has to knit the sweater. The Legislature is charged with knitting the sweater, the Governor doesn't know which threads unravel certain parts of the sweater, he doesn't know which thread holds the arm on the sweater.[90]

It was possible, as Lynde indicated, that the item veto could unravel a legislative compromise simply because the governor might be unaware of the negotiations that had produced a particular bill. This would be regrettable enough. But the item veto could also be exercised in this fashion intentionally and maliciously. George Rowe warned in the Michigan Convention of 1907–1908,

> It is a very dangerous thing to put into the hands of the Governor of the state; the power to disapprove of any portion of an appropriation bill would give him

power to control practically every man living or coming from a section of the
state where they want an appropriation for an institution in that particular section. If for example, I was in the senate and an appropriation was given for a
public institution in my city or in my county, it would be a very easy matter for
the Governor to hold me up on anything else that I might want with the threat
that he might veto the appropriation for that particular institution.[91]

In the view of these delegates, the item veto would upset the balance of power
not only by permitting the governor to wield undue influence over the legislature,
but also by enabling legislators to avoid responsibility for making tough budgeting
decisions. Walter Haynes argued in the Tennessee Convention of 1953 that

> with due regard to reasonable checks and balances I cannot concur in a proposal
> to put in the hands of the executive such power over the legislative branch of the
> government as I believe would be conferred by permitting the veto of separate
> items in a single appropriation bill. By the adoption of such a proposal I believe
> a considerable overbalance in favor of the executive would be produced which
> would eventually detract from the importance of the General Assembly and cor-
> respondingly augment beyond the limits of safety the power of the executive.

He was concerned with "the trading strength that would be placed in the hands
of the executive by this extensive power to punish or placate legislators." But he
also called particular attention to "a second effect of the item veto proposal that
is less apparent but nevertheless equally detrimental to orderly and responsible
government":

> That effect does not come about through executive coercion but through an-
> other very human and almost universal failing, namely the disposition to shirk
> unpleasant responsibility, or in well understood parlance, "to pass the buck."
> When a legislator knows that a Governor may remove an extravagant item of
> an appropriation bill by a veto which is in no practical danger of being over-
> ridden, there is the temptation to satisfy demanding special interests or unin-
> formed constituents by padding appropriation bills unconscionably, secure in
> the assumption that to keep within the cabletow of his budget the executive
> by the exercise of his item veto power must weed out the tares and accept for
> himself the resulting ill will of those deprived of their cherished projects.[92]

If the item veto attracted the most criticism because it was the most prominent of the three proposed reforms, the reduction veto was viewed by many

delegates as the most dangerous of these reforms. Even some advocates of the item veto had trouble supporting this proposal. William Trautmann argued in the Illinois Convention of 1920–1922, "There is a vast difference in reducing an item and vetoing an item. If the Governor objects to an item, he can eliminate it, but when he does eliminate it, he is not legislating. It does seem to me this is a very serious problem. This to my mind is a step in the wrong direction. It is consolidating, or the beginning of the consolidation of the legislative and the executive departments."[93] Not only would the reduction veto "give the Governor practically legislative power over appropriations matters,"[94] as his colleague David Shanahan explained, but it would also "encourage legislative carelessness," because "legislators, as individuals, would have less incentive to be fiscally responsible if the governor had the right and the power to reduce whatever appropriations they finally passed,"[95] as William Sommerschield argued when the issue resurfaced in the Illinois Convention of 1969–1970.

The amendatory veto, although a less important innovation than the reduction veto, also came under attack on the ground that it would disrupt legislative-executive relations. Robert Lowe in the Alabama Convention of 1901 thought that the amendatory veto was an "insidious innovation" that would permit "an ambitious and intriguing Governor . . . not merely to pass upon the laws the people's representatives have enacted, but . . . to shape, suggest, and frame those laws." He believed that it "seeks to remove the ancient landmarks, because it seeks to break down the wall that stands between the legislative and the executive." He concluded, "If the fathers were wise, if they builded wisely when they constructed the three departments and placed the walls high between them, it would be unwise in us to seek to tear down or lower those walls today."[96]

The Adoption of an Enhanced Executive Veto Power

Efforts to strengthen the executive veto met with mixed success in state conventions, with most states choosing to adopt the item veto and a modest number approving the reduction veto or amendatory veto. The item veto was the most popular of these reforms. It was first enacted by Georgia in its Constitution of 1865 and by Texas in its Constitution of 1866,[97] and then adopted by many other states in the late nineteenth century.[98] By the end of the twentieth century, only six states failed to permit the governor to exercise the item veto, with Maine in

1995 becoming the most recent state to provide for the power.[99] Although in nearly every case the item veto power is restricted to appropriations, the Washington Constitution of 1889, South Carolina Constitution of 1895, and Ohio Constitution (from 1903 to 1912) also permitted the item veto to be exercised on other bills.[100]

The reduction veto proved less popular. This power was first exercised by the governor of Pennsylvania in 1885 and affirmed by the Pennsylvania Supreme Court in 1901 and was also wielded by several other state governors in the early twentieth century. Although the use of this power was upheld by the courts in several of these states, it was frequently deemed an illegitimate extension of gubernatorial power.[101] In response to these judicial decisions and resulting uncertainty about the power, constitution makers in a total of ten states acted during the twentieth century to establish explicit constitutional authority for the reduction veto.[102]

The amendatory veto, which was first enacted in the Alabama Constitution of 1901 and Virginia Constitution of 1902,[103] was ultimately adopted in seven states during the twentieth century.[104] Although in South Dakota the amendatory veto may be exercised only to correct "errors in style or form,"[105] in the remaining states it can be used in a much broader fashion.[106]

Judicial Review

Whereas the executive veto was the subject of extensive discussion in the federal convention, the judicial veto received little attention.[107] As a result, Hamilton's defense of judicial review in Federalist No. 78, and to an extent in Federalist No. 81, serves as the principal guide to the framers' intentions. Hamilton made it clear in Federalist No. 78 that judges were expected to veto unconstitutional acts. In fact, he viewed it as axiomatic that "whenever a particular statute contravenes the Constitution, it will be the duty of the judicial tribunals to adhere to the latter and disregard the former."[108] As he explained, "The interpretation of the laws is the proper and peculiar province of the courts. A constitution is, in fact, and must be regarded by the judges as, a fundamental law. It therefore belongs to them to ascertain its meaning as well as the meaning of any particular act proceeding from the legislative body." In case of "an irreconcilable variance between the two, . . . the Constitution ought to be preferred to the statute."[109]

At the same time, Hamilton took note of the limited power of the judiciary, which he viewed as "beyond comparison the weakest of the three departments of power."[110] He thought it "of no weight to say that the courts, on the pretense of a repugnancy, may substitute their own pleasure to the constitutional intentions of the legislature."[111] Moreover, in Federalist No. 81 he dismissed as "false reasoning upon misconceived fact" any notion that "the power of construing the laws according to the *spirit* of the Constitution will enable that court to mould them into whatever shape it may think proper." Although confirming once again that the Court possessed the power of judicial review, he maintained that "there is not a syllable in the plan under consideration which *directly* empowers the national courts to construe the laws according to the spirit of the Constitution, or which gives them any greater latitude in this respect than may be claimed by the courts of every State."[112]

As Hamilton's comments indicated, state courts had been invalidating legislation for several years prior to the federal convention of 1787, and thus for several decades before *Marbury v. Madison* (1803), when the U.S. Supreme Court struck down an act of Congress for the first time. Although the exercise of judicial review at the federal level has occasioned much debate and has generated periodic, but unsuccessful, efforts to restrict its exercise through the years, state supreme courts' exercise of judicial review has also prompted much controversy and various restrictive proposals, with the main difference being that several of the state reforms were actually adopted. In fact, state conventions have considered, and in several cases enacted, a variety of proposals to limit judicial power, including abolishing judicial review, requiring a unanimous or supermajority vote of judges to invalidate a law, and subjecting judges or judicial decisions to popular recall.

Although scattered proposals to restrict judicial review were introduced in state conventions during the nineteenth century in response to particular events at the state and national level,[113] it was not until the early twentieth century that state constitution makers around the country undertook a thorough reassessment of judicial review and adopted several reforms, each of which was also considered but was never enacted at the national level. Critics of judicial review contended that judges were exceeding their proper role and that existing institutional arrangements were incapable of providing appropriate relief. Consequently, they supported institutional reforms that were designed to restore the original balance between the legislature and judiciary. Defenders of judicial review responded to these claims by arguing that existing mechanisms were fully

capable of addressing particular abuses of judicial review, and also by contending that the proposed reforms would do more to upset, than to restore, a proper
balance of power between the legislature and judiciary.[114]

The Case for Restricting Judicial Review

Early twentieth-century convention delegates who sought to limit judicial power
were reacting primarily to state and federal court decisions that they viewed
as representing a departure from the original purpose of judicial review.[115]
Several rulings were seen as particularly egregious and were cited repeatedly
by convention delegates.[116] On the state level, these decisions included *In re
Jacobs,* an 1885 New York Court of Appeals decision overturning a state law prohibiting the manufacture of cigars in tenement houses;[117] *Ritchie v. the People,*
an 1895 Illinois Supreme Court decision invalidating an eight-hour workday for
women in certain occupations;[118] and *Ives v. South Buffalo Railway Co.,* a 1911
New York Court of Appeals decision striking down a workers' compensation
law.[119] Among the U.S. Supreme Court decisions that drew the ire of Progressive Era convention delegates were the 1895 *Pollock v. Farmer's Loan & Trust
Co.* decision invalidating a national income tax;[120] the 1905 *Lochner* decision
overturning New York's ten-hour day for bakers;[121] a 1908 decision invalidating
a federal employers' liability law;[122] a pair of decisions striking down federal, as
well as state, prohibitions on yellow-dog contracts;[123] and several rulings that
prevented the federal government from regulating child labor.[124]

In the view of these early twentieth-century convention delegates, judges
who issued these decisions had gone far beyond interpreting the constitution
and were engaging in policy making of a kind not envisioned by the founders.
Herbert Kenny argued in the Massachusetts Convention of 1917–1919, "When
our courts were established they were meant to interpret the law, but to-day,
through their ability to declare laws unconstitutional they have become virtually a law-making body."[125] Moreover, in issuing repeated decisions of this kind,
the judiciary had shown itself to be far from the weakest of the three branches.
Harvey Watson in the Ohio Convention of 1912 argued,

> The courts have by a series of interpretations managed to write into the laws in
> many, and it must be said in most, important cases, interpretations which ma-
> terially and in some cases absolutely, ignore and reverse the will of the people

as expressed by their legislative branch. In short, the judicial branch of the government has gradually overshadowed until it has well-nigh overturned the function of the other branches of the government and made these two coordinate departments of government entirely subordinate and beneath and within the power and control of the judiciary.[126]

Certain courts, to be sure, were more active than others in blocking progressive legislation. Thus Harry Thomas in the Ohio Convention of 1912 viewed the Ohio Supreme Court as a frequent offender that had

practically nullified every safety law made for the protection of the workers in this state by their decisions on assumed risk, contributory negligence and fellow-servant rule. . . .

In reference to other laws passed for the benefit of the workers it is only necessary to call attention to the fact that the eight-hour law for public work was declared unconstitutional, the ten-hour law for train men declared unconstitutional, the law passed to regulate the sale of convict-made goods declared unconstitutional, the right of the poor litigant to attorney fees in appealed cases declared unconstitutional, the law weighing coal before screening for the coal miners; and the mechanic's lien law.[127]

On the other hand, after studying the reports of the Massachusetts Supreme Judicial Court, George Anderson in the Massachusetts Convention of 1917–1919 concluded that "Massachusetts has less call to complain of her judiciary than we have cause to complain of the Supreme Court of the United States, and than they have cause to complain in Illinois, Missouri, and New York."[128]

Nevertheless, and despite the varying records of particular courts, the view predominated in the early twentieth century that state and federal judges were frequently handing down decisions that failed to serve the public interest. Whether because the judicial process was so insulated that "the public are not represented at all,"[129] as Gerry Brown contended in the Massachusetts Convention of 1917–1919, or because the judges were, by virtue of their age or temperament, insufficiently attuned to "existing circumstances" and "progress,"[130] as Hiram Peck charged in the Ohio Convention of 1912, the conclusion was inescapable that judges were exceeding their charge and upsetting the traditional balance of power. J. A. Okey concluded in the Ohio Convention of 1912,

If you will examine the decisions of the supreme court you will find that very frequently courts have nullified laws for the alleged reason that the laws were in conflict with some provision of the constitution, but that was not the real reason that caused them to declare for the unconstitutionality. The real reason was that they didn't like the policy of the law and were not bold enough to come out and say they didn't like the policy of the law and they found an easier way by simply saying it conflicts with certain provisions of the constitution. That thing has gone entirely too far, and it has given far too much power to the court to nullify an act of the legislature.[131]

Delegates responded to these judicial rulings by proposing an assortment of reforms. One group of delegates was driven by dissatisfaction with the aggressive exercise of judicial review to undertake an historical analysis of the origin of the power, and, upon finding little support for judicial review in the founding era, concluded that it ought to be abolished. Thus, in the Massachusetts Convention of 1917–1919, Albert Bushnell Hart, a "life-long student of constitutional history," argued that "when the present Constitution of Massachusetts was framed it was not in the mind of any member of the original Convention that the courts of Massachusetts were to have the power to set aside acts of the General Court on the ground of unconstitutionality."[132] At the least, he argued, one would have to acknowledge that, contrary to Hamilton's claims in *The Federalist,* the power of judicial review did not follow inexorably from the creation of a constitutional form of government; therefore, it was "entirely possible to create democratic communities in which the courts have not the power to set aside the actions of the legislative or executive departments."[133] It was admittedly true, his colleague Charles Morrill argued, that judicial review had often been exercised through the years by federal and state courts, but the fact "that it has been usurped and now has been exercised for many years does not make it right."[134]

For the most part, delegates sought not to abolish judicial review, but rather to restrict its exercise. A leading proposal was to require a supermajority or unanimous vote of the judges to void a statute. To supporters of this reform proposal, it was disturbing enough that courts had overturned a number of popular statutes; however, as Isaiah Evans argued in the Nebraska Convention of 1919–1920, it was even worse that several of these controversial rulings had been decided by bare majorities, including U.S. Supreme Court decisions regarding the "Child Labor law," the "Income Tax Law," and the New York "bakery case." Insofar as one was convinced, as Evans was, that "the legislative branch of the Government, originating policies and passing laws, is the direct representative of the people," then it only made sense that "unless their work is clearly and plainly and palpably unconstitutional, in the language of Justice Harlan, it should remain as the law of the State, and it is no injustice and no reflection on the courts to say that they should have more than a mere majority behind their decision."[135] An additional concern, as Joseph Beeler argued in the same convention, was that "in many instances decisions of a court by a bare majority were afterwards, by the court, overturned because those decisions were not considered by the courts themselves of any very great binding effect by reason of the fact that they were rendered by a bare majority." Beeler pointed, in particular, to the U.S. Supreme Court "cases of the legal tender act and the income tax act," and he concluded that requiring more than a bare majority to strike down a legislative act would tend to "lend stability to that decision," and would in no way "detract from the independence of the Supreme Court."[136] His colleague Emile Fauquet made clear that it was

> not that the people want a law passed which is contrary to the Constitution, but where there is a doubt, and there seems to be a doubt, where the Supreme Court itself is divided, where there is a doubt about the constitutionality of the law, they want the people to have the advantage of that doubt, and that the law be left in effect until it is clearly unconstitutional as shown by a report of more than a bare majority of the Judges of the Supreme Court.[137]

Several of these delegates wanted to go so far as to require a unanimous vote of the justices to invalidate a law. Thus Patrick Broderick in the Massachusetts Convention of 1917–1919 argued that a clearly unconstitutional law would easily be recognized as such and would "be held by a unanimous opinion of the court to be unconstitutional." But when "the question is so close that any Justice of the court, for instance, a Justice like former Chief Justice Ho[l]mes, should hold such law to be constitutional, then, in my opinion, that law should continue to have full force and effect until it shall be declared to be unconstitutional by a unanimity of opinion of the Supreme Judicial Court."[138] For the most part, though, delegates advocated some sort of supermajority requirement. For instance, George Anderson in the same convention did "not now see a better way than to say two-thirds."[139] Meanwhile, Wilbur Bryant in the Nebraska Convention of 1919–1920 recommended that

> if a law is unconstitutional, out of seven it should require at least five men to say it is. Otherwise it is just the caprice of the odd man. A legislature has declared a law constitutional and a governor has declared a law constitutional,

and three judges have said it was constitutional and three do not think it is, and this odd man,—this one man,—that is all a majority is,—just the caprice of the odd fellow. He holds up his hand and bawls out "Whoa."[140]

Another group of delegates took a different approach and sought to permit the people to recall judges who issued errant decisions, or even to recall the decisions themselves. The recall of judges enjoyed the strong backing of William Jennings Bryan, who argued in an address to the Nebraska Convention of 1919–1920 that "a judge is the servant of the people just as every other official is. Judges are not only public servants, but they are human beings and liable to err."[141] At a time when several states were beginning to permit the recall of legislative and executive officials, the question naturally arose as to whether the recall should also apply to judges. Several delegates, such as Thomas Feeney in the Arizona Convention of 1910, were strongly in favor of the recall as a general principle, and saw no reason to exempt judges from its operation. By his reasoning, "The object and aim of the government was that it be constituted in triangular form, the legislative, and judicial, and the only method we have found whereby we can retain that triangle without making a right angled triangle and following the hypotenuse, is to put a recall on the judiciary and all public officials."[142] His colleague Michael Cunniff was of a similar mind and argued that the recall was a reformative, rather than a revolutionary, step, given that it was "simply extending to the people the power of the impeachment which has been in our government ever since the beginning, . . . with the mere exception of making the people the impeaching body . . . and making the people the court."[143] Other delegates supported the recall of judges not just as part of a general effort to democratize governing institutions, but for the specific purpose of restraining judges and restoring a balance between the legislative and judicial branches. Along these lines, Mr. Watson of Ohio argued, "The recall of the judiciary is not an agency to withdraw the judicial powers from that function, but to enliven and inspirit the judiciary with the spirit of the times and to make it as responsive to the public welfare as the spirit and will of vested property and gigantic vested interests."[144]

Whereas William Jennings Bryan was the most prominent proponent of the recall of judges, Theodore Roosevelt was the most notable supporter of the recall of judicial decisions, by which the people could disapprove of an errant judicial decision and reinstate an invalidated statute. In an address to the Ohio Convention of 1912 that generated controversy throughout his presidential campaign that year,[145] Roosevelt maintained that the recall of judges should be viewed "as a last resort, when it has become clearly evident that no other course will achieve the desired result."[146] But he argued that

> there is one kind of recall in which I very earnestly believe, and the immediate adoption of which I urge. There are sound reasons for being cautious about the recall of a good judge who has rendered an unwise and improper decision. . . . But when a judge decides a constitutional question, when he decides what the people as a whole can or cannot do, the people should have the right to recall that decision—not the judge—if they think it wrong.[147]

He explained, "If you don't like the word recall, say that the people will reserve for themselves their right to decide whether the legislature or the judiciary take the right view of the constitution if the two bodies clash."[148] It was not "that the people are infallible," but rather

> that our whole history shows that the American people are more often sound in their decisions than is the case with any of the government bodies to whom, for their convenience, they have delegated portions of their power. . . . Just as the people, and not the supreme court under Chief Justice Taney, were wise in their decisions of the vital questions of their day, so I hold that now the American people as a whole have shown themselves wiser than the courts in the way they have approached and dealt with such vital questions of our day as those concerning the proper control of big corporations and of securing their rights to industrial workers.[149]

For delegates such as Mr. Kenny of Massachusetts, the recall of judicial decisions was not only a means of applying democratic principles to the judicial branch, but it would also have the practical effect of enabling the people to overturn errant rulings without waiting for judges to reverse themselves or for the constitutional amendment process to play out. Referring to the length of time that it took for the Illinois Supreme Court to reverse its 1895 *Ritchie* decision and finally permit an eight-hour-day for women, Kenny complained, "It took that Supreme Court sixteen years to find that out. Was this justice? Would it not be better, after a Supreme Court has declared such a law unconstitutional upon precedents established in medieval times, to give the people a chance to decide in the light of present conditions?"[150]

The Case against Restricting Judicial Review

It was left to supporters of judicial review to rebut these critiques and defend the federal model against the various reform proposals. Many of these delegates began by questioning whether recent court behavior actually constituted such a clear departure from the traditional understanding of the judicial role. Along these lines, James Halfhill argued in the Ohio Convention of 1912 that the rulings that attracted so much criticism during this period were a relatively small set of decisions and were not representative of the overall work of the judiciary. In his view, "these cases that have been cited here, some thirty in number, to show that individual rights have been transgressed by the supreme court of Ohio are a slander upon the courts of the state of Ohio, unless you take into account the hundreds of other cases where the rights of the individuals have been fully and fairly protected by holding statutes unconstitutional."[151]

Not only had the extent of judicial overreaching been exaggerated, these delegates argued, but the people and the legislature were fully capable of responding to any errant decisions without resorting to the proffered reforms. There was, for instance, the impeachment power, which could be used to target cases of persistent judicial intransigence. In fact, several delegates during this period sought to make the impeachment process even more readily available, as a way of forestalling the need for radical reforms of judicial review. Thus Elihu Root, president of the New York Convention of 1915, argued in regard to the impeachment power, "We would have had a better government and a more contented people if this remedy had been more practical and available so that more unfaithful officers should have been called to account." He thought that "it is the inadequacy of the remedy of impeachment which has led to the widespread demand for recall and those of us who believe that that would be a great misfortune are bound to make the legal remedy . . . so adequate that we will hear no more of this demand for recall."[152] The people could also make use of, and on several occasions had made use of, the constitutional amendment process to overturn particular decisions with which they disagreed. This was the route that New York had taken in overcoming the 1911 *Ives* decision regarding that state's workers' compensation law, and that Congress had taken in proposing the Sixteenth Amendment to the U.S. Constitution and reauthorizing a national income tax. Joseph Votava in the Nebraska Convention of 1919–1920 therefore thought that "as a matter of fact, the Supreme Court of this State, if it has erred at all, has erred in not declaring enough laws unconstitutional." But "if there is an overwhelming demand for any law the people can always amend the Constitution just the same as they have done in the Income Tax controversy. If there is not an overwhelming demand for it, the people will not amend the Constitution and they will adhere to the rule of the Supreme Court."[153]

In the view of defenders of judicial review, then, the balance of power between the legislative and judicial branches had not been unduly disturbed by recent court decisions; but it would most assuredly be upset by the adoption of any of the proposed reforms. The general concern was that the reforms would all sweep too broadly. The intent might well be to prevent judges from engaging in policy making, but, as several delegates pointed out, the proposed reforms would apply to all judicial decisions, and they contained no means of distinguishing policy-making decisions from decisions that properly secured individual rights. Thus the same reform proposal that might inhibit the former ruling would be just as capable of preventing the latter. Francis Balch in the Massachusetts Convention of 1917–1919 called particular attention to this problem and complained that

> this debate has been almost wholly confined to that one aspect of the matter, to so-called social welfare legislation.
>   Have we sufficiently considered, all of us, that the prime constitutional function of the courts is not to pass on those social welfare matters under the police power, but to safeguard our fundamental rights. . . . I submit that in concentrating our attention exclusively on one narrow aspect of the constitutional aspects of the work of our courts, the gentleman has caused us dangerously to lose sight of the broader and more truly typical aspects of that work,—aspects which absolutely require that the courts should retain the power of giving *prompt*, as well as full, protection to our fundamental liberties.[154]

In addition to this general concern, supporters of judicial review also pointed to particular problems with each of the proposed reforms. Proposals to abolish judicial review stood little chance of passage, and therefore delegates devoted most of their efforts to critiquing the remaining reforms. However, supporters of judicial review took the opportunity to respond to what they considered to be several incorrect assumptions about the origin of judicial review on the part of delegates who would abolish the power. Albert Washburn in the Massachusetts Convention of 1917–1919 argued that, far from being an "act of judicial usurpation" on the part of John Marshall, "judicial review was the natural outgrowth of beliefs that were common property at the time the different Constitutions were being framed."[155] He was of the view that "the doctrine of judicial control naturally and logically results from a system of government which rests on a written Constitution."[156] In addition, his colleague John Merriam argued that the claim on the part of critics of judicial review that "the Legislature is the representative of the people and the only representative of the people" was "an assumption which is not sound." It was more accurate to say that "in our Constitution the courts are created as creatures of the people," and thus judicial review was "the legitimate function of the courts acting not in defiance of the people, not in defiance of the Legislature, but in behalf of the people, by means of a Constitution which the people have established."[157]

Supporters of judicial review also raised questions about the consequences of requiring a supermajority or unanimous vote for the exercise of judicial review. In particular, these delegates argued that such a requirement would make it more difficult for judges to issue the sorts of rights-protecting decisions that all agreed should be encouraged and preserved. Andrew Oleson in the Nebraska Convention of 1919–1920 contended, "If it were not for the safeguards that the courts give to us, the written statements in a Constitution would amount to nothing. We have had in the past, and we may have in the future, on account of the present troublous times, conditions which maintain here in this capital building where members of the legislature in open public statement consign the Constitution to perdition." He therefore urged the retention of a majority requirement, just as was recognized "in all of our other acts of life, in all other proceedings, as far as government is concerned."[158] In similar fashion, George Harris in the Ohio Convention of 1912 argued,

> If you vote away your sacred rights by demanding a unanimous decision of the supreme court to overturn a statutory law, you may be chaining yourselves and your posterity to something you do not dream of now. It is not difficult to foresee that in the not far distant future some particular sect may be dominant in the legislature and may secure the enactment of a statute which deprives all other sects of certain rights or burdens them, and yet by this original proposal you would make it impossible, unless you were strong enough to get a constitutional amendment by means of the initiative and referendum, to shake off those fetters.[159]

Several delegates went on to point out that this proposal might actually be seen as inconsistent with republican government, in that it would permit rule by a minority. As John McAnarney argued in regard to a proposed supermajority requirement in the Massachusetts Convention of 1917–1919, "Stripped of all verbiage, this amendment proposes that a minority of two may prevent the Supreme Judicial Court from declaring a statute unconstitutional. If that be so, that in effect is giving a minority of two the power to declare a statute constitutional. That would be unique."[160]

Proposals for the recall of judges or judicial decisions were seen as having similarly inhibiting effects on judicial decision making. Once again, defenders of judicial review argued that these proposals would likely work, as intended, to forestall rulings striking down social welfare legislation, but they would also have the unintended consequence of leading judges to stay their hand when reviewing legislation that clearly infringed on civil rights and liberties. Thus Alexander Tuthill in the Arizona Convention of 1910 did "not believe you will have an impartial judge if you hold the club of recall over him. I think if you pass the recall, you make the judgeship a travesty."[161] Meanwhile, to suggest that the work of judges should be subject to popular review, Mr. Harris of Ohio argued, was to misconceive the judicial role, which was "solely to expound the law, and this expounding of the law has absolutely no connection whatsoever with the wishes or political ideals of either the majority or minority." He explained that "in reference to the recall of the judiciary my opposition to this is as irrevocable as were the laws of the Medes and Persians," and he concluded, "Any other view would mean anarchy, socially and politically."[162]

The Adoption of Restrictions on Judicial Review

The rebuttals from supporters of judicial review had some effect, in that proposals for the abolition of judicial review were uniformly rejected. Nevertheless, several states adopted some version of each of the remaining proposals, thereby rejecting the federal model in certain respects.

Supermajority requirements were adopted in three states.[163] Ohio in 1912 stipulated that statutes could be held unconstitutional by the supreme court only with the concurrence of all but one of the seven justices.[164] North Dakota in 1919 required four of the five justices to approve the invalidation of a statute.[165] Nebraska in 1920 adopted a requirement that five of seven justices concur in the exercise of judicial review.[166] Although the Ohio supermajority requirement was eliminated by a 1968 amendment,[167] the North Dakota and Nebraska provisions remain in effect.[168]

The recall of judges proved to be the most popular of these reforms.[169] Oregon in 1908 was the first state to permit the recall of judges, along with other elected officials,[170] and by the end of the twentieth century, such a provision had been adopted in twelve states.[171] Although the judicial recall was the subject of much controversy in Arizona, where the adoption of the provision initially threatened the bid for statehood,[172] in most states, it was considered a logical extension of general provisions for the recall of legislative and executive officials, and was adopted at the same time as these provisions.[173]

The recall of judicial decisions was the least well-received of these proposals.[174] Colorado was the only state to adopt such a provision, which was implemented through the constitutional initiative process in 1912.[175] Nine years later, however, and before the procedure could actually be put to use, it was declared unconstitutional by the Colorado Supreme Court.[176]

Conclusion

The principal benefit of examining these state convention debates is that it becomes clear that the executive veto and judicial review have been the subject of considerable debate and substantial revision during the course of the American regime. At various times, state and national developments created doubts about whether these institutions were still carrying out their intended purposes, and this in turn generated reform proposals that were designed to enable these institutions to fulfill their original functions. These reforms were introduced by members of Congress and by state constitution makers, but the rigidity of the federal amendment process prevented these proposals from receiving serious consideration in Congress. At the state level, however, the flexibility of amendment processes not only ensured that these reforms received consideration, but it also permitted their adoption in varying degrees.

The chief concern about the executive veto, after an initial period when states gradually came to adopt the basic outlines of the federal model, was that legislators' increasing use of riders and omnibus bills was preventing the executive from wielding the veto in an effective fashion. This concern was not unique to state governments. In fact, item-veto amendments to the U.S. Constitution have been proposed from the 1870s onward in an effort to restore the original purpose of the veto. However, state constitution makers not only debated the item veto at great length during this same period, but also adopted this device in most cases.

The main concern about judicial review was that state and federal judges were increasingly engaging in policy making, particularly in the late nineteenth and early twentieth centuries, and in such a way as to prevent the enactment of progressive legislation. Once again, amendments were occasionally introduced in Congress to restrict judicial power, but they received little consideration and were never adopted. State constitution makers, by contrast, engaged in extended debates about supermajority requirements and the recall of judges and judicial decisions, and each of these was adopted in some form in the early twentieth century.

5

BICAMERALISM

For the past several centuries, bicameralism has been the sub-ject of considerable debate around the world. Political theorists have been led to discourse on the relative merits of bicameralism and unicameralism, to the point that John Stuart Mill remarked in the mid-nineteenth century that "of all topics relating to the theory of representative government, none has been the subject of more discussion, especially on the Continent, than what is known as the question of the Two Chambers."[1] Constitution makers have been no less concerned with the question. In fact, during the twentieth century, several countries made the move from bicameralism to unicameralism, such that by the start of the twenty-first century, a majority of countries operated unicameral legislatures.[2]

The United States is thought to constitute an important exception in that there has been little debate about the wisdom of maintaining two chambers in Congress. As Richard Fenno has argued, "Bicameralism is a political com-monplace in the United States. The division of our national legislature into two separate bodies was little debated in 1787, and it has been taken for granted ever since."[3] Moreover, save for the Seventeenth Amendment, which brought about direct senatorial elections,[4] few formal changes have been made in the composition and organization of the two chambers.[5]

In one sense, it is unsurprising that bicameralism has been so entrenched in the U.S. Congress, given the strong correlation around the world between the presence of a federal system and the decision to adopt a bicameral legislature.[6] It is less apparent why bicameralism has prevailed in the states, which might have been expected to follow the many other unitary polities around the world, as well as the many subnational polities in federations, that have adopted unicameralism.[7]

Scholars have occasionally turned their attention to state-level debates over bicameralism and noted that four states have established unicameral legislatures at various times. Several scholars have been drawn to the initial wave of state constitution making, when Pennsylvania, Georgia, and Vermont each operated unicameral legislatures,[8] with Pennsylvania's experiment running until 1790,[9] Georgia's experiment lasting until 1789,[10] and Vermont's unicameral legislature lasting until 1836.[11] Other scholars have studied Nebraska's experience with unicameralism, which began in 1937 and continues to this day.[12]

What has not received sufficient attention is the full extent of the challenge mounted against bicameralism in state conventions across the country during the last two centuries. At times, convention delegates mounted a direct challenge to bicameralism by proposing that the two-house system be eliminated and replaced by unicameralism.[13] At other times, delegates were led to reconsider the need for and purpose of bicameralism during various debates about the organization of the two houses, whether regarding the size and basis of apportionment of the two houses,[14] the term lengths of legislators in each house,[15] the different qualifications for serving in or voting for the members of the two houses,[16] or the distinctive powers of the houses.[17]

In fact, state constitution makers have engaged in extensive debates about the wisdom and purpose of bicameralism. After the founding era, when state constitution makers grappled with whether to adopt bicameralism and eventually did so (sometimes belatedly), challenges to bicameralism have been prevalent during three periods. The first challenge took place in the mid-nineteenth century, when one of the initial purposes of creating a senate—providing representation for property holders—came to be seen as an increasingly unpersuasive justification by Jacksonian Era convention delegates. Then, in the final decade of the nineteenth century and first two decades of the twentieth century, bicameralism was subject to another challenge, as Progressive Era constitution makers questioned the legitimacy of all governing institutions, including the senate, that were seen as inhibiting the direct expression of public opinion. Bicameralism then became the subject of controversy yet again in the second half of the twentieth century, when the U.S. Supreme Court prevented the states from apportioning either house on the basis of political subdivisions, thereby removing yet another justification for a second chamber.

In analyzing the debates stimulated by each of these challenges, it becomes clear that state constitution makers' conceptions of bicameralism have undergone several important changes. From the beginning, it was understood that a second house is valuable as a deliberative check on the passage of hasty or ill-advised legislation. It has also been understood that the two houses should be organized in a distinct manner, so as to represent different interests in the lawmaking process. During the course of American history, both of these justifications have been called into question, as constitution makers from the Progressive Era onward began to doubt whether a second house was necessary to promote deliberation, and as various distinctions between the houses were rendered unavailable, first during the Jacksonian Era and then after the Reapportionment Revolution. In one sense, bicameralism has survived these challenges intact, in that all but one state has retained its second chamber. In another sense, bicameralism has evolved considerably, in that the arguments advanced on its behalf have changed during the course of the American regime, and insofar as fewer such arguments are now available than in previous years.

The principal lesson to be drawn from these state convention debates is that bicameralism is less firmly entrenched in the American constitutional tradition than one would conclude from a study of the federal constitution alone. The periodic reconsideration of bicameralism by state constitution makers, in contrast with the inattention to the issue at the federal level, is due in part to the more frequent opportunities for such deliberation at the state level. In addition, state constitution makers have concluded that the rationale for bicameralism is not as clear or compelling at the state level, in light of the different structure of federal and state governments. That is, bicameralism at the national level has gone unchallenged primarily because the states are seen as sovereign and therefore provide a basis for distinguishing between the houses. At the state level, however, local governments do not enjoy a similar status, and as a result, state constitution makers have been led to search, not always successfully, for an alternative means of supplying a ground of distinction between the chambers.

The Founding

In drafting their initial constitutions in the 1770s and 1780s, state constitution makers had before them examples of both unicameral and bicameral legislatures. At the time that the Continental Congress issued its call for the states to draft their own constitutions, both Delaware and Pennsylvania (which had operated a bicameral system in the late seventeenth century and then shifted to unicameralism at the turn of the eighteenth century) had unicameral legislatures.[18] Other states—Massachusetts, Connecticut, New Hampshire, Rhode Island, Maryland, and Virginia—had initially operated unicameral legislatures in the seventeenth century, but were solidly in the bicameral camp by the start of the Revolution.[19] Other states—New Jersey, New York, North Carolina, South Carolina, and Georgia—essentially operated bicameral legislatures from the beginning.[20]

Given the opportunity to redesign their governing institutions in the 1770s and 1780s, a number of constitution makers urged the retention or adoption of single-chamber legislatures, most notably Benjamin Franklin.[21] As Franklin argued in 1789, by which time Pennsylvania's unicameral system had come under attack, "If one part of the legislature may control the operations of the other, may not the impulses of passion, the combinations of interest, the intrigues of faction, the haste of folly, or the spirit of encroachment in one of those bodies obstruct the good proposed by the other, and frustrate its advantages to the public."[22] The master of the pithy phrase and instructive anecdote, Franklin, who on an earlier occasion had likened a two-house legislature to "putting one horse before a cart and one behind it, both pulling in opposite directions,"[23] took this opportunity to tell the "fable of the snake, with two heads and one body." As he explained, "She was going to a brook to drink, and in her way was to pass through a hedge, a twig of which opposed her direct course; one head chose to go on the right side of the twig, the other on the left; so that time was spent in the contest, and, before the decision was completed, the poor snake died with thirst."[24]

In the belief that a second chamber contributed to unnecessary delay, superfluous expense, and additional opportunities for corruption, three states adopted unicameralism during their initial forays into constitution making. At the urging of Franklin, among others, Pennsylvania retained its unicameral legislature when adopting its Constitution of 1776; Georgia adopted unicameralism when drafting its Constitution of 1777; and Vermont followed Pennsylvania's lead in this area, as in so many others, when it drafted its Constitution of 1777. Although Georgia and Pennsylvania soon chose to add a second house, in 1789 and 1790, respectively, Vermont's unicameral legislature lasted until 1836.[25]

All of the other states rejected unicameralism. Delaware switched to bicameralism. Rhode Island and Connecticut declined to revise their constitutions and thus left their bicameral legislatures undisturbed. Each of the remaining states drafted constitutions that continued their existing bicameral systems.[26] To some extent, these decisions can be attributed to a reluctance to depart from long-standing precedent, given that many of these states boasted more than a century of experience with both an upper and a lower house. At the same time, state constitution makers were quite willing to deviate from precedents in other areas, and therefore individuals who favored retaining the bicameral system were required to articulate a persuasive justification for this position.

For most constitution makers during this period, the case for bicameralism began with the argument that a second chamber provided a necessary check on a single chamber. It was thought that members of a single body would invariably misuse their power, whether by enacting measures that failed to serve the public good or by exercising powers that properly belonged to other institutions. As John Adams explained in his *Thoughts on Government,* a single assembly would be "subject to fits of humor, starts of passion, flights of enthusiasm, partialities, or prejudice—and consequently productive of hasty results and absurd judgments"; it was "apt to be avaricious, and in time will not scruple to exempt itself from burdens which it will lay without compunction upon its constituents"; and it would be likely to "grow ambitious, and after a time will not hesitate to vote itself perpetual."[27] It was equally evident to supporters of bicameralism that a second house would go a long way toward improving the deliberative character of the lawmaking process. Thus when George Washington was asked to defend the provision for a senate in the federal constitution, he responded with an anecdote that was equally applicable to state constitutions of the day. As the story goes, Washington had been handed a cup of tea and proceeded to pour the tea into a saucer. He explained, "This cup is the House of Representatives. Its contents have come directly from the people, who may be in a state of great excitement. This saucer is the Senate, in which I can hold the scalding liquid till its heat has subsided enough to make it safe to drink."[28]

Supporters of a bicameral system were generally not content, however, to rest their case for a second chamber solely on its capacity to serve as a deliberative check. In their view, it was not enough merely to create a second house; this house had to be composed in a distinct manner from the first. As Thomas Jefferson wrote in his *Notes on the State of Virginia,* in the course of critiquing the composition of the Virginia senate, "The purpose of establishing different houses of legislation is to introduce the influence of different interests or different principles." Although "in some of the American states the delegates and senators are so chosen, as that the first represent the persons, and the second the property of the state," Virginia had made the mistake of providing for a senate that was "too homogenous with the house of delegates," and thereby failed to "derive from the separation of our legislature into two houses, those benefits which a proper complication of principles is capable of producing, and those which alone can compensate the evils which may be produced by their dissensions."[29]

This concern with distinguishing the two houses was not confined to Jefferson and other state constitution makers during this period. James Madison advanced a similar argument when defending the composition of the U.S. Senate. As he argued in Federalist No. 62, because "the improbability of sinister combinations will be in proportion to the dissimilarity in the genius of the two bodies, it must be politic to distinguish them from each other by every circumstance which will consist with a due harmony in all proper measures, and with the genuine principles of republican government."[30] But whereas delegates to the federal convention supplied several clear distinctions between the two houses of the U.S. Congress, most notably the apportionment of the Senate by states and the House by population, the proper basis for distinguishing the two houses of state legislatures was less certain.[31]

There was general agreement among early state constitution makers that the principal means of distinguishing the two houses was to provide that the senate would, to a certain extent, embody aristocratic virtues. There was some disagreement, though, about the precise manner of defining and protecting the aristocracy and about the specific way in which the senate ought to be structured so as to embody their virtues.[32] In terms of which individuals embodied aristocratic virtues, there was scattered support for recognition of a hereditary aristocracy, but for the most part delegates sought to take account of a natural aristocracy. As Benjamin Rush argued in a 1777 discourse on the Pennsylvania Constitution,

> It has often been said, that there is but one rank of men in America, and therefore, that there should be only one representation of them in a government. I agree, that we have no artificial distinctions of men into noblemen and

commoners among us, but it ought to be remarked, that superior degrees of industry and capacity, and above all, commerce, have introduced inequality of property among us, and these have introduced natural distinctions of rank in Pennsylvania, as certain and general as the artificial distinctions of men in Europe. This will ever be the case while commerce exists in this country.[33]

The general understanding, as Jackson Turner Main later concluded in his review of these debates, was that "a senate should consist of wise, and preferably disinterested, men," and these "men of wisdom would most likely be found among property holders who would then quite correctly defend property rights against the onslaught of numbers."[34]

As for the way to structure the senate to take account of these aristocratic virtues, several individuals argued that the main goal should be to *limit* the power of property holders. As Rush argued, "The men of middling property and poor men can never be safe in a mixed representation with the men of over-grown property. Their liberties can only be secured by having exact bounds prescribed to their power, in the fundamental principles of the Constitution. By a representation of the men of middling fortunes in one house, their *whole* strength is collected against the influence of wealth," and "would enable them to check that lust for dominion which is always connected with opulence."[35] More frequently, though, constitution makers sought to *secure* the interests of property holders. Theophilus Parsons, reputed author of the "Essex Result," argued in a 1778 assessment of the proposed Massachusetts Constitution, that the failure to provide adequate representation for property holders would mean that "some members enjoy greater benefits and powers in legislation than others," insofar as "the property-holder parts with the control over his person, as well as he who hath no property, and the former also parts with the control over his property, of which the latter is destitute."[36] It was therefore important that "representation of property be attended to" in the selection of the senate.[37]

State constitution makers differed in the specific ways that they sought to secure representation of property interests. Each state that drafted a constitution during the founding era provided for a senate that was much smaller than the house.[38] Nearly all of these states provided that revenue bills could only originate in the house, and several states also stipulated that revenue bills could not even be amended in the senate.[39] The majority of these states provided for longer terms of office for senators than representatives.[40] Many of these states also imposed different requirements for members of the house and senate. In addition to requiring a higher minimum age for service in the senate, most of these states—Delaware, Maryland, Massachusetts, New Hampshire, New Jersey, New York, North Carolina, and South Carolina—required senators to meet higher property requirements.[41] Finally, another group of states distinguished between the electorates that selected members of the two houses. Two states—New York and North Carolina—achieved such a distinction by imposing different property requirements on voters in house and senate elections.[42] Another two states—Massachusetts and New Hampshire—achieved such a distinction by apportioning senate seats based on the proportion of taxes paid by the residents of each district.[43] Two states—New York and Virginia—established quite large senate districts.[44] Maryland provided that senators would be selected by an electoral college mechanism.[45]

It is true, as Marc Kruman has noted, that these distinctions were used in different degrees in different states, and that states generally "refused to make senates too different and too independent" from the lower houses.[46] It is also true that these distinctions had varying degrees of effectiveness in creating senates that actually behaved in a distinct manner from the lower houses. As Main has shown, with the exception of Maryland, and to a certain degree South Carolina and Virginia, most senates "failed adequately to embody the aristocratic principle" that constitution makers envisioned, whether because property requirements were set at such a low level that few individuals were excluded from the upper house or because these requirements were not rigidly enforced.[47] Nevertheless, the fact remains that constitution makers in a majority of states sought to achieve such a distinction between the two houses, and, as Main concluded, even if senates did not always "become elite bodies, they did contain strong aristocratic elements that occasionally succeeded in checking the more popular branch."[48]

The Jacksonian Era

Beginning in the 1820s, and continuing throughout the nineteenth century, states were quite active in revising their original constitutions, and other states drafted constitutions for the first time. Constitution makers during this period came under pressure to eliminate any distinctions grounded in property holdings, and this had implications for many institutions, including bicameralism. As a result, delegates were led to reconsider the purpose, and occasionally the wisdom, of maintaining a second chamber.[49]

Although constitution makers in a few states maintained that a second chamber was still needed to represent property interests, by the mid-nineteenth century, these arguments had been overcome in nearly all states. With the elimination of property-based distinctions, the question inevitably arose as to whether the upper house should be retained and how it could be justified. The responses took three principal forms. First, scattered calls were heard for the elimination of the upper house, from delegates who argued that if the sole purpose of the senate was to protect property, then once property distinctions were rejected, the senate should be dispensed with as well. Another, much larger, group of delegates responded that the senate should be retained because it still served as a deliberative check on the passage of ill-advised legislation, even if senators and representatives no longer represented distinct interests. In fact, many delegates in this second group viewed the remaining distinctions between the two houses as remnants of an outdated belief that the senate should embody aristocratic virtues; therefore, they advocated the elimination of as many distinctions as possible. Although this position attracted a fair amount of support, the majority of delegates in nineteenth-century conventions ultimately supported a third position. On this view, the senate should be retained in order to promote deliberation, but this goal would be best achieved by organizing the two chambers so as to provide distinct perspectives in the lawmaking process. Therefore, this final group of delegates sought to retain, and occasionally enhance, the distinctive characteristics of the senate.

The Elimination of Property Distinctions

One of the first questions taken up in many nineteenth-century conventions was whether to retain the original property-based distinctions between the two houses. Although several states that entered the union in the nineteenth century adopted these distinctions, most declined to do so, and by the mid-nineteenth century, virtually all of the original states had eliminated these provisions. This is not to say, though, that delegates to these nineteenth-century conventions were completely and immediately persuaded of the wisdom of this course of action. In fact, property-based distinctions attracted a fair amount of support in several conventions and were occasionally retained for several decades after they were initially challenged.

Daniel Webster issued the most forceful defense of the need to take account of property in designing the senate. Webster argued that there were two main questions that faced the Massachusetts Convention of 1820–1821: "The first is, shall the legislative department be constructed with any other *check*, than such as arises simply from dividing the members of this department into two houses? The second is, if such other and further check ought to exist, *in what manner* shall it be created?"[50] It was clear to Webster that such a check was needed, insofar as there was "little of real utility" in any system in which "members of both houses are to be chosen at the same time, by the same electors, in the same districts, and for the same term of office."[51] He was therefore convinced that "if it be wise to give one agent the power of checking or controlling another, it is equally wise, most manifestly, that there should be some difference of character, sentiment, feeling, or origin, in that agent, who is to possess this control."[52] He was thus led to pose "the great question" of "where to find, or how to create this difference, in governments entirely elective and popular?"[53]

Webster concluded, along with several other early nineteenth-century delegates, that the best means of creating this difference was on the basis of property. William Prescott argued in the same Massachusetts convention that "the design of government was the protection of property as well as of personal rights—that there should be a representation of property as well as of persons. This must be done, either by giving the power of voting only to persons possessed of property, . . . or by giving a greater representation to the parts of the state where there was the greatest accumulation of property." In his view, "the senate, constituted in this manner, formed a more effectual check upon the house of representatives. If there were two bodies elected by the same persons, in the same districts, and in the same proportions, although they sat in different chambers, they would not act in an equal degree as a check upon each other."[54] As William Sullivan explained in the same convention, "The principle of the house of representatives is *equality,* perfect equality as to numbers which are to be represented." But the senate "was necessarily founded on some other principle; and none was more obvious than that of *property.*"[55] Although it might be possible to devise other means of distinguishing the two houses so "that they should in truth operate as checks—that they should not be liable to feel at the same moment that impulse or excitement which leads to haste and improvidence," it was clear to William Gaston in the North Carolina Convention of 1835 that "the only interests likely to be often arrayed against each other" at the state level "are those of *property* and of *persons.* Such a Government is formed for the purpose of protecting property and persons, and would be inadequate to its end, if left either at the mercy of the other."[56]

There was little question, in the view of these delegates, that society derived great benefits from the accumulation of property. Joseph Story was moved at one point in the Massachusetts Convention of 1820–1821 to consider "the blessings which property bestows," and he could not believe that several of his fellow delegates were "serious in their views, that it does not deserve our utmost protection." After recounting the many "general blessings, which prosperity diffuses through the whole mass of the community," he concluded that "every man, from him who possesses but a single dollar up to him who possesses the greatest fortune, is equally interested in its security and its preservation."[57] In light of the benefits that accrued to the state from the accumulation of property—Ambrose Spencer in the New York Convention of 1821 pointed out that "churches and hospitals are erected, and schools established by property, and every government that has the interest and prosperity of the governed at heart, must feel bound to protect it"[58]—delegates thought it was eminently reasonable for the state to provide special representation for property holders. Abel Upshur argued in the Virginia Convention of 1829–1830,

> If men enter into the social compact upon unequal terms; if one man brings into the partnership, his rights of person alone, and another brings into it, equal rights of person and all the rights of property beside, can they be said to have an equal interest in the common stock? Shall not he who has most at stake; who has, not only a *greater* interest, but a *peculiar* interest in society, possess an authority proportioned to that interest, and adequate to its protection?[59]

These delegates were particularly fearful of the consequences that would follow from eliminating property-based distinctions between the house and senate. During a debate in the New York Convention of 1821 about whether to retain a higher property requirement for voters in senate elections, James Kent referred to the senate "as the sheet anchor of the people's safety," and he sought to ensure that it would continue to be "the representative of the landed interest, and its security against the caprice of the motley assemblage of paupers, emigrants, journeyman manufacturers, and those undefinable classes of inhabitants which a state and city like ours is calculated to invite."[60] And when the question arose in the New Jersey Convention of 1844 as to whether to retain a property requirement for senators, James Parker made it clear that he

> wished to hold fast to that feature in one branch at least, so that if anything injurious to the landed interest should be attempted in the lower House, the

council might have some check upon them. Our laws were made in a great measure to affect property, and he questioned whether the whole landed interest should be left to hold their tenures subject to the legislation of those who have no interest in the land.[61]

Several delegates conjured up all sorts of dire consequences that might follow upon the elimination of higher property requirements in the senate. Willard Hall in the Delaware Convention of 1831 argued,

> If you take off the property qualification for Senator, I fear we shall run down hill rapidly. . . . No property qualification is to be required of members of the House of Representatives. This is correct. . . . But if we make the Senate the same in this respect as the House of Representatives, we may have a Legislature who may have no interest in regard to the manner in which taxes shall be laid—we may be giving away the power of taxation, and the taxes themselves, to men who have nothing to be taxed.[62]

Other delegates maintained that there was no need to engage in speculation; one need only peruse the historical record to see the disastrous consequences of upsetting the balance between people and property. John Adams in the Massachusetts Convention of 1820–1821 pointed out that "Aristides ruined the constitution of Solon, by destroying the balance between property and numbers, and, in consequence, a torrent of popular commotion broke in and desolated the republic. Let us come to Rome; property was infinitely more regarded than here, and it was only while the balance was maintained, that the liberties of the people were preserved." Turning to the present, he asked, "How many persons are there, even in this country, who have no property? Some think there are more without it, than with it. If so, and it were left to mere numbers, those who have no property would vote us out of our houses."[63]

These arguments had proved persuasive to a majority of state constitution makers in the late eighteenth century, and they occasionally carried the day in nineteenth-century conventions, including several conventions called for the purpose of writing inaugural constitutions[64] and others held to revise existing documents.[65] For the most part, though, nineteenth-century constitution makers came to view all property-based distinctions as illegitimate, and they increasingly voted to eliminate them.

In the view of an increasing number of convention delegates during this period, it was no longer possible to equate the accumulation of property with wisdom and prudence. As John Cramer proclaimed during a debate in the New York Convention of 1821 about whether to remove the higher property requirement for voters in senate elections, "Virtue is not synonymous with wealth. It resides not exclusively in the turreted palace. It descends to the straw-built cot, and the rude log cabin of our western wilds." He therefore urged the assembled delegates not to "degrade the deliberations of this assembly in the eyes of the world, by representing this class of our citizens as base and profligate, who are chargeable with no crime but that of poverty. Let us not brand this convention with a retention of this aristocratic feature in our constitution."[66] In the words of John Clayton during a debate over senate property requirements in the Delaware Convention of 1831, "It was not republican to make the possession of land, the qualification for an office."[67] Moreover, even if it were admitted that property holders were entitled to some influence in legislative deliberations, delegates began to follow Jacob Radcliff in the New York Convention of 1821 in arguing that "property will always carry with it an influence sufficient for its own protection," and it was therefore unnecessary to "give it an artificial aid, that may be dangerous to the rights of the community."[68] Finally, even if there might be legitimate concerns about preserving the rights of property holders against determined popular majorities, delegates responded that property requirements for electors or officeholders in one legislative chamber were unlikely, by themselves, to provide much protection. As Martin Van Buren argued in the same convention,

> When the people of this State shall have so far degenerated—when the principles of good order and good government which now happily characterize our people, and afford security to our institutions, shall have so far given way to anarchy and violence as to lead to an attack on private property either by an agrarian law . . . or by an attempt to throw all the public burthens on any particular class of men, then all constitutional provisions will be idle and unavailing, because they will have lost all their force and influence.[69]

The Search for a New Defense of the Bicameral Principle

One response to the elimination of property distinctions was to call for the abolition of the senate. In the view of several mid-nineteenth-century delegates, the sole reason for creating a senate had been to represent property interests; now that property interests were no longer entitled to representation, there was no need for a second chamber. Thus Christian Nave in the Indiana Convention of 1850–1851 wanted to "ask the reason why we should continue this aristocratic body in the organic law of the State?" He thought that the senate was "opposed in principle to our republican habits" and was "a badge of tyranny borrowed from our mother country, Great Britain." He could not understand why "a nation should have resorted to a Revolution to rid themselves of tyranny, and continue to adhere to any of the features of that Government, which have for their object the concentration of power in the few, to guard over the people's representatives; aye, sir, over the people themselves." He was therefore led to "conclude that there is no necessity for a Senate in this State."[70] Daniel Robertson in the Ohio Convention of 1850–1851 was of a similar mind, and he asked the assembled delegates, "Why *shall* we not dispense with the Senate?" In his view, "The progress of the Democratic principle has been such, that the reason for a State Senate has passed away, for the Senate was established originally, as I have shown in almost every state of the Union, to represent the landed interest."[71] Given that this was no longer a legitimate justification, Robertson considered whether any legitimate reasons remained for retaining the bicameral system. Unable to come up with a justification, he concluded that "like the fictions in law, the Senate is retained by the influence of custom and precedent, when the reason for it has passed away."[72] In a similar fashion, William Snyder in the Illinois Convention of 1869–1870 argued that although bicameralism might still serve a purpose at the national level, this purpose was inapplicable to the states, and therefore bicameralism ought to be rejected at the state level:

> There is an indispensable reason why the United States senate should exist, and that is the necessity of protection, somewhere, of the small sovereignties which compose our union, against the encroachment and oppression of the large ones. It is peculiar to our system and circumstances. But what reason can we give for the existence of the little conclave which meets in the other end of this building, or for the institution of any such body as a State senate? It is elected by the same voters, at the same time with the members of the other house. . . . Can any one point out what good the senate has ever done—of what benefit it has ever been?[73]

To be sure, several of these delegates proposed a unicameral legislature only in passing, and without offering a sustained defense of the position. This was the case, for instance, when Thomas Smith concluded a speech in the Indiana Convention of 1850–1851 by saying, "You might dispense with the Senate altogether if you thought proper. Greater men than I am have proposed but a single legislative branch. Benjamin Franklin was opposed to having any such body as a Senate in the legislative department of the Federal Government."[74] Still other delegates stressed that they were seeking primarily to stimulate debate on the subject; they were willing to be persuaded of the need for such an institution, but they wanted someone to make this case. It was in this spirit that Joseph McCormick addressed the Ohio Convention of 1850–1851. He argued that state senates had been retained merely because state constitution makers had "found such a provision in the constitution of the United States. I can see no other reason for it."[75] It was not that he was "so entirely satisfied that but one House is sufficient, as to declare [his] adhesion to such a provision firmly."[76] But he was unwilling to retain the institution unless "paramount reasons are given" and until he was shown that "some great good may be attained."[77]

Ultimately, few individuals went so far as to oppose bicameralism during this period, and these delegates constituted a distinct minority in nineteenth-century conventions. Nevertheless, they had the effect of compelling their colleagues to reconsider the purpose of bicameralism and to articulate a defense of the institution that could take account of the changed circumstances since the founding era.[78]

One group of delegates responded to this challenge by arguing that the senate should be retained because it still promoted deliberation in the lawmaking process. These delegates fully supported the elimination of property distinctions between the two houses, but they did not believe that the protection of property interests exhausted the justifications for retaining the senate. As George Hoadly explained in the Ohio Convention of 1873–1874, it was true that upper houses in other countries had been designed to "represent, in some form or other, the aristocratic and monarchical elements in society. In this country, if I am right, we have maintained the double-chamber system because we have found that it was not exposed to the evils that have been found abroad, and because it secures us, to some extent, against the mischief of hasty legislation, over-legislation, or too much legislation."[79]

This was not, in and of itself, a novel argument. Such an argument had been advanced by several individuals during the initial wave of eighteenth-century constitution making. At that time, though, arguments about the benefits of deliberation were usually advanced in tandem with arguments about the benefits of representing different interests. What was distinctive about this argument as it was advanced in mid-nineteenth-century conventions was that deliberation was now considered by several delegates to be the sole and sufficient justification for bicameralism, and, moreover, distinctions between the two houses were now deemed unnecessary and even illegitimate.

This view was perhaps best expressed by Augustus Reese in the Georgia Convention of 1877:

> There is some idea that the senate should be on a different basis from the house, derived probably from the idea that in congress senators and representatives stand upon a different basis. That is true, but the senators there represent sovereignties. Upon what basis do you put them in the state? Do they not represent the same interests, and the same constituencies? If they do, why shall there be any difference in the basis of choosing the two bodies? They have the same interest and constituencies to represent, and there is no reason for putting them on a different basis—no reason that will hold good either in practice or in policy. What is the use of two legislative bodies in the state at all? There is a vague, indefinite idea that the senate is a conservative body. Not so. Practically it amounts simply to this: that it is intended to prevent hasty and unwise legislation. If a bill passes the house to-day, it will be two or three days before it reaches the governor because it has to pass the senate first, and in that time any errors or hastily adopted provisions may be detected and corrected. If that were not reason for having the senate there would be no use for it at all in any state in the union.[80]

Delegates such as Mr. Reese could conceive of only two possible ways of distinguishing the house and senate. One might structure the upper house so as to represent the interests of property holders, or one could design the upper house so that it represented sovereign territories. As P. L. Mynatt argued in the same convention, it was clear by this point in time that "property cannot be represented." Moreover, although "in congress we have representation of people and of sovereign states," and "in England they have representations of property, of institutions, and of counties . . . [w]e cannot have any such thing under our form of government. Ours is a purely democratic government." He was therefore led to conclude, in the absence of any financial or territorial interests to be represented in the states, that "we have no use for a senate except for the purpose of checking the house in hasty legislation. That is the only reason for such a body."[81]

This view of bicameralism was put forward not only to justify the retention of the senate, but also to defend a particular conception of the way the senate should be constituted. In the view of many of these delegates, the deliberative function of the two houses could be fulfilled even in the absence of any differences in their composition. In fact, many of these delegates argued that existing distinctions were vestiges of earlier efforts to create an aristocratic upper house, and that they served primarily to perpetuate an outdated notion that the senate was intended to check the popular will.

Therefore, when questions arose in the nineteenth century about the wisdom of retaining various distinctions—whether regarding the number of members, size of constituencies, length of terms, qualifications of office holders, or powers of the two houses—many of these delegates urged that these distinctions be eliminated. In the New York Convention of 1846, for instance, James Forsyth sought to increase the size of the senate so that it would be brought more in line with the size of the house. He argued,

> In the early history of our Republic, it was thought necessary to interpose that body as a barrier between the property holders of the state and the great body of the people. This was the reason that that body was constituted of a small number. It was necessary for that object that it be small. But now that the doctrine of checks and bits and bridles upon the people was no longer tolerated, the time had come when this body must be made more representative and more assimilated to the wants of the people.[82]

Benjamin Platt Carpenter in the New York Convention of 1867–1868 similarly sought to reduce the size of senate districts, on the grounds that the purpose of a second house was to "be a check upon the other, not to contravene the popular will, but to prevent inconsiderate and hasty legislation." In his view, those who preferred to elect senators from large constituencies were seeking not so much to prevent ill-advised legislation as to create "a magnificent body, figuratively on stilts, far above the people, knowing nothing of the wants of localities, or the demands of the people."[83] Mr. Hoadly of Ohio had similar reasons for urging a reduction in the length of senate terms. In his view, lengthy senate terms were borne of the same aristocratic theories that were prevalent in Europe, where senates were designed to "represent landed, territorial, moneyed, or hereditary aristocracies." He argued that "when you make the term of office of one body longer than the other, you are going in the direction of the evil as it exists abroad," and he was led to "protest against every proposition which shall build up one House as a chamber having more dignity than the other."[84] Similarly, John Dickey in the Pennsylvania Convention of 1837–1838 sought to eliminate the higher senate age qualifications, as a means of breaking down

"the aristocracy of the Senate." He noted that "as we were now making innovations on the theory of the Constitution, by cutting down the independence of
the Senate, shortening its term, destroying its influence, and, in fact, making
it a popular branch, assimilated to the other House, he had proposed, by way
of carrying out this theory, to reduce the qualification of age."[85] Finally, William
Merrick in the Maryland Convention of 1850–1851 had similar motivations for
overturning the rule that revenue bills must originate in the house. He thought
that "this notion of denying to the Senate the privilege of originating money-
bills, was an obsolete idea. It was behind the times, and originated in a jealousy
of an aristocratic branch. There was such a branch in England, and probably
there had been similar branches here. But things were all changed. Here we
were now all democratic."[86]

Although this view of bicameralism was advanced at conventions and occasionally proved persuasive, it was not the dominant view during the nineteenth
century. Ultimately, a majority of convention delegates rejected the idea that
two similarly constituted houses could supply the deliberative check desired in
a bicameral system. This final group of delegates had no interest in reviving the
older notion that the senate represented a distinct societal interest, whether of
property holders or any other group; but they argued that the senate should still
be constituted so as to bring a distinct perspective to the lawmaking process.

It was not enough, this final group of delegates argued, to defend bicameralism merely by arguing that two houses would be more effective than one in
preventing the passage of hasty or ill-advised legislation. This was certainly a
purpose of creating two houses; but this purpose could not be achieved if the
two houses were mirror images of one another. As Abner Harding argued in the
Illinois Convention of 1847,

> Why incur the many inconveniences, and the expenses necessarily incident
> to such a form of government, unless the benefits which ought to be derived
> therefrom could be secured. If the members of the two branches of the legis-
> lature were to possess like qualifications, to be vested with like powers on all
> subjects of legislation, to be elected upon precisely the same basis of popula-
> tion, by the same electors, in the same manner, and for the same term, why
> should they be divided into two branches?

In his view, "It was not enough to be told that one branch was intended to be a
check upon the other, unless by their different characters and constituency this
desirable result was to be secured." He concluded, "I admit, Sir, that by the divi-

sion of the legislative department into two branches, those branches may have a tendency to check the action of each other; but, Sir, that tendency is as chaff before the wind, when they are all elected upon the same basis of representation, and two of them according to the same apportionment."[87]

The question was how to constitute the two houses in order to achieve the desired distinct institutional perspectives. Peter Van Winkle argued in the inaugural West Virginia Convention of 1861–1863 that "there should be a considerable distinction between the members of the two houses. It is entirely useless to have two houses of the legislature if they are both constituted in the same way precisely. There is no chance that you get a different opinion from one from what you get of the other." He argued that "it is not necessary to constitute a house of lords, or constitute an aristocracy who make a house of lords." Rather, it would be possible to "in some way introduce a principle which will make this second house as valuable to us as the principle of the house of lords is in the legislature of Great Britain." Thus the challenge was to

> create a senate here for this new state that shall necessarily from the mode in which it is constituted be compelled to regard these questions which will come up for legislation from a different standpoint from the house of delegates. If we can create such a body we make two houses who must approach the consideration of these questions by different roads; look at them in different aspects; be governed by different but not antagonistic interests; and then when an act passes both houses, we have some guaranty that it is more than the effervescence of the moment; not passed upon from impulse, but well considered and weighed; and that objections that may arise, not only from one point of view but from the other, have been obviated before it was permitted to pass.[88]

Fortunately, in the view of this group of delegates, there were a variety of ways of supplying such different perspectives. Their chief concern was to retain, reconceptualize, and occasionally augment existing institutional differences between the house and senate, so as to provide sufficiently distinct perspectives in the lawmaking process. In each case—regarding the size of the body, size of the constituency, length of terms, qualifications for membership, and powers of the chamber—these distinctions were seen as a way of differentiating the two chambers and serving additional goals quite apart from any desire to represent aristocratic virtues.

One way of obtaining distinct perspectives was to follow the long-standing practice of creating different-sized houses. Although efforts were occasionally made to increase the size of the senate on the grounds that smaller senates were relics of earlier efforts to create an aristocratic upper house, every state chose during the nineteenth century to continue its traditional policy of differentiating the size of the two houses.[89] One reason for maintaining different-sized chambers, as Francis Kernan explained in the New York Convention of 1867–1868, was simply that "the Senate, the smaller body, should be so constituted . . . as that it shall possess different characteristics from the House."[90] The idea, as A. R. Lawton argued in the Georgia Convention of 1877, was that chambers of different sizes would bring different perspectives to the legislative process: "Certain classes of legislation shall come from the house solely because it comes more directly from the people, in smaller numbers, and from the neighborhoods. It is to be hoped as the number is decreased we will find the legislature composed of better men, with larger views, and who will be more especially the representatives of the people."[91]

A related way of obtaining distinct perspectives was to elect senators and representatives from different-sized constituencies. Originally, some states provided that representatives and senators were selected by the same constituency; in these states, the different-sized chambers were created by permitting these constituencies to select several representatives to the lower house.[92] Although during the nineteenth century several states continued this policy, most took a different approach and created senate districts that were larger—sometimes considerably larger—than house districts.[93] At one level, larger senate districts had the virtue of distinguishing the two chambers. Thus John Grymes complained in the Louisiana Convention of 1845 that if the senate "is to be constituted upon the same model—if there is to be no dissimilarity in the constituency or in the territory it represents, what becomes of the theory of the government that it is a check to guard against the results of hasty and inconsiderate legislation."[94] He argued that at the present time, "the only distinction now remaining" in regard to the senate "is that they are called from a greater constituency. Destroy that difference, and the theory of our government is at an end."[95] As George Barker cautioned in the New York Convention of 1867–1868, to the extent that house and senate constituencies were made too similar, then the members "are often nominated by the influence of the same public men, are controlled by the same political considerations, and are elected at the same election every other year, and in spirit, in policy and effect, the same as if the legislative power was vested in one legislative body."[96] At another level, larger senate districts were valuable in that they compelled senators to take a broader perspective on policy making.

Robert McClelland in the Michigan Convention of 1850 had "always supposed a Senate should be differently constituted from the House," and it was evident to him that a senator who represented a large district would be "more competent and better fitted to represent the whole people calmly and dispassionately." He argued, "Make him responsible to a large extent of territory, and although he may reside in the midst of the popular excitement, yet he will generally survey the whole district, and act in accordance with the desires and interests of all. Representatives have charge of particular localities; but Senators should have their attention directed to large districts, and to the interests of the whole State."[97]

Another means of securing distinct perspectives was to establish longer terms for senators than representatives. Although states occasionally chose during the course of the nineteenth century to eliminate longer senate terms, for the most part states retained—and in some cases increased—the differential between house and senate terms.[98] Once again, longer senate terms were supported in part out of a desire simply to establish another distinction between the two chambers. During a debate in the Delaware Convention of 1831 over whether to adopt two- or six-year senate terms, Henry Rodney explained his preference for a six-year term by saying that he was "under the impression that property qualification" would be eliminated, "and thinking it necessary in that case to give more stability to the Senate."[99] In similar fashion, John Bartow in the Michigan Convention of 1850 announced his preference for a three-year rather than a one-year senate term, on the grounds that "if we were to have a Senate at all, and preserve its identity, the members should be elected in a different manner from the representatives. If the same mode is adopted, it does away with the Senate as a Senate, and makes it an adjunct of the House."[100] Aside from a general concern with distinguishing the two houses, delegates were also intent on obtaining certain advantages associated with longer terms of office in one house. James Brown in the West Virginia Convention of 1861–1863 was one of a number of delegates who expressed a desire "to furnish a body of mature years, of long experience, and whose term of office by being longer removed from the electors will constitute them something of a check balancing the other house which is always emphatically influenced by an expression of popular sentiment."[101]

Another means of distinguishing the two houses was to secure a greater degree of continuity for the members of one chamber. By providing longer senate terms and stipulating that only a portion of the senators would stand for office each election, states sought, once again, to distinguish the character of the two houses.[102] Thus Thomas Powell in the Ohio Convention of 1873–1874 argued that "there should be a great difference between the character of the Senate and that of the House of Representatives," and, among other grounds of distinction, "one half of [the senators] should be elected in a different year from the other half, so that the Senate may not be all elected at one time."[103] Among the reasons for permitting rotation in one house, according to Erastus Root in the New York Convention of 1821, was that it would make the senate "a stable and permanent body." As he explained, "It was advisable to have it divided into classes, by which a certain number of seats might become vacant, and be filled annually, preserving at all times a majority of old members, by whose experience the new ones might annually be benefited—the whole serving as a salutary check upon the other branch of the legislature."[104]

Another distinction was achieved by maintaining different qualifications for membership in the two houses. In this regard, property requirements were no longer an option; but age requirements were still a possibility. Although nearly half of the states chose not to adopt different age requirements for the two houses, many older states chose during the nineteenth century to retain their different age requirements, and some new states followed suit.[105] Once again, delegates viewed this provision as yet another means of providing some sort of difference in the character of the two houses. As Silas Bryan explained in the Illinois Convention of 1869–1870, in response to a motion to eliminate the higher age qualification for senators, "The distinction between the qualifications of senators and representatives is well founded; and so long as we keep up the distinction of the two houses, there should be this distinction of age." He made it clear that he was "not contending for any particular number of years, but for the justness of the distinction between the qualifications of the members of these different bodies."[106] Delegates also followed M. M. McCarver of the California Convention of 1849 in concluding that it was "but reasonable to suppose that maturity of judgment is acquired by the experience that age affords." He explained that "when the young and inexperienced members of the lower House passed laws, he desired that those laws should be reconsidered and amended by older and wiser heads."[107] Moreover, as John Chandler argued in the Pennsylvania Convention of 1837–1838, "if he understood the definition of 'senator,' it meant an old man, and was derived from the Latin word 'senex.' Therefore, sending *young* men to the senate, would be a contradiction in terms."[108]

A final ground of distinction concerned the powers of the two chambers. Most states assigned different responsibilities to the two houses in the impeachment and confirmation process and in regard to originating revenue bills. From time to time, though, delegates were led to reconsider the revenue-bill requirement, which was seen as stemming from an outdated notion that the two houses represented different classes of citizens. Once again, nineteenth-century constitution makers generally retained this provision, in part out of a desire to secure sufficient distinctions between the two chambers. Moreover, at times, delegates even sought to go further in sharpening the distinctions between the two houses. Thus James Dunlop argued, in an effort to augment the existing distinctions during the Pennsylvania Convention of 1837–1838, "The senate could only be an effectual check on the house of representatives, either by being organized in a different manner, or having different powers conferred on them." He noted that several recent changes had reduced the differences between the two chambers, and "there was, consequently, between the two bodies, no rivalry of opinion—no *esprit de corps*—no anxiety to watch and check each other." But "if the senate had somewhat different powers conferred on them, they would feel themselves more of a revising body," and this would help to ensure that "one body should be distinct from the other, in order that one might be a check on the other."[109] Although Dunlop's particular proposal was unsuccessful—he wanted to prevent the senate from originating appropriations as well as revenue bills[110]—two-thirds of the states did opt to retain their requirement that revenue bills must originate in the house, thereby maintaining yet another distinction between the two chambers.[111] In fact, several states considered going further and requiring that all bills originate in the house. In part, this was seen as yet another way of distinguishing the two chambers. As John Ritchie argued in the Kansas Convention of 1859, which went on to adopt this proposal,[112] "If the Senate is to have the same power with the House in originating bills, I would be in favor of but one body."[113] An additional reason, as James Winchell, president of the same convention, explained, was that this "would secure to the Senate a higher character. They would act as a board of censors, criticizing and amending the acts of the lower House."[114]

During the course of the nineteenth century, then, state constitution makers' conception of bicameralism evolved considerably. Forced by the elimination of property-based requirements to articulate a new defense of the bicameral principle, several delegates sought, unsuccessfully, to abolish the senate. Another group of delegates sought, with somewhat more success in certain states, to retain the senate but to eliminate many of its distinctive features. On this view, the deliberative purpose of the senate could be achieved without these distinctions.

Most states, however, decided not only to keep the senate, but also to maintain and even enhance its distinctive features. According to this prevailing view, distinctions between the house and senate were an essential means of producing different institutional perspectives and contributing to a more deliberative legislative process.

The Progressive Era

During the final decade of the nineteenth century and first two decades of the twentieth century, changing economic conditions and political doctrines led constitution makers to undertake a fundamental reassessment of state governing institutions. Convention delegates who had once been concerned with restraining the legislature out of a belief that legislation frequently advanced the cause of powerful economic interests now sought to remove barriers to an efficient legislative process, in the belief that legislation was often necessary to restrain corporate interests and protect individuals from corporate domination. Whether the concern was with enacting maximum-hours laws, minimum-wage provisions, workers' compensation acts, or social insurance measures, convention delegates frequently complained about the difficulty of securing the speedy passage of legislation, and they often attributed the difficulties to the influence of corporate interests. As a result, Progressive Era constitution makers were led to consider a variety of institutional reforms and to look with disfavor on any institutions that were seen as standing in the way of efficient legislative action or giving comfort to special interests.[115]

Bicameralism was one of the institutions that was called into question on these grounds during the Progressive Era. In the view of many delegates, the second chamber was no longer providing a brake on the passage of hasty and ill-advised legislation; rather, it was enabling special interests to prevent the passage of popular statutes. In fact, dissatisfaction with bicameralism became so widespread during this period that it was the rare convention that did not consider dispensing with the senate. In the ensuing debates, delegates who supported bicameralism were again compelled to defend the institution, and this time, they confronted a more serious and sustained challenge than in previous years. The mid-nineteenth-century critique had charged that the elimination of property-based distinctions rendered the second chamber superfluous; the challenge for defenders of bicameralism at that time had been to show that it was still possible to distinguish the two houses in important ways. During the Progressive Era, critics contended that the second chamber was actually harmful to the lawmaking process; supporters were thus forced to demonstrate that two chambers did, in fact, promote deliberation in the legislative process. Ultimately, these unicameralism proposals attracted some support in several conventions, but in each instance, convention delegates turned back these challenges.[116]

In regard to the existence of a second chamber, then, Progressive Era conventions featured extensive debates but few changes. However, the composition of the second chamber not only provoked much debate, but also led to the adoption of several changes during this period. Although there had been some discussion during the nineteenth century about distinguishing the houses by apportioning one by population and the other by political subdivision, these proposals had usually, although not always, been rejected. To the extent that nineteenth-century constitution makers had taken account of counties or towns in drawing legislative districts, such as by ensuring that each county could elect at least one member of the upper house, these provisions had generally not had much effect on the character of the two chambers. Beginning in the final decade of the nineteenth century, though, state constitution makers undertook a series of increasingly successful efforts to apportion one house by population and the other by political subdivision. At the same time, long-standing apportionment provisions in some states began to have the effect, as a result of changing population patterns, of creating two houses that were responsive to different interests. These developments were not without their critics, who in several instances defeated proposals to distinguish between the two houses in this fashion. In other states, however, convention delegates prevailed on their colleagues to adopt different bases of apportionment and thus to distinguish in yet another way between the house and senate.[117]

The Debate about the Need for a Second Chamber

Critics of bicameralism were convinced that even if two chambers had once served to promote deliberation in the lawmaking process, by the turn of the twentieth century, they were no longer serving this purpose.[118] Rather than giving two groups of legislators the opportunity to correct each other's mistakes, bicameralism actually permitted both houses to avoid taking responsibility for any mistakes. Thus Francis Jones in the inaugural Arizona Convention of 1910 was concerned about the "shifting from one house to the other of responsibilities" that accompanied a bicameral system. He was "very much in favor of eliminating the senate," and he argued "that almost all the states in the union are trying to get rid of their senates, and we ought not to try and create one."[119] Similarly, Roland Sawyer in the Massachusetts Convention of 1917–1919 argued that "by jockeying matters between the two branches it is possible for Representatives and Senators equally to escape responsibility for the enactment of legislation or the killing of legislation in a way detrimental to the people's interests."[120] The ultimate effect of a two-house legislature, as Charles Morrill argued in the same convention, was to "[make] it difficult to place the responsibility for legislative action. In Massachusetts as well as in other States we repeatedly see popular legislation,—what might be termed progressive legislation and labor legislation,—defeated by what is known as 'falling between the two branches;' that is, one branch will pass favorably upon a popular measure, often knowing that the other branch is 'fixed' in advance by the political machine of invisible government."[121] Moreover, rather than affording adequate time for the full consideration of legislative proposals, the bicameral system was actually having the opposite effect. According to the Minority Report of the Legislative Committee in the New York Convention of 1915, "The present method accentuates the congestion of important legislation which occurs at the end of a session when many important bills are amended and passed with scant attention. Bills are rushed from one house to another in the few days before adjournment and in the confusion much undesirable legislation is passed and becomes law."[122]

To the extent that two chambers did prevent the passage of legislation, these delegates argued, the bills that were defeated were the very ones that the public desired to see passed. Harry Thomas quoted from a newspaper editorial to this effect during the Ohio Convention of 1912. Echoing the argument of the eighteenth-century French philosopher Abbé de Sieyès—"if the second chamber agrees with the first, it is useless, and if not, it is bad"[123]—Thomas explained, "If the two bodies agree, one is sufficient, and if they disagree, then both might as well be abolished. They tell us that one serves as a check on the other; but oftener than otherwise the check is placed just where the people do not want it and where they would not have it if they had a single legislature."[124] John Norton in the Nebraska Convention of 1919–1920 was of the same mind. After taking note of the usual claim "that we need a check," he responded, "Is it not a fact that we get check of the wrong sort? Does not your two-house system more often check desirable legislation than undesirable legislation." During the previous legislative session, in particular, he thought that delegates would agree that there had been "a little too much check, if anything."[125] Even when the second chamber served only to delay, rather than defeat, the passage of legislation, these delegates argued that more often than not, this turned out to do more harm than good. As Hiram Peck argued in the Ohio Convention of 1912, "The two bodies are simply an obstacle to prompt action when it is often needed, and promote dickerings and discord when unity is wanted."[126] It was not that these delegates saw no need for a check on the passage of hasty and ill-advised legislation. They simply did not believe that the bicameral legislature was performing this function appropriately, and they were prepared, along with George Anderson in the Massachusetts Convention of 1917–1919, to put their faith in alternative checks such as "the new compulsory referendum" and "the Governor with his veto."[127]

Although these delegates were critical of the general concept of bicameralism, their particular target was the senate, which had come to be seen as "the graveyard of popular legislation," according to Mr. Morrill of Massachusetts.[128] His colleague George Webster recounted the story that George Washington had once defended the senate by arguing that it served to cool legislation, much as a saucer cooled one's tea. Webster went on to complain that "the senatorial saucer, sir, has reached such a degree of refrigeration that it freezes every beneficial piece of legislation that is brought up in the Commonwealth."[129] The obstructionist character of the senate was largely attributed to several of its distinctive features that had been celebrated, and occasionally augmented, during the course of the nineteenth century.[130] For instance, the small size of the senate was seen as rendering it more susceptible to corruption. Albert Parsons argued in the North Dakota Convention of 1889 that, for the most part, "corporate influence simply asks the absence of legislation," and so "the rule has been, for the corporations to direct their influence towards the upper house. It is much easier to control a small majority in that house than to control a majority in the lower house, and having a majority there they can check any legislation that they regard as being injurious to them."[131] The large size of senate districts also contributed to the problem, because, as Mr. Morrill explained, it was "impossible for the majority of their constituents—of the people—to keep close oversight of their activities; but in the popular branch, elected from smaller districts, where the members are better known and are more intimately acquainted with their constituents, it is possible for the public to have more control."[132] Compounding these problems were the lengthy senate terms, which made it less likely that senators would respond to public pressure and more difficult for constituents to punish senators for errant votes. As G. W. King argued in the Idaho Convention of 1889, "If you elect a class of men that will not obey the wishes of the people you have got to wait four years to turn them out."[133]

When these delegates canvassed the historical record, they were further fortified in their judgment that the senate could be safely dispensed with. Mr. Peck of Ohio pointed out that the "Constitutional Convention in which we are now sitting has only one chamber. Why haven't we two bodies? Are we of less importance than the general assembly? Is the work we are doing here less important? No it is more so; and every constitution that has ever been made in the United States has been made by a single body."[134] Mr. Norton of Nebraska pointed to city councils. He noted that although "in the early history of this country, many of the larger cities had bicameral councils," nearly all of these cities had changed course, so that "today there are very few large cities that have other than the one legislative body in their form of city government."[135] Mr. Morrill of Massachusetts called attention to the experiences of other countries, many of which had moved away from bicameralism in recent years. When he looked to the east, he found that "in England the House of Lords has been made subordinate to the House of Commons. In France the Senate has become more and more subordinate to the Chamber of Deputies. This is true also of Swiss governments, both National and cantonal. In Norway there is practically a one-House system." When he looked to the north, he noted that "all the provinces of the Dominion of Canada, except Quebec and Nova Scotia have one-House Legislatures." He was led to conclude that "the tendency in all countries having popular government is toward the abolition of the upper house."[136]

Although these delegates succeeded in placing unicameralism proposals on the agenda of nearly all of the Progressive Era conventions and securing varying degrees of support from the assembled delegates, the defenders of bicameralism ultimately prevailed in every instance. In response to critics who contended that changing economic conditions eliminated the need for a senate, defenders replied that the need for a deliberative check transcended these particular circumstances. Robert Luce, a delegate to the Massachusetts Convention of 1917–1919 and an academic authority on legislatures, was the most articulate defender of this position. Drawing on his extensive research into other countries' experiences with unicameralism, including the record of the late eighteenth-century French National Assembly, Luce argued,

Human nature is the same to-day that it was in the National Assembly. There are still the same reasons why one legislative body should be checked by another, and the reasons are familiar. You, sir, in the years of your presidency over this House saw times when gusts of passion swept through its ranks. You saw men carried away by the mob spirit; you knew occasions when, if one House could have acted without check, it would have perpetrated injustice; you and I, going home to the solitude of our chambers, have wondered that we could have been swept off our feet by some stirring speech or by some wave of sympathy. So it is we have found that it is not prudent on these great questions that may affect the destinies of millions, that may spread unhappiness through every corner of the State—we have found that it is not wise to allow one body, without the mature second consideration of another body, to decide our fate.[137]

John Carland offered a similar argument in the North Dakota Convention of 1889, and, in much the same fashion as Mr. Luce, he contended that the benefits of a deliberative check were timeless. It was true that a second chamber occasionally frustrated the immediate expression of the popular will, he argued, but in these instances, the system was generally operating as it should in securing the deliberate sense of the public:

It must be admitted that the people themselves sometimes make mistakes. The people have their flatterers as well as kings, but it may be as well admitted right here that the people make mistakes, and are often led away by passion, prejudice, self-interest—by thinking of the interest of the state last, and history has shown that wherever the legislative power has been vested in a single body they have been carried away by passion, and their proceedings have been so irregular as to cause an inadversion of mankind upon their proceedings.[138]

Defenders of bicameralism also maintained that the need for a deliberative check had, with only a few exceptions, been universally acknowledged in the United States and generally accepted around the world. It was true that constitutional conventions had always consisted of a single house, but the analogy to legislative bodies was imperfect. As George Knight explained in the Ohio Convention of 1912, "This constitutional convention is not the final body on anything. Everything it does is referred to the people—it has a very large second house, and that is not true with regard to legislation."[139] Nor was the example of city councils any more pertinent. Mr. Luce of Massachusetts argued, "A city government is not a Legislature, it does not legislate,—so our courts have held, and so our observation shows."[140] In addition, Mr. Carland of North Dakota argued that some of the examples of polities around the world that had recently adopted unicameralism, such as "the Swiss Republic, Norway, and of Ontario," should "be looked at under the conditions of things which exist in those countries."[141] Moreover, Mr. Luce pointed out that the international trend was not necessarily in the direction of unicameralism but was actually rather mixed, given that "when Australia recently gave the most earnest consideration to its new Constitution there was no serious argument in favor of abandoning the two-chamber system, and the decision of Japan might be cited also."[142]

Although this defense of bicameralism was not nearly as compelling to the assembled delegates as in earlier eras as a result of the newfound concern with securing rather than preventing legislative action, delegates were ultimately successful in turning back each of the unicameral challenges during the Progressive Era. The closest that any convention came to adopting unicameralism was in Arkansas in 1918 (where delegates initially voted to eliminate one chamber but then reversed themselves later in the proceedings) and in Nebraska in 1919–1920 (where a unicameralism proposal failed on a tie vote).[143] In each of the other conventions held during this era, advocates of unicameralism were unable to obtain broad-based support for their position.[144] To be sure, in several states—Oregon in 1912 and 1914, Oklahoma in 1914, and Arizona in 1916—supporters of unicameralism were able to make use of the initiative process to present these measures to the people, but in each case, the measures were easily defeated.[145] In addition, governors George Hodges of Kansas, George Hunt of Arizona, Ernest Lister of Washington, and Peter Norbeck of South Dakota each urged the adoption of unicameralism during this period, but legislators in each of these states took a different view of the merits of the proposal.[146]

The Debate about the Representation of Political Subdivisions

At the same time that one group of Progressive Era convention delegates was mounting an ultimately unsuccessful challenge to the existence of the senate, another group was seeking, with varying degrees of success, to alter the composition of the senate by taking account of political subdivisions in apportioning senate districts. This was not a novel proposition. Nineteenth-century constitution makers had frequently enacted apportionment provisions that deviated from a pure population basis, whether by providing equal representation for each political unit, awarding each unit at least one representative, or setting a limit on the total number of representatives from any one unit.[147] As Robert G. Dixon described the prevailing practice during the nineteenth century, "During this period relatively few states, concentrated mainly in the Northeast, used the 'federal' principle of straight county equality regardless of population differentials as the basis of representation in one legislative house. But during this same period a great many states—both old and new—mixed the population principle with provisions giving some voice to each political subdivision in at least one house of the legislature."[148] However, for the better part of the nineteenth century, as Gordon E. Baker noted, "these deviations seemed to do little violence to the population principle when the distribution of a state's inhabitants was fairly equal and the number of counties comparatively few."[149]

Before the late nineteenth century, therefore, legislative apportionment provisions had taken account of political subdivisions, but in practice, these provisions had not produced important disparities in the representation of various regions. Between 1889 and 1920, several developments led to a change in this state of affairs. First, as Royce Hanson explained, increasing migration to urban areas in older states, together with growth in the number of counties in newer states, meant that "restrictions on equal representation, such as minimum guarantees for all counties or maximum limits on the representation of any county, which had been of little consequence when adopted, were beginning to have a noticeable, if not appreciable effect by the end of the second decade of the 20th century."[150] In addition, as Baker noted, "a distrust of growing cities" led rural counties to push for the adoption of minimum- or maximum-county representation requirements in states that had not previously adopted these provisions.[151] Finally, as Dixon pointed out, although the concept of apportioning one house by population and the other by political subdivision "had been appealed to frequently, but usually unsuccessfully, in state constitutional conventional debates in the early decades of the nineteenth century," the Progressive Era "was marked by a frequently successful appeal to the 'federal' principle."[152]

Delegates who supported distinct bases of apportionment in the two houses did so for a variety of reasons, but a leading argument was that this would enhance the distinctiveness of the two chambers. Several delegates argued that the reliance on different bases of representation ought to be seen as one among several distinctions between the two houses. Ezekiel Cooper argued in this fashion in the Delaware Convention of 1896–1897, when he noted that the purpose of having two houses, made up "of different numbers" and with "longer term of service," was that they "are not only a check upon each other but they represent different lines of state government." He wanted to maintain a distinct basis of apportionment in the senate, because otherwise "we twist the idea that is now in my mind with reference to the composition for a special line of work—if you will allow the expression—of two bodies."[153]

Other delegates went further and suggested that a different basis of representation was now the only available distinction of any importance between the two houses. Mr. Parsons of North Dakota was particularly explicit about the connection between his support for bicameralism and the establishment of equal-county representation in the senate. He argued, "Inasmuch as I have been quoted as supporting one house, I would like to say that my choice and preference would be two houses of the legislature, with the upper house containing one Representative from each county, irrespective of the number of inhabitants. But if it were to be between two houses of the legislature as we have had them in the past, and one house, I should most emphatically vote for one house."[154] Melville Brown, president of the Wyoming Convention of 1889, reached the same conclusion and offered an even more detailed defense of this position. "If the principle of representation in proportion to population was to be adopted [for the senate], I would be in favor of a legislature composed of a single branch, because I can see no need of two houses in any legislative body if you are going to pursue that theory as to representation." After alluding to the ongoing debates about "the propriety of two houses in legislative bodies," he explained,

> I believe myself in having two branches or two houses in the legislative department of our state, and of all the states in this union, and I believe also in following the general principle that has been referred to as the American principle, namely, that the [senate] should be so constructed that it will work as a check upon the will of the popular majority in the lower house, or the house of representatives, and if it is not so constructed that it shall form a check upon the will of the popular house, it will be of no advantage to the people of Wyoming, and we might as well wipe it out as a useless and unnecessary thing. It becomes a mere figurehead, a thing to be looked at, wholly useless, and a matter of some expense to the people.[155]

Moreover, these delegates contended that if states were to take the step of apportioning one house by population and the other by political subdivision, they would merely be adhering to the long-standing precedent of the U.S. Congress. Charles Scott argued in the New Hampshire Convention of 1902, where towns were the relevant political unit, that "the principles of representation should be applied to the towns of this state as are applied by the government of the United States in dealing with the various states. Can we not afford to be as charitable towards them, the little towns, as the general government is towards the little state of New Hampshire in allowing her equal representation in the United States senate[?]"[156] C. R. Middleton acknowledged in the Montana Convention of 1889 that counties—the relevant political unit in most states—might not be sovereign in the same sense as states were sovereign. Nevertheless, the county

> has an individual existence; it can sue and be sued; it can and is placed in a position to acquire property and hold it in the name of the county; it has to build and own courthouses, jails and all that sort of thing; it has to provide for the levying and collection of taxes, for the payment of its debts, for the payment of judgments that are brought into court and sued, and it has obligations in the shape of bonds of a market value in the markets of the world. Will it be contended that it has no existence, that it has nothing in the shape of a sovereignty? I submit that so far as a county's relations to a state are concerned, it stands relatively and identically in the same position that a state does to the government of the United States, and that there is every reason and every argument to be used in favor of each county having the same consideration and the same representation in one house of the Legislature that a state has in the legislature of the nation.[157]

These delegates also took note of various advantages of representing political subdivisions in one legislative chamber. In some states, delegates sought to prevent sparsely populated rural areas and agricultural interests from being dominated by growing metropolitan areas, with their concentration of manufacturing interests. In the Delaware Convention of 1896–1897, Woodburn Martin expressed his concern about the power wielded by Wilmington residents, many of whom were in that city "to work in the manufactures, and when the work is good they are there, and if the work is not good, they may be somewhere else tomorrow." It was his belief "that the interests of the State of Delaware will be best protected by people who are the owners of the soil of this State; people who will see to it that the government is well managed, rather than those who have no community of interests, nothing to fix them here, but are free to go wherever their fancy chooses to carry them."[158] Other states were divided not so much along urban-rural lines, but rather by various commercial interests; accordingly, delegates in these states sought to ensure that one of these interests did not always prevail over the others. Mr. Middleton of Montana argued that if you "place the entire matter of both houses of this legislature upon a basis of popular representation [then], Mr. President, you know that the mining interests and the mining localities and sections of this state will forever dictate to the rest of the state and to the other industries and interests, what legislation they shall have and what they shall not." He thought that "there should be in one house of the Legislature a representation based upon the counties; so that although the population house might desire to have everything in the interest of the mining localities, that house could say to them, 'gentlemen you cannot have things your way entirely without conceding something to us.'"[159]

These arguments in favor of equal-county senate representation did not go unanswered in Progressive Era conventions. Some delegates responded that population was the only legitimate basis for apportioning state legislative districts. It was one thing for the federal convention in the late eighteenth century to have provided for equal-state representation in the U.S. Senate, but that decision had been the product of particular circumstances that were no longer present at the turn of the twentieth century. Asbury Conaway pointed out in the Wyoming Convention of 1889 that "the formation of the general government and of the senate of the United States was a series of compromises. It was necessary in order to get the original states, or a majority of them to bind themselves by the constitution of the United States that some things should be inserted in that constitution which were not exactly republican, not democratic."[160] Moreover, as Weldon Heyburn explained in the Idaho Convention of 1889, even if a legitimate case could still be made on the merits for representing the states in the U.S. Senate—and this was an open question—the same reasoning did not apply to the representation of counties in state senates: "There is a certain sovereignty about a state; it may frame its own constitution, within certain limits it has its own separate government, and it is in its essential being a state. No such character can be attached to the existence of a county. We have heard of state sovereignty, but I never heard of county sovereignty."[161] Similarly, Charles Varian concluded in the Utah Convention of 1895,

> A county in that sense bears no relation at all to the sovereign state in its connection with the other states of the Union. A county is simply a governmental agency, if you please, adapted in the aid of the purpose of the state government. There is no analogy whatever between the counties of the state and the states of this Union in their several relations to each other—no analogy at all in the system provided for under the Constitution of the United States

giving an equal representation to sovereign states as distinct empires, units by themselves. And the argument is misleading and far fetched that seeks to draw comparisons between the two classes of cases.[162]

In the words of George Baxter in the Wyoming Convention of 1889, "A man is not a resident or citizen of any county, but he is a citizen of the state, and it seems to me that every citizen should have an equal voice, equal representation in the legislature of the state which governs them."[163]

Insofar as it was conceded that individuals, not political units, were the only legitimate basis of representation in state legislatures, these delegates contended that there was no legitimate justification for the overrepresentation of certain citizens and underrepresentation of others. Several of these delegates appealed to the interests of residents from underrepresented areas. Thus Joseph Toole in the Montana Convention of 1889 appealed "to gentlemen representing counties that represent the wealth, that represent the manufacturing interests, that represent the commercial interests and the mining interests of this Territory" and urged them not "to sit silently by and see this matter of representation wrested from them and placed in the hands and power of those who do not proximate them in numbers."[164] Other delegates, such as William Claggett, president of the Idaho Convention of 1889, sought to demonstrate the illegitimacy of the principle of equal-county apportionment. He argued, "When we get down to the merits of the proposition, it is nothing more or less than a proposition to give one county that votes 500 votes the same political strength as another one that votes ten thousand." He thought the proposition was "in direct violation of every rule and principle upon which representative government is based in the United States."[165]

Ultimately, these appeals, whether to interest or principle, persuaded delegates at many Progressive Era conventions to continue apportioning both legislative houses on the basis of population.[166] In several other states, however, constitution makers concluded that it was appropriate to take account of political subdivisions in drawing district lines for at least one chamber. The New York Convention of 1894 was one of several conventions during this period to impose a limit on the number of senators from any one county.[167] Meanwhile, the Montana Convention of 1889 was the first in this period to go so far as to provide equal-county representation in the senate alongside of population-based representation in the house, and once this precedent was established, several other states followed suit.[168]

The Reapportionment Revolution

Debates about bicameralism continued in the several decades following the Progressive Era. Beginning in 1921 and continuing through the mid-twentieth century, the National Municipal League advocated a unicameral legislature in its Model State Constitution.[169] Then, in 1934 supporters of unicameralism realized their only twentieth-century success when Nebraska voters eliminated their second house via the initiative process. Nebraska senator George Norris had been a long-standing supporter of the one-house legislature, and after several particularly unpopular legislative sessions in 1931 and 1933, he was able to secure far more than the required number of signatures to place a unicameralism initiative on the ballot. When Nebraskans went to the polls to vote on Norris' unicameralism measure, which was placed alongside several popular measures to repeal prohibition and permit parimutuel betting, they easily approved all three measures.[170] In the aftermath of Nebraska's implementation of unicameralism in 1937, the issue attracted renewed attention among the public[171] and in several legislatures and conventions.[172]

It was not until the 1960s, however, that bicameralism reemerged as a leading issue for state constitution makers across the country. The impetus for this renewed interest was a series of U.S. Supreme Court decisions regarding state legislative apportionment. In 1962, in *Baker v. Carr*, the Court held that legislative reapportionment was a justiciable, rather than a political, question.[173] Then, in 1964, the Court held in *Reynolds v. Sims* that states were required to "make an honest and good faith effort to construct districts, in both houses of the legislature, as nearly of equal population as is practicable." Chief Justice Earl Warren declared that "political subdivisions of States—counties, cities, or whatever—never were and never have been considered as sovereign entities," and therefore the federal analogy was "inapposite and irrelevant to state legislative districting schemes." He made it clear, though, that he did

> not believe that the concept of bicameralism is rendered anachronistic and meaningless when the predominant basis of representation in the two legislative bodies is required to be the same—population. A prime reason for bicameralism, modernly considered, is to insure mature and deliberate consideration of, and to prevent precipitate action on, proposed legislative measures. Simply because the controlling criterion for apportioning representation is required to be the same in both houses does not mean that there will be no differences in the composition and complexion of the two bodies.

Warren listed several possible differences, such as the number of members, size of the constituencies, and length of the terms, and he concluded that "these and other factors could be, and are presently, in many States, utilized to engender different complexion and collective attitudes in the two bodies of a state legislature."[174]

These Supreme Court rulings prompted widespread constitutional revision during the next two decades, as all but a few states found it necessary to bring their apportionment provisions into compliance with the Court's one person–one vote standard.[175] In the conventions that followed, delegates were frequently led to consider whether the Court's decision had removed the last remaining justification for bicameralism by rendering illegitimate an important means of distinguishing between the two houses. In addition, delegates were led to consider, once again, whether two chambers served to promote deliberation in the lawmaking process, and by this point in time, they were able to draw lessons from the ongoing Nebraska experience with unicameralism. Defenders of bicameralism once again prevailed in the face of each of these challenges, but it was evident that the force of several traditional justifications for bicameralism had been weakened by these twentieth-century developments.

The Case against Bicameralism

From the 1920s to the early 1960s, the number of states adopting the "federal" principle of apportioning one house by population and the other by political subdivision,[176] or some variation on this model,[177] continued to grow.[178] Moreover, even in many states that did not formally adopt the federal principle, changing population patterns and the failure of legislatures to undertake a timely reapportionment led to an overrepresentation of rural counties in both houses, but especially in the senate.[179] W. Kingsland Macy may have overstated the case when he claimed in the New York Convention of 1938 that "we are in a bicameral system and in every bicameral system one house is usually determined by geography and one is determined by population."[180] But this sentiment was typical of a growing number of state constitution makers who came to associate bicameralism with distinct bases of legislative apportionment.[181]

Consequently, in the 1960s and 1970s, many convention delegates were left unpersuaded by Chief Justice Warren's argument that bicameralism could survive the *Reynolds v. Sims* decision. In the view of these delegates, the Court's ruling had, in fact, eliminated the principal justification for the bicameral system.[182] Richard Dobson in the North Dakota Convention of 1971–1972 was one of many delegates who argued, "Originally the upper house of a two-house legislative body was constituted of property-owners, and the lower house of so-called commoners." After a time, though, the states had followed the federal model in basing "their upper houses on area and their lower houses on population. But the U.S. Supreme Court knocked out the last remaining reason for a bicameral body for state legislatures with its one man one vote decision in 1964."[183] John Knuppel displayed a similar understanding of the purpose of bicameralism during the Illinois Convention of 1969–1970: "It used to be that there was a reason for two houses. One represented geography, the other represented people." But "under the concept of one man–one vote, there is no longer the reason for geographic representation. The reason now is to represent one man, and he doesn't need to be represented in two different houses."[184] Thomas Hamilton acknowledged in the Hawaii Convention of 1978 that bicameralism "still makes a kind of sense on the national level," but "it no longer makes any sense in terms of state government, because by constitutional decision there is only one thing that can be represented and if there is only one thing that can be represented, you need only one house to represent it."[185] As Robert Canfield concluded in the Illinois Convention of 1969–1970, "With one man–one vote there is absolutely no reason at all for having two houses of the legislature. It is purely duplicative. It is purely running over the same track twice with two different groups of people."[186]

Several of these delegates acknowledged that the Court had not eliminated all possible means of differentiating the house and senate; these delegates were simply not persuaded that the remaining distinctions were sufficiently meaningful to justify retaining the bicameral system. Dennis Roberts, chairman of the Rhode Island Convention of 1964–1969, took note of the Court's one man–one vote decision and argued that "it is obvious, that the justification for the second branch becomes very apparent, very unreal." He noted that the convention was left with no choice but of "resorting to the type of character for it as an extended term, dividing the membership into different kinds of election, the numbers." In the end, though, he had his doubts about the significance of any of these remaining distinctions, and therefore he wanted to "give the people of the State of Rhode Island the opportunity of making a decision as to what the form of legislative branch will be, either one house or two houses."[187] In similar fashion, Newman Marsilius argued in the Connecticut Convention of 1965, "Over the great

many years of the past the arguments that a bicameral set-up has been, we have
. . . one house on population, and one based on geographical units. This argument has now been destroyed, and the basis of support for the bicameral system
is now shifted." In assessing various arguments that might still be put forward,
he noted, "Now the major argument for a two house arrangement is that it may
permit in some limited way within the stricture of the Supreme Court ruling a
method by which one house can represent the smaller units, population, the
towns and the other house our metropolitan districts." But although this was
the "most persuasive" of the various remaining justifications and might be "a
good transition from what we have had to the future," he still had his "doubts,"
because such an "attempt to structure our legislature for the future on something that is out of the past is a bit of nostalgia." He therefore concluded that a
"one house legislature is the natural way for people to work."[188]

At the same time that the Court's removal of an important distinction between the two houses was prompting a reconsideration of the need for a second
chamber, delegates were also led to reconsider whether two houses were still
promoting deliberation in the lawmaking process. Many delegates advanced the
same kinds of arguments that had been advanced by Progressive Era critics of
bicameralism. Rather than promoting deliberation, they argued, a second house
merely increased the amount of "buck-passing," end-of-session "logjams," and
"duplicate" expenses, in the words of George Loo in the Hawaii Convention of
1968.[189] Moreover, the complexity of the bicameral system made it more difficult for citizens to keep watch over legislators and hold them accountable and
therefore made it too easy for special interests to wield undue influence in the
lawmaking process.[190]

Critics of bicameralism in the 1960s and 1970s also supplemented these
long-standing arguments by criticizing the conference committees that were frequently called on to settle disputes between the two houses. Concerns about the
secretive and undemocratic character of conference committees were a staple
of Senator Norris's campaign against bicameralism in the 1930s, and these
concerns only grew during the course of the twentieth century.[191] Thus Arlyne
Reichert in the Montana Convention of 1971–1972 argued that "under no circumstances in government is so much power invested in so few individuals"
as in the "notorious conference committee."[192] Mr. Loo of Hawaii thought that
the conference committee was "the villain of bicameralism." He was bothered
not only by the power wielded by such a small number of individuals, but also
by the fact that the conference committee "operates away from the public view,

provides no opportunity for citizens to testify, keeps no records of its votes and offers its results during the last days or hours of a session."[193] Some delegates therefore agreed with Mr. Knuppel of Illinois, who argued, "I'll tell you what the conference committee is. It's a unicameral body created out of the two houses to solve the inadequacies of the bicameral system."[194] For each of these reasons, it became clear to many delegates that two houses—and for all practical purposes a third—were no longer contributing to deliberation in the lawmaking process.

Mid-twentieth-century convention delegates also had the benefit of studying Nebraska's several decades of experience with unicameralism, and many delegates concluded from this experience that deliberation could be adequately secured without a second chamber.[195] Clinton Winslow in the Maryland Convention of 1967–1968 quoted from one study of the performance of Nebraska's unicameral legislature, and he concluded that "in Nebraska the general population has pretty well accepted the idea that what they have there is better than what they had before."[196] Royce Hanson, a delegate to the same convention and an academic authority on state legislatures, argued that if the primary concern was with preventing the passage of ill-advised legislation, then the Nebraska experience demonstrated that "the death rate of unwise legislation is as high in a unicameral body as it is in a bicameral body."[197] Moreover, Betty Howard argued in the Illinois Convention of 1969–1970 that the Nebraska experiment "demonstrate[s] that unicameralism can run with efficiency. It is free from log jams and deadlocks and recurrent crises as we have in our bicameral legislature."[198] In addition to showing that unicameralism had not given rise to any of the disasters foreseen by its critics, the Nebraska experience also demonstrated to many delegates that unicameralism had lived up to the advantages envisioned by its supporters. As Mrs. Reichert of Montana noted, "Nebraska ranked number one in accountability in the impartial survey conducted by the citizens' committee on state legislatures," and it was therefore reasonable to conclude that "a one house legislature would fix responsibility" in other states as well.[199]

The Case for Bicameralism

No other state followed Nebraska in adopting unicameralism, and in this sense, critics of bicameralism failed once again to achieve their goal. In another sense, though, supporters of unicameralism mounted their most serious challenge during this period, and defenders of bicameralism were forced to respond by articulating a justification that took account of both the Court's reapportionment decisions and the ongoing Nebraska experiment.

Several defenders of bicameralism in the 1960s and 1970s responded that there were some remaining important differences between the two chambers, and these differences continued to produce sufficiently distinct perspectives in the lawmaking process. Therefore, just as the decline of property qualifications in the mid-nineteenth century prompted defenders of bicameralism to place added emphasis on other differences in the composition of the two houses, the Court's reapportionment decisions led mid-twentieth-century defenders of the institution to enhance, and in some cases create, other grounds of distinction.[200]

Thus, several delegates noted that the reapportionment decisions left undisturbed the differences in the size of the chambers, and this remained a viable way of securing distinct perspectives in lawmaking. Penn Kimball therefore argued in the Connecticut Convention of 1965, "Now there are other reasons in the area of diversity for having a two house legislature," including the fact that "houses of different size behave differently. We have many members of this Convention who have been in Washington and I'm sure that they can testify that the deliberations in the House of Representatives and the deliberations in the Senate are very different in character."[201]

Other delegates pointed out that states could continue to elect representatives and senators from different constituencies. Thus, even if both houses had to be apportioned by population, senate districts could still encompass far more persons than house districts. This was the approach taken by J. Irwin Shapiro in the New York Convention of 1967, when he argued that there was still "a complete dissimilarity between the Senate and the Assembly. There is no need for unicameralism on the present basis of one-man, one-vote, because the State Senator and the Assemblyman do not represent the same people. There is one-man, one-vote, but the Senator represents two and a half times the population ratio of the Assemblyman."[202] In addition, states could still create noncoterminous house and senate districts. Several states at the time did not distinguish between house and senate constituencies, whether because "house members are elected at large from within the senate district" or because "house districts are individually established within the senate district."[203] Thus, one option for these states was to begin drawing noncoterminous districts. It was true, George Lewis acknowledged in the Illinois Convention of 1969–1970, that the Court's reapportionment decision "diminishes and almost abolishes the reasoning and the foundation for the bicameral system" because "the less items we have different in the two houses, the less reason for the two houses." Nevertheless, he believed that steps could be taken to ensure that there were "two different vantage points," and "certainly one of the most unique and one of the best differences would be achieved by noncoterminous districts." In this way, "the different combinations of interest groups, the different combinations of political groups, the different combinations of minority groups would be found in the two varying systems."[204]

Several delegates also argued that different term lengths would still produce distinct types of legislative behavior. Dwight Friedrich argued in the same convention, "The senate, with a four-year term, has a great deal more stability. If I had a choice, I would have the senate on an area basis; but that's out. But it still has the element of more stability than the house because of the smaller number, the longer terms, and the fewer members that turn over between sessions." He thought that "it would be a tremendous mistake for Illinois to go to a one-house legislature."[205] Similarly, John Lodge concluded in the Connecticut Convention of 1965 that "the one-man, one-vote decision does not remove the need for a bi-cameral legislature. Those who are elected to the Senate are apt to be animated by less parochial considerations. They are apt to take a more regional view[,] and furthermore if we change the term of election of the Senators to lengthen it, to stagger it, they will also have a slower pulse with which to confront the question of good legislation."[206]

As Mr. Lodge's comments suggest, one approach taken by convention delegates who sought to buttress bicameralism, especially in states that had previously eliminated differences between the two houses, was to try to enhance or recreate these distinctions, particularly differences in term lengths. Joseph Carlino in the New York Convention of 1967 set out one possible strategy. He argued,

Once you have removed every consideration in structuring of a legislative body, other than the criterion of population, as does *Reynolds v. Simms* [sic], you must consider what changes you make in the legislative structure in order to accommodate to the dictates of that decision. Some have argued belatedly and without success that [if] population be the sole criteria, unicameralism is the only answer. I think that question is behind us. It is not being considered by this Chamber, but once you discard the notion of unicameralism in a legislature based solely on the population consideration, I think it is essential that we develop, insofar as possible, different concepts in the bicameral system to justify and to make meaningful a bicameral system. That is why I propose this amendment to increase the term of the state Senate from two to four years and to leave the term of the Assembly as is.[207]

Efforts to lengthen senate terms to shore up the justification for bicameralism were undertaken on several occasions in the 1960s, although ultimately without much success.[208] Edward Corcoran in the Rhode Island Convention of 1964–1969 argued that "one of the most salient things is the fact that now we have got both houses by Supreme Court mandate that have to be created on the same basic representation." As a result, "the only distinction between the two houses is the fact that you have different persons occupying the seat. It seems to me that if we are going to keep the two houses, there should be a good reason for it. For that reason, I feel that there should definitely be a greater distinction between the personality involved." He therefore sought to provide for "a two-year term for the members of the house, whereas you have a four-year term for the members of the senate."[209] As his colleague Robert Pickard explained, "The theory of bicameralism in this Convention . . . would call for a substantial difference between the Senate and the House. The only way to establish that difference would be to have four-year terms for the Senate and two years for the House."[210]

In one sense, these arguments harked back to arguments that were put forth with such effectiveness by mid-nineteenth-century defenders of bicameralism. In another sense, though, the idea that senators should represent political subdivisions had assumed such prominence in the intervening years that it was difficult for mid-twentieth-century delegates to accommodate themselves to the removal of this distinction and to be content with the remaining distinctions. To be sure, differences in the number of members, size of constituencies, and length of terms were still in effect in many states. It was also true that states that had previously eliminated these distinctions could reintroduce them. However, in the view of some delegates, these differences were no longer sufficiently meaningful to carry the burden of justifying bicameralism.

One possible response, which was discussed by several political scientists in the mid-twentieth century but did not attract much support from constitution makers, was to develop new grounds of distinction between the two houses. Along these lines, a 1954 report of the American Political Science Association Committee on American Legislatures concluded that "the democratic ideal of equal representation and our traditional acceptance of bicameralism are in conflict" and that "it may be necessary to abandon the second if the first is accepted." At the least, "if we are to retain and invigorate bicameralism, there may

have to be a modification or rethinking of the theory of popular representation."
Among the "possibilities for a different basis of representation for the second
chamber" were "a shift to either occupational (or functional) representation,
or to various types of proportional representation."[211] Illinois had provided for
a version of proportional representation in its lower house since 1870, and so
there was some precedent for such a proposal, but no other states followed suit
during this period, and Illinois ended its experiment in 1970. Occupational representation had no precedent in the American political system, and no states
took this approach in the aftermath of the Court's reapportionment decisions.[212]
There were, of course, other ways by which delegates might have distinguished
the two houses, but none of these proved persuasive. As Jesse Turner argued in
the Tennessee Convention of 1965, where delegates devoted a good deal of effort to trying to both maintain a distinction between the two houses and comply
with the reapportionment decisions,

> If we here today are to use some factor other than population in apportion-
> ing our State Legislature, then I ask, what shall it be? Shall it be religion? Of
> course, most people say, "No, it should not." Then I would say that if we are
> going to use some factor other than religion, then religion is just about as good
> a factor to use as any other, so why not use religion. Shall it be geography? Shall
> it be economic interests? Shall it be education? Shall it be wealth? I think that
> we would come to the conclusion that perhaps the only true factor for us to
> measure in determining our Representatives in our State Government should
> be the matter of population.[213]

In the absence of any new grounds for distinguishing the two houses, state
constitution makers had to resort to either emphasizing the importance of existing distinctions, as delegates occasionally did, or highlighting the benefits of
providing a deliberative check, which was the more common approach. Thus
convention delegates who supported bicameralism during this period argued, in
much the same fashion as their Progressive Era predecessors, that there were
"advantages of having two forms of public debate,"[214] that it was "better to have
two eyes than one in this matter,"[215] and that a second chamber was essential
for promoting "deliberateness in legislation."[216] As for recent concerns about
the power wielded by conference committees, delegates responded that this was
merely a device "to bring about a compromise," and that all "legislation is compromise. What's evil about that?"[217]

Supporters of bicameralism could no longer rely solely on these traditional

theoretical arguments about deliberation, however, in light of the generally favorable reviews of Nebraska's ongoing experiment, which carried the implication that deliberation could be obtained without a second chamber. One group
of delegates responded that the lessons from the Nebraska experience were inapplicable to other states. Not only did Nebraska operate a nonpartisan legislature, in contrast with nearly all other states,[218] but, as Huanani Ching pointed
out in the Hawaii Convention of 1978, Nebraska was also more rural than most
states. He urged the delegates to be "cautious about making any assumptions
concerning the transfer of a unicameral system from one political environment,
like Nebraska's, to another, such as Hawaii's."[219] Other delegates highlighted
several unfavorable analyses of the Nebraska experience. For instance, Rudolf
Hildebrand in the North Dakota Convention of 1971–1972 pointed out that the
Citizens Conference on Legislatures had rated "the Nebraska Legislature thirty-
fifth in order for being functional."[220] Meanwhile, Jeannette Stanton argued in
the same convention that Nebraska was known to have inferior services in various areas, and that it had been the last state in the union to adopt at least one
kind of legislative reform. She concluded, "Now not being responsive about what
I've just mentioned means that they are not responsive to the people."[221]

There was no denying, however, that the Nebraska experiment exerted an
important influence on the debate in that delegates could no longer speak about
the negative consequences of adopting unicameralism with the same confidence as
in earlier years. As a result, supporters of bicameralism were often led to offer a more
modest defense, one primarily grounded in a need to respect tradition and precedent.
As Francis Gallagher argued in the Maryland Convention of 1967–1968, the bicameral system had withstood previous challenges, and it would be capable of sur-
viving this latest challenge. He argued, "Putting aside the crockery of the teacup
or the mug, I would say that the bicameral system is one which we have learned to
live with, and is one to which the people of Maryland are quite accustomed. It
is imbedded in our traditions and our history and it can be made to work sat-
isfactorily."[222] Moreover, it was telling, as Frederick Malkus argued in the same
convention, that no other states had chosen to follow Nebraska's lead, even in the
aftermath of the Court's reapportionment decisions. He asked the assembled delegates, "How many of these states since that historic decision and since the rewriting
of their constitution have provided for the unicameral system? The answer was
none. I know that Maryland should not follow the footsteps of other states for
the sake of following their footsteps. But you are a great lawyer, Mr. President,
you believe in precedent, and all other lawyers believe in precedent."[223]

Defenders of bicameralism thus did not lack for responses to their critics and for defenses of the institution, but these late twentieth-century defenses had evolved from the arguments put forth in previous years. Supporters of bicameralism occasionally still took note of the benefits of bringing distinct perspectives into the lawmaking process, but in the aftermath of *Reynolds v. Sims,* this argument was heard less frequently. Supporters also continued to argue that two houses were necessary to defeat hasty or ill-advised legislation, but this argument had to be tempered in light of generally favorable reports from Nebraska. As a result, supporters of bicameralism increasingly resorted to arguments from the weight of tradition and precedent.

Moreover, these arguments carried less force than in earlier eras, and as a result, critics of bicameralism garnered even more support than in previous eras. Whereas most unicameralism proposals in previous eras had been quickly disposed of without even coming to a vote, unicameralism was the subject of lengthy debates and numerous votes in conventions during the 1960s and 1970s, including in Michigan, Rhode Island, Connecticut, Tennessee, Hawaii, Maryland, and Illinois.[224] In fact, in Montana and North Dakota, convention delegates agreed to submit the matter to an ultimately unsuccessful popular vote.[225] Moreover, in subsequent years, the issue continued to attract support from the public, governors, and members of constitutional revision commissions.[226]

Conclusion

A principal benefit of examining the state convention debates regarding bicameralism is that it becomes clear that an institution that has been relatively uncontested at the national level has been the subject of frequent reconsideration at the state level. If one were to assess the degree of support for bicameralism in the American constitutional tradition by focusing solely on the federal constitution, one might conclude that the existence and purpose of a second chamber have gone unchallenged. In fact, the relative merits of bicameralism and unicameralism have been the subject of frequent debate in state conventions, and defenders of bicameralism have been forced to undertake a sustained reconsideration and defense of the institution.

Another benefit of examining these state convention debates is that one gains an appreciation for the evolving character of bicameralism throughout

American history. On one level, the institution of bicameralism could be considered relatively stable throughout state constitutional development, in that all but three states entered the union with a bicameral legislature, and only one state currently operates without a bicameral legislature. On another level, though, bicameralism has undergone important changes in that the system has been defended in several different ways throughout the course of the American regime.

Thus, for the better part of American history, bicameralism was thought to be valuable primarily insofar as it rested on important distinctions in the composition of the house and senate. At one point, constitution makers sought to balance the interests of the general public and of property holders. At another point, the principal concern was with representing political subdivisions in one house and population in the other house. At other times, convention delegates have sought to arrange the two houses so as to bring distinct perspectives to the lawmaking process. At the turn of the twenty-first century, however, only the last of these arguments still has any legitimacy.

Consequently, the defense of bicameralism has come to be waged almost entirely on a second front: on the grounds that it provides a check on the passage of hasty or ill-advised legislation. This long-standing justification has also been called into question on several occasions, though, first in response to the increasingly popular view that the public interest is better served by designing institutions so as to secure, rather than prevent, the passage of legislation, and second in response to the generally favorable reviews of the only ongoing state experiment with unicameralism. As a result, delegates have been increasingly led to defend the institution by invoking tradition and precedent.

In the early twenty-first century, therefore, the principle of bicameralism may be solidly entrenched and easily justified at the federal level, but the situation is quite different in the states, where bicameralism has been the subject of a series of challenges, and where several traditional justifications have been eliminated and the force of several others has been called into question during the course of the American regime.

6

RIGHTS

Do individuals possess positive rights that depend for their enforcement on governmental action, as distinct from negative rights that limit the scope of governmental action? The issue did not arise at the federal convention. Nor did it surface during the drafting of the federal Bill of Rights, which was concerned with defining civil rights and liberties and ensuring their protection against governmental action. Since that time, various efforts have been made to secure federal constitutional protection for social, economic, and environmental rights, but with little success.

Thus, during the Progressive Era, several federal amendments were introduced for the purpose of protecting workers' rights. Prompted by U.S. Supreme Court decisions that imposed constitutional barriers to the regulation of child labor, work hours, wages, and employment conditions, amendments were proposed that would have authorized Congress, and in some cases the states, to legislate in these areas.[1] However, only the child-labor amendment emerged from Congress, and it did not obtain the necessary support from state legislatures for ratification.[2]

Franklin Roosevelt went on to argue in his 1944 State of the Union address that the country had "accepted, so to speak, a second Bill of Rights under which a new basis of security and prosperity can be established for all."[3] Moreover, during his presidency he signed into law several measures that were intended to achieve economic security, to the point that the New Deal has been described by certain scholars as bringing about a constitutional transformation.[4] However, Roosevelt made no effort to secure passage of amendments to the Constitution to attain his goals of securing the right of an individual to a "useful and remunerative job" or to "earn enough to provide adequate food and clothing and recreation" or "to adequate medical care" or "to adequate protection from the economic fears of old age, sickness, accident, and unemployment," or the right of a family to "a decent home."[5]

Then, in the 1960s, prominent legal scholars began to argue that various clauses in the U.S. Constitution might be interpreted as securing protection for social and economic rights. In a pair of articles published in the 1960s in the *Yale Law Journal,* Charles Reich urged support for the concept of entitlement, which would require that "when individuals have insufficient resources to live under conditions of health and decency, society has obligations to provide support, and the individual is entitled to that support as of right."[6] Several years later, in the *Harvard Law Review,* Frank Michelman sought to build support for the concept of "minimum protection against economic hazard," by which "persons are entitled to have certain wants satisfied—certain existing needs fulfilled—by government, free of any direct charge over and above the obligation to pay general taxes."[7]

Although legal scholars continued to argue in subsequent years that these rights might be seen as implicit in various constitutional clauses,[8] these arguments have had little lasting impact on U.S. Supreme Court decision making. The closest the Court came to recognizing *constitutional* rights in this area came in two welfare benefits decisions—*Shapiro v. Thompson* (1969) and *Goldberg v. Kelly* (1970)—which overturned a residence requirement and required a pre-termination hearing, respectively. In his majority opinion in the latter case, Justice William J. Brennan quoted one of Reich's articles and cited another, and he went on to argue, "It may be realistic today to regard welfare entitlements as more like 'property' than a 'gratuity.'" He concluded, "Public assistance, then, is not mere charity, but a means to 'promote the general Welfare, and secure the Blessings of Liberty to ourselves and our Posterity.'"[9] However, the Court was quick to make it clear in *Dandridge v. Williams* (1970), in upholding a maximum limit on aid to families, that "the Constitution may impose certain procedural safeguards upon systems of welfare administration. But the Constitution does not empower this Court to second-guess state officials charged with the difficult responsibility of allocating limited public welfare funds among the myriad of potential recipients."[10] Moreover, in *DeShaney v. Winnebago* (1989) the Court was even more explicit in rejecting any notion that the Fourteenth Amendment might be read as guaranteeing positive rights. Chief Justice William Rehnquist wrote for the Court:

> Nothing in the language of the Due Process Clause itself requires the State to protect the life, liberty, and property of its citizens against invasion by private actors. The Clause is phrased as a limitation on the State's power to act, not as a guarantee of certain minimal levels of safety and security. It forbids the State itself to deprive individuals of life, liberty, or property without "due process of law," but its language cannot fairly be extended to impose an affirmative obligation on the State to ensure that those interests do not come to harm through other means.

He therefore concluded that "the Due Process Clauses generally confer no affirmative right to governmental aid, even where such aid may be necessary to secure life, liberty, or property interests of which the government itself may not deprive the individual."[11]

Similar efforts have been undertaken, with no more success, to persuade federal courts to recognize a constitutional right to a clean environment, and efforts to secure passage of a federal constitutional amendment guaranteeing such a right have been no more successful. In 1968, and then again in 1970 on the eve of the first Earth Day, Wisconsin senator Gaylord Nelson introduced the first such federal amendment, which would have provided that "every person has the inalienable right to a decent environment."[12] Meanwhile, New York representative Richard Ottinger proposed a more detailed amendment that would have provided, in part, that "the right of the people to clean air, pure water, freedom from excessive and unnecessary noise, and the natural, scenic, historic and esthetic qualities of their environment shall not be abridged."[13] These measures failed to obtain much support, though, and subsequent environmental amendments have also been defeated rather easily.[14]

The absence of any social, economic, or environmental rights in the U.S. Constitution is especially notable when one considers how frequently these rights have been recognized in other countries' constitutions and in international treaties. The Irish Constitution of 1937 was one of the first constitutions to include declaratory provisions of this kind, when it committed the government to "direct its policy toward securing: That the citizens (all of whom, men and women equally, have the right to an adequate means of livelihood) may through their occupations find the means of making reasonable provision for their domestic needs."[15] The Indian Constitution of 1949 also included such a provision, and it further directed the state, "within the limits of its economic capacity and development, [to] make effective provision for securing the right to work, to education and to public assistance in cases of unemployment, old age, sickness and disablement, and in other cases of undeserved want."[16] Since that time, these sorts of declaratory provisions have become commonplace in constitutions around the world; some countries have also enacted more explicit rights guarantees in these and other areas.[17] The South African Constitution of 1996 is among the most comprehensive, guaranteeing workers "the right to form and join a trade union" and "to strike"[18] and guaranteeing everyone the "right to have access to adequate housing,"[19] "the right to have access to health care services, including reproductive health care[,] sufficient food and water[,] and social security, including, if they are unable to support themselves and their dependants, appropriate social assistance,"[20] and "the right to an environment that is not harmful to their health or well-being."[21] Similar provisions can be found in the Universal Declaration of Human Rights (adopted in 1948) and the International Covenant on Economic, Cultural, and Social Rights (drafted in 1966), the first of which was signed by the United States, and the second of which was ratified by nearly every other country except the United States.[22]

When we turn to the state constitutional tradition, we find that state convention delegates have engaged in numerous debates about whether to include social, economic, and environmental rights in their constitutions, and they have frequently answered these questions in the affirmative, by adopting *permissive* provisions authorizing governmental action, *declaratory* provisions mandating governmental action, as well as *rights* provisions requiring governmental responsiveness in certain areas. One type of positive-rights provision that was widely adopted, particularly in the late nineteenth and early twentieth centuries, concerns the right of individuals to enjoy reasonable work hours, a minimum wage, safe work conditions, and compensation for workplace injuries.[23] Second, during the twentieth century, state constitution makers also adopted union rights provisions, whether in the form of clauses protecting the right to organize and bargain collectively or quite different clauses guaranteeing individuals a "right to work" and thus not to be required to join unions.[24] A third type of constitutional provision, which was occasionally adopted during the second half of the twentieth century, commits states to ensuring various kinds of economic and social security.[25] Finally, the late twentieth century saw the enactment of a fourth type of positive-rights provision guaranteeing the right to a clean and healthful environment.[26]

The principal lesson to be drawn from these state convention debates is that the absence of any positive rights provisions in the U.S. Constitution should not be viewed as the definitive expression of the accumulated wisdom and experience of the American constitutional tradition.[27] State constitution makers have had more frequent opportunities to revise their foundational documents from the late nineteenth century onward, at a time when concerns about social, economic, and environmental rights assumed increasing prominence. And in the course of these debates, state constitution makers have frequently deemed unpersuasive the arguments traditionally advanced for excluding social, economic, and environmental rights from the constitutional corpus. Whereas critics have traditionally argued that social, economic, and environmental rights are less fundamental than political and civil rights, state convention delegates have frequently responded that in the contemporary era these rights are just as important as traditional rights. In addition, whereas critics have argued that social, economic, and environmental rights provisions are less susceptible to judicial enforcement than political and civil rights, supporters have responded that these new rights are not so different in this respect from traditional rights; moreover, enshrining these rights in a constitution can serve other purposes aside from giving rise to judicial decision making.

Workers' Rights

Changing industrial conditions during the nineteenth century generated numerous concerns about the plight of workers and various attempts to secure protection for workers' rights. The first such efforts, beginning in the mid-nineteenth century, were aimed at setting minimum age and maximum-hours requirements for children.[28] Efforts were also made to limit the workday for adults, particularly for women, on public works, or in particular occupations.[29] Still other steps were taken to guarantee compensation for workplace injuries, whether by abrogating the fellow-servant, contributory-negligence, and assumption-of-risk doctrines that were commonly used to reduce employers' liability or by establishing workmen's compensation systems.[30] Finally, beginning in the early twentieth century, efforts were undertaken to establish a minimum wage for some or all workers.[31] For the most part, supporters of these workers' rights tried to achieve their goals by securing state legislation, and in many cases they were successful. But they also raised many of these issues in state conventions, whether out of a desire to enact permissive provisions, declaratory provisions, or rights provisions.

The Case for and against Workers' Rights

Although supporters and critics of workers' rights provisions naturally disagreed about the substantive merits of establishing these rights, the convention debates tended to revolve around the propriety of elevating these rights to constitutional status. Critics claimed that workers' rights did not belong in the constitution alongside traditional civil and political rights, and could be adequately secured through legislation. Supporters responded that there was no legitimate reason to distinguish between workers' rights and civil and political rights and that the former, no less than the latter, could only be rendered truly secure by adopting constitutional provisions.

Critics of constitutional workers' rights provisions contended that these rights were best secured through legislation rather than constitutional provisions. In their view, it was one thing to adopt constitutional provisions for the protection of civil and political rights, which were thought to have an enduring, and even permanent, character. Constitutional protection for workers' rights was a quite different matter, because such rights were expected to evolve over time. As Milton Hay argued in the Illinois Convention of 1869–1870 in regard to a proposed miners' safety clause,

> Law-making in a Constitution is always to be deprecated. What may be very good legislation to-day may not be good legislation five or ten years hence. It is a mere matter of experiment—a matter about which there may be honest differences of opinion as to whether it will work well to-day or not. Although a majority of us may so consider, it would not be proper to insert this into a Constitution, because experiment or time might prove that we were in error in regard to it. If left as a matter of legislation, when the error was discovered it could be amended.[32]

According to this view, deferring workers' rights issues to legislative resolution would accomplish something other than merely adhering to an abstract distinction between constitutional and statutory issues; it would benefit workers themselves by making it easier for them to secure future enhancements of these rights. As W. Gordon Robertson argued in the Virginia Convention of 1901–1902 in regard to a motion to limit the contributory-negligence doctrine,

> I do not think there is any man in this Convention who is opposed to giving to the railroad employees the relief this article calls for. I, for one, certainly am not opposed to it. I have stated, time and time again, that I am opposed to putting these things into the Constitution because I do not believe it is in the interest of the employees of the railroad companies any more than it is to the interest of the railroad companies to put it into our permanent law, that which, in its nature, is a legislative enactment.[33]

After all, as Wilfred Webb argued when a child-labor provision surfaced in the Arizona Convention of 1910, if such measures enjoyed majority support in the convention, they would likely command equally strong support in the legislature. He proclaimed that he was "willing to trust the first legislature of Arizona, and I am willing to leave legislative matters to that legislature and I do not suppose that all the virtues are possessed by this convention, and the next legislature may be just as desirous of enacting these measures as the gentlemen of this convention."[34]

Supporters of constitutional workers' rights provisions responded to these arguments by questioning the utility of the statutory/constitutional distinction that was so frequently invoked during these debates. Martin Foran argued in the Ohio Convention of 1873–1874, while supporting a miners' safety provision, "It has been said that this is properly a subject upon which the Legislature should alone act; but, Mr. Chairman, if the line of demarcation between organic or fundamental law, and legislative law, was closely drawn, nearly half the provisions in our present Constitution would have to be rejected, as not being within the legitimate scope of constitutional law."[35] After all, as Charles Meredith argued in the Virginia Convention of 1901–1902, while supporting a limitation of the contributory-negligence doctrine, this would be far from the first constitutional provision to deal with these sorts of matters:

> You are putting it in your Constitution, just as properly and with just as high a motive, as when you say a man's property shall not be taken for public purposes

without due compensation. Surely, if it is necessary to put in the Constitution some provision to protect a man's property, if you find the whole tendency or doctrine of the courts is to allow a man's life to be taken without due compensation, it is necessary to have a Constitutional protection to stop that evil also.[36]

Nor were workers' rights that different from many civil and political rights that were already receiving constitutional protection. Along these lines, Thomas Farrell argued in the Ohio Convention of 1912, "The right of the worker to be guaranteed a living wage by his state or his government will soon take rank with such axioms as the right of trial by jury, the right to bear arms, the right of petition and the right of speech, and though you may not see the necessity of the adoption of this governmental right to establish a minimum wage, yet such a crisis may arise at any moment."[37] The logic of this position, according to Aaron Hahn in the same convention, was that eighteenth and early nineteenth-century constitution makers had been concerned with protecting one set of rights, but a new set of rights had now assumed prominence:

We live in a time different from that of sixty years ago when our constitution was made. Take the constitution of 1851, look it through from beginning to end and you will not find the word "labor" or any provision for labor there. Now, would you, my friends, be willing to let the constitution of Ohio go out into the world without giving proper recognition to free labor, the brightest jewel in civilization? That would be wrong. We must not allow that. Whether it partakes of the legislative character or not, we must have certain regulations relative to labor inserted in our new constitution.[38]

Supporters argued that workers' rights should be constitutionalized because they were particularly at risk in the political process. In the late eighteenth century, religious freedom had been threatened by popular majorities who were intent on enacting legislation to achieve their ends. Consequently, religious-liberty clauses had been adopted in state constitutions. By the late nineteenth century, workers' rights were now under threat from corporate interests who wielded enough influence to block the passage of protective legislation. Therefore, it was only fitting that workers' rights clauses now be added to state constitutions. As Joseph Medill argued in the Illinois Convention of 1869–1870, while supporting a miners' safety provision,

It is true the Legislature has the power to pass such laws, even though the Constitution may be silent upon the subject; but the Legislature has neglected to perform this duty; session after session has passed, but no law has been enacted to secure the life and health of the miners. Opposition on account of the expense is made by the proprietors, and the Legislature, after wrangling and disputing, adjourns without doing anything. . . . I maintain that it is the bounden duty of this Convention to insert a clause making it obligatory upon the Legislature to provide for their protection; for, unless we do, there is very little likelihood that they will take any effectual action whatever.[39]

In the view of the supporters, legislators had not earned the people's trust on these issues, and in fact had turned out to be more responsive to special interests than to the public interest. Thomas Ewing noted in the Ohio Convention of 1873–1874 that "the miners, through their organizations, winter before last, brought this subject [of miners' safety] to the attention of the Legislature," but it was "defeated by the efforts of the owners of coal mines. . . . It is proper that this Convention should right this wrong by making it obligatory upon the Legislature to enact and provide for the execution of such laws as will secure safety and health to miners, without needlessly burdening their employers."[40] Nor could this corporate influence on the legislative process be easily overcome, even through repeated political pressure. As Thomas Feeney recounted in the Arizona Convention of 1910, "For twenty-five years labor has been knocking at the doors of the legislature for an employers' liability act, and has not gotten it, and this is one method of impressing it upon them that we want it. Gentlemen claim it would not be constitutional, but I would like to know what is constitutional and what is legislative; where should the line of demarcation go?"[41]

Supporters argued that workers' rights were at risk not only in the legislature, but also, and especially, in the judiciary, because even when legislators enacted workers' rights statutes, there was still a possibility of their being overturned in the courts. Therefore, the only way to ensure that these measures would survive judicial scrutiny was to enshrine them in the constitution. In some instances, convention delegates were responding to state court rulings that had already invalidated workers' rights statutes. Such was the case, Percy Tetlow argued in the Ohio Convention of 1912, with a measure establishing an eight-hour day on public works:

We desire this proposition to become a constitutional provision to safeguard this right, and to circumvent the decisions rendered by courts of this state. Many of you will remember that in 1900 a state law was passed in this state providing for an eight-hour day on public works, and also an eight-hour day on all contracts and subcontracts for and in behalf of the state and its political subdivisions. That law was declared unconstitutional by the supreme court of this state.[42]

On other occasions, state courts had not yet struck down a particular workers' rights measure, but delegates feared that such a decision might be handed down, and they sought to head off any such ruling. This was the reason why Henry Cordes supported a workmen's compensation provision in the same convention. He explained that the proposal "undertakes to write into the constitution of Ohio a constitutional provision making secure the workmen's compensation law passed by the last legislature, and declared constitutional by the Ohio Supreme Court by a vote of 4 to 2. Labor asks that this proposal be adopted, because we believe that by writing it into the constitution it will make it possible to continue this beneficial measure without any further fear of a constitutional question being raised again on this matter."[43] On still other occasions, legislatures had not yet enacted workers' rights statutes, but delegates proposed constitutional provisions in order to remove any uncertainty about their constitutionality, especially when this uncertainty might have accounted for legislators' hesitation to act in this area. Thus John Bodfish argued in the Massachusetts Convention of 1917–1919,

> You all are familiar with the constitutional argument of the right to contract freely, of taking property without due process and of exercising the taxing power for private ends. Because of the attitude of our courts and the judgments rendered by some of them and the discussions which we find in the opinions of our judges, it seems certain that there is grave doubt as to whether the Legislature can deal with these questions as changing conditions may seem to require.[44]

As his colleague Edward Carr concluded, "We are sitting to remove any doubts from our present Constitution, if there are any doubts as to the constitutionality of these proposed laws."[45]

The Adoption of Workers' Rights Provisions

Supporters of workers' rights provisions prevailed on many occasions in the late nineteenth and early twentieth centuries. In a few cases, convention delegates adopted general provisions committing the state to the protection of workers rights.[46] The Wyoming Constitution of 1889, for instance, provided in its Declaration of Rights that "the rights of labor shall have just protection through laws calculated to secure to the laborer proper rewards for his service and to promote the industrial welfare of the state."[47]

As for particular rights provisions, child-labor restrictions were enacted in a variety of forms, beginning with the Colorado Constitution of 1876.[48] Several states, such as New Mexico, chose to set out general principles of policy regarding child labor, to the effect that "the legislature shall enact suitable laws for the regulation of the employment of children."[49] Other states, such as Utah, offered more explicit directives, to the effect that "the legislature shall prohibit . . . the employment of . . . children under the age of fourteen years in underground mines."[50] Still other states, such as Idaho, simply proclaimed that "the employment of children under the age of fourteen years in underground mines is prohibited."[51]

Maximum-hours provisions were also enacted in various states, beginning with the California Constitution of 1879.[52] On one hand, states such as Michigan enacted permissive provisions, which gave the legislature "the power to enact laws relative to the hours and conditions under which men, women and children may be employed."[53] Other states, such as Wyoming, simply declared that "eight hours actual work shall constitute a lawful day's work in all mines, and on all State and municipal works."[54] Minimum wage provisions were also adopted in several states, beginning with the Ohio Constitution, as amended in 1912,[55] and in each case these provisions took the form of permissive clauses, such that "laws may be passed . . . establishing a minimum wage."[56]

The most popular workers' rights clauses during this period were concerned with guaranteeing workers' safety and ensuring compensation for workplace injuries. Workers' safety provisions generally took the form of declaratory clauses, albeit with varying levels of specificity.[57] Several of these clauses were quite detailed, such as in the Illinois Constitution of 1870, which was the first to contain a provision of this sort: "It shall be the duty of the general assembly to pass such laws as may be necessary for the protection of operative miners, by providing for ventilation, when the same may be required, and the construction of escapement shafts, or such other appliances as may secure safety in all coal mines, and to provide for the enforcement of said laws by such penalties and punishments as may be deemed proper."[58] Other workers' safety clauses were more general, such as in the Utah Constitution of 1895, which declared that "the legislature shall pass laws to provide for the health and safety of employees in factories, smelters, and mines."[59]

Employer-liability provisions first appeared in the Colorado Constitution of 1876 and took various forms in the states.[60] Some states chose to abrogate one or more of the various common law doctrines relied on by employers to escape judgments of liability for workplace injuries. Other states made it illegal for employers to force workers to forego liability claims as a condition of their contracts. Still other states chose to permit or require state legislatures to establish workmen's compensation funds. And several states enacted each of these types of provisions. The Arizona Constitution, for instance, provided that "the common law doctrine of fellow servants, so far as it affects the liability of a master for injuries to his servants resulting from the acts or omissions of any other servant or servants of the common master is forever abrogated."[61] In addition, "The defense of contributory negligence or of assumption of risk shall, in all cases whatsoever, be a question of fact and shall, at all times, be left to the jury."[62] Moreover, "It shall be unlawful for any person, company, association, or corporation to require of its servants or employees as a condition of their employment, or otherwise, any contract or agreement whereby such person, company, association, or corporation shall be released or discharged from liability or responsibility on account of personal injuries which may be received by such servants or employees while in the service or employment of such person, company, association, or corporation."[63] Finally, "The Legislature shall enact a Workmen's Compulsory Compensation law."[64]

Union Rights and the Right to Work

Another approach to improving working conditions was to secure the right to organize and bargain collectively so that workers could secure future gains on their own initiative. This took the form in the late nineteenth century of efforts to prohibit employers from blacklisting union members or preventing workers from joining unions (yellow-dog contracts), and in the early twentieth century of efforts to secure the right to organize and bargain collectively.[65] These efforts then produced a backlash in the mid-twentieth century, at which point business interests moved to secure adoption of right-to-work provisions prohibiting closed-shop arrangements and ensuring that workers could not be required to join unions as a condition of employment.[66] As much as these pro- and anti-union movements differed in their substantive goals, there is a strong similarity in the arguments advanced for and against the constitutionalization of both types of proposals. In both cases, critics argued that these rights were not properly constitutional because they were not as enduring or fundamental as traditional political and civil rights. Meanwhile, supporters, who were at times strong union advocates and at other times ardent union foes, responded that these rights were actually quite similar to long-standing rights in character and purpose.

The Case for and against Union Rights

Critics of constitutionalizing union rights argued that these rights were too ill-defined to be included in constitutions. Thus, in the Illinois Convention of 1920–1922, during a debate about a proposal declaring that "the labor of a human being is an attribute of life and is not property" and protecting "the right of workmen to organize into trade and labor unions," Charles Hamill argued,

> I am unwilling to give my assent to writing into the Constitution a sentence the meaning of which is so obscure. I conceive that it is the function of the Convention to write law—rules governing human conduct. It is not the function of the Convention to put forth abstract propositions of philosophy. If we are going to write a treatise on philosophy, let us write something that is at least as clear as ordinary metaphysics. What do we mean by the "labor of a human being" being an "attribute of life"?[67]

Similarly, Robert Carey in the New Jersey Convention of 1947 argued that the right to organize and bargain collectively was susceptible to different interpretations and therefore ill-suited for a constitutional provision. He argued,

> We are doing a dangerous thing. In the first place, we are using language in our Constitution that no man really understands. We will not know just what it means until some day some judge in some court somewhere in our State will tell us what we meant by this paragraph in our Constitution. It will be argued that it must have been put in for some vital purpose, to give us some rights that we haven't got today. It must be that, but who will answer the query then?[68]

He disclaimed any "disposition to be untoward toward the interests of labor." He simply believed that such a provision "has no proper place in the Constitution of our State. If it has a place anywhere, it is in the legislative program of our State."[69]

Critics argued that even if union rights could be assigned a precise meaning at this particular point in time, such a meaning was bound to evolve over time in response to changing conditions. As Elizabeth Kellerman explained in the Hawaii Convention of 1950,

> Suppose circumstances arise whereby it becomes definitely a matter necessary to the public interest to alter materially the meaning of the language, "right to bargain collectively." Suppose labor in a certain group attains such a monopoly over a full industry that it becomes as harmful to the public as the public has decreed such monopolies to be harmful when held entirely by industry, by management. . . . I don't think we want to preclude our legislature from redefining the language of collective bargaining as the ever changing relationships of industry and labor present themselves. . . . . I submit that it is a matter of definition and the definition should be subject to growth, to change to fit the needs of the people.[70]

Several delegates argued that the federal model was instructive in this regard, in that Congress had secured collective-bargaining rights on a statutory basis in the National Labor Relations Act of 1935 (the Wagner Act) and then had been able to modify these rights a dozen years later in the Taft-Hartley Act. Joseph Sherbow argued in the Maryland Convention of 1967–1968,

> In Congress they adopted, and very properly and undoubtedly belatedly, the National Labor Relations Act. All of this was statutory. When it was necessary to bring it closer to center because it was going too far, other statutes were passed. . . . In other words, this is properly regulated by statute at the national level, and this is the way it ought to be handled at the state level as well, because there you can make necessary changes when you go too far to the liberal or conservative side.[71]

Alfred Scanlan reached a similar conclusion in the same convention, and he argued that the right to bargain collectively was in this sense different from traditional constitutional rights. He explained that the right to bargain collectively, as secured through the Wagner Act, "is a fundamental statutory right, but since it was in the statute and not the constitution, the Congress was not precluded in the Taft-Hartley Act, and some others that have followed, from laying down restrictions upon carrying that right to the nth power. Unlike freedom of assembly and freedom of religion, the right to bargain collectively must be limited in some respects and on many occasions."[72]

These critics did not necessarily object to the recognition of union rights. Rather, they objected to securing these rights in the constitution, alongside enduring rights such as freedom of speech and religion, rather than by statute, as was proper for evolving rights and as had been the usual practice. Richard Kiefer explained in the same convention, "They are fine principles with which I am a hundred percent and wholly in agreement; but I do not think this provision belongs in the constitution. . . . It is not the kind of inalienable, natural permanent right that we should freeze into this constitution, particularly when this can be put on the statute books and is on the statute books in many states and in this State."[73]

Supporters of union rights responded that these rights were no less defined than many long-standing provisions whose constitutional status had never been questioned. Matsuki Arashiro in the Hawaii Convention of 1950 pointed out that the paradigmatic constitutional rights of free speech and religion were themselves phrased in rather vague and general terms. "Answering the lady delegate from the fourth district who said that word 'collective bargaining' is not clear, well, when we wrote our Constitution, our Federal Constitution, I don't think the freedom of speech and freedom of religion and all those things were clear then, but it has been regulated and it's still not clear as to its interpretation. It has been always brought to court for a clear definition."[74] Meanwhile, his colleague Yasutaka Fukushima called attention to the open-ended nature of due process clauses, which were a fixture in both federal and state bills of rights. He argued that the right to bargain collectively "may be undefined, but so are a lot of the other rights which we have written into our Constitution. Certainly the word 'collective bargaining' is not a word of art; certainly the words 'due process of law' are not words of art. It's subject to interpretation, and simply because we cannot define it categorically and state collective bargaining is this, does not mean that it is an undefined right."[75] In the view of these delegates, then, courts were frequently called on to interpret open-ended constitutional provisions, and in this respect, union rights could be viewed as a continuation of, rather than a departure from, traditional practices.

In fact, supporters argued that union rights were now even more fundamental than many traditional rights. Harry Bard argued in the Maryland Convention of 1967–1968 that union rights were the contemporary equivalent of traditional private property rights:

> In the 18th and 19th centuries, we accorded man the right of protection to operate as a free individual. We have seen the problems that came to man in society because man was free and creative, but in this century, particularly in this latter third of the 20th century, it is impossible for man to be free when acting alone in the economic realm. The nature of our society demands man's

freedom to act in groups when dealing with his economic requirements. Within this frame of reference, this right does deserve constitutional status.[76]

Elsbeth Bothe reached a similar conclusion in the same convention, though she preferred to view union rights as the modern embodiment of nineteenth-century prohibitions against involuntary servitude. In her mind, union rights were "as fundamental, as necessary, as any of those contained in the Declaration of Rights which we have for the most part adopted in this Convention; that it is coextensive and correlated with the rights of free speech and assembly; and that it is just as necessary and more so today than the prohibitions in our Constitution written 100 years ago against involuntary servitude and other direct means of keeping people under the domination of others."[77]

It was true, the supporters acknowledged, that earlier constitution makers had failed to recognize these types of rights, but this was because previous generations had encountered a different set of economic conditions. Arthur Harriman explained in the Massachusetts Convention of 1917–1919, "It is inconceivable, sir, that those men who formed the first Constitution could have conceived of the industrial conditions which have come to exist in our present life. We then had an individualistic system which has gone on until it has become collective, and capital has organized upon the one side and labor on the other."[78] By the twentieth century, though, new economic conditions dictated the recognition of new rights. In the view of Ronald Glass in the New Jersey Convention of 1947,

> These rights are well-established basic rights, and any delegate to this Convention who opposes inclusion of this clause doesn't understand the new world in which he lives, the highly industrialized world, so vastly different from the world he lived in only a few decades ago when sweat shops and 72 hours a week and other abuses were the order of the day and labor had no recourse. The right to organize and bargain collectively is a deep, inalienable right, as inalienable as the right of free speech and freedom to worship the way you please.[79]

As Lawrence Park concluded in the same convention, traditional civil and political rights had themselves been newly recognized at one point and had only become firmly established through the passage of time. He had no doubt that the right to organize and bargain collectively would undergo a similar evolution:

> When we look at our Constitution we find in it the right to trial by jury, the right of the writ of habeas corpus, and many other particular privileges which we

have had so long now that most of us cannot help but wonder when there was a time that those rights were not recognized. . . . It is a newly acquired right, but I say it is a right that is just as important in the origin and development of law as the right to trial by jury, the writ of habeas corpus, and so forth.[80]

Insofar as union rights were understood to be fundamental, as supporters believed them to be, then their security could not be made to depend on the vagaries of the political process. It was true, as the critics claimed, that legislatures could secure union rights by statute; that they had done so in many cases; and that this approach permitted the modification of these rights in response to changing conditions. However, the same argument could just as easily be advanced in regard to freedom of speech and religion, the supporters responded; and yet few would claim that these rights were undeserving of constitutional protection. According to Robert F. Wagner, principal author of the National Labor Relations Act and delegate to the New York Convention of 1938, the right to bargain collectively was "so fundamental that no court, no judge, no Legislature in the future should ever again deprive the workers of that freedom to exercise the same rights as other citizens in other economic activities, and to insure that the place to put it is in the Constitution of the State of New York, so that no temporary reactionary court or reactionary Legislature can deprive the wage earners of our State of that fundamental right."[81]

A principal concern, as Wagner suggested, was that legislatures could not be trusted to resist temporary passions that might lead to a curtailment of union rights. As Frank Eggers argued in the New Jersey Convention of 1947, labor rights, no less than civil rights, were susceptible to legislative encroachments:

I ask you who say you are sympathetic to labor, I ask you who want labor's right to organize never to be impaired, to look at recent history and judge for yourselves as to how much labor can trust the legislative body. Labor is merely asking this Convention to guarantee to it for the future the inherent right to organize and bargain collectively, so that during emotional crises, during times when public opinion might be swayed against labor, that a Legislature amenable to such emotional public opinion will not deprive labor of the inherent right that it has always had.[82]

An additional concern was that courts might strike down the protective statutes that had been enacted. James Bennett pointed out in the Maryland Convention of 1967–1968 that "the history of labor legislation shows the importance of having something of this kind in the constitution. Courts have been notably conservative, not to say reactionary, in interpreting the rights of the laboring people and the rights of the General Assembly in enacting such legislation."[83] In fact, in many instances when union rights proposals were introduced in conventions, legislatures had already secured these rights, and the chief aim of going further and constitutionalizing these rights was to provide a clear directive to judges. Murray Gootrad in the New York Convention of 1938 acknowledged that union rights had already been secured in that state by legislation. But, he argued,

> notwithstanding these laws, the necessity remains for incorporating an industrial Bill of Rights into the organic law of this State. I believe that my proposal should go into our Constitution, first, because I would like to restate the established law of this State, setting down such laws in a more fundamental and permanent form for the future guidance of our judges and legislatures. Secondly, to the extent that some of the proposed guarantees are today protected solely by virtue of legislative enactments, the constitutionality of which has not as yet been determined and which therefore are subject to harmful modification or outright repeal by judicial decision or future act of Legislature. Thirdly, because the present silence of the Constitution regarding the fundamental rights of labor has deprived the courts and other law-enforcement agencies of standards upon which to exercise a uniform discretion.[84]

The Case for and against the Right to Work

During the 1940s and for the next several decades, union rights continued to be debated, but counter-proposals were also introduced to combat the power of unions, by stipulating that workers could not be required to join unions as a condition of employment. As one would expect, the supporters of these right-to-work measures were frequently the same individuals who opposed collective-bargaining rights, and vice versa. Although the politics of the right-to-work issue therefore reflected a complete reversal of the positions in the collective-bargaining debates, the arguments for and against the constitutionalization of both measures were quite similar.

Critics maintained, in the same fashion as critics of collective-bargaining rights, that the right to work was of an evolving, rather than a permanent, character, and therefore best left to legislative regulation. As Ralph Maxwell argued in the North Dakota Convention of 1971–1972, there was no precedent for such a right in the U.S. Constitution:

> I have heard, and so have you—and we've heard it again this morning—that the right to work is a basic right and, therefore, it should be in the Constitution. I don't know what the authority is for the proposition that this is a basic right. It's not found in the common law or in the Magna Carta or in the Declaration of Independence. You won't find it in the Constitution of the United States or any of the amendments to that document.[85]

Nor, as Nicholas Schmit argued in the same convention, could delegates have any assurance, if they did adopt such a constitutional right, that its meaning would remain constant in future years: "How can we, in good conscience, lock into our Bill of Rights the so-called 'right-to-work' law, which meant one thing yesterday and means something else today, and probably will mean something different tomorrow."[86] Finally, as Sylvan Hubrig maintained in the same convention, this was just the sort of area in which legislatures would benefit from experimenting with various specifications and modifications of the right. He cautioned,

> Just a short time ago, this body objected to locking in the grand jury system into the Constitution. Are we going to today lock in the right-to-work section to the point that the Legislature cannot change the statute as they want to—would want to? Stop and think! Are we being consistent with our argument that the legislative matters should not be in the Constitution? Now is the time for us to draw the line in keeping legislation out of the Constitution.[87]

Supporters of constitutional right-to-work provisions responded, again in much the same fashion as supporters of collective-bargaining rights, by questioning the purported distinction between statutory and constitutional rights, and by arguing that the right to work was just as worthy of constitutional protection as many traditional rights. Arden Burbridge argued in the same convention,

> I am aware that some learned and sincere people have become such constitutional purists—on this issue, at least—that they would delete "right-to-work" from our Constitution because it offends their sensitivities on their definition of what is constitutional material. . . . I respectfully disagree. There is room in our Constitution to deal with such basic people-to-people rights as the freedom of religion and the freedom of the press. There was room in our old Constitution to deal with "right-to-work." Have we suddenly become so sophisticated

that we cannot acknowledge this basic right because it doesn't fit into our narrow definition of constitutional matter?[88]

Moreover, supporters argued that the right to work was just as insecure in the political process as were other established rights, and this was especially true on account of the disproportionate influence wielded by unions in many state legislatures. As Don Seyferth argued in the Michigan Convention of 1961–1962, "Today the right of Michigan workers to join and support a union is protected by law. This is as it should be. However, today Michigan workers' right to refrain from joining and supporting a union is not protected by law. This is not as it should be. The amendment before us, if adopted, will correct this flagrant violation of individual rights." He concluded, "This statement is nothing more nor nothing less than a simple reiteration of our basic fundamental individual rights as already constitutionally declared in our behalf."[89]

The Adoption of Union Rights and Right-to-Work Provisions

Union rights advocates and right-to-work supporters were each successful to some degree in securing enactment of their preferred provisions. The late nineteenth century and early twentieth century saw the adoption of several constitutional provisions prohibiting the keeping and sharing of blacklists.[90] Typical of these provisions were the ones found in the North Dakota Constitution of 1889, which was the first to adopt clauses of this sort. A provision in the North Dakota bill of rights states that "every citizen of this state shall be free to obtain employment wherever possible, and any person, corporation, or agent thereof, maliciously interfering or hindering in any way, any citizen from obtaining or enjoying employment already obtained, from any other corporation or person, shall be deemed guilty of a misdemeanor."[91] An additional provision in the body of the North Dakota Constitution declares that "the exchange of 'black lists' between corporations shall be prohibited."[92]

Beginning with the New York Convention of 1938, several states went on to protect the right of workers to organize and bargain collectively.[93] These states differ in some respects in their treatment of private and public employees, but the language in the New York bill of rights is typical insofar as it declares, "Employees shall have the right to organize and to bargain collectively through representatives of their own choosing."[94]

Beginning with amendments that were added in 1944 to the Florida and Arkansas Constitutions, several states followed a different path and enacted right-to-work provisions.[95] The Arkansas provision is typical in that it declares,

> No person shall be denied employment because of membership in or affiliation with or resignation from a labor union, or because of refusal to join or affiliate with a labor union; nor shall any corporation or individual or association of any kind enter into any contract, written or oral, to exclude from employment members of a labor union or persons who refuse to join a labor union, or because of resignation from a labor union; nor shall any person against his will be compelled to pay dues to any labor organization as a prerequisite to or condition of employment.[96]

Still other states have chosen to protect both the right to bargain collectively and the right to work. According to the relevant section of the Florida Declaration of Rights, "The right of persons to work shall not be denied or abridged on account of membership or non-membership in any labor union or labor organization. The right of employees, by and through a labor organization, to bargain collectively shall not be denied or abridged. Public employees shall not have the right to strike."[97]

Social and Economic Rights

State constitution makers have also considered another set of positive-rights provisions permitting, and in some cases requiring, the government to provide for the economic and social security of the citizenry.[98] The earliest proposals of this sort were introduced in the immediate aftermath of the Civil War in several southern conventions and mandated adequate treatment for the poor. These proposals continued to be debated during the twentieth century, as were additional efforts to ensure a degree of economic and social security for the citizenry. As the twentieth century progressed, measures were also proposed to secure a right to adequate health care and to protect the rights of consumers, among other provisions.

As in the previous debates over workers' rights and union rights, supporters and critics sparred primarily over whether social and economic rights were deserving of inclusion in the constitution, with critics arguing that these rights were properly regulated by statute and supporters responding that these rights were now as fundamental as traditional civil and political rights. This debate also turned on the question of what purpose would be served by recognizing social and economic rights, with critics contending that these provisions could not be enforced through the judicial process and supporters responding that constitutional rights served important purposes aside from giving rise to judicial interpretation.

The Case against Social and Economic Rights

Critics argued that social and economic rights were of a different character than traditional civil and political rights. For one thing, the precise meaning of terms such as "economic security" was difficult to pin down. Warren Taylor argued in the Alaska Convention of 1955–1956,

> It would be a dangerous thing to put that word in there because I don't believe it appears in any constitution that I have read, neither does it appear in the Federal Constitution. Economic right can be construed in many different ways, and, if we would adopt that word in this particular article, we are getting our-selves into a morass of doubt in which we may . . . [get] into soft going, and it may take a considerable amount of litigation to have the courts establish what economic right was guaranteed under the constitution.[99]

Moreover, the meaning of these rights was likely to evolve over time, and such changes could be best registered through legislative statutes. As W. O. Smith argued in the Hawaii Convention of 1950 in regard to a proposal committing the legislature to protect and promote public health, "Looking over these sections I cannot help but feel that we would be adding a lot of things to our Constitution which, when you put it in your Constitution, right now might be perfectly O.K., but in the future they might be subject to some change."[100] John Phillips pointed out in the same convention,

> In the next ten years there may be a different way of promoting health, a different method, a different means. Now doesn't that itself prove that this is an ephem-eral law which—man is constantly trying to solve and he does it best with the device known as the legislative process. Wouldn't it be better that we leave it up to the legislature to take up these problems of public health and have them work them out as they have been doing anyway and which is absolutely necessary to let them do, because only they can set forth the standards that are in there?[101]

Critics also questioned whether these rights commanded sufficient public support to be included in the constitution. Although freedom of speech and religion were well entrenched in the public mind, economic rights proposals were rather controversial and, for this reason, less deserving of constitutional status. As John Dyer argued in the Hawaii Convention of 1968, while responding to a proposal that "the right of the people to economic security, sufficient to live with dignity, shall not be violated" and that "the legislature shall provide protection against the loss or inadequacy of income," "I consider this the most fantastic proposal that hit the floor of this Convention. Actually what this proposal does is to provide a guaranteed income to everybody in the state."[102] Richard Bartlett had a similar reaction to a consumers' rights proposal in the New York Convention of 1967. He thought it was "demeaning to the dignity of a Bill of Rights" and was "the very kind of thing that has got to be dealt with by statute."[103]

Critics also questioned the purpose that would be served by adopting social and economic rights provisions. It was one thing to prohibit government from violating freedom of speech or religion; convention delegates assumed that violations of these guarantees would be remedied through judicial decisions. It was quite another matter to guarantee a right to economic security, or to direct the state to provide for the poor, or to promote public health. Some delegates were unclear as to how these provisions would be enforced, and they asked for clarification on this point. Thus Yasutaka Fukushima argued in regard to a public health proposal in the Hawaii Convention of 1950, "As I read this section here and the following section, it is a mandate upon the legislature. . . . How does the committee propose to enforce the mandate?"[104] Still other delegates needed no clarification on this point; they were convinced that it would be impossible to enforce these provisions, because of the absence of concrete standards that could serve as the basis for judicial decisions. As Woody Jenkins argued in the Louisiana Convention of 1973–1974, a proposed right to economic security "really accomplishes nothing other than to make a policy statement. Wouldn't it be better then to leave such things out of the constitution rather than trying to put them into a constitution that is already burdened with too much verbiage?"[105] Insofar as these provisions were unenforceable, Alfred Scanlan argued in the Maryland Convention of 1967–1968, appending them to the constitution might do more harm than good by giving citizens false hope about the possibility of government solving the enduring problems of poverty and unemployment: "Here we have a platitude that no state action could ever achieve. To put it in our Constitution is to delude the people who most need it."[106] After all, as Mr. Dyer of Hawaii argued, the common-sense understanding was that "if you got a right, surely you must be able to enforce it."[107]

Moreover, to the extent that social and economic rights might in fact be enforceable through judicial decisions, this only raised additional problems, such as fears that judges would interpret open-ended clauses to require legislators to adopt all sorts of programs and make costly expenditures. Gary O'Neill in the Louisiana Convention of 1973–1974 was concerned that an economic security provision would "allow any citizen to sue the state at any time because he thinks he's economically insecure."[108] His colleague Lantz Womack argued that such a provision would lead the state to "get caught in a trap to where the court would tell you that economic security's term is much broader than we have been led to believe the intent of this article is, and it would take far more money from the state treasury to do it than is provided today, then who will you take it away from?"[109]

The Case for Social and Economic Rights

Supporters responded that social and economic rights were no less fundamental than civil and political rights. It was true that social and economic rights had gone unrecognized by drafters of the U.S. Constitution and previous state constitution makers. However, by the mid-twentieth century, conditions had changed to the point that social and economic rights were now sufficiently important to be entitled to constitutional status. According to Harry Bard in the Maryland Convention of 1967–1968,

> Eighteenth and nineteenth century man needed political security, and so freedoms to vote, hold office, and to speak one's mind were concerns of our earlier Maryland Constitutions. The fathers of the Constitution of 1776, 1851, 1864 and 1867 recognized that if man were to be free he had to have these political securities. . . . But our times and those ahead of us require us to establish economic securities. If man cannot be free economically from want, of what avail is the ballot?[110]

In fact, these delegates argued, economic rights could be considered in some ways even more fundamental than political rights. As Addie Key argued in the same convention,

> There is no freedom without economic freedom. There is no liberty without economic freedom, and there is no life, real life, without economic security.

So having recognized in our constitution that political power originates in the people and that all government is instituted to secure these rights of life, liberty, and the pursuit of happiness, I want you also to recognize the same political power and the same government has to work to secure that economic freedom that is necessary before any other can be secured.[111]

Lloyd Taylor argued in the same convention that, by the mid-twentieth century, citizens were likely to appreciate the importance of economic rights even more so than political rights. Disappointed by the absence of any economic rights in the final draft of the proposed constitution, he complained, "The constitution does not have any guts. It has a certain number of political rights, but people cannot eat political rights. They need something for their stomachs, and people throughout the State of Maryland, want something they can see and something they can really put their teeth into, but they cannot put their teeth into this constitution."[112]

To be sure, there were different understandings among these various delegates as to which social and economic rights were entitled to constitutional protection. Some delegates were prepared to recognize a right to economic subsistence. For instance, Lyle Monroe in the Montana Convention of 1971–1972 argued that "all persons have [an] inalienable right to pursue the basic necessities of life, that there can be no right to life apart from the possibility of existence."[113] Other delegates sought to recognize a right to adequate health care. As Kenneth Urdahl argued in the North Dakota Convention of 1971–1972, "There is a growing recognition today of health as an important [right]—that's important to the pursuit of other rights. . . . It was for these reasons that the committee felt it important at this time to add the 'pursuit of health' as a basic right."[114] Still other delegates sought to protect consumers' rights. As David Stahl explained in the Illinois Convention of 1969–1970,

Most citizens of Illinois will never serve on a grand jury, be guilty of libel, be tried by a jury, require bail, be convicted of a serious crime, or have his life directly affected by some of the provisions we have properly adopted in our bill of rights. But virtually every citizen is almost daily a consumer, concerned with his economic well-being. If you want a provision for all of the people, please support this amendment.[115]

Along these lines, Earl Koger argued in the Maryland Convention of 1967–1968, "Every great constitution guarantees the people basic rights, and here is a basic right that is badly needed." In particular, "people need the right not to be deliberately deceived," and they also need "rights against fraud, not to be subjected to criminals in the market place," and "rights against psychological subjugation."[116]

Supporters also responded to the critics' concerns that social and economic rights provisions would serve no purpose because they were not judicially enforceable. Their principal response was that these constitutional provisions might serve other purposes, aside from empowering judges to hold public officials accountable for violations of rights. For one thing, as Edward Corsi argued in the New York Convention of 1938, constitutional provisions could help to prevent judges from overturning legislative efforts to secure social and economic rights. He explained, "This amendment . . . is an empowering clause which enables the Legislature to go ahead and meet the challenge of insecurity with such wisdom as it may have. Nothing in the Constitution, we say, shall prevent the Legislature from providing against poverty, sickness, old age, from protecting the blind, the deaf, the dumb, the physically handicapped, and the multitude of our citizens of tomorrow whose needs are the duty and responsibility of government."[117] He went on to proclaim, "Here are words which set forth a definite policy of government, a concrete social obligation which no court may ever misread."[118] His colleague James McNally offered a similar explanation of a proposal authorizing the legislature to promote public health: "That is the only purpose of the committee in offering this proposal to the delegates: So that, in the event at some future time or place the Legislature of this State sees fit to pass a health insurance measure, that measure would be constitutional."[119]

Supporters also argued that these provisions were valuable in setting out standards for legislators to strive to attain. It was true that federal constitution makers had eschewed provisions of this kind. But the federal model, with its emphasis on clearly defined, judicially enforceable provisions, was not the only legitimate approach. As Nils Larsen explained in the Hawaii Convention of 1950, if the U.S. Constitution offered the final word on these questions, then "we really don't need to do the job that we are doing. We should have quit the first day and accepted the United States Constitution." In his view, state constitutions had always served a quite different purpose: that of "indicat[ing] the philosophy and thinking of the people." And one virtue of this approach was that state constitutions had traditionally set a "path of philosophy along which the legislature could provide legislation. It's true they don't have to do it, but I believe the Constitution very definitely indicates a pathway on which—along which we might march. And also, gives us, perhaps, a handle or a suggestion along which, if we are really interested and we find a group of people unprotected, where we can ask for protection under the Constitution."[120] Nadao Yoshinaga acknowledged in the Hawaii Convention of 1968, during a debate over an economic security provision, that the state constitutional approach occasionally led to the drafting of "rights that sometimes are difficult to understand," but he maintained that these rights provisions nevertheless served an important function:

> Among these rights are the enjoyment of life, liberty, and the pursuit of happiness which may not necessarily always be mathematically definable and enforceable in court. I think that all this amendment intends, as it stands before this body now, is that there is at least a strong expression of the people of Hawaii as to the kind of economic right we believe that each and every one of us in the State of Hawaii is entitled to.[121]

At times, the expression of such rights in the constitution might serve as a goal for legislators to keep in view; at other times, these provisions might serve as a goad to legislators, by forcing them to go further in guaranteeing economic and social security than they would otherwise be inclined. Lyle Monroe explained, in regard to one such provision in the Montana Convention of 1971–1972 that "this is more or less a constitutional sermon so that maybe the Legislature, from time to time, can improve and update—update and upgrade our public assistance programs from time to time as they see fit."[122] At still other times, the adoption of these constitutional provisions might serve to caution legislators against the temptation to reduce protection for social and economic rights during periods of budget shortfalls. As Ann Corbett argued in the Hawaii Convention of 1950, "It's my belief that these advances have been won by the people of the territory over the past 50 years by battles in court and in the legislature, and that if we don't reiterate and re-emphasize them at this time, we might conceivably lose them at some future date."[123]

Finally, supporters argued that economic and social rights provisions would assist the citizenry, by establishing standards by which they could judge the performance of legislators and hold accountable legislators who failed to meet their charge. As Charles Figy explained in the Michigan Convention of 1961–1962, "We think it necessary that this convention not pass over the thought of giving some recognition to the importance of public health. . . . We think it is a declaratory statement, it is calling the attention of the people and the legislature to the problems as they exist today, and as the problems may arise in the next several years to come."[124] In this regard, state constitutional provisions might serve a purpose similar to the Declaration of Independence at the federal level, by setting out enduring principles that the people would be committed and inspired to honor. As Nicholas Schloeder argued in the Maryland Convention of 1967–1968 in regard to an economic security provision,

> For many of us the real history of this country is the fulfillment of the promises of the Declaration of Independence, a fulfillment of the promise that all men are created equal. It is the life, liberty, and the pursuit of happiness. Pursuit of happiness means an equal chance of all people to set for themselves goals and to move positively toward the attainment of those goals. A constitution is a basic and fundamental law of the state, and goes far beyond the question of judicial pensions or whether or not a comptroller will, in fact, control. A constitution is an instrument of government and as such it is a social as well as a legal document and should provide in part at least for a promise of enlightenment.[125]

The Adoption of Social and Economic Rights

Ultimately, state constitution makers were sufficiently persuaded by the critics' arguments that they rejected the more open-ended and expansive of these social and economic rights proposals. For instance, the Maryland Convention of 1967–1968 chose not to approve a proposal that would have stated that "it is the policy of the State that all persons shall have economic security and the opportunity for employment, in order that they may live in decency, dignity, and health."[126] And a proposal in the Texas Convention of 1974 to the effect that "every person is entitled to adequate, comprehensive health care" was also ultimately rejected.[127] Similarly, the Illinois Convention of 1969–1970 turned down proposals that "each person shall have the right to conscionable treatment in the market place,"[128] and that "it shall be the public policy of the state that all persons shall have adequate nourishment, housing, medical care, and other needs of human life and dignity."[129]

At the same time, some state convention delegates were sufficiently impressed by the arguments in favor of various social and economic rights that they enacted several of these provisions. Several states, beginning with Alabama, Arkansas, North Carolina, and South Carolina in 1868, have enacted provisions committing state or local governments to address the needs of the poor, disabled, or elderly.[130] In several instances, these provisions are admonitory, as in the Illinois Constitution of 1970, whose preamble listed as one of several purposes the intent to "eliminate poverty and inequality."[131] In several other instances, these provisions are permissive, such as in the Louisiana Constitution of 1974, which provided that "the legislature may establish a system of economic and social welfare,"[132] or in the Hawaii Constitution, as amended in 1978, which established that "the State shall have the power to provide financial assistance, medical assistance and social services for persons who are found to be in need of and are eligible for such assistance and services as provided by law."[133] In most cases, though, the provisions are declaratory, such as in the Alabama Constitution of 1868, which proclaimed, "It shall be the duty of the General Assembly to make adequate provisions in each county for the maintenance of the poor of this State."[134] Several of these declaratory provisions are quite specific in their direction to the legislature, such as the North Carolina Constitution of 1868, which provided, in part, that "beneficent provision for the poor, the unfortunate, and orphan being one of the first duties of a civilized and Christian State, the general assembly shall, at its first session, appoint and define the duties of a board of public charities."[135] Still other of these declaratory provisions set out broad goals and then permit the legislature to determine the specific means of satisfying them, as in the New York Constitution, as amended in 1938, which stated, "The aid, care and support of the needy are public concerns and shall be provided by the state and by such of its subdivisions, and in such manner and by such means, as the legislature may from time to time determine."[136]

Several states also adopted provisions committing the legislature to provide for the health of the citizenry.[137] The New York Constitution, as amended in 1938, was the first to adopt such a provision, which was in the form of a declaratory clause but permitted the legislature to determine the precise means of following the directive. The provision stated, "The protection and promotion of the health of the inhabitants of the state are matters of public concern and provision therefore shall be made by the state and by such of its subdivisions and in such manner, and by such means as the legislature shall from time to time determine."[138] Other states chose to enact pure declaratory provisions, including the Alaska Constitution of 1956, which stated simply, "The Legislature shall provide for the promotion and protection of public health."[139] Still other states adopted permissive provisions, such as the Louisiana Constitution of 1974, which provided, "The Legislature may establish a system of . . . public health."[140]

Environmental Rights

The same sort of changing economic conditions and increasing rates of industrialization that led to the adoption of workers' rights, union rights, and social and economic rights also gave rise in the latter part of the twentieth century to proposals for the enactment of environmental rights provisions.[141] States have considered a variety of measures in this area, including guarantees of fishing and hunting rights (which first appeared in the Vermont Constitution of 1777)[142] and protection for state land preserves (typified by the Forever Wild forest-preserve provision that appeared in the New York Constitution of 1894),[143] among other provisions.[144] However, the environmental provisions that have generated the most debate in state conventions, particularly during the second half of the twentieth century, have been concerned with committing the state to the protection of the environment and, in some cases, to guaranteeing an individual right to a healthful environment. Critics once again questioned whether such environmental rights were deserving of constitutional status and were skeptical about how environmental rights provisions could be enforced. Meanwhile, supporters sought to explain why environmental rights were just as entitled to constitutional status as traditional rights; supporters also called attention to various beneficial purposes that might be served by including environmental rights provisions in a constitution.

The Case against Environmental Rights

Critics argued that the right to a "clean" or "healthful" environment was too ill-defined to be guaranteed in the constitution. Wade Dahood complained in the Montana Convention of 1971–1972, "I've listened to arguments with respect to what a healthy environment is and what [it] is not; and let me tell you here and now, there is no one that [can] come forward and tell you what a healthy environment is. I have listened to doctors who have tried to define what a healthy environment is, and not one has yet succeeded."[145] Meanwhile, Edward Lennox was led to ask in the Louisiana Convention of 1973–1974, "Who would decide if this amendment were adopted, where a healthful environment begins and/or ends?"[146] If the lack of a precise definition for these rights counseled against including them in the constitution, their technical character provided another reason for leaving them to be secured by legislation. John Lord Jr. in the New

Hampshire Convention of 1974 pointed out, "There are some fairly loose defini-
tions in this resolution. For instance, what is 'protection of air'? Does that mean
we can't [breathe] it? Certainly not. But that is a fairly loose definition. What is
'protection of land'? Does that mean that paving it over is protecting it from the
rain washing it away?" He therefore concluded that environmental rights were
different in kind from traditional constitutional rights: "Natural resources are
tangible things unlike life, liberty and the pursuit of happiness. They should be
protected by specific, qualified regulations through the application of standards,
through statutory law. Environmental problems are often technical, engineering
and social problems and they should be dealt with in that way, not through a
Constitutional amendment to the Bill of Rights."[147]

Critics were equally concerned about the consequences of adopting such
provisions. Some delegates argued against their adoption on the grounds that
these provisions would have no effect and therefore would be at best useless and
at worst misleading to the citizenry. Thus Billy Williamson argued in the Texas
Convention of 1974 in regard to an environmental policy provision, "This is
some more of this word count malarky that's being put in the constitution that
really doesn't say anything." He preferred that the constitution remain "silent,"
in which case advances in environmental protection could still be achieved
through "the statute books." As things stood, the proposed measure was "completely superfluous and it is totally unnecessary in the constitution."[148] In the
view of these critics, to adopt constitutional provisions out of a desire to bring
about political change was to subscribe to a mistaken view of how political reform was actually achieved. As George Lewis argued in the Illinois Convention
of 1969–1970 in regard to an environmental protection measure,

> These things are not conquered by constitutional provisions. Safety in mines
> were really not conquered by constitutional provisions. They were conquered
> by an enlightened legislature which were enlightened by public interest, and
> certainly the public interest is growing. So I believe that the place where this
> properly belongs is in the legislature. It is a legislative problem to cope with
> that issue in good time, and I think that we are making a mistake by putting it
> in the constitution.[149]

Mr. Scanlan in the Maryland Convention of 1967–1968 made a similar point
about the questionable historical value of such constitutional clauses, but in his
case with reference to the ineffectiveness of clean election clauses:

My point is, no matter how noble the aspirations or the exhortations that the various groups have—and I certainly sympathize with the conservationists, and I hope that everything they aspire to in this statement is ultimately done by the legislature of this state—I do not believe the exhortation to that effect has any place in the constitution. You can look at the old constitution and see exhortations, the one in which the legislature was exhorted to guarantee the purity of the election laws. I suggest that the presence of that or the absence of that exhortation had no effect whatsoever on the ultimate involvement of the present Corrupt Practices Act.[150]

Other delegates opposed these provisions for precisely the opposite reason: out of a fear that their adoption would have important and quite harmful effects. In particular, several delegates were concerned that if environmental provisions were framed as judicially enforceable rights rather than mere statements of policy, that this would empower judges to overturn decisions made through the democratic process. Geoffrey Brazier in the Montana Convention of 1971–1972 was especially troubled by this possibility, and he quoted at length from the work of an environmental scholar, Joseph Sax, in an effort to persuade his fellow delegates to reject an environmental rights proposal. Quoting Sax, he argued, "'There is an important and insufficiently understood distinction between a declaration of the right to a decent environment appearing in a statute and one appearing in a constitution. A right with constitutional status does indeed create the opportunity for its enforcement in the courts, but it also—and herein lies the danger,' says the author—'gives courts ultimate authority.'" According to Brazier (again quoting Sax), this was to be feared because "a court, even with the best motive, should not be authorized to function as an environmental czar against the clear wishes of the public and its elected representatives." On the other hand, "a statutory declaration of rights can open environmental matters fully to judicial attention but still leave ultimate decisionmaking power in the hands of the elected representatives of the public." In this way, Brazier argued (still quoting Sax), environmental rights could be distinguished from traditional rights that deserved to be constitutionalized:

There is a fundamental difference between almost all environmental problems and the issues to which the Bill of Rights so often used as an analogy is addressed. Essentially the Bill of Rights deals with the problems of permanent minorities and with government oppression of unpopular individual groups. For such problems, where the danger is tyranny by the majority, some foil is needed to the majoritarian rule that governs the legislative process. Giving ultimate constitutional authority to the courts in the matter of free speech and the rights of the criminal defendant or the religious dissenter is most appropriate, but environmental questions are preeminently problems caused by powerful and well-organized minorities who have managed to manipulate governmental agencies to their own ends.

Therefore, the principal need in regard to environmental issues was "for a forum that can help to even the political and administrative leverage of the adversaries," and although courts might play some role in securing such an "equalization," it would be best to "leave the ultimate decision to a truly democratized, democratic process."[151]

At the least, then, the critics argued that there were good reasons to be cautious about adopting open-ended environmental rights provisions, especially when litigants and judges might make use of them to tilt public policy away from the intent of the people and their elected representatives. As John Paulson concluded during the North Dakota Convention of 1971–1972 in regard to an environmental provision,

> The proposal as it stands only opens a Pandora's box of troubles. The sponsors cannot tell what will happen, we cannot tell the public what will happen. They say they are giving the citizens a right to sue. What they are doing is giving the peculiar limited interest people a chance to go into court and raise trouble and stop the state from carrying on programs which the state has already deemed to be in the public interest.[152]

The Case for Environmental Rights

Supporters responded that environmental rights were no less defined and every bit as important as a number of traditional constitutional rights. As Mary Lee Leahy argued in the Illinois Convention of 1969–1970, the federal constitution contained open-ended rights guarantees, yet there were few calls to eliminate these provisions: "We do define in the report what we mean by healthful environment, but ultimately, it would be the courts in the same way that the courts have decided over the years what the terms 'due process' and 'equal protection' mean."[153] James Derbes in the Louisiana Convention of 1973–1974 referred to these same federal constitutional clauses, along with several others, in an effort to demonstrate that an open-ended state constitutional rights provision would hardly be a novelty in the American constitutional tradition. He thought that "it would be a matter of judicial interpretation as much as the due process clause of the United States Constitution, the equal protection clause of the United States Constitution, the right against self incrimination, the right to trial by jury, etc. are also provided therein."[154] In fact, as Harold Arbanas argued in the Montana Convention of 1971–1972, practically all of the clauses in the federal Bill of Rights had been framed in general terms and then given particular meaning in subsequent court cases. Responding to a colleague who criticized state constitutional environmental rights as being ill-defined, he therefore argued,

> I couldn't help thinking, when Mr. Dahood was speaking this afternoon, that if you'd put the word "liberty" in the place of "clean environment," that practically everything he said would have rung true—that the same kind of talk could be given with regard to the great American ideal of liberty—you know, that we can't define it and there'd be all sorts of litigation. What does liberty mean? . . . If I took away your liberty, we could have days and days saying what that means; and yet these are the things that have been the ideal of our country.[155]

Nor were environmental rights any less fundamental than traditional rights, in the eyes of the supporters. It was true that the federal constitution did not provide for environmental rights, but this was because environmental problems were not yet acute when the federal convention delegates assembled in the late eighteenth century. As Mr. Derbes of Louisiana argued, "The framers of the Constitution of the United States of America, when they met almost two hundred years ago, failed to so provide because this country had not at that time entered into a stage of industrial development equivalent to that of today."[156] By the late twentieth century, the country had reached a stage of development that a right to a healthful environment could be viewed as a perfection of, rather than a departure from, the founders' handiwork. Along these lines, Mr. Derbes argued that environmental rights were an appropriate counterpart to long-standing property rights. Given that "we have provided for the right of the individual to use and to control and to dispose of his private property," he argued, "I say to you that there is a legitimate personal right of the individual to enjoy, wherever possible and insofar as possible, a healthful environment." He urged delegates "to make a twentieth century provision in this constitution," one "which reflects the problems of our twentieth century industrial society."[157] John Fay in the New York Convention of 1967 argued, similarly, that a conservation bill of rights was "something that is basically fundamental, as a necessary extension to the due process clause[;] due process to me requires that every citizen of the State must have the right to protection of those resources which alone can make life worthwhile in an age of increasing mechanism."[158] In fact, supporters argued that environmental rights were not only a logical extension of traditional constitutional rights but were actually a prerequisite for the enjoyment of these rights. Mrs. Leahy of Illinois explained:

> We believe that this is a fundamental right—an extension of the right to life—and that it is made operable in this particular section. We believe that at this time, in this society, it is important that this be stressed. We've heard a lot of discussion in here about the problems Illinois faces at this time—problems of race relations, problems in education, and so on—and yet the testimony that we heard would lead us to believe that unless we solve the problem of the environment, we won't be around in fifty years to see the results of the solutions to the other problems.[159]

Supporters were also prepared to respond to the critics' concerns about the consequences of placing environmental rights provisions in the constitution. Supporters had little doubt that such provisions would have important and beneficial consequences, although they differed among themselves about the precise nature of these benefits. Several supporters expected that environmental rights would serve as the basis for judicial decisions and therefore would be enforced in the same way as traditional constitutional rights. As Thomas McCracken argued in the Illinois Convention of 1969–1970, "This language, if adopted as part of our constitution, would give an individual the right to challenge the legislature's definition of the word 'healthful,' very definitely. A person could go into court . . . and if his complaint stated that the statute was inconsistent with the common understanding of the word 'healthful' as used in the constitution, then the court would have the power to declare that particular legislation unconstitutional."[160]

For the most part, though, supporters contended that the consequences of environmental rights provisions would be felt in ways other than through judicial enforcement, and that the critics failed to appreciate these various other purposes. One such purpose would be to exhort legislators to take action in this area. Thus John Lyman in the New Hampshire Convention of 1984 argued, "This Resolution is a statement of principle. It belongs in our Constitution, Part 1st of which is mainly a litany of principles. . . . It would provide a solid foundation for legislation, calculated to protect and conserve our common natural resources."[161] Frank Millard in the Michigan Convention of 1961–1962 expressed a similar view: that environmental rights provisions would call the attention of legislators to issues that might not otherwise press immediately upon them. He argued, "This is more or less just a memorializing of the legislature, that they have the right, the power. We are not giving them any power. They have that power. We are just telling them to look out into the future for our natural resources, the air and the water, and to make some regulations so that they will not be used up for the other generations that are to follow."[162] To view constitutional provisions as serving a hortatory function was, to be sure, to adhere to a different understanding than prevailed at the federal level. But this merely pointed to an important difference between the purposes of state and federal constitutions. As John Hardwicke argued during a debate over an environmental rights proposal in the Maryland Convention of 1967–1968,

> I have no objection whatsoever to exhortatory language in our constitution, and I hope when the time comes to consider other exhortatory language that we will give consideration to it not on the basis that it is exhortatory or not exhortatory, but on the basis of the language in the case. I hope we will not set out here an antiseptic constitution which will be so sterile, which will consist of such meaningless and dried, hard, legal phrases that it will make such dull reading that nobody will look at it. I do not object to exhortatory language in the constitution. It has a good effect, sets guidelines.[163]

A final purpose of elevating environmental rights to constitutional status, in the view of supporters, would be to give expression to the fundamental goals and values of the people. Once again, this was quite different from the arrangement at the federal level, where the Declaration of Independence articulated the principles and purposes of the polity and the Constitution outlined powers and rights. State constitutions, though, were seen as fulfilling both of these functions. Thus Harold Norris asked and answered his own question in the Michigan Convention of 1961–1962: "Does this particular formulation belong in a constitution? I submit that it does. A constitution is a design for government, an ordering of values. It sets forth here a value upon the health, safety and welfare of the people in terms of preserving the air, water and natural resources of the state, and I think that we do proclaim by this constitution a high value on these matters, and it is germane to our concern."[164] To add an environmental provision to the state constitution, as Peter Tomei argued in the Illinois Convention of 1969–1970, was therefore perfectly in keeping with the state constitutional tradition, in that

> one of the jobs of a state constitution is to set out, not only the legal framework of government, but also to capture the hopes and aspirations of the people. . . . I think perhaps more than anything else we may do in this Convention to capture the hopes and aspirations of the people is to adopt this provision in its entirety

as proposed by the committee. To do that, I believe, we will have done a great thing for the state of Illinois and for the people.[165]

The Adoption of Environmental Rights

Supporters of environmental provisions generally prevailed in the conventions that were held during the second half of the twentieth century.[166] The resulting provisions vary in their specific form, but beginning with the drafting of the Alaska Constitution of 1956, state constitution makers have enacted many environmental policy provisions.[167] Several of these provisions are permissive, such as in the Georgia Constitution, which provides that "the General Assembly shall have the power to provide by law for . . . restrictions upon land use in order to protect and preserve the natural resources, environment, and vital areas of this state."[168] Most of these provisions are declaratory, such as in the Florida Constitution, which states, "It shall be the policy of the state to conserve and protect its natural resources and scenic beauty. Adequate provision shall be made by law for the abatement of air and water pollution and of excessive and unnecessary noise and for the conservation and protection of natural resources."[169]

Several states have gone so far as to frame their environmental provisions as guarantees of individual rights. For instance, the Illinois Constitution provides that "each person has the right to a healthful environment."[170] Hawaiians, meanwhile, are guaranteed "the right to a clean and healthful environment."[171] Pennsylvanians are guaranteed "a right to clean air, pure water, and to the preservation of the natural, scenic, historic and esthetic values of the environment."[172] The Massachusetts Constitution goes a step further in stating that "the people shall have the right to clean air and water, freedom from excessive and unnecessary noise, and the natural, scenic, historic, and esthetic qualities of their environment."[173]

Conclusion

The benefit of analyzing these state convention debates is that it becomes possible to appreciate the logic underlying state constitution makers' adoption of workers' rights, union rights and the right to work, social and economic rights, and environmental rights. The federal constitution was drafted before these rights assumed prominence, and even when changing conditions generated calls to recognize these rights at the federal level, the rigidity of the federal amendment process prevented these proposals from being given serious consideration. As a result, there has been little opportunity at the federal level (outside of a few U.S. Supreme Court cases) to assess the case for and against the constitutionalization of these rights. The situation has been quite different at the state level, though, where positive-rights proposals have been advanced, and in many cases, adopted. Given an opportunity to confront the two principal arguments advanced against the recognition of these rights, state convention delegates have frequently found these arguments unpersuasive, thereby suggesting that these arguments may not be sufficiently compelling in the contemporary era to disqualify positive rights from inclusion in constitutions, whether at the state or federal level.

First, whereas critics have argued that many of these positive rights are not as clearly defined or as fundamental as civil and political rights, state constitution makers have frequently responded that these rights can reasonably be viewed as a logical continuation of, rather than a dramatic departure from, traditional rights in these respects. In particular, provisions guaranteeing adequate treatment for the poor, for instance, or a right to a healthful environment, are no less defined than the due process and equal protection clauses, among other long-standing rights clauses. Moreover, though these modern rights are in one sense quite different from the political and civil rights secured by the founding generation, in another sense they can be seen as the contemporary equivalent, counterpart, or embodiment of these rights.

Second, whereas critics have argued that these positive rights are not as susceptible to judicial enforcement as traditional civil and political rights, state constitution makers have responded by calling attention to several other important purposes that might be served by constitutional provisions. In particular, the adoption of constitutional provisions can empower legislators and permit them to secure these rights in the face of contrary judicial decisions. Such provisions can also serve to inspire or admonish legislators to take action in a particular area. Finally, these provisions can give expression to the fundamental goals and values of a polity.

CITIZEN CHARACTER

The idea that government should take an active role in forming the character of the citizenry is generally seen as inconsistent with the principles underlying the American constitutional tradition. There is, to be sure, a good amount of disagreement about whether the drafters of the U.S. Constitution presupposed or sought to encourage in the citizenry a degree of *civic* virtue. In fact, over the last three decades, many scholars have been persuaded that the American regime is predicated on the maintenance of some sort of civic virtue, whether defined as active participation in governance or the willingness to sacrifice private interest for the sake of the public interest.[1] However, any role for government in encouraging the development of *moral* virtue is thought to have received little support in the American constitutional tradition, whether from the founders or succeeding generations.

In regard to the founders' view of the role of the federal government in fostering moral virtue, one group of scholars argues that the founders simply did not address the issue in a comprehensive fashion, in part because state governments may have been expected to perform this function.[2] Another group of scholars concludes that the founders presupposed certain moral virtues but expected these virtues to be formed indirectly, whether through the structure of the polity or through nongovernmental institutions.[3] Still other scholars have gone so far as to contend that the founders rejected any governmental role in character formation altogether.[4]

Nor do the federal constitutional records of the last two centuries yield much more evidence of a commitment to encouraging the moral development of the citizenry. The outstanding exception is, of course, the Eighteenth Amendment; however, the ensuing decade-and-a-half-long experiment with national prohibition is now widely viewed as an aberrant case. As a result, we are left primarily with assorted U.S. Supreme Court opinions that have given an imprimatur to governmental efforts to shape citizen character and that have occasionally addressed issues of character formation in a tangential fashion.[5] In terms of federal constitutional provisions currently dedicated to the formation of citizen character, the record is barren.[6]

When we turn to the state constitutional tradition,[7] however, where the U.S. Supreme Court's traditionally quite broad reading of the police power for many years gave the states sweeping power to regulate the health, safety, and welfare of their citizens, we find that state constitution makers have been intimately concerned with the formation of citizen character.[8] This state constitutional commitment to the superintendence of citizen character is demonstrated most clearly in four principal areas.[9] The earliest, and for a long time most prominent, way that state constitution makers sought to encourage virtuous behavior was by supporting religious institutions, particularly by providing financial assistance to religious societies, schools, and charitable organizations.[10] A second way in which state constitution makers sought to shape citizen character was through the creation of public school systems and, particularly, the enactment of compulsory schooling laws, which were expected to contribute not only to students' intellectual growth but also to their moral development.[11] A third perennial source of concern for state convention delegates has been games of chance, particularly lotteries. During long periods of American history, lotteries have been constitutionally prohibited on the grounds that gambling is inconsistent with the moral development of the citizenry.[12] Finally, state constitution makers have been concerned, for the better part of the country's history, with restricting the sale, manufacture, and consumption of liquor. Once again, an issue that was the subject of frequent debates in state legislatures and courts also attracted the interest of convention delegates, many of whom sought to stamp out the liquor traffic along with its attendant vices.[13]

What emerges from these convention debates is a state constitutional commitment to the formation of citizen character that stands in marked contrast to the dominant understanding of the American constitutional tradition. Regardless of the reason for the absence of a commitment to character formation in the U.S. Constitution—whether because the founders did not envision any such role for the national government, or because they disdained such a role for any level of government, or because they rejected the constitutionalization of such a governmental role—the fact remains that federal convention delegates did not adopt any constitutional provisions in this area. By contrast, in their exercise of their police power, state constitution makers frequently concluded, after lengthy debates and in the face of powerful and occasionally effective rebuttals, that government should be committed to encouraging virtue and discouraging vice. Moreover, state constitution makers determined, again after an extensive consideration of contrary arguments, that it is necessary and proper to express this commitment through constitutional provisions.

Religion

The governmental role in supporting religious institutions has been the subject of extensive discussion in state conventions, and for a time, several state constitutions affirmed such a role. From the beginning, as Chester Antieau et al. noted, constitution makers held a "firm belief that good government was dependent on the development of good moral character, and said so frequently in their early constitutional documents. They believed also that moral behavior stemmed from the inculcation of strong religious values."[14] Consequently, the issue of whether to require individuals to support religious societies was an open question in several state conventions in the late eighteenth and early nineteenth centuries, and it was not until 1833 that every state ended this practice. Convention delegates then proceeded, beginning in the mid-nineteenth century, to consider extending public support to religious schools, and, beginning in the late nineteenth century, whether to support religious orphanages and other charitable institutions. Although state constitution makers differed in their particular answers to these later questions, the nineteenth-century trend was generally in the direction of not only disapproving any governmental role in supporting religious institutions, but also occasionally imposing even more restrictions against governmental action than are found in the federal constitution.

Public Support of Religious Societies

Before the Revolutionary War, established churches were more the norm than the exception, but the degree and nature of the establishment varied throughout the colonies. As Antieau et al. explained, "In some colonies only the Anglican Church was established; in others the local church, such as the Congregationalist, might be established, or a combination of churches might be established. In some colonies an established church was intended to make religious liberty more meaningful. On the other hand, an establishment could well be used to curtail political as well as religious liberty."[15] Furthermore, in some colonies, the establishment consisted of stipulating that only ministers of a certain faith could perform marriages. Other colonies went further and imposed religious tests on officeholders. Still others went so far as to compel financial support of, and attendance at, a particular church.[16]

Although in the initial wave of eighteenth-century constitution making many states moved to eliminate these requirements and achieve some sort of disestablishment, other states retained these provisions. As a result, convention delegates were still debating many questions concerning the proper relationship between political and religious institutions well into the early nineteenth century. In some of these nineteenth-century conventions, the principal question was whether to maintain religious tests for holding office. On certain occasions, as in the Maine Convention of 1819, delegates considered whether it was a duty of all individuals to take part in religious worship. On other occasions, as in the Connecticut Convention of 1818 and Massachusetts Convention of 1820–1821, the principal question was whether to maintain compulsory taxation in support of religious societies. Running through each of these particular debates were the fundamental questions of whether religious worship was a matter of public concern and, if so, whether it ought to be encouraged by the government.[17]

Many convention delegates answered this pair of questions in the affirmative: religious worship provided essential support to republican government, and governmental encouragement of religious worship was wise and proper. It was indisputable, this group of delegates argued, that republican government required the support of religion. Most important, individuals who were strong in their religious faiths were likely to be better citizens than those who were unable to draw on such support. As Warren Dutton argued in the Massachusetts Convention of 1820–1821, religious worship aided the highest and best purposes of the State—its tendency was to make better subjects and better magistrates, better husbands, parents and children. It enforced the duties of imperfect obligations which human laws could not reach—it inculcated all the domestic and social virtues, frugality and industry, prudence, kind and charitable feeling—it made men just and honest in their dealings as individuals, and by diffusing the sentiments of equity and benevolence, its tendency was to make states and communities just towards each other. . . . Are not these effects good for the State?[18]

Religious worship was also seen as improving the character of governing officials. Ezekiel Whitman in the Maine Convention of 1819 emphasized that religious worship was "conducive to the best interests of civil society. The government which *is best administered is best;* and government cannot be well administered where the morals of the people and their rulers are corrupt; and in what way can we be sure of good morals without the aid of religion? It not only inculcates the best of principles, but rivets them upon the mind."[19] Still other delegates stressed the way that religion contributed to the successful operation of the legal system, particularly by maintaining the integrity of oaths. Benjamin Greene argued in the same convention, "And what, Sir, is man without religion? Ourselves, our property and reputation, are not safe without it. Destroy religion, and you impair the obligation of an oath. I am sensible religion exists no where, but between a man's conscience and his God. But it must exist somewhere—it is our duty to encourage it every where—it is the best security of man."[20]

Moreover, these delegates maintained that there was simply no substitute for the support offered by religious faith, because morality was dependent on religion and could be formed in no other way. Although contrary arguments were occasionally encountered to the effect that individuals might be capable of abiding by moral precepts regardless of whether they were embedded in religious doctrine, Samuel Wilde in the Massachusetts Convention of 1820–1821 maintained that this was assuredly not the case:

Morality cannot exist without religion. There may be a kind of morality with a false religion; it will be more or less pure according to the approach of religion to the truth; but without religion it has no sanction or power; it can have no influence. Without the sanctions of religion, men will follow their own desires, their pleasures, the dictates of their passions. Morality has no sanctions, and can be no check. Take away religion, and you take away all restraints on the passions, on vice, on immorality.[21]

If morality in the absence of religion was inadequate, reason supplied an even weaker foundation. According to Joseph Stone in the same convention,

> Without religion we have no standard for governing the conduct. Gentlemen may say that reason should be our guide. It is no guide—it sometimes directs one thing, sometimes another; it is not to be trusted without the aid of religion, and some general system should be recognized by the government. A particular system was not wanted; they had been in other countries the cause of bloodshed and numerous evils. But some general system was demanded.[22]

From these premises, the conclusion necessarily followed, at least for these delegates, that government should encourage religious worship. Such a conclusion was evident to Mr. Whitman of Maine, who reasoned, "If then, morals depend on religion and the support of civil government upon morals, is it not the duty of every government, by all suitable means, to *uphold* and *encourage* the institutions for public instruction in the principles of religion?"[23] After all, as Leverett Saltonstall argued in the Massachusetts Convention of 1820–1821, the fundamental purpose of government was to

> adopt such measures as will promote the happiness of the people and the good order and preservation of civil society. Whatever tends to promote these great objects, it is the duty of government to cherish and support, because these are the objects for which government is instituted. The design of government is not merely the security of life against those who would attack it, and property against those who would plunder it, but to improve the character and condition of those who are subject to it.[24]

The legitimacy of governmental efforts to encourage virtuous behavior by supporting religious worship was all the more evident, according to these delegates, once one considered that states were already in the business of making moral judgments insofar as they outlawed behavior that was deemed vicious. As long as it was permissible for the state to punish vicious behavior, Samuel Hoar reasoned in the same convention, there should be no hesitation about supporting virtuous activity:

> To say that the Legislature shall not regulate anything relating to religion, was to say that they shall not encourage any virtues or punish any vices or crimes. If we could trust to anything in history, it was to this, that our prosperity, and

what most distinguishes Massachusetts, is owing to our provision for the support of religion and morality. [Mr. Hoar] considered these a great support of
civil society. He believed the only alternative was, to support it by religion and
morality, or by a standing army.[25]

If government was empowered to encourage religious worship, then the next
logical step, in the view of many delegates, was to compel individuals to support religious societies. Although it was occasionally argued "that religion is so
important that men will voluntarily support it," and therefore that compulsory
taxation was unnecessary, Mr. Dutton of Massachusetts thought that such an
argument "proceed[ed] wholly on a mistake" and was inconsistent with human
nature. Even if individuals could be counted on to recognize their duty to support religious societies, he argued, it was quite another thing to expect them to
actually do their duty:

> It was dangerous to place the duty and the pecuniary interest of men in com-
> petition with each other. There was enough of disinclination to moral duty,
> without adding the sordid aid of money. Place the duty of men in one scale,
> their disinclination and money in the other, and which will preponderate? The
> tendency of such a competition was to weaken or sever the last ties that bind
> men to their highest duties.[26]

On this view of the matter, requiring individuals to contribute to religious societies was not so different from levying taxes for the support of all sorts of other
necessary governmental functions, ranging from the administering of judicial and
school systems to the waging of war. Joseph Tuckerman in the Massachusetts Convention of 1820–1821 viewed the judicial system as a comparable case. He argued
that "as no state ever did or can flourish without religion, any more than without
a judiciary, it was quite as reasonable that every individual should be obliged to
support religion in some form, as that he should contribute to the support of the
established courts of law."[27] Meanwhile, Mr. Hoar of Massachusetts

> compared the provision for religious worship to that for town schools: those
> who have no children pay as great a tax as if they had; and if any person, having
> children, is not satisfied with the schoolmaster appointed by the town, he takes
> away his children, but never thinks of withholding his money from the support
> of the town schools; and yet the principle is the same; it is in fact a stronger
> case; for a man may withdraw to any religious society, and pay his money where
> he pleases, only he must pay somewhere.[28]

As Nathaniel Terry pointed out in the Connecticut Convention of 1818,

> This law is to be established for the health of the *community*—we are taxed
> to support many things which we don't like; suppose I do not like a particular
> religious denomination, and am taxed to support it, unless I unite myself to
> some other; does this interfere with my rights of conscience? no more Sir, I
> beg leave to say, than it does to be taxed for the support of a war, which I don't
> approve of.[29]

In fact, several delegates argued that the case for compulsory support of religious societies was, if anything, even stronger than the case for compulsory
taxation to support these other public functions. George Blake reasoned in the
Massachusetts Convention of 1820–1821, "If there was any subject in relation to
which there should be an injunction on all to contribute their aid, this merited
the highest place; in relation to all other institutions—courts of justice, schools,
highways, etc.—it was admitted that every individual should be compelled to
contribute towards their support. If religious institutions should be left to the
voluntary support of individuals, it should be so with all others."[30]

It is significant that convention delegates who opposed religious establishments rarely disagreed with the premise that religious worship improved the
character of the citizenry and, by extension, the polity. For the most part, the
critics of religious establishment accepted this contention, or at least chose not
to dispute it, preferring instead to challenge the propriety and effectiveness of
governmental efforts to compel individuals to support religious societies.

The critics doubted that it was a legitimate function of government to compel
support of religion. Even if the polity did benefit from religious worship, it was
quite a leap—and, to their mind, an illegitimate one—to therefore conclude that
government could use the force of law to require support for religious societies.
John Chandler argued in the Maine Convention of 1819 that "there is a difference between religious duties, and political duties. One may be a proper subject
of legislation, and not the other. We were not sent here to prescribe the religious
duties, but to determine the rights of the people. This is a religious duty, but not
in my opinion a political duty."[31] In similar fashion, Joshua Stow explained in
the Connecticut Convention of 1818, "It is the duty of *all* to worship in sincerity
and in truth; but I deny the right of any power to make a man worship."[32] Moreover, any effort to transgress the proper boundary between these two realms, as
Enoch Mudge argued in the Massachusetts Convention of 1820–1821, "had a
tendency to produce strife and contention."[33] Consequently, these critics argued

that it was a far safer course of action, and one that republican governments were gradually coming around to adopting, to refrain from exercising any power over religious affairs. John Holmes in the Maine Convention of 1819 therefore argued,

> Give your Legislature a power to *uphold* religion, and trust to their discretion for the *suitable means,* and you arm them with a weapon which might prostrate in the dust, your religious liberties. It is the same power, which in other countries, and other times, has sanctioned the most inveterate and cruel persecutions. . . . It does not satisfy my mind to be told merely, that neither we nor our posterity shall probably abuse this power; and this is all that can be promised. I would not give the power, and then only can we be sure it will not be abused.[34]

Critics were also concerned about the effectiveness of governmental efforts to support religious worship. Some of these delegates were skeptical that individuals could in fact be compelled to support religious societies. Thus Henry Childs in the Massachusetts Convention of 1820–1821 took note of the argument that "if we abandon the means of supporting religious instruction, we should be obliged to resort to a standing army to enforce obedience to the laws." Childs, though, "would reverse the proposition. Establish the principle that government has a right to compel the support of public worship, and a standing army will be necessary to carry it into effect."[35] Moreover, to the extent that legislatures might try to enforce these laws, this would actually reduce the power of religious leaders to improve the character of the citizenry and polity. Ward Locke in the Maine Convention of 1819 noted that "if we appeal to history, we shall find little encouragement for legislating on this subject. Pure religion always flourishes most, when it is left most free."[36] Similarly, Mr. Mudge of Massachusetts explained that once ministers became allied with the state, they would lose the power to influence their congregations in healthy directions. He pointed out, in relation to compulsory taxation for religious societies, that "the ministers in many instances do not wish it. They had rather labor with their own hands for their support, than that the stock and property of their flock should be taken and sold for their maintenance."[37] In fact, these delegates argued, history had proven that religion was quite capable of securing adequate support without any governmental assistance. According to Ebenezer Nelson in the Massachusetts Convention of 1820–1821, "It had been objected that the Christian religion would go down, if not supported by the civil arm. It had stood on its own broad basis for two thousand years, and it had been as prosperous the last twenty years as ever it had been. It was the safest and most honorable way to leave it to voluntary support."[38]

This argument between the supporters and critics of religious establishment was, over time, resolved in all states in favor of the critics.[39] To be sure, throughout the nineteenth century, supporters prevailed in certain states on certain issues, particularly regarding religious tests for office holding.[40] In regard to compulsory taxation for support of religious societies, however, every state had eliminated the practice by the end of the first third of the nineteenth century. Virginia effected a complete disestablishment through a series of statutes culminating in the enactment of an 1802 statute,[41] as did Vermont through an 1807 statute.[42] Connecticut disestablished when it drafted a constitution in 1818.[43] Disestablishment was accomplished in New Hampshire by an 1819 statute.[44] Finally, Massachusetts voters, after initially rejecting a disestablishment proposal that emerged from the Convention of 1820–1821, eventually approved such an amendment in 1833.[45]

Public Support of Religious Schools

The question of the proper governmental role in supporting religious institutions was by no means concluded in the early nineteenth century. It is true that no further consideration was given to providing direct aid to churches, but many convention delegates were still committed to supporting religious schools, on the grounds that such schools played an important role in forming citizen character. In fact, beginning in the 1840s and continuing for the better part of the next century, this issue surfaced frequently at state conventions.[46] Although the outcomes were invariably consistent with expected voting patterns, with Catholics supporting such aid and Protestants objecting, the convention debates were frequently elevated to a theoretical level, as delegates were forced to articulate and defend their views on the governmental role in supporting religious institutions.[47]

Delegates who advocated governmental support of religious schools contended—in much the same fashion as defenders of governmental support of religious societies—that religious training was essential for the formation of good citizens. Joseph Carbery in the Ohio Convention of 1873–1874 quoted at length from various articles to the effect that "if we consult the masters of thought, and those who shape the destinies of nations, we shall be surprised to find how unanimously they hold moral training paramount to intellectual culture, and how strongly they insist on making the latter always subservient to the former."[48] In his view, the facts were "sufficient to convince any impartial mind that there can be no social virtue, no morality, no true and lasting greatness, without religion," and therefore students would benefit from attending schools where religious principles could be "laid broad and deep." He explained, "Men do not seek grapes from thorns, nor figs from thistles. Yet, by a strange inconsistency, some would expect virtuous youth from godless schools. But the order of nature cannot be reversed. Like generates like."[49] The conclusion was readily apparent: "It is, then, absurd to devote six days of the week to the teaching of human learning, and trust to a hurried hour in the Sunday-school for the imparting of religious knowledge. By such a system we may make expert shop-boys, first-rate accountants, shrewd and thriving 'earthworms,' as Bishop Berkeley says, but it would be presumption to think of thus making good citizens, much less virtuous Christians."[50] According to this line of reasoning, the state would do well "to encourage such schools as may be established by the spontaneous action of the people, or any division of the people, and to sustain the same in exact proportion to the number of children under instruction."[51]

Moreover, proponents of governmental assistance to religious schools argued—again, in the same manner as delegates had justified governmental support of religious societies—that there was nothing illegitimate about the state extending such aid. So important was the moral instruction of youth, in the view of these delegates, that the state should be supportive of practically any institution willing to undertake this responsibility. William Woodbridge therefore concluded in the Michigan Convention of 1835 that

> virtue and liberty were the only bonds which can keep society together, and he was unwilling to deprive it of any institution which might strengthen their bonds. If the Catholics for instance should establish a college here, as was proposed, should not the legislature have authority to replenish the Treasury of such an institution, if it was found conducive to the general good, as it assuredly would be? He was unwilling to deprive them of a single aid, even of a Theological seminary.[52]

Additionally, these delegates argued that governmental assistance could be offered in a manner that did not run afoul of established views on the relationship between church and state. In their view, by providing aid to all schools, public and private, the state was treating citizens equally by taking no account of the religious character of their educational institution of choice. T. B. Thorpe in the Louisiana Convention of 1864 explained, "The idea is to afford succor to all institutions of whatever creed. . . . Now, while I think it is our duty to discountenance, in any possible way, anything that leads to sectarianism, it is also our duty to look beyond the fact that these schools are under the support of religious denominations."[53] Furthermore, distributing aid to schools without regard to their religious character would be far preferable to the alternative of prohibiting aid to religious schools, especially when delegates were well aware that this would work to the disadvantage of one particular group of citizens. As Francis Bird argued in the Massachusetts Convention of 1853 in regard to one such anti-aid proposal, "Every-body knows this resolution appears to be aimed at one class of our citizens, one denomination of religion. Nobody has intimated any apprehension that money would be used for the benefit of Protestant sectarianism." Rather the question had been raised solely "in relation to the support of Catholic schools."[54]

Delegates who took the contrary view and opposed governmental support for religious schools did not necessarily deny that these schools contributed to improving the character of the citizenry. To be sure, some delegates occasionally expressed doubts about whether a religious education was in fact beneficial, and these doubts were especially prevalent during periods of high rates of Catholic immigration. For instance, Samuel Lothrop in the Massachusetts Convention of 1853 wanted "all our children, the children of our Catholic and Protestant population, to be educated together in our public schools. . . . I wish all children to be educated, not as members of religious sects, not as belonging to one religious party or another, but to come together on one common ground, as children of the State, to be educated together in mutual respect, forbearance, and good will, so far as differences of religious opinion are concerned."[55] For the most part, though, critics acknowledged the benefits of religious training and chose to raise other concerns about public assistance to parochial schools.

Some delegates contended that governmental support of religious schools, no matter how beneficial to the students in attendance, constituted an impermissible intrusion into religious affairs. In the words of William Spruance in the Delaware Convention of 1896–1897, "The policy of our government should be, not only to establish no religion and no sect, but not directly to contribute to the maintenance of any sect or denomination. I think, to be consistent with the provisions of the bill of rights, we ought not to give our public money to religious schools."[56] The chief concern, as George Cornwell made clear in the

New York Convention of 1894, was that these appropriations would "build up and strengthen denominational and church interests at the expense of popular education."[57] Moreover, these delegates argued, anti-aid provisions were consistent not only with long-standing constitutional guarantees but also with sound public policy precepts. Were the state to distribute aid to religious denominations, there would be no end to the claims that would be made on the treasury, nor to the resulting political controversies. As Nathaniel Cogswell explained in the Massachusetts Convention of 1853, the effort to prohibit aid to religious schools was "not aimed at any particular sect, but was intended to cut off all sectional and denominational disputes on the subject of the distribution of the money raised for the support of schools."[58] After all, as his colleague Amariah Chandler argued, "If we take the position that a part of this fund may be given to one denomination, another may come in and claim the same privilege, and another, and another, until the fund is completely exhausted, and perverted from its original design."[59]

Furthermore, critics argued that governmental support of religious schools was unnecessary and counterproductive. Isaac Crary in the Michigan Convention of 1835 was convinced that "religion and virtue were amply sufficient for their own protection" and that religious schools were well positioned to secure adequate support for their work without need of any governmental assistance.[60] In fact, some delegates followed George Coleman of the Massachusetts Convention of 1917–1919 in arguing that "the educational institutions that are advocating these amendments in favor of themselves are making a serious mistake, not only with reference to the great issue that is before us but also with reference to their own interest in the long run."[61] Not the least of these fears was the concern that once religious schools became allied with and dependent for support on the state, they would be deprived of their independence and, possibly, their effectiveness in guiding the development of citizens in their preferred manner. As Frederick Anderson argued in the same convention, "The prohibition of sectarian appropriations is just as good for the church as it is for the State. We are not opposed to religion because we say that the State shall not give appropriations to religious bodies or institutions. We are helping religion by that proposition. It has been the history from the very beginning that it has been good both for the church and for the State that they should be separate."[62]

When these questions of state assistance to religious schools arose in the latter half of the nineteenth century and early twentieth century, as they frequently did, especially in states with a large Catholic population, state constitution makers resolved uniformly against permitting such assistance.[63] Critics of such assistance had already enjoyed success in enacting state constitutional prohibitions before 1875, when President Ulysses S. Grant advocated and Maine representative James Blaine formally introduced a federal constitutional anti-aid amendment.[64] However, the attention drawn to the ultimately unsuccessful federal Blaine Amendment gave additional impetus to state constitution makers' efforts to enact anti-aid provisions, which came to be known as State Blaine Amendments.[65] In some states, public assistance had not yet been extended to any schools, and a state constitutional provision was adopted to forestall any such possibility. In other states, religious schools had for some time been the beneficiary of public funds, and constitutional provisions were enacted so as to prohibit any further aid.[66] In any case, as Anson Phelps Stokes concluded, "By the close of the century few states continued to give any direct aid to private or denominational schools."[67]

Public Support of Religious Charitable Institutions

The debate about the governmental role in supporting religious institutions arose in still another form in the late nineteenth and early twentieth centuries, when states faced the question of whether governmental assistance should be extended to religious orphanages and other charities.[68] The arguments advanced during these convention debates were similar to the arguments put forth regarding public support of religious societies and schools. Delegates who supported governmental assistance to religious charities emphasized their contribution to the development of citizen character and stressed the costs of inhibiting such work. As Edward Lauterbach argued in the New York Convention of 1894, "Do not put in jeopardy 145 orphan asylums, the protectories so noble in their beneficence, all these institutions that it is conceded on all hands do so much good as the servants and agents of the State; do not, in the interest of morality, endeavor to enact into your Constitution that which will not only prevent education, but which may make these unfortunates houseless and homeless."[69] In similar fashion, James Shafter argued in the California Convention of 1878–1879 that "it is far cheaper and much better to have these orphans taken care of in this way than it would be to have them all in one institution, under the charge of State officers. I believe that moral training is as necessary to a child, in order to make a good citizen out of him, as food and clothes, I care not what creed they belong to."[70] Along these same lines, William McEwen in the Illinois Convention of 1920–1922 thought it would be "a great loss to the children of this State if we lost the mothering effect and the character building force of these sectarian institutions."[71]

In addition, supporters such as Charles Daly in the New York Convention of 1867–1868 argued that once the state decided to "bestow donations upon other institutions, which relieve the State of a trust otherwise imposed upon it, . . . there is no justice in excluding from the operations of its bounty any institution which comes under the denomination of religious." If anything, Daly believed, the state ought to be supporting, rather than inhibiting, the work of religious charities:

> No man in the present age is bold enough, I apprehend, to say that, any education which is bestowed upon our youth should be wanting in the religious element. If there is any thing in our civilization which tends to elevate us, and distinguish us from the ages that have preceded us, it is the fact of the large amount of religious education instilled in our youth, and the beneficial influence of it during the after stages of life.[72]

On the other hand, delegates who opposed such governmental expenditures argued that these services could and should be performed by the state. James Reynolds in the California Convention of 1878–1879 objected to "state support to sectarian institutions" and argued,

> Now, sir, it is no doubt true that these institutions take very good care of the orphans. We are told that the State cannot take care of them because she is not prepared, and therefore the only thing to do is to aid these societies in caring for them. Now, we propose, by this amendment, to put an end to this in the near future, and to put it far enough off so that the State can make the necessary provisions.[73]

In addition, William Gray in the Illinois Convention of 1920–1922 argued that state aid to religious charities constituted just as serious a violation of church-state boundaries as other forms of assistance to religious institutions:

> I am opposed to a continuation of the principle in which the State is now engaged, in contributing public funds for the support or aid in any way of sectarian institutions. That these institutions are doing a noble and grand work no one can question . . . , but I am actuated by an altogether different motive.

From my earliest youth I have been taught and now believe that the policy of the separation of church and State is the very wisest one possible for this country to sustain.[74]

In the end, the outcome of this debate was somewhat different than on the previous issues. Although the precise wording of the ensuing constitutional provisions varied, a fair number of states chose to distinguish between governmental assistance to religious societies and schools (which was deemed impermissible) and aid to religious charities (which was occasionally permitted).[75] The logic underlying this distinction as well as the ultimate decision to permit state aid to certain religious charities was best expressed by Amos Miller in the Illinois Convention of 1920–1922. After noting that the policy of providing public assistance to religious charities had been in place for some time, he asked, "Has any tendency grown up toward giving any one religious institution or any combinations of religious institutions control over the State government? Personally I do not know of any such tendency. . . . Now, if I am right on that, it would seem to me that there is no principle involved of connecting up the church and the State."[76]

Although twentieth-century convention delegates continued to debate these types of questions, there has been a shift in the range of these debates and the forum in which they are conducted. Since the 1940s, the U.S. Supreme Court has been primarily responsible for resolving the various issues concerning the relationship between political and religious institutions. Additionally, these issues have been, on the whole, more narrow than the fundamental questions that were debated by state convention delegates throughout the nineteenth and early twentieth centuries.

Education

Education has long been considered the responsibility of state and local governments, and so it is no surprise that the governmental role in this area has received extensive treatment in state conventions.[77] In the course of these conventions, state constitution makers have naturally been led to consider a wide range of issues concerning public schooling, including the relative degree of state and local control over schooling, the means of financing the schools, the content of the curriculum and textbooks, the certification of teachers, and attendance policies, each of which has received much scholarly attention.[78]

For purposes of this analysis, however, what stands out from a review of the state convention debates regarding education is the extent of state constitution makers' concern not only with students' intellectual training, but also with their moral development. This issue was raised to some extent during the initial debates about the creation of state public school systems, which took place before the Civil War in many northern states and after the war in most southern states. The issue was then raised even more directly during debates over compulsory-attendance requirements, which were adopted in the late nineteenth century in the North and the early twentieth century in the South. In each of these debates, and especially regarding compulsory-attendance provisions, state legislators, judges, and, inevitably, convention delegates grappled with the extent to which government should assume responsibility for the intellectual and moral education of the citizenry.

The creation of statewide public school systems in the nineteenth century was itself not without controversy.[79] Legislators and convention delegates sparred frequently over how to finance these schools. Whereas supporters favored compulsory school taxation on the grounds that it would equalize education opportunity for all citizens, critics charged that this infringed on the rights of citizens who had no schoolchildren or who were already providing for their children's education in some other manner.[80]

An equally enduring point of controversy concerned the moral content of the school curriculum. The leading supporters of public schools were motivated in no small part by a desire to impart certain character traits to a wide range of students, including, but not limited to, predominantly Catholic immigrants. According to Michael Katz, "For reformers like Horace Mann and Henry Barnard, the common school movement became a moral crusade. In their view, free publicly supported common schools would unite Christian morality with democratic patriotism; the common school would stamp out the evils of ignorance, crime, vice, and aristocratic privilege; and finally, the common school would not only assimilate the immigrants but also transform them into virtuous, productive American citizens."[81] It was precisely because many individuals—especially Irish Catholics—recognized that the public school curriculum would have such a moral content that they initially opposed the creation of a public school system. As David Nasaw has written, "The Irish believed that the common schools had been invented for the express purpose of turning their children against them. In these schools, Irish children would be forced to read from a Protestant Bible. Their teachers would be Protestant and their school books would be filled with slurs against the Irish character, history, culture, and religion. The Irish were correct in their evaluation of the schooling their children would receive."[82]

Despite these controversies, support was gradually obtained for the establishment of public schools and for the moral character of the instruction in these schools. The process of creating state school systems began with New England states in the first few decades of the nineteenth century, then spread to mid-Atlantic and midwestern states in the decades preceding the Civil War, and finally came to southern states in the war's aftermath.[83] In each of these areas, the shaping of moral character was understood to be at the heart of these schools' mission. In fact, as Carl Kaestle has written, "intellectual education did not receive as high a priority as moral education in discussions of the purposes of common schools. Far more emphasis was placed on character, discipline, virtue, and good habits than on literacy, arithmetic skills, analytical ability, or knowledge of the world."[84]

Requiring individuals to pay taxes to support public schools was one thing; it was another matter entirely to require parents to send their children to schools, whether public or private. Leaders of the common school movement saw this as the next logical step, which they urged states to take beginning in the 1840s. In the view of others, however, this exceeded the proper governmental role. As in the debate over compulsory taxation to support public schools, supporters and critics of compulsory schooling were motivated by a complex mix of concerns, including efforts to reduce child labor, "Americanize" recent immigrants, and reform juvenile delinquents. At the heart of the issue, however, and running throughout these arguments, was the question of the proper governmental role in shaping the character of the citizenry.[85]

The Case for Compulsory Education

Supporters of compulsory schooling argued that the benefits of school attendance for the citizenry were clear enough. These delegates focused most of their attention on the benefits for poor children, whose parents frequently permitted, and in some cases required, them to absent themselves from school. As Samuel Wherry argued in the Pennsylvania Convention of 1872–1873,

> The question as it presents itself in the proposition now under consideration is narrowed down to this: the right and duty of the State to secure the moral,

mental and industrial training of orphan, destitute, neglected, vagrant, tru-
ant, incorrigible, apprenticed, pauper and criminal children; children whom
parents and guardians, society, the church and the schools fail to educate and
train to usefulness and happiness, and who are learning in the streets, from
countless teachers of vice.[86]

Wherry cautioned that, although it was tempting to "comfort ourselves with the
thought that most of these illiterate persons are foreigners, immigrants, old persons, too, who will soon die off and leave behind them more intelligent children
. . . it is a thin delusion, perfectly transparent in the light of truth and fact."[87]

To consign these children to a life of ignorance, supporters of compulsory
education argued, would have consequences not just for the children themselves but for the polity as a whole. Several delegates, including Charles Bowman in the same Pennsylvania convention, called attention to the connection
between ignorance and crime, and concluded that compulsory education would
help to prevent future generations of lawbreakers. He argued that "the safety
of the state depends upon it. The welfare and future prosperity of the people
depend upon it. . . . Does not that ignorance and crime entail upon the State an
expense far greater than would be the cost of their education."[88] Other delegates
emphasized the connection between ignorance and the corruption of the political process. Mr. Wherry argued, "It is of the highest interest to you and to me
whether our fellow-citizens are ignorant or intelligent. We stand with shame at
the ballot-box and see our ballot cancelled by some ragged sot too ignorant to
comprehend the ballot he casts."[89] Meanwhile, Stephen Hand in the New York
Convention of 1867–1868 took an even broader view and supported compulsory
education out of a belief that

it is because the very administration of the laws of the State depends for its
security upon the public virtue and the public intelligence of the citizen; so
that our government may have a standing on a sure basis and exist in any
degree of safety. In order that republicanism may live, in order that the people
may be qualified for self government, it is absolutely essential that the people
themselves shall be so educated as to be qualified to be citizens under a free
government.[90]

Given that the public interest was served by a broad diffusion of education,
it was appropriate for government to do everything it could to compel youth to
receive an education, whether in public schools or in some other fashion. J. E.
Philpott in the Nebraska Convention of 1871 argued that "the government has

a right to exercise all those means which are necessary to assure its permanence and stability. Now it cannot be denied that the success of a republican government is largely dependent upon the intelligence of the people." Therefore, it was entirely proper that government provide for compulsory education: "It has this right, as much as to draft its citizens into the army and send them out after a few months drill, to meet the enemy, and no one will deny this right."[91] Drawing on a wide array of philosophical resources to defend the legitimacy of compulsory-education measures, including the works of political theorists who were not seen as generally friendly to expansive views of government power, George Curtis argued in the New York Convention of 1867–1868,

> I will cite, for instance, John Stuart Mill, who, of all the distinguished English publicists is, probably, the one who asserts the small function of government as strongly as any man who insists that government should interfere in the individual action as little as may be; and yet Mr. Mill, after the greatest consideration, does not hesitate to say, with his characteristic caution, that it is a just exercise of the power of government to furnish opportunity to every parent in the State to have his children educated, and then to require that those children shall receive an elementary education.[92]

These delegates were well aware of the various charges leveled against compulsory-education policies, including the claim that they "militate[d] against the great and comprehensive principles of republicanism" and were "a subversion of the rights and liberties of the people."[93] In the view of supporters of compulsory education, though, these claims were grounded in an impoverished conception of liberty. It was true that parents had a right to raise their children as they saw fit; however, parental rights were not unlimited. J. K. Jillson argued in the South Carolina Convention of 1868, "I am willing to accept the widest, highest, and most expansive definition of freedom, but I am not disposed to accept the term as synonymous with unbridled license."[94] Moreover, as G. B. Lake explained in the Nebraska Convention of 1871, these parental rights could be forfeited. He took "the high ground that no parent has the right to bring up his children in ignorance, profligacy and vice. If he do so he has forfeited his right, as a parent, to the custody and care of that child."[95] Nor were parental rights the only rights in the balance. Milton Burtch in the Michigan Convention of 1867 noted that "if parents have rights, children also have rights."[96] In the words of Mr. Wherry of Pennsylvania, "The child himself has a right to such training as will fit him for usefulness and enjoyment in life, just as much as he has a right to care and protection and food and raiment."[97] The rights of the community also merited consideration. William Ramsey argued in the Kentucky Convention of 1890–1891, "Parents should not imagine that, because the children are theirs, they can do with them as they please. They are members of the Commonwealth. The whole community is interested, because it is a public benefit, and protests against the ignorance and selfishness of parents. It is true individuals and personal rights are concerned, but society has a right to be protected against vice, ignorance and crime."[98] In light of these various considerations, A. J. Weaver concluded in the Nebraska Convention of 1871 that compulsory-attendance requirements were in no way an infringement on individual liberty: "I claim there can be no reasonable or sound argument against the proposition that the state has property in the individuals composing the state to the extent of being justifiable in forcing upon them certain duties and compelling them to perform certain acts which from a logical stand point would not only be highly beneficial to the individual himself but redound to the good of the state at large."[99]

Finally, there was the matter of whether these measures were deserving of constitutional status. Although some supporters of this policy were content to leave the question to be resolved by the legislature, others believed that the governmental commitment to compulsory education should be expressed in the constitution. In some cases, these delegates supported the adoption of constitutional provisions empowering legislatures to enact compulsory-attendance laws. The logic of this position, as Ezekiel Cooper explained in the Delaware Convention of 1896–1897, was that "in the permission to do it, it carries the sanction of the Constitutional Convention in the fact that it ought to be done."[100] His colleague Charles Richards believed, similarly, that "it will amount to something if we put this in the Constitution. It will show, beyond a shadow of a doubt, that this Convention had considered this question," and therefore it "will be more likely to be brought to the attention of the Legislature."[101] Other delegates supported constitutional provisions that required legislatures to adopt compulsory-education laws. Such provisions were intended not only to ease any concerns about the constitutionality of such laws, but also to express the importance of the issue to the polity. George Opdyke explained in the New York Convention of 1867–1868,

> If we want to elevate the moral character of our people, and qualify them for usefulness, we can take no better means, in my judgment, than to adopt this rule of compulsory education. It has been said here this evening that these are proper questions for the Legislature. On the contrary, I believe it to be the duty of those who frame the fundamental law, thus to lay down the principles which

shall govern legislation. . . . Here is a rule which I believe to be of the best, and as fundamental as any. If there be a proper place for it anywhere, that place is in the fundamental law.[102]

The Case against Compulsory Education

Critics of compulsory-attendance provisions responded that no matter how impressive the benefits of education for children, government had no power to compel parents to make this choice. J. G. McClinton argued in the Nevada Convention of 1864 that he was

> willing, therefore, to do all I can to encourage common schools; all I can for the encouragement of every species of educational improvement and morality; but I am not willing to carry my own desires so far as to bring them in conflict with what I consider one of the fundamental principles of our government. I cannot resist the conviction in my own mind, that the proposition to compel parents to send their children to our public schools, or to any other schools, is inimical to the spirit of our Republican institutions.[103]

Certainly, these delegates argued, the advantages of an education were widely acknowledged, and the state would be well advised to encourage parents to take advantage of the public schools or other schools. However, insofar as parents might reach a different conclusion about the value of an education for their own children, these delegates contended that the state should defer to the parents' judgment. Thus B. S. Newsom argued in the Nebraska Convention of 1871,

> I believe in education as much as any one here, but when you say that you shall take the child from the parent as you would take property by process of law, and compel him to go where, perhaps, the parent would not like to have him go, you take away certain indefeasible rights. For if the parent has not a right to his own child, what in the name of Heaven, can he have a right to?[104]

In the view of these delegates, to tolerate the infringement on individual liberty that would necessarily accompany compulsory education would only set a precedent for future invasions of liberty. E. L. Dohoney in the Texas Convention of 1875 argued, "They had no right to invade the mansion of the parent and take from him or her their bright-eyed child, and turn him over to the State. Whenever they should do that they could do anything. When that was done the science of free government was trodden under foot; the liberties of the country gone."[105] Phillip Pipkin suggested in the Missouri Convention of 1875 that the same reasoning that was used to support compulsory education could just as easily be applied to other areas, with regrettable consequences:

> Now sir, it is claimed here that it is necessary for the good of the Republic that all should be educated. Granted. Is it not equally necessary that all should be cleanly, that health may prevail? Is not it equally necessary that all the people of the country shall be well fed, that they may be comfortable & happy. Is not it equally necessary that all the domestic relations between all members of families should be harmonious that the good of the Republic may exist? Now sir, if it is necessary that these things should exist, why should not the Republic regulate these things?[106]

In similar fashion, John Develin in the New York Convention of 1867–1868 argued,

> You might as well undertake to compel parents to teach their children trades, or to follow a certain profession, or oblige our citizens to go to church every Sunday, because it is supposed that such visits improve the morals of the attendants at church, as to adopt this; but does this, in our country, justify the interference of the Legislature? Certainly not. This amendment violates one of the first and most important principles upon which our government is founded—the right of personal and social liberty.[107]

Moreover, critics argued that compulsory schooling laws could never be enforced, and to the extent that they might be enforced would lead to even greater violations of individual liberty. Thus S. A. Strickland called attention to the vagueness of the phrasing in a compulsory schooling proposal that came before the Nebraska Convention of 1871. He complained that it would be difficult for a government official to determine what constituted an acceptable education other than attendance at a public school. In order to enforce this law in any sort of fair and effective manner, he maintained, "you will have to have a police force larger than enough to enforce the Ku Klux bill, it is plain to be seen."[108] Furthermore, if the state did hire police to patrol for violations of the law, it was inconceivable that such officers would go so far as to arrest parents for failing to send their children to a proper school. Robert DeLarge in the South Carolina Convention of 1868 therefore considered this "a proviso that can never be enforced. It is just as impossible to put such a section in practical operation, as it would be for a man to fly to the moon."[109]

At the same time, these delegates feared the consequences if legislatures might somehow try to enforce the law. William Kerr in the Ohio Convention of 1873–1874 lamented, "The spectacle of constables entering the family to search for children not in school, dragging parents before magistrates, and imposing penalties on them for not keeping their children in school, when, perhaps, they are able neither to subsist without their service, nor to feed and clothe them while in school, is a scene I never want to witness in our beloved land."[110] Other delegates conjured up all sorts of scenarios that might occur if the state was given license to enforce laws of this kind. John Campbell in the Pennsylvania Convention of 1872–1873 was one of several delegates to point out the dangerous ways in which government officials might make use of this discretionary enforcement power. He argued,

It will, under the color of reclaiming vagrant, abandoned and neglected children, allow your State agents, who may become the mere officers of religious denominations, to go into the houses of private citizens, and on the plea that the fathers or the mothers or the guardians do not educate in the proper way the children entrusted to their care, take them out of their homes and put them into the proposed prison schools. Will you permit that? Will you permit the State to be turned into a machine for religious persecution? That will be the effect of it.[111]

Meanwhile, Nathaniel Daniells argued in the Michigan Convention of 1867, "We do not live in Prussia; and I do not believe it is worth while for us to enact in the fundamental law of the State, a provision savoring so much of imperial power. . . . I am opposed to a provision of this sort, which would aim to establish a system of espionage and tyranny for the purpose of enforcing attendance in our schools."[112]

As Mr. Daniells's comments indicated, critics maintained that their fears about the consequences of compulsory schooling were not merely speculative, but had already been borne out to some degree in polities that had enacted such policies. Two examples dominated the discussion: Prussia, whose compulsory-attendance policy dated back to the eighteenth century,[113] and Massachusetts, which in 1852 became the first state to adopt a compulsory schooling law and remained the only state to do so for the next fifteen years.[114] In the view of the critics, neither of these cases inspired confidence. Richard Sansom, a delegate to the Texas Convention of 1875, believed that both systems could be traced back to the Spartan regime, which he was disinclined to imitate. He argued,

And what are its concomitants [in Sparta]? Iron money, the murder by the state of children on account of deformity. Adultery and theft are made virtuous. Then we follow it down to Prussia and what are its concomitants there? Absolute dominion of the government over the person of the subject from birth to the grave. The government registering his birth, the government putting him into the schools, the government putting him into the army, and when too old and infirm for service in the fields the Government putting him into the arsenals, dock yards, or fortifications, his place in the regiment never empty, the yoke never thrown off his weary neck until he goes to the grave or comes to America. Now let us follow it to New England and see what were its concomitants there—men fined for kissing their wives on Sunday, Quakers whipped out of the colony at the cart's tail on account of their religious opinions, poor wretches burned at the stake for supposed dealings with the devil.[115]

According to this line of reasoning, the virtues fostered by polities that had enacted compulsory schooling laws were not necessarily suitable for all polities. The Prussian system was thought to rely too heavily on martial virtues. In the words of J. C. Campbell in the Nebraska Convention of 1871, "That is a monarchical government, this is republican. In Prussia every man is forced to serve in the army for seven years. Are we going to force every man to serve in the army, whether there is war or peace? No sir!"[116] As for Massachusetts, its school curriculum was viewed by the critics as too imbued with Puritan virtues and, according to certain delegates around the country, with an excessive intellectualism. Along these lines, C. F. Manderson, who was not opposed in principle to compulsory-attendance requirements but was concerned about particular aspects of this policy, took the opportunity in the same convention to recount a tragic tale about the ill effects of New England educational systems. He told the assembled delegates,

I have no children, but there died at my house in Ohio, some years ago, a beautiful accomplished girl, some 16 years of age. The disease of which she died was a puzzle to the physicians, but upon a full investigation of her history, they came to the conclusion that she was a victim to that hot bed of education in New England which has driven many to idiocy or the grave. At 16 years of age, she had an amount of knowledge that would be a credit to an adult.

The cause of her death, according to Manderson, was that "she had been kept constantly at school from a very early age."[117]

Finally, these delegates argued that even if compulsory schooling policies were desirable, there was no warrant for placing such policies in the constitution. According to Fred Nye in the Nebraska Convention of 1919–1920, this was purely "a matter of legislation," which "had received the complete consideration of the Legislature at the last session." There was no need "to burden our Constitution with the legislative matter," especially when the legislature was well positioned to legislate on this subject and to take account of changing conditions and sentiments.[118] After all, as William Saulsbury noted in the Delaware Convention of 1896–1897, it was "a settled principle of Constitutional law that the General Assembly may take such action now," and there was no sense that legislatures had failed to act out of a fear that compulsory education violated existing constitutional provisions.[119] Consequently, there was no reason to remove this issue from legislative control.

Ultimately, the arguments advanced by supporters of compulsory schooling proved persuasive, at least as to the merits of the policy. Nearly all of the northern states adopted compulsory attendance laws by the close of the nineteenth century; southern states followed in the early twentieth century; and once Mississippi adopted its compulsory education law in 1918, these policies were in effect in every state.[120] The constitutionalization of these policies was another matter. On this point, the critics prevailed more often than not. All told, ten states adopted constitutional provisions regarding compulsory attendance, with these states evenly divided over whether to permit or require legislatures to adopt such policies.[121]

The legitimacy of compulsory-attendance policies resurfaced on several occasions after these nineteenth-century convention debates. Beginning in the final decade of the nineteenth century and continuing through the first part of the twentieth century, states took various steps to strengthen the often lax enforcement of their laws.[122] Then, in the 1920s, during a period of increased concern about the need to "Americanize" recent immigrants, several states considered, and Oregon went so far as to enact, a law requiring attendance at *public* schools—a law that was subsequently overturned by the Supreme Court in *Pierce v. Society of Sisters*.[123] In the 1970s, a U.S. Supreme Court decision in *Wisconsin v. Yoder* in favor of the Amish and against Wisconsin's postsecondary compulsory-attendance law also led to renewed discussion of the legitimacy of these policies.[124] However, throughout these later developments—and even as scholarly attention has shifted in the aftermath of the U.S. Supreme Court's decision in *San Antonio v. Rodriguez* (1973) to other aspects of state constitutional education clauses, such as requirements for equity and adequacy in school financing[125]—the commitment to compulsory education policies that was established in the nineteenth century has remained relatively unchallenged.

Lotteries

The question of whether to permit state-run or independent gambling operations has been a recurring issue in state conventions, with lotteries providing the most enduring source of controversy. Beginning in the late eighteenth century and continuing to the present, reformers have mounted a series of efforts to persuade state governments to prohibit games of chance, on the grounds that these games promote character traits inconsistent with the virtues required to sustain a republican regime. Although reformers frequently advanced their cause in state legislatures, they also sought to adopt constitutional prohibitions on the subject, so as to remove any possibility that future legislators would give in to the ever-present temptation to renew gambling operations.[126]

The Nineteenth-Century Abolition of Lotteries

During the colonial era, lotteries flourished throughout the country. In fact, by the 1770s, as John Ezell has noted, "all of the colonies had had experience with lotteries, either licensed, unlicensed, or both. In general the inhabitants had shown no disposition to disapprove of the practice, but on the contrary, had welcomed drawings, particularly when they benefited schools, churches, or the residents of particular areas."[127] Although some individuals—most notably Quakers—raised concerns about the proliferation of lotteries in the late eighteenth and early nineteenth centuries, they were unsuccessful in putting a stop to a practice that raised large sums of money for a variety of causes, ranging from the outfitting of Revolutionary War soldiers, to the support of educational institutions, to the construction of roads, bridges, and canals.[128]

    It was not until the 1820s that public opinion began to turn against lotteries, at which time lottery opponents began to press their case in state legislatures and conventions. This shift was partly the result of concerns about the corrupt administration of private lotteries. New Yorkers were treated to a particularly revealing exposé of the inner workings of private lotteries in 1818, when newspaper editor Charles Baldwin leveled charges of corruption at lottery administrators and then provided all sorts of details when he was brought up on libel charges.[129] During the next decade, legislative committees in several northern states conducted additional investigations and brought forth similar charges.[130] Public opposition was also driven by fears that gambling was becoming increasingly associated with other types of criminal activity. Residents of states bordering the Mississippi River were particularly shocked in 1835 by the death of a prominent citizen of Vicksburg at the hands of a den of gamblers, as well as the subsequent lynching of those men at the hands of an antigambling mob. As a result, in the ensuing years, several southern states moved to tighten their gambling laws.[131]

For the most part, though, opposition to lotteries during this period was fueled by concerns about the vices they fostered. When the lottery issue arose in state conventions, as it did in nearly every convention held during the antebellum era, delegates who favored banning lotteries repeatedly detailed their harmful effects on the citizenry.[132] Many delegates feared that lotteries led to the financial ruin of individuals who became ensnared in these games, and moreover, that these individuals were frequently among the poorest citizens. Martin Bates argued in the Delaware Convention of 1852–1853, "I go upon the ground that lotteries are an evil, and a great evil. The sums of money which are raised by them to drain your creeks, build your seminaries, help to pay for your steamboats, or pay the debts of your churches, comes out of the labor of the poor, who oftentimes send their children supperless to bed, in order to get money to buy lottery tickets."[133] Jacob Hoppe in the California Convention of 1849 was of a similar mind-set. He was well aware of the revenue that could be raised through lotteries, but he argued that "there is another question involved in the adoption of this section—a question of far greater importance than money. It concerns the well-being of society, and the permanent industrial interests of the State." In particular, he argued that "the effects are most deeply felt by those who are least able to sustain them. It penetrates to the domestic circle; it destroys the happiness of families, and falls with a particular weight upon the widow and the orphan."[134]

Delegates also argued that lottery playing led to the acquisition of all sorts of moral vices. John Duer in the New York Convention of 1821 was one of many delegates who opposed lotteries because they encouraged speculation. He argued,

The principal evil, was their tendency to promote and encourage a spirit of rash and wild speculation amongst the poor and labouring classes—to fill their minds with absurd and extravagant hopes, which diverted them from the regular pursuits of industry; and the continued indulgence of which was seen to be destructive to those principles and habits which it should be the object of every wise government to cultivate and preserve. . . . He hoped he might concur with other gentlemen, in seeking to prevent a practice productive of these consequences, without subjecting himself to the imputation of affecting an extraordinary purity, or leaning to a Pharisaical rigour of morals.[135]

Other delegates were particularly concerned about the undermining of the work ethic. Kimball Dimmick in the California Convention of 1849 argued that the lottery "encourages habits of idleness, and a distaste for those industrial pursuits best calculated to promote the wealth and prosperity of the mass." He challenged the assembled delegates, "Shall this State, which is to introduce our great republican principles of government to the nations of the Pacific, derive its means of support from the ruin of individuals? Shall the State of California give its sanction to an institution which can only be sustained by producing degradation, poverty, and crime?" He trusted not.[136]

Delegates were concerned about the demoralizing effects of all lotteries, but they were particularly troubled by state-run lotteries, which were viewed as encouraging and profiting from vice. Lewis Dent in the California Convention of 1849 argued that "the State should be prohibited from indulging in a practice which was condemned in individuals. The State should not be permitted to derive its nourishment from the destruction of its members. If the practice is objectionable in individuals, it is still more so in a Government, which professes to be the guardian of individuals, and the protector of their interests."[137] William Dodge argued in similar fashion in the New York Convention of 1821:

> The evil consequence of lotteries is more extensive than we can at first imagine. It tends to demoralize the state—it sets an example which is followed by every class of society—it loosens the moral obligations of society, and corrupts and adulterates the source—and the branches and streams which emanate from it become, of necessity, adulterated also. By establishing this principle as legal and constitutional, you afford an example more powerful to excite, than all your laws are to deter, from the commission of this species of crime.[138]

Finally, these delegates argued that it was not enough to rely on legislators to ban lotteries, and that it was appropriate and necessary to constitutionalize these bans. To some extent, this was because delegates thought it was fitting for those drafting a constitution to express their firm opposition to "any injurious or immoral practice," as Mr. Dimmick of California explained. "Gentlemen assert that we are not here to make laws. He would ask are we not here to make a Constitution—the strongest law known under our system of government."[139]

However, the primary reason for "not leav[ing] the subject to the discretion of the legislature," Mr. Duer of New York explained, was that

> this was exactly one of the subjects on which the discretion of an ordinary legislature was not to be trusted. Legislatures were always under a strong temptation to resort to lotteries as a mode of raising revenue; and from a temptation to which it was more than probable they would yield, the constitution should preserve them. Lotteries, although taxes in effect, were not such in appearance and form, they were not so considered or felt by the people, or even by that portion of the community by whom they were paid: they were not considered as forming any addition to the public burthens, and could therefore be laid without any hazard to the popularity of those by whom they were imposed. Experience justified the assertion that this motive was too strong to be resisted by the virtue of any popular assembly, and the safest course to preserve their integrity was to remove the temptation.[140]

Lotteries were not without their defenders—or, better stated, lottery bans were not without their critics. A few critics expressed doubts about whether lotteries were quite as immoral as they had been portrayed. James Kent argued in the New York Convention of 1821, for instance, that he was

> no friend to lotteries in general, but he could not admit that they were *per se* criminal or immoral when authorized by law. If they were nuisances, it was in the manner in which they were managed. . . . The American congress, in 1776, instituted a national lottery, and perhaps no body of men ever surpassed them in intelligence and virtue. Lotteries had been authorized by congress under the present constitution of the United States, and very frequently by the legislature of this state. He was unwilling to say all these had been from the beginning immoral acts.[141]

His colleague John Cramer concurred; he "did not consider this practice any more immoral than many others which were permitted and encouraged by our legislature."[142]

For the most part, critics acknowledged the immoral character of lottery playing and chose to contest the proposed bans on other grounds. Many of these delegates emphasized the financial benefits of lotteries. Samuel Young in the New York Convention of 1821 noted that

> large sums of money had been raised to improve the navigation of the Hudson, and for the erection of colleges within this state. There had, to be sure,

been some failures and defalcations, but nothing compared with the amount received by the State; and the legislature had learnt a lesson on this subject, which would enable them to avoid future losses in the same way. The state received, in one year, over and above all losses, more than thirty thousand dollars, from this very source.[143]

Meanwhile, Wilkins Updike in the Rhode Island Convention of 1842 opposed a prohibition on lotteries because he "preferred that the income derived from lotteries should be appropriated to erecting a hospital for the insane."[144] Similarly, R. M. Price argued in the California Convention of 1849 that

> he was opposed to the system himself, and would be sorry to see it legalized; but he believed it was a necessary evil in California at this time. Three hundred thousand dollars could be raised annually by the State for the privilege of lotteries. This would be a great relief under the embarrassing position that the State will be placed in when the new government goes into operation, owing to the difficulty of organizing a perfect system of taxation.[145]

In addition, several delegates opposed lottery bans on the grounds that although such bans might make for good policy in an ideal world, they could never be enforced in an effective manner. Ambrose Spencer, New York chief justice and delegate to the New York Convention of 1821, was particularly concerned about the difficulties of enforcement, noting, "Should our legislature hereafter see fit to pass a law, that no foreign tickets should be sold within this state, agents will be appointed to go to other states and purchase them; for the inducement is such, that they will not be restrained."[146] In fact, some of these delegates maintained that enacting an unenforceable provision would be worse than remaining silent on the matter, for this would give the state less power to supervise the practice. In this vein, Mr. Price of California noted that "however objectionable the principle was, yet he believed it was better in some cases to legalize immoral acts than to have them done in secret."[147]

Several of these delegates also argued that even if a lottery ban was desirable, it was inadvisable to place such a ban in the constitution. In some cases, delegates professed to be agnostic about the propriety of lotteries; they simply believed that legislators were better positioned than convention delegates to make such a decision. Thus W. E. Shannon in the California Convention of 1849 "thought it should be left to the Legislature. He did not conceive that there was a greater amount of wisdom, including the gray hairs, in this Convention, than there would be in the future Legislatures of the State; nor was it proper to prevent those bodies from adopting such measures of general policy as they might deem expedient. He desired to leave the Legislature untrammelled."[148] In other cases, delegates "had no objection to prohibiting lotteries," but preferred, in the words of Matthew Deady in the Oregon Convention of 1857, to "leave it to be regulated by law, like other crimes."[149] In still other cases, delegates did not believe that lotteries were necessarily in need of prohibition; they opposed a constitutional ban, as Chancellor Kent explained, because "there might be occasions in the future progress of society, in which a resort to lotteries to raise necessary funds might be expedient, and he doubted the policy of thus abridging the power of the legislature upon ethical theories."[150]

Despite the force of these objections, in virtually every convention in which this debate was joined between 1820 and 1860, these concerns were met and overcome by delegates who were intent on securing constitutional prohibitions against state-administered and privately run lotteries.[151] Consequently, by the start of the Civil War, lotteries had been eliminated in all states but Delaware, Kentucky, and Missouri, and frequently through adoption of constitutional provisions.[152]

Although the Civil War led some states to consider repealing their lottery bans—several southern and western states relied on lotteries to raise revenue to fight the war and then rebuild in its aftermath—the postbellum era represented more of a continuation of, rather than a departure from, the reigning opposition to lotteries. Most important, this lottery revival was short-lived, so that by 1878 all but one of the states that had turned to lotteries to raise revenues had reversed course.[153] Additionally, even the infamous Louisiana Lottery, which originated when the Louisiana Convention of 1864 repealed its previous ban and permitted the licensing of lotteries, was eventually shut down at the end of 1894.[154] Moreover, Louisiana was an exceptional case, in this as in so many other areas. None of the states that joined the union in the closing decades of the nineteenth century chose to permit lotteries, and this decision was usually approved by a wide margin.

With the expiration of all lottery charters in Louisiana after 1894, not a single state permitted lotteries.[155] Although the first half of the twentieth century witnessed somewhat of a relaxation of public attitudes toward other forms of gambling such as parimutuel betting, states maintained a steadfast opposition to lotteries during this period.[156]

The Late Twentieth-Century Resurgence of Lotteries

The lottery debate reemerged in the mid-1960s, and during the next four decades most states reversed course and eliminated their lottery bans. To be sure, supporters of these bans continued to advance the traditional nineteenth-century arguments in favor of constitutional prohibitions on lotteries. Delegates such as George Harper in the Montana Convention of 1971–1972 continued to emphasize the vices associated with lotteries and to express doubt that anyone could "make a case for gambling on the basis that it's helpful in personal character-building, or in creating a strong society."[157] Other supporters of lottery bans followed their nineteenth-century predecessors in emphasizing the impropriety of permitting government to raise revenue by encouraging unhealthy character traits. Along these lines, Donald McKiernan reminded the Rhode Island Convention of 1964–1969 that "we have experienced a lottery in Rhode Island before. It did provide to us revenue in time of scarcity." But "what happens when the evils of [the] system become even more apparent[,] when we see as we saw in Rhode Island that that is a tax paid by the poor. Indeed, the poorest of the poor, those that have nothing but dreams and illusions? What happens when we see the morals and the ethics of not only our legislature but our state at large undermined?"[158] Still other delegates reminded their colleagues of the long-appreciated virtues of constitutionalizing these bans. As Frank Millard argued in the Michigan Convention of 1961–1962, the lottery issue did not deserve to be thrown "back into the legislature where it would be subject to, maybe, a lot of abuses or there might be pressures brought to bear which should not be brought to bear in a matter like this."[159] And as Leo Graybil emphasized in the Montana Convention of 1971–1972, "Gambling is a constitutional issue. It's one of the fundamental principles of governmental structure that a constitution should include—things which protect the ethical and the moral rights of people."[160]

However, these traditional arguments simply did not carry the same weight in the late twentieth century as in previous eras. Most important, delegates were no longer confident in declaring that certain character traits should be discouraged, much less that government should be doing the discouraging. Thus Frank Stemberk in the Illinois Convention of 1969–1970 complained, "It just seems that certain people would like to legislate morality, and you just can't legislate morality. . . . As far as the moral issue is concerned of a lottery or a bingo-type game, I am not a moralist. I don't have any divine revelation, and I don't mean to say it's right or it's wrong; but I don't think any of us, at this point, is here to say that this is right and this is wrong. And it is not our position."[161] Late twentieth-century convention delegates acknowledged that their predecessors had been prepared to make such determinations about immoral behavior; they were simply no longer prepared to do so. Nor, these modern delegates suggested, would citizens in the contemporary era consent any longer to public officials making such determinations. As Hugo Ricci argued in the Rhode Island Convention of 1964–1969, in seeking to overturn a long-standing lottery ban in place from the original Rhode Island Constitution of 1842, "This is 122 years later. Times have changed. We live in a free democracy. Our people want to do anything that they possibly can do within the confines of the law. They don't want to be repressed in any manner, shape, or form, and certainly they will have a right in a sovereign state to buy a lottery ticket and to partake from a lottery program if they so wish."[162]

Additionally, late twentieth-century delegates were generally more enamored than their predecessors of the funds that could be raised through lotteries. More to the point, these delegates were less prepared to view lotteries as an inappropriate means of generating such revenue. And any remaining inhibitions were frequently overcome by reassurances, as Ricci provided, that such revenues "will be used for educational purposes," or, as Raul Longoria urged in the Texas Convention of 1974, "for good causes such as for the hospitals or the mentally retarded or the old-age pensioners."[163]

Finally, these delegates were no longer persuaded that the lottery question deserved to be withdrawn from legislative control. In part, this was a logical consequence of the growing acceptance of the morality of lottery playing during this period. As John Hardwicke explained in the Maryland Convention of 1967–1968, "It is not the apparent kind of evil obvious on the face of it, a per se evil which should be banned by the constitution. I urge you, therefore, to leave this constitution silent on the subject and let the legislature consider it from time to time."[164] In part, also, this was a product of the growing acceptance of lotteries as instruments of fund-raising. As long as the overriding goal had been to prevent legislatures from succumbing to the temptation to plug budget gaps by resorting to lotteries, then it made sense to constitutionalize the issue. Once lotteries were viewed as a legitimate means of raising revenue, then it was appropriate to give free rein to legislators to determine whether to tap this source. As Charles Dukes argued in the same convention, "Of all the areas in this constitution in which we should not be restrictive to the legislature, finance more than any other single item should be unrestricted." He explained, "It is not the purpose nor the wisdom of this Convention to forestall forever the opportunity of the legislature of the State of Maryland, the political subdivisions and the people of the State of Maryland to use some form of gambling device which may be used to raise money."[165]

No longer convinced that government had any role to play in discouraging lottery playing, and attracted by the promise of financial support for education and other public functions, state constitution makers therefore came full circle during this period. After an initial period in the late eighteenth and early nineteenth centuries when lotteries were abundant, and then another period lasting from the mid-nineteenth through the mid-twentieth centuries when lotteries were virtually prohibited, lotteries were again very much in favor during the late twentieth century. New Hampshire's adoption of a lottery in 1964—a full seven decades after the end of the Louisiana Lottery and the effective abolition of legal lotteries across the country, and over a century after their near abolition in the antebellum era—heralded a national resurgence of support for lotteries,[166] and by the early twenty-first century, lotteries were legal in all but nine states.[167]

Liquor

Liquor regulation is the best-known example of a way that federal constitution makers during the early twentieth century sought to shape citizen character, but it is not always appreciated that state constitution makers have also been intimately concerned with this issue, and in an even more sustained fashion. Although the enactment and repeal of a national prohibition amendment from 1919 to 1933 is now widely understood to be "a pathological fluke or an accident—certainly not an accurate expression of the American tradition of progress and reform,"[168] liquor prohibition is very much in keeping with a long-standing state constitutional tradition.

To be sure, for the first fifty years after the Revolutionary Era, state constitution makers evinced little concern with liquor regulation. In fact, as William J. Rorabaugh has written, during this early period,

> alcohol was pervasive in American society; it crossed regional, sexual, racial, and class lines. Americans drank at home and abroad, alone and together, at work and at play, in fun and in earnest. They drank from the crack of dawn to the crack of dawn. At nights taverns were filled with boisterous, mirth-making

tipplers. Americans drank before meals, with meals, and after meals. They drank while working in the fields and while travelling across half a continent. They drank in their youth, and, if they lived long enough, in their old age. They drank at formal events, such as weddings, ministerial ordinations, and wakes, and on no occasion—by the fireside of an evening, on a hot afternoon, when the mood called.[169]

With the exception of religious denominations such as the Puritans and Quakers, as well as individuals such as Dr. Benjamin Rush and Rev. Lyman Beecher, each of whom mounted campaigns against intemperance in these early years, there was little in the way of an organized movement to counter this excessive dependence on alcohol. As a result, governmental regulation of liquor was modest in scope throughout this early period.[170]

It was not until the 1820s and 1830s, with the formation of several statewide temperance societies, that groups began to promote temperance on a grand scale and that these nascent efforts at moral suasion came to be supplemented by a call for restrictive legislation. Reformers enjoyed one of their first important political victories in 1838 with the passage of a Massachusetts law banning the sale of distilled liquor in any quantity less than fifteen gallons.[171] Although this statute was repealed after only two years, temperance societies continued to press their case in other states, and in Maine in 1851, Neal Dow was responsible for securing passage of the first statewide prohibition law.[172]

From that point, and continuing for the better part of the next eight decades, the regulation of liquor became a dominant issue in state politics, especially during 1851–1855, 1880–1889, and 1907–1919. Throughout these periods, groups such as the American Temperance Union, Washington Temperance Society, Women's Christian Temperance Union, and Anti-Saloon League pressed state legislatures, and at times, state conventions, to take steps to reduce consumption of intoxicating beverages.[173] Temperance supporters sought either to prohibit governments from issuing liquor licenses (known as a no-license policy), to permit localities to prohibit liquor sales within their boundaries (referred to as local option), or to prohibit the sale and manufacture of liquor across the state (referred to as prohibition). Individuals who opposed these measures occasionally argued against any liquor regulations whatsoever; more frequently, they sought to retain the traditional policy of licensing liquor establishments, which was much less intrusive than the leading alternatives.

What stands out from a review of these continuing battles between temperance supporters and critics is the extent to which the debates turned on fundamental questions about the proper governmental role in shaping the character of the citizenry. Thus, as Ernst Freund once remarked,

> it is certainly the more conservative view to look upon the control of the liquor traffic as a means of protecting the community from crime and the financial burdens of pauperism, but it is also clear that the police power, resting upon this incontestable ground, in reality is turned into a power to protect the weak individual from his own weakness, into a power to prevent the wasteful expenditure of money and time, and finally into a power to impose upon the minority the sentiments or prejudices of the majority of the community, as to what is morally right and good.[174]

The ensuing debates over the proper extent of liquor regulation and the appropriate governmental role in shaping citizen character went on to produce, in the words of William Novak, "a public discussion of the principles and practices of early American governance second only to that other great constitutional crisis of the nineteenth century—slavery and Civil War."[175]

The Case for Prohibition

Convention delegates who supported temperance provisions often began by detailing the costs associated with the consumption of alcohol. There was no disputing that many lives had been cut short by excessive drinking. Jacob Van Valkenburgh argued in the Michigan Convention of 1867, "It is now admitted by all men not influenced by mercenary motives, everywhere on all occasions, that its use is evil and only evil; that it has made more victims than famine, pestilence or the sword; that it has caused more sighs and tears and groans—that it has blasted more prospects, blighted more hopes, and crushed more hearts than all the other agencies for evil on earth."[176] Nor could one ignore the effects of alcohol use on families, particularly on the wives and children of men who frequented saloons and then squandered their salaries and deserted their homes. According to Alvin Voris in the Ohio Convention of 1873–1874,

> It not only destroys the individual who indulges in the habit, but blights all the properly recognized feelings, obligations and functions of the family relation; natural affection flees before it; and common decency is trampled under its feet. Its very breath, like the sirocco, causes every human impulse to wither and die within its dominion. It revels in human depravity, and the utter de-

struction of everything that is good or pure, and is pleased to leave society a howling waste.[177]

Also to be reckoned with were the financial costs borne by society as a whole. Thus John Holmes in the Michigan Convention of 1907–1908 argued,

> The cost to the state of the liquor traffic is a sum so stupendous that any figures I should dare to give would convict me of trifling with the facts. The amount of human life absolutely destroyed, the amount of industry sacrificed, the shame, sorrow, crime, poverty, pauperism, and the wild waste of physical and financial resources make an aggregate so vast as to stagger computation and beggar description in addition to the fifty thousand yearly sacrificed to this traffic. It is estimated that five hundred thousand dissolute men are idle as a direct result of the intemperate use of intoxicating liquors. And this army of idle men at a salary of four hundred dollars a year would amount to two hundred million dollars annually lost as a direct result of the use of intoxicating liquors.[178]

Although delegates referred repeatedly to these social and financial costs, they were even more concerned with the moral consequences of permitting trafficking in intoxicating liquors. Temperance supporters spoke constantly of the frailty of human nature and of individual susceptibility to the temptations posed by alcoholic beverages. For the state to permit individuals to succumb to these temptations by legalizing the sale of liquor was to contribute not only to the ruin of families and lost productivity but also to the demoralization of individuals themselves. Thus Herbert Freeman argued in the Michigan Convention of 1907–1908, "We know there are thousands of men who at one time could control and govern their appetites and habits, but who have now sunk so low in their downward career that it is impossible for them to longer resist the temptations of the saloon and other places of vice, and they can only be rescued from a drunkard's or felon's doom by the removal of the saloon and its influence from their midst."[179] As George Miller explained in the Utah Convention of 1895, "If a man has contracted the habit and love for intoxicating liquors, it is impossible for that man through his own individual power of will power to release himself from that habit. Hence, we that advocate prohibition do it from a humane standpoint and from a desire to help our fellowmen."[180] In fact, several delegates argued that it was for precisely this reason that some of the same individuals who were the most afflicted by alcoholism were also the most fervent supporters of prohibition. David Clark, for instance, told the delegates in the Delaware Convention of 1896–1897 that, during his campaign for membership in the convention, he had encountered a young man "who was addicted to the use of this evil stuff" and who implored Clark to "do something to give the people a chance to vote on this question." Clark noted, "Now this very man had a horse blanket hanging up in his room, which had a picture of a horse on it, and he shot at it, as he said he saw on it things which he thought were demons after him. He had been drinking. And that man said he wanted a chance to vote on this question. Let us give that man a chance to vote on this question."[181]

Temperance supporters argued that the liquor traffic also had a demoralizing effect on the state itself as a result of governmental participation in licensing liquor establishments. Thus Wilmer Walker in the Ohio Convention of 1912 argued, "The state cannot afford to temporize with organized lawlessness, or compromise on matters universally recognized as basically immoral. When it becomes partner in iniquity, sharing its unholy profits, and winking at violations of what even the courts have universally declared to be illegal and without right to exist, it has no guarantee of either perpetuity or continued prosperity."[182] Although licensing was defended by some delegates as a pragmatic way of limiting the ill effects of liquor, and occasionally as a means of raising needed revenue, temperance supporters contended that such a policy rendered the state complicit in a business with which it ought not to be associated. Joseph Bagg argued in the Michigan Convention of 1850, "If it were right to legalize the traffic in liquor, why not legalize houses of ill fame, for the support of ministers of the gospel? It could be done on the same principle, for it was no worse than to give a license to a man to murder with liquor."[183] His colleague, Lorenzo Mason, argued that revenues gained from liquor licenses were "the price of blood, and on the same principle brothels, gambling houses, lotteries, or any other vice in community, could be licensed by the Legislature."[184] Meanwhile, William Smithers in the Delaware Convention of 1896–1897 likened the licensing of saloons to the propagation of disease:

If the State of Delaware draws its life's breath from the atmosphere of the saloon; if it leans for its support upon the rum traffic; if it be dependent upon a revenue that brings along with it trembling sots, pale-faced women, and pauperized children, then God help her. The apple of Sodom is luscious fruit compared with her. If a man should propose to open a place for the dissemination of Asiatic cholera, and offer to share the proceeds with the State, would you go into partnership with him for the dissemination of any disease? I think not. Why not, when you seek to foster that which not only kills, but destroys utterly.[185]

These delegates had no illusions that a prohibition policy would eradicate every last use of liquor and make every man temperate. At the least, though, as Ephraim Hall argued in the West Virginia Convention of 1861–1863, by refusing to permit the operation of saloons, the state would "put the temptation where it will not stare them in the face. You can by wholesome laws, and the people will sustain you in it, provide against building up a school to teach them to be intemperate."[186]

These delegates were cognizant of claims that enactment of a prohibition policy would be inconsistent with traditional conceptions of individual liberty, but they argued that governmental regulation in this area was well supported by long-standing precedents. Thus David White in the Pennsylvania Convention of 1872–1873 was unimpressed by the objection that government has "no right to prohibit a citizen from manufacturing and selling liquor." He noted, "Gambling and lotteries were, at one time, openly practiced, and protected by law. Now they are forbidden and punished. . . . Are not the evils arising from the traffic in alcoholic liquors ten-fold worse than the evils arising from gambling?"[187] His colleague Thomas Hazzard offered a similar defense of liquor regulation, arguing, "We already have many sorts of regulations which are called for, in order to promote the public health. We regulate the sale of stale meat. We say that there shall be no unwholesome food exposed in the market. Now, is it not equally right and just that we should regulate the sale of this unwholesome stuff?"[188] It was true that governmental prohibition of alcohol was rooted in a desire to protect the moral, as well as physical, health of individuals, whereas governmental regulation of adulterated food was grounded solely in a concern with physical health. Nevertheless, delegates argued that the same general principle applied in both cases. Henry Elson therefore concluded in the Ohio Convention of 1912 that it is "only partially true" to say "that society as a whole has no right to act for the individual, that the individual's morality is not a matter of public policy." He reasoned,

> We know there are laws against the use of cocaine. We know that there are laws against the use of opium. There are laws against attempted suicide. Now these are laws that prove that society does sometimes interfere with the individual to save him. And, as stated, society is acting for itself when it does this, because he is a member of society and, especially if he is young, he is a future citizen, and it is society's business to make the future citizenship as strong as it possibly can. Then I say society has not only the rights, but it is its duty, to do just as much as possible towards training of the young in such a way that they will be strong and self-reliant when they grow to maturity."[189]

Delegates argued that prohibition could also be viewed as a logical continuation of long-standing governmental efforts to ward off threats to the social order. On this view, government had as much of an interest in preventing a coarsening of social mores as in preventing individuals from engaging in unhealthy acts. Thus Mr. Voris of Ohio argued,

> All recognize that public virtue is essential to the well-being of any people. So fundamental is this idea, that it is adopted as a principle in politics, that whatever corrupts public virtue should be prohibited, and whatever is necessary to its development should be fostered by the State. Whatever is subversive of the public peace or good order of society is inimical to the just rights of mankind, dangerous to the State, and ought not to be tolerated, much less protected, by the sanctions of law.[190]

To conclude otherwise, Simeon Nash argued in the Ohio Convention of 1850–1851, would give undue weight to one particular conception of individual liberty and would place insufficient emphasis on the need to maintain the social order. In opposing the liquor traffic, which he saw as "corrupting the morals of society," he asked, "Are the morals of society a matter of no moment? Rather are they not in all governments the one thing needful to be cared for? Can society remain organized, and its progress continue onward, if its morals are undermined and degraded? Above all, can a government, resting upon the popular will, like ours, last a day after public virtue has become extinct?"[191]

Finally, temperance supporters frequently argued that prohibition measures belonged in the constitution rather than in ordinary statute law. In part, this was because legislatures were thought to be incapable of acting in the public interest in this area, on account of what Mr. Clark of Delaware referred to as "the mighty influence and the mighty power that is wielded by the liquor people."[192] His colleague James Gilchrist explained, "As the influence of the liquor interest has been powerful enough in the past to defeat proposed Local Option in the General Assembly, . . . if we depend upon the General Assembly hereafter to grant us the privilege of voting on the License Question, we will never get it."[193]

Another reason for placing prohibition in the constitution was to signal to the people the importance of this issue by enshrining it in their fundamental law. John Coats argued in the Ohio Convention of 1873–1874,

> The first principles, powers, and duties of legislation consist in commanding what is right, and prohibiting what is wrong; and it will not be claimed that the

principles applied to general legislation are not equally applicable to the work of forming the fundamental law, to become the basis of legislation. A stream cannot rise above its fountain head by its own inherent force; hence arises the necessity of so framing and shaping the fundamental law as to meet these and all just requirements.[194]

In fact, several delegates argued that an additional benefit of elevating prohibition to constitutional status was that citizens would likely treat a constitutional provision on this subject more seriously than they would a legislative statute. Thus in the New Hampshire Convention of 1889, where legislative prohibition was already in effect, William Manahan sought to go further and place the measure on a constitutional basis, on the grounds that a "constitutional prohibition, being the direct work of the people, will be more vigorously followed up and fully enforced."[195] Meanwhile, George Willard in the Michigan Convention of 1867 thought that

there can be no greater moral influence exerted, than by putting in the Constitution of the State this declaration, that no man whatever shall be licensed to sell intoxicating drinks. Why? Because the people have pronounced it a great moral wrong. Every one throughout the State will regard this declaration as the expression of the moral sentiment of the people. Our children will grow up under the influence of this Constitution. As they read this provision in the organic law, they will be led to see what the people have pronounced to be a wrong.[196]

The Case against Prohibition

Delegates who opposed temperance measures put forth various rebuttals, including many that paralleled arguments first advanced in the debate over lottery bans. Most important, critics argued that prohibition was inconsistent with fundamental regime principles. Edward Morton in the Michigan Convention of 1867 was one of several delegates who believed that these measures constituted a threat to individual liberty, insofar as they exceeded the traditional understanding of limited governmental power. He argued that "the personal liberty of the citizen is infringed upon by any act which steps between him and his right to judge for himself in regard to what he may use as a beverage."[197] Meanwhile, Jacob Mueller in the Ohio Convention of 1873–1874 argued that the prohibition movement was animated by an excessive concern for superintending moral behavior, and that this was inconsistent with principles of self-government. He argued that "this prohibition and suppression theory is more than an absurdity; it is a violation of the spirit of our Constitution, and against human nature. . . . Because some weak specimens of humanity are allowing themselves to be brutalized by their passion for stimulants, it does not follow that the whole people should be treated as imbeciles, needing to be humiliated by being placed under guardianship." He thought that the proper approach was to treat this problem "like all moral and religious questions, . . . by moral suasion."[198] Daniel Lamb in the West Virginia Convention of 1861–1863 offered perhaps the most theoretical critique of prohibition policies, when he argued that sumptuary measures such as prohibition were inconsistent with a Millian conception of liberty, which he took to be the conception that should guide the American regime. Lamb was

> utterly opposed to this system of legislating for the purpose of compelling men to be good. I do not believe the legislature are a proper tribunal to take care of the morals of a people in reference to matters of this kind. There are a great many things that ought not to be regulated by legislative action, that must be left to a man's own judgment and conscience, and the legislature cannot even interfere with him when he does wrong. . . . If a man does direct wrong to another, there the legislature ought to interfere by its laws. But you cannot prescribe a set of laws that will protect a man against himself.[199]

Critics were also concerned about the difficulty of enforcing temperance measures. In their view, even if it was within the proper domain of the state to adopt measures prohibiting liquor consumption, these measures would never achieve their desired effect. As Stanley Bowdle argued in the Ohio Convention of 1912, the law

> merely registers in a formal manner what has already become the custom of the people of the state. Mark you, one of the implications of that is that a law which has force behind it is no law. It is the law which does not force that is the law, for if a law is effective because it has a prior custom then we get rid of the element of force altogether. . . . What is the logic of all this? It is that the appeal of the drys to force is a ridiculous appeal.[200]

According to this line of reasoning, the desire for the stimulation afforded by alcoholic beverages was so firmly rooted in human nature that it could never be eradicated. Therefore efforts to stamp out this habit would merely succeed in driving it underground. For instance, John Campbell, despite being a self-proclaimed "temperance man," nevertheless argued in the Pennsylvania Convention of 1872–1873 that he did "not believe the vice of intemperance can be reached by means of legislation of this character. All sumptuary laws—and a law of this kind is a sumptuary law of the worst character—have been found to fail always in the past and I think will always be found to fail in the future." He opposed prohibition because he thought that "the very effect of it is the contrary of that which the persons urging this kind of legislation desire. . . . A man who has the appetite for intoxicating drinks now goes to the public house; adopt a proposition of this kind and he will make his own house a tavern, and the very evils that these mistaken friends of temperance complain of will be rendered far worse."[201] James Caples in the California Convention of 1878–1879 was of a similar mind-set. He argued,

If it was possible for us to secure morality and the just deportment of the people by legislative enactment, it would be desirable to do it, and I would be the first to advocate it. But, Mr. Chairman, if we could do this we could do more, and I should be in favor of going back and repealing original sin; wipe it all out at one fell blow. Why not? Let us repeal the fall of man, and transfer mankind back into the garden of Eden. But . . . we have got to accept the world as we find it. I deny utterly that it is within the range of possibility to legislate to secure and enforce morality.[202]

Additionally, these delegates argued that the enactment of prohibitory measures would have various adverse consequences for the state. Insofar as enforcement of these measures would be ineffective, this would in turn lead to reduced respect for all laws. Thus Wellington Burt argued in the Michigan Convention of 1907–1908, "A law placed upon the statute book that cannot be enforced is worse than no law at all."[203] Additionally, as James Birney explained in the Michigan Convention of 1867, an unenforced law "will have a greatly demoralizing effect; it tends to affect every other law on the statute book. If there is any one law which is notoriously not observed, it tends to lessen in the minds of the people their respect for every other law."[204] Moreover, to the extent that prohibition would bring an end to the licensing of liquor establishments, this would lead to reduced state revenues. Robert Dasey in the Delaware Convention of 1896–1897 noted, "For a considerable length of time the liquor traffic was a questionable one, but after awhile the people decided to legalize it as a source of revenue, and that the revenue derived therefrom should be converted into the school fund. Some people claim that an education which is obtained from the revenue derived from the granting of licenses is an immoral education. But I never looked at it in that light."[205]

Finally, some delegates argued that even if prohibition was conceded to be a wise and legitimate policy, there was no warrant for constitutionalizing such a policy. Solon Thacher, a delegate to the Kansas Convention of 1859, claimed to be "as strong a temperance man as there is upon this floor," but he thought it was "unwise for us to incorporate a provision of this nature into the Constitution"; he preferred to "leave these vexed questions to one side, trusting to the Legislature to regulate all these things."[206] Similarly, William Ladd explained in the New Hampshire Convention of 1889 that he was "not on the side of free rum," but he thought that the virtue of leaving the liquor question to "be regulated by statute" was that "the people may try one thing, and if it does not accomplish the desired object that they may not have their hands tied so that they cannot try another thing." He "would not put it into the fundamental law of the State, for the reason already suggested,—that times change, interests change, business changes, the feelings of the people change."[207]

The Adoption of Prohibition

Although the critics of prohibition carried the day in various conventions, particularly in the mid-nineteenth century, temperance supporters enjoyed increasing success in the late nineteenth and early twentieth centuries. Nevertheless, states varied throughout this time in the types of temperance measures that they adopted and in their willingness to constitutionalize these policies.

Several of the earliest constitutional temperance measures, which were adopted in the constitutions of Michigan (1850) and Ohio (1851), called simply for the abolition of the license system.[208] As William Bates explained in the Ohio Convention of 1850–1851, "The temperance men of the state—those who have been long engaged in the cause, think that in order to put down intemperance, you must abolish the license system, and so far take away the respectability of the business of making men drunkards." The intent was "that this monopoly shall be put down—that the protection shall be taken away, so that public opinion may be brought to bear directly upon the subject."[209] In this way, Mr. Bagg of Michigan argued, "the State may cut loose from all responsibility—all participation in the system of licensing the sale of intoxicating drinks." This measure, which was a rather modest reform that did not call for the actual abolition of liquor, appealed to those who did "not wish the State to give a moral tone to the traffic, to legalize it," and yet who were "too sensible to ask anything more."[210]

Another approach, which also fell short of statewide prohibition, called for local option in regard to liquor regulation. Mr. Gilchrist of Delaware explained the appeal of this policy by arguing, "I am in favor of Prohibition wherever a prohibitory law can be enforced. My motto is 'Prohibition for the State; total abstinence for the individual.' As Prohibition is not yet practicable in Delaware; therefore I am in favor of Local Option, which is simply 'Local Prohibition.' It is to give the qualified electors of certain districts the privilege of expressing by their votes, whether they are in favor of, or against the manufacture and sale of intoxicating liquors in such districts. Is there anything unreasonable in this?"[211] Because of the capacity of local option policies to bridge differences among a wide spectrum of views on the liquor question, these measures proved particularly popular. During the nineteenth century, temperance supporters often saw local option as the most stringent policy that could be achieved at the time, and they were often forced to settle for such a policy instead of their preferred policy of statewide prohibition. By the end of the century, local option had been adopted in thirty-seven states, and had been placed in the constitutions of Texas (1876), Florida (1885), Kentucky (1891), and Delaware (1897).[212] During the early twentieth century, local option attracted even more support and received an additional impetus, as temperance supporters came to view this policy not merely as a less than desirable compromise, but rather as an attractive first step toward enacting statewide prohibition.[213]

Finally, statewide prohibition was, for many years, less popular than local option, but it enjoyed increasing success as the nineteenth century progressed. Not surprisingly, prohibition was the preferred policy of the most committed temperance supporters, including, for instance, Mr. Valkenburgh, who argued in the Michigan Convention of 1850, "Let us not stop at any half-way house in this business. Let us be thorough, radical, ultra if you please. . . . Tell me not of moral suasion with liquor vendors in this age of the world; the law, the *law* is the only agent that can reach their sympathies."[214] The effectiveness of these sorts of appeals was at its highest during a series of prohibitory waves during the late nineteenth and early twentieth centuries. During an initial wave in the 1850s, thirteen states adopted statewide prohibition, in all cases through legislation rather than constitutional provisions.[215] Although many of these states soon repealed their prohibition laws, a second prohibition wave emerged in the 1880s. Eight states provided for statewide prohibition at some point during this period, including six states—Kansas (1880), Iowa (1882), Maine (1884), Rhode Island (1886), South Dakota (1889), and North Dakota (1889)—that placed prohibition clauses in their constitutions.[216] The adoption of the inaugural Oklahoma constitution in 1907 then signaled the start of a third wave of prohibition measures, and by 1919, the list of dry states had grown to thirty-three. Moreover, nineteen of these states constitutionalized their policies, including Maine, Kansas, and North Dakota (each of whose provisions were still in effect from the nineteenth century), as well as Oklahoma (1907), West Virginia (1912), Oregon (1914), Colorado (1914), Arizona (1914), Idaho (1916), South Dakota (1916), Michigan (1916), Nebraska (1916), New Mexico (1917), Utah (1918), Ohio (1918), Wyoming (1918), Florida (1918), Texas (1919), and Kentucky (1919).[217]

At this point, the prohibition movement took on a national character, culminating in the ratification of the Eighteenth Amendment to the U.S. Constitution in 1919. Although some states chose to continue their policies of local option or statewide prohibition even after the repeal of national prohibition in 1933, liquor regulation never again assumed the prominent role that it enjoyed for the final two-thirds of the nineteenth century and the first third of the twentieth century. As Jack Blocker has written, "Although the old debates continued, their context changed dramatically. In its heyday the temperance cause attracted mass participation as have few issues in American history. . . . During the period since Repeal, however, the significant debates over liquor policy have occurred among elites in business, government, and the professions. The liquor issue has been largely removed from the public arena."[218]

Conclusion

There are important differences in the ways that these four issues regarding character formation unfolded in the course of state constitutional development. The effort to permit governmental support for religious institutions was the most short-lived, in that all states decided by the early nineteenth century to prohibit public support of religious societies and, by the close of the nineteenth century, to ban public support for religious schools. The compulsory-education movement proceeded in a quite different manner. Although certain states acted more quickly than others, there was a steady trend in the direction of adopting this policy and occasionally placing it on a constitutional basis. By 1920, the states had uniformly chosen not only to require taxpayer support of public school systems, but also to compel student attendance at a school of some sort, whether at public schools or in some other fashion. The movements to regulate lotteries and liquor, by contrast, both proceeded in a cyclical fashion. Lotteries were prevalent before 1820. Then they were gradually eliminated through constitutional provisions adopted between 1820 and 1860 and, with several late nineteenth-century exceptions, were banned completely until 1964. After this time, states returned to the pre-1820 status of near-universal acceptance of lotteries. The regulation of liquor proceeded similarly. Before the 1830s, liquor was relatively unregulated. Then in the 1850s, 1880s, and 1910s, states adopted increasingly restrictive liquor regulations that were frequently elevated to constitutional status. Since the enactment and repeal of national prohibition, however, there has been a marked reduction in state temperance policies.

Despite these differences in the particular patterns of state constitutional development in each of these areas, it is possible to advance several general conclusions about the lessons that can be drawn from examining the state convention debates regarding character formation. Although federal constitution makers have, with one notable exception, declined to enact constitutional provisions of this sort, state constitution makers have frequently determined that a polity should not only be concerned about the character of the citizenry, but should take active steps to form certain character traits, and that this should be done through constitutional provisions. Contrary arguments have been frequently advanced—with increasing success through the years—to the effect that governmental efforts to form citizen character are inconsistent with republicanism and are not a suitable subject of constitutional provisions. However, state constitution makers have on many occasions rejected both of these positions, and in the process, they have demonstrated a commitment to the constitutionalization of character formation that stands in marked contrast to the dominant understanding of the American constitutional tradition in this area.

Two particular conclusions can therefore be drawn from these state convention debates as to the reasons why state constitution makers were for many years prepared to adopt constitutional provisions designed to shape the character of the citizenry. First, state constitution makers have frequently concluded that it is necessary and proper for republican governments to promote character traits that are conducive to the well-being of individual citizens and the polity as a whole. At times, this has taken the form of encouraging behavior that is seen as beneficial for individuals themselves and the health of the polity. At other times, this has led to prohibiting behavior that is viewed as unhealthy for individuals, detrimental to the social order, and demoralizing to the state.

Second, state constitution makers have frequently deemed it appropriate to constitutionalize this commitment to character formation. At times, constitutional provisions have been seen as necessary to guarantee the legitimacy of these efforts against contrary court decisions. At other times, constitutional provisions have served to express to the people the importance of the issue and perhaps to influence individual behavior as a result. On still other occasions, constitutional provisions have removed from legislative control issues on which legislators had shown themselves to be overly susceptible to powerful self-interests or special interests and therefore incapable of legislating in the public interest.

Conclusion

The principal benefits of analyzing the extant state convention debates are threefold. First, it becomes possible to explain many of the distinctive features of state constitutional development and to view these distinctive state institutions as the product of state constitution makers' sustained reconsideration of the logic of the federal model. Second, these debates can contribute to a better understanding of the entirety of the American constitutional tradition by making it possible to view the debates surrounding the federal convention of 1787 as only one component of an experience with constitution making that also includes the deliberations undertaken in numerous state constitutional conventions throughout American history. Third, these debates might also provide lessons for constitution makers in emerging democracies who currently seek to draw lessons from the American experience, and who might benefit from encountering the arguments of state constitution makers who have grappled over the past several centuries with how to best address perennial institutional problems.

In terms of providing an explanation for state constitutional development, these debates make it clear that state constitution makers' decisions to depart from the federal model in various respects are not the result of an impoverished grasp of constitution making or a lack of reflection about institutional alternatives and consequences. As we have seen, state constitution makers were well aware of the various arguments in favor of the federal model, given that plenty of delegates were on hand at these conventions to articulate the merits of the federal approach. Nor has there been any shortage of deliberation about the relative merits of the federal approach and the alternative approaches that were eventually adopted by a number of state constitution makers. Rather, state constitution makers over the last several centuries have departed from the decisions made by the eighteenth-century framers of the federal constitution because the greater flexibility of state amendment procedures enabled state convention delegates to continually respond to problems that arose in the course of governance, and to reassess and occasionally reject the capacity of the federal model to permit a resolution of these problems in a manner consistent with the public interest. Although several of these problems were especially prominent (such as the need to overcome unresponsive legislatures and obstructionist judges) and state conventions were particularly numerous in certain periods (such as during the Jacksonian Era, Progressive Era, and Reapportionment Revolution), state constitution makers' rejection of the federal model was by no means confined to these issues or eras, but rather was a product of a wide-ranging and continual reexamination of governing principles and institutions.

Regarding the design of amendment and revision processes, state constitution makers gave due consideration to Madisonian arguments about the dangers of frequent constitutional change, but they gradually rejected this position and adopted more flexible procedures. Not only did many states make it easier to enact amendments than at the federal level, but they also established additional mechanisms of constitutional change, including the constitutional initiative and the periodic convention referendum. The adoption of these more flexible procedures was due in part to the need to overcome various problems that were thought to be exacerbated by a rigid amendment process, such as entrenched geographic interests in the nineteenth century and activist judges in the twentieth century. In addition, state constitution makers concluded in the course of their deliberations that the framers of the federal constitution did not fully appreciate the benefits of a more flexible process, such as the opportunities to take account of progress, educate citizens about the fundamental law, and encourage change through constitutional channels rather than extraconstitutional or even revolutionary actions.

As for the concept of representation, state constitution makers were well versed in Madisonian arguments against direct democracy, but they gradually decided to permit citizens to play a direct role in governance. In the nineteenth century, this led to the adoption in many states of the mandatory legislative referendum and optional legislative referendum. Then, in the twentieth century, just under half of the states provided for the popular initiative and/or referendum. These institutional innovations were adopted primarily in response to various problems of governance that arose during the nineteenth and early twentieth centuries, such as the need to overcome self-interested legislators and powerful interest groups and the need to resolve controversial moral issues in a manner that would be viewed by the people as legitimate. Throughout the ensuing convention debates, state constitution makers concluded that the founders had been overly sanguine about the capacity of representative institutions to address each of these problems, and so they turned to various direct democratic institutions to provide a more effective response.

When state constitution makers turned to consider the separation of powers system, and particularly the executive veto and judicial review, they sought to design these institutions in such a way as to restore what they understood to be an original balance of power that had been upset by intervening developments. In the late nineteenth century, legislative riders and omnibus bills were seen as preventing the executive from wielding the veto effectively, and therefore the item veto, and occasionally the reduction veto and amendatory veto, were adopted as a means of restoring the executive to its original position. Then, in the early twentieth century, judges were thought to be engaging in policy making rather than constitutional interpretation, and steps were occasionally taken to restore the judiciary to its intended role by limiting the exercise of judicial review, whether by adopting supermajority requirements or by permitting the recall of judges or judicial decisions. In each of these cases, parallel proposals were introduced and considered at the state and federal level in response to problems that were common to both levels. However, the rigidity of the federal amendment process led to the defeat of these reform proposals at the federal level, whereas the flexibility of state amendment processes permitted their enactment in the states in varying degrees.

In terms of bicameralism, state constitution makers have engaged in a series of debates about whether to retain the senate, and if so, how it might be distinguished from the house. This repeated questioning of bicameralism at the state level, in contrast with the virtual absence of any such debate at the federal level, is due in large part to the greater opportunity to raise such questions as a result of the more flexible state amendment processes. However, it can also be attributed to differences in the structure of state and federal governments. In particular, local governments enjoy a different status in state governments than the states themselves enjoy in the federal government, thereby rendering unavailable to state constitution makers the most enduring basis for distinguishing the two chambers at the federal level and thus for justifying the need for a second chamber in the U.S. Congress. As a result, state constitution makers have engaged in periodic debates about the need for a second chamber, including during the Jacksonian Era, the Progressive Era, and the Reapportionment Revolution. Ultimately, bicameralism has survived in all but one state, albeit on a less firm footing and with a less compelling justification than at the federal level.

In terms of individual rights, the eighteenth-century framers of the federal Constitution and Bill of Rights gave little thought to securing positive rights, but nineteenth- and twentieth-century state constitution makers have had frequent occasion to reconsider this decision. The adoption of social, economic, and environmental rights provisions in many state constitutions can be explained in part by the fact that flexible amendment procedures permitted these issues to be reconsidered at a time when individuals were more conscious of and concerned about securing these rights. Additionally, when these issues have been raised in state conventions from the late nineteenth century to the present, state constitution makers have frequently deemed unpersuasive the reasons given by defenders of the federal model for excluding these rights from the constitutional corpus. In the view of many state constitution makers, it is no longer possible to consider social, economic, and environmental rights to be less fundamental than civil and political rights. Moreover, even if these rights cannot be judicially enforced in the same fashion as traditional rights, this does not exhaust the purposes that might be served by placing these rights in the constitution, such as inspiring legislators to secure their protection and expressing their importance in the people's fundamental charter.

In regard to the formation of citizen character, although delegates to the federal convention declined to enact any constitutional provisions on the subject, state constitution makers have frequently concluded that government should take an active role in shaping citizen character and that this role should be constitutionalized. In adopting constitutional provisions of this sort—whether in regard to support for religious institutions, compulsory education, prohibition of lotteries, and regulation of liquor—state constitution makers might be said to be have fulfilled, rather than departed from, the expectations of their federal counterparts, insofar as some of the founders likely counted on the states to perform such a role. In another sense, though, the absence of such provisions in the federal constitution has at times been interpreted by scholars in a quite different manner: as demonstrating that character formation should not be the concern of a republican polity, and certainly not a concern of constitution makers in such a polity. This position has often been rejected by state constitution makers, who have concluded that it is necessary and proper for government to superintend the character of the people, whether for the welfare of the citizenry, the maintenance of the social order, or the upholding of certain standards of behavior on the part of the state itself. Moreover, state constitution makers have determined that such provisions deserve to be placed in the constitution, whether out of a desire to remove the regulation of certain matters from legislators who cannot be trusted to handle them in a responsible fashion, or to demonstrate to the people the importance of certain virtues and thereby guide them in their attainment of these virtues.

An analysis of the state convention debates on each of these issues can help to explain the distinctive aspects of state constitutional development; it can also contribute to a better understanding of the American constitutional tradition as a whole. The general scholarly tendency has been to view the federal constitution as representing the entirety of the American constitutional tradition, or at least as offering the best expression of that tradition. In light of the analysis of state convention debates in this book, it would be important to modify this received wisdom. As we have seen, the stability of the federal constitution in regard to certain governing principles and institutions turns out not to be attributable to the fact that these principles and institutions represent the considered judgment of American constitution makers on these issues. Rather, such stability at the federal level is due in many respects to the rigidity of the federal amendment process, which has prevented the federal constitution from reflecting many institutional innovations that were considered at both the state and federal levels and widely adopted by state constitution makers; therefore, these state institutions are entitled to be considered as expressing the evolving understanding of the American constitutional tradition through the years. The implication is that if the federal amendment process had only been more flexible, many of these innovations would likely have been adopted at the federal level as well. Consequently, the federal constitution ought properly be viewed as representing only one part of the American constitutional tradition, and, in some cases, as not necessarily the best expression of the accumulated wisdom and experience of American constitution makers.

Thus in one case—bicameralism—the American constitutional tradition should be understood as encompassing two different approaches that can each lay claim to representing one strand of the American constitutional tradition. In this instance, the state and federal traditions have diverged primarily because of the different situations in which the respective constitution makers found themselves. Therefore, the American constitutional tradition ought to be seen in this case as making equal room for both approaches: the unchallenged commitment to bicameralism at the federal level, and the continuing questioning of the wisdom and purpose of bicameralism at the state level.

In another case—the formation of citizen character—the state approach is best understood as complementing the federal approach, and therefore as representing one important component of the American constitutional tradition. Although there are various ways to interpret the silence of federal constitution makers on the issue of character formation, one conclusion that clearly cannot be drawn from the absence of such provisions in the federal constitution is that the American constitutional tradition has therefore rejected a constitutional commitment to character formation. In fact, once we take account of the state approach in this area, it becomes clear that constitution makers in the American regime have been intimately concerned with character formation, albeit at the state rather than federal level.

In each of the other cases—concerning amendment and revision, representation, separation of powers, and individual rights—the American constitutional tradition is best understood as encompassing two different approaches, with the state approach offering the more authentic expression of the considered judgment of American constitution makers. In these cases, the greater flexibility of state constitutions permitted more frequent opportunities to reconsider the logic and consequences of various institutional arrangements during the past two centuries, and the approach followed by state constitution makers is entitled to be viewed as the better expression of the accumulated wisdom and experience of American constitution makers. This is the case, for instance, in regard to the design of amendment and revision procedures, where states have invariably provided for more flexible processes, and where federal proposals were introduced, but never enacted, to create similarly flexible processes. This judgment also applies to the concept of representation, where states have generally adopted various direct democratic institutions, and where such proposals were introduced at the federal level for similar reasons, but were unsuccessful due to the rigidity of the federal amendment process. A similar conclusion can be drawn in regard to the separation of powers system, especially the adoption at the state level of the item veto power and, to some extent, the various restrictions on judicial review. Similar proposals to change the executive and judicial veto powers were, again, considered at the federal level but failed to overcome the barriers that the federal amendment process has placed in the way of constitutional changes. Finally, this conclusion is applicable to the constitutionalization of social, economic, and environmental rights. When these rights came to prominence in the late nineteenth and twentieth centuries, the flexibility of state amendment processes permitted a full debate on their legitimacy and often led to their adoption. Parallel proposals were introduced and occasionally debated at the federal level during this period, but they were unable to survive the rigid federal amendment process.

Ultimately, this study of state convention debates has implications not only for scholars who seek a comprehensive understanding of the American constitutional tradition, but also for constitution makers who seek to draw lessons from the American experience as they go about designing institutions for emerging democracies. To the extent that constitution makers in other countries might seek to benefit from the American experience—and it must be admitted that in the contemporary era the American experience is often less sought after than the experiences of various other countries—it would be important to consider the logic of both the federal and state approaches. To be sure, a complete evaluation of these approaches would require a comprehensive assessment of the consequences of adopting the respective institutional arrangements at the state and federal level, and this would demand an analysis that goes beyond the current study. Nevertheless, as constitution makers in emerging democracies consider the merits of various institutions of governance, and as they look to the United States for guidance, they would do well to examine the arguments in the extant state convention debates that illuminate the origin and development of the distinctive institutions that have been adopted in the American states. The arguments in *Madison's Notes, Elliot's Debates,* and *The Federalist* certainly deserve the continued attention of constitution makers in other countries, and these sources will continue to illuminate the logic of the federal approach to various institutions of governance. However, the state convention debates throughout American history ought to at least be placed alongside, and in many cases should take precedence over, these classic eighteenth-century federal sources, so that officials charged with framing new constitutions in the twenty-first century might best appreciate the accumulated wisdom and experience of the American constitutional tradition.

Appendix

Extant State Convention Debate Records

Alabama: *The History and Debates of the Convention of the People of Alabama [1861]*, by William R. Smith (Montgomery: White, Pfister, 1861); *Official Proceedings of the Constitutional Convention of the State of Alabama [1901]*, 4 vols. (Wetumpka: Wetumpka Printing, 1940).

Alaska: *Minutes of the Daily Proceedings, Alaska Constitutional Convention, 1955–56*, 6 vols. (Juneau: Alaska Legislative Council, 1965).

Arizona: *The Records of the Arizona Constitutional Convention of 1910*, ed. John S. Goff (Phoenix: Supreme Court of Arizona, 1991).

Arkansas: *Debates and Proceedings of the Convention Which Assembled at Little Rock [1868] . . . to Form a Constitution for the State of Arkansas* (Little Rock: J. G. Price, 1868).

California: *Report of the Debates in the Convention of California on the Formation of the State Constitution [1849]*, by J. Ross Browne (Washington, D.C.: J. T. Towers, 1850); *Debates and Proceedings of the Constitutional Convention of the State of California [1878]*, E. B. Willis and P. K. Stockton, Official Stenographers, 3 vols. (Sacramento: J. D. Young, 1880–1881).

Connecticut: Wesley W. Horton, "Annotated Debates of the 1818 Constitutional Convention," *Connecticut Bar Journal* 65 (January 1991): 1–104; *The Third Constitutional Convention of the State of Connecticut: Proceedings [1965]*, 3 vols. (Hartford: Connecticut State Library, 1966).

Delaware: *Debates of the Delaware Convention, for Revising the Constitution [1831]* (Wilmington: Samuel Harker, 1831); *Debates and Proceedings of the Constitutional Convention of the State of Delaware [1852–1853]* (Dover: G. W. S. Nicholson, Printer and Publisher, 1853); *Debates and Proceedings of the Constitutional Convention of the State of Delaware [1896]*, reported by Charles G. Guyer and Edmond C. Hardesty, 5 vols. (Milford: Milford Chronicle Publishing Company, 1958).

Georgia: *A Stenographic Report of the Proceedings of the Constitutional Convention held in Atlanta, Georgia, 1877* (Atlanta: Constitution Publishing, 1877).

Hawaii: *Proceedings of the Constitutional Convention of Hawaii, 1950*, vol. 2 (Honolulu: State of Hawaii, 1961); *Proceedings of the Constitutional Convention of Hawaii of 1968*, vol. 2 (Honolulu: State of Hawaii, 1972); *Proceedings of the Constitutional Convention of Hawaii, 1978*, vol. 2 (Honolulu: State of Hawaii, 1980).

Idaho: *Proceedings and Debates of the Constitutional Convention of Idaho, 1889,* ed. I. W. Hart, 2 vols. (Caldwell: Caxton Printers, 1912).

Illinois: *The [Illinois] Constitutional Debates of 1847,* ed. Arthur Charles Cole (Springfield: Illinois State Historical Society Library, 1919); *Debates and Proceedings of the Constitutional Convention of the State of Illinois [1869],* Ely, Burnham, & Bartlett, Official Stenographers, 2 vols. (Springfield: E. L. Merritt & Brother, 1870); *Proceedings of the Constitutional Convention of the State of Illinois, Convened January 6, 1920,* 5 vols. (Springfield: Illinois State Journal, 1920–1922); *Record of Proceedings: Sixth Illinois Constitutional Convention [1969]: Verbatim Transcripts,* vols. 2–5 (Springfield: John W. Lewis, 1972).

Indiana: *Report of the Debates and Proceedings of the Convention for the Revision of the Constitution of the State of Indiana, 1850,* H. Fowler, Official Reporter, 2 vols. (Indianapolis: A. H. Brown, 1850).

Iowa: *Fragments of the Debates of the Iowa Constitutional Conventions of 1844 and 1846,* comp. and ed. by Benjamin F. Shambaugh (Iowa City: State Historical Society of Iowa, 1900); *The Debates of the Constitutional Convention of the State of Iowa [1857],* W. Blair Lord, Reporter, 2 vols. (Davenport: Luse, Lane, 1857).

Kansas: *A Reprint of the Proceedings and Debates of the Convention Which Framed the Constitution of Kansas at Wyandotte in July, 1859* (Topeka: Kansas State Printing Plant, 1920).

Kentucky: *Report of the Debates and Proceedings of the Convention for the Revision of the Constitution of the State of Kentucky, 1849,* R. Sutton, Official Reporter to the Convention (Frankfort: A. G. Hodges, 1850); *Official Report of the Proceedings and Debates in the Convention . . . of September, 1890, To Adopt, Amend or Change the Constitution of the State of Kentucky,* 4 vols. (Frankfort: E. Polk Johnson, 1890).

Louisiana: *Proceedings and Debates of the Convention of Louisiana [1845]* (New Orleans: Besancon, Ferguson, 1845); *Debates in the Convention for the Revision and Amendment of the Constitution of the State of Louisiana [1864],* Albert O. Bennett, Official Reporter (New Orleans: W. R. Fish, 1864); *Records of the Louisiana Constitutional Convention of 1973: Convention Transcripts,* vols. 5–9 (Louisiana Constitutional Convention Records Commission, 1977).

Maine: *The Debates and Journal of the Constitutional Convention of the State of Maine, 1819–20* (Augusta: Maine Farmers' Almanac Press, 1894).

Maryland: *Debates and Proceedings of the Maryland Reform Convention to Revise the State Constitution [1851],* 2 vols. (Annapolis: W. M'Neir, 1851); *The Debates of the Constitutional Convention of the State of Maryland [1864],* Wm. Blair Lord, Reporter, 3 vols. (Annapolis: Richard P. Bayly, 1864); *Debates of the Maryland Constitutional Convention of 1867* (as reprinted from articles reported in The Baltimore Sun), comp. by Philip B. Perlman (Baltimore: Hepbron and Haydon Publishers, 1923); *Debates of the [Maryland] Constitutional Convention of 1967–1968* (Annapolis: Hall of Records Commission, 1982).

Massachusetts: *Journal of Debates and Proceedings in the Convention of Delegates, Chosen to Revise the Constitution of Massachusetts [1820–21],* reported for the Boston Daily Advertiser (Boston: Daily Advertiser, 1853); *Official Report of the Debates and Proceedings in the State Convention to Revise and Amend the Constitution of the Commonwealth of Massachusetts [1853],* 3 vols. (Boston: White & Potter, 1853); *Debates in the Massachusetts Constitutional Convention, 1917–1918,* 3 vols. (Boston: Wright and Potter, 1919).

Michigan: *The Michigan Constitutional Conventions of 1835–36: Debates and Proceedings,* ed. Harold M. Dorr (Ann Arbor: University of Michigan Press, 1940); *Report of the Proceedings and Debates in the Convention to Revise the Constitution of the State of Michigan, 1850* (Lansing: R. W. Ingals, 1850); *The Debates and Proceedings of the Constitutional Convention of the State of Michigan [1867],* Official Report by Wm. Blair Lord and David Wolfe Brown, 2 vols. (Lansing: John A. Kerr, Printers to the State, 1867); *Proceedings and Debates of the Constitutional Convention of the State of Michigan [1907],* Official Report by Joseph H. Brewer, Chas. H. Bender, and Chas. H. McGurrin, 2 vols. (Lansing: Wynkoop, Hallenbeck, Crawford Co., State Printers, 1908); *Official Record, State of Michigan Constitutional Convention, 1961,* 2 vols. (Lansing, 1964).

Minnesota: *The Debates and Proceedings of the Minnesota Constitutional Convention [1857],* reported officially by Francis H. Smith (St. Paul: Earle S. Goodrich, Territorial Printers, 1857); *Debates and Proceedings of the Constitutional Convention for the Territory of Minnesota [1857],* T. F. Andrews, Official Reporter to the Convention (St. Paul: George W. Moore, Printer, 1858).

Mississippi: *Journal of the Proceedings and Debates in the Constitutional Convention of the State of Mississippi, August, 1865* (Jackson: E. M. Yerger, State Printer, 1865).

Missouri: *Journal and Proceedings of the Missouri State Convention, Held at Jefferson City and St. Louis, March, 1861* (St. Louis: George Knapp, 1861); *Proceedings of the Missouri State Convention, Held at Jefferson City, July 1861* (St. Louis: George Knapp, 1861); *Proceedings of the Missouri State Convention, Held at the City of St. Louis, October, 1861* (St. Louis: George Knapp, 1861); *Proceedings of the Missouri State Convention, Held in Jefferson City, June, 1862* (St. Louis: George Knapp, 1862); *Proceedings of the Missouri State Convention, Held in Jefferson City, June, 1863* (St. Louis: George Knapp, 1863); *Debates of the Missouri Constitutional Convention of 1875,* eds. Isidor Loeb and Floyd C. Shoemaker, 12 vols. (Columbia: The State Historical Society of Missouri, 1930–1944).

Montana: *Proceedings and Debates of the Constitutional Convention Held in the City of Helena, Montana [1889]* (Helena: State Publishing, 1921); *Montana Constitutional Convention, 1971–1972: Verbatim Transcript,* vols. 3–7 (Helena: Montana Legislature, 1981).

Nebraska: *Official Report of the Debates and Proceedings in the Nebraska Constitutional Convention [1871],* revised, edited, and indexed for publication by

Addison E. Sheldon, 3 vols. (York: T. E. Sedgwick, 1906–1913); *Journal of the Nebraska Constitutional Convention [1919],* 2 vols. (Lincoln: Kline Publishing, 1921).

Nevada: *Official Report of the Debates and Proceedings in the Constitutional Convention of the State of Nevada [1864],* Andrew J. Marsh, Official Reporter (San Francisco: Frank Eastman, Printer, 1866).

New Hampshire: *Journal of the Constitutional Convention of the State of New Hampshire, December 1876* (Concord: Edward A. Jenks, 1877); *Journal of the Constitutional Convention of the State of New Hampshire, January 1889* (Manchester: John B. Clarke, 1889); *Journal of the [New Hampshire] Constitutional Convention of 1902* (Concord: Rumford Press, 1903); *Journal of the Convention to Revise the [New Hampshire] Constitution, June 1912* (Manchester: John B. Clarke, 1912); *Journal of the Convention to Revise the [New Hampshire] Constitution, June, 1918* (Manchester: John B. Clarke, 1918); *Journal of the Convention to Revise the [New Hampshire] Constitution, January 20, 1920* (Manchester: John B. Clarke, 1920); *Journal of the Convention to Revise the [New Hampshire] Constitution, February, 1923* (Concord: Evans Printing, 1923); *Journal of the Convention to Revise the [New Hampshire] Constitution, June, 1930* (Manchester: Granite State Press, 1930); *Journal of the Convention to Revise the [New Hampshire] Constitution, May, 1938* (Manchester: Granite State Press, 1938); *Journal of the Convention to Revise the [New Hampshire] Constitution, September, 1941* (Manchester: Granite State Press, 1941); *Journal of the Convention to Revise the [New Hampshire] Constitution, May 1948* (Manchester: Granite State Press, 1948); *Journal of the Convention to Revise the [New Hampshire] Constitution, May 1956* (Manchester: Granite State Press, 1956); *Journal of the Convention to Revise the [New Hampshire] Constitution, December 1959* (Peterborough: Transcript Printing Company, 1959); *Journal of the Convention to Revise the [New Hampshire] Constitution, May 1964* (Concord: Evans Printing, 1964); *Journal of the Convention to Revise the [New Hampshire] Constitution, May 1974* (Concord: Evans Printing, 1974); *Journal of the Convention to Revise the [New Hampshire] Constitution, May 1984* (Concord, 1984).

New Jersey: *Proceedings of the New Jersey State Constitutional Convention of 1844,* comp. and ed., New Jersey Writers' Project of the Work Projects Administration (Trenton: New Jersey State Historical Society, 1942); *[New Jersey] Constitutional Convention of 1947,* vol. 1 (Bayonne: Jersey Printing, 1949).

New York: *Report of the Debates and Proceedings of the Convention of the State of New York [1821],* by L. H. Clarke (New York: J. Seymour, 1821); *Reports of the Proceedings and Debates of the [New York] Convention of 1821,* by Nathaniel H. Carter and William L. Stone, Reporters (Albany: E. and E. Hosford, 1821); *Report of the Debates and Proceedings of the Convention for the Revision of the Constitution of the State of New York, 1846,* reported by William G. Bishop and William H. Attree (Albany: Office of the Evening Atlas, 1846); *Debates and Proceedings in the New York State Convention, for the Revision of the Constitution*

[1846], by S. Croswell and R. Sutton, reporters for the Argus (Albany: Office of the Albany Argus, 1846); *Proceedings and Debates of the Constitutional Convention of the State of New York Held in 1867 and 1868*, reported by Edward F. Underhill, 5 vols. (Albany: Weed, Parsons and Company, 1868); *Revised Record of the Constitutional Convention of the State of New York [1894]*, 5 vols. (Albany: Argus Company, 1900); *Revised Record of the Constitutional Convention of the State of New York [1915]*, 4 vols. (Albany: J. B. Lyon Company, 1916); *Revised Record of the Constitutional Convention of the State of New York [1938]*, 4 vols. (Albany: J. B. Lyon, Company, 1938); *Proceedings of the Constitutional Convention of the State of New York [1967]*, vols. 2–4 (Albany: New York State Constitutional Convention, 1967).

North Carolina: *Proceedings and Debates of the Convention of North Carolina [1835]* (Raleigh: Joseph Gales and Son, 1836).

North Dakota: *Official Report of the Proceedings and Debates of the First Constitutional Convention of North Dakota [1889]*, R. M. Tuttle, Official Stenographer (Bismarck: Tribune, State Printers and Binders, 1889); *Debates of the North Dakota Constitutional Convention of 1972*, ed. Dean F. Bard, 2 vols. (Bismarck: Quality Printing Service, 1972).

Ohio: *Report of the Debates and Proceedings of the Convention for the Revision of the Constitution of the State of Ohio, 1850–51*, J. V. Smith, Official Reporter to the Convention, 2 vols. (Columbus: S. Medary, 1851); *Official Report of the Proceedings and Debates of the Third Constitutional Convention of Ohio [1873]*, 2 vols. (Cleveland: W. S. Robison, 1873–1874); *Proceedings and Debates of the Constitutional Convention of the State of Ohio [1912]*, 2 vols. (Columbus: F. J. Heer Printing, 1912).

Oregon: *The Oregon Constitution and Proceedings and Debates of the Oregon Convention of 1857*, ed. Charles H. Carey (Salem: State Printing Department, 1926).

Pennsylvania: *Proceedings and Debates of the Convention of the Commonwealth of Pennsylvania [1837]*, reported by John Agg, 14 vols. (Harrisburg: Packer, Barrett, and Parke, 1837–1839); *Debates of the Convention to Amend the Constitution of Pennsylvania [1872–1873]*, 9 vols. (Harrisburg: Benjamin Singerly, 1873); *Debates of the Pennsylvania Constitutional Convention of 1967–1968*, 2 vols. (Harrisburg: Commonwealth of Pennsylvania, 1969).

Rhode Island: *Journal of the Convention Assembled to Frame a Constitution for the State of Rhode Island [1842]* (Providence: Anthony, State Printers, 1859); *Proceedings of the Limited Constitutional Convention of the State of Rhode Island [1944]* (Providence: Secretary of State, 1944); *Proceedings of the Limited Constitutional Convention of the State of Rhode Island [1951]* (Providence: Secretary of State, 1951); *Proceedings of the Limited Constitutional Convention of the State of Rhode Island [1955]* (Providence: Secretary of State, 1955); *Proceedings of the Limited Constitutional Convention of the State of Rhode Island [1958]* (Providence: Secretary of State, 1958); *State of Rhode Island*

and Providence Plantations: Constitutional Convention [1964–1969]: Report of Proceedings, 3 vols. (Providence, 1969); *The Proceedings of the Rhode Island Constitutional Convention of 1973*, comp. and ed. Patrick T. Conley (Providence: The Oxford Press, 1973).

South Carolina: *Proceedings of the Constitutional Convention of South Carolina [1868]*, 2 vols. (Charleston: Denny & Perry, 1868).

South Dakota: *Dakota Constitutional Convention [1885, 1889]*, ed. Doane Robinson, 2 vols. (Huron: Huronite Printing, 1907).

Tennessee: *Journal and Proceedings of the [Tennessee] Constitutional Convention [1953]* (Nashville: The Limited Constitutional Convention, State of Tennessee, 1954); *Journal and Transcript of the Proceedings of the [Tennessee] Constitutional Convention [1959]* (Nashville: Limited Constitutional Convention, State of Tennessee, 1959); *Journal and Proceedings of the [Tennessee] Limited Constitutional Convention [1965]* (Nashville: Limited State Constitutional Convention, State of Tennessee, 1965); *Journal and Debates of the [Tennessee] Limited Constitutional Convention of 1971* (Nashville: Limited State Constitutional Convention, State of Tennessee, 1971); *Journal and Proceedings of the Limited Constitutional Convention, State of Tennessee [1977]* (Nashville: Limited Constitutional Convention, State of Tennessee, 1977).

Texas: *Debates of the Texas Convention [1845]* (Houston: J. W. Cruger, 1846); *Debates in the Texas Constitutional Convention of 1875*, ed. and comp. Seth Shepard McKay (Austin: University of Texas, 1930); *Texas Constitutional Convention [1974]: Official Proceedings*, 2 vols. (Austin: Constitutional Convention of Texas, 1974).

Utah: *Official Report of the Proceedings and Debates of the Convention . . . to Adopt a Constitution for the State of Utah [1895]*, 2 vols. (Salt Lake City: Star Printing, 1898).

Virginia: *Proceedings and Debates of the Virginia State Convention of 1829–30* (Richmond: Samuel Shepherd & Co. for Ritchie & Cook, 1830); *Register of the Debates and Proceedings of the Va. Reform Convention [1850–1851]* (Richmond: R. H. Gallagher, 1851); *Proceedings of the Virginia State Convention of 1861*, ed. George H. Reese, 4 vols. (Richmond: Virginia State Library, 1965); *The Debates and Proceedings of the Constitutional Convention of the State of Virginia [1867–1868]*, vol. 1 (Richmond: Office of the New Nation, 1868); *Report of the Proceedings and Debates of the Constitutional Convention, State of Virginia [1901–1902]*, 2 vols. (Richmond: Hermitage Press, 1906); *Journal of the Constitutional Convention of the Commonwealth of Virginia to Amend the Constitution of Virginia for Voting by Certain Members of the Armed Forces . . . 1945* (Richmond: Commonwealth of Virginia, 1945); *Journal of the Constitutional Convention of the Commonwealth of Virginia to Revise and Amend Sec. 141 of the Constitution of Virginia . . . 1956* (Richmond: Commonwealth of Virginia, 1956).

West Virginia: *Debates and Proceedings of the First Constitutional Convention of West Virginia (1861–1863)*, ed. Charles H. Ambler, Frances Haney Atwood, and William B. Mathews, 3 vols. (Huntington: Gentry Brothers, Printers, 1939).

Wisconsin: *The [Wisconsin] Convention of 1846*, ed. Milo M. Quaife (Madison: State Historical Society of Wisconsin, 1919); *Journal of the Convention to Form a Constitution for the State of Wisconsin [1847–1848]* (Madison: W. T. Tenney, Smith, and Holt, Printers, 1848).

Wyoming: *Journal and Debates of the Constitutional Convention of the State of Wyoming [1889]* (Cheyenne: Daily Sun, 1893).

Notes

Introduction

1. For much of the nineteenth century, the leading study of state constitutional conventions was John A. Jameson, *A Treatise on Constitutional Conventions, Their History, Powers, and Modes of Proceeding*, 4th ed. (1887; reprint, New York: Da Capo Press, 1972), which was stimulated by the author's concern about an attempt in the Illinois Convention of 1862 to "set up for that body, in debate, a claim of inherent powers amounting almost to absolute sovereignty" (iii). Accordingly, Jameson set out "to inquire into the history, powers, and modes of proceeding of the constitutional convention," and to demonstrate that conventions did not possess unlimited powers (1). The leading twentieth-century study of state conventions is Albert L. Sturm, *Thirty Years of State Constitution-Making, 1938–1968* (New York: National Municipal League, 1970), which analyzed "the principal methods and techniques employed by the states in revising their constitutions" (v) and was explicitly "not concerned with substantive constitutional change and development" (vi). See also Albert L. Sturm, "The Development of American State Constitutions," *Publius* 12 (Winter 1982): 57–98. Other comprehensive studies of state conventions published in the twentieth century include Walter F. Dodd, *The Revision and Amendment of State Constitutions* (Baltimore: Johns Hopkins Press, 1910); Roger S. Hoar, *Constitutional Conventions: Their Nature, Powers, and Limitations* (Boston: Little, Brown, 1917); Elmer E. Cornwell Jr., Jay S. Goodman, and Wayne R. Swanson, *Constitutional Conventions: The Politics of Revision* (New York: National Municipal League, 1974); and Elmer E. Cornwell Jr., Jay S. Goodman, and Wayne R. Swanson, *State Constitutional Conventions: The Politics of the Revision Process in Seven States* (New York: Praeger, 1975).

2. Notable studies of particular conventions, in addition to the many articles and unpublished dissertations of this sort, include Ralph C. McDanel, *The Virginia Constitutional Convention of 1901–1902* (Baltimore: Johns Hopkins Press, 1928); Carl Brent Swisher, *Motivation and Technique in the California Constitutional Convention, 1878–1879* (1930; reprint, New York: Da Capo Press, 1969); Vernon A. O'Rourke and Douglas W. Campbell, *Constitution-Making in a Democracy: Theory and Practice in New York State* (Baltimore: Johns Hopkins Press, 1943); Richard N. Baisden, *Charter for New Jersey: The New Jersey Constitutional Convention of 1947* (Trenton: New Jersey Department of Education, 1952); Albert L. Sturm, *Constitution-Making in Michigan, 1961–1962* (Ann Arbor: Institute of Public Administration, University of Michigan, 1963); Elmer E. Cornwell Jr. and Jay S. Goodman, *The Politics of the Rhode Island Constitutional Convention* (New York: National Municipal League, 1969); George D. Wolf, *Constitutional Revision in Pennsylvania: The Dual Tactic of Amendment and Limited Convention* (New York: National Municipal League, 1969); Richard J. Connors, *The Process of Constitutional Revision in New Jersey, 1940–1947* (New York: National Municipal League, 1970); John P. Wheeler Jr. and Melissa Kinsey,

Magnificent Failure: The Maryland Constitutional Convention of 1967–1968 (New York: National Municipal League, 1970); Martin L. Faust, *Constitution Making in Missouri: The Convention of 1943–1944* (New York: National Municipal League, 1971); Norman Meller, *With an Understanding Heart: Constitution Making in Hawaii* (New York: National Municipal League, 1971); Donna E. Shalala, *The City and the Constitution: The 1967 New York Convention's Response to the Urban Crisis* (New York: National Municipal League, 1972); Walter H. Nunn and Kay G. Collett, *Political Paradox: Constitutional Revision in Arkansas* (New York: National Municipal League, 1973); Samuel K. Gove and Thomas R. Kitsos, *Revision Success: The Sixth Illinois Constitutional Convention* (New York: National Municipal League, 1974); Victor Fischer, *Alaska's Constitutional Convention* (Fairbanks: University of Alaska Press, 1975); Thomas Schick, *The New York State Constitutional Convention of 1915 and the Modern State Governor* (New York: National Municipal League, 1978); Elmer Gertz and Joseph P. Pisciotte, *Charter for a New Age: An Inside View of the Sixth Illinois Constitutional Convention* (Urbana: University of Illinois Press, 1980); Dennis C. Colson, *Idaho's Constitution: The Tie That Binds* (Moscow: University of Idaho Press, 1991); Henrik N. Dullea, *Charter Revision in the Empire State: The Politics of New York's 1967 Constitutional Convention* (Albany, N.Y.: Rockefeller Institute Press, 1997); and Ernest C. Reock Jr., *Unfinished Business: The New Jersey Constitutional Convention of 1966* (New Brunswick, N.J.: Center for Urban Policy Research Press, 2003).

3. Many studies have drawn on convention proceedings in tracing the broad sweep of constitutional development in particular states. In addition to the contributions to the projected fifty-volume series edited by G. Alan Tarr for Greenwood Press, other notable studies of the constitutional development of particular states include Charles Z. Lincoln, *The Constitutional History of New York,* 5 vols. (Rochester, N.Y.: Lawyers Co-operative Publishing, 1906); Charles Kettleborough, *Constitution Making in Indiana,* 2 vols. (Indianapolis: Indiana Historical Commission, 1916); Wallace McClure, *State Constitution-Making, with Especial Reference to Tennessee* (Nashville, Tenn.: Marshall and Bruce, 1916); William Anderson, *A History of the Constitution of Minnesota* (Minneapolis: University of Minnesota, 1921); Benjamin F. Shambaugh, *The Constitutions of Iowa* (Iowa City: State Historical Society of Iowa, 1934); Ethel K. Ware, *A Constitutional History of Georgia* (New York: Columbia University Press, 1947); Albert B. Saye, *A Constitutional History of Georgia, 1732–1945* (Athens: University of Georgia Press, 1948); Malcolm C. McMillan, *Constitutional Development in Alabama, 1789–1901: A Study in Politics, the Negro, and Sectionalism* (Chapel Hill: University of North Carolina Press, 1955); Rosalind L. Branning, *Pennsylvania Constitutional Development* (Pittsburgh: University of Pittsburgh Press, 1960); Janet Cornelius, *Constitution Making in Illinois, 1818–1970* (Urbana: University of Illinois Press, 1972); A. E. Dick Howard, *Commentaries on the Constitution of Virginia,* 2 vols. (Charlottesville: University Press of Virginia, 1974); Joan Wells Coward, *Kentucky in the New Republic: The Process of Constitution Making* (Lexington: University Press of Kentucky, 1979); Peter J. Galie, *Ordered Liberty: A Constitutional History of New York* (New York: Fordham University Press, 1996); Harvey Bernard Rubenstein, ed., *The Delaware Constitution of 1897: The First One Hundred Years* (Wilmington: Delaware State Bar Association, 1997); Bailey Thomson, ed., *A Century of Controversy: Constitutional Reform in Alabama* (Tuscaloosa: University of Alabama Press, 2002).

4. Studies that have drawn on convention proceedings in multiple states or in various regions include John D. Hicks, *The Constitutions of the Northwest States* (Lincoln: University Studies of the University of Nebraska, 1924); Gordon M. Bakken, *Rocky Mountain Constitu-*

tion Making, 1850–1912 (Westport, Conn.: Greenwood Press, 1987); Don E. Fehrenbacher, *Constitutions and Constitutionalism in the Slaveholding South* (Athens: University of Georgia Press, 1989), 1–32; David Alan Johnson, *Founding the Far West: California, Oregon, and Nevada, 1840–1890* (Berkeley: University of California Press, 1992); James T. McHugh, *Ex Uno Plura: State Constitutions and Their Political Cultures* (Albany: State University of New York Press, 2003).

5. Studies that have drawn on convention proceedings during particular eras include Francis N. Thorpe, *A Constitutional History of the American People, 1776–1850,* 2 vols. (New York: Harper & Brothers, 1898); Gordon S. Wood, *The Creation of the American Republic, 1776–1787* (Chapel Hill: University of North Carolina Press, 1969); Cecelia M. Kenyon, "Constitutionalism in Revolutionary America," in *Constitutionalism: Nomos XX,* ed. J. Roland Pennock and John W. Chapman (New York: New York University Press, 1979), 84–121; Willi Paul Adams, *The First American Constitutions: Republican Ideology and the Making of the State Constitutions in the Revolutionary Era* (Chapel Hill: University of North Carolina Press, 1980); Donald S. Lutz, *Popular Consent and Popular Control: Whig Political Theory in the Early State Constitutions* (Baton Rouge: Louisiana State University Press, 1980); Marc W. Kruman, *Between Authority and Liberty: State Constitution Making in Revolutionary America* (Chapel Hill: University of North Carolina Press, 1997); Fletcher M. Green, *Constitutional Development in the South Atlantic States, 1776–1860: A Study in the Evolution of Democracy* (Chapel Hill: University of North Carolina Press, 1930); Gregory Glen Schmidt, "Republican Visions: Constitutional Thought and Constitutional Revision in the Eastern United States, 1815–1830" (Ph.D. diss., University of Illinois, 1981); Merrill D. Peterson, ed., *Democracy, Liberty, and Property: The State Constitutional Conventions of the 1820s* (Indianapolis, Ind.: Bobbs-Merrill, 1966); Laura J. Scalia, "The Many Faces of Locke in America's Early Nineteenth-Century Democratic Philosophy," *Political Research Quarterly* 49 (December 1996): 807–835; Laura J. Scalia, *America's Jeffersonian Experiment: Remaking State Constitutions, 1820–1850* (DeKalb: Northern Illinois University Press, 1999); George Philip Parkinson Jr., "Antebellum State Constitution-Making: Retention, Circumvention, Revision" (Ph.D. diss, University of Wisconsin, 1972); Ralph A. Wooster, *The Secession Conventions of the South* (Princeton, N.J.: Princeton University Press, 1962); John Luther Bell Jr., "Constitutions and Politics: Constitutional Revision in the South Atlantic States, 1864–1902" (Ph.D. diss., University of North Carolina, 1969); Richard L. Hume, "The 'Black and Tan' Constitutional Conventions of 1867–1869 in Ten Former Confederate States: A Study of Their Membership" (Ph.D. diss. University of Washington, 1969); Michael Perman, *The Road to Redemption: Southern Politics, 1869–1879* (Chapel Hill: University of North Carolina Press, 1984); Michael Perman, *Struggle for Mastery: Disfranchisement in the South, 1888–1908* (Chapel Hill: University of North Carolina Press, 2001).

6. Studies that have drawn on convention proceedings regarding particular issues include Kirk H. Porter, *A History of Suffrage in the United States* (Chicago: University of Chicago Press, 1918); Robert J. Steinfeld, "Property and Suffrage in the Early American Republic," *Stanford Law Review* 41 (January 1989): 335–376; Jacob Katz Cogan, "The Look Within: Property, Capacity, and Suffrage in Nineteenth-Century America," *Yale Law Journal* 107 (November 1997): 473–498; Laura J. Scalia, "Who Deserves Political Influence? How Liberal Ideals Helped Justify Mid Nineteenth-Century Exclusionary Policies," *American Journal of Political Science* 42 (April 1998): 349–376; Alexander Keyssar, *The Right to Vote: The Contested History of Democracy in the United States* (New York: Basic Books, 2000); Kermit L. Hall, "The Judiciary on Trial: State Constitutional Reform and the Rise

of an Elected Judiciary, 1846–1860," *Historian* 45 (May 1983): 337–354; Caleb Nelson, "A Re-Evaluation of Scholarly Explanations for the Rise of the Elective Judiciary in Antebellum America," *American Journal of Legal History* 37 (April 1993): 190–224; Daniel T. Rodgers, *Contested Truths: Keywords in American Politics since Independence* (1987; reprint, Cambridge, Mass.: Harvard University Press, 1998); and John Dinan, "The Pardon Power and the American State Constitutional Tradition," *Polity* 35 (April 2003): 389–418.

7. This view of state conventions, it should be noted, has not always been the dominant view. At the end of the nineteenth century, Francis N. Thorpe set out to document "the evidence of changes—and, it is believed, of progress—which the American people have held respecting the principles, the organization, and the administration of their civil institutions." He noted that "the principal authorities upon which the evidence rests are the laws and constitutions of the country, and the journals, proceedings, and debates of constitutional conventions." Francis N. Thorpe, *Constitutional History*, 1:v, viii. Several decades later, Walter F. Dodd noted, "Through constitutional conventions, or the process of individual amendment, the American states are constantly reexamining and changing their political institutions. These changes relate chiefly to matters of detail, but in the development of state constitutions since 1776 many fundamental changes have taken place. The American state constitution is a human document; and the development of popular government and popular sentiment can to a large extent be traced in the changing character of state constitutional provisions." Walter F. Dodd, *State Government*, 2nd ed. (New York: The Century Co., 1928), 108. Around the same time, James Q. Dealey argued in regard to state constitutions more generally: "One might almost say that the romance, the poetry, and even the drama of American politics are deeply embedded in the many state constitutions promulgated since the publication of Paine's Common Sense, the Declaration of Independence, and the Virginia Bill of Rights," which convinced him that state constitutions would be "among our most valued records of social, political, and constitutional history." James Q. Dealey, *Growth of American State Constitutions from 1776 to the End of the Year 1914* (Boston: Ginn, 1915), 11–12, cited in G. Alan Tarr, ed., introduction to *Constitutional Politics in the States: Contemporary Controversies and Historical Patterns* (Westport, Conn.: Greenwood Press, 1996), xxi n10. Dealey noted, for instance, that during the Jacksonian Era, "interest in state constitutions had been aroused and debates in conventions in the discussion of constitutional points at times rivaled the writers of the *Federalist* in their clear enunciation of fundamental principles" (51). Moreover, James Schouler commented during this same period, in regard to state constitutional development more generally, that "the study of republican institutions is an exceedingly interesting one which these several commonwealths furnish," and "while the Federal constitution has yielded but little to structural reform for more than a hundred years, State instruments abound in improved ideas of government which deserve to be nationalized." James Schouler, *Constitutional Studies: State and Federal* (1897; reprint, New York: Da Capo Press, 1971), 305, 306.

Moreover, this view of state constitutional conventions does not command universal agreement even in the contemporary era. Several scholars have suggested in recent years that there is much to be learned from studying state convention debates. Michael Kammen has argued, for instance, that "another section of the submerged iceberg may be found in constitutionalism at the state level, notably in the many revisions that have been made in our state constitutions[,] in the conventions held for that purpose, and, once again, in the chimerical influence of ideas that were discussed extensively yet never implemented." Michael Kammen, *A Machine That Would Go of Itself: The Constitution in American Culture* (New

York: Alfred A. Knopf, 1986), 11. In addition, Daniel T. Rodgers has written, "Too many of our assumptions about the frame of American political argument have been shaped by the debates peculiar to national politics, at the expense of the sort of political talk that flourished closer to home—and nowhere so freely as in the state constitutional conventions of the nineteenth century" (*Contested Truths,* 255). Similarly, Daniel J. Elazar took note, in a more general sense, of the benefit of studying the political theory underlying state constitutions: "The tendency has been to assume either that the philosophic assumptions of the state constitutions are the same as those of the United States Constitution or that state constitutions are wordy patchworks of compromises having little, if any, rhyme or reason. Neither assumption is accurate, and even those constitutions which can be said to be a bundle of compromises reflect the political struggle between representatives of competing conceptions of government within particular states." Daniel J. Elazar, "The Principles and Traditions Underlying State Constitutions," *Publius* 12 (Winter 1982): 11. In a similar vein, Helen Hershkoff has written that "constitutional theorists are as unlikely to consider the Utah Constitution as they are the Swiss Constitution. This scholarly gap reflects an intellectual bias: the tendency to conflate questions of how a civil society can and should constitute itself with the more specific questions of how the Federal Constitution does and should resolve this problem." Helen Hershkoff, "Positive Rights and State Constitutions: The Limits of Federal Rationality Review," *Harvard Law Review* 112 (April 1999): 1131, 1195.

8. James Willard Hurst, *The Growth of American Law: The Law Makers* (Boston: Little, Brown, 1950), 224.

9. James A. Gardner, "What Is a State Constitution?" *Rutgers Law Journal* 24 (Summer 1993): 1025, 1025–1026. Gardner went on to say that the greater detail and frequency of amendment of state constitutions "undermine any sense of a state constitution as a deliberate, considered expression of fundamental values; moreover, to the extent that state constitutions can be said to reveal the character of the polity, the character so revealed is hardly the sober and reflective one contemplated by constitutionalism" (1027).

10. Morton Keller, "The Politics of State Constitutional Revision, 1820–1930," in *The Constitutional Convention as an Amending Device,* ed. Kermit L. Hall, Harold M. Hyman, and Leon V. Sigal (Washington, D.C.: American Historical Association and American Political Science Association, 1981), 69. At the same time, Keller, who viewed the Massachusetts Conventions of 1820–1821 and 1917–1919, the New York Conventions of 1821, 1846, and 1915, and the Virginia Convention of 1829–1830 as exceptions to this statement, also wrote in regard to state conventions that "surely few themes in the history of American government have been less adequately studied" (68).

11. Christian G. Fritz, "The American Constitutional Tradition Revisited: Preliminary Observations on State Constitution-Making in the Nineteenth-Century West," *Rutgers Law Journal* 25 (Summer 1994): 945, 952–953. Fritz has done as much as anyone to begin to remedy this situation and to draw attention to the way in which "the states' experience" might "prompt us to rethink a top-heavy (federal constitutional) view of American constitutional history and constitutionalism" (956), including in articles such as Christian G. Fritz, "Rethinking the American Constitutional Tradition: National Dimensions in the Formation of State Constitutions," *Rutgers Law Journal* 26 (Summer 1995): 969–992; Christian G. Fritz, "Alternative Visions of American Constitutionalism: Popular Sovereignty and the Early American Constitutional Debate," *Hastings Constitutional Law Quarterly* 24 (Winter 1997): 287–357; Marsha L. Baum and Christian G. Fritz, "American Constitution-Making: The Neglected State Constitutional Sources," *Hastings Constitutional Law Quarterly* 27

(Winter 2000): 199–242; and Christian G. Fritz, "Fallacies of American Constitutionalism," *Rutgers Law Journal* 35 (Summer 2004): 1327–1369.

12. The literature on this phenomenon of independent state court interpretation of state bills of rights is voluminous. For present purposes, it will be sufficient to take note of several of the leading works. State supreme court judges such as Hans A. Linde of Oregon pioneered this movement and have discussed these efforts in articles such as Hans A. Linde, "First Things First: Rediscovering the State's Bill of Rights," *University of Baltimore Law Review* 9 (Spring 1980): 379–396. U.S. Supreme Court Justice William J. Brennan Jr. took note of this movement and gave it a significant boost with the publication of his article, "State Constitutions and the Protection of Individual Rights," *Harvard Law Review* 90 (January 1977): 489–504.

Meanwhile, legal scholars have analyzed these developments in a variety of articles, including A. E. Dick Howard, "State Courts and Constitutional Rights in the Day of the Burger Court," *Virginia Law Review* 62 (June 1976): 873–944; Robert F. Williams, "In the Supreme Court's Shadow: Legitimacy of State Court Rejection of Supreme Court Reasoning and Result," *South Carolina Law Review* 35 (Spring 1984): 353–404; James A. Gardner, "The Failed Discourse of State Constitutionalism," *Michigan Law Review* 90 (February 1992): 761–837; Paul W. Kahn, "Interpretation and Authority in State Constitutionalism," *Harvard Law Review* 106 (March 1993): 1147–1168; and Robert A. Schapiro, "Identity and Interpretation in State Constitutional Law," *Virginia Law Review* 84 (April 1998): 389–457. For a comprehensive treatment, which also examines a wide range of issues other than judicial protection of individual rights, see Robert F. Williams, *State Constitutional Law: Cases and Materials,* 3rd ed. (Charlottesville, Va.: Lexis Law Publishing, 1999).

Finally, in *Understanding State Constitutions* (Princeton, N.J.: Princeton University Press, 1998), G. Alan Tarr, although he ultimately concludes by providing guidance for judicial interpretation of state constitutions, has done more than anyone, both in this book and in his other writings, to call attention to the ways in which political scientists and constitutional historians might profit from studying state constitutions other than by focusing on the manner in which state bills of rights are interpreted by state courts. Scholars in these fields are in his debt for his wide-ranging and illuminating work in this regard.

13. It is worth noting that American state constitutions at one time attracted a great deal of interest from constitution makers in other countries. As George Athan Billias has written, although by the mid-nineteenth century "the Federal Constitution increasingly became the model that foreign countries looked to," "the influence of the first state constitutions in Europe had been truly remarkable during the early years of the republic." George Athan Billias, "American Constitutionalism and Europe, 1776–1848," in *American Constitutionalism Abroad: Selected Essays in Comparative Constitutional History,* ed. George Athan Billias (Westport, Conn.: Greenwood Press, 1990), 23. The influence of the early state constitutions was felt not only in France, where these documents were widely circulated, but also to varying degrees in Belgium, the Netherlands, Norway, Greece, and Russia. See Billias, "American Constitutionalism and Europe," 19–23; Robert R. Palmer, *The Age of the Democratic Revolution: A Political History of Europe and America,* 2 vols. (Princeton, N.J.: Princeton University Press, 1959–1964), 1:263–282; and Robert R. Palmer, "The Impact of the American Revolution Abroad," in *The Impact of the American Revolution Abroad,* Library of Congress Symposia on the American Revolution (Washington, D.C.: Library of Congress, 1976), 12–15.

14. Comprehensive analyses of state convention debates regarding suffrage requirements are found in Porter, *History of Suffrage;* and Keyssar, *Right to Vote.* The debates over suffrage distinctions based on property, wealth, and race in early nineteenth-century state conventions are analyzed in Peterson, *Democracy, Liberty, and Property;* Steinfeld, "Property and Suffrage"; Cogan, "Look Within"; and Scalia, "Who Deserves Political Influence?" Additionally, Perman, *Struggle for Mastery,* draws on several southern state convention debates in explaining the turn-of-the-twentieth-century adoption of provisions that disenfranchised many African Americans.

15. For representative studies, see the contributions to Paul Finkelman and Stephen E. Gottlieb, eds., *Toward a Usable Past: Liberty under State Constitutions* (Athens: University of Georgia Press, 1991); and John J. Dinan, *Keeping the People's Liberties: Legislators, Citizens, and Judges as Guardians of Rights* (Lawrence: University Press of Kansas, 1998).

16. The leading study is Howard Lee McBain, *The Law and the Practice of Municipal Home Rule* (New York: Columbia University Press, 1916).

17. The principal effort to identify patterns within the state constitutional tradition is Elazar, "Principles and Traditions."

18. Various studies of this sort have been conducted in regard to particular state conventions, and many of these analyses have followed in the tradition of Swisher, *Motivation and Technique.*

Chapter 1: State Constitutional Conventions

1. In sketching the basic features of state conventions in this chapter, I have benefited from various studies that have examined the broad sweep of state constitutional development, including Francis N. Thorpe, *A Constitutional History of the American People, 1776–1850,* 2 vols. (New York: Harper & Brothers, 1898); James Q. Dealey, *Growth of American State Constitutions from 1776 to the End of the Year 1914* (Boston: Ginn, 1915); Sister M. Barbara McCarthy, *The Widening Scope of American Constitutions* (Washington, D.C.: Catholic University of America, 1928); Albert L. Sturm, *Thirty Years of State Constitution-Making, 1938–1968* (New York: National Municipal League, 1970); Morton Keller, "The Politics of State Constitutional Revision, 1820–1930," in *The Constitutional Convention as an Amending Device,* eds. Kermit L. Hall, Harold M. Hyman, and Leon V. Sigal (Washington, D.C.: American Historical Association and American Political Science Association, 1981); Daniel J. Elazar, "The Principles and Traditions Underlying State Constitutions," *Publius* 12 (Winter 1982): 11–25; Albert L. Sturm, "The Development of American State Constitutions," *Publius* 12 (Winter 1982): 57–98; John Kincaid, "State Constitutions in the Federal System," *Annals of the American Academy of Political and Social Science* 496 (March 1988): 12–22; Lawrence M. Friedman, "State Constitutions in Historical Perspective," *Annals of the American Academy of Political and Social Science* 496 (March 1988): 33–42; Kermit L. Hall, "Mostly Anchor and Little Sail: The Evolution of American State Constitutions," in *Toward a Useable Past: Liberty under State Constitutions,* ed. Paul Finkelman and Stephen E. Gottlieb (Athens: University of Georgia Press, 1991), 388–417; and G. Alan Tarr, *Understanding State Constitutions* (Princeton, N.J.: Princeton University Press, 1998). Although many of these studies have concentrated on the various formal mechanisms through which constitutional change has taken place in the states, Michael Besso has properly called attention to the ways in which state constitutional development has also taken place through informal

constitutional construction. Michael Besso, "Constitutional Amendment Procedures and the Informal Political Construction of Constitutions," *Journal of Politics* 67 (February 2005): 69–87.

2. These conventions are discussed in William C. Morey, "The First State Constitutions," *Annals of the American Academy of Political and Social Science* 4 (September 1893): 201–232; William C. Webster, "Comparative Study of the State Constitutions of the American Revolution," *Annals of the American Academy of Political and Social Science* 9 (May 1897): 380–420; Thorpe, *Constitutional History*, 1:29–132; Walter F. Dodd, *The Revision and Amendment of State Constitutions* (Baltimore: Johns Hopkins Press, 1910), 1–29; Dealey, *Growth of American State Constitutions*, 24–39; Allan Nevins, *The American States during and after the Revolution, 1775–1789* (New York: Macmillan, 1924), 117–205; Willi Paul Adams, *The First American Constitutions: Republican Ideology and the Making of the State Constitutions in the Revolutionary Era* (Chapel Hill: University of North Carolina Press, 1980); Donald S. Lutz, *Popular Consent and Popular Control: Whig Political Theory in the Early State Constitutions* (Baton Rouge: Louisiana State University Press, 1980); Sturm, "Development of American State Constitutions," 60–63; Gordon S. Wood, "Foreword: State Constitution-Making in the American Revolution," *Rutgers Law Journal* 24 (Summer 1993): 911–926; Robert F. Williams, "The State Constitutions of the Founding Decade: Pennsylvania's Radical 1776 Constitution and Its Influences on American Constitutionalism," *Temple Law Review* 62 (Summer 1989): 541–585; Marc W. Kruman, *Between Authority and Liberty: State Constitution Making in Revolutionary America* (Chapel Hill: University of North Carolina Press, 1997); and Tarr, *Understanding State Constitutions*, 60–93.

3. On these conventions, see Thorpe, *Constitutional History*, 1:240–486, 2:1–501; Dealey, *Growth of American State Constitutions*, 47–55; George Philip Parkinson Jr., "Antebellum State Constitution-Making: Retention, Circumvention, Revision" (Ph.D. diss., University of Wisconsin, 1972); Sturm, "Development of American State Constitutions," 63–66; and Laura J. Scalia, *America's Jeffersonian Experiment: Remaking State Constitutions, 1820–1850* (DeKalb: Northern Illinois University Press, 1999).

4. For discussions of southern constitution making during this period, see Dealey, *Growth of American State Constitutions*, 56–79; Ralph A. Wooster, *The Secession Conventions of the South* (Princeton, N.J.: Princeton University Press, 1962); Richard L. Hume, "The 'Black and Tan' Constitutional Conventions of 1867–1869 in Ten Former Confederate States: A Study of Their Membership" (Ph.D. diss., University of Washington, 1969); Michael Perman, *The Road to Redemption: Southern Politics, 1869–1879* (Chapel Hill: University of North Carolina Press, 1984); Michael Les Benedict, "The Problem of Constitutionalism and Constitutional Liberty in the Reconstruction South," in *An Uncertain Tradition: Constitutionalism and the History of the South*, ed. Kermit L. Hall and James W. Ely Jr. (Athens: University of Georgia Press, 1989), 225–249; Donald E. Fehrenbacher, *Constitutions and Constitutionalism in the Slaveholding South* (Athens: University of Georgia Press, 1989), 1–32; and Tarr, *Understanding State Constitutions*, 130–132.

5. On this era of constitution making, see Dealey, *Growth of American State Constitutions*, 89–113; Sturm, "Development of American State Constitutions," 68–71; Francis N. Thorpe, "Recent Constitution Making in the United States," *Annals of the American Academy of Political and Social Science* 2 (September 1891): 145–201; Amasa M. Eaton, "Recent State Constitutions," *Harvard Law Review* 6 (25 May and 15 October 1892): 53–72, 109–124; John D. Hicks, *The Constitutions of the Northwest States* (Lincoln: University Studies of the University of Nebraska, 1924); J. Morgan Kousser, *The Shaping of Southern Politics:*

Suffrage Restriction and the Establishment of the One-Party South, 1880–1910 (New Haven, Conn.: Yale University Press, 1974), 139–181; Tarr, *Understanding State Constitutions,* 60–93; John Dinan, "Framing a 'People's Government': State Constitution-Making in the Progressive Era," *Rutgers Law Journal* 30 (Summer 1999): 933–985; Michael Perman, *Struggle for Mastery: Disfranchisement in the South, 1888–1908* (Chapel Hill: University of North Carolina Press, 2001).

6. This period of constitutional revision is discussed in Sturm, "Development of American State Constitutions," 71–74; Hall, "Mostly Anchor and Little Sail," 407–410; Tarr, *Understanding State Constitutions,* 153–157.

7. On the growing reliance on other mechanisms to bring about constitutional change during this period, see Thomas Gais and Gerald Benjamin, "Public Discontent and the Decline of Deliberation: A Dilemma in State Constitutional Reform," *Temple Law Review* 68 (Fall 1995): 1291–1315; Robert F. Williams, "Are State Constitutional Conventions Things of the Past? The Increasing Role of the Constitutional Commission in State Constitutional Change," *Hofstra Law and Policy Symposium* 1 (1996): 1–26; Janice C. May, "Trends in State Constitutional Amendment and Revision," in *The Book of the States, 2003 Edition,* vol. 35 (Lexington, Ky.: Council of State Governments, 2003), 3–9.

8. States holding limited conventions during this period include Louisiana (1973–1974), Rhode Island (1973), Tennessee (1971 and 1977), and Texas (1974).

9. Alaska, Arizona, Colorado, Idaho, Maine, Minnesota, Oklahoma, Oregon, Utah, and Wyoming.

10. William C. Hill, *The Vermont State Constitution: A Reference Guide* (Westport, Conn.: Greenwood Press, 1992), 12–18.

11. Lewis L. Laska, *The Tennessee State Constitution: A Reference Guide* (Westport, Conn.: Greenwood Press, 1990), 19.

12. Susan E. Marshall, *The New Hampshire State Constitution: A Reference Guide* (Westport, Conn.: Praeger, 2004), 17–18.

13. Elazar, "Principles and Traditions," 21.

14. Mark T. Carleton, "Elitism Sustained: The Louisiana Constitution of 1974," *Tulane Law Review* 54 (April 1980): 560, quoted in Tarr, *Understanding State Constitutions,* 142–143.

15. See Janice C. May, *The Texas Constitutional Revision Experience in the '70s* (Austin, Tex.: Sterling Swift, 1975).

16. The Louisiana Convention, which has been referred to by Janice C. May as "of questionable pedigree" and which was "regarded by Louisianans as a special legislative session in disguise," is noted in "State Constitutional Reforms: Recent Experiences" (paper presented at a Symposium on the Alabama Constitution, Montgomery, Ala., December 13–15, 1995).

17. William Anderson, *A History of the Constitution of Minnesota* (Minneapolis: University of Minnesota, 1921), 75–114.

18. *Proceedings and Debates of the Virginia State Convention of 1829–1830,* iii. Madison's presence at this convention made for some quite interesting moments, particularly in light of the fact that the Federalist Papers were quoted frequently by various delegates in support of their positions. At a time when the authorship of several of the eighty-five Federalist Papers was still in some doubt, it became necessary on several occasions for Madison to clarify his role in the project and to distinguish his contributions from those of John Jay and Alexander Hamilton. On one occasion, Benjamin Watkins Leigh began an argument by stating, "Sir, I refer the Committee to the 54th number of The Federalist (I know not who was the author of it)" (165). Some time later, Charles Mercer also quoted from Federalist No. 54, and he

said that according to his edition, it had been written by Hamilton. Philip Doddridge rose to correct him and to say that "the paper from which the extract had been read, was attributed in some of the editions of the Federalist, to Mr. Jay." At that point, "Mr. Madison then rose and said, that although he was not desirous to take part in this discussion, yet under all the circumstances he was, perhaps, called on to state, that the paper in question was not written by Mr. Hamilton or Mr. Jay, but by the third person connected with that work" (188).

19. *Official Report of the Proceedings and Debates of the Third Constitutional Convention of Ohio [1873]*, 2:769.

20. For an analysis of notable delegates who participated in early nineteenth-century conventions in particular, see Thorpe, *Constitutional History*, 2:395–499.

21. *Report of the Debates in the Convention of California on the Formation of the State Constitution [1849]*, 28.

22. *Official Report of the Debates and Proceedings in the Constitutional Convention of the State of Nevada [1864]*, 16.

23. *Report of the Proceedings and Debates in the Convention to Revise the Constitution of the State of Michigan, 1850*, 7.

24. This approach is described in Christian G. Fritz, "The American Constitutional Tradition Revisited: Preliminary Observations on State Constitution-Making in the Nineteenth-Century West," *Rutgers Law Journal* 25 (Summer 1994): 945, 975–984; Tarr, *Understanding State Constitutions*, 50–55.

25. For a comprehensive list of these compilations of state constitutions, see Marsha L. Baum and Christian G. Fritz, "American Constitution-Making: The Neglected State Constitutional Sources," *Hastings Constitutional Law Quarterly* 27 (Winter 2000): 199–242.

26. For several instances where conventions purchased compilations for the delegates, see *Debates and Proceedings of the Constitutional Convention of the State of Delaware [1896]*, 111; *The Debates and Proceedings of the Constitutional Convention of the State of Michigan [1867]*, 1:47–50; *Journal of the Nebraska Constitutional Convention [1919]*, 87–112; *Official Report of the Proceedings and Debates of the Third Constitutional Convention of Ohio [1873]*, 1:72–74.

27. *Official Report of the Proceedings and Debates of the Third Constitutional Convention of Ohio [1873]*, 1:73.

28. *Proceedings and Debates of the Constitutional Convention of the State of Ohio, 1912*, 378–387.

29. See his speeches at *Proceedings and Debates of the Constitutional Convention of the State of Ohio [1912]*, 663–670; *Journal of the Nebraska Constitutional Convention [1919]*, 304–331; *Proceedings of the Constitutional Convention of the State of Illinois, Convened January 6, 1920*, 657–672.

30. *Official Record, State of Michigan Constitutional Convention, 1961*, 384–390.

31. *Proceedings of the Constitutional Convention of the State of New York, 1967*, 2:21–24.

32. *Official Report of the Proceedings and Debates of the First Constitutional Convention of North Dakota [1889]*, 65–67. In a much quoted statement, both in future conventions and later scholarship, Cooley, who at the time was chairman of the Interstate Commerce Commission, urged the delegates, "Don't in your constitution-making legislate too much. In your Constitution you are tying the hands of the people. Don't do that to any such extent as to prevent the Legislature hereafter from meeting all evils that may be within the reach of proper legislation. Leave something for them" (67).

33. See, for instance, the speech of California Governor Hiram Johnson, at the Ohio

Convention of 1912. *Proceedings and Debates of the Constitutional Convention of the State of Ohio [1912]*, 544–549.

34. See, for instance, the speech of former Nebraska Insurance Commissioner Thomas R. Pansing to the Rhode Island Convention of 1964–1969, at *State of Rhode Island and Providence Plantations: Constitutional Convention [1964–1969]: Report of Proceedings*, 466–480.

35. *Proceedings of the Constitutional Convention of the State of Illinois, Convened January 6, 1920*, 105–129, 309–337.

36. See *Minutes of the Daily Proceedings, Alaska Constitutional Convention, 1955–56*, 314, 329.

37. *State of Rhode Island and Providence Plantations: Constitutional Convention [1964–1969]: Report of Proceedings*, 522–525.

38. *Journal and Proceedings of the [Tennessee] Limited Constitutional Convention [1965]*, 478–485.

39. This list includes the Mississippi Convention of 1890, South Carolina Convention of 1895, Delaware Convention of 1896–1897, Virginia Convention of 1901–1902, and the Louisiana Conventions of 1898, 1913 and 1921.

40. See, for instance, the Tennessee Conventions of 1953, 1959, 1965, 1971, and 1977.

41. See, for instance, the Massachusetts Conventions of 1820–1821 and 1853.

42. For recent examples, see the Montana Convention of 1971–1972 and North Dakota Convention of 1971–1972.

43. This was the case, for instance, in Iowa, Kansas, Nevada, and Wisconsin.

44. Nineteenth-century conventions that experienced such rejections included the Delaware Convention of 1852–1853, Massachusetts Convention of 1853, Michigan Convention of 1867, Nebraska Convention of 1871, New York Convention of 1867–1868, and Ohio Convention of 1873–1874. Among the twentieth-century conventions whose recommendations met such a fate are the New York Convention of 1915, Illinois Convention of 1920–1922, Missouri Convention of 1922–1923, Rhode Island Convention of 1964–1969, New York Convention of 1967, Maryland Convention of 1967–1968, New Mexico Convention of 1969, Arkansas Convention of 1969–1970, North Dakota Convention of 1971–1972, and Arkansas Convention of 1978–1980.

45. *Debates of the Convention to Amend the Constitution of Pennsylvania [1872–1873]*, 1:85.

46. *Debates in the Massachusetts Constitutional Convention, 1917–1918*, 1:15.

47. *Debates and Proceedings of the Constitutional Convention of the State of California [1878]*, 1:127.

48. *Official Report of the Proceedings and Debates of the Third Constitutional Convention of Ohio [1873]*, 1:92.

49. *Proceedings and Debates of the Constitutional Convention of the State of Ohio [1912]*, 114.

50. *Proceedings of the New Jersey State Constitutional Convention of 1844*, 32.

51. *Report of the Debate and Proceedings of the Convention for the Revision of the Constitution of the State of Indiana, 1850*, 26–27.

52. *Official Proceedings of the Constitutional Convention of the State of Alabama [1901]*, 72.

53. Ibid., 58–59.

54. Ibid., 71.

55. *Proceedings and Debates of the Constitutional Convention Held in the City of Helena, Montana [1889]*, 55.

56. *The [Illinois] Constitutional Debates of 1847*, 76–77.

57. *Debates in the Texas Constitutional Convention of 1875*, 24.

58. *Debates in the Massachusetts Constitutional Convention, 1917–1918*, 1:14–15.

59. *Proceedings of the New Jersey State Constitutional Convention of 1844*, 34.

60. *Debates and Proceedings of the Constitutional Convention of the State of California [1878]*, 1:33.

61. *Debates and Proceedings of the Constitutional Convention of the State of Delaware [1896]*, 215.

62. Ibid., 215–216.

63. *Official Report of the Proceedings and Debates of the Third Constitutional Convention of Ohio [1873]*, 1:91.

64. *The Oregon Constitution and Proceedings and Debates of the Oregon Convention of 1857*, 137.

65. *Debates in the Texas Constitutional Convention of 1875*, 26.

66. *Journal of the Proceedings and Debates in the Constitutional Convention of the State of Mississippi, August, 1865*, 26–27.

67. *Journal and Debates of the Constitutional Convention of the State of Wyoming [1889]*.

68. The printer, Robert Gallagher, "had difficulty obtaining what he considered proper payment from the convention, and therefore refused to carry out all the terms of the agreement," and as a result he only published one volume of the debates, covering only two months of the proceedings. Francis Pendleton Gaines, "The Virginia Constitutional Convention of 1850–51: A Study in Sectionalism" (Ph.D. diss., University of Virginia, 1950), 120n60. The debates are contained in *Register of the Debates and Proceedings of the Va. Reform Convention [1850–1851]*.

69. Delegates to the Idaho Convention of 1889 provided enough funds to hire a stenographer, but it was several decades before the legislature appropriated funds for the publication of the debates in 1912. Similar delays occurred in the publication of the debates of the Kansas Convention of 1859 (which were eventually reprinted and made widely available in 1920), the Montana Convention of 1889 (published in 1921), the South Dakota Conventions of 1885 and 1889 (published in 1907), and the West Virginia Convention of 1861–1863 (published in 1939).

70. In the case of the Nebraska Convention of 1871, for instance, a record of the debates was found in a statehouse vault nearly three decades later, and after much pleading, the legislature eventually provided for their publication in three volumes issued between 1906 and 1913. *Official Report of the Debates and Proceedings in the Nebraska Constitutional Convention [1871]*, 1:7.

71. For instance, the Missouri Historical Society undertook the task of publishing the debates of the Missouri Convention of 1875 in twelve volumes that appeared between 1930 and 1944. Similarly, the Delaware Supreme Court made possible the publication of the debates in the Delaware Convention of 1896–1897 in 1958.

72. *The Debates and Journal of the Constitutional Convention of the State of Maine, 1819–20*, iii–iv.

73. *Proceedings and Debates of the Virginia State Convention of 1829–30*, iv.

74. *The History and Debates of the Convention of the People of Alabama [1861]*, iii.

75. *Report of the Debates and Proceedings of the Convention of the State of New York [1821]; Reports of the Proceedings and Debates of the [New York] Convention of 1821*.

NOTES TO PAGES 26-30   299

76. *Report of the Debates and Proceedings of the Convention for the Revision of the Constitution of the State of New York, 1846; Debates and Proceedings in the New York State Convention, for the Revision of the Constitution [1846].*

77. I have not included in this study several other conventions, such as the New Hampshire Convention of 1850–1851, whose debates were reported in contemporaneous newspaper accounts but have not been published in book form (see Thorpe, *Constitutional History,* 2:398), or the Washington Convention of 1889, where contemporary newspaper accounts have been compiled but not assembled in narrative form. See Beverly Rosenow, *Washington State Constitutional Convention 1889: Contemporary Newspaper Articles,* vol. 2 (Buffalo, N.Y.: William S. Hein, 1999). In several cases, such as the North Carolina Convention of 1868, scholars are in the process of assembling and publishing these newspaper accounts in narrative form, and so it is likely that future scholars will have the benefit of additional convention debates. See John V. Orth, *The North Carolina State Constitution: A Reference Guide* (Westport, Conn.: Greenwood Press, 1993), 173.

78. Included in this list is the Connecticut Convention of 1818, whose debates are the oldest to have survived and were finally published in 1991, as well as the Massachusetts Convention of 1820–1821 (published in 1853), the Michigan Convention of 1835 (published in 1940), the New Jersey Convention of 1844 (published in 1942), the Iowa Conventions of 1844 and 1846 (published in 1900), the Wisconsin Convention of 1846 (published in 1919), the Illinois Convention of 1847 (published in 1919), the Oregon Convention of 1857 (published in 1926), the Maryland Convention of 1867 (published in 1923), the Texas Convention of 1875 (published in 1930), and the Arizona Convention of 1910 (published in 1991).

Chapter 2: Amendment and Revision

1. On the debates about the creation of the federal amendment process, see Sanford Levinson, "'Veneration' and Constitutional Change: James Madison Confronts the Possibility of Constitutional Amendment," *Texas Tech Law Review* 21 (1990): 2443–2460; John R. Vile, *The Constitutional Amending Process in American Political Thought* (Westport, Conn.: Praeger, 1992), 23–46; Richard B. Bernstein with Jerome Agel, *Amending America: If We Love the Constitution So Much, Why Do We Keep Trying to Change It?* (Lawrence: University Press of Kansas, 1993), 14–30; and David E. Kyvig, *Explicit and Authentic Acts: Amending the U.S. Constitution, 1776–1995* (Lawrence: University Press of Kansas, 1996), 42–65.

2. "Letter to James Madison" (6 September 1789), in *The Life and Selected Writings of Thomas Jefferson,* eds. Adrienne Koch and William Peden (New York: Modern Library, 1944), 491; see also his "Letter to Samuel Kercheval" (12 July 1816), 673–676. For additional treatments of the Jeffersonian approach to constitutional revision, see Vile, *Constitutional Amending Process,* 59–78; and David N. Mayer, *The Constitutional Thought of Thomas Jefferson* (Charlottesville: University Press of Virginia, 1994), 295–319.

3. Alexander Hamilton et al., *The Federalist Papers,* ed. Clinton Rossiter (1961; reprint, New York: Mentor, 1999), 246.

4. Ibid., 282, 283.

5. Herman Ames, *The Proposed Amendments to the Constitution of the United States during the First Century of Its History* (1896; reprint, New York: Burt Franklin, 1970), 292.

6. Among the more notable proposals, Missouri senator John Henderson in 1864 wanted to permit amendments to be proposed by a majority of each house of Congress or on the peti-

tion of a majority of states, and then to be ratified by two-thirds of state legislatures or conventions. Wisconsin senator Robert La Follette in 1912 and 1913 wanted amendments to be proposed by a majority of each house or on the petition of ten states, and then to be ratified by a majority vote of the people in a majority of states. New York representative Walter Chandler in 1913 and 1916 proposed, among other things, that Congress should call a convention every thirty years. Several members of Congress in the 1920s proposed that amendments could be initiated by a petition signed by 500,000 citizens and then ratified by a majority of voters in the country. These various efforts to craft a more flexible federal amendment process are discussed in Ames, *Proposed Amendments,* 281–304; M. A. Musmanno, *Proposed Amendments to the Constitution* (Washington, D.C.: U.S. Government Printing Office, 1929), 189–206; Lester B. Orfield, *The Amending of the Federal Constitution* (Ann Arbor: University of Michigan Press, 1942), 168–221; Peter Suber, *The Paradox of Self-Amendment: A Study of Logic, Law, Omnipotence, and Change* (New York: Peter Lang, 1990), 322–326; and John R. Vile, *Encyclopedia of Constitutional Amendments, Proposed Amendments, and Amending Issues, 1789–1995* (Santa Barbara, Calif.: ABC-CLIO, 1996), 9–11.

7. As one would expect, there has been a fair amount of variation in the amendment and revision procedures employed by particular states through the years. Several of these differences among states have over time been eliminated. For instance, Pennsylvania (until 1790) and Vermont (until 1870) permitted councils of censors to recommend constitutional changes. In addition, in Rhode Island (until 1935), the lack of a specific constitutional provision was interpreted as prohibiting the calling of conventions, and the only means of constitutional change was through legislative-initiated amendments. Conversely, in New Hampshire (until 1964), the legislature was unable to submit amendments to the people for ratification, and the only way to change the constitution was through a convention.

Several other unique features of particular state amendment processes are still in place. Delaware is the only state whose legislature may enact amendments without submitting them for popular ratification. In addition, although a number of states permit revision commissions to make recommendations and conduct research in preparation for constitutional changes, Florida alone empowers its revision commission to submit amendments directly to the people.

8. For a treatment of the changes in each state's amendment and revision procedures through the early 1980s, see Suber, *Paradox of Self-Amendment,* 333–355. For a current listing of state amendment and revision procedures, see *The Book of the States, 2004 Edition,* vol. 36 (Lexington, Ky.: Council of State Governments, 2004), 12–16.

9. On the unreflective nature of state constitutional revision processes, see the comments of James Willard Hurst, *The Growth of American Law: The Law Makers* (Boston: Little, Brown, 1950), 201–204, 237. For a sustained critique of flexible state amendment procedures, see Michael G. Colantuono, "The Revision of American State Constitutions: Legislative Power, Popular Sovereignty, and Constitutional Change," *California Law Review* 75 (July 1987): 1473, 1499–1511. For additional critical comments, see the quotations reported in Peter J. Galie and Christopher Bopst, "Changing State Constitutions: Dual Constitutionalism and the Amending Process," *Hofstra Law and Policy Symposium* 1 (1996): 27, 29. For a comprehensive discussion (and critique) of these negative assessments, see Christian G. Fritz, "The American Constitutional Tradition Revisited: Preliminary Observations on State Constitution-Making in the Nineteenth-Century West," *Rutgers Law Journal* 25 (Summer 1994): 945, 957–960.

These negative assessments are, admittedly, not universally held. Scholars who have questioned the merits of the rigid federal approach and/or who have taken note of advantages of the state approach include Donald S. Lutz, "Toward a Theory of Constitutional Amendment," in *Responding to Imperfection: The Theory and Practice of Constitutional Amendment,* ed. Sanford Levinson (Princeton, N.J.: Princeton University Press, 1995), 251, 265; Stephen Holmes and Cass R. Sunstein, "The Politics of Constitutional Revision in Eastern Europe," in Levinson, *Responding to Imperfection,* 275–306; Laura J. Scalia, *America's Jeffersonian Experiment: Remaking State Constitutions, 1820–1850* (Dekalb: Northern Illinois University Press, 1999), 156–167; and Sanford Levinson, "Designing an Amendment Process," in *Constitutional Culture and Democratic Rule,* eds. John Ferejohn, Jack N. Rakove, and Jonathan Riley (New York: Cambridge University Press, 2001), 281, 285.

10. Stephen M. Griffin has suggested that the adoption of state amendment procedures may be attributable to the influence of anti-Federalist beliefs. Citing Michael Lienesch, *New Order of the Ages: Time, the Constitution, and the Making of Modern American Political Thought* (Princeton, N.J.: Princeton University Press, 1988), 148–149, Griffin wrote, "We know very little about how this permissive attitude toward constitutional amendment developed, but it is possible it is the descendant of Anti-Federalist beliefs that limits on government should be as specific as possible." Stephen M. Griffin, *American Constitutionalism: From Theory to Politics* (Princeton, N.J.: Princeton University Press, 1996), 35. Christian G. Fritz is one of several scholars to call attention to the influence of Jefferson's belief in the need for periodic constitutional revision. As Fritz has argued, "While Jefferson's constitutional vision gradually faded from discussions of the Federal Constitution and today is considered an anachronism in constitutional theory and practice, his vision assumed considerable importance in the intellectual life of state constitution-making." Fritz, "American Constitutional Tradition Revisited," 973.

11. On the periodic submission of the question of whether to call a constitutional convention, see Robert J. Martineau, "The Mandatory Referendum on Calling a State Constitutional Convention: Enforcing the People's Right to Reform Their Government," *Ohio State Law Journal* 31 (Spring 1970): 421–455. On the approach to constitutional revision in the late eighteenth century, see Christian G. Fritz, "Alternative Visions of American Constitutionalism: Popular Sovereignty and the Early American Constitutional Debate," *Hastings Constitutional Law Quarterly* 24 (Winter 1997): 287–357; and Marc W. Kruman, *Between Authority and Liberty: State Constitution Making in Revolutionary America* (Chapel Hill: University of North Carolina Press, 1997), 53–59. On the approach to constitutional revision in the western states in the nineteenth century, see Fritz, "American Constitutional Tradition Revisited," which makes extensive use of convention debates.

12. The leading nineteenth-century account, which does make extensive use of convention debates, is John A. Jameson, *A Treatise on Constitutional Conventions, Their History, Powers, and Modes of Proceeding,* 4th ed. (1887; reprint, New York: Da Capo Press, 1972). Another exhaustive account of nineteenth (and early twentieth) century developments is Walter F. Dodd, *The Revision and Amendment of State Constitutions* (Baltimore: Johns Hopkins Press, 1910). See also Ellis Paxson Oberholtzer, *The Referendum in America, Together with Some Chapters on the Initiative and Recall* (New York: Charles Scribner's Sons, 1911), 128–172; James Q. Dealey, *Growth of American State Constitutions from 1776 to the End of the Year 1914* (Boston: Ginn, 1915), 139–149; and James W. Garner, "Amendment of State Constitutions," *American Political Science Review* 1 (February 1907): 213–247. Twentieth-century developments are taken into account in Thomas R. White, "Amendment and Revision of State Constitutions," *University of Pennsylvania Law Review* 100 (June 1952):

1132–1152; Ernest R. Bartley, "Methods of Constitutional Change," in *Major Problems in State Constitutional Revision*, ed. W. Brooke Graves (Chicago: Public Administration Service, 1960), 21–37; John P. Wheeler, "Changing the Fundamental Law," in *Salient Issues of Constitutional Revision*, ed. John P. Wheeler (New York: National Municipal League, 1961), 49–62; Albert L. Sturm, *Thirty Years of State Constitution-Making, 1938–1968* (New York: National Municipal League, 1970); Albert L. Sturm, "The Development of American State Constitutions," *Publius* 12 (Winter 1982): 57–98; Janice C. May, "Constitutional Amendment and Revision Revisited," *Publius* 17 (Winter 1987): 153–179; and Galie and Bopst, "Changing State Constitutions."

13. These debates are contained in the following sources:

Alabama: *Official Proceedings of the Constitutional Convention of the State of Alabama [1901]*, 3906–3929.

Alaska: *Minutes of the Daily Proceedings, Alaska Constitutional Convention, 1955–56*, 1242–1280, 3424–3441.

Arizona: *The Records of the Arizona Constitutional Convention of 1910*, 189–190, 686–691.

California: *Report of the Debates in the Convention of California on the Formation of the State Constitution [1849]*, 166–167, 354–361; *Debates and Proceedings of the Constitutional Convention of the State of California [1878]*, 1276–1278, 1445.

Connecticut: "Annotated Debates of the 1818 Constitutional Convention," 75–76; *The Third Constitutional Convention of the State of Connecticut: Proceedings [1965]*, 813–826.

Delaware: *Debates of the Delaware Convention, for Revising the Constitution [1831]*, 224–228, 232–234; *Debates and Proceedings of the Constitutional Convention of the State of Delaware [1852–1853]*, 3–68, 119–123, 148–150; *Debates and Proceedings of the Constitutional Convention of the State of Delaware [1896]*, 2393–2439, 2456–2463, 2476–2536, 2971–3006.

Georgia: *A Stenographic Report of the Proceedings of the Constitutional Convention Held in Atlanta, Georgia, 1877*, 429–430.

Hawaii: *Proceedings of the Constitutional Convention of Hawaii, 1950*, 2:744–780; *Proceedings of the Constitutional Convention of Hawaii of 1968*, 2:526–532, 540–541; *Proceedings of the Constitutional Convention of Hawaii, 1978*, 2:106–112.

Idaho: *Proceedings and Debates of the Constitutional Convention of Idaho, 1889*, 1696–1700.

Illinois: *The [Illinois] Constitutional Debates of 1847*, 199–201, 927–928; *Debates and Proceedings of the Constitutional Convention of the State of Illinois [1869]*, 391–392, 424–429, 1309–1320, 1591–1595; *Proceedings of the Constitutional Convention of the State of Illinois, Convened January 6, 1920*, 239–342, 715–780, 2475–2522, 4378–4413, 4527–4546; *Record of Proceedings: Sixth Illinois Constitutional Convention [1969]: Verbatim Transcripts*, 442–462, 472–479, 483–506, 516–566, 577–587, 2710–2712, 2911–2915, 3598–3615.

Indiana: *Report of the Debates and Proceedings of the Convention for the Revision of the Constitution of the State of Indiana, 1850*, 1258–1260, 1913–1919, 1938–1941.

Iowa: *The Debates of the Constitutional Convention of the State of Iowa [1857]*, 603–626, 638–640, 1030–1033.

Kansas: *A Reprint of the Proceedings and Debates of the Convention Which Framed the Constitution of Kansas at Wyandotte in July, 1859*, 270, 307–308, 554.

Kentucky: *Report of the Debates and Proceedings of the Convention for the Revision of the Constitution of the State of Kentucky, 1849,* 841–843, 862, 947–952, 987–994; *Official Report of the Proceedings and Debates in the Convention . . . of September, 1890, To Adopt, Amend or Change the Constitution of the State of Kentucky,* 1534–1561, 1583–1587, 1593–1672, 1709–1733, 1736–1784, 5234–5263.

Louisiana: *Proceedings and Debates of the Convention of Louisiana [1845],* 404–420, 843–845; *Debates in the Convention for the Revision and Amendment of the Constitution of the State of Louisiana [1864],* 100–107, 480–481; *Records of the Louisiana Constitutional Convention of 1973: Convention Transcripts,* 2808–2810, 3113–3177.

Maine: *The Debates and Journal of the Constitutional Convention of the State of Maine, 1819–20,* 345–347.

Maryland: *Debates and Proceedings of the Maryland Reform Convention to Revise the State Constitution [1851],* 2:359–388; *The Debates of the Constitutional Convention of the State of Maryland [1864],* 387–391, 1080–1083, 1831–1833; *Debates of the Maryland Constitutional Convention of 1867,* 271–272, 380; *Debates of the [Maryland] Constitutional Convention of 1967–1968,* 2583–2608, 3022–3026, 3034–3036, 3142–3151, 3155–3160.

Massachusetts: *Journal of Debates and Proceedings in the Convention of Delegates, Chosen to Revise the Constitution of Massachusetts [1820–21],* 188, 403–407, 413–415; *Official Report of the Debates and Proceedings in the State Convention to Revise and Amend the Constitution of the Commonwealth of Massachusetts [1853],* 2:562–567, 714–725; 3:118–125, 290–310, 312–318, 341–351, 489–496, 517–534; *Debates in the Massachusetts Constitutional Convention, 1917–1918,* 2:1–1062; 3:1279–1307.

Michigan: *The Michigan Constitutional Conventions of 1835–36: Debates and Proceedings,* 361–362, 382; *Report of the Proceedings and Debates in the Convention to Revise the Constitution of the State of Michigan, 1850,* 465–467; *The Debates and Proceedings of the Constitutional Convention of the State of Michigan [1867],* 2:605–609, 760, 851–852; *Proceedings and Debates of the Constitutional Convention of the State of Michigan [1907],* 546–570, 577–686, 932–939, 960–965, 1167–1171, 1255–1256, 1358–1360, 1392–1395; *Official Record, State of Michigan Constitutional Convention, 1961,* 2452–2490, 3003–3013, 3198–3206.

Minnesota: *The Debates and Proceedings of the Minnesota Constitutional Convention [1857],* 453; *Debates and Proceedings of the Constitutional Convention for the Territory of Minnesota [1857],* 387–390.

Missouri: *Debates of the Missouri Constitutional Convention of 1875,* 10:479–483; 11:363–413.

Montana: *Proceedings and Debates of the Constitutional Convention Held in the City of Helena, Montana [1889],* 576–578, 647–655; *Montana Constitutional Convention, 1971–1972: Verbatim Transcript,* 453–532, 1187–1197.

Nebraska: *Official Report of the Debates and Proceedings in the Nebraska Constitutional Convention [1871],* I: 406–414; II: 29–30; III: 25–29; *Journal of the Nebraska Constitutional Convention [1919],* 258–261, 455–459, 473–484, 494–517, 662–668, 1408–1410, 2482–2484, 2647–2651, 2777–2778.

Nevada: *Official Report of the Debates and Proceedings in the Constitutional Convention of the State of Nevada [1864],* 526–532, 540, 810–811.

New Hampshire: *Journal of the Constitutional Convention of the State of New Hampshire, December 1876,* 227–229, 254–256; *Journal of the Constitutional Convention of the State of New Hampshire, January 1889,* 116–127; *Journal of the [New Hampshire] Constitutional Convention of 1902,* 626–641; *Journal of the Convention to Revise the [New*

Hampshire] Constitution, June 1912, 446–452, 499–509; *Journal of the Convention to Revise the [New Hampshire] Constitution, January 20, 1920*, 204–216; *Journal of the Convention to Revise the [New Hampshire] Constitution, June, 1930*, 72–80, 87–101, 122–124; *Journal of the Convention to Revise the [New Hampshire] Constitution, May, 1938*, 186–205; *Journal of the Convention to Revise the [New Hampshire] Constitution, May 1948*, 123–139, 181–185, 280–282; *Journal of the Convention to Revise the [New Hampshire] Constitution, May 1956*, 173–183; *Journal of the Convention to Revise the [New Hampshire] Constitution, December 1959*, 49–51; *Journal of the Convention to Revise the [New Hampshire] Constitution, May 1964*, 108–118, 157–171; *Journal of the Convention to Revise the [New Hampshire] Constitution, May 1974*, 194–197; *Journal of the Convention to Revise the [New Hampshire] Convention, May 1984*, 94–100.

New Jersey: *Proceedings of the New Jersey State Constitutional Convention of 1844*, 54–75, 575–579; *[New Jersey] Constitutional Convention of 1947*, 1:692–699, 728–737.

New York: *Reports of the Proceedings and Debates of the [New York] Convention of 1821*, 291–294, 553; *Report of the Debates and Proceedings of the Convention for the Revision of the Constitution of the State of New York, 1846*, 772, 1038; *Proceedings and Debates of the Constitutional Convention of the State of New York Held in 1867 and 1868*, 1349–1352, 2804–2814; *Revised Record of the Constitutional Convention of the State of New York [1894]*, 2:4–25; 4:826–833, 897–901, 1102–1107; *Revised Record of the Constitutional Convention of the State of New York [1915]*, 3250–3312, 3759–3775; *Revised Record of the Constitutional Convention of the State of New York [1938]*, 2525–2530; *Proceedings of the Constitutional Convention of the State of New York [1967]*, 3:6–54, 700; 4:144–164.

North Carolina: *Proceedings and Debates of the Convention of North Carolina [1835]*, 345–350, 369–373.

North Dakota: *Official Report of the Proceedings and Debates of the First Constitutional Convention of North Dakota [1889]*, 497–503, 624–625; *Debates of the North Dakota Constitutional Convention of 1972*, 511–513, 721–728, 922–926, 1030–1032.

Ohio: *Report of the Debates and Proceedings of the Convention for the Revision of the Constitution of the State of Ohio, 1850–51*, 2:427–436; *Official Report of the Proceedings and Debates of the Third Constitutional Convention of Ohio [1873]*, 2:2808–2813, 2835–2842, 2846–2853, 2855–2861, 3498–3505; *Proceedings and Debates of the Constitutional Convention of the State of Ohio [1912]*, 552–555, 671–717, 726–744, 756–944, 1365–1372, 1882–1902, 1906–1913, 1933–1943.

Pennsylvania: *Proceedings and Debates of the Convention of the Commonwealth of Pennsylvania [1837]*, 12:49–50, 55–56, 58–102, 225–237, 242–262, 307–322; 13:53–54; *Debates of the Convention to Amend the Constitution of Pennsylvania [1872–1873]*, 5:6–15; 6:161–165, 193–195; 8:74–75.

Rhode Island: *Journal of the Convention Assembled to Frame a Constitution for the State of Rhode Island [1842]*, 39; *State of Rhode Island and Providence Plantations: Constitutional Convention [1964–1969]: Report of Proceedings*, 1299–1312, 1329–1336, 2091–2094, 2098–2105; *Proceedings of the Rhode Island Constitutional Convention of 1973*, 122–123, 135–139.

Tennessee: *Journal and Proceedings of the [Tennessee] Constitutional Convention [1953]*, 733–794, 801–808, 814–827, 851–857, 862–902.

Texas: *Debates of the Texas Convention [1845]*, 84–85, 471–473; *Debates in the Texas Constitutional Convention of 1875*, 134–142, 325–326; *Texas Constitutional Convention [1974]: Official Proceedings*, 715–739, 2137–2141.

Utah: *Official Report of the Proceedings and Debates of the Convention . . . To Adopt a Constitution for the State of Utah [1895]*, 406–407, 674–679.

Virginia: *Proceedings and Debates of the Virginia State Convention of 1829–30*, 621, 789–791; *Report of the Proceedings and Debates of the Constitutional Convention, State of Virginia [1901–1902]*, 2610–2624, 2752–2759.

West Virginia: *Debates and Proceedings of the First Constitutional Convention of West Virginia (1861–1863)*, 2:68–106, 348–371.

Wisconsin: *Journal of the Convention to Form a Constitution for the State of Wisconsin [1847–1848]*, 474–475, 480, 513.

Wyoming: *Journal and Debates of the Constitutional Convention of the State of Wyoming [1889]*, 316.

14. On the evolving understanding of constitutions during this period, see Gordon S. Wood, *The Creation of the American Republic, 1776–1787* (Chapel Hill: University of North Carolina Press, 1969), esp. 306–389; and Fritz, "Alternative Visions."

15. Maryland, Delaware, and South Carolina (1778) provided, in varying fashions, for legislative amendments that required public notice and a particular vote requirement (as in South Carolina) or a supermajority vote (as in Delaware) or approval in consecutive sessions (as in Maryland), over and above what was required for enacting statutes. Georgia, Massachusetts, and New Hampshire (1784) provided, in various fashions, for the calling of constitutional conventions, whether upon a petition of voters (as in Georgia), by a vote of the people held fifteen years after the adoption of the constitution (as in Massachusetts), or every seven years (as in New Hampshire). Pennsylvania and Vermont each provided that a council of censors would convene every seven years and would have the power to call a constitutional convention. New Jersey, New York, North Carolina, and Virginia did not provide for a formal amendment and revision procedure. Finally, Connecticut and Rhode Island did not draft constitutions during this period. These late eighteenth-century amendment and revision procedures are discussed in Dodd, *Revision and Amendment of State Constitutions*, 27–29; Garner, "Amendment of State Constitutions," 214–219; Willi Paul Adams, *The First American Constitutions: Republican Ideology and the Making of the State Constitutions in the Revolutionary Era* (Chapel Hill: University of North Carolina Press, 1980), 139–144; and Kruman, *Between Authority and Liberty*, 53–59.

16. On the relationship between the distribution of geographic power and constitutional revision and for citations to the literature on this connection, see Fritz, "Alternative Visions," 355. See Fletcher M. Green, *Constitutional Development in the South Atlantic States, 1776–1860: A Study in the Evolution of Democracy* (Chapel Hill: University of North Carolina Press, 1930), esp. 142–170; George Philip Parkinson Jr., "Antebellum State Constitution-Making: Retention, Circumvention, Revision" (Ph.D. diss., University of Wisconsin, 1972), esp. 35–42, 51–56, 66–72, 99–102, 133–143; James A. Henretta, "Foreword: Rethinking the State Constitutional Tradition," *Rutgers Law Journal* 22 (Summer 1991): 819, 826–829; and G. Alan Tarr, *Understanding State Constitutions* (Princeton, N.J.: Princeton University Press, 1998), 102–105.

17. *Proceedings and Debates of the Convention of North Carolina [1835]*, 372.

18. *Debates and Proceedings of the Maryland Reform Convention to Revise the State Constitution [1851]*, 2:361, 362.

19. *Proceedings of the New Jersey State Constitutional Convention of 1844*, 74.

20. On the interest in taking account of progress in constitution making during this period, see Gregory Glen Schmidt, "Republican Visions: Constitutional Thought and Constitutional

Revision in the Eastern States, 1815–1830" (Ph.D. diss., University of Illinois, 1981), 54–63; and Fritz, "American Constitutional Tradition Revisited," 973–975.

21. *Proceedings and Debates of the Convention of Louisiana [1845]*, 415.

22. *Report of the Debates and Proceedings of the Convention for the Revision of the Constitution of the State of Indiana, 1850*, 1917.

23. *Debates of the Missouri Constitutional Convention of 1875*, 11:394.

24. *Official Report of the Proceedings and Debates of the Third Constitutional Convention of Ohio [1873]*, 2:2847.

25. *Proceedings and Debates of the Convention of Louisiana [1845]*, 415.

26. *Proceedings and Debates of the Convention of the Commonwealth of Pennsylvania [1837]*, 12:231.

27. See Marvin E. Gettleman, *The Dorr Rebellion: A Study in American Radicalism, 1833–1849* (New York: Random House, 1973); and George M. Dennison, *The Dorr War: Republicanism on Trial, 1831–1861* (Lexington: University Press of Kentucky, 1976).

28. *Proceedings of the New Jersey State Constitutional Convention of 1844*, 58.

29. *Official Report of the Proceedings and Debates in the Convention . . . of September, 1890, to Adopt, Amend or Change the Constitution of the State of Kentucky*, 1659–1660 (quotations transposed).

30. *Proceedings and Debates of the Convention of North Carolina [1835]*, 348–349.

31. *Proceedings and Debates of the Virginia State Convention of 1829–30*, 321, 791.

32. *Debates and Proceedings of the Constitutional Convention of the State of Delaware [1896]*, 2398–2399.

33. *Debates and Proceedings of the Maryland Reform Convention to Revise the State Constitution [1851]*, 363, 364.

34. *Report of the Debates and Proceedings of the Convention for the Revision of the Constitution of the State of Kentucky, 1849*, 948.

35. *Debates of the Texas Convention [1845]*, 472.

36. *Proceedings of the New Jersey State Constitutional Convention of 1844*, 60–61.

37. *Journal of Debates and Proceedings in the Convention of Delegates, Chosen to Revise the Constitution of Massachusetts [1820–21]*, 405.

38. Ibid., 404.

39. *Proceedings and Debates of the Convention of the Commonwealth of Pennsylvania [1837]*, 12:236–237.

40. *Debates and Proceedings of the Constitutional Convention of the State of Delaware [1852–1853]*, 5.

41. *Debates of the Delaware Convention, for Revising the Constitution [1831]*, 233.

42. *Official Report of the Proceedings and Debates of the Third Constitutional Convention of Ohio [1873]*, 2:3504.

43. *Debates and Proceedings of the Maryland Reform Convention to Revise the State Constitution [1851]*, 2:364.

44. Maryland Constitution (1776), Art. LIX; Delaware Constitution (1776), Art. 30; South Carolina Constitution (1778), Art. XLIV. See Dodd, *Revision and Amendment of State Constitutions*, 120.

45. *Report of the Debates and Proceedings of the Convention for the Revision of the Constitution of the State of Indiana, 1850*, 1258.

46. Ibid., 1259.

47. *Proceedings and Debates of the Virginia State Convention of 1829–30*, 789.

48. *Report of the Debates and Proceedings of the Convention for the Revision of the Constitution of the State of Indiana, 1850,* 1259.

49. Connecticut Constitution (1818), Art. XI. The Connecticut provision required a majority of the house to approve an amendment in one session, and then two-thirds of both the house and senate to approve the amendment in the next session, followed by popular ratification. See Dodd, *Revision and Amendment of State Constitutions,* 125.

50. Alabama Constitution (1819), "Mode of Amending and Revising the Constitution." See Dodd, *Revision and Amendment of State Constitutions,* 123.

51. Massachusetts Constitution (1780), Articles of Amendment, Art. IX (adopted 1821). See Dodd, *Revision and Amendment of State Constitutions,* 131.

52. *The Debates of the Constitutional Convention of the State of Iowa [1857],* 617.

53. *Report of the Proceedings and Debates in the Convention to Revise the Constitution of the State of Michigan, 1850,* 466.

54. *Official Report of the Debates and Proceedings in the Constitutional Convention of the State of Nevada [1864],* 528 (quotations transposed).

55. Maine Constitution (1819), Art. X, Sec. 2. See Dodd, *Revision and Amendment of State Constitutions,* 126. On the influence of Maine's approach in the second half of the nineteenth century, see Dodd, *Revision and Amendment of State Constitutions,* 130.

56. *A Stenographic Report of the Proceedings of the Constitutional Convention Held in Atlanta, Georgia, 1877,* 430.

57. *Proceedings and Debates of the Convention of the Commonwealth of Pennsylvania [1837],* 12:98.

58. *Report of the Debates in the Convention of California on the Formation of the State Constitution [1849],* 357.

59. *Debates and Proceedings of the First Constitutional Convention of West Virginia (1861–1863),* 2:105.

60. *Proceedings and Debates of the Convention of the Commonwealth of Pennsylvania [1837],* 12:252.

61. At the end of the nineteenth century, the states that permitted amendments upon a vote in one legislative session but required a supermajority legislative vote were: Alabama Constitution (1875), Art. XVII, Sec. 1; California Constitution (1879), Art. XVIII, Sec. 1; Colorado Constitution (1876), Art. XIX, Sec. 2; Florida Constitution (1885), Art. XVII, Sec. 1; Georgia Constitution (1877), Art. XIII, Sec. I, Para. I; Idaho Constitution (1889), Art. XX, Sec. 1; Illinois Constitution (1870), Art. XIV, Sec. 2; Kansas Constitution (1859), Art. 14, Sec. 1; Kentucky Constitution (1891), Sec. 256; Louisiana Constitution (1898), Art. 321; Maine Constitution (1819), Art. X, Sec. 2; Maryland Constitution (1867), Art. XIV, Sec. 1; Michigan Constitution (1850), Art. XX, Sec. 1; Montana Constitution (1889), Art. XIX, Sec. 9; Nebraska Constitution (1875), Art. XV, Sec. 1; North Carolina Constitution (1868), Art. XIII, Sec. 2 (as amended 1876); Ohio Constitution (1851), Art. XVI, Sec. 1; Texas Constitution (1876), Art. XVII, Sec. 1; Utah Constitution (1895), Art. XXIII, Sec. 1; Washington Constitution (1889), Art. XXIII, Sec. 1; West Virginia Constitution (1872), Art. XIV, Sec. 2; Wyoming Constitution (1889), Art. XX, Sec. 1.

62. At the end of the nineteenth century, the states that permitted amendments upon a majority vote in two legislative sessions were: Indiana Constitution (1851), Art. XVI, Sec. 1; Iowa Constitution (1857), Art. X, Sec. 1; Nevada Constitution (1864), Art. XVI, Sec. 1; New Jersey Constitution (1844), Art. IX; New York Constitution (1894), Art. XIV, Sec. 1; North Dakota Constitution (1889), Art. 15, Sec. 202; Oregon Constitution (1857), Art. XVII, Sec.

1; Pennsylvania Constitution (1874), Art. XVIII, Sec. 1; Rhode Island Constitution (1842), Art. XIII; Virginia Constitution (1870), Art. XII; Wisconsin Constitution (1848), Art. XII, Sec. 1.

63. At the end of the nineteenth century, the states that required action by two legislative sessions, with a supermajority vote in at least one house in at least one session, were: Connecticut Constitution (1818), Art. XI; Delaware Constitution (1897), Art. XVI, Sec. 1; Massachusetts Constitution (1780), Articles of Amendment, Art. IX (adopted 1821); Mississippi Constitution (1890), Art. 15, Sec. 273; South Carolina Constitution (1895), Art. XVI, Sec. 1; Tennessee Constitution (1870), Art. XI, Sec. 3; Vermont Constitution (1793), Articles of Amendment, Art. 25, Sec. 1 (adopted 1870).

64. The states that permitted amendments by a majority vote in one legislation session were: Arkansas Constitution (1874), Art. XIX, Sec. 22; Minnesota Constitution (1857), Art. XIV, Sec. 1 (as amended 1898); Missouri Constitution (1875), Art. XV, Sec. 2; South Dakota Constitution (1889), Art. XXIII, Sec. 1.

65. Dodd, *Revision and Amendment of State Constitutions,* 50.

66. Massachusetts Constitution (1780), Part II, Ch. VI, Art. X; New Hampshire Constitution (1784), Part II; Kentucky Constitution (1792), Art. XI; Indiana Constitution (1816), Art. VIII, Sec. 1; New York Constitution (1846), Art. XIII, Sec. 2; Michigan Constitution (1850), Art. XX, Sec. 2; Maryland Constitution (1851), Art. XI; Ohio Constitution (1851), Art. XVI, Sec. 3; Iowa Constitution (1857), Art. X, Sec. 3; Virginia Constitution (1870), Art. XII. On the origin of these provisions, see Martineau, "Mandatory Referendum," 424–425.

67. *Debates and Proceedings of the Maryland Reform Convention to Revise the State Constitution [1851],* 373.

68. *The Debates and Journal of the Constitutional Convention of the State of Maine, 1819–20,* 346.

69. *The Debates of the Constitutional Convention of the State of Iowa [1857],* 640.

70. *Report of the Debates and Proceedings of the Convention for the Revision of the Constitution of the State of Ohio, 1850–51,* 2:430.

71. *Report of the Proceedings and Debates in the Convention to Revise the Constitution of the State of Michigan, 1850,* 466–467.

72. *Debates of the Missouri Constitutional Convention of 1875,* 11:393.

73. The interval was twenty years in Maryland, New York, Ohio, and Virginia; sixteen years in Michigan; twelve years in Indiana; ten years in Iowa; and seven years in New Hampshire.

74. On the general decline of interest in state constitutions during the twentieth century, see Henretta, "Foreword," 836–837. On the relative lack of interest in reforming state constitutional amendment and revision procedures in particular, see Sturm, "Development of American State Constitutions," 95.

75. These reform measures are discussed in Frank J. Goodnow, *Social Reform and the Constitution* (New York: Macmillan, 1911), 242–328; S. J. Duncan-Clark, *The Progressive Movement: Its Principles and Its Programme* (Boston: Small, Maynard, 1913), 109–167; Benjamin Parke De Witt, *The Progressive Movement: A Non-Partisan, Comprehensive Discussion of Current Tendencies in American Politics* (New York: Macmillan, 1915), 244–273.

76. For a comprehensive discussion, see Paul S. Reinsch, *American Legislatures and Legislative Methods* (New York: The Century Co., 1907), 228–274.

77. *Proceedings and Debates of the Constitutional Convention of the State of Michigan [1907],* 592.

78. For contrasting views of the significance of the decisions, see Melvin I. Urofsky, "State Courts and Protective Legislation during the Progressive Era: A Reevaluation," *Journal of American History* 72 (June 1985): 63–91; Paul Kens, "The Source of a Myth: Police Powers of the States and Laissez-Faire Constitutionalism, 1900–1937," *American Journal of Legal History* 35 (January 1991): 70–98.

79. *Debates in the Massachusetts Constitutional Convention, 1917–1918,* 2:739.

80. For contemporaneous critiques of these state court rulings, see William L. Ransom, *Majority Rule and the Judiciary: An Examination of Current Proposals for Constitutional Change Affecting the Relation of Courts to Legislation* (New York: Scribner's Sons, 1912); Gilbert E. Roe, *Our Judicial Oligarchy* (New York: B. W. Huebsch, 1912).

81. *Debates in the Massachusetts Constitutional Convention, 1917–1918,* 2:48.

82. On the strategy of adopting piecemeal amendments, see William Allen White, *The Old Order Changeth: A View of American Democracy* (New York: Macmillan, 1912), 54–56; and Charles E. Merriam, *American Political Ideas: Studies in the Development of American Political Thought, 1865–1917* (New York: Macmillan, 1920), 190.

83. On the efforts to adopt institutional reforms to rein in legislators, see Charles A. Beard and Birl E. Schultz, *Documents on the State-Wide Initiative, Referendum, and Recall* (New York: Macmillan, 1912); William Bennett Munro, ed., *The Initiative, Referendum and Recall* (New York: D. Appleton, 1912); and Delos F. Wilcox, *Government by All the People, or The Initiative, the Referendum, and the Recall as Instruments of Democracy* (1912; reprint, New York: Da Capo Press, 1972). On the efforts to adopt institutional reforms to rein in the judiciary, see J. Patrick White, "Progressivism and the Judiciary: A Study of the Movement for Judicial Reform, 1901–1917" (Ph.D. diss., University of Michigan, 1957); and William G. Ross, *A Muted Fury: Populists, Progressives, and Labor Unions Confront the Courts, 1890–1937* (Princeton, N.J.: Princeton University Press, 1994).

84. On the turn to the reform of state amendment procedures during this period, see Oberholtzer, *Referendum in America,* 156. On the way in which reforms of state amendment procedures were seen as one aspect of an overall strategy to secure political reforms, see Merriam, *American Political Ideas,* 225.

85. *Revised Record of the Constitutional Convention of the State of New York [1915],* 3278.

86. Ibid., 3265.

87. Ibid., 3283 (quotations transposed).

88. *Debates in the Massachusetts Constitutional Convention, 1917–1918,* 2:26, 27.

89. This relationship between the rigidity of constitutional amendment procedures and the power of the judiciary was discussed by several individuals, primarily in regard to the national government, but with implications for state governments as well. See Herbert Croly, *Progressive Democracy* (New York: Macmillan, 1914), 232, 237; and Munroe Smith, "Shall We Make Our Constitution Flexible?" *North American Review* 194 (November 1911): 657, 662, 663; both cited in Vile, *Constitutional Amending Process,* 144–145.

90. *Proceedings and Debates of the Constitutional Convention of the State of Ohio [1912],* 378–379.

91. *Proceedings and Debates of the Constitutional Convention of the State of Michigan [1907],* 566 (quotations transposed).

92. James Bryce, "Flexible and Rigid Constitutions," *Studies in History and Jurisprudence* (New York: Oxford University Press, 1901): 124–213.

93. *Proceedings and Debates of the Constitutional Convention of the State of Michigan [1907],* 641.

94. Ibid., 615.

95. Ibid., 599.

96. Ibid., 580.

97. Ibid., 599.

98. *Debates in the Massachusetts Constitutional Convention, 1917–1918*, 2:739.

99. Ibid., 2:229.

100. *Revised Record of the Constitutional Convention of the State of New York [1915]*, 3251.

101. *Proceedings and Debates of the Constitutional Convention of the State of Michigan [1907]*, 558.

102. Ibid., 556.

103. *Debates in the Massachusetts Constitutional Convention, 1917–1918*, 2:51.

104. *Proceedings and Debates of the Constitutional Convention of the State of Ohio [1912]*, 664.

105. The original provision that emerged from the New Mexico Convention of 1910 was complicated. Under this original plan, amendments would have generally required a two-thirds vote in the legislature and a majority vote of the people. But there were several twists. First, amendments needed only a majority vote in the legislature in the second year after the adoption of the constitution, and then in every eighth year afterward. Second, the popular vote in favor of the amendment had to equal at least 40 percent of the overall votes cast in the election, and half of all counties had to approve of the amendment. The substitute provision that was eventually approved by the voters in 1911, at Congress's urging, eliminated all of these extra requirements and permitted amendments upon a mere majority vote in the legislature and a majority vote of the people. See Thomas C. Donnelly, *The Government of New Mexico* (Albuquerque: University of New Mexico Press, 1953), 48n42, 50.

106. The four states that retained both requirements are Delaware (which does not require popular ratification), South Carolina (which requires a two-thirds vote in the first session and a majority vote in the second session), Tennessee (which requires a majority vote in the first session and a two-thirds vote in the second session), and Vermont (which requires a two-thirds vote of the senate and a majority vote of the house in the first session and a majority vote of both houses in the second session). See Delaware Constitution (1897), Art. XVI, Sec. 1; South Carolina Constitution (1895), Art. XVI, Sec. 1; Tennessee Constitution (1870), Art. XI, Sec. 3 (as amended 1953); Vermont Constitution (1793), Articles of Amendment, Art. 45 (adopted 1974).

107. The twenty-five states that permitted amendments by a supermajority legislative vote in a single legislative session are Alabama, Alaska, California, Colorado, Florida, Georgia, Idaho, Illinois, Kansas, Kentucky, Louisiana, Maine, Maryland, Michigan, Mississippi, Montana, Nebraska, New Hampshire, North Carolina, Ohio, Texas, Utah, Washington, West Virginia, and Wyoming. See Alabama Constitution (1901), Art. XVIII, Sec. 284; Alaska Constitution (1956), Art. XIII, Sec. 1; California Constitution (1879), Art. XVIII, Sec. 1 (as amended 1970); Colorado Constitution (1876), Art. XIX, Sec. 2 (as amended 1994); Florida Constitution (1968), Art. XI, Sec. 1; Georgia Constitution (1983), Art. X, Sec. I, Para. II; Idaho Constitution (1889), Art. XX, Sec. 1 (as amended 1974); Illinois Constitution (1970), Art. XIV, Sec. 2(a); Kansas Constitution (1859), Art. 14, Sec. 1 (as amended 1980); Kentucky Constitution (1891), Sec. 256 (as amended 1979); Louisiana Constitution (1974), Art. XIII, Sec. 1; Maine Constitution (1819), Art. X, Sec. 4; Maryland Constitution (1867), Art. XIV, Sec. 1 (as amended 1978); Michigan Constitution (1963), Art. XII, Sec. 1; Mississippi Constitution (1890), Art. 15, Sec. 273 (as amended 1959); Montana Constitution (1972), Art. XIV, Sec.

8; Nebraska Constitution (1875), Art. XVI, Sec. 1 (as amended 1920); New Hampshire Constitution (1784), Part II, Art. 100 (as amended 1964 and 1980); North Carolina Constitution (1971), Art. XIII, Sec. 4; Ohio Constitution (1851), Art. XVI, Sec. 1 (as amended 1974); Texas Constitution (1876), Art. 17, Sec. 1 (as amended 1972); Utah Constitution (1895), Art. XXIII, Sec. 1 (as amended 1976); Washington Constitution (1889), Art. XXIII, Sec. 1 (as amended 1962); West Virginia Constitution (1872), Art. XIV, Sec. 2 (as amended 1972); Wyoming Constitution (1889), Art. 20, Sec. 1.

The eight states that permitted amendments upon a majority vote in consecutive legislative sessions are Indiana, Iowa, Massachusetts, Nevada, New York, Pennsylvania, Virginia, and Wisconsin. See Indiana Constitution (1851), Art. 16, Sec. 1 (as amended 1998); Iowa Constitution (1857), Art. X, Sec. 1; Massachusetts Constitution (1780), Articles of Amendment, Art. XLVIII (adopted 1918); Nevada Constitution (1864), Art. 16, Sec. 1 (as amended 1998); New York Constitution (1894), Art. XIX, Sec. 1 (as amended 1938); Pennsylvania Constitution (1968), Art. XI, Sec. 1; Virginia Constitution (1971), Art. XII, Sec. 1; Wisconsin Constitution (1848), Art. XII, Sec. 1.

The three states that permitted amendments upon either a supermajority vote in a single session or a majority vote in two sessions are Connecticut, Hawaii, and New Jersey. See Connecticut Constitution (1965), Art. XII; Hawaii Constitution (1950), Art. XVII, Sec. 3 (as amended 1978); New Jersey Constitution (1947), Art. IX, Para. 1.

108. The ten states are Arizona, Arkansas, Minnesota, Missouri, New Mexico, North Dakota, Oklahoma, Oregon, Rhode Island, and South Dakota. See Arizona Constitution (1911), Art. XXI, Sec. 1; Arkansas Constitution (1874), Art. 19, Sec. 22 (as amended 1920); Minnesota Constitution (1857), Art. IX, Sec. 1 (as amended 1898); Missouri Constitution (1945), Art. XII, Sec. 2(a); New Mexico Constitution (1911), Art. XIX, Sec. 1 (as amended 1911); North Dakota Constitution (1889), Art. IV, Sec. 16 (as amended 1978); Oklahoma Constitution (1907), Art. XXIV, Sec. 1 (as amended 1974); Oregon Constitution (1857), Art. XVII, Sec. 1 (as amended 1906); Rhode Island Constitution (1986), Art. XIV, Sec. 1; South Dakota Constitution (1889), Art. XXIII, Sec. 1 (as amended 1972).

109. New Hampshire (where amendments could only be submitted by conventions) required a two-thirds popular vote. Rhode Island required a three-fifths vote. The provisions in the Alabama, Arkansas, Illinois, Indiana, Minnesota, Mississippi, Nebraska, Ohio, Oregon, Tennessee, and Wyoming constitutions were all interpreted as requiring a majority vote in the election. See Alabama Constitution (1875), Art. XVII, Sec. 1; Arkansas Constitution (1874), Art. XIX, Sec. 22; Illinois Constitution (1870), Art. XIV, Sec. 2; Indiana Constitution (1851), Art. XVI, Sec. 1; Minnesota Constitution (1857), Art. XIV, Sec. 1 (as amended 1898); Mississippi Constitution (1890), Art. 15, Sec. 273; Nebraska Constitution (1875), Art. XV, Sec. 1; New Hampshire Constitution (1784), Part II, Sec. 99 (as amended 1792); Ohio Constitution (1851), Art. XVI, Sec. 1; Oregon Constitution (1857), Art. XVII, Sec. 1; Rhode Island Constitution (1842), Art. XIII; Tennessee Constitution (1870), Art. XI, Sec. 3; Wyoming Constitution (1889), Art. XX, Sec. 1.

110. *The Records of the Arizona Constitutional Convention of 1910,* 687.

111. For discussions of the importance of the problem, as well as various efforts to get around this requirement during the late nineteenth and early twentieth centuries, see Dodd, *Revision and Amendment of State Constitutions,* 188–202; Charles V. Laughlin, "A Study in Constitutional Rigidity. I," *University of Chicago Law Review* 10 (January 1943): 142–176; and Kenneth C. Sears and Charles V. Laughlin, "A Study in Constitutional Rigidity. II," *University of Chicago Law Review* 11 (June 1944): 374–442.

112. *Journal of the Nebraska Constitutional Convention [1919]*, 667.

113. *Revised Record of the Constitutional Convention of the State of New York [1915]*, 3255.

114. Ibid., 3268.

115. New Hampshire requires a two-thirds vote. See New Hampshire Constitution (1784), Part II, Art. 100 (as amended 1792, 1964, and 1980). The states with majority-in-the-election requirements are Hawaii, Illinois (a majority in the election or three-fifths of voters on the question), Minnesota, Tennessee (a majority of those voting for governor), and Wyoming. See Hawaii Constitution (1950), Art. XVII, Sec. 2; Illinois Constitution (1970), Art. XIV, Sec. 2(b); Minnesota Constitution (1857), Art. XIV, Sec. 1 (as amended 1898); Tennessee Constitution (1870), Art. XI, Sec. 3 (as amended 1953); Wyoming Constitution (1889), Art. XX, Sec. 1. In addition, Nebraska requires that the majority of voters who support an amendment must equal at least 35 percent of voters in the election. Nebraska Constitution (1875), Art. XVI, Sec. 1 (as amended 1920).

116. For discussions of periodic convention questions in the twentieth century, see Gerald Benjamin, "The Mandatory Constitutional Convention Question Referendum: The New York Experience in National Context," *Albany Law Review* 65 (2002): 1017–1050; and May, "Constitutional Amendment and Revision Revisited," 155–156.

117. *Records of the Louisiana Constitutional Convention of 1973: Convention Transcripts*, 3171.

118. *[New Jersey] Constitutional Convention of 1947*, 1:731–732.

119. States that adopted this procedure during the twentieth century include Oklahoma (1907), Missouri (1920), Hawaii (1950), Alaska (1956), Connecticut (1965), Illinois (1970), Montana (1972), and Rhode Island (1973). For the provisions in states that allowed for a periodic convention referendum at the end of the twentieth century, see Alaska Constitution (1956), Art. XIII, Sec. 3; Connecticut Constitution (1965), Art. XIII, Sec. 2; Hawaii Constitution (1950), Art. XV, Sec. 2; Illinois Constitution (1970), Art. XIV, Sec. 1(b); Iowa Constitution (1857), Art. X, Sec. 3; Maryland Constitution (1867), Art. XIV, Sec. 2; Michigan Constitution (1963), Art. XII, Sec. 3; Missouri Constitution (1945), Art. XII, Sec. 3(a); Montana Constitution (1972), Art. XIV, Sec. 3; New Hampshire Constitution (1784), Part II, Sec. 100 (as amended 1792, 1964, and 1980); New York Constitution (1894), Art. XIX, Sec. 2 (as renumbered 1938); Ohio Constitution (1851), Art. XVI, Sec. 3 (as amended 1912); Oklahoma Constitution (1907), Art. XXIV, Sec. 2; Rhode Island Constitution (1986), Art. XIV, Sec. 2.

120. *Minutes of the Daily Proceedings, Alaska Constitutional Convention, 1955–56*, 1264–1265.

121. *Debates of the [Maryland] Constitutional Convention of 1967–1968*, 2601.

122. On the adoption of the constitutional initiative, see Dealey, *Growth of American State Constitutions*, 147–149; Sturm, *Thirty Years of State Constitution-Making*, 26–27; Janice C. May, "The Constitutional Initiative: A Threat to Rights?" in *Human Rights in the States: New Directions in Policymaking*, ed. Stanley H. Friedelbaum (Westport, Conn.: Greenwood Press, 1988), 163–184; and John F. Cooper, "The Citizen Initiative Petition to Amend State Constitutions: A Concept Whose Time Has Passed, or a Vigorous Component of Participatory Democracy at the State Level?" *New Mexico Law Review* 28 (Spring 1998): 227, 229–237.

123. *Proceedings and Debates of the Constitutional Convention of the State of Michigan [1907]*, 661.

124. *Debates in the Massachusetts Constitutional Convention, 1917–1918*, 2:414.

125. *Proceedings and Debates of the Constitutional Convention of the State of Ohio [1912],* 664.

126. *Debates in the Massachusetts Constitutional Convention, 1917–1918,* 2:295.

127. *Record of Proceedings: Sixth Illinois Constitutional Convention [1969]: Verbatim Transcripts,* 2710.

128. Ibid., 583.

129. *Debates of the [Maryland] Constitutional Convention of 1967–1968,* 2588.

130. *Proceedings and Debates of the Constitutional Convention of the State of Michigan [1907],* 578.

131. *Texas Constitutional Convention [1974]: Official Proceedings,* 736.

132. The states that adopted the constitutional initiative between 1900 and 1920 are Oregon (1902), Oklahoma (1907), Michigan (1908), Missouri (1908), Arkansas (1910), Colorado (1910), California (1911), Arizona (1911), Nebraska (1912), Nevada (1912), Ohio (1912), North Dakota (1914), and Massachusetts (1918). The states that adopted the constitutional initiative later in the twentieth century are Florida (1968), Illinois (1970), Montana (1972), South Dakota (1972), and Mississippi (where it was originally adopted in 1914, only to be invalidated by the state supreme court in 1922, then reenacted in 1992).

These states vary in their requirements for initiating and ratifying amendments, but two distinctive requirements particularly deserve mention. Illinois permits the constitutional initiative to be used only to amend the legislative article. Meanwhile, Massachusetts and Mississippi both provide for the indirect initiative, whereby initiated measures must first be submitted to the legislature. In Massachusetts, an initiated measure must be approved by one-fourth of both houses in two sessions before popular ratification. In Mississippi, an initiated measure must first be submitted to the legislature and may be amended, but in this case, the original measure must also be placed on the ballot for the consideration of the people.

For the current provisions, see Arizona Constitution (1911), Art. XXI, Sec. 1; Arkansas Constitution (1874), Amendment 7 (adopted 1920); California Constitution (1879), Art. XVIII, Sec. 3 (as amended 1970); Colorado Constitution (1876), Art. V, Sec. 1(5) (as amended 1910); Florida Constitution (1968), Art. XI, Sec. 3; Illinois Constitution (1970), Art. XIV, Sec. 3; Massachusetts Constitution (1780), Articles of Amendment, Art. XLVIII (adopted 1918), Amendment LXXXI (adopted 1950); Michigan Constitution (1963), Art. XII, Sec. 2; Mississippi Constitution (1890), Art. 15, Sec. 273 (as amended 1992); Missouri Constitution (1945), Art. XII, Sec. 2(b); Montana Constitution (1972), Art. XIV, Sec. 9; Nebraska Constitution (1875), Art. III, Sec. 2, 4 (adopted 1912); Nevada Constitution (1864), Art. 19, Sec. 2 (adopted 1912); North Dakota Constitution (1889), Art. III, Sec. 9 (as amended 1914 and 1918); Ohio Constitution (1851), Art. II, Sec. 1a (as amended 1912); Oklahoma Constitution (1907), Art. XXIV, Sec. 3; Oregon Constitution (1857), Art. IV, Sec. 1(2)(c) (as amended 1902); South Dakota Constitution (1889), Art. XXIII, Sec. 1 (as amended 1972).

Chapter 3: Representation

1. Much of this commentary has been quite critical of the states' approach, particularly regarding the popular initiative and referendum. See, for instance, David B. Magleby, *Direct Legislation: Voting on Ballot Propositions in the United States* (Baltimore: Johns Hopkins University Press, 1984); California Commission on Campaign Financing, *Democracy by Initiative: Shaping California's Fourth Branch of Government* (Los Angeles: Center for Responsive

Government, 1992); John Haskell, *Direct Democracy or Representative Government: Dispelling the Populist Myth* (Boulder, Colo.: Westview Press, 2001); John M. Allswang, *The Initiative and Referendum in California, 1898–1998* (Stanford, Calif.: Stanford University Press, 2000); and Richard J. Ellis, *Democratic Delusions: The Initiative Process in America* (Lawrence: University Press of Kansas, 2002). For exceptions, see Laura Tallian, *Direct Democracy* (Los Angeles: People's Lobby Press, 1977); Joseph F. Zimmerman, *Participatory Democracy: Populism Revived* (Westport, Conn.: Praeger, 1986); David D. Schmidt, *Citizen Lawmakers: The Ballot Initiative Revolution* (Philadelphia: Temple University Press, 1989); Thomas E. Cronin, *Direct Democracy: The Politics of Initiative, Referendum, and Recall* (Cambridge, Mass.: Harvard University Press, 1989); M. Dane Waters, ed., *The Battle over Citizen Lawmaking* (Durham, N.C.: Carolina Academic Press, 2001); and John G. Matsusaka, *For the Many or the Few: The Initiative, Public Policy, and American Democracy* (Chicago: University of Chicago Press, 2004).

2. Federalist No. 63, in Alexander Hamilton et al., *The Federalist Papers*, ed. Clinton Rossiter (1961; reprint, New York: Mentor, 1999), 355.

3. Federalist No. 10, ibid., 46.

4. Ibid., 48.

5. Ibid., 49.

6. Ibid., 49–50. For discussions of the logic underlying the Madisonian preference for republicanism over direct democracy, see Joseph M. Bessette, *The Mild Voice of Reason: Deliberative Democracy and American National Government* (Chicago: University Press of Chicago, 1994), 6–39; and Charles R. Kesler, "The Founders' Views of Direct Democracy and Representation," in *Democracy: How Direct? Views from the Founding Era and the Polling Era*, ed. Elliot Abrams (Lanham, Md.: Rowman & Littlefield, 2002): 1–18.

7. The leading source is Ellis Paxson Oberholtzer, *The Referendum in America, Together with Some Chapters on the Initiative and Recall* (New York: Charles Scribner's Sons, 1911). Several other useful accounts are Frederick A. Cleveland, *The Growth of Democracy in the United States* (Chicago: Quadrangle Press, 1898); Charles S. Lobingier, *The People's Law, or Popular Participation in Law-Making* (New York: Macmillan, 1909); Arthur N. Holcombe, *State Government in the United States*, 2nd ed. (New York: Macmillan, 1926), 132–141, 478–520; James Bryce, *The American Commonwealth* (1914; reprint, Indianapolis, Ind.: Liberty Fund, 1995), 1:400–426; and Steven L. Piott, *Giving Voters a Voice: The Origins of the Initiative and Referendum in America* (Columbia: University of Missouri Press, 2003).

8. For contemporaneous accounts, see William Bennett Munro, ed., *The Initiative, Referendum and Recall* (New York: D. Appleton, 1912); Edwin M. Bacon and Morrill Wyman, *Direct Elections and Law-Making by Popular Vote* (Boston: Houghton Mifflin, 1912); Herbert Croly, *Progressive Democracy* (New York: Macmillan, 1914); and Benjamin Parke De Witt, *The Progressive Movement: A Non-Partisan, Comprehensive Discussion of Current Tendencies in American Politics* (New York: Macmillan, 1915). For several recent accounts of this period, see Sarah M. Henry, "Progressivism and Democracy: Electoral Reform in the United States, 1888–1919" (Ph.D. diss., Columbia University, 1995); and Thomas Goebel, *A Government by the People: Direct Democracy in America, 1890–1940* (Chapel Hill: University of North Carolina Press, 2002). For a brief account that stretches back to the founding era, see G. Alan Tarr, "For the People: Direct Democracy in the State Constitutional Tradition," in Abrams, *Democracy: How Direct?*, 87–99.

9. Thomas Goebel took note of this inattention to state convention debates in his recent account of direct democracy, when he noted that at the federal level, various institutional

devices "slowed down the pace of constitutional change," but "the situation was strikingly different at the state level, an arena of constitutional experimentation that has received little attention from historians and legal scholars." Goebel, *Government by the People,* 49. For studies that have made use of convention debates in analyzing the origin of direct democracy at the state level, see Henry, "Progressivism and Democracy," 474–497; John J. Dinan, *Keeping the People's Liberties: Legislators, Citizens, and Judges as Guardians of Rights* (Lawrence: University Press of Kansas, 1998), 60–79; and John Dinan, "Framing a 'People's Government': State Constitution-Making in the Progressive Era," *Rutgers Law Journal* 30 (Summer 1999): 933, 964–974.

10. For a debate about the right of citizens to instruct their representatives, see *Report of the Debates in the Convention of California on the Formation of the State Constitution [1849],* 294–297.

11. The debates about compulsory voting are found in the following sources:

Massachusetts: *Debates in the Massachusetts Constitutional Convention, 1917–1918,* 3:20–83.

Nebraska: *Journal of the Nebraska Constitutional Convention [1919],* 537–540.

New York: *Revised Record of the Constitutional Convention of the State of New York [1894],* 1:1058–1100.

Ohio: *Proceedings and Debates of the Constitutional Convention of the State of Ohio [1912],* 1192–1195.

12. The debates about adopting proportional representation in state legislative elections are found in the following sources:

Illinois: *Debates and Proceedings of the Constitutional Convention of the State of Illinois [1869],* 175–176, 561–564, 1191–1193, 1726–1729; *Record of Proceedings: Sixth Illinois Constitutional Convention [1969]: Verbatim Transcripts,* 2657–2666, 2744–2776, 2781–2810, 4048–4058, 4063–4066, 4070–4072, 4089–4101, 4107–4118, 4314–4333, 4345–4399, 4407–4416, 4462–4468, 4553–4563, 4574–4604.

Massachusetts: *Debates in the Massachusetts Constitutional Convention, 1917–1918,* 3:202–207.

Michigan: *Proceedings and Debates of the Constitutional Convention of the State of Michigan [1907],* 902–906.

Missouri: *Debates of the Missouri Constitutional Convention of 1875,* 6:274–278.

Nebraska: *Official Report of the Debates and Proceedings in the Nebraska Constitutional Convention [1871],* 1:304–308; 2:121–134; 3:259–265, 341–348.

New Hampshire: *Journal of the Constitutional Convention of the State of New Hampshire, December 1876,* 166–173.

North Dakota: *Official Report of the Proceedings and Debates of the First Constitutional Convention of North Dakota [1889],* 347–349.

Ohio: *Official Report of the Proceedings and Debates of the Third Constitutional Convention of Ohio [1873],* 2:1577–1591, 1680–1694, 3517–3526.

South Dakota: *Dakota Constitutional Convention [1885, 1889],* 1:381–382.

13. These debates about the popular recall are found in the following sources:

Alaska: *Minutes of the Daily Proceedings, Alaska Constitutional Convention, 1955–56,* 1207–1217, 1221–1240.

Arizona: *The Records of the Arizona Constitutional Convention of 1910,* 242–246, 260–270, 800–812, 920–922, 925–929.

Hawaii: *Proceedings of the Constitutional Convention of Hawaii, 1978,* 2:851–854.

Michigan: *Official Record, State of Michigan Constitutional Convention, 1961,* 2263–2267.

Nebraska: *Journal of the Nebraska Constitutional Convention [1919],* 1526–1541.

Ohio: *Proceedings and Debates of the Constitutional Convention of the State of Ohio [1912],* 1291–1311, 1773–1775.

14. The debates about mandatory referendums generally occurred in the course of wide-ranging debates about restricting legislative power in particular areas, such as banking, making internal improvements, extending loans of state credit, incurring state debt, or increasing taxes.

The debates about restrictions on legislative power regarding banking are found in the following sources:

California: *Report of the Debates in the Convention of California on the Formation of the State Constitution [1849],* 108–121, 124–135, 324–329; *Debates and Proceedings of the Constitutional Convention of the State of California [1878],* 421–429.

Delaware: *Debates and Proceedings of the Constitutional Convention of the State of Delaware [1852–1853],* 246–247, 257.

Illinois: *The [Illinois] Constitutional Debates of 1847,* 85–89, 164–170, 251–283, 641–694, 703–719; *Record of Proceedings: Sixth Illinois Constitutional Convention [1969]: Verbatim Transcripts,* 1110–1114, 1118–1150, 1164–1168.

Indiana: *Report of the Debates and Proceedings of the Convention for the Revision of the Constitution of the State of Indiana, 1850,* 1414–1420, 1426–1429, 1436–1649, 1779–1787, 1919–1928, 1983–1996.

Iowa: *Fragments of the Debates of the Iowa Constitutional Conventions of 1844 and 1846,* 67–102, 141–150, 195–204; *The Debates of the Constitutional Convention of the State of Iowa [1857],* 344–360, 373–394, 404–407, 773–775, 785–794.

Kansas: *A Reprint of the Proceedings and Debates of the Convention Which Framed the Constitution of Kansas at Wyandotte in July, 1859,* 84–94, 96–112, 553–554.

Maryland: *The Debates of the Constitutional Convention of the State of Maryland [1864],* 832–845, 851–858.

Massachusetts: *Official Report of the Debates and Proceedings in the State Convention to Revise and Amend the Constitution of the Commonwealth of Massachusetts [1853],* 3:318–336, 351–360.

Michigan: *The Michigan Constitutional Conventions of 1835–36: Debates and Proceedings,* 389–392; *Report of the Proceedings and Debates in the Convention to Revise the Constitution of the State of Michigan, 1850,* 555–583, 691–697; *The Debates and Proceedings of the Constitutional Convention of the State of Michigan [1867],* 1:146–148.

Minnesota: *The Debates and Proceedings of the Minnesota Constitutional Convention [1857],* 397, 399–417; *Debates and Proceedings of the Constitutional Convention for the Territory of Minnesota [1857],* 141–146, 307–329.

Missouri: *Debates of the Missouri Constitutional Convention of 1875,* 11:215–225.

Nevada: *Official Report of the Debates and Proceedings in the Constitutional Convention of the State of Nevada [1864],* 451–458.

New Jersey: *Proceedings of the New Jersey State Constitutional Convention of 1844,* 311–323.

New York: *Report of the Debates and Proceedings of the Convention for the Revision of the Constitution of the State of New York, 1846,* 182–185, 985–1005.

Pennsylvania: *Proceedings and Debates of the Convention of the Commonwealth of*

Pennsylvania [1837], 1:358–391; 5:473–513; 6:34–202, 206–339, 350–369, 372–469; 7:5–138, 154–383, 411–430; 8:5–38, 50–71; 9:104–217.

Wisconsin: *The [Wisconsin] Convention of 1846*, 84–87, 98–134, 138–143, 147–187, 200–204, 462–465, 470–478, 508–510, 690–697; *Journal of the Convention to Form a Constitution for the State of Wisconsin [1847–1848]*, 265–290, 295–318.

The debates about restrictions on legislative power regarding internal improvements are found in the following sources:

Alabama: *Official Proceedings of the Constitutional Convention of the State of Alabama [1901]*, 2631–2643.

Delaware: *Debates of the Delaware Convention, for Revising the Constitution [1831]*, 160–161; *Debates and Proceedings of the Constitutional Convention of the State of Delaware [1852–1853]*, 213–214.

Illinois: *Debates and Proceedings of the Constitutional Convention of the State of Illinois [1869]*, 311–320, 323–343, 347–365, 368–389, 395–424, 429–451, 453–479, 484–486; *Proceedings of the Constitutional Convention of the State of Illinois, Convened January 6, 1920*, 1052–1069, 1075–1099, 1108–1121, 1984–2052, 3893–3894, 4414–4439.

Iowa: *Fragments of the Debates of the Iowa Constitutional Conventions of 1844 and 1846*, 52–54.

Maryland: *Debates and Proceedings of the Maryland Reform Convention to Revise the State Constitution [1851]*, 1:338–355.

Minnesota: *Debates and Proceedings of the Constitutional Convention for the Territory of Minnesota [1857]*, 462–466, 471–475.

New York: *Revised Record of the Constitutional Convention of the State of New York [1894]*, 4:327–329.

West Virginia: *Debates and Proceedings of the First Constitutional Convention of West Virginia (1861–1863)*, 2:396–410; 3:2–43, 127–135, 144–276.

Wisconsin: *The [Wisconsin] Convention of 1846*, 323–324, 487–489; *Journal of the Convention to Form a Constitution for the State of Wisconsin [1847–1848]*, 207–212, 345–352.

The debates about restrictions on legislative power regarding the loaning of state credit are located in the following sources:

Illinois: *Debates and Proceedings of the Constitutional Convention of the State of Illinois [1869]*, 214–222, 284–289, 294–305.

Indiana: *Report of the Debates and Proceedings of the Convention for the Revision of the Constitution of the State of Indiana, 1850*, 644–652.

Massachusetts: *Official Report of the Debates and Proceedings in the State Convention to Revise and Amend the Constitution of the Commonwealth of Massachusetts [1853]*, 2:281–314, 638–683; 3:2–26.

Nevada: *Official Report of the Debates and Proceedings in the Constitutional Convention of the State of Nevada [1864]*, 166–192, 203–218, 387–404, 458–464, 467–477, 494–498.

New York: *Report of the Debates and Proceedings of the Convention for the Revision of the Constitution of the State of New York, 1846*, 54–61.

North Dakota: *Official Report of the Proceedings and Debates of the First Constitutional Convention of North Dakota [1889]*, 437–438.

Utah: *Official Report of the Proceedings and Debates of the Convention . . . To Adopt a Constitution for the State of Utah [1895]*, 894–929.

The debates about restrictions on legislative power regarding the incurring of state debt are located in the following sources:

Alabama: *The History and Debates of the Convention of the People of Alabama [1861]*, 281–292.

Alaska: *Minutes of the Daily Proceedings, Alaska Constitutional Convention, 1955–56*, 2416–2447, 3402–3407.

California: *Report of the Debates in the Convention of California on the Formation of the State Constitution [1849]*, 165–166.

Delaware: *Debates and Proceedings of the Constitutional Convention of the State of Delaware [1852–1853]*, 213–214; *Debates and Proceedings of the Constitutional Convention of the State of Delaware [1896]*, 1417–1422, 1487–1497, 1520–1529, 1563–1565.

Georgia: *A Stenographic Report of the Proceedings of the Constitutional Convention held in Atlanta, Georgia, 1877*, 295–299.

Idaho: *Proceedings and Debates of the Constitutional Convention of Idaho, 1889*, 561–584.

Illinois: *The [Illinois] Constitutional Debates of 1847*, 353–355; *Debates and Proceedings of the Constitutional Convention of the State of Illinois [1869]*, 615–617, 636–642.

Indiana: *Report of the Debates and Proceedings of the Convention for the Revision of the Constitution of the State of Indiana, 1850*, 652–715, 725–741, 916–917.

Iowa: *Fragments of the Debates of the Iowa Constitutional Conventions of 1844 and 1846*, 47–49; *The Debates of the Constitutional Convention of the State of Iowa [1857]*, 260–275.

Kansas: *A Reprint of the Proceedings and Debates of the Convention Which Framed the Constitution of Kansas at Wyandotte in July, 1859*, 327–328.

Kentucky: *Report of the Debates and Proceedings of the Convention for the Revision of the Constitution of the State of Kentucky, 1849*, 753–777, 781–786.

Louisiana: *Proceedings and Debates of the Convention of Louisiana [1845]*, 838–840, 878–880; *Records of the Louisiana Constitutional Convention of 1973: Convention Transcripts*, 2800–2807.

Maryland: *Debates and Proceedings of the Maryland Reform Convention to Revise the State Constitution [1851]*, 1:338–355; *The Debates of the Constitutional Convention of the State of Maryland [1864]*, 802; *Debates of the [Maryland] Constitutional Convention of 1967–1968*, 1791–1815, 2859–2861.

Michigan: *Official Record, State of Michigan Constitutional Convention, 1961*, 602–629, 2620–2627.

Minnesota: *The Debates and Proceedings of the Minnesota Constitutional Convention [1857]*, 393–396; *Debates and Proceedings of the Constitutional Convention for the Territory of Minnesota [1857]*, 462–466, 471–475.

Missouri: *Debates of the Missouri Constitutional Convention of 1875*, 7:326–352, 368–376.

Nebraska: *Official Report of the Debates and Proceedings in the Nebraska Constitutional Convention [1871]*, 2:387–389; *Journal of the Nebraska Constitutional Convention [1919]*, 1308–1312, 2536–2538.

New Hampshire: *Journal of the Convention to Revise the [New Hampshire] Constitution, May 1984*, 253–259, 268–271.

New Jersey: *Proceedings of the New Jersey State Constitutional Convention of 1844*, 310–311.

New York: *Report of the Debates and Proceedings of the Convention for the Revision of the Constitution of the State of New York, 1846,* 943–950; *Proceedings and Debates of the Constitutional Convention of the State of New York Held in 1867 and 1868,* 790–812, 1852–1862, 2246–2248, 3747–3755; *Revised Record of the Constitutional Convention of the State of New York [1915],* 1254–1325, 2366–2370; *Proceedings of the Constitutional Convention of the State of New York [1967],* 4:72–120.

North Dakota: *Official Report of the Proceedings and Debates of the First Constitutional Convention of North Dakota [1889],* 426–430; *Debates of the North Dakota Constitutional Convention of 1972,* 1256–1264, 1332–1342, 1479–1494.

Ohio: *Report of the Debates and Proceedings of the Convention for the Revision of the Constitution of the State of Ohio, 1850–51,* 1:466–472; *Official Report of the Proceedings and Debates of the Third Constitutional Convention of Ohio [1873],* 2:2511–2541; *Proceedings and Debates of the Constitutional Convention of the State of Ohio [1912],* 207–224, 259–289, 295–317, 320–328, 343–351, 1777–1784.

Pennsylvania: *Proceedings and Debates of the Convention of the Commonwealth of Pennsylvania [1837],* 12:110–113.

Rhode Island: *Proceedings of the Limited Constitutional Convention of the State of Rhode Island [1951],* 70–75.

South Carolina: *Proceedings of the Constitutional Convention of South Carolina [1868],* 656–658.

South Dakota: *Dakota Constitutional Convention [1885, 1889],* 2:494–531.

Texas: *Debates in the Texas Constitutional Convention of 1875,* 114–115; *Texas Constitutional Convention [1974]: Official Proceedings,* 863–889.

Utah: *Official Report of the Proceedings and Debates of the Convention . . . To Adopt a Constitution for the State of Utah [1895],* 1116–1142, 1184–1201.

Virginia: *Register of the Debates and Proceedings of the Va. Reform Convention [1850–1851],* 285–287; *Report of the Proceedings and Debates of the Constitutional Convention, State of Virginia [1901–1902],* 2891–2901.

Wisconsin: *The [Wisconsin] Convention of 1846,* 322–323; *Journal of the Convention to Form a Constitution for the State of Wisconsin [1847–1848],* 195–197, 203–204.

Debates about restricting legislative power to increase taxes are located in the following sources:

New Hampshire: *Journal of the Convention to Revise the [New Hampshire] Constitution, May 1974,* 366–376; *Journal of the Convention to Revise the [New Hampshire] Constitution, May 1984,* 76–78.

New York: *Proceedings and Debates of the Constitutional Convention of the State of New York Held in 1867 and 1868,* 1799–1827.

For a proposed mandatory referendum on *all* legislation, see South Dakota: *Dakota Constitutional Convention [1885, 1889],* 1:113.

15. For the most part, these debates concerned the legitimacy of optional referendums for any subject. These debates are located in the following sources:

Indiana: *Report of the Debates and Proceedings of the Convention for the Revision of the Constitution of the State of Indiana, 1850,* 1256–1257, 1269.

Iowa: *The Debates of the Constitutional Convention of the State of Iowa [1857],* 140, 801–805.

Massachusetts: *Debates in the Massachusetts Constitutional Convention, 1917–1918,* 3:381–382.

Michigan: *Proceedings and Debates of the Constitutional Convention of the State of Michigan [1907]*, 1215–1216, 1372–1377.

Minnesota: *Debates and Proceedings of the Constitutional Convention for the Territory of Minnesota [1857]*, 204–205, 517.

New York: *Revised Record of the Constitutional Convention of the State of New York [1894]*, 2:798–817; 3:106–109.

Ohio: *Report of the Debates and Proceedings of the Convention for the Revision of the Constitution of the State of Ohio, 1850–51*, 1:259–260, 2:215–219, 221–228; *Official Report of the Proceedings and Debates of the Third Constitutional Convention of Ohio [1873]*, 2:248–249, 1492–1498.

Oregon: *The Oregon Constitution and Proceedings and Debates of the Oregon Convention of 1857*, 316, 330.

Rhode Island: *State of Rhode Island and Providence Plantations: Constitutional Convention [1964–1969]: Report of Proceedings*, 1197–1198.

On several occasions, these debates concerned the legitimacy of optional referendums on particular subjects such as liquor prohibition or the extension of the suffrage. These debates are located in the following sources:

Delaware: *Debates and Proceedings of the Constitutional Convention of the State of Delaware [1896]*, 2281–2377, 2951–2964.

New Hampshire: *Journal of the [New Hampshire] Constitutional Convention of 1902*, 460–490, 691–709.

Ohio: *Official Report of the Proceedings and Debates of the Third Constitutional Convention of Ohio [1873]*, 2:2888–2912, 2918–2944, 2996–3094, 3162–3185.

Oregon: *The Oregon Constitution and Proceedings and Debates of the Oregon Convention of 1857*, 163–171.

Pennsylvania: *Debates of the Convention to Amend the Constitution of Pennsylvania [1872–1873]*, 3:39–73; 5:314–326.

West Virginia: *Debates and Proceedings of the First Constitutional Convention of West Virginia (1861–1863)*, 2:410–437.

16. The debates about the popular initiative and referendum are located in the following sources:

Alaska: *Minutes of the Daily Proceedings, Alaska Constitutional Convention, 1955–56*, 928–982, 993–1088, 1121–1142, 1167–1207, 2947–2992.

Arizona: *The Records of the Arizona Constitutional Convention of 1910*, 175–234, 379–382, 734–751.

Connecticut: *The Third Constitutional Convention of the State of Connecticut: Proceedings [1965]*, 283–292.

Hawaii: *Proceedings of the Constitutional Convention of Hawaii, 1950*, 2:774–780; *Proceedings of the Constitutional Convention of Hawaii of 1968*, 2:520–523; *Proceedings of the Constitutional Convention of Hawaii, 1978*, 2:808–851.

Illinois: *Proceedings of the Constitutional Convention of the State of Illinois, Convened January 6, 1920*, 239–342, 715–780, 2475–2522.

Maryland: *Debates of the [Maryland] Constitutional Convention of 1967–1968*, 644–669, 671–732.

Massachusetts: *Debates in the Massachusetts Constitutional Convention, 1917–1918*, 2:1–1062.

Michigan: *Proceedings and Debates of the Constitutional Convention of the State of*

Michigan [1907], 546–686, 1372–1377; *Official Record, State of Michigan Constitutional Convention, 1961*, 2390–2397.

Montana: *Montana Constitutional Convention, 1971–1972: Verbatim Transcript*, 2695–2720, 2823–2825.

Nebraska: *Journal of the Nebraska Constitutional Convention [1919]*, 258–261, 455–459, 473–484, 494–517, 1408–1410, 2647–2651.

New Hampshire: *Journal of the [New Hampshire] Constitutional Convention of 1902*, 782–790; *Journal of the Convention to Revise the [New Hampshire] Constitution, June 1912*, 152–199, 342–379; *Journal of the Convention to Revise the [New Hampshire] Convention, January 20, 1920*, 306–333; *Journal of the Convention to Revise the [New Hampshire] Constitution, May, 1938*, 118–122; *Journal of the Convention to Revise the [New Hampshire] Constitution, May 1948*, 99–103; *Journal of the Convention to Revise the [New Hampshire] Constitution, May 1984*, 79–84.

North Dakota: *Debates of the North Dakota Constitutional Convention of 1972*, 885–929, 1391–1394, 1623–1626, 1635–1650.

Ohio: *Proceedings and Debates of the Constitutional Convention of the State of Ohio [1912]*, 552–555, 671–717, 726–744, 756–954, 1882–1902, 1906–1909, 1933–1943.

Rhode Island: *State of Rhode Island and Providence Plantations: Constitutional Convention [1964–1969]: Report of Proceedings*, 1198–1199.

Texas: *Texas Constitutional Convention [1974]: Official Proceedings*, 1287–1293, 2028–2048.

17. Proposals to institute direct democracy at the federal level were introduced in Congress on three principal occasions. Several proposals were introduced along these lines during the Populist and Progressive eras, including an 1895 amendment advanced by Kansas senator William Peffer that would have permitted the people or state legislatures to force the submission of various measures to a national popular vote. Then, before and during World War I, and again in the years preceding World War II, various amendments were proposed that would have required a national popular referendum on whether the United States should enter or continue a war, including an amendment by Indiana representative Louis Ludlow that was defeated in the House in 1938. Finally, in 1977, South Dakota senator James Abourezk introduced a national initiative and referendum amendment that was the subject of several Senate subcommittee hearings. See Robert Allen, "National Initiative Proposal: A Preliminary Analysis," *Nebraska Law Review* 58 (1979): 965–1052; Cronin, *Direct Democracy*, 157–195; John R. Vile, *Encyclopedia of Constitutional Amendments, Proposed Amendments, and Amending Issues, 1789–1995* (Santa Barbara, Calif.: ABC-CLIO, 1996), 164–166; and Donald R. Wolfensberger, *Congress and the People: Deliberative Democracy on Trial* (Washington, D.C.: Woodrow Wilson Center Press, 2000), 71–85, 129–146.

18. Cleveland, *Growth of Democracy*, 173.

19. Lobingier, *People's Law*, 349–350.

20. Holcombe, *State Government in the United States*, 133.

21. Cleveland, *Growth of Democracy*, 182.

22. Texas was the first state to provide for a referendum on the location of the capital, and during the course of the nineteenth century, several other states adopted a similar policy. See Texas Constitution (1845), Art. III, Sec. 35. For a discussion, see Cleveland, *Growth of Democracy*, 215–216.

23. Wisconsin was the first state to include in its constitution a clause providing that the legislature could extend the suffrage but only upon the approval of a popular majority. See

Wisconsin Constitution (1848), Art. III, Sec. 1. For a discussion, see Oberholtzer, *Referendum in America,* 193–195.

24. Among the more interesting provisions of this sort was a clause in the Virginia Constitution (1851), Art. IV, Sec. 5, providing that in case of a failure of the legislature to agree on a principle of legislative apportionment, voters would have the opportunity to make the selection from among four possible apportionment rules.

25. The 1848 Constitutions of Illinois and Wisconsin each prohibited the removal of a county seat without the consent of the voters in the county, and many other states adopted similar requirements. See Illinois Constitution (1848), Art. VII, Sec. 5; Wisconsin Constitution (1848), Art. XIII, Sec. 8. For a discussion, see Cleveland, *Growth of Democracy,* 225–227.

26. Tennessee in its Constitution of 1835 was the first state to require popular approval of any changes in county boundaries, and many states followed this precedent. See Tennessee Constitution (1835), Art. X, Sec. 4. For a discussion, see Cleveland, *Growth of Democracy,* 222–225.

27. For discussions of state efforts to respond to these problems, see William J. Shultz, "Limitations on State and Local Borrowing Powers," *Annals of the American Academy of Political and Social Science* 181 (September 1935): 118–119; B. U. Ratchford, *American State Debts* (Durham, N.C.: Duke University Press, 1941), 73–134; Carter Goodrich, "The Revulsion against Internal Improvements," *Journal of Economic History* 10 (November 1950): 145–169; James Roger Sharp, *The Jacksonians versus the Banks: Politics in the States after the Panic of 1837* (New York: Columbia University Press, 1970); John Lauritz Larson, *Internal Improvement: National Public Works and the Promise of Popular Government in the Early United States* (Chapel Hill: University of North Carolina Press, 2001), 195–224; and John Joseph Wallis, "Constitutions, Corporations, and Corruption: American States and Constitutional Change, 1842 to 1852," *Journal of Economic History* 65 (March 2005): 211–256. For a discussion of the mid-nineteenth-century debates over the legislative referendum in New York in particular, see L. Ray Gunn, *The Decline of Authority: Public Economic Policy and Political Development in New York State, 1800–1860* (Ithaca, N.Y.: Cornell University Press, 1988), 153–158, 170–196.

28. *Report of the Debates and Proceedings of the Convention for the Revision of the Constitution of the State of Kentucky, 1849,* 757.

29. *Journal of the Convention to Form a Constitution for the State of Wisconsin [1847–1848],* 208.

30. *Register of the Debates and Proceedings of the Va. Reform Convention [1850–1851],* 286.

31. *Report of the Debates and Proceedings of the Convention for the Revision of the Constitution of the State of New York, 1846,* 949.

32. *Report of the Debates and Proceedings of the Convention for the Revision of the Constitution of the State of Indiana, 1850,* 683.

33. *Report of the Debates and Proceedings of the Convention for the Revision of the Constitution of the State of New York, 1846,* 943.

34. Charles A. Beard and Birl E. Schultz, *Documents on the State-Wide Initiative, Referendum, and Recall* (New York: Macmillan, 1912), 6. For a comprehensive treatment of these state-debt limitations, see A. James Heins, *Constitutional Restrictions against State Debt* (Madison: University of Wisconsin Press, 1963).

35. *Report of the Proceedings and Debates in the Convention to Revise the Constitution of the State of Michigan, 1850,* 562.

36. *The [Illinois] Constitutional Debates of 1847*, 165.

37. *Report of the Proceedings and Debates in the Convention to Revise the Constitution of the State of Michigan, 1850*, 562–563.

38. *Report of the Proceedings and Debates in the Convention to Revise the Constitution of the State of Michigan, 1850*, 583.

39. Ibid., 562.

40. See, for instance, the West Virginia Constitution (1863), Art. XI, Sec. 5.

41. See, for instance, the Delaware Constitution (1897), Art. VIII, Sec. 3.

42. See, for instance, the Alabama Constitution (1875), Art. IV, Sec. 54.

43. *Journal of the Convention to Form a Constitution for the State of Wisconsin [1847–1848]*, 208, 209.

44. *Official Report of the Debates and Proceedings in the Constitutional Convention of the State of Nevada [1864]*, 175, 176.

45. *Report of the Debates and Proceedings of the Convention for the Revision of the Constitution of the State of Indiana, 1850*, 662.

46. *A Reprint of the Proceedings and Debates of the Convention Which Framed the Constitution of Kansas at Wyandotte in July, 1859*, 85.

47. *Report of the Proceedings and Debates in the Convention to Revise the Constitution of the State of Michigan, 1850*, 583.

48. *Report of the Debates and Proceedings of the Convention for the Revision of the Constitution of the State of New York, 1846*, 948.

49. *Report of the Debates and Proceedings of the Convention for the Revision of the Constitution of the State of Indiana, 1850*, 666.

50. *Fragments of the Debates of the Iowa Constitutional Conventions of 1844 and 1846*, 48.

51. *The Debates of the Constitutional Convention of the State of Iowa [1857]*, 269.

52. *Report of the Proceedings and Debates in the Convention to Revise the Constitution of the State of Michigan, 1850*, 561.

53. *Report of the Debates and Proceedings of the Convention for the Revision of the Constitution of the State of Kentucky, 1849*, 785.

54. *Fragments of the Debates of the Iowa Constitutional Conventions of 1844 and 1846*, 49.

55. *The Debates of the Constitutional Convention of the State of Iowa [1857]*, 265.

56. *Report of the Proceedings and Debates in the Convention to Revise the Constitution of the State of Michigan, 1850*, 561.

57. *Report of the Debates and Proceedings of the Convention for the Revision of the Constitution of the State of New York, 1846*, 945.

58. Ibid., 945.

59. *Report of the Proceedings and Debates in the Convention to Revise the Constitution of the State of Michigan, 1850*, 558.

60. *Report of the Debates and Proceedings of the Convention for the Revision of the Constitution of the State of New York, 1846*, 947.

61. Ibid., 945.

62. *Official Report of the Debates and Proceedings in the State Convention to Revise and Amend the Constitution of the Commonwealth of Massachusetts [1853]*, 2:307.

63. Ibid., 2:675.

64. *Official Report of the Proceedings and Debates of the Third Constitutional Convention of Ohio [1873]*, 2:2641.

65. Ibid., 2:2528.

66. See the Rhode Island Constitution (1842), Art. IV, Sec. 13. For discussions of Rhode Island's leadership role on this issue, see Cleveland, *Growth of Democracy*, 213; Oberholtzer, *Referendum in America*, 183; Lobingier, *People's Law*, 353; Holcombe, *State Government in the United States*, 136; and Ratchford, *American State Debts*, 122.

67. States that followed suit during the nineteenth century included Michigan, New Jersey, New York, Iowa, Illinois, California, Kentucky, Kansas, North Carolina, Arkansas, Missouri, Colorado, Idaho, Montana, Washington, Wyoming, and South Carolina. For discussions, see Cleveland, *Growth of Democracy*, 213–215; Oberholtzer, *Referendum in America*, 183–186; and Goodrich, "Revulsion against Internal Improvements," 156–161. For these constitutional provisions, which required referendums on the incurring of state debt and/ or the loaning of state credit, depending on the particular state, see Arkansas Constitution (1868), Art. X, Sec. 6; California Constitution (1849), Art. VIII; Colorado Constitution (1876), Art. XI, Sec. 5; Idaho Constitution (1889), Art. VIII, Sec. 1; Illinois Constitution (1848), Art. III, Sec. 37; Iowa Constitution (1846), Art. 7; Kansas Constitution (1859), Art. 11, Sec. 6; Kentucky Constitution (1850), Art. II, Sec. 36; Michigan Constitution (1836), Amendment No. II (adopted 1844); Missouri Constitution (1875), Art IV, Sec. 44; Montana Constitution (1889), Art. XIII, Sec. 2; New Jersey Constitution (1844), Art. IV, Sec. VI(4); New York Constitution (1846), Art. VII, Sec. 12; North Carolina Constitution (1868), Art. V, Sec. 5; South Carolina Constitution (1868), Art. 16 (adopted 1873); Washington Constitution (1889), Art. VIII, Sec. 3; Wyoming Constitution (1889), Art. XVI, Sec. 2.

68. Illinois Constitution (1848), Art. III, Sec. 37. On Illinois's leadership role, see Cleveland, *Growth of Democracy*, 220.

69. States that adopted these provisions in the nineteenth century included Minnesota, Colorado, Idaho, Montana, and Utah. For a discussion, see Cleveland, *Growth of Democracy*, 220–221; and Oberholtzer, *Referendum in America*, 189–190. For the specific constitutional provisions, see the Colorado Constitution (1876), Art. X, Sec. 11; Idaho Constitution (1889), Art. VII, Sec. 9; Minnesota Constitution (1857), Art. IX, Sec. 2; Montana Constitution (1889), Art. XII, Sec. 9; Utah Constitution (1895), Art. XIII, Sec. 7.

70. In the case of the Iowa provision, contained in the proposed Iowa Constitution (1844), Art. IV, Sec. 3, the voters rejected the work of the 1844 Convention, and another convention held in 1846 reported a somewhat different provision on the subject. See Jack Stark, *The Iowa State Constitution: A Reference Guide* (Westport, Conn.: Greenwood Press, 1998), 2–4. On Iowa's leadership role in this area, see Cleveland, *Growth of Democracy*, 216–217; Oberholtzer, *Referendum in America*, 191; and Holcombe, *State Government in the United States*, 137. A provision of this kind in the Wisconsin Constitution (1848), Art. XI, Sec. 5, was approved by the voters. For a discussion of Wisconsin's leadership role in this regard, see Bryce, *American Commonwealth*, 1:418.

71. States that followed suit over the next three decades included Illinois, Michigan, Ohio, Kansas, and Missouri. By the 1870s, federal assumption of this banking function made these provisions unnecessary. See Cleveland, *Growth of Democracy*, 217–218; and Oberholtzer, *Referendum in America*, 191–193. For the specific constitutional provisions, see Illinois Constitution (1848), Art. X, Sec. 5; Kansas Constitution (1859), Art. 13, Sec. 8; Michigan Constitution (1850), Art. XV, Sec. 2; Missouri Constitution (1875), Art. XII, Sec. 26; Ohio Constitution (1851), Art. XIII, Sec. 7.

72. *Report of the Debates and Proceedings of the Convention for the Revision of the Constitution of the State of New York, 1846*, 944. See the New York Constitution (1846), Art. VII,

Sec. 12, as well as a similar provision in the Oklahoma Constitution (1907), Art. X, Sec. 25.

73. For examples of supermajority requirements, see South Carolina Constitution (1868), Art. 16 (adopted 1873); Wyoming Constitution (1889), Art. XVI, Sec. 6.

74. On the origin of these referendums, see Holcombe, *State Government in the United States*, 134–139.

75. Oberholtzer, *Referendum in America*, 288; Cleveland, *Growth of Democracy*, 185.

76. Oberholtzer, *Referendum in America*, 205–206.

77. *Rice v. Foster*, 4 Harr. 479 (1847).

78. *Parker v. Commonwealth*, 6 Barr. 507 (1847).

79. There had been scattered court decisions regarding the referendum before this time, including a Massachusetts case, *Wales v. Belcher*, 3 Pick. 508 (1826); a Virginia case, *Goddin v. Crump*, 8 Leigh 120 (1837); and a Maryland case, *Burgess v. Pue*, 2 Gill. 11 (1844); but in every case the state court had upheld the referendum, and as a result, there had not been much further litigation on this subject. See Cleveland, *Growth of Democracy*, 191–193.

80. Decisions striking down statewide referendums include a New York case, *Barto v. Himrod*, 4 Seld. 483 (1853); an Iowa case, *Santo v. State*, 2 Iowa 165 (1855); a Rhode Island case, *Brown v. Copeland*, 3 R.I. 33; a Michigan case, *People v. Collins*, 3 Mich. 343 (1855); and a New Hampshire case, *State v. Hayes*, 61 N.H. 264 (1881). The contrary Vermont Supreme Court decision was rendered in *State v. Parker*, 26 Vt. 357 (1854). See Oberholtzer, *Referendum in America*, 210–216.

81. Oberholtzer, *Referendum in America*, 321.

82. Ibid.

83. *Debates and Proceedings of the Constitutional Convention of the State of Delaware [1896]*, 2289, 2290.

84. *Debates and Proceedings of the First Constitutional Convention of West Virginia (1861–1863)*, 2:410.

85. *The Oregon Constitution and Proceedings and Debates of the Oregon Convention of 1857*, 165.

86. *Report of the Debates and Proceedings of the Convention for the Revision of the Constitution of the State of Ohio, 1850–51*, 2:219.

87. *Debates and Proceedings of the Constitutional Convention for the Territory of Minnesota [1857]*, 205.

88. On this argument, see Zimmerman, *Participatory Democracy*, 45.

89. *Official Report of the Proceedings and Debates of the Convention . . . To Adopt a Constitution for the State of Utah [1895]*, 1451.

90. *Debates and Proceedings of the Constitutional Convention of the State of Delaware [1896]*, 2295.

91. *Report of the Debates and Proceedings of the Convention for the Revision of the Constitution of the State of Ohio, 1850–51*, 2:224.

92. On this justification, see Holcombe, *State Government in the United States*, 484–485.

93. *Official Report of the Proceedings and Debates of the Third Constitutional Convention of Ohio [1873]*, 2:2894 (quotations transposed).

94. Ibid., 2:3172.

95. *Report of the Debates and Proceedings of the Convention for the Revision of the Constitution of the State of Ohio, 1850–51*, 2:223, 224.

96. Ibid., 2:222.

97. *Debates and Proceedings of the First Constitutional Convention of West Virginia (1861–1863)*, 2:428.

98. *Official Report of the Proceedings and Debates of the Third Constitutional Convention of Ohio [1873]*, 2:2909–2910.

99. Ibid., 2:2910.

100. *Report of the Debates and Proceedings of the Convention for the Revision of the Constitution of the State of Ohio, 1850–51*, 2:225.

101. *The Oregon Constitution and Proceedings and Debates of the Oregon Convention of 1857*, 330.

102. *Report of the Debates and Proceedings of the Convention for the Revision of the Constitution of the State of Indiana, 1850*, 1256.

103. *Revised Record of the Constitutional Convention of the State of New York [1894]*, 2:801.

104. *Report of the Debates and Proceedings of the Convention for the Revision of the Constitution of the State of Ohio, 1850–51*, 2:217, 224.

105. Ibid., 2:217.

106. Ibid., 2:218–219.

107. Ibid., 2:224–225.

108. It is worth noting, however, that the exceptions to these general prohibitions were often quite significant. See the Ohio Constitution (1851), Art. II, Sec. 26; Oregon Constitution (1857), Art. I, Sec. 22; and Kentucky Constitution (1891), Sec. 60, for a wide range of issues that were explicitly exempt from these prohibitions.

109. On the limited use of the binding statewide referendum, see Oberholtzer, *Referendum in America*, 200–205. On the use of the local referendum, see 279–310. On the use of the advisory referendum, see 205–208.

110. In regard to explicit provision for local referendums, see the Delaware Constitution (1897), Art. XIII, Sec. 1; Florida Constitution (1885), Art. XIX, Sec. 1; Kentucky Constitution (1891), Sec. 61; Texas Constitution (1876), Art. XVI, Sec. 20.

111. In regard to statewide referendums, see the Massachusetts Constitution (1780), Articles of Amendment, Art. XLII (adopted 1913); Michigan Constitution (1908), Art. IV, Sec. 38.

112. For discussions of the late-nineteenth-century movement for the adoption of the initiative and referendum, see Schmidt, *Citizen Lawmakers*, 3–14, 217–285; Ellis, *Democratic Delusions*, 26–34; and Goebel, *Government by the People*, 25–47. There is some difference of opinion about the extent to which late nineteenth-century supporters of the initiative and referendum drew on foreign versus domestic precedents. Edwin M. Bacon and Morrill Wyman chose to emphasize the foreign origin of these institutions, and in particular the Swiss decisions in 1848 to permit the popular referendum and in 1891 to permit the popular initiative. Bacon and Wyman, *Direct Elections and Law-Making*, 44. By contrast, Ellis Paxson Oberholtzer called attention to the way in which initiative and referendum supporters relied on precedents from existing referendum provisions in American state constitutions. Oberholtzer, *Referendum in America*, 100.

113. *Debates in the Massachusetts Constitutional Convention, 1917–1918*, 2:175.

114. *Proceedings and Debates of the Constitutional Convention of the State of Michigan [1907]*, 560.

115. *Debates in the Massachusetts Constitutional Convention, 1917–1918*, 2:946–947.

116. *Proceedings and Debates of the Constitutional Convention of the State of Michigan [1907]*, 592.

117. *Proceedings of the Constitutional Convention of the State of Illinois, Convened January 6, 1920,* 241.

118. *Journal of the [New Hampshire] Constitutional Convention of 1902,* 756.

119. *Journal of the Convention to Revise the [New Hampshire] Convention, January 20, 1920,* 318.

120. Ibid., 310.

121. *Proceedings and Debates of the Constitutional Convention of the State of Michigan [1907],* 640.

122. *Proceedings of the Constitutional Convention of the State of Illinois, Convened January 6, 1920,* 244.

123. *Journal of the Convention to Revise the [New Hampshire] Constitution, June 1912,* 344.

124. *Debates in the Massachusetts Constitutional Convention, 1917–1918,* 2:282.

125. Ibid., 2:94.

126. *Proceedings and Debates of the Constitutional Convention of the State of Michigan [1907],* 572.

127. *Proceedings of the Constitutional Convention of the State of Illinois, Convened January 6, 1920,* 2490.

128. *Journal of the [New Hampshire] Constitutional Convention of 1902,* 784.

129. Ibid., 789.

130. *Journal of the Nebraska Constitutional Convention [1919],* 497 (quotations transposed).

131. *Journal of the Convention to Revise the [New Hampshire] Constitution, June 1912,* 355.

132. *Proceedings of the Constitutional Convention of the State of Illinois, Convened January 6, 1920,* 267.

133. *Journal of the Convention to Revise the [New Hampshire] Convention, January 20, 1920,* 319.

134. *Journal of the Convention to Revise the [New Hampshire] Constitution, June 1912,* 154.

135. *Debates in the Massachusetts Constitutional Convention, 1917–1918,* 2:514.

136. *Proceedings and Debates of the Constitutional Convention of the State of Ohio [1912],* 839. It should be noted that several individuals outside of the convention halls occasionally went so far as to speak of the need to completely break with the founding conception of representation by raising the possibility of bypassing or eventually eliminating the legislature. See, for instance, the comments in James Q. Dealey, *Growth of American State Constitutions from 1776 to the End of the Year 1914* (Boston: Ginn, 1915), 182; and Frank Parsons, *The City for the People* (Philadelphia: C. F. Taylor, 1901), 375–376. For a discussion of this strand of the direct democracy movement, see Dinan, *Keeping the People's Liberties,* 85; and Goebel, *Government by the People,* 54–55.

137. *The Records of the Arizona Constitutional Convention of 1910,* 198.

138. *Proceedings and Debates of the Constitutional Convention of the State of Ohio [1912],* 803.

139. *Journal of the Nebraska Constitutional Convention [1919],* 510.

140. *Proceedings and Debates of the Constitutional Convention of the State of Michigan [1907],* 586 (quotations transposed).

141. For early assessments of the Oregon experience with the initiative and referendum, some of which reached favorable conclusions and others of which were unfavorable, see Burton J. Hendrick, "Law-Making by the Voters," *McClure's* 37 (September 1911): 435–450;

George H. Haynes, "'People's Rule' in Oregon, 1910," *Political Science Quarterly* 26 (March 1911): 32–62; Samuel W. McCall, "Representative as against Direct Democracy," *Atlantic Monthly* 108 (October 1911): 454–466; Jonathan Bourne Jr., "Initiative, Referendum, and Recall," *Atlantic Monthly* 109 (January 1912): 122–131; Frederick V. Holman, "The Unfavorable Results of Direct Legislation in Oregon," in Munro, *Initiative, Referendum and Recall,* 279–297; George H. Haynes, "'People's Rule' on Trial," *Political Science Quarterly* 28 (March 1913): 18–33; Allen H. Eaton, *The Oregon System: The Story of Direct Legislation in Oregon* (Chicago: A. C. McClurg, 1912); James D. Barnett, *The Operation of the Initiative, Referendum, and Recall in Oregon* (New York: Macmillan, 1912); and Gilbert Hedges, *Where the People Rule* (San Francisco: Bender-Moss, 1914).

142. *Debates in the Massachusetts Constitutional Convention, 1917–1918,* 2:55–56.

143. *Proceedings and Debates of the Constitutional Convention of the State of Ohio [1912],* 824.

144. *Proceedings and Debates of the Constitutional Convention of the State of Michigan [1907],* 548.

145. *Journal of the Nebraska Constitutional Convention [1919],* 510–511.

146. *Proceedings and Debates of the Constitutional Convention of the State of Ohio [1912],* 801.

147. *Proceedings of the Constitutional Convention of the State of Illinois, Convened January 6, 1920,* 773.

148. *Proceedings and Debates of the Constitutional Convention of the State of Ohio [1912],* 690.

149. *Debates in the Massachusetts Constitutional Convention, 1917–1918,* 2:509.

150. Ellis, *Democratic Delusions,* 39.

151. The order of adoption of the initiative and referendum was as follows: South Dakota (1898), Utah (1900), Oregon (1902), Nevada (1905) (the referendum only), Montana (1906), Oklahoma (1907), Maine (1908), Missouri (1908), Arkansas (1910), Colorado (1910), California (1911), Arizona (1911), New Mexico (1911) (the referendum only), Idaho (1912), Nebraska (1912), Ohio (1912), Washington (1912), Nevada (1912) (the initiative, to go along with the existing referendum), Michigan (1913), Mississippi (1914) (later invalidated by the Mississippi Supreme Court), North Dakota (1914), Maryland (1915) (the referendum only), Kentucky (1915) (the referendum only, and solely in regard to legislation classifying personal property for purposes of taxation), and Massachusetts (1918). Between 1918 and 1956, not a single state adopted the initiative. Then, between 1956 and 1970, two other states adopted the initiative and referendum: Alaska (1956) and Wyoming (1968). See Schmidt, *Citizen Lawmakers,* 16–17. For the current constitutional provisions, see Alaska Constitution (1956), Art. XI; Arizona Constitution (1911), Art. IV, Part 1, Sec. 1; Arkansas Constitution (1874), Amendment 7 (adopted 1920); California Constitution (1879), Art. II, Sec. 8, 9 (as amended 1976); Colorado Constitution (1876), Art. V, Sec. 1 (as amended 1910); Idaho Constitution (1889), Art. III, Sec. 1 (as amended 1912); Kentucky Constitution (1891), Sec. 171 (as amended 1915); Maine Constitution (1819), Art. IV, Part Third, Sec. 17–20 (adopted 1908); Maryland Constitution (1867), Art. XVI (as amended 1915); Massachusetts Constitution (1780), Articles of Amendment, Art. XLVIII (adopted 1918); Art. LXXXI (adopted 1950); Michigan Constitution (1963), Art. II, Sec. 9; Missouri Constitution (1945), Art. III, Sec. 49–53; Montana Constitution (1972), Art. III, Sec. 4–5; Nebraska Constitution (1875), Art. III, Sec. 2–4 (as amended 1912); Nevada Constitution (1864), Art. 19 (as amended 1904 and 1912); New Mexico Constitution (1911), Art. IV, Sec. 1; North Dakota Constitution (1889), Art. III (as amended 1914 and 1918); Ohio Constitution (1851), Art. II, Sec. 1 (as amended 1912); Oklahoma Constitution (1907), Art. V, Sec. 2;

Oregon Constitution (1857), Art. IV, Sec. 1 (as amended 1902); South Dakota Constitution (1889), Art. III, Sec. 1 (as amended 1898); Utah Constitution (1895), Art. VI, Sec. 1(2) (as amended 1900); Washington Constitution (1889), Art. II, Sec. 1 (as amended 1912); Wyoming Constitution (1889), Art. III, Sec. 52 (as amended 1968).

152. Wyoming Constitution (1889), Art. III, Sec. 52 (as amended 1968).

153. See, for instance, Massachusetts Constitution (1780), Articles of Amendment, Art. XLVIII (adopted 1918).

154. Ohio Constitution (1851), Art. II, Sec. 1 (as amended 1912).

155. Massachusetts Constitution (1780), Articles of Amendment, Art. XLVIII (adopted 1918).

Chapter 4: Separation of Powers

1. Academic challenges that have been mounted against the separation of powers system at the national level are discussed in M. J. C. Vile, *Constitutionalism and the Separation of Powers* (Oxford: Clarendon Press, 1967), 263–314.

2. For an overview of state constitutional development in this area, see G. Alan Tarr, "Interpreting the Separation of Powers in State Constitutions," *New York University Annual Survey of American Law* 59 (2003): 329–340.

3. The tendency to elect many executive department heads reached its height during the nineteenth century but then gave way to a "short ballot" movement in the early twentieth century. See Charles A. Beard, "The Ballot's Burden," *Political Science Quarterly* 24 (December 1909): 589–614; and John N. Mathews, "State Administrative Reorganization," *American Political Science Review* 16 (August 1922): 387–398.

4. This aspect of state separation of powers systems has been particularly well studied by scholars, several of whom have made significant use of state convention debates in tracing the origin of an elected judiciary. See especially Kermit L. Hall, "The Judiciary on Trial: State Constitutional Reform and the Rise of an Elected Judiciary, 1846–1860," *Historian* 44 (May 1983): 337–354; Kermit L. Hall, "Progressive Reform and the Decline of Democratic Accountability: The Popular Election of State Supreme Court Judges, 1850–1920," *American Bar Foundation Research Journal* (Spring 1984): 345–369; and Caleb Nelson, "A Re-Evaluation of Scholarly Explanations for the Rise of the Elective Judiciary in Antebellum America," *American Journal of Legal History* 37 (April 1993): 190–224. Studies that have drawn on selected state convention debates in this area include Francis N. Thorpe, *A Constitutional History of the American People, 1776–1850,* 2 vols. (New York: Harper & Brothers, 1898), 2:34–65; John V. Orth, "Tuesday, February 11, 1868: The Day North Carolina Chose Direct Election of Judges," *North Carolina Law Review* 70 (September 1992): 1825–1851; and Alex B. Long, "An Historical Perspective on Judicial Selection Methods in Virginia and West Virginia," *Journal of Law and Politics* 18 (Summer 2002): 691–772.

5. There have also been challenges to other aspects of the separation of powers system, including scattered calls to move from a presidential to a parliamentary system at the state level. These debates are contained in the following sources:

Illinois: *Record of Proceedings: Sixth Illinois Constitutional Convention [1969]: Verbatim Transcripts,* 2730–2732.

Massachusetts: *Debates in the Massachusetts Constitutional Convention, 1917–1918,* 3:887–930, 977–1003.

Montana: *Montana Constitutional Convention, 1971–1972: Verbatim Transcript,* 749–759.

6. These debates are contained in the following sources:

Alabama: *Official Proceedings of the Constitutional Convention of the State of Alabama [1901],* 618–684.

Alaska: *Minutes of the Daily Proceedings, Alaska Constitutional Convention, 1955–56,* 1738–1746, 1757–1759, 1806–1814, 1819–1823, 3102–3104.

Connecticut: *The Third Constitutional Convention of the State of Connecticut: Proceedings [1965],* 975–983, 1000–1019.

Delaware: *Debates and Proceedings of the Constitutional Convention of the State of Delaware [1852–1853],* 124–126, 128–129; *Debates and Proceedings of the Constitutional Convention of the State of Delaware [1896],* 209–210, 225–243, 247–285.

Hawaii: *Proceedings of the Constitutional Convention of Hawaii, 1950,* 2:215–219, 263–267, 450–451, 459.

Illinois: *The [Illinois] Constitutional Debates of 1847,* 404–442; *Debates and Proceedings of the Constitutional Convention of the State of Illinois [1869],* 151–153, 791–792, 1375–1378; *Proceedings of the Constitutional Convention of the State of Illinois, Convened January 6, 1920,* 1548–1562; *Record of Proceedings: Sixth Illinois Constitutional Convention [1969]: Verbatim Transcripts,* 885–888, 901–912, 1337–1357, 4081–4085.

Indiana: *Report of the Debates and Proceedings of the Convention for the Revision of the Constitution of the State of Indiana, 1850,* 1322–1330, 1345–1351.

Iowa: *Fragments of the Debates of the Iowa Constitutional Conventions of 1844 and 1846,* 58–63; *The Debates of the Constitutional Convention of the State of Iowa [1857],* 525–527, 567.

Kansas: *A Reprint of the Proceedings and Debates of the Convention Which Framed the Constitution of Kansas at Wyandotte in July, 1859,* 129–132.

Kentucky: *Official Report of the Proceedings and Debates in the Convention . . . of September, 1890, To Adopt, Amend or Change the Constitution of the State of Kentucky,* 1053–1056, 1478–1490.

Louisiana: *Records of the Louisiana Constitutional Convention of 1973: Convention Transcripts,* 445–451, 600–601.

Maryland: *Debates and Proceedings of the Maryland Reform Convention to Revise the State Constitution [1851],* 2:348–355; *The Debates of the Constitutional Convention of the State of Maryland [1864],* 897–899; *Debates of the Maryland Constitutional Convention of 1867,* 182–190; *Debates of the [Maryland] Constitutional Convention of 1967–1968,* 1370–1373, 1390–1391, 1448–1456.

Massachusetts: *Debates in the Massachusetts Constitutional Convention, 1917–1918,* 3:930–955.

Michigan: *Report of the Proceedings and Debates in the Convention to Revise the Constitution of the State of Michigan, 1850,* 134–135, 452–453; *The Debates and Proceedings of the Constitutional Convention of the State of Michigan [1867],* 2:84–88; *Proceedings and Debates of the Constitutional Convention of the State of Michigan [1907],* 492–494; *Official Record, State of Michigan Constitutional Convention, 1961,* 1653–1657.

Minnesota: *Debates and Proceedings of the Constitutional Convention for the Territory of Minnesota [1857],* 134–135.

Missouri: *Debates of the Missouri Constitutional Convention of 1875,* 2:153; 5:178–191; 7:319–321.

Montana: *Proceedings and Debates of the Constitutional Convention Held in the City of Helena, Montana [1889]*, 433–434; *Montana Constitutional Convention, 1971–1972: Verbatim Transcript*, 842, 948–958, 1701.

Nevada: *Official Report of the Debates and Proceedings in the Constitutional Convention of the State of Nevada [1864]*, 312–314.

New Hampshire: *Journal of the Convention to Revise the [New Hampshire] Constitution, May 1948*, 93–95, 143–152; *Journal of the Convention to Revise the [New Hampshire] Constitution, May 1964*, 91–105; *Journal of the Convention to Revise the [New Hampshire] Constitution, May 1974*, 210–218, 344–360; *Journal of the Convention to Revise the [New Hampshire] Constitution, May 1984*, 62–64, 105–106, 279–296, 332–333.

New Jersey: *Proceedings of the New Jersey State Constitutional Convention of 1844*, 175–206; *[New Jersey] Constitutional Convention of 1947*, 1:213–220.

New York: *Reports of the Proceedings and Debates of the [New York] Convention of 1821*, 44–121; *Report of the Debates and Proceedings of the Convention for the Revision of the Constitution of the State of New York, 1846*, 152–153, 324–337, 360–371; *Proceedings and Debates of the Constitutional Convention of the State of New York Held in 1867 and 1868*, 894–895, 1109–1131, 3619–3621.

North Dakota: *Debates of the North Dakota Constitutional Convention of 1972*, 328–331, 383–384, 998–1003.

Ohio: *Report of the Debates and Proceedings of the Convention for the Revision of the Constitution of the State of Ohio, 1850–51*, 1:72–75, 110–125, 308–313; 2:292–293; *Official Report of the Proceedings and Debates of the Third Constitutional Convention of Ohio [1873]*, 2:296–309, 1023–1024, 1060–1146, 1498–1515, 1532–1543; *Proceedings and Debates of the Constitutional Convention of the State of Ohio [1912]*, 565–571, 1195–1204.

Pennsylvania: *Proceedings and Debates of the Convention of the Commonwealth of Pennsylvania [1837]*, 2:184–199, 203–218; *Debates of the Convention to Amend the Constitution of Pennsylvania [1872–1873]*, 2:384–385; 5:233–238.

Rhode Island: *State of Rhode Island and Providence Plantations: Constitutional Convention [1964–1969]: Report of Proceedings*, 931–970.

Tennessee: *Journal and Proceedings of the [Tennessee] Constitutional Convention [1953]*, 532–560, 581–604, 702–732; *Journal and Proceedings of the Limited Constitutional Convention, State of Tennessee [1977]*, 301–319, 519–521.

Texas: *Debates of the Texas Convention [1845]*, 134–146, 319; *Debates in the Texas Constitutional Convention of 1875*, 161–162; *Texas Constitutional Convention [1974]: Official Proceedings*, 653–663, 2223–2230, 2253–2256.

Utah: *Official Report of the Proceedings and Debates of the Convention . . . To Adopt a Constitution for the State of Utah [1895]*, 885–886, 1161–1163.

Virginia: *Report of the Proceedings and Debates of the Constitutional Convention, State of Virginia [1901–1902]*, 1027–1028, 1040–1043, 1874–1879.

Wisconsin: *Journal of the Convention to Form a Constitution for the State of Wisconsin [1847–1848]*, 72–73, 75, 87–90.

Wyoming: *Journal and Debates of the Constitutional Convention of the State of Wyoming [1889]*, 461–462.

7. These debates are contained in the following sources:

Arizona: *The Records of the Arizona Constitutional Convention of 1910*, 43, 242–246, 260–270, 800–812, 920–922, 925–929.

Massachusetts: *Debates in the Massachusetts Constitutional Convention, 1917–1918*, 1:453–541, 851–872.

Nebraska: *Journal of the Nebraska Constitutional Convention [1919]*, 1134–1148, 1526–1541, 2312–2323.

New York: *Proceedings and Debates of the Constitutional Convention of the State of New York Held in 1867 and 1868*, 3283–3285, 3356–3365.

North Dakota: *Debates of the North Dakota Constitutional Convention of 1972*, 1138–1144, 1394–1395.

Ohio: *Proceedings and Debates of the Constitutional Convention of the State of Ohio [1912]*, 1025–1130, 1140–1164, 1291–1311, 1773–1775, 1825–1834.

8. As Edward Campbell Mason noted, "Popular objections to the veto power date back to a very early time in our national history. In 1818 a resolution found its way into Congress calling for a total abolition of the veto power. . . . A second era of objection to the veto dates from about 1833. From this time until well down to 1850 the President's right to refuse his signature to bills was vigorously attacked." Edward Campbell Mason, *The Veto Power: Its Origin, Development and Function in the Government of the United States (1789–1889)* (Boston: Ginn, 1890), 135. All told, constitutional amendments to change the legislative override requirements from two-thirds to a mere majority were introduced in Congress on nine occasions in the nineteenth century (Mason, *Veto Power*, 137) and on assorted occasions in the twentieth century. John R. Vile, *Encyclopedia of Constitutional Amendments, Proposed Amendments, and Amending Issues, 1789–1995* (Santa Barbara, Calif.: ABC-CLIO, 1996), 245–246.

9. Ulysses S. Grant in 1873 was the first president to urge approval of a constitutional item-veto amendment, although certainly not the last. In fact, Russell M. Ross and Fred Schwengel refer to the item-veto amendment as "one of the most frequently suggested amendments to the United States Constitution" in "An Item Veto for the President?" *Presidential Studies Quarterly* 12 (Winter 1982): 66. Representative James Faulkner of West Virginia was the first to formally introduce such an amendment in Congress, in 1876, and many amendments along these lines have been introduced in subsequent Congresses, but "only one of these proposals was ever reported favorably out of congressional committee, and that occurred in 1884." Robert J. Spitzer, *The Presidential Veto: Touchstone of the American Presidency* (Albany: State University of New York Press, 1988), 127. As late as 1982, Ross and Schwengel could still write that "Congress has paid scant attention to most of the more than one hundred and forty proposals that would vest this authority in the hands of the President of the United States." Ross and Schwengel, "An Item Veto for the President?," 67. In the mid-1980s and then again in the mid-1990s, the issue attracted renewed attention, and Congress approved an item-veto statute in 1996, only to see it invalidated by the Supreme Court two years later in *Clinton v. City of New York*, 524 U.S. 417 (1998).

10. The first effort to restrict judicial review by requiring that it be exercised by a supermajority of the justices took place in the 1820s, in response to the U.S. Supreme Court's invalidation of several state statutes. Although most amendments introduced in Congress at this time applied only to invalidations of state laws, several others, including a proposal in 1823 by Kentucky senator Richard Johnson, also applied to invalidations of congressional laws. Similar proposals, which occasionally required not just a supermajority but a unanimous vote of the justices, were introduced in Congress in the late 1860s out of a fear that the Court would strike down Reconstruction legislation, and at various times from the 1890s to the 1930s, including most notably by Idaho senator William Borah, at a time when the Court was particularly active in striking down economic legislation. Maurice S. Culp, "A Survey of the Proposals to Limit or Deny the Power of Judicial Review by the Supreme Court of the United States," *Indiana Law Journal* 4 (March 1929): 386–398, 5 (April 1929): 474–490; Charles

Warren, *The Supreme Court in United States History,* rev. ed. (Boston: Little, Brown, 1935), 1:652–685, 2:455–497; Charles Warren, *Congress, the Constitution, and the Supreme Court,* rev. ed. (Boston: Little, Brown, 1935), 179–221; Evan H. Caminker, "Thayerian Deference to Congress and Supreme Court Supermajority Rule: Lessons from the Past," *Indiana Law Journal* 78 (Winter/Spring 2003): 73, 117–122.

Proposals to abolish judicial review were introduced on occasion during the nineteenth century but enjoyed particular prominence during the Progressive Era, when in 1917 and then again in 1923 Oklahoma senator Robert Owen introduced resolutions that would have prohibited the Supreme Court from invalidating congressional statutes, and then again in the New Deal Era when several such bills and amendments were introduced in Congress. Culp, "Survey of the Proposals," 488; William G. Ross, *A Muted Fury: Populists, Progressives, and Labor Unions Confront the Courts, 1890–1937* (Princeton, N.J.: Princeton University Press, 1994), 164–165, 169–170; Katherine B. Fite and Louis Baruch Rubinstein, "Curbing the Supreme Court—State Experiences and Federal Proposals," *Michigan Law Review* 35 (March 1937): 762, 764–765.

Proposals to restrict the exercise of judicial review by permitting the recall of judges or judicial decisions were advanced in the Progressive Era by several prominent officials, including Theodore Roosevelt and Robert La Follette, but few of these proposals were actually introduced in Congress. Measures that were formally introduced include a 1911 bill proposed by Senator Owen that would have permitted Congress to recall federal judges, a 1912 resolution sponsored by Kansas senator Joseph Bristow that would have permitted Congress to refer to the people any congressional law that had been invalidated by the Court, and a 1923 amendment proposed by Wisconsin representative James Frear that would have given Congress the power to reenact invalidated laws by a two-thirds vote and would have also permitted the recall of federal judges. Ross, *Muted Fury,* 114, 153, 199–200.

11. The federal convention debates regarding these issues are discussed in Mason, *Veto Power,* 20–22; Spitzer, *Presidential Veto,* 10–20; Joseph E. Kallenbach, *The American Chief Executive: The Presidency and the Governorship* (New York: Harper & Row, 1966), 58–59, 61–62, 64; and Ronald C. Moe, "The Founders and Their Experience with the Executive Veto," *Presidential Studies Quarterly* 17 (Spring 1987): 413–432.

12. As Spitzer has written, "Again and again in the convention's consideration of the veto power, one central theme persistently surfaced: the veto as a device of executive self-protection against encroachments of the legislature." Spitzer, *Presidential Veto,* 15.

13. Alexander Hamilton et al., *The Federalist Papers,* ed. Clinton Rossiter (1961; reprint, New York: Mentor, 1999), 411.

14. Ibid., 410.

15. Ibid., 411.

16. Ibid.

17. John A. Fairlie, "The Veto Power of the State Governor," *American Political Science Review* 11 (August 1917): 473, 476; Arthur Holcombe, *State Government in the United States,* 2nd ed. (New York: Macmillan, 1926), 114–115.

18. *Proceedings of the New Jersey State Constitutional Convention of 1844,* 202–203.

19. *Debates and Proceedings of the Constitutional Convention of the State of Delaware [1896],* 226.

20. *Proceedings of the New Jersey State Constitutional Convention of 1844,* 204.

21. *Reports of the Proceedings and Debates of the [New York] Convention of 1821,* 51.

22. Ibid., 79.

23. *Report of the Debates and Proceedings of the Convention for the Revision of the Constitution of the State of Indiana, 1850,* 1326.

24. *Official Report of the Proceedings and Debates of the Third Constitutional Convention of Ohio [1873],* 2:1093.

25. According to Mason, "Down through Jackson's administration twenty-one bills were vetoed, and only five or six were based upon other than constitutional grounds." Mason, *Veto Power,* 129.

26. As Spitzer commented in regard to Jackson's bank veto, "Supplementing the constitutional rationale was a loudly broadcast subtext—that the president need only rely on his political judgment in making a veto decision. Though this conclusion was not inconsistent with the intent of the framers, nor even with the vetoes of some of Jackson's predecessors, it was a view that had never been so broadly and baldly articulated by a sitting president." Spitzer, *Presidential Veto,* 34. For treatments of presidential vetoes from Jackson to Johnson, as well as the controversies generated by these vetoes, see 33–59; and Richard A. Watson, *Presidential Vetoes and Public Policy* (Lawrence: University Press of Kansas, 1993), 29–127.

27. *Debates of the Texas Convention [1845],* 145.

28. Ibid., 146.

29. *The [Illinois] Constitutional Debates of 1847,* 408.

30. *Report of the Debates and Proceedings of the Convention for the Revision of the Constitution of the State of New York, 1846,* 361.

31. *The [Illinois] Constitutional Debates of 1847,* 420.

32. *Debates and Proceedings of the Constitutional Convention of the State of Illinois [1869],* 791.

33. *Proceedings of the New Jersey State Constitutional Convention of 1844,* 203–204.

34. *Debates of the Maryland Constitutional Convention of 1867,* 184.

35. *Debates and Proceedings of the Constitutional Convention of the State of Delaware [1852–1853],* 124.

36. *Report of the Debates and Proceedings of the Convention for the Revision of the Constitution of the State of Ohio, 1850–51,* 1:112.

37. *Report of the Debates and Proceedings of the Convention for the Revision of the Constitution of the State of Indiana, 1850,* 1325, 1326.

38. *Debates and Proceedings of the Constitutional Convention of the State of Delaware [1896],* 226–227, 230.

39. *The Debates and Proceedings of the Constitutional Convention of the State of Michigan [1867],* 2:88.

40. *Official Report of the Proceedings and Debates in the Convention . . . of September, 1890, To Adopt, Amend or Change the Constitution of the State of Kentucky,* 1488.

41. *Debates and Proceedings of the Constitutional Convention of the State of Delaware [1896],* 269.

42. *Reports of the Proceedings and Debates of the [New York] Convention of 1821,* 116.

43. Ibid., 118.

44. *The [Illinois] Constitutional Debates of 1847,* 411, 412.

45. *Proceedings of the New Jersey State Constitutional Convention of 1844,* 190.

46. *A Reprint of the Proceedings and Debates of the Convention Which Framed the Constitution of Kansas at Wyandotte in July, 1859,* 130.

47. *Debates and Proceedings of the Constitutional Convention of the State of Delaware [1896],* 239.

48. Ibid., 275.

49. *Official Report of the Proceedings and Debates of the Third Constitutional Convention of Ohio [1873]*, 2:1113.

50. *Reports of the Proceedings and Debates of the [New York] Convention of 1821*, 84.

51. *Proceedings and Debates of the Convention of the Commonwealth of Pennsylvania [1837]*, 2:193.

52. On President Washington's issuance of the veto for policy reasons in this instance, see Carlton Jackson, *Presidential Vetoes: 1792–1945* (Athens: University of Georgia Press, 1967), 3–4.

53. *Fragments of the Debates of the Iowa Constitutional Conventions of 1844 and 1846*, 61.

54. *Journal of the Convention to Form a Constitution for the State of Wisconsin [1847–1848]*, 72.

55. *The [Illinois] Constitutional Debates of 1847*, 433.

56. Ibid., 440.

57. *Fragments of the Debates of the Iowa Constitutional Conventions of 1844 and 1846*, 60.

58. *Debates and Proceedings of the Constitutional Convention of the State of Delaware [1852–1853]*, 125.

59. *Reports of the Proceedings and Debates of the [New York] Convention of 1821*, 63.

60. Ibid., 64.

61. *Debates of the Maryland Constitutional Convention of 1867*, 186–187.

62. Fairlie, "Veto Power," 476–477.

63. Ibid., 477. On the gradual adoption of the gubernatorial veto, see Gerald Benjamin, "The Diffusion of the Governor's Veto Power," *State Government* 55 (1982): 99, 101.

64. Holcombe, *State Government*, 115.

65. Fairlie, "Veto Power," 480.

66. Ibid., 481–482.

67. The majority-override states are Alabama, Arkansas, Indiana, Kentucky, Tennessee, and West Virginia (except in regard to budget or supplementary appropriations bills, which require a two-thirds override). The three-fifths-override states are Delaware, Illinois, Maryland, Nebraska, North Carolina, and Ohio. Alaska, on the other hand, goes even further than the federal model by requiring a three-fourths override on vetoes of money bills.

The veto-override provisions in the fifty states can be found at: Alabama Constitution (1901), Art. V, Sec. 125; Alaska Constitution (1956), Art. II, Sec. 16; Arizona Constitution (1911), Art. V, Sec. 7; Arkansas Constitution (1874), Art. 6, Sec. 15; California Constitution (1879), Art. IV, Sec. 10(a); Colorado Constitution (1876), Art. IV, Sec. 11; Connecticut Constitution (1965), Art. IV, Sec. 15; Delaware Constitution (1897), Art. III, Sec. 18; Florida Constitution (1968), Art. III, Sec. 8; Georgia Constitution (1983), Art. III, Sec. V, Para. XIII(d); Hawaii Constitution (1950), Art. III, Sec. 17 (as renumbered 1978); Idaho Constitution (1889), Art. IV, Sec. 10; Illinois Constitution (1970), Art. IV, Sec. 9(b); Indiana Constitution (1851), Art. 5, Sec. 14(a)(2)(C) (as amended 1990); Iowa Constitution (1857), Art. III, Sec. 16; Kansas Constitution (1859), Art. 2, Sec. 14(a) (as amended 1974); Kentucky Constitution (1891), Sec. 88; Louisiana Constitution (1974), Art. III, Sec. 18(C); Maine Constitution (1819), Art. IV, Part Third, Sec. 2; Maryland Constitution (1867), Art. II, Sec. 17; Massachusetts Constitution (1780), Part the Second, Ch. I, Sec. 1, Art. II; Michigan Constitution (1963), Art. IV, Sec. 33; Minnesota Constitution (1857), Art. IV,

Sec. 23 (as reorganized 1974); Mississippi Constitution (1890), Art. 4, Sec. 72; Missouri Constitution (1945), Art. III, Sec. 32; Montana Constitution (1972), Art. VI, Sec. 10(3); Nebraska Constitution (1875), Art. IV, Sec. 15; Nevada Constitution (1864), Art. 4, Sec. 35; New Hampshire Constitution (1784), Part Second, Art. 44 (as amended 1792); New Jersey Constitution (1947), Art. V, Sec. I, Para. 14(e); New Mexico Constitution (1911), Art. IV, Sec. 22; New York Constitution (1894), Art. IV, Sec. 7 (as renumbered 1938); North Carolina Constitution (1971), Art. II, Sec. 22(1) (as amended 1996); North Dakota Constitution (1889), Art. V, Sec. 9; Ohio Constitution (1851), Art. II, Sec. 16 (as amended 1912); Oklahoma Constitution (1907), Art. VI, Sec. 11; Oregon Constitution (1857), Art. V, Sec. 15b(2) (adopted 1916); Pennsylvania Constitution (1968), Art. IV, Sec. 15; Rhode Island Constitution (1986), Art. IX, Sec. 14; South Carolina Constitution (1895), Art. IV, Sec. 21; South Dakota Constitution (1889), Art. IV, Sec. 4; Tennessee Constitution (1870), Art. III, Sec. 18 (as amended 1953); Texas Constitution (1876), Art. 4, Sec. 14; Utah Constitution (1895), Art. VII, Sec. 8; Vermont Constitution (1793), Ch. II, Sec. 11 (as amended 1836 and 1913); Virginia Constitution (1971), Art. V, Sec. 6; Washington Constitution (1889), Art. III, Sec. 12 (as amended 1974); West Virginia Constitution (1872), Art. VI, Sec. 51D(11) (as amended 1968); Art. VII, Sec. 14 (as amended 1970); Wisconsin Constitution (1848), Art. V, Sec. 10(2)(a); Wyoming Constitution (1889), Art. 4, Sec. 8.

68. On Smith's role in the creation of the item veto, see Roger H. Wells, "The Item Veto and State Budget Reform," *American Political Science Review* 18 (November 1924): 782–783. For an extended excerpt of Smith's defense of the item veto, see U.S. Congress, House, Committee on Rules, *Item Veto: State Experience and Its Application to the Federal Situation,* 99th Cong., 2nd sess. (Washington, D.C.: Government Printing Office, 1986), 206–210.

69. The debate over a federal item veto, which began with the initial expression of support for the device by President Grant and its formal proposal by Representative Faulkner in the 1870s, is chronicled in, among other works: Vernon L. Wilkinson, "The Item Veto in the American Constitutional System," *Georgetown Law Journal* 25 (November 1936): 106–133; Judith A. Best, "The Item Veto: Would the Founders Approve?" *Presidential Studies Quarterly* 14 (Spring 1984): 183–188; Thomas E. Cronin and Jeffrey J. Weill, "An Item Veto for the President?" *Congress and the Presidency* 12 (Autumn 1985): 127–151; "Symposium on the Line-Item Veto," *Notre Dame Journal of Law, Ethics and Public Policy* 1 (1985): 157–283; Louis Fisher and Neal Devins, "How Successfully Can the States' Item Veto Be Transferred to the President?" *Georgetown Law Journal* 75 (October 1986): 159–197; and Ronald C. Moe, *Prospects for the Item Veto at the Federal Level: Lessons from the States* (Washington, D.C.: National Academy of Public Administration, 1988).

70. *Proceedings and Debates of the Constitutional Convention of the State of New York Held in 1867 and 1868,* 1110.

71. *Official Report of the Proceedings and Debates in the Convention . . . of September, 1890, To Adopt, Amend or Change the Constitution of the State of Kentucky,* 1054.

72. *Official Proceedings of the Constitutional Convention of the State of Alabama [1901],* 664–665.

73. *Debates of the Missouri Constitutional Convention of 1875,* 2:153.

74. *Report of the Proceedings and Debates of the Constitutional Convention, State of Virginia [1901–1902],* 1875.

75. *Journal of the Convention to Revise the [New Hampshire] Constitution, May 1984,* 281.

76. On the evolution of the arguments in support of the item veto throughout each of these periods, see Ronald C. Moe and Louis Fisher, "Item Veto as a State Reform: Its Origin and Evolution," in U.S. Congress, House, Committee on Rules, *Item Veto*, 5–47; and Moe, *Prospects for the Item Veto*, 5–13.

77. *Debates and Proceedings of the Constitutional Convention of the State of Delaware [1896]*, 232.

78. This point is made in Wells, "Item Veto and State Budget Reform."

79. *Proceedings and Debates of the Constitutional Convention of the State of Michigan [1907]*, 494.

80. *Proceedings and Debates of the Constitutional Convention of the State of Ohio [1912]*, 569–570.

81. *Journal and Proceedings of the [Tennessee] Constitutional Convention [1953]*, 546. See also Frank W. Prescott, "The Executive Veto in the Southern States," *Journal of Politics* 10 (November 1948): 659–675; Frank W. Prescott, "The Executive Veto in American States," *Western Political Quarterly* 3 (March 1950): 98–112; and Frank W. Prescott and Joseph F. Zimmerman, *The Politics of the Veto of Legislation in New York State*, 2 vols. (Washington, D.C.: University Press of America, 1980).

82. *Journal of the Convention to Revise the [New Hampshire] Constitution, May 1948*, 145.

83. On the origin and early development of the reduction veto, see Fairlie, "Veto Power," 486–488; and Holcombe, *State Government*, 324–325.

84. *Proceedings of the Constitutional Convention of Hawaii, 1950*, 2:450.

85. *Proceedings of the Constitutional Convention of the State of Illinois, Convened January 6, 1920*, 1552–1553.

86. *Official Record, State of Michigan Constitutional Convention, 1961*, 1654.

87. *Official Proceedings of the Constitutional Convention of the State of Alabama [1901]*, 675–676 (quotations transposed).

88. *Journal of the Convention to Revise the [New Hampshire] Constitution, May 1974*, 354–356.

89. *Report of the Proceedings and Debates of the Constitutional Convention, State of Virginia [1901–1902]*, 1879.

90. *Journal of the Convention to Revise the [New Hampshire] Constitution, May 1984*, 285.

91. *Proceedings and Debates of the Constitutional Convention of the State of Michigan [1907]*, 493.

92. *Journal and Proceedings of the [Tennessee] Constitutional Convention [1953]*, 534–535.

93. *Proceedings of the Constitutional Convention of the State of Illinois, Convened January 6, 1920*, 1560.

94. Ibid., 1548.

95. *Record of Proceedings: Sixth Illinois Constitutional Convention [1969]: Verbatim Transcripts*, 907.

96. *Official Proceedings of the Constitutional Convention of the State of Alabama [1901]*, 630.

97. Wells, "Item Veto and State Budget Reform," 783.

98. See Benjamin, "Diffusion of the Governor's Veto Power," 103.

99. The states without an item veto are Indiana, Nevada, New Hampshire, North

Carolina, Rhode Island, and Vermont. The item veto provisions in the forty-four states that do provide for the power are found at: Alabama Constitution (1901), Art. V, Sec. 126; Alaska Constitution (1956), Art. II, Sec. 15; Arizona Constitution (1911), Art. V, Sec. 7; Arkansas Constitution (1874), Art. 6, Sec. 17; California Constitution (1879), Art. IV, Sec. 10(e) (adopted 1908); Colorado Constitution (1876), Art. IV, Sec. 12; Connecticut Constitution (1965), Art. IV, Sec. 16; Delaware Constitution (1897), Art. III, Sec. 18; Florida Constitution (1968), Art. III, Sec. 8; Georgia Constitution (1983), Art. III, Sec. V, Para. XIII(e); Hawaii Constitution (1950), Art. III, Sec. 16 (as amended 1974 and renumbered 1978); Idaho Constitution (1889), Art. IV, Sec. 11; Illinois Constitution (1970), Art. IV, Sec. 9(d); Iowa Constitution (1857), Art. III, Sec. 16 (as amended 1968); Kansas Constitution (1859), Art. 2, Sec. 14(b) (as amended 1974); Kentucky Constitution (1891), Sec. 88; Louisiana Constitution (1974), Art. IV, Sec. 5(G); Maine Constitution (1819), Art. IV, Part Third, Sec. 2-A (adopted 1995); Maryland Constitution (1867), Art. II, Sec. 17 (as amended 1890); Massachusetts Constitution (1780), Articles of Amendment, Art. LXIII, Sec. 5 (adopted 1918); Michigan Constitution (1963), Art. V, Sec. 19; Minnesota Constitution (1857), Art. IV, Sec. 23 (as amended 1876 and reorganized 1974); Mississippi Constitution (1890), Art. 4, Sec. 73; Missouri Constitution (1945), Art. IV, Sec. 26; Montana Constitution (1972), Art. VI, Sec. 10(5); Nebraska Constitution (1875), Art. IV, Sec. 15 (as amended 1976); New Jersey Constitution (1947), Art. V, Sec. I, Para. 15; New Mexico Constitution (1911), Art. IV, Sec. 22; New York Constitution (1894), Art. IV, Sec. 7 (as renumbered 1938); North Dakota Constitution (1889), Art. V, Sec. 9; Ohio Constitution (1851), Art. II, Sec. 16 (as amended 1912); Oklahoma Constitution (1907), Art. VI, Sec. 12; Oregon Constitution (1857), Art. V, Sec. 15a (adopted 1916); Pennsylvania Constitution (1968), Art. IV, Sec. 16; South Carolina Constitution (1895), Art. IV, Sec. 21; South Dakota Constitution (1889), Art. IV, Sec. 4; Tennessee Constitution (1870), Art. III, Sec. 18 (as amended 1953); Texas Constitution (1876), Art. 4, Sec. 14; Utah Constitution (1895), Art. VII, Sec. 8; Virginia Constitution (1971), Art. V, Sec. 6; Washington Constitution (1889), Art. III, Sec. 12 (as amended 1974); West Virginia Constitution (1872), Art. VI, Sec. 51D(11) (as amended 1968); Wisconsin Constitution (1848), Art. V, Sec. 10(1)(b) and (c) (as amended 1930 and 1990); Wyoming Constitution (1889), Art. 4, Sec. 9.

100. For the Washington provision, which permits the governor to object to "sections or appropriation items," see Washington Constitution (1889), Art. III, Sec. 12 (as amended 1974). For the South Carolina provision, which permits the governor to "not approve any one or more of the items or Sections contained in any Bill appropriating money," see South Carolina Constitution (1895), Art. IV, Sec. 21. In addition, Oregon permits the item veto to be exercised on any items contained in emergency bills. See Oregon Constitution (1857), Art. V, Sec. 15a (adopted 1916). See Niels H. Debel, *The Veto Power of the Governor of Illinois* (Urbana: University of Illinois, 1917), 23; and Timothy P. Burke, "The Partial Veto Power: Legislation by the Governor," *Washington Law Review* 49 (1974): 603, 604.

101. Wells, "Item Veto and State Budget Reform," 784–785.

102. These states are Alaska, California, Hawaii, Illinois, Massachusetts, Missouri, Nebraska, New Jersey, Tennessee, and West Virginia. See Moe and Fisher, "Item Veto as a State Reform," 47. For the reduction veto provisions in these states, see Alaska Constitution (1956), Art. II, Sec. 15; California Constitution (1879), Art. IV, Sec. 10(e) (adopted 1922); Hawaii Constitution (1950), Art. III, Sec. 16; Illinois Constitution (1970), Art. IV, Sec. 9(d); Massachusetts Constitution (1780), Articles of Amendment, Art. LXIII, Sec. 5 (adopted 1918); Missouri Constitution (1945), Art. IV, Sec. 26; Nebraska Constitution (1875), Art. IV, Sec.

15 (as amended 1972); New Jersey Constitution (1947), Art. V, Sec. I, Para. 15; Tennessee Constitution (1870), Art. III, Sec. 18 (as amended 1953); West Virginia Constitution (1872), Art. VI, Sec. 51D(11) (as amended 1968). Although in Illinois the reduction veto may be overridden by a mere majority, rather than the usual three-fifths vote, in other states the override provisions for item and reduction vetoes are the same.

103. Fairlie, "Veto Power," 483.

104. The states are Alabama, Illinois, Massachusetts, Montana, New Jersey, South Dakota, and Virginia. See Moe and Fisher, "Item Veto as a State Reform," 47. For these states' amendatory veto provisions, see Alabama Constitution (1901), Art. V, Sec. 125; Illinois Constitution (1970), Art. IV, Sec. 9(e); Massachusetts Constitution (1780), Articles of Amendment, Art. LVI (adopted 1918); Montana Constitution (1972), Art. VI, Sec. 10(2); New Jersey Constitution (1947), Art. V, Sec. 1, Para. 14(f); South Dakota Constitution (1889), Art. IV, Sec. 4 (as amended 1972); Virginia Constitution (1971), Art. V, Sec. 6. See John Nelson Walters, "The Illinois Amendatory Veto," *John Marshall Journal of Practice and Procedure* 11 (1978): 415, 420.

105. See South Dakota Constitution (1889), Art. IV, Sec. 4 (as amended 1972).

106. Benjamin, "Diffusion of the Governor's Veto Power," 102–104. On the use of the amendatory veto, see Kallenbach, *American Chief Executive*, 365–366.

107. The issue of the judicial role in reviewing legislation surfaced primarily during discussions about the composition of the proposed council of revision, and, particularly, about whether judges should participate in such a council. A number of delegates objected to the inclusion of judges on the council of revision, but they advanced different reasons for this conclusion, and with different implications for the power of judicial review. On the one hand, Elbridge Gerry "doubt[ed] whether the Judiciary ought to form a part of it, as they will have a sufficient check against encroachments on their own department by their exposition of the laws, which involved a power of deciding on their Constitutionality." Adrienne Koch, ed., *Madison's Notes of Debates in the Federal Convention of 1787* (New York: W. W. Norton, 1966), 61. On the other hand, John Mercer, in the course of rejecting any role for the judiciary in the council of revision, explained that he "disapproved of the Doctrine that the Judges as expositors of the Constitution should have authority to declare a law void." Koch, *Madison's Notes,* 462.

108. *Federalist Papers,* 436.

109. Ibid., 435.

110. Ibid., 433–434.

111. Ibid., 436–437.

112. Ibid., 450 (quotations transposed).

113. For instance, at the same time in the late 1860s that Congress was considering, and the House was approving, a measure to require two-thirds of Supreme Court justices to strike down legislation, largely out of a desire to protect the Reconstruction Acts, delegates at the New York Convention of 1867–1868 were debating, and ultimately rejecting, a parallel proposal regarding their state high court. This congressional effort to require a supermajority vote for the exercise of judicial review, which failed in the Senate, is discussed in Culp, "Survey of the Proposals," 395; Warren, *Supreme Court in United States History,* 466–471; and William Lasser, *The Limits of Judicial Power: The Supreme Court in American Politics* (Chapel Hill: University of North Carolina Press, 1988), 106–107. The New York Convention debates are found in *Proceedings and Debates of the Constitutional Convention of the State of New York Held in 1867 and 1868,* 3283–3285, 3356–3365. Both the chief supporter

of the New York proposal, Elbridge Lapham, and the main opponent, George Comstock, acknowledged in the convention debates that this state proposal was an outgrowth of the contemporary debate in Congress over preventing the Supreme Court from overturning the Reconstruction Acts. See *Proceedings and Debates of the Constitutional Convention of the State of New York Held in 1867 and 1868*, 3361, 3364.

114. For discussions of the early twentieth-century movement to limit the power of judicial review at both the state and federal level, see Ross, *Muted Fury;* Warren, *Congress, the Constitution, and the Supreme Court*, 128–245; William L. Ransom, *Majority Rule and the Judiciary: An Examination of Current Proposals for Constitutional Change Affecting the Relation of Courts to Legislation* (New York: Scribner's Sons, 1912); Charles E. Merriam, *American Political Ideas: Studies in the Development of American Political Thought, 1865–1917* (New York: Macmillan, 1920), 187–211; J. Patrick White, "Progressivism and the Judiciary: A Study of the Movement for Judicial Reform, 1901–1917" (Ph.D. diss., University of Michigan, 1957); and John Dinan, "Framing a 'People's Government': State Constitution-Making in the Progressive Era," *Rutgers Law Journal* 30 (Summer 1999): 933, 949–957.

115. For discussions of these decisions, see Louis B. Boudin, "Government by Judiciary," *Political Science Quarterly* 26 (June 1911): 238, 266–270; Gilbert E. Roe, *Our Judicial Oligarchy* (New York: B. W. Huebsch, 1912); and Walter F. Dodd, "Social Legislation and the Courts," *Political Science Quarterly* 28 (March 1913): 1–17.

116. See, for instance, the cases cited by Herbert Kenny in *Debates in the Massachusetts Constitutional Convention, 1917–1918*, 1:478–483.

117. 98 N.Y. 98 (1885).

118. 155 Ill. 98 (1895).

119. 201 N.Y. 271 (1911).

120. *Pollock v. Farmers Loan & Trust Co.*, 158 U.S. 601 (1895).

121. *Lochner v. New York*, 198 U.S. 45 (1905).

122. *First Employers' Liability Cases*, 207 U.S. 463 (1908).

123. *Adair v. U.S.*, 208 U.S. 161 (1908); *Coppage v. Kansas*, 236 U.S. 1 (1915).

124. *Hammer v. Dagenhart*, 247 U.S. 251 (1918); *Bailey v. Drexel Furniture Co.*, 259 U.S. 20 (1922).

125. *Debates in the Massachusetts Constitutional Convention, 1917–1918*, 1:481.

126. *Proceedings and Debates of the Constitutional Convention of the State of Ohio [1912]*, 1304.

127. Ibid., 1117.

128. *Debates in the Massachusetts Constitutional Convention, 1917–1918*, 1:490.

129. Ibid., 1:458.

130. *Proceedings and Debates of the Constitutional Convention of the State of Ohio [1912]*, 1028.

131. Ibid., 1107.

132. *Debates in the Massachusetts Constitutional Convention, 1917–1918*, 1:495.

133. Ibid., 1:500.

134. Ibid., 1:464.

135. *Journal of the Nebraska Constitutional Convention [1919]*, 1140.

136. Ibid., 1147.

137. Ibid., 1145.

138. *Debates in the Massachusetts Constitutional Convention, 1917–1918*, 1:540.

139. Ibid., 1:531.

140. *Journal of the Nebraska Constitutional Convention [1919]*, 1138.

141. Ibid., 319.

142. *The Records of the Arizona Constitutional Convention of 1910*, 920.

143. Ibid., 265.

144. *Proceedings and Debates of the Constitutional Convention of the State of Ohio [1912]*, 1305.

145. For the political context and aftermath of Roosevelt's Columbus speech, see Ross, *Muted Fury*, 134–148; and Stephen Stagner, "The Recall of Judicial Decisions and the Due Process Debate," *American Journal of Legal History* 24 (1980): 257–272.

146. Ibid., 384.

147. Ibid.

148. Ibid., 385.

149. Ibid.

150. *Debates in the Massachusetts Constitutional Convention, 1917–1918*, 1:480.

151. *Proceedings and Debates of the Constitutional Convention of the State of Ohio [1912]*, 1144.

152. *Revised Record of the Constitutional Convention of the State of New York [1915]*, 2669–2670.

153. *Journal of the Nebraska Constitutional Convention [1919]*, 1141.

154. *Debates in the Massachusetts Constitutional Convention, 1917–1918*, 1:493–494.

155. Ibid., 1:867–868.

156. Ibid., 1:503.

157. Ibid., 1:465, 466 (quotations transposed).

158. *Journal of the Nebraska Constitutional Convention [1919]*, 1135.

159. *Proceedings and Debates of the Constitutional Convention of the State of Ohio [1912]*, 1112–1113.

160. *Debates in the Massachusetts Constitutional Convention, 1917–1918*, 1:456.

161. *The Records of the Arizona Constitutional Convention of 1910*, 920.

162. *Proceedings and Debates of the Constitutional Convention of the State of Ohio [1912]*, 1295 (quotations transposed).

163. For additional discussion of the debate over supermajority requirements during this period, see Ross, *Muted Fury*, 218–232; Robert E. Cushman, "Constitutional Decisions by a Bare Majority of the Court," *Michigan Law Review* 19 (June 1921): 771–803; Warren, *Congress, the Constitution, and the Supreme Court*, 178–221; Caminker, "Thayerian Deference."

164. See the Ohio Constitution (1851), Art. IV, Sec. 2 (as amended 1912), which went on to make an exception for decisions involving "the affirmance of a judgment of the court of appeals declaring a law unconstitutional and void." On the adoption of the Ohio provision, see Edwin O. Stene, "Is There Minority Control of Court Decisions in Ohio?" *University of Cincinnati Law Review* 9 (January 1935): 23–40; Carl L. Meier, "Power of the Ohio Supreme Court to Declare Laws Unconstitutional," *University of Cincinnati Law Review* 5 (May 1931): 293–310; W. Rolland Maddox, "Minority Control of Court Decisions in Ohio," *American Political Science Review* 24 (August 1930): 638–648; and Jonathan L. Entin, "Judicial Supermajorities and the Validity of Statutes: How *Mapp* Became a Fourth Amendment Landmark Instead of a First Amendment Footnote," *Case Western Reserve Law Review* 52 (Winter 2001): 441, 443–452.

165. North Dakota Constitution (1889), Art. VI, Sec. 4 (as amended 1919).

166. Nebraska Constitution (1875), Art. V, Sec. 2 (as amended 1920). On the adoption of the Nebraska provision, see Paul W. Madgett, "The 'Five-Judge' Rule in Nebraska," *Creighton Law Review* 2 (1969): 329, 329–334; and William Jay Riley, "To Require That a Majority of the Supreme Court Determine the Outcome of Any Case Before It," *Nebraska Law Review* 50 (Summer 1971): 622, 624–627.

167. Entin, "Judicial Supermajorities," 465–466.

168. On the operation of each of these supermajority requirements, see Fite and Rubinstein, "Curbing the Supreme Court," 773–780; Robert L. Hausser, "Limiting the Voting Power of the Supreme Court: Procedure in the States," *Ohio State Law Journal* 5 (December 1938): 54–86; William W. Redmond, "Note: Constitutional Law—Requirement in State Constitution of More Than a Majority of Supreme Court to Invalidate Legislation," *Nebraska Law Bulletin* 19 (March 1940): 32–35; Madgett, "'Five-Judge' Rule," 338–348; Riley, "To Require That a Majority," 631–635; Robert A. Schapiro, "Judicial Deference and Interpretive Coordinacy in State and Federal Constitutional Law," *Cornell Law Review* 85 (March 2000): 656, 691–692; Entin, "Judicial Supermajorities," 452–465; and Caminker, "Thayerian Deference," 90–93.

Other states considered adopting similar measures, including Minnesota, where voters in 1914 rejected a supermajority requirement that was submitted by the legislature; however, none of these other proposals was enacted. See Cushman, "Constitutional Decisions," 797.

169. For additional discussion of the recall of judges during this period, see Walter F. Dodd, "The Recall and the Political Responsibility of Judges," *Michigan Law Review* 10 (December 1911): 79–92; Delos F. Wilcox, *Government by All the People, or The Initiative, the Referendum, and the Recall as Instruments of Democracy* (1912; reprint, New York: Da Capo Press, 1972), 211–227; and Ross, *Muted Fury,* 110–129.

170. See James D. Barnett, "The Operation of the Recall in Oregon," *American Political Science Review* 6 (February 1912): 41–53.

171. These states are: Arizona, California, Colorado, Georgia, Minnesota, Montana, Nevada, New Jersey, North Dakota, Oregon, Rhode Island, and Wisconsin. For these states' recall provisions, see Arizona Constitution (1911), Art. 8, Sec. 1; California Constitution (1879), Art. II, Sec. 13–19 (as amended 1911 and renumbered 1976); Colorado Constitution (1876), Art. XXI (adopted 1912); Georgia Constitution (1983), Art. II, Sec. II, Para. IV; Minnesota Constitution (1857), Art. VIII, Sec. 6 (adopted 1996); Nevada Constitution (1864), Art. 2, Sec. 9 (adopted 1912); New Jersey Constitution (1947), Art. I, Sec. 2; North Dakota Constitution (1889), Art. III, Sec. 10 (adopted 1920); Oregon Constitution (1857), Art. II, Sec. 18 (adopted 1908); Rhode Island Constitution (1986), Art. IV, Sec. 1; Wisconsin Constitution (1848), Art. XIII, Sec. 12 (adopted 1926).

172. The Arizona Convention of 1910 originally approved a judicial recall provision despite the fear of some delegates that President William Howard Taft would veto the Arizona statehood bill. As Wilfred Webb warned during the convention, "If the judiciary is included in the recall, it will be one of the strongest arguments with the President of the United States against the approval of our constitution." *The Records of the Arizona Constitutional Convention of 1910,* 806. When Taft made good on this threat, the people responded by removing the recall provision and resubmitting their proposal to Congress. Then, at the first election after the state's admission to the union, Arizona voters promptly reinstated the original judicial recall provision (1475–1476). See also John D. Leshy, "The Making of the Arizona Constitution," *Arizona State Law Journal* 20 (1988): 1, 100–106; and Ross, *Muted Fury,* 111–113.

173. See Rod Farmer, "Power to the People: The Progressive Movement for the Recall, 1890s–1920," *New England Journal of History* 57 (Winter 2001): 59–83. On the dates of adoption of the general recall of public officials, see Frederick L. Bird and Frances M. Ryan, *The Recall of Public Officers: A Study of the Operation of the Recall in California* (New York: Macmillan, 1930), 5–6; and Joseph F. Zimmerman, *The Recall: Tribunal of the People* (Westport, Conn.: Praeger, 1997), 14–15. The six states that provide for the recall but exclude judges from its operation are Alaska, Idaho, Kansas, Louisiana, Michigan, and Washington.

174. For additional discussion of the recall of judicial decisions during the Progressive era, see Elihu Root, "Judicial Decisions and Public Feeling," *Case and Comment* 19 (1912): 666–671; Daniel W. Baker, "The Recall of Judicial Decisions," *Georgetown Law Journal* 1 (January 1912): 1–12; James B. McDonough, "The Recall of Decisions—A Fallacy," *Central Law Journal* 75 (12 July 1912): 35–40; Rome G. Brown, "The Judicial Recall—A Fallacy Repugnant to Constitutional Government," *Annals of the American Academy of Political and Social Science* 43 (September 1912): 239–277; James A. Metcalf, "Dangers That Lurk in the Recall of the Judiciary," *Annals of the American Academy of Political and Social Science* 43 (September 1912): 278–285; William Draper Lewis, "A New Method of Constitutional Amendment by Popular Vote," *Annals of the American Academy of Political and Social Science* 43 (September 1912): 311–325; John G. Palfrey, "The Constitution and the Courts," *Harvard Law Review* 26 (April 1913): 507–530; Dodd, "Social Legislation and the Courts"; and Ross, *Muted Fury,* 130–154.

175. Colorado Constitution (1876), Art. VI, Sec. 1 (as amended 1912). For additional background on the adoption of this measure, see Duane A. Smith, "Colorado and Judicial Recall," *American Journal of Legal History* 7 (1963): 199–209.

176. On the invalidation of the Colorado provision by the Colorado Supreme Court in *The People v. Western Union,* 70 Colo. 90 (1921) and *The People v. Max,* 70 Colo. 100 (1921), see Smith, "Colorado and Judicial Recall"; Fite and Rubinstein, "Curbing the Supreme Court," 772–773; and Ross, *Muted Fury,* 152.

Chapter 5: Bicameralism

1. John Stuart Mill, *Representative Government,* ed. Herbert Acton (London: Everyman's Library, 1972), 352. This question, which was once taken up by political theorists such as Mill and Jeremy Bentham, has more recently attracted the attention of political scientists and other students of legislative institutions. See, for instance, Saul Levmore, "When Are Two Decisions Better Than One?" *International Review of Law and Economics* 12 (June 1992): 145–162; William H. Riker, "The Merits of Bicameralism," *International Review of Law and Economics* 12 (June 1992): 166–168; William H. Riker, "The Justification of Bicameralism," *International Political Science Review* 13 (1992): 101; George Tsebelis and Jeannette Money, *Bicameralism* (New York: Cambridge University Press, 1997); and James R. Rogers, "An Information Rationale for Congruent Bicameralism," *Journal of Theoretical Politics* 13 (April 2001): 123–151.

2. For a discussion of three countries that shifted to unicameralism during the second half of the twentieth century, see Lawrence D. Longley and David M. Olson, eds., *Two into One: The Politics and Processes of National Legislative Cameral Change* (Boulder, Colo.: Westview Press, 1991). For a recent discussion, see Louis Massicotte, "Legislative Unicameralism: A Global Survey and a Few Case Studies," *Journal of Legislative Studies* 7 (Spring

2001): 151–170. According to Massicotte, the general trend has been in the direction of uni-cameralism, but this tailed off slightly at the end of the twentieth century: "Over the last 20 years, bicameralism has thrived far more than during the previous three decades. Between 1950 and 1979, more countries abolished their second chamber (19) than created one or restored it (17), with nine countries creating a second chamber but abolishing it within the period. However, from 1980 to 1999, only six second chambers were abolished, while 11 were restored and 14 created anew, for a total of 25. Among countries with working parliaments, the proportion having unicameral legislatures has decreased from 67.5 per cent in 1980 to 64 per cent today" (154).

3. Richard Fenno, *The United States Senate: A Bicameral Perspective* (Washington, D.C.: American Enterprise Institute for Public Policy Research, 1982), vii, quoted in Samuel C. Patterson and Anthony Mughan, "Senates and the Theory of Bicameralism," in *Senates: Bicameralism in the Contemporary World,* ed. Samuel C. Patterson and Anthony Mughan (Columbus: Ohio State University Press, 1997), 9. On the debates about bicameralism that did take place in the founding era, see Daniel Wirls and Stephen Wirls, *The Invention of the United States Senate* (Baltimore: Johns Hopkins University Press, 2004). Since the founding era, there has been relatively little discussion about the existence or composition of the U.S. Senate. Bentham's "Anti-Senatica," a sustained attack on the U.S. Senate that was sent to President Andrew Jackson in 1830 but apparently received no response, stands as a notable exception (see Alfred De Grazia, *Public and Republic: Political Representation in America* [New York: Alfred A. Knopf, 1951], 122–123), as does a congressional resolution introduced in 1911 by Wisconsin representative Victor Berger that called for the elimination of the Senate and received no more attention (see John R. Vile, *Encyclopedia of Constitutional Amendments, Proposed Amendments, and Amending Issues, 1789–1995* [Santa Barbara, Calif.: ABC-CLIO, 1996], 273). For a rare critique of the existence of the Senate in the contemporary era, see Lynn A. Baker and Samuel H. Dinkin, "The Senate: An Institution Whose Time Has Gone?" *Journal of Law and Politics* 13 (Winter 1997): 21–103. Critiques of the equal-state apportionment of the Senate have been somewhat more common. See, for instance, William N. Eskridge Jr., "The One Senator, One Vote Clauses," and Suzanna Sherry, "Our Unconstitutional Senate," both in *Constitutional Stupidities, Constitutional Tragedies,* ed. William N. Eskridge Jr. and Sanford Levinson (New York: New York University Press, 1998), 35–39, 95–97; and Frances E. Lee and Bruce I. Oppenheimer, *Sizing Up the Senate: The Unequal Consequences of Equal Representation* (Chicago: University of Chicago Press, 1999).

4. The debates surrounding the Seventeenth Amendment essentially served to confirm a change that had already taken place in the relationship between state legislatures and U.S. senators, as William Riker has shown in "The Senate and American Federalism," *American Political Science Review* 49 (June 1955): 452–469. See George H. Haynes, *The Election of Senators* (New York: Henry Holt, 1912); C. H. Hoebeke, *The Road to Mass Democracy: Original Intent and the Seventeenth Amendment* (New Brunswick, N.J.: Transaction Publishers, 1995); and Ralph Rossum, *Federalism, the Supreme Court, and the Seventeenth Amendment: The Irony of Constitutional Democracy* (Lexington, Mass.: Lexington Books, 2002).

5. One would, of course, have to take account of various changes in regard to the work and operation of the second chamber, as Elaine Swift has shown regarding the early part of the nineteenth century in *The Making of an American Senate: Reconstitutive Change in Congress, 1787–1841* (Ann Arbor: University of Michigan Press, 1996), and as Barbara Sin-

clair, among others, has shown regarding the late twentieth century, in *The Transformation of the U.S. Senate* (Baltimore: Johns Hopkins University Press, 1989).

6. See Arend Lijphart, *Patterns of Democracy: Government Forms and Performance in Thirty-Six Democracies* (New Haven, Conn.: Yale University Press, 1999), 213; Massicotte, "Legislative Unicameralism," 152. For a discussion of the various ways in which other federal systems provide for the representation of subnational polities, see Meg Russell, "The Territorial Role of Second Chambers," *Journal of Legislative Studies* 7 (Spring 2001): 105–118.

7. According to Massicotte, "Even among federations, the almost universal acknowledgment that second chambers are appropriate, indeed indispensable, at the national level often obscures the fact that at the subnational level of federal countries, only 73 state legislatures are bicameral out of over 450. Bicameralism prevails only in the United States and in Australia (except for a single state in each case) and survives in a minority of units in Argentina (nine provinces out of 23), in India (five states out of 25), in Russia (four units out of 89) and in Micronesia (one state out of 4), while unicameral state legislatures are the rule in all other existing federations, including Germany, Austria, Belgium, Switzerland, and Canada." Massicotte, "Legislative Unicameralism," 151.

8. On the late eighteenth-century state debates about bicameralism, see William C. Morey, "The First State Constitutions," *Annals of the American Academy of Political and Social Science* 4 (September 1893): 201, 212–224; Thomas F. Moran, *The Rise and Development of the Bicameral System in America* (Baltimore: Johns Hopkins University Press, 1895); Ellis Paxson Oberholtzer, *The Referendum in America, Together with Some Chapters on the Initiative and Recall* (New York: Charles Scribner's Sons, 1911), 1–68; Jackson Turner Main, *The Upper House in Revolutionary America, 1763–1788* (Madison: University of Wisconsin Press, 1967), 99–191; Gordon S. Wood, *The Creation of the American Republic, 1776–1787* (Chapel Hill: University of North Carolina Press, 1969), 206–255; Willi Paul Adams, *The First American Constitutions: Republican Ideology and the Making of the State Constitutions in the Revolutionary Era* (Chapel Hill: University of North Carolina Press, 1980), 262–266; Donald S. Lutz, *The Origins of American Constitutionalism* (Baton Rouge: Louisiana State University Press, 1988), 91–92; and Marc W. Kruman, *Between Authority and Liberty: State Constitution Making in Revolutionary America* (Chapel Hill: University of North Carolina Press, 1997), 131–154.

9. On the Pennsylvania experiment, see Joseph B. Kingsbury, "Unicameral Legislatures in Early American States," *Washington University Studies* 13 (October 1925): 95, 96–104; J. Paul Selsam, *The Pennsylvania Constitution of 1776: A Study in Revolutionary Democracy* (Philadelphia: University of Pennsylvania Press, 1936), 183–187, 213–216; Irma A. Watts, "Why Pennsylvania Abandoned Unicameralism," *State Government* 9 (March 1936): 54–55; Alvin W. Johnson, *The Unicameral Legislature* (Minneapolis: University of Minnesota Press, 1938), 33–37; John Nees Shaeffer, "Constitutional Change in the Unicameral States, 1776–1793" (Ph.D. diss., University of Wisconsin, 1968), 36–88, 190–237, 332–369.

10. On the Georgia experiment, see Kingsbury, "Unicameral Legislatures," 104–105; Johnson, *Unicameral Legislature,* 32–33; Albert B. Saye, *A Constitutional History of Georgia, 1732–1945* (Athens: University of Georgia Press, 1948), 102–103, 142–143; and Shaeffer, "Constitutional Change," 89–133, 238–331.

11. On the Vermont experiment, see Kingsbury, "Unicameral Legislatures," 105–117; Daniel B. Carroll, *The Unicameral Legislature of Vermont* (Montpelier: Vermont Historical Society, 1933); Johnson, *Unicameral Legislature,* 37–44; and Shaeffer, "Constitutional Change," 134–189, 370–397.

12. On the adoption of unicameralism in Nebraska, see George W. Norris, "One House Legislature," *Annals of the American Academy of Political and Social Science* 181 (September 1935): 50–58; John P. Senning, *The One-House Legislature* (New York: McGraw-Hill, 1937), 50–74; and Johnson, *Unicameral Legislature*, 132–148.

13. These debates are contained in the following sources:

Alaska: *Minutes of the Daily Proceedings, Alaska Constitutional Convention, 1955–56*, 419–467.

Arizona: *The Records of the Arizona Constitutional Convention of 1910*, 580–581.

Connecticut: *The Third Constitutional Convention of the State of Connecticut: Proceedings [1965]*, 200–242.

Hawaii: *Proceedings of the Constitutional Convention of Hawaii of 1968*, 2:120–138; *Proceedings of the Constitutional Convention of Hawaii, 1978*, 2:276–288.

Idaho: *Proceedings and Debates of the Constitutional Convention of Idaho, 1889*, 454–464.

Illinois: *The [Illinois] Constitutional Debates of 1847*, 285; *Debates and Proceedings of the Constitutional Convention of the State of Illinois [1869]*, 141–144, 497; *Record of Proceedings: Sixth Illinois Constitutional Convention [1969]: Verbatim Transcripts*, 2724–2730.

Indiana: *Report of the Debates and Proceedings of the Convention for the Revision of the Constitution of the State of Indiana, 1850*, 980–981.

Louisiana: *Records of the Louisiana Constitutional Convention of 1973: Convention Transcripts*, 225–226.

Maryland: *Debates of the [Maryland] Constitutional Convention of 1967–1968*, 410–412, 431–456.

Massachusetts: *Debates in the Massachusetts Constitutional Convention, 1917–1918*, 3:211–233.

Michigan: *Proceedings and Debates of the Constitutional Convention of the State of Michigan [1907]*, 407; *Official Record, State of Michigan Constitutional Convention, 1961*, 2154–2157.

Montana: *Montana Constitutional Convention, 1971–1972: Verbatim Transcript*, 728–734, 747–749, 759–760, 775–779, 785–789.

Nebraska: *Journal of the Nebraska Constitutional Convention [1919]*, 2124–2145.

New Hampshire: *Journal of the Convention to Revise the [New Hampshire] Constitution, May 1984*, 105–106.

New York: *Revised Record of the Constitutional Convention of the State of New York [1915]*, 348–351, 426–432, 476–499.

North Dakota: *Official Report of the Proceedings and Debates of the First Constitutional Convention of North Dakota [1889]*, 102–128; *Debates of the North Dakota Constitutional Convention of 1972*, 290–323, 1581–1596, 1708–1719.

Ohio: *Report of the Debates and Proceedings of the Convention for the Revision of the Constitution of the State of Ohio, 1850–51*, 1:143–144, 147–149, 153–155, 168–171; *Proceedings and Debates of the Constitutional Convention of the State of Ohio [1912]*, 864–865, 1132–1133.

Pennsylvania: *Debates of the Pennsylvania Constitutional Convention of 1967–1968*, 33.

Rhode Island: *State of Rhode Island and Providence Plantations: Constitutional Convention [1964–1969]: Report of Proceedings*, 988–992, 1171–1197.

Tennessee: *Journal and Proceedings of the [Tennessee] Limited Constitutional Convention [1965]*, 478–494.

14. The debates about the size and apportionment of the two houses are found in the following sources:

Alabama: *Official Proceedings of the Constitutional Convention of the State of Alabama [1901]*, 2343–2355, 3966–3972.

Alaska: *Minutes of the Daily Proceedings, Alaska Constitutional Convention, 1955–56,* 1553–1580, 1834–1977, 3373–3378.

Arizona: *The Records of the Arizona Constitutional Convention of 1910*, 572–581, 796–799.

California: *Report of the Debates in the Convention of California on the Formation of the State Constitution [1849]*, 400–415; *Debates and Proceedings of the Constitutional Convention of the State of California [1878]*, 747, 749–761, 768–777, 1246–1252, 1254–1258.

Connecticut: "Annotated Debates of the 1818 Constitutional Convention," 39–50; *The Third Constitutional Convention of the State of Connecticut: Proceedings [1965]*, 872–899.

Delaware: *Debates of the Delaware Convention, for Revising the Constitution [1831]*, 118–122; *Debates and Proceedings of the Constitutional Convention of the State of Delaware [1852–1853]*, 180–190, 193–201, 204–205, 215–219, 230–238, 242–246; *Debates and Proceedings of the Constitutional Convention of the State of Delaware [1896]*, 2003–2085, 2586–2612, 2615–2636, 2814–2842.

Georgia: *A Stenographic Report of the Proceedings of the Constitutional Convention Held in Atlanta, Georgia, 1877*, 340–368.

Hawaii: *Proceedings of the Constitutional Convention of Hawaii, 1950*, 2:66–142, 156–176, 760; *Proceedings of the Constitutional Convention of Hawaii of 1968*, 2:192–315; *Proceedings of the Constitutional Convention of Hawaii, 1978*, 2:317–331.

Idaho: *Proceedings and Debates of the Constitutional Convention of Idaho, 1889*, 464–474, 486–506, 1202–1211, 1898–1913, 1918–1927.

Illinois: *The [Illinois] Constitutional Debates of 1847*, 124–158, 293–298; *Debates and Proceedings of the Constitutional Convention of the State of Illinois [1869]*, 491–495, 696–702, 704–724, 728–743, 917–928; *Proceedings of the Constitutional Convention of the State of Illinois, Convened January 6, 1920*, 1610–1663, 1694–1731, 2696–2835, 2973–3090, 4238–4254; *Record of Proceedings: Sixth Illinois Constitutional Convention [1969]: Verbatim Transcripts*, 2654–2666, 2676–2683, 2732–2776, 2781–2810, 2935–2961, 2964–2986, 4070–4078, 4109–4113, 4406–4407.

Indiana: *Report of the Debates and Proceedings of the Convention for the Revision of the Constitution of the State of Indiana, 1850*, 262–276, 981–1050, 1241–1247.

Iowa: *The Debates of the Constitutional Convention of the State of Iowa [1857]*, 541–549, 553–555, 577–578, 1013–1016.

Kansas: *A Reprint of the Proceedings and Debates of the Convention Which Framed the Constitution of Kansas at Wyandotte in July, 1859*, 115–120, 357–361, 475–481.

Kentucky: *Report of the Debates and Proceedings of the Convention for the Revision of the Constitution of the State of Kentucky, 1849*, 444–617, 632–639, 937–947, 953–987, 994–1002; *Official Report of the Proceedings and Debates in the Convention . . . of September, 1890, To Adopt, Amend or Change the Constitution of the State of Kentucky*, 3807–3839, 3962–3989, 4385–4424, 4445–4452, 4608–4630.

Louisiana: *Proceedings and Debates of the Convention of Louisiana [1845]*, 128–163, 305–391, 420–482, 489–659; *Debates in the Convention for the Revision and Amendment of the Constitution of the State of Louisiana [1864]*, 235–238, 245–247, 250–252; *Records of the Louisiana Constitutional Convention of 1973: Convention Transcripts,* 219–225, 312–316, 354–368.

Maine: *The Debates and Journal of the Constitutional Convention of the State of Maine, 1819–20,* 130–196, 202–208, 242–250, 294–343.

Maryland: *Debates and Proceedings of the Maryland Reform Convention to Revise the State Constitution [1851],* 1:106–112, 115–122, 127–137, 284–288; 2:15–200, 706–713, 718–726, 819–823; *The Debates of the Constitutional Convention of the State of Maryland [1864],* 1032–1076, 1655–1676; *Debates of the Maryland Constitutional Convention of 1867,* 297–300; *Debates of the [Maryland] Constitutional Convention of 1967–1968,* 412–417, 462–476, 479–526, 528–597, 1542–1616, 3067–3075.

Massachusetts: *Journal of Debates and Proceedings in the Convention of Delegates, Chosen to Revise the Constitution of Massachusetts [1820–21],* 227–235, 240–249, 257–332, 495–519, 533–537; *Official Report of the Debates and Proceedings in the State Convention to Revise and Amend the Constitution of the Commonwealth of Massachusetts [1853],* 1:190–213, 218–232, 809–950; 2:38–59, 127–248, 267–269, 314–325, 332–384, 392–432, 437–468, 576–638; 3:570–577, 580–613; *Debates in the Massachusetts Constitutional Convention, 1917–1918,* 3:159–189.

Michigan: *The Michigan Constitutional Conventions of 1835–36: Debates and Proceedings,* 366–368, 386–387; *Report of the Proceedings and Debates in the Convention to Revise the Constitution of the State of Michigan, 1850,* 111–129, 348–357, 359–383, 414–424, 449–458, 795–799; *The Debates and Proceedings of the Constitutional Convention of the State of Michigan [1867],* 2:7–15, 693–704, 982–986; *Proceedings and Debates of the Constitutional Convention of the State of Michigan [1907],* 238–240, 261–264, 901–906, 911–914; *Official Record, State of Michigan Constitutional Convention, 1961,* 2014–2030, 2034–2153, 2157–2158, 2163–2180, 2799–2822, 3100–3103, 3113–3116.

Minnesota: *The Debates and Proceedings of the Minnesota Constitutional Convention [1857],* 234–238, 252–254, 271–273; *Debates and Proceedings of the Constitutional Convention for the Territory of Minnesota [1857],* 198–200.

Missouri: *Debates of the Missouri Constitutional Convention of 1875,* 2:15–23; 3:204–360; 4:349–360; 5:193–504; 6:20–290, 406–433.

Montana: *Proceedings and Debates of the Constitutional Convention Held in the City of Helena, Montana [1889],* 597–600, 622–640, 649–655; *Montana Constitutional Convention, 1971–1972: Verbatim Transcript,* 680–681, 742–746, 760–770, 779–785, 1596–1614.

Nebraska: *Official Report of the Debates and Proceedings in the Nebraska Constitutional Convention [1871],* 1:531–541, 561–582; 2:288–298, 304–329, 372–374, 568–581, 624–628; 3:146–156, 305–318; *Journal of the Nebraska Constitutional Convention [1919],* 755–758, 1017–1049, 1577–1583, 2005–2064, 2651–2655.

Nevada: *Official Report of the Debates and Proceedings in the Constitutional Convention of the State of Nevada [1864],* 632–638.

New Hampshire: *Journal of the Constitutional Convention of the State of New Hampshire, December 1876,* 59–78, 129–142, 147–165, 176–188, 196–225, 231–252; *Journal of the Constitutional Convention of the State of New Hampshire, January 1889,* 239–249; *Journal of the [New Hampshire] Constitutional Convention of 1902,* 103–181, 196–204, 268–331, 338–459, 641–650, 720–746; *Journal of the Convention to Revise the [New Hampshire] Constitution, June 1912,* 72–78, 99–106, 118–144, 316–336, 390–400, 515–539; *Journal of the Convention to Revise the [New Hampshire] Convention, January 20, 1920,* 220–281, 295–300, 416–425; *Journal of the Convention to Revise the [New Hampshire] Constitution,*

May, 1938, 168–186; *Journal of the Convention to Revise the [New Hampshire] Convention, September, 1941, 63–88; Journal of the Convention to Revise the [New Hampshire] Constitution, May 1948, 236–263; Journal of the Convention to Revise the [New Hampshire] Constitution, May 1956, 124–126, 143–153; Journal of the Convention to Revise the [New Hampshire] Constitution, December 1959, 65–76, 84–91; Journal of the Convention to Revise the [New Hampshire] Constitution, May 1964, 221–261, 265–276; Journal of the Convention to Revise the [New Hampshire] Constitution, May 1974, 225–229; Journal of the Convention to Revise the [New Hampshire] Constitution, May 1984,* 135–145.

New Jersey: *Proceedings of the New Jersey State Constitutional Convention of 1844,* 282–287, 512–513.

New York: *Report of the Debates and Proceedings of the Convention of the State of New York [1821],* 200–212, 216, 237–245, 257–259, 273, 295–296; *Report of the Debates and Proceedings of the Convention for the Revision of the Constitution of the State of New York, 1846,* 373–383, 401–429, 444–469, 477–479; *Revised Record of the Constitutional Convention of the State of New York [1894],* 3:343–348, 987–1242; 4:6–96, 359–376, 654–694; *Revised Record of the Constitutional Convention of the State of New York [1915],* 426–432, 446–448, 476–499, 532–678, 3951–3960, 3990–4033; *Revised Record of the Constitutional Convention of the State of New York [1938],* 1146–1149, 1317–1325, 2841–2956, 3279–3326; *Proceedings of the Constitutional Convention of the State of New York [1967],* 2:659–662.

North Carolina: *Proceedings and Debates of the Convention of North Carolina [1835],* 32–60, 82–162, 204–212, 359–366.

North Dakota: *Official Report of the Proceedings and Debates of the First Constitutional Convention of North Dakota [1889],* 284–288, 323–339, 540–541, 544–548; *Debates of the North Dakota Constitutional Convention of 1972,* 269–270, 1172–1198, 1328–1332, 1503–1513.

Ohio: *Report of the Debates and Proceedings of the Convention for the Revision of the Constitution of the State of Ohio, 1850–51,* 1:99–104, 130–137, 140–157, 168–172, 271–273, 460–461; 2:748–753, 756–787; *Official Report of the Proceedings and Debates of the Third Constitutional Convention of Ohio [1873],* 2:1577–1628, 1644–1654, 1666–1698, 1704–1734, 3239–3300, 3304–3321, 3326–3348; *Proceedings and Debates of the Constitutional Convention of the State of Ohio [1912],* 1683–1690.

Pennsylvania: *Proceedings and Debates of the Convention of the Commonwealth of Pennsylvania [1837],* 2:57–138, 157–161, 166–168; 8:141–160, 198–236, 242–252; 12:140–164, 174–175, 180–196; *Debates of the Convention to Amend the Constitution of Pennsylvania [1872–1873],* 2:165–182, 186–248, 250–281, 284–301, 309–326; 5:362–373, 407–467, 501–559, 638–715, 752–757; 7:21–50, 58–116, 155–218, 305–312; 8:76–79, 96–121, 382–385, 447–458; *Debates of the Pennsylvania Constitutional Convention of 1967–1968,* 451–564, 1178–1197.

Rhode Island: *Journal of the Convention Assembled to Frame a Constitution for the State of Rhode Island [1842],* 31–35, 39–42; *State of Rhode Island and Providence Plantations: Constitutional Convention [1964–1969]: Report of Proceedings,* 1213–1216, 1419–1433.

South Carolina: *Proceedings of the Constitutional Convention of South Carolina [1868],* 364–375, 529–536.

South Dakota: *Dakota Constitutional Convention [1885, 1889],* 1:177–182, 227.

Tennessee: *Journal and Proceedings of the [Tennessee] Limited Constitutional Convention [1965],* 854–903, 946–952.

Texas: *Debates of the Texas Convention [1845]*, 213–222, 230–252, 531–558; *Debates in the Texas Constitutional Convention of 1875*, 97–99, 262–263; *Texas Constitutional Convention [1974]: Official Proceedings*, 1099–1113, 1159–1173, 1330–1332.

Utah: *Official Report of the Proceedings and Debates of the Convention . . . To Adopt a Constitution for the State of Utah [1895]*, 175–187, 819–864.

Virginia: *Proceedings and Debates of the Virginia State Convention of 1829–30*, 53–345, 361–362, 446–455, 494–502, 537–575, 654–671, 672–705, 750–762, 798–799, 808–812, 820–821, 828–854; *Register of the Debates and Proceedings of the Va. Reform Convention [1850–1851]*, 100–101, 144–148, 278–285, 287–305, 307–358, 363–504; *Proceedings of the Virginia State Convention of 1861*, 4:290–303, 307–311; *The Debates and Proceedings of the Constitutional Convention of the State of Virginia [1867–1868]*, 372–378.

West Virginia: *Debates and Proceedings of the First Constitutional Convention of West Virginia (1861–1863)*, 2:110–341, 1151–1183.

Wisconsin: *The [Wisconsin] Convention of 1846*, 466–469, 480–482, 620–625, 628–629; *Journal of the Convention to Form a Constitution for the State of Wisconsin [1847–1848]*, 216–225, 252–255, 320–321, 360–370, 379–390.

Wyoming: *Journal and Debates of the Constitutional Convention of the State of Wyoming [1889]*, 409–427, 455–460, 539–547, 552–575.

15. The debates about the term lengths of legislators in the two houses are found in the following sources:

Alabama: *Official Proceedings of the Constitutional Convention of the State of Alabama [1901]*, 2236–2253, 4706–4713.

Alaska: *Minutes of the Daily Proceedings, Alaska Constitutional Convention, 1955–56*, 1784–1793.

Delaware: *Debates of the Delaware Convention, for Revising the Constitution [1831]*, 38–41, 122–123, 161–163.

Hawaii: *Proceedings of the Constitutional Convention of Hawaii of 1968*, 2:283–290; *Proceedings of the Constitutional Convention of Hawaii, 1978*, 2:332–339.

Idaho: *Proceedings and Debates of the Constitutional Convention of Idaho, 1889*, 474–485, 1192–1201.

Illinois: *The [Illinois] Constitutional Debates of 1847*, 284–292; *Record of Proceedings: Sixth Illinois Constitutional Convention [1969]: Verbatim Transcripts*, 2654–2655.

Indiana: *Report of the Debates and Proceedings of the Convention for the Revision of the Constitution of the State of Indiana, 1850*, 1050–1051.

Iowa: *Fragments of the Debates of the Iowa Constitutional Conventions of 1844 and 1846*, 57–58.

Kentucky: *Official Report of the Proceedings and Debates in the Convention . . . of September, 1890, To Adopt, Amend or Change the Constitution of the State of Kentucky*, 3799–3804, 4249–4269.

Maryland: *Debates and Proceedings of the Maryland Reform Convention to Revise the State Constitution [1851]*, 1:246–283; *Debates of the [Maryland] Constitutional Convention of 1967–1968*, 418.

Michigan: *The Debates and Proceedings of the Constitutional Convention of the State of Michigan [1867]*, 2:724–726.

Minnesota: *The Debates and Proceedings of the Minnesota Constitutional Convention [1857]*, 254–262.

Montana: *Montana Constitutional Convention, 1971–1972: Verbatim Transcript,* 770–775.

Nebraska: *Official Report of the Debates and Proceedings in the Nebraska Constitutional Convention [1871],* 1:575–576.

Nevada: *Official Report of the Debates and Proceedings in the Constitutional Convention of the State of Nevada [1864],* 138–140.

New Hampshire: *Journal of the Constitutional Convention of the State of New Hampshire, December 1876,* 83–95.

New Jersey: *Proceedings of the New Jersey State Constitutional Convention of 1844,* 124–138, 287–296, 511–513.

New York: *Report of the Debates and Proceedings of the Convention for the Revision of the Constitution of the State of New York, 1846,* 373–383, 401–414; *Proceedings and Debates of the Constitutional Convention of the State of New York Held in 1867 and 1868,* 650–665, 677–716, 758–789, 819–848, 852–876, 3586–3591, 3678–3682; *Revised Record of the Constitutional Convention of the State of New York [1894],* 3:343–348, 987–1242; 4:6–96, 359–376, 654–694; *Proceedings of the Constitutional Convention of the State of New York [1967],* 2:646–656, 664–668.

North Dakota: *Debates of the North Dakota Constitutional Convention of 1972,* 847–854, 1208–1223.

Ohio: *Report of the Debates and Proceedings of the Convention for the Revision of the Constitution of the State of Ohio, 1850–51,* 1:218–226; 2:142–148; *Official Report of the Proceedings and Debates of the Third Constitutional Convention of Ohio [1873],* 2:263–365, 1025–1048.

Pennsylvania: *Proceedings and Debates of the Convention of the Commonwealth of Pennsylvania [1837],* 2:162–165; 8:169–193; *Debates of the Convention to Amend the Constitution of Pennsylvania [1872–1873],* 1:331–334, 337–347, 355–361, 364–374, 380–430, 433–450; 5:338–349.

Rhode Island: *Journal of the Convention Assembled to Frame a Constitution for the State of Rhode Island [1842],* 37; *State of Rhode Island and Providence Plantations: Constitutional Convention [1964–1969]: Report of Proceedings,* 1365–1368, 1849–1857, 1869–1875, 2037–2041, 2111–2115.

Tennessee: *Journal and Proceedings of the [Tennessee] Limited Constitutional Convention [1965],* 502–519, 540–556.

Texas: *Debates of the Texas Convention [1845],* 509–517; *Debates in the Texas Constitutional Convention of 1875,* 94–96; *Texas Constitutional Convention [1974]: Official Proceedings,* 1142–1159, 2277–2287.

Virginia: *Report of the Proceedings and Debates of the Constitutional Convention, State of Virginia [1901–1902],* 459–471, 488–598, 606–615, 1844–1869, 3091–3096.

West Virginia: *Debates and Proceedings of the First Constitutional Convention of West Virginia (1861–1863),* 1:716–752.

16. The debates about the qualifications for members of the two houses are found in the following sources:

Alabama: *Official Proceedings of the Constitutional Convention of the State of Alabama [1901],* 2260–2268.

Arizona: *The Records of the Arizona Constitutional Convention of 1910,* 582.

California: *Report of the Debates in the Convention of California on the Formation of the State Constitution [1849],* 83–84; *Debates and Proceedings of the Constitutional Convention of the State of California [1878],* 745–747.

Delaware: *Debates of the Delaware Convention, for Revising the Constitution [1831],* 41, 125–128; *Debates and Proceedings of the Constitutional Convention of the State of Delaware [1852–1853],* 101–102, 116–118, 238; *Debates and Proceedings of the Constitutional Convention of the State of Delaware [1896],* 2238–2253.

Hawaii: *Proceedings of the Constitutional Convention of Hawaii of 1968,* 2:179–189.

Idaho: *Proceedings and Debates of the Constitutional Convention of Idaho, 1889,* 506–507, 1211–1214.

Illinois: *The [Illinois] Constitutional Debates of 1847,* 292; *Debates and Proceedings of the Constitutional Convention of the State of Illinois [1869],* 499–508, 939–940; *Record of Proceedings: Sixth Illinois Constitutional Convention [1969]: Verbatim Transcripts,* 2666–2667, 2814–2819, 4058–4063.

Indiana: *Report of the Debates and Proceedings of the Convention for the Revision of the Constitution of the State of Indiana, 1850,* 1051–1052.

Iowa: *Fragments of the Debates of the Iowa Constitutional Conventions of 1844 and 1846,* 56–57; *The Debates of the Constitutional Convention of the State of Iowa [1857],* 515–516, 567–573.

Kentucky: *Official Report of the Proceedings and Debates in the Convention . . . of September, 1890, To Adopt, Amend or Change the Constitution of the State of Kentucky,* 3804–3805, 4270–4272.

Louisiana: *Proceedings and Debates of the Convention of Louisiana [1845],* 52–94; *Records of the Louisiana Constitutional Convention of 1973: Convention Transcripts,* 316–347.

Maine: *The Debates and Journal of the Constitutional Convention of the State of Maine, 1819–20,* 196–201.

Maryland: *Debates and Proceedings of the Maryland Reform Convention to Revise the State Constitution [1851],* 1:303–304; *Debates of the [Maryland] Constitutional Convention of 1967–1968,* 417–418.

Michigan: *The Debates and Proceedings of the Constitutional Convention of the State of Michigan [1867],* 2:15–22.

New Hampshire: *Journal of the Convention to Revise the [New Hampshire] Constitution, May 1974,* 218–220; *Journal of the Convention to Revise the [New Hampshire] Constitution, May 1984,* 151–157.

New Jersey: *Proceedings of the New Jersey State Constitutional Convention of 1844,* 104–110.

Ohio: *Report of the Debates and Proceedings of the Convention for the Revision of the Constitution of the State of Ohio, 1850–51,* 1:217–218, 226–228; *Official Report of the Proceedings and Debates of the Third Constitutional Convention of Ohio [1873],* 2:265–268.

Pennsylvania: *Proceedings and Debates of the Convention of the Commonwealth of Pennsylvania [1837],* 2:42–55, 168–170; 8:106–112, 119–141, 252–261; 12:165–167; *Debates of the Convention to Amend the Constitution of Pennsylvania [1872–1873],* 1:452–354; 5:350–353.

South Carolina: *Proceedings of the Constitutional Convention of South Carolina [1868],* 184–185.

South Dakota: *Dakota Constitutional Convention [1885, 1889],* 1:182–184.

Texas: *Debates of the Texas Convention [1845],* 525–526; *Debates in the Texas Con-*

stitutional Convention of 1875, 94–96; *Texas Constitutional Convention [1974]: Official Proceedings*, 1114–1122.

Utah: *Official Report of the Proceedings and Debates of the Convention . . . To Adopt a Constitution for the State of Utah [1895]*, 867.

Virginia: *Proceedings and Debates of the Virginia State Convention of 1829–30*, 461–464, 671–672, 799.

West Virginia: *Debates and Proceedings of the First Constitutional Convention of West Virginia (1861–1863)*, 1:786–803.

The debates about different qualifications for voting for members of the two houses are found in the following source:

New York: *Report of the Debates and Proceedings of the Convention of the State of New York [1821]*, 113–137.

17. The debates about the different legislative powers of the two houses are found in the following sources:

Alabama: *Official Proceedings of the Constitutional Convention of the State of Alabama [1901]*, 2435–2446, 2485–2490, 2499–2511.

Delaware: *Debates and Proceedings of the Constitutional Convention of the State of Delaware [1896]*, 1412–1415.

Indiana: *Report of the Debates and Proceedings of the Convention for the Revision of the Constitution of the State of Indiana, 1850*, 2009–2010.

Kansas: *A Reprint of the Proceedings and Debates of the Convention Which Framed the Constitution of Kansas at Wyandotte in July, 1859*, 126–129.

Maryland: *Debates and Proceedings of the Maryland Reform Convention to Revise the State Constitution [1851]*, 1:309–310.

Michigan: *The Debates and Proceedings of the Constitutional Convention of the State of Michigan [1867]*, 2:82–83.

Minnesota: *The Debates and Proceedings of the Minnesota Constitutional Convention [1857]*, 238–239.

New York: *Report of the Debates and Proceedings of the Convention of the State of New York [1821]*, 212–213.

Pennsylvania: *Proceedings and Debates of the Convention of the Commonwealth of Pennsylvania [1837]*, 2:175–182; 9:51–60.

South Dakota: *Dakota Constitutional Convention [1885, 1889]*, 1:232–234.

Virginia: *Proceedings and Debates of the Virginia State Convention of 1829–30*, 801–804, 856–857.

West Virginia: *Debates and Proceedings of the First Constitutional Convention of West Virginia (1861–1863)*, 1:896–905.

18. See Moran, *Rise and Development*, 38–42.

19. See ibid., 8–26, 43–47.

20. Ibid., 27–38, 47–50.

21. Although there is no doubt about Franklin's support for unicameralism in the 1780s, there has been some dispute about the extent of his backing for a unicameral legislature in the 1770s. For further discussion, see Robert Luce, *Legislative Assemblies* (Boston: Houghton Mifflin, 1924), 26–27; and Selsam, *Pennsylvania Constitution*, 185–187.

22. Benjamin Franklin, "Queries and Remarks Respecting Alterations in the Constitution of Pennsylvania," in *The Writings of Benjamin Franklin*, ed. Albert Henry Smyth, 10 vols.

(New York: Macmillan, 1905–1907), 10:55–60, excerpted in Philip B. Kurland and Ralph Lerner, eds., *The Founders' Constitution*, 5 vols. (Chicago: University of Chicago Press, 1987), 1:376.

23. Selsam, *Pennsylvania Constitution*, 186.

24. Franklin, "Queries and Remarks Respecting Alterations in the Constitution of Pennsylvania," in *The Founders' Constitution*, 1:376.

25. See Shaeffer, "Constitutional Change," on the adoption and subsequent rejection of unicameralism in Pennsylvania (36–88, 277–331), Georgia (89–133, 332–369), and Vermont (134–189, 370–397).

26. Tennessee came the closest of any of the other states to adopting unicameralism in the late eighteenth century. The Convention of 1796 that was charged with drafting the state's inaugural constitution initially approved a motion to adopt a single-chamber legislature but then reversed itself and decided to provide a second chamber. See Lewis L. Laska, *The Tennessee State Constitution: A Reference Guide* (Westport, Conn.: Greenwood Press, 1990), 3.

27. John Adams, "Thoughts on Government," in *The Political Writings of John Adams,* ed. George A. Peek Jr. (New York: Macmillan, 1985), 87. For additional discussions of Adams's views on bicameralism, see Correa Moylan Walsh, *The Political Science of John Adams: A Study in the Theory of Mixed Government and the Bicameral System* (New York: G. P. Putnam's Sons, 1915); and C. Bradley Thompson, *John Adams and the Spirit of Liberty* (Lawrence: University Press of Kansas, 1998), 175–185, 216–222.

28. Quoted in Luce, *Legislative Assemblies*, 36.

29. *The Portable Thomas Jefferson,* ed. Merrill D. Peterson (New York: Penguin, 1975), 164 (quotations transposed). Jefferson's views on this point evolved during the course of his life, to the point that he "abandoned altogether the idea that there should be any distinction whatsoever in the character and functions of the two houses." Frances Harrold, "The Upper House in Jeffersonian Political Theory," *Virginia Magazine of History and Biography* 78 (July 1970): 281, 286.

30. Alexander Hamilton et al., *The Federalist Papers,* ed. Clinton Rossiter (1961; reprint, New York: Mentor, 1999), 347.

31. James Wilson represents an important exception to the general understanding that bicameralism presupposed significant distinctions in the composition of the two houses. In his "Lectures on Law," delivered in 1791 in the immediate aftermath of Pennsylvania's shift from unicameralism to bicameralism, he noted, "To choose the senators by the same persons, by whom the members of the house of representatives are chosen, is, we are told, to lose the material distinction, and, consequently, all the benefits which would result from the material distinction, between the two branches of the legislature." He responded, "But many and strong reasons, we think, may be assigned, why all the advantages, to be expected from two branches of a legislature, may be gained and preserved, though those two branches derive their authority from precisely the same source." James Wilson, *The Works of James Wilson,* ed. Robert G. McCloskey, 2 vols. (Cambridge, Mass.: Belknap Press, 1967), 1:414–415, excerpted in Kurland and Lerner, *Founders' Constitution,* 1:378.

32. On this point, see G. Alan Tarr, *Understanding State Constitutions* (Princeton, N.J.: Princeton University Press, 1998), 85–86.

33. Benjamin Rush, "Observations on the Government of Pennsylvania," in *The Selected Writings of Benjamin Rush,* ed. Dagobert D. Runes (New York: Philosophical Library, 1947), 57–64, excerpted in Kurland and Lerner, *Founders' Constitution,* 1:364.

34. Main, *Upper House,* 215.

35. Rush, "Observations on the Government of Pennsylvania," in Kurland and Lerner, *Founders' Constitution,* 1:364.

36. Theophilus Parsons, "Essex Result," in *American Political Writings during the Founding Era, 1760–1805,* ed. Charles S. Hyneman and Donald S. Lutz (Indianapolis, Ind.: Liberty Fund, 1983), 1:493.

37. Ibid., 511. For further discussion of Parsons's views on bicameralism and the importance of the "Essex Result," see Elisha P. Douglass, *Rebels and Democrats: The Struggle for Equal Political Rights and Majority Rule* (Chapel Hill: University of North Carolina Press, 1955), 180–183.

38. The provisions for the original states that drafted state constitutions during this period are as follows: Delaware (1776) provided seven representatives for each county and three senators for each county; Georgia (1789) provided a fixed number of representatives for each county and one senator for each county; Maryland (1776) provided for 24 representatives and for 15 senators; Massachusetts (1780) provided one representative for roughly every 150 inhabitants in each town and for 40 senators; New Hampshire (1784) provided one representative for roughly every 150 inhabitants in each town and for 12 senators; New Jersey (1776) provided three representatives for each county and one senator for each county; New York (1777) provided for 70 representatives and 24 senators; North Carolina (1776) provided two representatives for each county (as well as one representative for each of six cities), and one senator for each county; Pennsylvania (1790) provided for at least 60, but no more than 100 representatives, and for the number of senators to be no less than one-fourth, but no greater than one-third, of the number of representatives; South Carolina (1778) provided for 202 representatives and 13 senators; and Virginia (1776) provided two representatives for each county (plus one representative each for two cities) and 24 senators.

39. The requirement that revenue bills originate in the house was adopted in Delaware (1776); Maryland (1776); New Hampshire (1784); New Jersey (1776); Pennsylvania (1990); South Carolina (1776), and Virginia (1776). In addition, New Jersey (1776), Virginia (1776), and South Carolina (1778; but not 1790) prevented the senate from amending revenue bills; the senates in these states were thus required to approve or reject the entire bills. Virginia (1776) went so far as to prevent the senate from introducing *any* bills.

40. All of the states that drafted state constitutions during this period provided for annual elections for seats in the lower house. Seven of the states that drafted constitutions during this period provided for longer terms of office for their senators, including Delaware (1776) and Georgia (1789), each of which provided for senatorial elections every three years; New York (1777), Pennsylvania (1790), South Carolina (1790), and Virginia (1776), each of which provided for senatorial elections every four years; and Maryland (1776), which provided for senatorial elections every five years. The other four states provided for annual senatorial elections.

41. Delaware (1792), whose Constitution of 1776 had provided for no such distinction, required that house members be freeholders and that senators possess a freehold of 200 acres of land or an estate in real and personal property of 1,000 pounds. Georgia (1789) required that house members possess 200 acres of land or other property worth 150 pounds and that senators possess 250 acres of land or other property worth 250 pounds. Maryland (1776) required that house members possess real or personal property worth 500 pounds, and that senators possess real and personal property worth 1,000 pounds. Massachusetts (1780) stipulated that house members have either a freehold worth 100 pounds in the town

from which they were elected or any ratable estate worth 200 pounds; senators were required to have a freehold of 300 pounds or personal estate of 600 pounds. New Hampshire (1784) required house members to have an estate of 100 pounds, half of which must be a freehold, whereas senators were required to have a freehold estate valued at 200 pounds. New Jersey (1776) required house members to possess 500 pounds in real and personal estate, and senators to possess 1,000 pounds in real and personal estate. New York (1777) placed no property requirements on house members but required senators to be freeholders. In North Carolina (1776), house members were required to possess 100 acres of land, and senators were required to possess 300 acres of land. South Carolina (1790) provided that house members who were residents of the district from which they were elected must have either 500 acres of land and ten slaves or real estate valued at 150 pounds, and that house members who did not reside in their district must have a freehold estate worth 500 pounds; resident senators were required to have a freehold estate worth 300 pounds, and nonresident senators had to have an estate worth 1,000 pounds. Of the states that drafted constitutions during this period, Virginia and Pennsylvania were the only ones that failed to provide distinct property requirements for members of the two houses. On the rejection of a proposed distinction in the Virginia Constitution of 1776, see Kruman, *Between Authority and Liberty*, 136.

42. New York (1777) required voters in House elections to have a freehold estate worth 20 pounds or to rent a tenement worth 40 shillings and to be a taxpayer; voters in senate elections were required to have an estate worth 100 pounds. North Carolina (1776) imposed a taxpaying requirement on voters in house elections, but required voters in senate elections to own 50 acres of land.

43. Both Massachusetts (1780) and New Hampshire (1784) required legislators, in drawing senate districts, to "govern themselves by the proportion of public taxes paid by the said districts."

44. New York (1777) divided the state into four "great" districts, which were responsible for selecting nine, six, six, and three senators, respectively. Virginia (1776) divided the state into twenty-four districts, each of which was responsible for selecting a member of the senate.

45. In Maryland (1776), voters from each county selected two electors, who then convened with other electors from around the state and chose a slate of fifteen senators (six from the eastern shore and nine from the western part of the state). Kentucky (1792) adopted a similar electoral college system for the selection of its senators, and it remained in effect until the adoption of its 1799 constitution. In a somewhat different fashion, South Carolina (1776) provided, for a two-year period, that members of the upper house would be selected by the lower house.

46. Kruman, *Between Authority and Liberty*, 153. In fact, Kruman concludes that "most state constitutions did *not* require senators to possess greater wealth; most did *not* grant senators longer terms; and most did *not* create special senatorial constituencies" (154). These conclusions notwithstanding, it is nevertheless the case that every one of the original bicameral states that drafted a constitution during this period adopted at least one of these distinctions, and most of these states adopted several of these distinctions. For further discussions of the distinctions that were established in each of these states, see Dudley O. McGovney, *The American Suffrage Medley: The Need for a National Uniform Suffrage* (Chicago: University of Chicago Press, 1949), 11–25; Arthur N. Holcombe, *State Government in the United States*, 2nd ed. (New York: Macmillan, 1926), 67–68; Fletcher M. Green, *Constitutional Development in the South Atlantic States, 1776–1860: A Study in the Evolution*

of Democracy (Chapel Hill: University of North Carolina Press, 1930), 84–88; William C. Webster, "Comparative Study of the State Constitutions of the American Revolution," *Annals of the American Academy of Political and Social Science* 9 (May 1897): 390–392; and Morey, "First State Constitutions," 221–225.

47. Main, *Upper House*, 190.

48. Ibid., 236.

49. On the various ways in which nineteenth-century state constitution makers sought to remove property distinctions and democratize governing institutions, especially during the Jacksonian Era, see Alexander Keyssar, *The Right to Vote: The Contested History of Democracy in the United States* (New York: Basic Books, 2000), 26–52; De Grazia, *Public and Republic*, 113–145; Chilton Williamson, *American Suffrage: From Property to Democracy, 1760–1860* (Princeton, N.J.: Princeton University Press, 1960), 138–280; Kirk H. Porter, *A History of Suffrage in the United States* (Chicago: University of Chicago Press, 1918), 20–111; Daniel T. Rodgers, *Contested Truths: Keywords in American Politics since Independence* (1987; reprint, Cambridge, Mass.: Harvard University Press, 1998), 80–111; Rogers M. Smith, *Civic Ideals: Conflicting Visions of Citizenship in U.S. History* (New Haven, Conn.: Yale University Press, 1997), 212–216; George Philip Parkinson Jr., "Antebellum State Constitution-Making: Retention, Circumvention, Revision" (Ph.D. diss, University of Wisconsin, 1972); and Gregory Glen Schmidt, "Republican Visions: Constitutional Thought and Constitutional Revision in the Eastern United States, 1815–1830" (Ph.D. diss, University of Illinois, 1981).

50. *Journal of Debates and Proceedings in the Convention of Delegates, Chosen to Revise the Constitution of Massachusetts [1820–21]*, 305.

51. Ibid. (quotations transposed).

52. Ibid., 307.

53. Ibid.

54. Ibid., 229.

55. Ibid., 268.

56. *Proceedings and Debates of the Convention of North Carolina [1835]*, 132.

57. *Journal of Debates and Proceedings in the Convention of Delegates, Chosen to Revise the Constitution of Massachusetts [1820–21]*, 285–286.

58. *Report of the Debates and Proceedings of the Convention of the State of New York [1821]*, 115.

59. *Proceedings and Debates of the Virginia State Convention of 1829–30*, 71.

60. *Report of the Debates and Proceedings of the Convention of the State of New York [1821]*, 115.

61. *Proceedings of the New Jersey State Constitutional Convention of 1844*, 105.

62. *Debates of the Delaware Convention, for Revising the Constitution [1831]*, 127.

63. *Journal of Debates and Proceedings in the Convention of Delegates, Chosen to Revise the Constitution of Massachusetts [1820–21]*, 278.

64. The inaugural Louisiana Constitution of 1812 required representatives to possess landed property worth 500 dollars, and senators to possess landed property worth 1,000 pounds; these provisions were eliminated in the 1845 constitution. The inaugural Mississippi Constitution of 1817 provided that representatives must hold 150 acres of land or have an interest in real estate valued at 500 dollars, and senators must hold 300 acres of land or have an interest in real estate valued at 1,000 dollars; with the adoption of the 1832 constitution, these provisions were eliminated. A number of other states that drafted constitutions

during the first part of the nineteenth century adopted property requirements for service in their legislatures, but they declined to distinguish between the requirements for senators and representatives.

65. In regard to the apportionment of senate districts on the basis of taxation, delegates to the Massachusetts Convention of 1820–1821 initially voted to eliminate this provision but then turned around and, after hearing the speeches of Adams, Webster, Story, and others, voted by a wide margin to retain the provision, which survived until 1857. For the final vote, see *Journal of Debates and Proceedings in the Convention of Delegates, Chosen to Revise the Constitution of Massachusetts [1820–21]*, 322. For a discussion of these debates, see Luce, *Legislative Assemblies*, 76–83. The North Carolina Convention of 1835 adopted such a provision, and it was retained until 1868. New Hampshire's similar provision, which had been adopted in 1784, survived a number of nineteenth- and twentieth-century conventions and was not replaced until 1964. The Mississippi Convention of 1817 adopted a slightly different provision, by which house districts were apportioned by the number of free white inhabitants and senate districts were apportioned according to the number of free white taxable inhabitants; this provision survived until the adoption of the 1832 constitution. Several other states, including Pennsylvania and South Carolina, decided at various times in the nineteenth century to apportion their legislatures according to the number of taxable inhabitants or according to the portion of taxes paid by inhabitants in a given area, but these states applied these measures to both the house and senate and did not use them as a basis of distinction between the two houses.

In regard to distinct requirements for voting for members of the two houses, the North Carolina Convention of 1835 opted to retain distinct property requirements for voting in house and senate elections, and it was not until 1857 that this provision was finally eliminated. The different property requirements for voting in house and senate elections in New York were eliminated in the 1821 convention.

In regard to distinct requirements for holding office in the two houses, the Delaware Convention of 1831 voted to retain distinct property requirements for holding office, and this provision was not eliminated until 1897. The Georgia Convention of 1798 modified but ultimately retained distinct property requirements for holding office, and this provision was only eliminated in 1835. Maryland eliminated its distinct property requirements by an amendment enacted in 1810. The Massachusetts Convention of 1820–1821 did not disturb the distinct property requirements; they survived until 1840. New Hampshire's distinct property requirements survived until 1852. New Jersey eliminated its distinct requirements in its first revision convention in 1844. New York's distinct property requirements were retained in the Convention of 1821 and were not eliminated until an amendment was enacted for this purpose in 1845. The North Carolina Convention of 1835 maintained distinct property requirements for serving in the senate, and these were not eliminated until the adoption of the Constitution of 1868. South Carolina eliminated its distinct property requirements for officeholding in its Convention of 1865.

66. *Report of the Debates and Proceedings of the Convention of the State of New York [1821]*, 122.

67. *Debates of the Delaware Convention, for Revising the Constitution [1831]*, 41.

68. *Report of the Debates and Proceedings of the Convention of the State of New York [1821]*, 118.

69. Ibid., 131.

70. *Report of the Debates and Proceedings of the Convention for the Revision of the Constitution of the State of Indiana, 1850*, 980–981.

71. *Report of the Debates and Proceedings of the Convention for the Revision of the Constitution of the State of Ohio, 1850–51,* 1:153.

72. Ibid.

73. *Debates and Proceedings of the Constitutional Convention of the State of Illinois [1869],* 144.

74. *Report of the Debates and Proceedings of the Convention for the Revision of the Constitution of the State of Indiana, 1850,* 270.

75. *Report of the Debates and Proceedings of the Convention for the Revision of the Constitution of the State of Ohio, 1850–51,* 1:143.

76. Ibid., 1:144.

77. Ibid.

78. The Ohio Convention of 1850–1851, Indiana Convention of 1850–1851, and Illinois Convention of 1869–1870 featured speeches in favor of unicameralism during this period, but in none of these instances was the matter brought to a vote. See *Report of the Debates and Proceedings of the Convention for the Revision of the Constitution of the State of Ohio, 1850–51,* 1:143–144, 153–155, 168–171; *Report of the Debates and Proceedings of the Convention for the Revision of the Constitution of the State of Indiana, 1850,* 980–981; *Debates and Proceedings of the Constitutional Convention of the State of Illinois [1869],* 141–144. Meanwhile, a motion in favor of unicameralism was put to a vote in the Illinois Convention of 1847 but was easily rejected. See *The [Illinois] Constitutional Debates of 1847,* 285. For a discussion of the Indiana debates, see Val Nolan Jr., "Unicameralism and the Indiana Constitutional Convention of 1850," *Indiana Law Journal* 26 (Winter 1951): 349–359. For a general discussion of the treatment of unicameralism in these mid-nineteenth-century conventions, see Laura J. Scalia, *America's Jeffersonian Experiment: Remaking State Constitutions, 1820–1850* (DeKalb: Northern Illinois University Press, 1999), 106–108.

79. *Official Report of the Proceedings and Debates of the Third Constitutional Convention of Ohio [1873],* 2:1047.

80. *A Stenographic Report of the Proceedings of the Constitutional Convention Held in Atlanta, Georgia, 1877,* 345.

81. Ibid., 346.

82. *Report of the Debates and Proceedings of the Convention for the Revision of the Constitution of the State of New York, 1846,* 398–399.

83. *Proceedings and Debates of the Constitutional Convention of the State of New York Held in 1867 and 1868,* 698.

84. *Official Report of the Proceedings and Debates of the Third Constitutional Convention of Ohio [1873],* 2:1047–1048.

85. *Proceedings and Debates of the Convention of the Commonwealth of Pennsylvania [1837],* 2:169.

86. *Debates and Proceedings of the Maryland Reform Convention to Revise the State Constitution [1851],* 1:310.

87. *The [Illinois] Constitutional Debates of 1847,* 294.

88. *Debates and Proceedings of the First Constitutional Convention of West Virginia (1861–1863),* 1:747–749.

89. This policy had been followed by all of the states that drafted constitutions in the eighteenth century, and it was adhered to by all states during the nineteenth century. A number of states fixed the sizes of the house and senate in the constitution, and in every one of these instances the number of house members exceeded the number of senators, usually by a ratio

in the neighborhood of 3 to 1. Other states did not provide specific numbers of representatives and senators; rather, they provided that the numbers of representatives and senators must fall within a certain range. Once again, in every case, the range for the house exceeded the range for the senate. Still other states fixed the size of the house of representatives and then provided that the number of members of the senate could vary, as long as it did not exceed a certain fraction of the number of representatives. See Luce, *Legislative Assemblies*, 86–97.

90. *Proceedings and Debates of the Constitutional Convention of the State of New York Held in 1867 and 1868*, 693.

91. *A Stenographic Report of the Proceedings of the Constitutional Convention Held in Atlanta, Georgia, 1877*, 351.

92. The eighteenth-century constitutions in Delaware, Georgia, New Jersey, North Carolina, and South Carolina provided that representatives and senators were to be selected from the same constituencies. The eighteenth-century constitutions in Maryland, Massachusetts, New Hampshire, New York, Pennsylvania, and Virginia provided that representatives and senators would be selected from different constituencies.

93. Delaware, Kansas, Maryland, New Jersey, and South Carolina each provided during the nineteenth century that representatives and senators were to be selected from the same constituencies, either by the counties, in several of these states, or by special electoral districts, as in several other of these states. Georgia, Iowa, and North Carolina began by providing that representatives and senators were to be selected from the same constituencies, but each of these states moved during the nineteenth century to create senate districts that were larger than house districts (Georgia created larger districts beginning with its 1865 constitution; Iowa made such a change in its 1857 constitution; North Carolina did so in a series of amendments adopted in 1835). Illinois took the opposite approach; it began by providing for different-sized constituencies for senators and representatives, but with the adoption of a system of cumulative voting in the house of representatives in its 1870 constitution, it provided that members of both houses would represent the same constituencies.

The remaining states all provided for senate districts that were larger than house districts, and of this group, both New York and Michigan experimented with extremely large senate districts. New York, which began with four multimember senate districts, moved to adopt eight multimember senate districts in 1821, and then finally adopted thirty-two single-member senate districts in 1846. Michigan, which borrowed considerably from the New York Constitution, began in 1835 by providing for between four and eight multimember senate districts, and then moved in 1850 to create thirty-two single-member senate districts.

94. *Proceedings and Debates of the Convention of Louisiana [1845]*, 621.

95. Ibid.

96. *Proceedings and Debates of the Constitutional Convention of the State of New York Held in 1867 and 1868*, 659.

97. *Report of the Proceedings and Debates in the Convention to Revise the Constitution of the State of Michigan, 1850*, 353, 354.

98. This policy of distinguishing between the term lengths of senators and representatives, which had first been adopted by Virginia in its 1776 constitution, was adopted in most, but not all, states during the nineteenth century. Several states—Maine, Massachusetts, Nebraska, New Hampshire, North Carolina, Rhode Island, Tennessee, and Vermont—were consistent in their preference for *not* distinguishing between the term lengths of senators and representatives. Several other states—Georgia, Michigan, Mississippi, and Ohio—fluctuated between support for different-length terms and same-length terms, eventually settling

on same-length terms. All of the remaining states were more or less consistent during the nineteenth century in their preference *for* distinguishing the term lengths for members of the two houses, and nearly all of these states—save New Jersey, whose representatives served for one year and whose senators served for three years—adopted two-year terms for representatives and four-year terms for senators. See Luce, *Legislative Assemblies,* 119–121.

99. *Debates of the Delaware Convention, for Revising the Constitution [1831],* 161–162.

100. *Report of the Proceedings and Debates in the Convention to Revise the Constitution of the State of Michigan, 1850,* 351.

101. *Debates and Proceedings of the First Constitutional Convention of West Virginia (1861–1863),* 1:744.

102. The principle of rotation in the senate, which was inaugurated by Virginia in its 1776 constitution, was adopted by a significant majority of states during the nineteenth century. At the same time, a number of states declined to distinguish between the house and senate in this fashion, whether because the senate terms were not long enough to permit the principle of rotation to operate, or because they did not agree with the logic underlying the policy. A number of the states in this latter group—Georgia, Kansas, Maine, Massachusetts, Nebraska, Nevada, New Hampshire, North Carolina, Rhode Island, Tennessee, and Vermont—were consistent in declining to adopt the principle of rotation in the senate. Several of these states—Michigan, New York, and Ohio—began by adopting the principle of rotation but then rejected it during the course of the nineteenth century.

103. *Official Report of the Proceedings and Debates of the Third Constitutional Convention of Ohio [1873],* 2:1027.

104. *Report of the Debates and Proceedings of the Convention of the State of New York [1821],* 201.

105. A number of states—California, Colorado, Connecticut, Kansas, Massachusetts, Minnesota, Nebraska, Nevada, New York, Oregon, Rhode Island, West Virginia, and Wisconsin—were consistent in their preference for *not* distinguishing between the house and senate in this manner, whether by not requiring any minimum age for service in either house or by requiring the same minimum age for service in both houses. Several states—Florida, Ohio, and Virginia—began by distinguishing between the age requirements for service in the two houses but ultimately eliminated this distinction during the nineteenth century. Most states were consistent in their preference *for* distinguishing between the age requirements for service in the house and senate, and several states—New Jersey, North Carolina and Tennessee—began by not making any distinction but moved during the course of the nineteenth century to adopt such distinctions.

106. *Debates and Proceedings of the Constitutional Convention of the State of Illinois [1869],* 504.

107. *Report of the Debates in the Convention of California on the Formation of the State Constitution [1849],* 84 (quotations transposed).

108. *Proceedings and Debates of the Convention of the Commonwealth of Pennsylvania [1837],* 8:254.

109. Ibid., 9:54–55.

110. See the objections and subsequent vote in ibid., 9:55–60. Such a provision was adopted in the Louisiana Constitution of 1879, where all revenue and appropriation bills were required to originate in the house.

111. Nearly one-third of the states—California, Connecticut, Florida, Maryland, Massachusetts, Missouri, Nevada, New York, North Carolina, Ohio, Rhode Island, Tennessee, and

West Virginia—declined to make any distinction between the ability of the house and senate to originate revenue bills. Two states—Arkansas and Nebraska—began by declining to make any such distinction but decided during the nineteenth century to adopt such a distinction. One state, New Jersey, which originally prevented the senate from altering any revenue bills, eliminated this provision in the middle of the nineteenth century. The remaining states were consistent in prohibiting the senate from originating revenue bills.

112. The Virginia Constitution included such a requirement from the beginning, but it was eliminated in the early nineteenth century. The requirement in the Kansas Constitution was eliminated five years after its adoption.

113. *A Reprint of the Proceedings and Debates of the Convention Which Framed the Constitution of Kansas at Wyandotte in July, 1859*, 128.

114. Ibid., 127.

115. For general treatments of these concerns, see Charles E. Merriam, *American Political Ideas: Studies in the Development of American Political Thought, 1865–1917* (New York: Macmillan, 1920); Benjamin Parke De Witt, *The Progressive Movement: A Non-Partisan, Comprehensive Discussion of Current Tendencies in American Politics* (New York: Macmillan, 1915); J. Allen Smith, *The Spirit of American Government* (New York: Macmillan, 1907); and Hoebeke, *Road to Mass Democracy*. On the way in which the movement toward direct democracy raised questions about the future of the bicameral system, see Alfred Zantziger Reed, *The Territorial Basis of Government under the State Constitutions* (1911; reprint, New York: AMS Press, 1968), 215.

116. This late nineteenth- and early twentieth-century activity in regard to unicameralism is discussed in Luce, *Legislative Assemblies*, 34–35; John D. Hicks, *The Constitutions of the Northwest States* (Lincoln: University of Nebraska, 1924), 42–52; Senning, *One House Legislature*, 39–49; Johnson, *Unicameral Legislature*, 95–109; James D. Barnett, "The Bicameral System in State Legislation," *American Political Science Review* 9 (August 1915): 449, 453; and John Dinan, "Framing a 'People's Government': State Constitution-Making in the Progressive Era," *Rutgers Law Journal* 30 (Summer 1999): 933, 958–963.

117. On the way that this issue came to the forefront of state constitutional politics in the late nineteenth and early twentieth centuries, see Tarr, *Understanding State Constitutions*, 103–105, 145; Advisory Commission on Intergovernmental Relations, *Apportionment of State Legislatures* (Washington, D.C.: U.S. Government Printing Office, 1962), 19. On the way in which this issue became intertwined with the question of the value of bicameralism, see Holcombe, *State Government*, 253–256.

118. Critics of bicameralism during this period included not only state constitution makers, but also various academic commentators. For scholarly critiques of bicameralism during this period, see Barnett, "Bicameral System"; and James Q. Dealey, *Growth of American State Constitutions from 1776 to the End of the Year 1914* (Boston: Ginn, 1915), 278–279. For a scholar who was open to considering the abolition of the bicameral system, see Holcombe, *State Government*, 274–275. For a scholarly analysis of the working of the bicameral system that concluded that a second house was not essential to securing effective lawmaking, see David Leigh Colvin, *The Bicameral Principle in the New York Legislature* (New York: Columbia University, 1913).

119. *The Records of the Arizona Constitutional Convention of 1910*, 577 (quotations transposed).

120. *Debates in the Massachusetts Constitutional Convention, 1917–1918*, 3:232.

121. Ibid., 3:212.

122. *Revised Record of the Constitutional Convention of the State of New York [1915]*, 349.

123. Quoted in Tsebelis and Money, *Bicameralism*, 1.

124. *Proceedings and Debates of the Constitutional Convention of the State of Ohio [1912]*, 1132–1133.

125. *Journal of the Nebraska Constitutional Convention [1919]*, 2127, 2128.

126. *Proceedings and Debates of the Constitutional Convention of the State of Ohio [1912]*, 865.

127. *Debates in the Massachusetts Constitutional Convention, 1917–1918*, 3:215.

128. Ibid., 3:208.

129. Ibid., 2:268.

130. It is true that supporters of unicameralism during this period occasionally criticized the existence of a senate from a completely different angle, on the grounds that it was no longer sufficiently distinct from the house and therefore ceased to serve any purpose. See the comments to this effect by Albert Bushnell Hart in the Massachusetts Convention of 1917–1919 (*Debates in the Massachusetts Constitutional Convention, 1917–1918*, 3:212) and Wilbur Bryant in the Nebraska Convention of 1919–1920 (*Journal of the Nebraska Constitutional Convention [1919]*, 2133). For a scholarly argument along these lines, see J. H. Morgan, "Second Chambers," *Contemporary Review* 97 (May 1910): 533, 543–544.

131. *Official Report of the Proceedings and Debates of the First Constitutional Convention of North Dakota [1889]*, 112.

132. *Debates in the Massachusetts Constitutional Convention, 1917–1918*, 3:209.

133. *Proceedings and Debates of the Constitutional Convention of Idaho, 1889*, 458.

134. *Proceedings and Debates of the Constitutional Convention of the State of Ohio [1912]*, 865.

135. *Journal of the Nebraska Constitutional Convention [1919]*, 2127.

136. *Debates in the Massachusetts Constitutional Convention, 1917–1918*, 3:212 (quotations transposed).

137. Ibid., 3:218.

138. *Official Report of the Proceedings and Debates of the First Constitutional Convention of North Dakota [1889]*, 118.

139. *Proceedings and Debates of the Constitutional Convention of the State of Ohio [1912]*, 865.

140. *Debates in the Massachusetts Constitutional Convention, 1917–1918*, 3:218.

141. *Official Report of the Proceedings and Debates of the First Constitutional Convention of North Dakota [1889]*, 117.

142. *Debates in the Massachusetts Constitutional Convention, 1917–1918*, 3:217.

143. See Senning, *One-House Legislature*, 39, 45.

144. In the North Dakota Convention of 1889, a unicameralism proposal was debated but disposed of without taking a vote (*Official Report of the Proceedings and Debates of the First Constitutional Convention of North Dakota [1889]*, 103–128). In the Idaho Convention of 1889, a unicameralism measure was given some consideration but then rejected (*Proceedings and Debates of the Constitutional Convention of Idaho, 1889*, 454–463). In the New York Convention of 1915, the minority report of the Legislative Committee, which advocated unicameralism, was considered briefly and then disposed of quickly (*Revised Record of the Constitutional Convention of the State of New York [1915]*, 348–352). In the Massachusetts Convention of 1917–1919, the delegates debated the abolition of the senate at some length before rejecting the proposal (*Debates in the Massachusetts Constitutional Convention, 1917–1918*, 3:211–232). Massachusetts delegates also considered, and easily rejected,

a proposal to reduce the power of the senate by permitting bills that passed the house but died in the senate to still become law as long as they received the support of two-thirds of the members of the house (3:208–210). Recorded votes were taken in the Arizona Convention of 1910, where a unicameralism proposal was defeated by a vote of 39–10 (*The Records of the Arizona Constitutional Convention of 1910,* 581) and in the Ohio Convention of 1912, where a unicameralism measure was defeated 62–38 (*Proceedings and Debates of the Constitutional Convention of the State of Ohio [1912],* 1133).

145. The votes were as follows: Oregon, 1912: 71,183 (against)—31,020 (for); Oregon, 1914: 123,429 (against)—62,376 (for); Oklahoma, 1914: 94,686 (for)—71,742 (against) (the measure failed because of an Oklahoma requirement that initiatives receive a majority of all votes cast in the election, and a substantial number of voters declined to vote on this particular measure); Arizona, 1916: 22,286 (against)—11,631 (for). See Senning, *One-House Legislature,* 39–42; and N. D. Houghton, "Arizona's Adventure with Unicameralism—An Anti-Climax," *University of Kansas City Law Review* 11 (1942): 38–44.

146. Luce, *Legislative Assemblies,* 34–35; Johnson, *Unicameral Legislature,* 96–98, 103–108.

147. There is some dispute about the extent to which states deviated from population as a basis for apportionment during the nineteenth century. According to Robert B. McKay, "So widespread had been the original acceptance of the equality principle that no fewer than 36 of the original state constitutions provided that representation in both houses of the state legislatures would be based completely, or predominantly, on population. Between 1790 and 1889 no state was admitted to the Union in which the original constitution did not provide for representation principally based on population in both houses of the legislature." Robert B. McKay, *Reapportionment: The Law and Politics of Equal Representation* (New York: Twentieth Century Fund, 1965), 24–25. On the other hand, Robert G. Dixon Jr. referred to "the grossly misleading character of the figure 'thirty-six,'" and he argued that the claim that "between 1790 and 1889 no state was admitted to the union in which the original constitution did not provide for representation principally based on population in both houses of the legislature" is "seriously undercut by the evidence." According to his reading of the evidence, a number of states did make allowances for territorial representation during this period. Robert G. Dixon Jr., *Democratic Representation: Reapportionment in Law and Politics* (New York: Oxford University Press, 1968), 78, 81. At the end of the day, this dispute boils down to a disagreement over how to determine whether representation was based "predominantly" on population. There is little doubt that a significant number of states did deviate from population as the standard for apportionment, but reasonable persons can differ on whether these state legislatures were apportioned *predominantly* on the basis of population. For an argument that differences in the degree to which various states in the nineteenth century relied on population versus territory can be attributed in part to differences in state size (with smaller states relying more on territory and larger states relying more on population), see Rosemarie Zagarri, *The Politics of Size: Representation in the United States, 1776–1850* (Ithaca, N.Y.: Cornell University Press, 1987), 36–60.

148. Dixon, *Democratic Representation,* 82.

149. Gordon E. Baker, *Reapportionment Revolution: Representation, Political Power, and the Supreme Court* (New York: Random House, 1966), 20–21.

150. Royce Hanson, *The Political Thicket: Reapportionment and Constitutional Democracy* (Englewood Cliffs, N.J.: Prentice-Hall, 1966), 14.

151. Baker, *Reapportionment Revolution,* 21.

152. Dixon, *Democratic Representation,* 84 (quotations transposed). For earlier arguments

that appealed to the "federal analogy" in seeking support for representation of political sub-divisions in one house of the legislature, see *Journal of the Convention Assembled to Frame a Constitution for the State of Rhode Island [1842]*, 39–40 (James Simmons); *The [Illinois] Constitutional Debates of 1847*, 128 (James Davis); *Report of the Debates and Proceedings of the Convention for the Revision of the Constitution of the State of Kentucky, 1849*, 493 (Garrett Davis); *The Debates of the Constitutional Convention of the State of Iowa [1857]*, 546–547 (Daniel Solomon); *Official Report of the Debates and Proceedings in the Consti-tutional Convention of the State of Nevada [1864]*, 635–636 (Lloyd Frizell); *Proceedings of the Constitutional Convention of South Carolina [1868]*, 365 (L. S. Langley); *Debates of the Convention to Amend the Constitution of Pennsylvania [1872–1873]*, 5:453 (J. W. F. White); *Debates of the Missouri Constitutional Convention of 1875*, 3:253 (Robert Fyan).

153. *Debates and Proceedings of the Constitutional Convention of the State of Delaware [1896]*, 2025–2026 (quotations transposed).

154. *Official Report of the Proceedings and Debates of the First Constitutional Convention of North Dakota [1889]*, 127.

155. *Journal and Debates of the Constitutional Convention of the State of Wyoming [1889]*, 425–426.

156. *Journal of the [New Hampshire] Constitutional Convention of 1902*, 721.

157. *Proceedings and Debates of the Constitutional Convention Held in the City of Helena, Montana [1889]*, 631.

158. *Debates and Proceedings of the Constitutional Convention of the State of Delaware [1896]*, 2052.

159. *Proceedings and Debates of the Constitutional Convention Held in the City of Helena, Montana [1889]*, 630.

160. *Journal and Debates of the Constitutional Convention of the State of Wyoming [1889]*, 422.

161. *Proceedings and Debates of the Constitutional Convention of Idaho, 1889*, 473.

162. *Official Report of the Proceedings and Debates of the Convention . . . To Adopt a Con-stitution for the State of Utah [1895]*, 832.

163. *Journal and Debates of the Constitutional Convention of the State of Wyoming [1889]*, 568–569.

164. *Proceedings and Debates of the Constitutional Convention Held in the City of Helena, Montana [1889]*, 623.

165. *Proceedings and Debates of the Constitutional Convention of Idaho, 1889*, 470, 471.

166. In the Idaho Convention of 1889, for instance, the legislative committee proposed that the senate be apportioned equally by county, but the convention ultimately chose to apportion the senate by population. See Donald Crowley and Florence Heffron, *The Idaho State Constitution: A Reference Guide* (Westport, Conn.: Greenwood Press, 1994), 9. The Wyoming Convention of 1889 reached a similar conclusion. After much debate, the dele-gates voted to apportion both houses by population. See Robert B. Keiter and Tim Newcomb, *The Wyoming State Constitution: A Reference Guide* (Westport, Conn.: Greenwood Press, 1993), 82.

167. See the New York Constitution (1894), Art. III, Sec. 4. On this point, see Peter J. Galie, *The New York State Constitution: A Reference Guide* (Westport, Conn.: Greenwood Press, 1991), 82.

168. See Montana Constitution (1889), Art. V, Sec. 4. For the argument that the Montana Constitution of 1889 was the first of several state constitutions during this period to adopt

the "federal" principle, see McKay, *Reapportionment,* 26–29; and Dixon, *Democratic Representation,* 85. This policy was also adopted during the Progressive Era in Idaho, where the legislature in 1895 apportioned the senate equally by county, and then a constitutional amendment to this effect was enacted in 1912. Bernard C. Borning, "Idaho," in *Impact of Reapportionment on the Thirteen Western States,* ed. Eleanore Bushnell (Salt Lake City: University of Utah Press, 1970), 141. States that retained this policy during this period include South Carolina, which had provided since its Constitution of 1868 for equal-county representation in the senate, and where the Convention of 1895 provided for one senator for each county; New Jersey, which had provided for equal-county representation in the senate since its inaugural Constitution of 1776 and which rejected the efforts of Governor Woodrow Wilson and others to eliminate this requirement; and Vermont, which had provided since its Constitution of 1777 for equal representation of towns in the house, and which retained this policy throughout this period. For New Jersey, see Alan Shank, *New Jersey Reapportionment Politics: Strategies and Tactics in the Legislative Process* (Rutherford, N.J.: Fairleigh Dickinson University Press, 1969), 87–88. For Vermont, see Frank M. Bryan, "Vermont," in *Reapportionment Politics: The History of Redistricting in the 50 States,* ed. Leroy Hardy, Alan Heslop, and Stuart Anderson (Beverly Hills, Calif.: Sage Publications, 1981), 327.

169. See the series of Model State Constitution volumes produced between 1921 and 1968. On the support for unicameralism in the inaugural Model State Constitution, see Tarr, *Understanding State Constitutions,* 152–153.

170. The unicameralism initiative received 286,086 votes for and 193,512 votes against. See Senning, *One-House Legislature,* 50–75; Johnson, *Unicameral Legislature,* 129–148; Jack Rodgers, Robert Sittig, and Susan Welch, "The Legislature," in *Nebraska Government and Politics,* ed. Robert Miewald (Lincoln: University of Nebraska Press, 1984), 57–63; and Charlyne Berens, *One House: The Unicameral's Progressive Vision for Nebraska* (Lincoln: University of Nebraska Press, 2005), 18–41.

171. As one indication of the extent of popular interest in the issue, the national high school debate topic in 1937 focused on the issue of unicameralism. See Harrison Boyd Summers, comp., *Unicameral Legislatures* (New York: H. W. Wilson, 1936); and Harrison Boyd Summers, comp., *Unicameralism in Practice* (New York: H. W. Wilson, 1936).

172. On the debates in various state legislatures in the immediate aftermath of Nebraska's adoption of unicameralism, see Johnson, *Unicameral Legislature,* 152–155; and O. Douglas Weeks, *Two Legislative Houses or One* (Dallas: Arnold Foundation, 1938), 18–19. Among the various conventions that considered the issue was the Missouri Convention of 1943–1944, where the Committee on the Legislative Department issued a minority report in favor of unicameralism that was ultimately rejected, and where a unicameralism amendment that had been submitted by the initiative procedure lost by the narrow margin of 401,900–364,794 in a 1944 election that was held between the time that the convention adjourned and the ratification vote was held. See Martin L. Faust, *Constitution Making in Missouri: The Convention of 1943–1944* (New York: National Municipal League, 1971), 64–65. See also the Alaska Convention of 1955–1956, which debated a unicameralism proposal at some length; see their *Minutes of the Daily Proceedings: Alaska Constitutional Convention, 1955–56,* 419–467. There was a good deal of support for considering unicameralism at the New Jersey Convention of 1947, but the legislature explicitly prohibited convention delegates from considering the matter; see *[New Jersey] Constitutional Convention of 1947,* 2:936.

173. 369 U.S. 186 (1962).

174. 377 U.S. 533 (1964), 576–577.

175. On the "flurry of activity following the Supreme Court's reapportionment rulings," see Tarr, *Understanding State Constitutions*, 145. On the way in which these rulings forced a reconsideration of the need for a bicameral legislature, see A. E. Dick Howard, *Commentaries on the Constitution of Virginia*, 2 vols. (Charlottesville: University Press of Virginia, 1974), 1:467.

176. Three additional states adopted the federal model in its pure form—that is, equal-county representation in the senate: New Mexico (1949) (see Fernando V. Padilla, "New Mexico," in Hardy et al., *Reapportionment Politics*, 221); Nevada (1950), whose legislature had essentially adopted this policy in 1917 (see Eleanore Bushnell, "Nevada," in Hardy et al., *Reapportionment Politics*, 200); and Arizona (1952), whose initial Constitution of 1911 provided for a nineteen-member senate, with all fourteen counties permitted to elect one senator and the five largest counties permitted to each select another senator (see J. L. Polinard, "Arizona," in Hardy et al., *Reapportionment Politics*, 37). As a result, states that had adopted the federal principle by this time included Montana, Idaho, South Carolina, New Jersey, New Mexico, Nevada, Arizona, and Vermont.

177. For instance, in 1926, California voters approved an initiative that apportioned the house by population and provided that the senate would be apportioned primarily by county, in that no county was permitted to elect more than one senator, and no more than three counties could be included in any one senatorial district. See T. Anthony Quinn, "California," in Hardy et al., *Reapportionment Politics*, 53.

178. On the reapportionment provisions in place in the fifty state constitutions at the beginning of the 1960s, see Dixon, *Democratic Representation*, 86–87; and Advisory Commission on Intergovernmental Relations, *Apportionment of State Legislatures*, appendix A.

179. Baker, *Reapportionment Revolution*, 28–29.

180. *Revised Record of the Constitutional Convention of the State of New York [1938]*, 2909.

181. See, for instance, the comments of Cable Wirtz in the Hawaii Convention of 1950 (*Proceedings of the Constitutional Convention of Hawaii, 1950*, 2:760). See also the comments of Harold Norris in the Michigan Convention of 1961–1962 (*Official Record, State of Michigan Constitutional Convention, 1961*, 2156).

182. This point was made in a number of conventions held during this period. See, for instance, *Debates of the [Maryland] Constitutional Convention of 1967–1968*, 444 (Mary Bryson); *Proceedings of the Constitutional Convention of Hawaii of 1968*, 2:121 (George Loo); *Montana Constitutional Convention, 1971–1972: Verbatim Transcript*, 748 (Arlyne Reichert). Professors and politicians also advanced such an argument during this period. See Talbot D'Alemberte and Charles C. Fishburne Jr., "The Unicameral Legislature," *University of Florida Law Review* 17 (Winter 1964): 355, 355; Jesse Unruh, "Unicameralism—The Wave of the Future," in *Strengthening the States: Essays on Legislative Reform*, ed. Donald G. Herzberg and Alan Rosenthal (Garden City, N.Y.: Doubleday, 1971), 95; and Eugene DeClercq, "Inter-House Differences in American State Legislatures," *Journal of Politics* 39 (August 1977): 774, 775, 784.

183. *Debates of the North Dakota Constitutional Convention of 1972*, 309.

184. *Record of Proceedings: Sixth Illinois Constitutional Convention [1969]: Verbatim Transcripts*, 2725.

185. *Proceedings of the Constitutional Convention of Hawaii, 1978*, 2:281.

186. *Record of Proceedings: Sixth Illinois Constitutional Convention [1969]: Verbatim Transcripts*, 2726.

187. *State of Rhode Island and Providence Plantations: Constitutional Convention [1964–1969]: Report of Proceedings,* 1171, 1173–1174 (quotations transposed).

188. *The Third Constitutional Convention of the State of Connecticut: Proceedings [1965],* 220–222.

189. *Proceedings of the Constitutional Convention of Hawaii of 1968,* 2:121.

190. For a sampling of these types of arguments, see *Debates of the [Maryland] Constitutional Convention of 1967–1968,* 446 (John Hardwicke); *Debates of the North Dakota Constitutional Convention of 1972,* 299 (John Paulson); *Proceedings of the Constitutional Convention of Hawaii, 1978,* 2:286 (Alan Kimball).

191. On Norris's focus on the conference committee during the Nebraska campaign, see Senning, *One-House Legislature,* 57. See also Johnson, *Unicameral Legislature,* 132.

192. *Montana Constitutional Convention, 1971–1972: Verbatim Transcript,* 748.

193. *Proceedings of the Constitutional Convention of Hawaii of 1968,* 2:121.

194. *Record of Proceedings: Sixth Illinois Constitutional Convention [1969]: Verbatim Transcripts,* 2725.

195. A number of assessments were made of the performance of Nebraska's unicameral legislature during its first twenty-five years, including: Harry T. Dobbins, "Nebraska's One-House Legislature—After Six Years," *National Municipal Review* 30 (September 1941): 511–514; Lane W. Lancaster, "Nebraska's Experience with a One-House Legislature," *University of Kansas City Law Review* 11 (1942): 24–30; John P. Senning, "Unicameralism Passes Test," *National Municipal Review* 33 (February 1944): 60–65; Richard C. Spencer, "Nebraska Idea 15 Years Old," *National Municipal Review* 39 (February 1950): 83–86; Roger V. Shumate, "The Nebraska Unicameral Legislature," *Western Political Quarterly* 5 (September 1952): 504–512; Belle Zeller, ed., *American State Legislatures* (New York: Thomas Y. Crowell, 1954), 47–60, 240–255; Jack W. Rodgers, "One House for 20 Years," *National Municipal Review* 46 (July 1957): 338–342, 347; Adam C. Breckenridge, *One House for Two: Nebraska's Unicameral Legislature* (Washington, D.C.: Public Affairs Press, 1957); and Hugo F. Srb, "The Unicameral Legislature—A Successful Innovation," *Nebraska Law Review* 40 (1961): 626–633.

All of these studies reported favorably on the Nebraska experience, although several were more favorable than others. Among the more comprehensive analyses was one conducted by the Committee on American Legislatures of the American Political Science Association and reported in Zeller, *American State Legislatures.* The committee concluded that "many of the supposed checks and safeguards provided by a bifurcated legislature are more or less illusory" and that "unicameralism has proved to be successful in Nebraska, has improved the legislative process there, and has developed none of the evils anticipated for a one-house legislature" (59–60). Roger Shumate, in his analysis in the *Western Political Quarterly,* reached a generally similar conclusion. In answer to the question, "Has the removal of the check provided by a second chamber resulted in hasty and ill-considered legislation?" he answered, "Apparently not." In regard to other questions, though, such as whether there was any difference in the "quality of legislation produced under the two systems," or whether the legislature was "subject to more or less influence by lobbyists," he found that it was not possible to provide definitive conclusions (508–509). Additionally, in reviewing the available studies in the late 1960s, the National Municipal League argued in its *Model State Constitution,* 6th rev. ed. (New York: National Municipal League, 1968), that "most of the claimed virtues of unicameralism have been realized in the Nebraska experience during the past 30 years" (43).

More recent studies of the operation of Nebraska's unicameral legislature include Kim Robak, "The Nebraska Unicameral and Its Lasting Benefits," *Nebraska Law Review* 76 (1997): 791–818; Thomas Todd, "Nebraska's Unicameral Legislature" (Minnesota Legislature, House Research Department, January, 1998); and Berens, *One House*.

196. *Debates of the [Maryland] Constitutional Convention of 1967–1968*, 452.

197. Ibid., 432.

198. *Record of Proceedings: Sixth Illinois Constitutional Convention [1969]: Verbatim Transcripts*, 2728.

199. *Montana Constitutional Convention, 1971–1972: Verbatim Transcript*, 747.

200. A number of academic commentators took a similar approach during this period. See, for instance, Robert B. McKay, *Reapportionment and the Federal Analogy* (New York: National Municipal League, 1962), 9–10; Advisory Council on Intergovernmental Relations, *Apportionment of State Legislatures*, 38.

201. *The Third Constitutional Convention of the State of Connecticut: Proceedings [1965]*, 217.

202. *Proceedings of the Constitutional Convention of the State of New York [1967]*, 2:650.

203. *Record of Proceedings: Sixth Illinois Constitutional Convention [1969]: Verbatim Transcripts*, 2737 (David Davis).

204. Ibid., 2736.

205. Ibid., 2727.

206. *The Third Constitutional Convention of the State of Connecticut: Proceedings [1965]*, 240.

207. *Proceedings of the Constitutional Convention of the State of New York [1967]*, 2:648.

208. Michigan and Tennessee were the only states during this period to increase the length of the senate term. Both the Michigan Convention of 1961–1962 and Tennessee Convention of 1965 retained two-year terms for house members but increased senate terms from two to four years.

209. *State of Rhode Island and Providence Plantations: Constitutional Convention [1964–1969]: Report of Proceedings*, 1850–1851.

210. Ibid., 2038.

211. Zeller, *American State Legislatures*, 35–36, 39. For a proposal that some provision be made for functional representation, see Alfred De Grazia, *Essay on Apportionment and Representative Government* (Washington, D.C.: American Enterprise Institute for Public Policy Research, 1963), 169–174. For a discussion of functional representation, see Jefferson B. Fordham, *The State Legislative Institution* (Philadelphia: University of Pennsylvania Press, 1959), 38–39.

212. On the way in which proposals for proportional and functional representation have been treated in the course of the American regime, see De Grazia, *Public and Republic*, 184–204, 214–233.

213. *Journal and Proceedings of the [Tennessee] Limited Constitutional Convention [1965]*, 869.

214. *The Third Constitutional Convention of the State of Connecticut: Proceedings [1965]*, 215 (Penn Kimball).

215. *Montana Constitutional Convention, 1971–1972: Verbatim Transcript*, 776 (Magnus Aasheim).

216. *Debates of the [Maryland] Constitutional Convention of 1967–1968*, 444 (Alfred Scanlan, quoting Woodrow Wilson).

217. *Debates of the North Dakota Constitutional Convention of 1972*, 312 (George Long-mire).

218. Minnesota operated a non-partisan legislature through much of the twentieth century but then adopted a partisan system in the early 1970s. See Robak, "Nebraska Unicameral," 792n1.

219. *Proceedings of the Constitutional Convention of Hawaii, 1978*, 2:283.

220. *Debates of the North Dakota Constitutional Convention of 1972*, 294.

221. Ibid., 296.

222. *Debates of the [Maryland] Constitutional Convention of 1967–1968*, 456.

223. Ibid., 453.

224. Unicameralism measures failed by an 88–34 vote in the Michigan Convention of 1961–1962 (*Official Record, State of Michigan Constitutional Convention, 1961*, 2157); a 40–29 vote in the Rhode Island Convention of 1964–1969 (*State of Rhode Island and Providence Plantations: Constitutional Convention [1964–1969]: Report of Proceedings*, 1195–1197); a 71–4 vote in the Connecticut Convention of 1965 (*The Third Constitutional Convention of the State of Connecticut: Proceedings [1965]*, 241–242); a 76–9 vote in the Tennessee Convention of 1965 (*Journal and Proceedings of the [Tennessee] Limited Constitutional Convention [1965]*, 493); a 65–11 vote in the Hawaii Convention of 1968 (*Proceedings of the Constitutional Convention of Hawaii of 1968*, 2:138); a 75–19 vote in the Hawaii Convention of 1978 (*Proceedings of the Constitutional Convention of Hawaii, 1978*, 2:288); a 92–39 vote in the Maryland Convention of 1967–1968 (*Debates of the [Maryland] Constitutional Convention of 1967–1968*, 456); and a 65–18 vote in the Illinois Convention of 1969–1970 (*Record of Proceedings: Sixth Illinois Constitutional Convention [1969]: Verbatim Transcripts*, 2730). Meanwhile, unicameralism was also a subject of some debate in the New Jersey Convention of 1966, where a unicameralism proposal enjoyed significant support for a time before being eventually overtaken by support for the traditional bicameral system. Ernest C. Reock Jr., *Unfinished Business: The New Jersey Constitutional Convention of 1966* (New Brunswick, N.J.: Center for Urban Policy Research Press, 2003), 93–198.

The Michigan Convention of 1961–1962 also rejected, by an 87–35 vote, a proposal that would have permitted bills that passed the house but died in the senate to still become law if they repassed the house in the next legislative session or if they received the support of three-fifths of the members of the house. *Official Record, State of Michigan Constitutional Convention, 1961*, 2162.

225. In the Montana Convention of 1971–1972, delegates agreed, at an early stage of the proceedings, to place the issue of unicameralism before the voters as one of three separate measures; it was defeated at the polls, but it received the support of 44 percent of the voters. Thomas Todd, "History of Unicameralism in the United States," Minnesota Legislature, Committee on Governmental Operations and Veterans Affairs Policy, 13 October 1999. In the North Dakota Convention of 1971–1972, delegates expressed their support for the bicameral system by a 61–35 vote, but they nevertheless agreed to submit the measure to the people as an alternate proposal (*Debates of the North Dakota Constitutional Convention of 1972*, 322), which received 31 percent of the popular vote and therefore was defeated (Todd, "History of Unicameralism in the United States").

226. In regard to support from the voters, Alaska voters in 1976 approved an initiative by a margin of 58,782–55,204 that advised the legislature to adopt unicameralism, but the legislature declined to act on this advice. See Virginia Graham, *A Compilation of Statewide*

Initiative Proposals Appearing on Ballots through 1976 (Washington, D.C.: Congressional Research Service, 1976), 112.

In regard to constitutional revision commissions, the California Constitutional Revision Commission offered a preliminary recommendation in favor of unicameralism, but after further debate decided in 1996 not to submit this recommendation to the legislature in its final report. See California Constitution Revision Commission, *Final Report and Recommendations to the Governor and the Legislature* (Sacramento, Calif.: Forum on Government Reform, 1996); "State Panel Won't Push One-House Legislature," *San Francisco Chronicle*, 7 February 1996, A17. In 1997, a unicameralism proposal failed by a 19–14 vote in the Florida Revision Commission, which is the only such body in the country with the power to submit recommendations directly to the people for ratification. James R. Rogers, "Judicial Review Standards in Unicameral Legislative Systems: A Positive Theoretic and Historical Analysis," *Creighton Law Review* 33 (December 1999), 65, 74n48.

In regard to gubernatorial support, Minnesota governor Jesse Ventura made unicameralism a centerpiece of his reform program, and he had the support of House speaker Steve Sviggum, but a unicameralism proposal failed to gain much support in either chamber and failed in the 2000 legislative session. Robert Whereatt, "Ventura Not Happy Unicameral Plan Was Hung Out to Dry," *Minneapolis Star-Tribune*, 11 May 2000, 15A.

Not surprisingly, legislators have been less supportive of unicameralism proposals; nevertheless, these measures were considered in a variety of legislatures in the 1990s. See Rogers, "Judicial Review Standards," 73–74.

Chapter 6: Rights

1. On these various amendments, see John R. Vile, *Encyclopedia of Constitutional Amendments, Proposed Amendments, and Amending Issues, 1789–1995* (Santa Barbara, Calif.: ABC-CLIO, 1996), 47–49, 185, 207–208, 349–350.

2. See Stephen B. Wood, *Constitutional Politics in the Progressive Era: Child Labor and the Law* (Chicago: University of Chicago Press, 1968).

3. Franklin D. Roosevelt, *The Public Papers and Addresses of Franklin D. Roosevelt,* ed. Samuel Rosenman, 13 vols. (New York: Harper, 1938–1950): 13:40.

4. See Bruce A. Ackerman, *We the People: Foundations,* vol. 1 (Cambridge, Mass.: Belknap Press, 1991).

5. Roosevelt, *Public Papers and Addresses,* 13:41–42. For an extensive treatment of Roosevelt's call for a second bill of rights, see Cass R. Sunstein, *The Second Bill of Rights: FDR's Unfinished Revolution and Why We Need It Now More Than Ever* (New York: Basic Books, 2004).

6. Charles A. Reich, "Individual Rights and Social Welfare: The Emerging Legal Issues," *Yale Law Journal* 74 (June 1965): 1245, 1256. See also Charles A. Reich, "The New Property," *Yale Law Journal* 73 (April 1964): 733–787.

7. Frank I. Michelman, "The Supreme Court 1968 Term—Foreword: On Protecting the Poor throughout the Fourteenth Amendment," *Harvard Law Review* 83 (November 1969): 7, 13. Additional articles by Michelman on this topic include Frank I. Michelman, "In Pursuit of Constitutional Welfare Rights: One View of Rawls' Theory of Justice," *University of Pennsylvania Law Review* 121 (May 1973): 962–1019; and Frank I. Michelman, "Welfare

Rights in a Constitutional Democracy," *Washington University Law Quarterly* (Summer 1979): 659–693.

8. For examples of such arguments, which locate support for positive rights primarily in the due process or equal protection clauses of the Fourteenth Amendment or in the Thirteenth Amendment or in the General Welfare clause, but occasionally in other clauses, see David Currie, "Positive and Negative Constitutional Rights," *University of Chicago Law Review* 53 (Summer 1986): 864–890; Peter B. Edelman, "The Next Century of Our Constitution: Rethinking Our Duty to the Poor," *Hastings Law Journal* 39 (November 1987): 1–61; Susan Bandes, "The Negative Constitution: A Critique," *Michigan Law Review* 88 (August 1990): 2271–2347; Akhil Reed Amar, "Forty Acres and a Mule: A Republican Theory of Minimal Entitlements," *Harvard Journal of Law and Public Policy* 13 (Winter 1990): 37–43; and Sotirios A. Barber, *Welfare and the Constitution* (Princeton, N.J.: Princeton University Press, 2003).

9. *Goldberg v. Kelly,* 397 U.S. 254 (1970), 263n8, 265.

10. 397 U.S. 471 (1970), 487. For discussions of these decisions, see William E. Forbath, "Constitutional Welfare Rights: A History, Critique, and Reconstruction," *Fordham Law Review* 69 (April 2001): 1821, 1862–1867; Martha F. Davis, *Brutal Need: Lawyers and the Welfare Rights Movement, 1960–1973* (New Haven, Conn.: Yale University Press, 1993); and Elizabeth Bussiere, *(Dis)Entitling the Poor: The Warren Court, Welfare Rights, and the American Political Tradition* (University Park: Pennsylvania State University Press, 1997). For a discussion of a series of decisions in this area that rested on statutory grounds, see R. Shep Melnick, *Between the Lines: Interpreting Welfare Rights* (Washington, D.C.: The Brookings Institution, 1994), 83–111.

11. 489 U.S. 189 (1989), 195, 196. Judge Richard Posner offered an equally clear rejection of this view in his opinion in *Jackson v. City of Joliet,* when he argued that "the Constitution is a charter of negative rather than positive liberties. The men who wrote the Bill of Rights were not concerned that government might do too little for the people but that it might do too much to them. The Fourteenth Amendment, adopted in 1868 at the height of laissez-faire thinking, sought to protect Americans from oppression by state government, not to secure them basic governmental services." 715 F.2d 1200 (7th Cir. 1983), 1203 (citations omitted). Meanwhile, Roger Pilon recently offered a similarly sweeping rejection of the notion that the American constitutional tradition provides any support for positive rights, when he testified against a proposed victims rights constitutional amendment that was under consideration by the U.S. Senate Judiciary Committee. He argued, "This proposal has about it, then, the air of certain European, especially Eastern European, constitutions, which list 'rights' not as liberties that government must respect as it goes about its assigned functions but as 'entitlements' that government must affirmatively provide. We have thus far resisted that tradition in this nation. It would be unfortunate if we should begin it through this 'back door,' as it were." Roger Pilon, U.S. Congress, Senate, Committee on the Judiciary, "Hearing on Victims Rights Amendment," 107th Cong., 2nd sess., 27 July 2002.

12. H.R.J. Res. 1321, 90th Cong., 2nd Sess. (1968).

13. H.R.J. Res. 1205, 91st Cong., 2nd Sess. (1970).

14. For a discussion of these constitutional amendment proposals, see Vile, *Encyclopedia of Constitutional Amendments,* 118–119; Richard O. Brooks, "A Constitutional Right to a Healthful Environment," *Vermont Law Review* 16 (Spring 1992): 1063, 1063–1064, 1068; Carole L. Gallagher, "The Movement to Create an Environmental Bill of Rights: From Earth Day, 1970 to the Present," *Fordham Environmental Law Journal* 9 (Fall 1997): 107, 120–129.

15. Constitution of Ireland (1937), Art. 45, Sec 2(i).

16. Constitution of India (1949), Art. 41.

17. For discussions of the costs and benefits of adopting positive rights provisions in constitutions around the world, see Akira Osuka, "Welfare Rights," *Law and Contemporary Problems* 53 (Spring 1990): 13–28; Mary Ann Glendon, "Rights in Twentieth-Century Constitutions," *University of Chicago Law Review* 59 (Winter 1992): 519–538; Craig Scott and Patrick Macklem, "Constitutional Ropes of Sand or Justiciable Guarantees? Social Rights in a New South African Constitution," *University of Pennsylvania Law Review* 141 (November 1992): 1–147; Cass R. Sunstein, "Against Positive Rights," and Wiktor Osiatynski, "Social and Economic Rights in a New Constitution for Poland," in *Western Rights? Post Communist Application,* ed. Adras Sajo (Cambridge, Mass.: Kluwer Law International, 1996): 225–269; Mac Darrow and Philip Alston, "Bills of Rights in Comparative Perspective," in *Promoting Human Rights through Bills of Rights: Comparative Perspectives,* ed. Philip Alston (New York: Oxford University Press, 1999), 502–511; and Albie Sachs, "Social and Economic Rights: Can They Be Made Justiciable?" *SMU Law Review* 53 (Fall 2000): 1381–1391.

18. Constitution of South Africa (1966), Art. 23.

19. Ibid., Art. 26.

20. Ibid., Art. 27.

21. Ibid., Art. 24.

22. See, among other provisions, Art. 22, 24, and 25 of the Universal Declaration of Human Rights, and Art. 8, 9, 11, and 12 of the International Covenant on Human, Economic, and Cultural Rights.

23. These debates are contained in the following sources:

Arizona: *The Records of the Arizona Constitutional Convention of 1910,* 440–447, 542–549, 881–885.

Illinois: *Debates and Proceedings of the Constitutional Convention of the State of Illinois [1869],* 264–276.

Kentucky: *Official Report of the Proceedings and Debates in the Convention . . . of September, 1890, To Adopt, Amend or Change the Constitution of the State of Kentucky,* 4761–4766.

Massachusetts: *Debates in the Massachusetts Constitutional Convention, 1917–1918,* 3:543–618, 674–738.

Michigan: *Proceedings and Debates of the Constitutional Convention of the State of Michigan [1907],* 385–403, 1053–1056, 1108–1111, 1115–1117.

Nebraska: *Journal of the Nebraska Constitutional Convention [1919],* 1654–1676, 1679–1691, 1698–1717.

Montana: *Montana Constitutional Convention, 1971–1972: Verbatim Transcript,* 2316–2328.

New York: *Revised Record of the Constitutional Convention of the State of New York [1894],* 1:1101–1129; 2:612–626; 4:403–414; *Revised Record of the Constitutional Convention of the State of New York [1915],* 1874–1943, 2178–2224, 2248–2255, 3936–3951, 4204–4223; *Revised Record of the Constitutional Convention of the State of New York [1938],* 1216–1250, 2200–2254, 2663–2679.

North Dakota: *Official Report of the Proceedings and Debates of the First Constitutional Convention of North Dakota [1889],* 506–511.

Ohio: *Official Report of the Proceedings and Debates of the Third Constitutional Convention of Ohio [1873],* 1:345–358, 360–367, 596–616; 2:2867–2869; *Proceedings and*

Debates of the Constitutional Convention of the State of Ohio [1912], 1328–1347, 1707–1713, 1784–1786.

Pennsylvania: *Debates of the Convention to Amend the Constitution of Pennsylvania [1872–1873],* 5:470–481.

Utah: *Official Report of the Proceedings and Debates of the Convention . . . To Adopt a Constitution for the State of Utah [1895],* 1170–1173.

Virginia: *Report of the Proceedings and Debates of the Constitutional Convention, State of Virginia [1901–1902],* 2572–2573, 2833–2854.

Wyoming: *Journal and Debates of the Constitutional Convention of the State of Wyoming [1889],* 443–454, 606–611, 791–795.

24. These debates are contained in the following sources:

Alaska: *Minutes of the Daily Proceedings, Alaska Constitutional Convention, 1955–56,* 1380–1386.

Arizona: *The Records of the Arizona Constitutional Convention of 1910,* 831–835, 987.

Hawaii: *Proceedings of the Constitutional Convention of Hawaii, 1950,* 2:674–688; *Proceedings of the Constitutional Convention of Hawaii of 1968,* 2:476–498; *Proceedings of the Constitutional Convention of Hawaii, 1978,* 2:157–167.

Illinois: *Proceedings of the Constitutional Convention of the State of Illinois, Convened January 6, 1920,* 858–934, 942–963, 4619–4643, 4681–4690, 4717–4718; *Record of Proceedings: Sixth Illinois Constitutional Convention [1969]: Verbatim Transcripts,* 1487–1489, 1614–1630.

Maryland: *Debates of the [Maryland] Constitutional Convention of 1967–1968,* 2281–2325, 2336–2340, 2903–2906, 2921–2926, 3039–3061, 3297–3303.

Massachusetts: *Debates in the Massachusetts Constitutional Convention, 1917–1918,* 1:1041–1165.

Michigan: *Official Record, State of Michigan Constitutional Convention, 1961,* 2871–2880.

Montana: *Montana Constitutional Convention, 1971–1972: Verbatim Transcript,* 2328–2340, 2351–2367.

New Jersey: *[New Jersey] Constitutional Convention of 1947,* 1:308–331, 651–662.

New York: *Revised Record of the Constitutional Convention of the State of New York [1938],* 1216–1250, 2117–2124, 2200–2254, 2663–2679.

North Dakota: *Debates of the North Dakota Constitutional Convention of 1972,* 431–447, 552–559, 737–740, 1614–1621.

Texas: *Texas Constitutional Convention [1974]: Official Proceedings,* 988–990, 1971–1981.

25. These debates are contained in the following sources:

Alabama: *Official Proceedings of the Constitutional Convention of the State of Alabama [1901],* 2616–2624.

Alaska: *Minutes of the Daily Proceedings, Alaska Constitutional Convention, 1955–56,* 1298–1302, 1536–1546, 3317–3320.

Arkansas: *Debates and Proceedings of the Convention Which Assembled at Little Rock [1868] . . . to Form a Constitution for the State of Arkansas,* 286–293.

Hawaii: *Proceedings of the Constitutional Convention of Hawaii, 1950,* 2:543–579; *Proceedings of the Constitutional Convention of Hawaii of 1968,* 2:37–43; *Proceedings of the Constitutional Convention of Hawaii, 1978,* 2:123–128, 151–156.

Illinois: *Record of Proceedings: Sixth Illinois Constitutional Convention [1969]: Verbatim Transcripts,* 1577–1587, 1631–1633, 1721–1733.

Louisiana: *Records of the Louisiana Constitutional Convention of 1973: Convention Transcripts,* 2470–2485, 2545–2550.

Maryland: *Debates of the [Maryland] Constitutional Convention of 1967–1968,* 1204–1212, 1216–1229, 2364–2366, 2427–2441, 2475–2476, 2660–2664, 2889–2890, 2907–2909.

Massachusetts: *Debates in the Massachusetts Constitutional Convention, 1917–1918,* 1:632–850; 3:543–618.

Michigan: *Official Record, State of Michigan Constitutional Convention, 1961,* 2613–2618.

Montana: *Montana Constitutional Convention, 1971–1972: Verbatim Transcript,* 1636–1637.

New Hampshire: *Journal of the Convention to Revise the [New Hampshire] Constitution, May, 1938,* 78–94.

New York: *Revised Record of the Constitutional Convention of the State of New York [1938],* 1083–1086, 2125–2199, 3132–3135, 3159–3184; *Proceedings of the Constitutional Convention of the State of New York [1967],* 2:726–738; 3:819–833; 4:276–286, 293–303.

North Dakota: *Debates of the North Dakota Constitutional Convention of 1972,* 234–238.

Texas: *Texas Constitutional Convention [1974]: Official Proceedings,* 2013–2016, 2049–2053, 2396–2406.

26. These debates are contained in the following sources:

Hawaii: *Proceedings of the Constitutional Convention of Hawaii, 1978,* 2:128–132.

Illinois: *Record of Proceedings: Sixth Illinois Constitutional Convention [1969]: Verbatim Transcripts,* 2991–3021, 3931–3937.

Louisiana: *Records of the Louisiana Constitutional Convention of 1973: Convention Transcripts,* 1253–1255.

Maryland: *Debates of the [Maryland] Constitutional Convention of 1967–1968,* 735–759, 3113–3120, 3357–3360, 3362–3363.

Michigan: *Official Record, State of Michigan Constitutional Convention, 1961,* 2602–2612.

Montana: *Montana Constitutional Convention, 1971–1972: Verbatim Transcript,* 1198–1271, 1637–1640.

New Hampshire: *Journal of the Convention to Revise the [New Hampshire] Constitution, May 1974,* 141–146; *Journal of the Convention to Revise the [New Hampshire] Constitution, May 1984,* 174–178.

New York: *Proceedings of the Constitutional Convention of the State of New York [1967],* 2:938–949.

North Dakota: *Debates of the North Dakota Constitutional Convention of 1972,* 580–587, 831–836, 1739–1743.

Texas: *Texas Constitutional Convention [1974]: Official Proceedings,* 1645–1687, 2089–2096.

27. General treatments of state constitutional positive rights provisions include Burt Neuborne, "State Constitutions and the Evolution of Positive Rights," *Rutgers Law Journal* 20 (Summer 1989): 881–901; Jonathan Feldman, "Separation of Powers and Judicial Review of Positive Rights Claims: The Role of State Courts in an Era of Positive Government," *Rutgers*

Law Journal 24 (Summer 1993): 1057–1100; Helen Hershkoff, "Positive Rights and State Constitutions: The Limits of Federal Rationality Review," *Harvard Law Review* 112 (April 1999): 1131–1196; Helen Hershkoff, "Positive Rights and the Evolution of State Constitutions," *Rutgers Law Journal* 33 (Summer 2002): 799–833; Frank B. Cross, "The Error of Positive Rights," *UCLA Law Review* 48 (April 2001): 857, 893–899; and G. Alan Tarr, *Understanding State Constitutions* (Princeton, N.J.: Princeton University Press, 1998), 147–150.

For specific treatments of social and economic rights provisions in state constitutions, see Daan Braveman, "Children, Poverty, and State Constitutions," *Emory Law Journal* 38 (Summer 1989): 577–614; Adam S. Cohen, "More Myths of Parity: State Court Forums and Constitutional Actions for the Right to Shelter," *Emory Law Journal* 38 (Summer 1989): 615–660; Helen Hershkoff, "Rights and Freedoms under the State Constitution: A New Deal for Welfare Rights," *Touro Law Review* 13 (1997): 631–652; and Helen Hershkoff, "Welfare Devolution and State Constitutions," *Fordham Law Review* 67 (March 1999): 1403–1433.

For specific treatments of environmental rights provisions, see A. E. Dick Howard, "State Constitutions and the Environment," *Virginia Law Review* 58 (February 1972): 193–229; and Barton H. Thompson Jr., "Environmental Policy and State Constitutions: The Potential Role of Substantive Guidance," *Rutgers Law Journal* 27 (Summer 1996): 863–925.

Several scholars have made use of assorted state convention debates in analyzing several of these issues, including Cohen, "More Myths of Parity," 638–641; Hershkoff, "Rights and Freedoms," 643–647; Hershkoff, "Welfare Devolution and State Constitutions," 1418–1425; and Frank E. L. Deale, "The Unhappy History of Economic Rights in the United States and Prospects for Their Creation and Renewal," *Howard Law Journal* 43 (Spring 2000): 281, 330–335.

28. Elizabeth Brandeis, "Labor Legislation," in *History of Labor in the United States, 1896–1932,* ed. John R. Commons, 4 vols. (New York: Macmillan, 1935), 3:403–456.

29. Ibid., 3:457–500, 540–563.

30. Ibid., 3:501–539.

31. Ibid., 3:564–610.

32. *Debates and Proceedings of the Constitutional Convention of the State of Illinois [1869],* 274.

33. *Report of the Proceedings and Debates of the Constitutional Convention, State of Virginia [1901–1902],* 2853.

34. *The Records of the Arizona Constitutional Convention of 1910,* 444–445.

35. *Official Report of the Proceedings and Debates of the Third Constitutional Convention of Ohio [1873],* 1:600.

36. *Report of the Proceedings and Debates of the Constitutional Convention, State of Virginia [1901–1902],* 2841.

37. *Official Report of the Proceedings and Debates of the Third Constitutional Convention of Ohio [1873],* 1:1331.

38. *Proceedings and Debates of the Constitutional Convention of the State of Ohio [1912],* 1338.

39. *Debates and Proceedings of the Constitutional Convention of the State of Illinois [1869],* 271.

40. *Official Report of the Proceedings and Debates of the Third Constitutional Convention of Ohio [1873],* 1:348.

41. *The Records of the Arizona Constitutional Convention of 1910,* 545.

42. *Proceedings and Debates of the Constitutional Convention of the State of Ohio [1912]*, 1339.

43. Ibid., 1346.

44. *Debates in the Massachusetts Constitutional Convention, 1917–1918*, 3:551.

45. Ibid., 3:607.

46. These general commitments to the protection of workers rights are found in the following provisions: Utah Constitution (1895), Art. XVI, Sec. 1; Wyoming Constitution (1889), Art. I, Sec. 22.

47. Wyoming Constitution (1889), Art. I, Sec. 22.

48. These child labor protections are found in the following provisions: Arizona Constitution (1911), Art. XVIII, Sec. 2; Colorado Constitution (1876), Art. XVI, Sec. 2; Idaho Constitution (1889), Art. XIII, Sec. 4; Kentucky Constitution (1891), Sec. 243; Montana Constitution (1889), Art. XVIII, Sec. 3 (adopted 1904); New Mexico Constitution (1911), Art. XVII, Sec. 2; Art. XX, Sec. 10; North Dakota Constitution (1889), Art. XVII, Sec. 209; Oklahoma Constitution (1907), Art. XXIII, Sec. 3, 4; Utah Constitution (1895), Art. XVI, Sec. 3(1); Wyoming Constitution (1889), Art. IX, Sec. 3.

49. New Mexico Constitution (1911), Art. XX, Sec. 10.

50. Utah Constitution (1895), Art. XVI, Sec. 3.

51. Idaho Constitution (1889), Art. XIII, Sec. 4.

52. These maximum-hour protections are found in the following provisions: Arizona Constitution (1911), Art. XVIII, Sec. 1; California Constitution (1879), Art. XIV, Sec. 2 (adopted 1902 and renumbered 1976); Colorado Constitution (1876), Art. V, Sec. 25-A (adopted 1902); Idaho Constitution (1889), Art. XIII, Sec. 2; Michigan Constitution (1908), Art. V, Sec. 29 (as amended 1920); Montana Constitution (1889), Art. XVIII, Sec. 4 (as amended 1904); Nebraska Constitution (1875), Art. XV, Sec. 8 (as amended 1920); New Mexico Constitution (1911), Art. XX, Sec. 19; New York Constitution (1894), Art. I, Sec. 17 (as amended 1938); Ohio Constitution (1851), Art. II, Sec. 34, 37 (adopted 1912); Oklahoma Constitution (1907), Art. XXIII, Sec. 1; Utah Constitution (1895), Art. XVI, Sec. 6 (as amended 1920); Wyoming Constitution (1889), Art. XIX, Sec. 2.

53. Michigan Constitution (1908), Art. V, Sec. 29 (as amended 1920).

54. Wyoming Constitution (1889), Art. XIX, Sec. 2.

55. These minimum wage provisions are found in the following provisions: California Constitution (1879), Art. XIV, Sec. 1 (adopted 1914 and renumbered 1976); Nebraska Constitution (1875), Art. XV, Sec. 8 (as amended 1920); Ohio Constitution (1851), Art. II, Sec. 34 (adopted 1912); Utah Constitution (1895), Art. XVI, Sec. 8 (adopted 1933).

56. Ohio Constitution (1851), Art. II, Sec. 34 (adopted 1912).

57. These workers' safety provisions are found in the following provisions: Arizona Constitution (1911), Art. XIX; Arkansas Constitution (1874), Art. XIX, Sec. 18; Colorado Constitution (1876), Art. XVI, Sec. 2; Idaho Constitution (1889), Art. XIII, Sec. 2 (as amended 1902); Illinois Constitution (1870), Art. IV, Sec. 29; New Mexico Constitution (1911), Art. XVII, Sec. 2; Ohio Constitution (1851), Art. II, Sec. 34 (adopted 1912); Oklahoma Constitution (1907), Art. XXIII, Sec. 5; Utah Constitution (1895), Art. XVI, Sec. 6; Washington Constitution (1889), Art. II, Sec. 35; Wyoming Constitution (1889), Art. IX, Sec. 2.

58. Illinois Constitution (1870), Art. IV, Sec. 29.

59. Utah Constitution (1895), Art. XVI, Sec. 6.

60. These employer liability provisions are found in the following provisions: Arizona

Constitution (1911), Art. XVIII, Sec. 3–6, 8; California Constitution (1879), Art. XIV, Sec. 4 (adopted 1911 and renumbered 1976); Colorado Constitution (1876), Art. XV, Sec. 15; Kentucky Constitution (1891), Sec. 241; Louisiana Constitution (1974), Art. XII, Sec. 8; Mississippi Constitution (1890), Art. VII, Sec. 193; Montana Constitution (1889), Art. XV, Sec. 16; New Mexico Constitution (1911), Art. XX, Sec. 16; New York Constitution (1894), Art. I, Sec. 16 (renumbered 1938), Sec. 18 (as amended 1913 and renumbered 1938); Ohio Constitution (1851), Art. II, Sec. 35 (adopted 1912); Oklahoma Constitution (1907), Art. IX, Sec. 36; Art. XXIII, Sec. 6, 8; South Carolina Constitution (1895), Art. IX, Sec. 15; Utah Constitution (1895), Art. XVI, Sec. 5; Vermont Constitution (1793), Ch. II, Sec. 66 (as amended 1913); Virginia Constitution (1902), Art. XII, Sec. 162; Wyoming Constitution (1889), Art. IX, Sec. 4; Art. X, Sec. 4.

61. Arizona Constitution (1911), Art. XVIII, Sec. 4.

62. Ibid., Sec. 5.

63. Ibid., Sec. 3.

64. Ibid., Sec. 8.

65. For the development of state policies in these areas, see Commons, *History of Labor in the United States*, vols. 2–4; Charles C. Killingsworth, *State Labor Relations Acts: A Study of Public Policy* (Chicago: University of Chicago Press, 1948).

66. For the history of right-to-work measures, see Paul Sultan, *Right-to-Work Laws: A Study in Conflict* (Los Angeles: Institute of Industrial Relations, University of California, 1958); and Gilbert J. Gall, *The Politics of Right to Work* (Westport, Conn.: Greenwood Press, 1988).

67. *Proceedings of the Constitutional Convention of the State of Illinois, Convened January 6, 1920*, 4628.

68. *[New Jersey] Constitutional Convention of 1947*, 1:310.

69. Ibid.

70. *Proceedings of the Constitutional Convention of Hawaii, 1950*, 2:678–679.

71. *Debates of the [Maryland] Constitutional Convention of 1967–1968*, 2905.

72. Ibid., 2320.

73. Ibid., 2306.

74. *Proceedings of the Constitutional Convention of Hawaii, 1950*, 2:683.

75. *Ibid*, 2:685.

76. *Debates of the [Maryland] Constitutional Convention of 1967–1968*, 2305.

77. Ibid., 2281.

78. *Debates in the Massachusetts Constitutional Convention, 1917–1918*, 1:1047.

79. *[New Jersey] Constitutional Convention of 1947*, 1:654.

80. Ibid., 1:314.

81. *Revised Record of the Constitutional Convention of the State of New York [1938]*, 1246.

82. *[New Jersey] Constitutional Convention of 1947*, 1:325.

83. *Debates of the [Maryland] Constitutional Convention of 1967–1968*, 2307.

84. *Revised Record of the Constitutional Convention of the State of New York [1938]*, 1218.

85. *Debates of the North Dakota Constitutional Convention of 1972*, 433.

86. Ibid., 438.

87. Ibid., 436.

88. Ibid., 431.

89. *Official Record, State of Michigan Constitutional Convention, 1961*, 2871.

90. These prohibitions on blacklists are found in the following provisions: Arizona Constitution (1911), Art. XIX, Sec. 9; North Dakota Constitution (1889), Art. I, Sec. 23; Art. XVII, Sec. 212; Utah Constitution (1895), Art. XII, Sec. 19; Art. XVI, Sec. 4.

91. North Dakota Constitution (1889), Art. I, Sec. 23.

92. Ibid., Art. XVII, Sec. 212.

93. These protections for the right to organize and bargain collectively are found in the following provisions: Florida Constitution (1968), Art. I, Sec. 6; Hawaii Constitution (1950), Art. XIII, Sec. 1, 2 (as amended 1968 and renumbered 1978); Missouri Constitution (1945), Art. I, Sec. 29; New Jersey Constitution (1947), Art. I, Sec. 19; New York Constitution (1894), Art. 1, Sec. 17 (adopted 1938).

94. New York Constitution (1894), Art. I, Sec. 17 (adopted 1938).

95. These right-to-work clauses are found in the following provisions: Arizona Constitution (1911), Art. XXV (adopted 1946); Arkansas Constitution (1874), Amendment 34 (adopted 1944); Florida Constitution (1968), Art. I, Sec. 6; Kansas Constitution (1859), Art. 15, Sec. 12 (adopted 1958); Mississippi Constitution (1890), Art. 7, Sec. 198-A (adopted 1960); Nebraska Constitution (1875), Art. XV, Sec. 13 (adopted 1946); Oklahoma Constitution (1907), Art. XXIII, Sec. 1-A (adopted 2001); South Dakota Constitution (1889), Art. VI, Sec. 2 (as amended 1946).

96. Arkansas Constitution (1874), Amendment 34 (adopted 1944).

97. Florida Constitution (1968), Art. I, Sec. 6.

98. These provisions are discussed in Neuborne, "State Constitutions and the Evolution of Positive Rights"; Feldman, "Separation of Powers"; Hershkoff, "Positive Rights and State Constitutions"; Hershkoff, "Positive Rights and the Evolution of State Constitutions"; Braveman, "Children, Poverty, and State Constitutions"; Cohen, "More Myths of Parity."

99. *Minutes of the Daily Proceedings, Alaska Constitutional Convention, 1955–56*, 1301.

100. *Proceedings of the Constitutional Convention of Hawaii, 1950*, 2:544.

101. Ibid., 2:548.

102. *Proceedings of the Constitutional Convention of Hawaii of 1968*, 2:39.

103. *Proceedings of the Constitutional Convention of the State of New York [1967]*, 4:278.

104. *Proceedings of the Constitutional Convention of Hawaii, 1950*, 2:544.

105. *Records of the Louisiana Constitutional Convention of 1973: Convention Transcripts*, 2472.

106. *Debates of the [Maryland] Constitutional Convention of 1967–1968*, 2433.

107. *Proceedings of the Constitutional Convention of Hawaii of 1968*, 2:41.

108. *Records of the Louisiana Constitutional Convention of 1973: Convention Transcripts*, 2475.

109. Ibid., 2476.

110. *Debates of the [Maryland] Constitutional Convention of 1967–1968*, 1206.

111. Ibid., 2439.

112. Ibid., 2908.

113. *Montana Constitutional Convention, 1971–1972: Verbatim Transcript*, 1637.

114. *Debates of the North Dakota Constitutional Convention of 1972*, 234.

115. *Record of Proceedings: Sixth Illinois Constitutional Convention [1969]: Verbatim Transcripts*, 1724.

116. *Debates of the [Maryland] Constitutional Convention of 1967–1968*, 1220.

117. *Revised Record of the Constitutional Convention of the State of New York [1938]*, 2144.

118. Ibid., 2126.

119. Ibid., 2155.

120. *Proceedings of the Constitutional Convention of Hawaii, 1950,* 2:549.

121. *Proceedings of the Constitutional Convention of Hawaii of 1968,* 2:41.

122. *Montana Constitutional Convention, 1971–1972: Verbatim Transcript,* 1637.

123. *Proceedings of the Constitutional Convention of Hawaii, 1950,* 2:555.

124. *Official Record, State of Michigan Constitutional Convention, 1961,* 2614.

125. *Debates of the [Maryland] Constitutional Convention of 1967–1968,* 2434.

126. These debates are contained in ibid., 2427–2441, 2475–2476, 2889–2890, 2907–2909.

127. These debates are contained in *Texas Constitutional Convention [1974]: Official Proceedings,* 2013–2016, 2049–2053, 2396–2406.

128. These debates are contained in *Record of Proceedings: Sixth Illinois Constitutional Convention [1969]: Verbatim Transcripts,* 1721–1733.

129. These debates are contained in ibid., 1631–1633.

130. These social and economic security protections are found in the following provisions: Alabama Constitution (1901), Art. IV, Sec. 88; Alaska Constitution (1956), Art. VII, Sec. 5; Arkansas Constitution (1868), Art. V, Sec. 46; California Constitution (1879), Art. XVI, Sec. 3 (as amended 1974), Sec. 11 (as adopted 1938); Colorado Constitution (1876), Art. XXIV (adopted 1936); Georgia Constitution (1983), Art. IX, Sec. III, Para. I(c); Hawaii Constitution (1950), Art. IX, Sec. 2, 3, 4 (as amended 1978); Idaho Constitution (1889), Art. X, Sec. 1; Illinois Constitution (1970), Preamble; Indiana Constitution (1851), Art. IX, Sec. 3; Kansas Constitution (1859), Art. 7, Sec. 4; Louisiana Constitution (1974), Art. XII, Sec. 8; Massachusetts Constitution (1780), Articles of Amendment, Art. XLVII (adopted 1917); Mississippi Constitution (1890), Art. XIV, Sec. 262; Missouri Constitution (1945), Art. III, Sec. 38(a); Montana Constitution (1972), Art. XII, Sec. 3(3); Nevada Constitution (1864), Art. 13, Sec. 1; New Mexico Constitution (1911), Art. IX, Sec. 14; New York Constitution (1894), Art. XVII, Sec. 1 (adopted 1938); North Carolina Constitution (1868), Art. XI, Sec. 7, 8, 9, 10; Oklahoma Constitution (1907), Art. XVII, Sec. 3; Art. XXV, Sec. 1 (adopted 1936); South Carolina Constitution (1895), Art. XII, Sec. 1, 3; Texas Constitution (1876), Art. XVI, Sec. 8; Utah Constitution (1895), Art. XIX, Sec. 2; Wyoming Constitution (1889), Art. VII, Sec. 18.

131. Illinois Constitution (1970), Preamble.

132. Louisiana Constitution (1974), Art. XII, Sec. 8.

133. Hawaii Constitution (1950), Art. IX, Sec. 3 (as amended 1978).

134. Alabama Constitution (1868), Art. IV, Sec. 34.

135. North Carolina Constitution (1868), Art. XI, Sec. 7.

136. New York Constitution (1894), Art. XVII, Sec. 1 (adopted 1938).

137. These modern public health clauses, as distinct from the many state provisions establishing departments or boards of public health, are found in the following provisions: Alaska Constitution (1956), Art. VII, Sec. 4; Hawaii Constitution (1950), Art. IX, Sec. 1; Louisiana Constitution (1974), Art. XII, Sec. 8; Michigan Constitution (1963), Art. IV, Sec. 51; New York Constitution (1894), Art. XVII, Sec. 3 (adopted 1938).

138. New York Constitution (1894), Art. XVII, Sec. 3 (adopted 1938).

139. Alaska Constitution (1956), Art. VII, Sec. 4.

140. Louisiana Constitution (1974), Art. XII, Sec. 8.

141. The adoption of state constitutional environmental provisions is discussed in a num-

ber of articles, including Howard, "State Constitutions and the Environment"; Brooks, "Constitutional Right to a Healthful Environment"; Thompson, "Environmental Policy and State Constitutions"; Robert A. McLaren, "Environmental Protection Based on State Constitutional Law: A Call for Reinterpretation," *Hawaii Law Review* 12 (Summer 1990): 123–152; Mary Ellen Cusack, "Judicial Interpretation of State Constitutional Rights to a Healthful Environment," *Boston College Environmental Affairs Law Review* 120 (1993): 173–201; and Barton H. Thompson Jr., "Constitutionalizing the Environment: The History and Future of Montana's Environmental Provisions," *Montana Law Review* 64 (Winter 2003): 157–198.

142. Vermont Constitution (1777), Ch. II, Sec. XXXIX.

143. New York Constitution (1894), Art. VII, Sec. 7.

144. For a discussion and categorization of these and other types of environmental provisions in state constitutions, see Thompson, "Environmental Policy and State Constitutions."

145. *Montana Constitutional Convention, 1971–1972: Verbatim Transcript*, 1257.

146. *Records of the Louisiana Constitutional Convention of 1973: Convention Transcripts*, 1253.

147. *Journal of the Convention to Revise the [New Hampshire] Constitution, May 1974*, 143.

148. *Texas Constitutional Convention [1974]: Official Proceedings*, 2095 (quotations transposed).

149. *Record of Proceedings: Sixth Illinois Constitutional Convention [1969]: Verbatim Transcripts*, 3020.

150. *Debates of the [Maryland] Constitutional Convention of 1967–1968*, 744–745.

151. *Montana Constitutional Convention, 1971–1972: Verbatim Transcript*, 1225–1226, quoting Joseph L. Sax, *Defending the Environment: A Strategy for Citizen Action* (New York: Alfred A. Knopf, 1970).

152. *Debates of the North Dakota Constitutional Convention of 1972*, 833.

153. *Record of Proceedings: Sixth Illinois Constitutional Convention [1969]: Verbatim Transcripts*, 3000.

154. *Records of the Louisiana Constitutional Convention of 1973: Convention Transcripts*, 1253.

155. *Montana Constitutional Convention, 1971–1972: Verbatim Transcript*, 1259–1260.

156. *Records of the Louisiana Constitutional Convention of 1973: Convention Transcripts*, 1253.

157. Ibid., 1255.

158. *Proceedings of the Constitutional Convention of the State of New York [1967]*, 2:941.

159. *Record of Proceedings: Sixth Illinois Constitutional Convention [1969]: Verbatim Transcripts*, 2991.

160. Ibid., 3003.

161. *Journal of the Convention to Revise the [New Hampshire] Constitution, May 1984*, 175.

162. *Official Record, State of Michigan Constitutional Convention, 1961*, 2605.

163. *Debates of the [Maryland] Constitutional Convention of 1967–1968*, 751.

164. *Official Record, State of Michigan Constitutional Convention, 1961*, 2611.

165. *Record of Proceedings: Sixth Illinois Constitutional Convention [1969]: Verbatim Transcripts*, 3020.

166. According to Barton Thompson, "All state constitutions drafted since 1959 address modern concerns of pollution and preservation. Half a dozen states with pre-1960

constitutions also have amended their constitutions to address modern environmental issues. In total, more than a third of all state constitutions now contain environmental policy
provisions." Thompson, "Constitutionalizing the Environment," 160.

167. These environmental policy clauses, as distinct from guarantees of hunting and fishing rights and the protection of state land preserves, are found in the following provisions:
Alabama Constitution (1901), Amendment No. 543 (adopted 1992); Alaska Constitution
(1956), Art. VIII, Sec. 2; Florida Constitution (1968), Art. II, Sec. 7; Georgia Constitution
(1983), Art. III, Sec. VI, Para. II(a)(1); Hawaii Constitution (1950), Art. IX, Sec. 8; Art. XI,
Sec. 9 (adopted 1978); Illinois Constitution (1970), Art. XI, Sec. 1, 2; Louisiana Constitution (1974), Art. IX, Sec. 1; Massachusetts Constitution (1780), Articles of Amendment, Art.
XCVII (adopted 1972); Michigan Constitution (1963), Art. IV, Sec. 52; Montana Constitution (1972), Art. II, Sec. 3; Art. IX, Sec. 1; New Mexico Constitution (1911), Art. XX, Sec.
21 (adopted 1971); New York Constitution (1894), Art. XIV, Sec. 4 (adopted 1969); North
Carolina Constitution (1971), Art. XIV, Sec. 5; Ohio Constitution (1851), Art. II, Sec. 36
(adopted 1912); Pennsylvania Constitution (1968), Art. I, Sec. 27; Rhode Island Constitution (1986), Art. I, Sec. 17; Virginia Constitution (1971), Art. XI, Sec. 1, 2.

168. Georgia Constitution (1983), Art. III, Sec. 6, Para. 2(a)(1).

169. Florida Constitution (1968), Art. II, Sec. 7.

170. Illinois Constitution (1970), Art. XI, Sec. 2.

171. Hawaii Constitution (1950), Art. XI, Sec. 9 (adopted 1978).

172. Pennsylvania Constitution (1968), Art. I, Sec. 27.

173. Massachusetts Constitution (1780), Articles of Amendment, Art. XCVII (adopted
1972).

Chapter 7: Citizen Character

1. Among the first scholars to call attention to the founders' concern with civic virtue
were Hannah Arendt, *On Revolution* (New York: Viking Press, 1963); Bernard Bailyn, *The
Ideological Origins of the American Revolution* (Cambridge, Mass.: Belknap Press, 1967);
Gordon S. Wood, *The Creation of the American Republic, 1776–1787* (Chapel Hill: University of North Carolina Press, 1969); and J. G. A. Pocock, *The Machiavellian Moment: Florentine
Political Thought and the Atlantic Republican Tradition* (Princeton, N.J.: Princeton University Press, 1975). After the publication of these initial works, scholars have generally aligned
themselves with one of two camps. One group of "republican" theorists tends to emphasize the prominent place of civic virtue in the American political tradition. This includes,
among others, Lance Banning, *The Jeffersonian Persuasion: Evolution of a Party Ideology*
(Ithaca, N.Y.: Cornell University Press, 1978); Drew McCoy, *The Elusive Republic: Political
Economy in Jeffersonian America* (Chapel Hill: University of North Carolina Press, 1980);
and Michael J. Sandel, *Democracy's Discontent: America in Search of a Public Philosophy*
(Cambridge, Mass.: Belknap Press, 1996). Another group of "liberal" theorists contends that
the role of civic virtue has been overemphasized, to the point that scholars have lost sight of
the overriding influence of Lockean themes in the founding. These influences, which were
detailed most clearly in Louis Hartz, *The Liberal Tradition in America: An Interpretation of
American Political Thought since the Revolution* (New York: Harcourt, Brace, 1955), have
also been emphasized in recent years by John Patrick Diggins, *The Lost Soul of American
Politics: Virtue, Self-Interest, and the Foundations of Liberalism* (New York: Basic Books,

1984); Joyce Appleby, *Capitalism and a New Social Order: The Republican Vision of the 1790s* (New York: New York University Press, 1984); Thomas Pangle, *The Sprit of Modern Republicanism: The Moral Vision of the American Founders and the Philosophy of Locke* (Chicago: University of Chicago Press, 1988); Steven M. Dworetz, *The Unvarnished Doctrine: Locke, Liberalism, and the American Revolution* (Durham, N.C.: Duke University Press, 1990); Richard Sinopoli, *The Foundations of American Citizenship: Liberalism, the Constitution, and Civic Virtue* (New York: Oxford University Press, 1992); Jerome Huyler, *Locke in America: The Moral Philosophy of the Founding Era* (Lawrence: University Press of Kansas, 1995); and Michael Zuckert, *The Natural Rights Republic: Studies in the Foundation of the American Political Tradition* (Notre Dame, Ind.: Notre Dame University Press, 1996).

2. Daniel Walker Howe has argued that Publius "has little to say about the highest faculties of *private* morality and speculative reason, because the specific task before him did not require that he discuss them." Thus he concludes that "it is a mistake to try to extract from [The Federalist Papers] a complete theory or a comprehensive statement of the relation between government and virtue, such as one finds in Aristotle." Daniel Walker Howe, "The Language of Faculty Psychology in *The Federalist Papers*," in *Conceptual Change and the Constitution*, ed. Terence Ball and J. G. A. Pocock (Lawrence: University Press of Kansas, 1988), 127. In similar fashion, James W. Ceaser has argued that "*The Federalist* was not obliged to treat every major question about liberal democracy, and it was especially likely to avoid certain matters that were to be dealt with chiefly by the states or local governments. The means of promoting citizenship fall mainly in this area." James W. Ceaser, *Liberal Democracy and Political Science* (Baltimore: Johns Hopkins University Press, 1990), 15. Additionally, Leo Paul S. de Alvarez has argued that "the Framers thought that there was a responsibility on the part of the political order to provide for the religion, morality, and education of the people" and that "the choice was deliberately made to leave such matters to the States." Leo Paul S. de Alvarez, "The Constitution and American Character: The Framers' Views," in *Constitutionalism in Perspective: The United States Constitution in Twentieth Century Politics*, ed. Sarah Baumgartner Thurow (Lanham, Md.: University Press of America, 1988), 263.

3. Thus Robert Goldwin noted the importance of the separation of powers system and concluded that, in the design of this system, "the Framers did not seek to remake Americans, but rather to take them as they are and lead them to habits of right action. Their task was to direct the powerful American tendency to self-interest and self-advancement so that abuses would be controlled. More, they aimed not only to control these tendencies but actually to turn them to the benefit of the people." Robert Goldwin, "Of Men and Angels: A Search for Morality in the Constitution," in *The Moral Foundations of the American Republic*, ed. Robert H. Horwitz (Charlottesville: University Press of Virginia, 1977), 10. Similarly, Martin Diamond concluded that the founders expected that the design of the political system would foster certain "republican" virtues; that a commercial order would permit the full play of "bourgeois" virtues; and that a variety of "moral" virtues "would develop from religion, education, family upbringing, and simply out of the natural yearnings of human nature." Martin Diamond, "Ethics and Politics: The American Way," in Horwitz, *Moral Foundations of the American Republic*, 71. In addition, Jean Yarbrough has argued that "the Founders were indeed concerned with the character of the citizens." But "the Founders accepted the fundamental liberal premise that the perfection of the individual is not the task of government, but the concern of society and, more particularly, the family, the churches, and the school."

Jean Yarborough, "Republicanism Reconsidered: Some Thoughts on the Foundation and Preservation of the American Republic," *Review of Politics* 41 (January 1979): 61, 73–74 (quotations transposed).

4. For instance, Benjamin Barber argued that the founders "absolutely depended on a studied obliviousness to public purposes and public interests as defined by traditional republican formulas. To insist on discovering public goods was only to generate faction and occlude those private interests that alone, pitted against each other, promised the semblance of consensus." Benjamin Barber, "The Compromised Republic: Public Purposelessness in America," in Horwitz, *Moral Foundations of the American Republic*, 29. Similarly, Richard Hofstadter argued that the founders "accepted the mercantile image of life as an eternal battleground, and assumed the Hobbesian war of each against all; they did not propose to put an end to this war, but merely to stabilize it and make it less murderous. They had no hope and they offered none for any ultimate organic change in the way men conduct themselves." Richard Hofstadter, "The Founding Fathers: An Age of Realism," in Horwitz, *Moral Foundations of the American Republic*, 84–85. Peter S. Onuf went further and rejected the possibility that the framers of the federal constitution expected state governments to perform the role of character formation. After considering the possibility, advanced by some scholars, that "the federal Constitution was silent on questions of character and citizenship precisely because the state constitutions committed the states to support religion and public education," Onuf concluded, to the contrary, that "the founders did not rely on the states to foster virtue." Peter S. Onuf, "State Politics and Republican Virtue: Religion, Education, and Morality in Early American Federalism," in *Toward a Usable Past: Liberty under State Constitutions*, ed. Paul Finkelman and Stephen E. Gottlieb (Athens: University of Georgia Press, 1991), 92, 111.

5. These statements are found in nineteenth-century opinions upholding state liquor regulations (e.g., *Thurlow v. Commonwealth of Massachusetts*, 46 U.S. 504 [1847], 577), Progressive Era decisions upholding congressional regulation of lotteries and prostitution (e.g., *Champion v. Ames*, 188 U.S. 321 [1903], 356–357; *Hoke v. U.S.*, 227 U.S. 308 [1913], 322), and recent decisions upholding state regulation of obscenity and indecency (e.g., *Miller v. California*, 413 U.S. 15 [1973], 35; *Barnes v. Glen Theatre, Inc.*, 501 U.S. 560 [1991], 567).

6. In the federal Convention of 1787, George Mason tried to secure support for a provision that would have permitted Congress "to enact sumptuary laws," on the grounds that "no government can be maintained unless the manners be made consonant to it." However, this motion was rejected, partly on the grounds, as Oliver Ellsworth explained, that "as far as the regulation of eating & drinking can be reasonable, it is provided for in the power of taxation." Adrienne Koch, ed., *Madison's Notes of Debates in the Federal Convention of 1787* (New York: W. W. Norton, 1966), 488.

A number of federal constitutional amendments have been proposed in subsequent years regarding character formation. Several amendments were introduced in the late nineteenth and early twentieth centuries regarding marriage. Michigan representative Julius Caesar Burrows in 1879 proposed an amendment to restrict polygamy, and this was followed by similar proposals during the next four decades. Meanwhile, Louisiana senator Joseph Ransdell in 1914 introduced an amendment, one of several during this period, that would have prohibited divorce with the right to remarry. See M. A. Musmanno, *Proposed Amendments to the Constitution* (Washington, D.C.: U.S. Government Printing Office, 1929), 104–108; John R. Vile, *Encyclopedia of Constitutional Amendments, Proposed Amendments, and Amending Issues, 1789–1995* (Santa Barbara, Calif.: ABC-CLIO, 1996), 201–202; and Gaines M. Foster, *Moral Reconstruction: Christian Lobbyists and the Federal Legislation of Morality* (Chapel Hill: University of North Carolina Press, 2002), 68–70, 135–140. In regard to lotteries, amendments were proposed in 1890 and 1892 to institute a national prohibition on lotteries, and thereby ban the Louisiana Lottery Company. See Musmanno, *Proposed Amendments to the Constitution,* 145–146; Vile, *Encyclopedia of Constitutional Amendments,* 193; Foster, *Moral Reconstruction,* 125–126. In regard to religion, the most notable nineteenth-century proposal, which came close to receiving congressional approval, was the Blaine Amendment, advocated by President Ulysses S. Grant and introduced by Maine representative James Blaine in 1875, in an effort to prohibit public aid to religious schools. See Herman Ames, *The Proposed Amendments to the Constitution of the United States during the First Century of Its History* (1896; reprint, New York: Burt Franklin, 1970), 277–278; Vile, *Encyclopedia of Constitutional Amendments,* 35–36. The chief concern with regard to religion during the twentieth century, particularly from the 1960s to the present, has been with introducing amendments to permit prayer in public schools, in the face of contrary U.S. Supreme Court decisions. See Vile, *Encyclopedia of Constitutional Amendments,* 237–239. Similarly, amendments were proposed, beginning in the 1950s and 1960s, to empower state and federal governments to restrict obscene expression, again in the face of contrary court decisions (223). Amendments have also been introduced to prohibit abortion or permit states to make such a determination, in response to the Court's decision in *Roe v. Wade,* 410 U.S. 113 (1973). See Vile, *Encyclopedia of Constitutional Amendments,* 258–260.

7. In examining state constitutional developments in this area, I am following in the path of several scholars who have either suggested that the state constitutional tradition might be a profitable area of study for those interested in the topic of character formation or who have undertaken a study of some aspect of this tradition. Daniel J. Elazar, in his comprehensive and influential analysis of state politics, identified an influential strand of American political culture, which he refers to as "moralistic" and which is characterized by "a general commitment to utilizing communal—preferably nongovernmental, but government if necessary—power to intervene into the sphere of 'private' activities when it is considered necessary to do so for the public good or the well-being of the community." Daniel J. Elazar, *American Federalism: A View from the States,* 2nd ed. (New York: Crowell, 1972), 97. In addition, in his study of the principles that informed constitution making in the founding generation, Barry Alan Shain argued that although "at the national level, the ultimate end of public activity was limited to the promotion and protection of commercial activity and the securing of individual or minority rights," the states "continued to demonstrate a commitment to preserving their foundational Protestant cultures, to shaping the moral character of their residents, and to placing individual rights in an inferior position to those of the majority." Barry Alan Shain, *The Myth of American Individualism: The Protestant Origins of American Political Thought* (Princeton, N.J.: Princeton University Press, 1994), 143–144. Meanwhile, Donald Lutz, in his study of eighteenth-century state constitutions, concluded that "religious and secular thinkers could agree on what kind of behavior was essential. For instance, many public documents, including half a dozen state constitutions, listed the following virtues: justice, moderation, temperance, industry, frugality, and honesty." Donald Lutz, *The Origins of American Constitutionalism* (Baton Rouge: Louisiana State University Press, 1988), 87. Laura J. Scalia extended the time frame even further by examining state conventions held during the first half of the nineteenth century. She found a fair amount of evidence of state constitution makers' concern for citizen character, although this concern changed

386 NOTES TO PAGE 223

form during this period. She argued that although "no speaker claimed virtue had anything but instrumental value," it was still the case that "their comments reinforced their position that good citizenship and virtuous leadership . . . were not only instrumentally useful but absolutely necessary to the success of republican government." Laura J. Scalia, *America's Jeffersonian Experiment: Remaking State Constitutions, 1820–1850* (DeKalb: Northern Illinois University Press, 1999), 131. See also Laura J. Scalia, "Constitutions as Constituting People: The Interaction of Good Laws and Good Men—Massachusetts as a Case Study, 1641–1853," paper presented at the 1997 Annual Meeting of the American Political Science Association, Washington, D.C., 28–31 August 1997; and Laura J. Scalia, "Constitutions and the Formation of Public Communities," paper presented at the 1998 Annual Meeting of the American Political Science Association, Boston, Mass., 3–6 September 1998.

8. The decision to focus on state convention debates means that only cursory treatment is given to other political activity at the state level, such as legislative statutes and court decisions. Several of these developments have been explored in Ernst Freund, *The Police Power: Public Policy and Constitutional Rights* (Chicago: Callaghan and Company, 1904), 172–241; Clifford S. Griffin, *Their Brothers' Keepers: Moral Stewardship in the United States, 1800–1865* (New Brunswick, N.J.: Rutgers University Press, 1960); Morton Keller, *Affairs of State: Public Life in Late Nineteenth Century America* (Cambridge, Mass.: Belknap Press, 1977), 122–161, 473–521; Morton Keller, *Regulating a New Society: Public Policy and Social Change in America, 1900–1933* (Cambridge, Mass.: Harvard University Press, 1994), 13–215; William J. Novak, *The People's Welfare: Law and Regulation in Nineteenth-Century America* (Chapel Hill: University of North Carolina Press, 1996), 149–189; and James A. Morone, *Hellfire Nation: The Politics of Sin in American History* (New Haven, Conn.: Yale University Press, 2003), 222–344.

9. Admittedly, this study does not take account of every way in which state constitution makers evinced a concern for the character of the citizenry. Among the various other issues that surfaced in convention debates about citizen character and that led occasionally to the enactment of constitutional provisions were divorce (a number of late nineteenth-century state conventions placed strict limitations on the grounds for obtaining divorces, out of a desire to strengthen marital bonds); and tobacco (several conventions at the turn of the twentieth century considered restricting the sale of cigarettes, not so much for health reasons but rather because of concerns about the effect on the moral development of the citizenry).

The debates about proposals to limit or abolish the granting of divorces (as distinct from the even more common proposals to prohibit the *legislature* from granting divorces) are found in the following sources:

Alabama: *The History and Debates of the Convention of the People of Alabama [1861]* (Montgomery: White, Pfister, 1861), 368–371.

Georgia: *A Stenographic Report of the Proceedings of the Constitutional Convention held in Atlanta, Georgia, 1877*, 253–258.

Kentucky: *Official Report of the Proceedings and Debates in the Convention . . . of September, 1890, To Adopt, Amend or Change the Constitution of the State of Kentucky*, 3921–3960.

New Hampshire: *Journal of the Convention to Revise the [New Hampshire] Constitution, May 1956*, 205–210.

North Dakota: *Official Report of the Proceedings and Debates of the First Constitutional Convention of North Dakota [1889]*, 49–50.

Ohio: *Proceedings and Debates of the Constitutional Convention of the State of Ohio [1912]*, 1425–1428.

Pennsylvania: *Debates of the Convention to Amend the Constitution of Pennsylvania [1872–1873]*, 2:611–622.

The debates regarding cigarettes are found in the following sources:

Michigan: *Proceedings and Debates of the Constitutional Convention of the State of Michigan [1907]*, 477–483.

New York: *Revised Record of the Constitutional Convention of the State of New York [1915]*, 172–174.

10. The debates about governmental support of religious institutions are found in the following sources:

Alaska: *Minutes of the Daily Proceedings, Alaska Constitutional Convention, 1955–56*, 1509–1532.

California: *Debates and Proceedings of the Constitutional Convention of the State of California [1878]*, 1258–1266, 1272–1274.

Connecticut: "Annotated Debates of the 1818 Constitutional Convention," 25–30, 66–74; *The Third Constitutional Convention of the State of Connecticut: Proceedings [1965]*, 577–580, 587–596.

Delaware: *Debates and Proceedings of the Constitutional Convention of the State of Delaware [1896]*, 1248–1260.

Idaho: *Proceedings and Debates of the Constitutional Convention of Idaho, 1889*, 386–392.

Illinois: *Debates and Proceedings of the Constitutional Convention of the State of Illinois [1869]*, 617–626; *Proceedings of the Constitutional Convention of the State of Illinois, Convened January 6, 1920*, 1149–1205, 4081–4115, 4264–4276; *Record of Proceedings: Sixth Illinois Constitutional Convention [1969]: Verbatim Transcripts*, 780–789, 841–855, 4143–4144.

Louisiana: *Debates in the Convention for the Revision and Amendment of the Constitution of the State of Louisiana [1864]*, 490–500, 523–531.

Maine: *The Debates and Journal of the Constitutional Convention of the State of Maine, 1819–20*, 92–115.

Massachusetts: *Journal of Debates and Proceedings in the Convention of Delegates, Chosen to Revise the Constitution of Massachusetts [1820–21]*, 346–376, 381–402, 417–461, 557–565, 576–603; *Official Report of the Debates and Proceedings in the State Convention to Revise and Amend the Constitution of the Commonwealth of Massachusetts [1853]*, 2:543–550; 3:613–626; *Debates in the Massachusetts Constitutional Convention, 1917–1918*, 1:44–363.

Michigan: *Michigan Constitutional Conventions of 1835–36: Debates and Proceedings*, 285–286; *Report of the Proceedings and Debates in the Convention to Revise the Constitution of the State of Michigan, 1850*, 41–42; *The Debates and Proceedings of the Constitutional Convention of the State of Michigan [1867]*, 2:384–387, 726–727; *Proceedings and Debates of the Constitutional Convention of the State of Michigan [1907]*, 208–214; *Official Record, State of Michigan Constitutional Convention, 1961*, 473–476.

Missouri: *Debates of the Missouri Constitutional Convention of 1875*, 9:328–342.

Montana: *Montana Constitutional Convention, 1971–1972: Verbatim Transcript*, 2008–2035.

Nebraska: *Official Report of the Debates and Proceedings in the Nebraska Constitutional Convention [1871]*, 1:338–340.

Nevada: *Official Report of the Debates and Proceedings in the Constitutional Convention of the State of Nevada [1864]*, 660–661.

New Hampshire: *Journal of the Constitutional Convention of the State of New Hampshire, December 1876*, 126–128; *Journal of the Constitutional Convention of the State of New Hampshire, January 1889*, 219–233; *Journal of the [New Hampshire] Constitutional Convention of 1902*, 38–74, 183–196, 613–625.

New Jersey: *Proceedings of the New Jersey State Constitutional Convention of 1844*, 345–347, 401–407, 550–552; *[New Jersey] Constitutional Convention of 1947*, 1:704–727.

New York: *Reports of the Proceedings and Debates of the [New York] Convention of 1821*, 462–466, 574–577; *Proceedings and Debates of the Constitutional Convention of the State of New York Held in 1867 and 1868*, 2710–2754, 2815–2924; *Revised Record of the Constitutional Convention of the State of New York [1894]*, 3:739–762, 766–806, 961–986; 4:741–772, 777–813, 857–887; *Revised Record of the Constitutional Convention of the State of New York [1938]*, 1055–1056; *Proceedings of the Constitutional Convention of the State of New York [1967]*, 2:763–910; 3:493–511; 4:121–136, 397–408, 646–654, 659–661.

North Carolina: *Proceedings and Debates of the Convention of North Carolina [1835]*, 213–332, 382–397.

Ohio: *Official Report of the Proceedings and Debates of the Third Constitutional Convention of Ohio [1873]*, 2:2186–2260, 2267–2270, 2280–2286.

Pennsylvania: *Debates of the Convention to Amend the Constitution of Pennsylvania [1872–1873]*, 5:284–290; 7:386–388.

Virginia: *Report of the Proceedings and Debates of the Constitutional Convention, State of Virginia [1901–1902]*, 786–818, 1237–1244, 2005–2024.

11. The debates about compulsory-schooling provisions are found in the following sources:

Arizona: *The Records of the Arizona Constitutional Convention of 1910*, 534–537.

Delaware: *Debates and Proceedings of the Constitutional Convention of the State of Delaware [1896]*, 1237–1248.

Kentucky: *Official Report of the Proceedings and Debates in the Convention . . . of September, 1890, To Adopt, Amend or Change the Constitution of the State of Kentucky*, 1036, 1135–1146, 4520–4522, 4549–4550.

Michigan: *The Debates and Proceedings of the Constitutional Convention of the State of Michigan [1867]*, 2:305, 418–419, 514–516.

Missouri: *Debates of the Missouri Constitutional Convention of 1875*, 9:100–121.

Nebraska: *Official Report of the Debates and Proceedings in the Nebraska Constitutional Convention [1871]*, 1:269–291; 2:204–210, 218–262, 466–472; 3:395; *Journal of the Nebraska Constitutional Convention [1919]*, 434–451.

Nevada: *Official Report of the Debates and Proceedings in the Constitutional Convention of the State of Nevada [1864]*, 566–574.

New York: *Proceedings and Debates of the Constitutional Convention of the State of New York Held in 1867 and 1868*, 2916–2924, 3812–3813.

Ohio: *Official Report of the Proceedings and Debates of the Third Constitutional Convention of Ohio [1873]*, 2:2186–2260, 2270–2275.

Pennsylvania: *Debates of the Convention to Amend the Constitution of Pennsylvania [1872–1873]*, 2:470–473; 6:42–70; 7:681–694.

South Carolina: *Proceedings of the Constitutional Convention of South Carolina [1868]*, 655–656, 685–709.

Texas: *Debates in the Texas Constitutional Convention of 1875*, 100–113, 194–201, 212–234, 326–369.

Virginia: *Report of the Proceedings and Debates of the Constitutional Convention, State of Virginia [1901–1902]*, 1231–1237, 1835–1838.

12. The debates about restrictions on lotteries and other forms of gambling are found in the following sources:

California: *Report of the Debates in the Convention of California on the Formation of the State Constitution [1849]*, 90–93.

Delaware: *Debates and Proceedings of the Constitutional Convention of the State of Delaware [1852–1853]*, 207–211; *Debates and Proceedings of the Constitutional Convention of the State of Delaware [1896]*, 802, 820–823, 2871–2884.

Illinois: *Record of Proceedings: Sixth Illinois Constitutional Convention [1969]: Verbatim Transcripts*, 662–667, 670–684, 3701–3703.

Kentucky: *Official Report of the Proceedings and Debates in the Convention . . . of September, 1890, To Adopt, Amend or Change the Constitution of the State of Kentucky*, 443, 563, 627–630, 753–754, 784–785, 1019–1020, 1173–1175.

Louisiana: *Debates in the Convention for the Revision and Amendment of the Constitution of the State of Louisiana [1864]*, 398–407; *Records of the Louisiana Constitutional Convention of 1973: Convention Transcripts*, 3211–3237.

Maryland: *Debates and Proceedings of the Maryland Reform Convention to Revise the State Constitution [1851]*, 1:307–308; *Debates of the [Maryland] Constitutional Convention of 1967–1968*, 1677–1733, 2865–2868, 3377–3383.

Michigan: *Official Record, State of Michigan Constitutional Convention, 1961*, 2290–2309, 2931–2939.

Minnesota: *Debates and Proceedings of the Constitutional Convention for the Territory of Minnesota [1857]*, 111–112, 197.

Missouri: *Debates of the Missouri Constitutional Convention of 1875*, 7:386.

Montana: *Montana Constitutional Convention, 1971–1972: Verbatim Transcript*, 2728–2760.

New Jersey: *Proceedings of the New Jersey State Constitutional Convention of 1844*, 545–546; *[New Jersey] Constitutional Convention of 1947*, 1:267–277, 348–389, 427–448.

New York: *Reports of the Proceedings and Debates of the [New York] Convention of 1821*, 461–462, 566–572; *Revised Record of the Constitutional Convention of the State of New York [1894]*, 4:971–978, 1079–1088, 1110–1130; *Revised Record of the Constitutional Convention of the State of New York [1938]*, 637–640, 701–739, 763–786, 843–863, 2827–2837; *Proceedings of the Constitutional Convention of the State of New York [1967]*, 3:340–345.

North Dakota: *Debates of the North Dakota Constitutional Convention of 1972*, 142–146, 202–208, 1610–1613.

Oregon: *The Oregon Constitution and Proceedings and Debates of the Oregon Convention of 1857*, 367–368.

Pennsylvania: *Proceedings and Debates of the Convention of the Commonwealth of Pennsylvania [1837]*, 2:223–224; 12:45–49.

Rhode Island: *Journal of the Convention Assembled to Frame a Constitution for the State of Rhode Island [1842]*, 38–39, 65; *State of Rhode Island and Providence Plantations:*

Constitutional Convention [1964–1969]: Report of Proceedings, 1095–1121, 1152–1157, 1990–2006; *The Proceedings of the Rhode Island Constitutional Convention of 1973*, 98–99, 132–134.

Texas: *Texas Constitutional Convention [1974]: Official Proceedings*, 1872–1898, 1907–1934, 2382–2385.

Utah: *Official Report of the Proceedings and Debates of the Convention . . . To Adopt a Constitution for the State of Utah [1895]*, 937–938.

13. The debates about restrictions on liquor are found in the following sources:

California: *Debates and Proceedings of the Constitutional Convention of the State of California [1878]*, 1081–1086.

Delaware: *Debates and Proceedings of the Constitutional Convention of the State of Delaware [1896]*, 2281–2377, 2951–2964.

Idaho: *Proceedings and Debates of the Constitutional Convention of Idaho, 1889*, 113–124.

Indiana: *Report of the Debates and Proceedings of the Convention for the Revision of the Constitution of the State of Indiana, 1850*, 1434–1435.

Kansas: *A Reprint of the Proceedings and Debates of the Convention Which Framed the Constitution of Kansas at Wyandotte in July, 1859*, 457–459.

Michigan: *Report of the Proceedings and Debates in the Convention to Revise the Constitution of the State of Michigan, 1850*, 183–188, 397–414, 430–434, 766–770; *The Debates and Proceedings of the Constitutional Convention of the State of Michigan [1867]*, 2:199–205, 390–398, 517–544, 547–559, 631–688, 864–885, 888–895, 902–925; *Proceedings and Debates of the Constitutional Convention of the State of Michigan [1907]*, 1122–1134; *Official Record, State of Michigan Constitutional Convention, 1961*, 709–712.

Mississippi: *Journal of the Proceedings and Debates in the Constitutional Convention of the State of Mississippi, August, 1865*, 237–239.

Nebraska: *Official Report of the Debates and Proceedings in the Nebraska Constitutional Convention [1871]*, 2:565–568; 3:319–332, 349–352, 387–389.

New Hampshire: *Journal of the Constitutional Convention of the State of New Hampshire, January 1889*, 155–207.

New York: *Proceedings and Debates of the Constitutional Convention of the State of New York Held in 1867 and 1868*, 2129–2164, 2791–2795, 3265–3282, 3285–3296, 3666–3672; *Revised Record of the Constitutional Convention of the State of New York [1894]*, 2:87–90, 767–773, 791–797.

North Dakota: *Official Report of the Proceedings and Debates of the First Constitutional Convention of North Dakota [1889]*, 145–148.

Ohio: *Report of the Debates and Proceedings of the Convention for the Revision of the Constitution of the State of Ohio, 1850–51*, 2:436–461, 711–723; *Official Report of the Proceedings and Debates of the Third Constitutional Convention of Ohio [1873]*, 2:2888–2912, 2918–2944, 2996–3094, 3162–3185; *Proceedings and Debates of the Constitutional Convention of the State of Ohio [1912]*, 249–256, 354–376, 387–404, 416–433, 448–544, 571–598, 1800–1809.

Oregon: *The Oregon Constitution and Proceedings and Debates of the Oregon Convention of 1857*, 163–171.

Pennsylvania: *Debates of the Convention to Amend the Constitution of Pennsylvania [1872–1873]*, 3:39–73; 5:314–326.

Rhode Island: *State of Rhode Island and Providence Plantations: Constitutional Convention [1964–1969]: Report of Proceedings*, 597–608.

South Dakota: *Dakota Constitutional Convention [1885, 1889]*, 1:326–332, 367–379, 386–392.

Utah: *Official Report of the Proceedings and Debates of the Convention . . . To Adopt a Constitution for the State of Utah [1895]*, 1431–1464.

Virginia: *Report of the Proceedings and Debates of the Constitutional Convention, State of Virginia [1901–1902]*, 2108–2139, 2578–2610, 2750–2752.

West Virginia: *Debates and Proceedings of the First Constitutional Convention of West Virginia (1861–1863)*, 2:410–437.

14. Chester J. Antieau, Phillip M. Carroll, and Thomas C. Burke, *Religion under the State Constitutions* (New York: Central Book, 1965), 51.

15. Chester J. Antieau, Arthur T. Downey, and Edward C. Roberts, *Freedom from Federal Establishment: Formation and Early History of the First Amendment Religion Clauses* (Milwaukee, Wis.: Bruce Publishing, 1964), 2.

16. Ibid., 10–29. See also Gerard V. Bradley, *Church-State Relationships in America* (Westport, Conn.: Greenwood Press, 1987), 19–68; John K. Wilson, "Religion under the State Constitutions, 1776–1800," *Journal of Church and State* 32 (Autumn 1990): 753–767; and Mark Douglas McGarvie, *One Nation under Law: America's Early National Struggles to Separate Church and State* (DeKalb: Northern Illinois University Press, 2004), 21–31.

17. For a helpful treatment of the debates about this issue in the case of the Massachusetts Convention of 1820–1821, see Scalia, "Constitutions as Constituting People," 18–21.

18. *Journal of Debates and Proceedings in the Convention of Delegates, Chosen to Revise the Constitution of Massachusetts [1820–21]*, 369.

19. *The Debates and Journal of the Constitutional Convention of the State of Maine, 1819–20*, 111.

20. Ibid., 101.

21. *Journal of Debates and Proceedings in the Convention of Delegates, Chosen to Revise the Constitution of Massachusetts [1820–21]*, 373.

22. Ibid., 177.

23. *The Debates and Journal of the Constitutional Convention of the State of Maine, 1819–20*, 111.

24. *Journal of Debates and Proceedings in the Convention of Delegates, Chosen to Revise the Constitution of Massachusetts [1820–21]*, 386.

25. Ibid., 355.

26. Ibid., 370–371.

27. Ibid., 362.

28. Ibid., 355.

29. "Annotated Debates of the 1818 Constitutional Convention," 69–70.

30. *Journal of Debates and Proceedings in the Convention of Delegates, Chosen to Revise the Constitution of Massachusetts [1820–21]*, 349.

31. *The Debates and Journal of the Constitutional Convention of the State of Maine, 1819–20*, 103.

32. "Annotated Debates of the 1818 Constitutional Convention," 71.

33. *Journal of Debates and Proceedings in the Convention of Delegates, Chosen to Revise the Constitution of Massachusetts [1820–21]*, 356.

392 NOTES TO PAGES 230–232

34. *The Debates and Journal of the Constitutional Convention of the State of Maine, 1819–20*, 108.

35. *Journal of Debates and Proceedings in the Convention of Delegates, Chosen to Revise the Constitution of Massachusetts [1820–21]*, 359.

36. *The Debates and Journal of the Constitutional Convention of the State of Maine, 1819–20*, 101.

37. *Journal of Debates and Proceedings in the Convention of Delegates, Chosen to Revise the Constitution of Massachusetts [1820–21]*, 356.

38. Ibid., 363.

39. On the process of disestablishment in the original states, see Anson Phelps Stokes, *Church and State in the United States*, 3 vols. (New York: Harper and Brothers, 1950), 1:366–446; and McGarvie, *One Nation under Law*.

40. See Antieau et al., *Religion under the State Constitutions*, 102–104.

41. See Stokes, *Church and State*, 1:392–397.

42. See William G. McLoughlin, *New England Dissent, 1630–1833: The Baptists and the Separation of Church and State*, 2 vols. (Cambridge, Mass.: Harvard University Press, 1971): 2:789–812.

43. See Stokes, *Church and State*, 1:414–418; McLoughlin, *New England Dissent*, 2:1043–1062. The constitutional provision is found in Connecticut Constitution (1818), Art. VII, Sec. 1.

44. See Stokes, *Church and State*, 1:428–432; McLoughlin, *New England Dissent*, 2:894–911.

45. See Stokes, *Church and State*, 1:425–427; McLoughlin, *New England Dissent*, 2:1207–1262. The constitutional provision is found in Massachusetts Constitution (1780), Articles of Amendment, Art. XI (adopted 1833).

46. For discussions of the controversy that erupted over this issue in New York beginning particularly in the 1840s, see Vincent Lannie, *Public Money and Parochial Education: Bishop Hughes, Governor Seward, and the New York School Controversy* (Cleveland: Case Western Reserve University Press, 1968); Diane Ravitch, *The Great School Wars, New York City, 1805–1973: A History of the Public Schools as Battlefield of Social Change* (New York: Basic Books, 1974). For a treatment of the debate about this issue in the Massachusetts Convention of 1853 in particular, see Scalia, "Constitutions as Constituting People," 23–24.

47. This was, to be sure, merely one of several mid-nineteenth-century convention debates over the relationship between church and state regarding education. The concern for the formation of virtuous citizens also took the form of supporting Bible reading and the use of other religious materials in the public schools, with supporters and critics generally taking different sides than on the question of public support of religious schools. See Donald E. Boles, *The Bible, Religion, and the Public Schools*, 3rd ed. (Ames: Iowa State University Press, 1965), 48–57; and Stokes, *Church and State*, 2:549–572. For the political context of these debates, see John C. Jeffries Jr. and James E. Ryan, "A Political History of the Establishment Clause," *Michigan Law Review* 100 (November 2001): 279, 297–305.

48. *Official Report of the Proceedings and Debates of the Third Constitutional Convention of Ohio [1873]*, 2: 2197–2198.

49. Ibid., 2:2199.

50. Ibid.

51. Ibid., 2:2206.

52. *Michigan Constitutional Conventions of 1835–36: Debates and Proceedings*, 285.

53. *Debates in the Convention for the Revision and Amendment of the Constitution of the State of Louisiana [1864]*, 491.

54. *Official Report of the Debates and Proceedings in the State Convention to Revise and Amend the Constitution of the Commonwealth of Massachusetts [1853]*, 3:615.

55. Ibid., 3:617.

56. *Debates and Proceedings of the Constitutional Convention of the State of Delaware [1896]*, 1251.

57. *Revised Record of the Constitutional Convention of the State of New York [1894]*, 3:962.

58. *Official Report of the Debates and Proceedings in the State Convention to Revise and Amend the Constitution of the Commonwealth of Massachusetts [1853]*, 3:619.

59. Ibid., 3:620.

60. *Michigan Constitutional Conventions of 1835–36: Debates and Proceedings*, 285.

61. *Debates in the Massachusetts Constitutional Convention, 1917–1918*, 1:200.

62. Ibid., 1:161.

63. See generally Stokes, *Church and State*, 2:681–689.

64. On the federal Blaine Amendment, see Steven K. Green, "The Blaine Amendment Reconsidered," *American Journal of Legal History* 36 (1992): 38–69; Stephen Macedo, *Diversity and Distrust: Civic Education in a Multicultural Democracy* (Cambridge, Mass.: Harvard University Press, 2000), 76–80; and Philip Hamburger, *Separation of Church and State* (Cambridge, Mass.: Harvard University Press, 2002), 287–334.

65. In fact, "new states were typically required to implement a modified version of the Blaine amendment as a condition of joining the Union." In addition, "old and new states voluntarily added such restrictions to their state constitutions." Edward J. Larson, "The 'Blaine Amendment' in State Constitutions," in *The School-Choice Controversy: What Is Constitutional?*, ed. James W. Skillen (Grand Rapids, Mich.: Baker Books, 1993), 35, 40. See also Joseph Viteritti, "Blaine's Wake: School Choice, The First Amendment, and State Constitutional Law," *Harvard Journal of Law and Public Policy* 21 (Summer 1998): 657, 672–675; and Mark Edward DeForrest, "An Overview and Evaluation of State Blaine Amendments: Origins, Scope, and First Amendment Concerns," *Harvard Journal of Law and Public Policy* 26 (Spring 2003): 551–626.

66. For a compilation of state constitutional prohibitions on public support of religious schools, see Samuel W. Brown, *The Secularization of American Education* (New York: Teachers College, Columbia University, 1912), 103–119. These nineteenth- and early twentieth-century state constitutional prohibitions on public aid to religious schools are found at: Alabama Constitution (1875), Art. XII, Sec. 8; Arizona Constitution (1911), Art. IX, Sec. 10; Art. XI, Sec. 7; Arkansas Constitution (1868), Art. IX, Sec. 1; California Constitution (1879), Art. IX, Sec. 8; Colorado Constitution (1876), Art. V, Sec. 34; Art. IX, Sec. 7; Delaware Constitution (1897), Art. X, Sec. 3; Florida Constitution (1885), Art. XII, Sec. 13; Idaho Constitution (1889), Art. IX, Sec. 5; Illinois Constitution (1870), Art. VIII, Sec. 3; Kansas Constitution (1859), Art. 6, Sec. 8; Kentucky Constitution (1891), Sec. 189; Louisiana Constitution (1898), Art. 253; Massachusetts Constitution (1780), Articles of Amendment, Art. XVIII (adopted 1855); Michigan Constitution (1850), Art. IV, Sec. 40; Minnesota Constitution (1857), Art. VIII, Sec. 3 (adopted 1877); Mississippi Constitution (1890), Art. VIII, Sec. 208; Missouri Constitution (1875), Art. XI, Sec. 11; Montana Constitution (1889), Art. XI, Sec. 8; Nebraska Constitution (1875), Art. VIII, Sec. 11; Nevada Constitution (1864), Art. XI, Sec. 10 (adopted 1880); New Hampshire Constitution (1784), Part II, Art. 82 (adopted

1902); New Mexico Constitution (1911), Art. XII, Sec. 3; New York Constitution (1894), Art. IX, Sec. 4; North Dakota Constitution (1889), Art. VIII, Sec. 152; Ohio Constitution (1851), Art. VI, Sec. 2; Oklahoma Constitution (1907), Art. II, Sec. 5; Pennsylvania Constitution (1874), Art. X, Sec. 2; South Carolina Constitution (1868), Art. X, Sec. 5; South Dakota Constitution (1889), Art. VIII, Sec. 16; Texas Constitution (1876), Art. VII, Sec. 5; Utah Constitution (1895), Art. X, Sec. 13; Virginia Constitution (1902), Art. IX, Sec. 141; Washington Constitution (1889), Art. IX, Sec. 4; Wyoming Constitution (1889), Art. VII, Sec. 8. By the early twenty-first century, these provisions were in effect in more than thirty states, although not all of these provisions can be accurately termed "Blaine Amendments." On the different means of counting state Blaine Amendments, see Toby J. Heytens, "School Choice and State Constitutions," *Virginia Law Review* 86 (February 2000): 117, 123.

67. Stokes, *Church and State*, 2:686. For the range of state constitutional prohibitions regarding public aid to religious schools, see Antieau et al., *Religion under the State Constitutions*, 23–50.

68. For a treatment of the debates about this issue in the specific case of New York, see John Webb Pratt, *Religion, Politics, and Diversity: The Church-State Theme in New York History* (Ithaca, N.Y.: Cornell University Press, 1967), 204–270.

69. *Revised Record of the Constitutional Convention of the State of New York [1894]*, 3:771.

70. *Debates and Proceedings of the Constitutional Convention of the State of California [1878]*, 1273.

71. *Proceedings of the Constitutional Convention of the State of Illinois, Convened January 6, 1920*, 1178.

72. *Proceedings and Debates of the Constitutional Convention of the State of New York Held in 1867 and 1868*, 2750.

73. *Debates and Proceedings of the Constitutional Convention of the State of California [1878]*, 1266.

74. *Proceedings of the Constitutional Convention of the State of Illinois, Convened January 6, 1920*, 1175.

75. See generally Antieau et al., *Religion under State Constitutions*, 9–22. State constitutional provisions regarding aid to charitable organizations are found at: Alabama Constitution (1875), Art. IV, Sec. 34; California Constitution (1879), Art. IV, Sec. 22, 30; Colorado Constitution (1876), Art. V, Sec. 34; Louisiana Constitution (1898), Art. 53; Massachusetts Constitution (1780), Articles of Amendment, Art. XLVI (adopted 1917); Montana Constitution (1889), Art. V, Sec. 35; New Mexico Constitution (1911), Art. IV, Sec. 31; New York Constitution (1894), Art. VIII, Sec. 14; Pennsylvania Constitution (1874), Art. III, Sec. 17, 18; South Carolina Constitution (1895), Art. XI, Sec. 9; Virginia Constitution (1902), Art. IV, Sec. 67; Wyoming Constitution (1889), Art. III, Sec. 36.

76. *Proceedings of the Constitutional Convention of the State of Illinois, Convened January 6, 1920*, 1185.

77. Delegates to the federal convention gave brief consideration to a proposal to establish a national university, but it was rejected, and the federal constitution makes no mention of education. See Koch, *Madison's Notes*, 477–478, 639; and Paul Monroe, *Founding of the American Public School System: A History of Education in the United States* (New York: Hafner Publishing, 1971), 194–195, 199–200.

78. For a study that draws heavily on state constitutional convention debates regarding a number of these issues, see David Tyack, Thomas James, and Aaron Benavot, *Law and the*

Shaping of Public Education, 1785–1954 (Madison: University of Wisconsin Press, 1987). For analyses of the state constitutional education provisions that emerged from these various debates, see John Mathiason Matzen, *State Constitutional Provisions for Education: Fundamental Attitude of the American People Regarding Education as Revealed by State Constitutional Provisions, 1776–1929* (New York: Teachers College, Columbia University, 1931); and John C. Eastman, "When Did Education Become a Civil Right? An Assessment of State Constitutional Provisions for Education, 1776–1900," *American Journal of Legal History* 42 (January 1998): 1–34.

79. On the creation of state public school systems, see Edgar W. Knight, *Education in the United States,* 3rd rev. ed. (Boston: Ginn, 1951), 192–277; Harry G. Good, *A History of American Education,* 2nd ed. (New York: Macmillan, 1962), 134–170; R. Freeman Butts, *Public Education in the United States: From Revolution to Reform* (New York: Holt, Rinehart and Winston, 1978), 79–167; David Nasaw, *Schooled to Order: A Social History of Public Schooling in the United States* (New York: Oxford University Press, 1979), 29–84; and Ira Katznelson and Margaret Weir, *Schooling for All: Class, Race, and the Decline of the Democratic Ideal* (New York: Basic Books, 1985), 28–57.

80. Nasaw, *Schooled to Order,* 53.

81. Michael Katz, *A History of Compulsory Education Laws* (Bloomington, Ind.: Phi Delta Kappa Educational Foundation, 1976), 15.

82. Nasaw, *Schooled to Order,* 69.

83. Monroe, *Founding of the American Public School System,* 211–294.

84. Carl F. Kaestle, *Pillars of the Republic: Common Schools and American Society, 1780–1860* (New York: Hill and Wang, 1983), 100. For an extended discussion, see 75–103.

85. For discussions of the various issues that were implicated in the compulsory schooling debate, see Forest C. Ensign, *Compulsory School Attendance and Child Labor* (New York: Arno Press, 1969); Lawrence Kotin and William F. Aikman, *Legal Foundations of Compulsory School Attendance* (Port Washington, N.Y.: Kennikat Press, 1980), 24–29; and David B. Tyack, "Ways of Seeing: An Essay on the History of Compulsory Schooling," in *History, Education, and Public Policy: Recovering the American Educational Past,* ed. Donald R. Warren (Berkeley, Calif.: McCutchan Publishing, 1978), 56–89.

86. *Debates of the Convention to Amend the Constitution of Pennsylvania [1872–1873],* 6:42.

87. Ibid., 6:42–43.

88. Ibid., 6:65.

89. Ibid., 6:44.

90. *Proceedings and Debates of the Constitutional Convention of the State of New York Held in 1867 and 1868,* 2922.

91. *Official Report of the Debates and Proceedings in the Nebraska Constitutional Convention [1871],* 2:240.

92. *Proceedings and Debates of the Constitutional Convention of the State of New York Held in 1867 and 1868,* 2919.

93. *Proceedings of the Constitutional Convention of South Carolina [1868],* 696.

94. Ibid.

95. *Official Report of the Debates and Proceedings in the Nebraska Constitutional Convention [1871],* 1:274.

96. *The Debates and Proceedings of the Constitutional Convention of the State of Michigan [1867],* 2:515.

97. *Debates of the Convention to Amend the Constitution of Pennsylvania [1872–1873]*, 6:44.

98. *Official Report of the Proceedings and Debates in the Convention . . . of September, 1890, To Adopt, Amend or Change the Constitution of the State of Kentucky*, 4522.

99. *Official Report of the Debates and Proceedings in the Nebraska Constitutional Convention [1871]*, 2:231.

100. *Debates and Proceedings of the Constitutional Convention of the State of Delaware [1896]*, 1241.

101. Ibid., 1245–1246.

102. *Proceedings and Debates of the Constitutional Convention of the State of New York Held in 1867 and 1868*, 2918.

103. *Official Report of the Debates and Proceedings in the Constitutional Convention of the State of Nevada [1864]*, 571.

104. *Official Report of the Debates and Proceedings in the Nebraska Constitutional Convention [1871]*, 1:271.

105. *Debates in the Texas Constitutional Convention of 1875*, 225.

106. *Debates of the Missouri Constitutional Convention of 1875*, 9:113.

107. *Proceedings and Debates of the Constitutional Convention of the State of New York Held in 1867 and 1868*, 2921.

108. *Official Report of the Debates and Proceedings in the Nebraska Constitutional Convention [1871]*, 2:221.

109. *Proceedings of the Constitutional Convention of South Carolina [1868]*, 686.

110. *Official Report of the Proceedings and Debates of the Third Constitutional Convention of Ohio [1873]*, 2:2191.

111. *Debates of the Convention to Amend the Constitution of Pennsylvania [1872–1873]*, 6:57.

112. *The Debates and Proceedings of the Constitutional Convention of the State of Michigan [1867]*, 2:515.

113. James Van Horn Melton, *Absolutism and the Eighteenth-Century Origins of Compulsory Schooling in Prussia and Austria* (New York: Cambridge University Press, 1988).

114. See Ensign, *Compulsory School Attendance*, 46–86.

115. *Debates in the Texas Constitutional Convention of 1875*, 108–109.

116. *Official Report of the Debates and Proceedings in the Nebraska Constitutional Convention [1871]*, 2:225.

117. Ibid., 1:272.

118. *Journal of the Nebraska Constitutional Convention [1919]*, 450.

119. *Debates and Proceedings of the Constitutional Convention of the State of Delaware [1896]*, 1240.

120. For the dates of enactment of these measures, see William M. Landes and Lewis C. Solmon, "Compulsory Schooling Legislation: An Economic Analysis of Law and Social Change in the Nineteenth Century," *Journal of Economic History* 32 (March 1972): 54, 56–57. For a detailed treatment of each of these measures, see August W. Steinhilber and Carl J. Sokolowski, *State Law on Compulsory Attendance* (Washington, D.C.: U.S. Government Printing Office, 1966).

121. For a discussion of the states that elevated their compulsory schooling provisions to constitutional status at some point, see Kotin and Aikman, *Legal Foundations*, 195–202. The states that adopted permissive provisions are Colorado, Delaware, Idaho, and Nevada. The

states adopting mandatory provisions are New Mexico, North Carolina, Oklahoma, South Carolina, Virginia, and Wyoming (both North Carolina and Virginia had earlier adopted permissive provisions but then moved to adopt mandatory provisions in their most recent constitutions). These provisions are found at Colorado Constitution (1876), Art. IX, Sec. 11; Delaware Constitution (1897), Art. X, Sec. 1; Idaho Constitution (1889), Art. IX, Sec. 9; Nevada Constitution (1864), Art. XI, Sec. 2; New Mexico Constitution (1911), Art. XII, Sec. 5; North Carolina Constitution (1971), Art. IX, Sec. 3; Oklahoma Constitution (1907), Art. XIII, Sec. 4; South Carolina Constitution (1868), Art. X, Sec. 4; Virginia Constitution (1971), Art. VIII, Sec. 3; Wyoming Constitution (1889), Art. VII, Sec. 9.

122. For a discussion of the underenforcement of these laws, see U.S. Commissioner of Education, "Compulsory Attendance Laws in the United States," *Report for 1888–1889* (Washington, D.C.: Government Printing Office, 1889). On the strengthening of the enforcement of these laws, see Tyack, "Ways of Seeing," 60–64.

123. 268 U.S. 510 (1925). See David B. Tyack, "The Perils of Pluralism: The Background of the Pierce Case," *American Historical Review* 74 (October 1968): 74–98. For the connection between this case and the nineteenth-century debates about compulsory education, see Barbara Woodhouse, "Who Owns the Child? *Meyer* and *Pierce,* and the Child as Property," *William and Mary Law Review* 33 (Summer 1992): 995–1122.

124. 406 U.S. 205 (1972). On the debates stimulated by this decision, see Albert N. Keim, ed., *Compulsory Education and the Amish: The Right Not to Be Modern* (Boston: Beacon Press, 1975).

125. 411 U.S. 1 (1973).

126. For general analyses of state regulation of lotteries, see Herbert Asbury, *Sucker's Progress: An Informal History of Gambling in America from the Colonies to Canfield* (New York: Dodd, Mead, 1938), 72–87; David Weinstein and Lillian Deitch, *The Impact of Legalized Gambling: The Socioeconomic Consequences of Lotteries and Off-Track Betting* (New York: Praeger, 1974), 7–18; Charles T. Clotfelter and Philip J. Cook, *Selling Hope: State Lotteries in America* (Cambridge, Mass.: Harvard University Press, 1989); Richard McGowan, *State Lotteries and Legalized Gambling; Painful Revenue or Painful Mirage* (Westport, Conn.: Praeger, 1994), 3–21. For studies that take note of the nineteenth-century state constitutional debates about lotteries, see John S. Ezell, *Fortune's Merry Wheel: The Lottery in America* (Cambridge, Mass.: Harvard University Press, 1960), esp. 204–229; Christian G. Fritz, "The American Constitutional Tradition Revisited: Preliminary Observations on State Constitution-Making in the Nineteenth-Century West," *Rutgers Law Journal* 25 (Summer 1994): 945, 965–967.

127. Ezell, *Fortune's Merry Wheel,* 53.

128. See Henry Chafetz, *Play the Devil: A History of Gambling in the United States from 1492 to 1955* (New York: C. N. Potter, 1960), 28–50; Clotfelter and Cook, *Selling Hope,* 33–37.

129. Ezell, *Fortune's Merry Wheel,* 187–190.

130. Ibid., 192–203.

131. Chafetz, *Play the Devil,* 55–63.

132. For a helpful discussion of concerns about the effect of lotteries on citizen character during this period, see Ann Fabian, *Card Sharps, Dream Books, and Bucket Shops: Gambling in 19th-Century America* (Ithaca, N.Y.: Cornell University Press, 1990), 114–125.

133. *Debates and Proceedings of the Constitutional Convention of the State of Delaware [1852–1853],* 209.

398   NOTES TO PAGES 249-253

134. *Report of the Debates in the Convention of California on the Formation of the State Constitution [1849]*, 91.

135. *Reports of the Proceedings and Debates of the [New York] Convention of 1821*, 569–570.

136. *Report of the Debates in the Convention of California on the Formation of the State Constitution [1849]*, 93.

137. Ibid., 91.

138. *Reports of the Proceedings and Debates of the [New York] Convention of 1821*, 566.

139. *Report of the Debates in the Convention of California on the Formation of the State Constitution [1849]*, 93.

140. *Reports of the Proceedings and Debates of the [New York] Convention of 1821*, 571.

141. Ibid., 568.

142. Ibid., 569.

143. Ibid.

144. *Journal of the Convention Assembled to Frame a Constitution for the State of Rhode Island [1842]*, 38.

145. *Report of the Debates in the Convention of California on the Formation of the State Constitution [1849]*, 91.

146. *Reports of the Proceedings and Debates of the [New York] Convention of 1821*, 566.

147. *Report of the Debates in the Convention of California on the Formation of the State Constitution [1849]*, 90.

148. Ibid., 91.

149. *The Oregon Constitution and Proceedings and Debates of the Oregon Convention of 1857*, 368.

150. *Reports of the Proceedings and Debates of the [New York] Convention of 1821*, 568.

151. See Ezell, *Fortune's Merry Wheel*, 204–229.

152. Ibid., 228–229.

153. Ibid., 230–241.

154. The provision that legitimated lotteries was Louisiana Constitution (1864), Title VII, Art. 116. The Louisiana Constitution (1879), Art. 167, then permitted the legislature to continue granting lottery charters but stipulated that "all charters shall cease and expire on the first of January, 1895, from which time all lotteries are prohibited in the State." For discussions of the Louisiana Lottery, see Ezell, *Fortune's Merry Wheel*, 242–270; Asbury, *Sucker's Progress*, 83–87; Lee Hargrave, *The Louisiana State Constitution: A Reference Guide* (Westport, Conn.: Greenwood Press, 1991), 9–10.

155. On the elimination of all lotteries by the end of the nineteenth century, see Freund, *Police Power*, 181; and Clotfelter and Cook, *Selling Hope*, 38. The state constitutional prohibitions on lotteries are found at Alabama Constitution (1875), Art. IV, Sec. 26; Arkansas Constitution (1874), Art. XIX, Sec. 14; California Constitution (1879), Art. IV, Sec. 26; Colorado Constitution (1876), Art. XVIII, Sec. 2; Delaware Constitution (1897), Art. II, Sec. 17; Florida Constitution (1868), Art. V, Sec. 20; Georgia Constitution (1877), Art. I, Sec. II, Para. IV; Idaho Constitution (1889), Art. III, Sec. 20; Illinois Constitution (1870), Art. IV, Sec. 27; Indiana Constitution (1851), Art. XV, Sec. 8; Iowa Constitution (1857), Art. III, Sec. 28; Kansas Constitution (1859), Art. 15, Sec. 3; Kentucky Constitution (1891), Sec. 226; Louisiana Constitution (1898), Art. 178; Maryland Constitution (1867), Art. III, Sec. 36; Michigan Constitution (1850), Art IV, Sec. 27; Minnesota Constitution (1857), Art. IV, Sec. 31; Mississippi Constitution (1890), Art. 4, Sec. 98; Missouri Constitution (1875), Art. XIV, Sec. 10; Montana Constitution (1889), Art. XIX, Sec. 2; Nebraska Constitution (1875), Art.

III, Sec. 21; Nevada Constitution (1864), Art. IV, Sec. 24; New Jersey Constitution (1844), Art. IV, Sec. VII(2); New York Constitution (1894), Art. I, Sec. 9; North Dakota Constitution (1889), Amendments, Art. 1 (adopted 1894); Ohio Constitution (1851), Art. XV, Sec. 6; Oregon Constitution (1857), Art. XV, Sec. 4; Rhode Island Constitution (1842), Art. IV, Sec. 12; South Carolina Constitution (1895), Art. XVII, Sec. 7; South Dakota Constitution (1889), Art. III, Sec. 25; Tennessee Constitution (1870), Art. XI, Sec. 5; Texas Constitution (1876), Art. III, Sec. 47; Utah Constitution (1895), Art. VI, Sec. 28; Virginia Constitution (1870), Art. V, Sec. 18; Washington Constitution (1889), Art. II, Sec. 24; West Virginia Constitution (1872), Art. VI, Sec. 36; Wisconsin Constitution (1848), Art. IV, Sec. 24.

156. On the decision of several states to permit forms of gambling other than lotteries in the early twentieth century, see Weinstein and Deitch, *Impact of Legalized Gambling*, 13. On the unsuccessful efforts to permit lotteries in several states during this period, see Ezell, *Fortune's Merry Wheel*, 277–278.

157. *Montana Constitutional Convention, 1971–1972: Verbatim Transcript*, 2731.

158. *State of Rhode Island and Providence Plantations: Constitutional Convention [1964–1969]: Report of Proceedings*, 1097.

159. *Official Record, State of Michigan Constitutional Convention, 1961*, 2933.

160. *Montana Constitutional Convention, 1971–1972: Verbatim Transcript*, 2734.

161. *Record of Proceedings: Sixth Illinois Constitutional Convention [1969]: Verbatim Transcripts*, 680–681.

162. *State of Rhode Island and Providence Plantations: Constitutional Convention [1964–1969]: Report of Proceedings*, 1105–1106.

163. Ibid., 1106; *Texas Constitutional Convention [1974]: Official Proceedings*, 1874.

164. *Debates of the [Maryland] Constitutional Convention of 1967–1968*, 1720.

165. Ibid., 1697, 1698.

166. On the resurgence of support for the lottery during this period, see Clotfelter and Cook, *Selling Hope*, 139–159. For the dates of adoption of state lotteries in the late twentieth century, see Denise von Herrmann, *The Big Gamble: The Politics of Lottery and Casino Expansion* (Westport, Conn.: Praeger, 2002), 12.

167. The nonlottery states are Alabama, Alaska, Arkansas, Hawaii, Mississippi, Nevada, North Dakota, Utah, and Wyoming. Lotteries are prohibited by constitutional provision in six of these states. For the relevant provisions, see Alabama Constitution (1901), Sec. 65; Arkansas Constitution (1874), Art. XIX, Sec. 14; Mississippi Constitution (1890), Art. 4, Sec. 98; Nevada Constitution (1864), Art. 4, Sec. 24; North Dakota Constitution (1889), Art. XI, Sec. 25; Utah Constitution (1895), Art. VI, Sec. 27.

168. This is taken by Norman H. Clark to be the conventional view, to which, it should be noted, he did not subscribe. Norman H. Clark, *Deliver Us from Evil: An Interpretation of American Prohibition* (New York: W. W. Norton, 1976), 6.

169. W. J. Rorabaugh, *The Alcoholic Republic: An American Tradition* (New York: Oxford University Press, 1979), 20–21.

170. For a discussion of temperance activities during this period, see John A. Krout, *The Origins of Prohibition* (New York: Alfred A. Knopf, 1925), 51–123.

171. Ibid., 262–271.

172. Ibid., 283–295. For additional treatments of this early stage of the temperance movement, see also Robert L. Hampel, *Temperance and Prohibition in Massachusetts, 1813–1852* (Ann Arbor, Mich.: UMI Research Press, 1982); Frank L. Byrne, *Prophet of Prohibition: Neal Dow and His Crusade* (Madison: State Historical Society of Wisconsin, 1961); and Ian R.

Tyrell, *Sobering Up: From Temperance to Prohibition in Antebellum America, 1800–1860* (Westport, Conn.: Greenwood Press, 1979).

173. For a comprehensive discussion of these temperance movements and their successes at the state level, see Ernst H. Cherrington, *The Evolution of Prohibition in the United States of America* (Westerville, Ohio: American Issue Press, 1920). For additional analyses, see Clark, *Deliver Us from Evil;* David Leigh Colvin, *Prohibition in the United States: A History of the Prohibition Party and the Prohibition Movement* (New York: George H. Doran, 1926); Peter Odegard, *Pressure Politics: The Story of the Anti-Saloon League* (New York: Columbia University Press, 1928); Joseph R. Gusfield, *Symbolic Crusade: Status Politics and the American Temperance Movement* (Urbana: University of Illinois Press, 1963); K. Austin Kerr, *Organized for Prohibition: A New History of the Anti-Saloon League* (New Haven, Conn.: Yale University Press, 1985); Jack S. Blocker Jr., *American Temperance Movements: Cycles of Reform* (Boston: Twayne, 1989); Richard F. Hamm, *Shaping the 18th Amendment: Temperance Reform, Legal Culture, and the Polity, 1880–1920* (Chapel Hill: University of North Carolina Press, 1995); Thomas R. Pegram, *Battling Demon Rum: The Struggle for a Dry America, 1800–1933* (Chicago: Ivan R. Dee, 1998); and Ann-Marie E. Szymanski, *Pathways to Prohibition: Radicals, Moderates, and Social Movement Outcomes* (Durham, N.C.: Duke University Press, 2003).

174. Freund, *Police Power,* 193.

175. Novak, *People's Welfare,* 171.

176. *The Debates and Proceedings of the Constitutional Convention of the State of Michigan [1867],* 2:552.

177. *Official Report of the Proceedings and Debates of the Third Constitutional Convention of Ohio [1873],* 2:2908.

178. *Proceedings and Debates of the Constitutional Convention of the State of Michigan [1907],* 1126.

179. Ibid., 1132.

180. *Official Report of the Proceedings and Debates of the Convention . . . To Adopt a Constitution for the State of Utah [1895],* 1442.

181. *Debates and Proceedings of the Constitutional Convention of the State of Delaware [1896],* 2304.

182. *Proceedings and Debates of the Constitutional Convention of the State of Ohio [1912],* 455.

183. *Report of the Proceedings and Debates in the Convention to Revise the Constitution of the State of Michigan, 1850,* 186.

184. Ibid., 398.

185. *Debates and Proceedings of the Constitutional Convention of the State of Delaware [1896],* 2320.

186. *Debates and Proceedings of the First Constitutional Convention of West Virginia (1861–1863),* 2:427.

187. *Debates of the Convention to Amend the Constitution of Pennsylvania [1872–1873],* 3:49.

188. Ibid., 3:64.

189. *Proceedings and Debates of the Constitutional Convention of the State of Ohio [1912],* 422.

190. *Official Report of the Proceedings and Debates of the Third Constitutional Convention of Ohio [1873],* 2:2907.

191. *Report of the Debates and Proceedings of the Convention for the Revision of the Constitution of the State of Ohio, 1850–51*, 2:449.

192. *Debates and Proceedings of the Constitutional Convention of the State of Delaware [1896]*, 2307.

193. Ibid., 2288.

194. *Official Report of the Proceedings and Debates of the Third Constitutional Convention of Ohio [1873]*, 2:2905.

195. *Journal of the Constitutional Convention of the State of New Hampshire, January 1889*, 175.

196. *The Debates and Proceedings of the Constitutional Convention of the State of Michigan [1867]*, 2:651–652.

197. Ibid., 2:531.

198. *Official Report of the Proceedings and Debates of the Third Constitutional Convention of Ohio [1873]*, 2:2999.

199. *Debates and Proceedings of the First Constitutional Convention of West Virginia (1861–1863)*, 2:430.

200. *Proceedings and Debates of the Constitutional Convention of the State of Ohio [1912]*, 505.

201. *Debates of the Convention to Amend the Constitution of Pennsylvania [1872–1873]*, 5:316.

202. *Debates and Proceedings of the Constitutional Convention of the State of California [1878]*, 1082.

203. *Proceedings and Debates of the Constitutional Convention of the State of Michigan [1907]*, 1129.

204. *The Debates and Proceedings of the Constitutional Convention of the State of Michigan [1867]*, 2:535.

205. *Debates and Proceedings of the Constitutional Convention of the State of Delaware [1896]*, 2313.

206. *A Reprint of the Proceedings and Debates of the Convention Which Framed the Constitution of Kansas at Wyandotte in July, 1859*, 458.

207. *Journal of the Constitutional Convention of the State of New Hampshire, January 1889*, 172, 173 (quotations transposed).

208. These provisions are found at Michigan Constitution (1850), Art. IV, Sec. 47; Ohio Constitution (1851), Art. XV, Sec. 9. On the logic underlying these no-license policies, see Blocker, *American Temperance Movements*, 53–54; and Szymanski, *Pathways to Prohibition*, 96.

209. *Report of the Debates and Proceedings of the Convention for the Revision of the Constitution of Ohio, 1850–51*, 2:438.

210. *Report of the Proceedings and Debates of the Convention to Revise the Constitution of the State of Michigan, 1850*, 186.

211. *Debates and Proceedings of the Constitutional Convention of the State of Delaware [1896]*, 2286.

212. Clark, *Deliver Us from Evil*, 97–99; Hamm, *Shaping the 18th Amendment*, 133. For the relevant state constitutional provisions, see Delaware Constitution (1897), Art. XIII; Florida Constitution (1885), Art. XIX; Kentucky Constitution (1891), Sec. 61; Texas Constitution (1876), Art. XVI, Sec. 20.

213. Colvin, *Prohibition in the United States*, 355–379.

214. *Report of the Proceedings and Debates of the Convention to Revise the Constitution of the State of Michigan, 1850*, 406–408.

215. See Cherrington, *Evolution of Prohibition*, 136–145; Freund, *Police Power*, 202–203; Colvin, *Prohibition in the United States*, 31–35; Szymanski, *Pathways to Prohibition*, 128. The states and territories that adopted statewide prohibition statutes during this period are Connecticut, Delaware, Illinois, Indiana, Iowa, Maine, Massachusetts, Michigan, Nebraska, New Hampshire, New York, Rhode Island, and Vermont.

216. See Cherrington, *Evolution of Prohibition*, 176–181; and Colvin, *Prohibition in the United States*, 135–144, 202–227. Statewide prohibition was already in effect at the beginning of the decade in New Hampshire. The states that adopted prohibition at some point during the decade are Iowa, Kansas, Maine, North Dakota, Rhode Island, and South Dakota. For the state constitutional provisions adopted during this period, see Iowa Constitution (1857), Art. I, Sec. 26 (adopted 1882); Kansas Constitution (1859), Art. 15, Sec. 10 (adopted 1880); Maine Constitution (1819), Art. XXVI (adopted 1884); North Dakota Constitution (1889), Art. 20; Rhode Island Constitution (1842), Articles of Amendment, Art. V (adopted 1886); South Dakota Constitution (1889), Art. XXIV. Not all of these constitutional provisions survived for long, though. The Iowa provision was invalidated by the state supreme court shortly after its adoption. The Rhode Island provision was repealed by the people in 1889, as was the South Dakota provision in 1896.

217. See Colvin, *Prohibition in the United States*, 435. Statewide prohibition was in effect at the beginning of this period in Kansas, Maine, and North Dakota, and was adopted during this period in Alabama, Arizona, Arkansas, Colorado, Florida, Georgia, Idaho, Indiana, Iowa, Kentucky, Michigan, Mississippi, Montana, Nebraska, Nevada, New Hampshire, New Mexico, North Carolina, Ohio, Oklahoma, Oregon, South Carolina, South Dakota, Tennessee, Texas, Utah, Virginia, Washington, West Virginia, and Wyoming. For the state constitutional provisions that were adopted during this period, see Arizona Constitution (1911), Art. XXIII (adopted 1914), XXIV (adopted 1916); Colorado Constitution (1876), Art. XXII (adopted 1914); Florida Constitution (1885), Art. XIX (adopted 1918); Idaho Constitution (1889), Art. III, Sec. 26 (adopted 1916); Kentucky Constitution (1891), Sec. 226a (adopted 1919); Michigan Constitution (1908), Art. XVI, Sec. 11 (adopted 1916); Nebraska Constitution (1871), Art. XV, Sec. 10 (adopted 1916); New Mexico Constitution (1911), Art. XXIII (adopted 1917); Ohio Constitution (1851), Art. XV, Sec. 9 (adopted 1918); Oklahoma Constitution (1907), Art. I, Sec. 7; Oregon Constitution (1857), Art. I, Sec. 36 (adopted 1914); South Dakota Constitution (1889), Art. XXIV (adopted 1916); Texas Constitution (1876), Art. XVI, Sec. 20 (adopted 1919); Utah Constitution (1895), Art. XXII, Sec. 3 (as amended 1918); West Virginia Constitution (1872), Art. VI, Sec. 46 (adopted 1912); Wyoming Constitution (1889), Art. XIX, Sec. 10 (adopted 1918).

218. Blocker, *American Temperance Movements*, 160.

Selected Bibliography

Adams, Willi Paul. *The First American Constitutions: Republican Ideology and the Making of the State Constitutions in the Revolutionary Era.* Chapel Hill: University of North Carolina Press, 1980.

Adkinson, Danny M., and Lisa McNair Palmer. *The Oklahoma State Constitution: A Reference Guide.* Westport, Conn.: Greenwood Press, 2001.

Adrian, Charles R. "Trends in State Constitutions." *Harvard Journal on Legislation* 5 (March 1968): 311–341.

Anderson, William. *A History of the Constitution of Minnesota.* Minneapolis: University of Minnesota, 1921.

Antieau, Chester J., Arthur T. Downey, and Edward C. Roberts. *Freedom from Federal Establishment: Formation and Early History of the First Amendment Religion Clauses.* Milwaukee, Wis.: Bruce Publishing, 1964.

Antieau, Chester J., Phillip M. Carroll, and Thomas C. Burke. *Religion under the State Constitutions.* New York: Central Book, 1965.

Baisden, Richard N. *Charter for New Jersey: The New Jersey Constitutional Convention of 1947.* Trenton: New Jersey Department of Education, 1952.

Bakken, Gordon M. *Rocky Mountain Constitution Making, 1850–1912.* Westport, Conn.: Greenwood Press, 1987.

Barnett, James D. "The Bicameral System in State Legislation." *American Political Science Review* 9 (August 1915): 449–466.

Bastress, Robert M. *The West Virginia State Constitution: A Reference Guide.* Westport, Conn.: Greenwood Press, 1995.

Baum, Marsha L., and Christian G. Fritz. "American Constitution-Making: The Neglected State Constitutional Sources." *Hastings Constitutional Law Quarterly* 27 (Winter 2000): 199–242.

Bell, John Luther, Jr. "Constitutions and Politics: Constitutional Revision in the South Atlantic States, 1864–1902." Ph.D. diss., University of North Carolina, 1969.

Benjamin, Gerald. "The Diffusion of the Governor's Veto Power." *State Government* 55 (1982): 99–105.

———. "The Mandatory Constitutional Convention Question Referendum: The New York Experience in National Context." *Albany Law Review* 65 (2002): 1017–1050.

Besso, Michael. "A Study in Constitutional Development: The Effect of Political and Social Institutions on the Campaign for a Written Constitution in Connecticut." *Studies in American Political Development* 17 (Fall 2003): 117–148.

———. "Constitutional Amendment Procedures and the Informal Political Construction of Constitutions." *Journal of Politics* 67 (February 2005): 69–87.

Bowers, Michael W. *The Nevada State Constitution: A Reference Guide.* Westport, Conn.: Greenwood Press, 1993.

Branning, Rosalind L. *Pennsylvania Constitutional Development*. Pittsburgh: University of Pittsburgh Press, 1960.

Brown, Samuel W. *The Secularization of American Education*. New York: Teachers College, Columbia University, 1912.

Browne, Cynthia E., comp. *State Constitutional Conventions: From Independence to the Completion of the Present Union, 1776–1959, A Bibliography*. Westport, Conn.: Greenwood Press, 1973.

Bryce, James. "Flexible and Rigid Constitutions." *Studies in History and Jurisprudence*. New York: Oxford University Press, 1901.

———. *The American Commonwealth*. 2 vols. 1914. Reprint, Indianapolis, Ind.: Liberty Fund, 1995.

Burdine, J. Alton. "Basic Materials for the Study of State Constitutions and State Constitutional Development." *American Political Science Review* 48 (December 1954): 1140–1152.

Canning, Bonnie, comp. *State Constitutional Conventions, Revisions, and Amendments, 1959–1976: A Bibliography*. Westport, Conn.: Greenwood Press, 1977.

Cherrington, Ernst H. *The Evolution of Prohibition in the United States of America*. Westerville, Ohio: American Issue Press, 1920.

Cleveland, Frederick A. *The Growth of Democracy in the United States*. Chicago: Quadrangle Press, 1898.

Cogan, Jacob Katz. "The Look Within: Property, Capacity, and Suffrage in Nineteenth-Century America." *Yale Law Journal* 107 (November 1997): 473–498.

Colantuono, Michael G. "The Revision of American State Constitutions: Legislative Power, Popular Sovereignty, and Constitutional Change." *California Law Review* 75 (July 1987): 1473–1512.

Colson, Dennis C. *Idaho's Constitution: The Tie That Binds*. Moscow: University of Idaho Press, 1991.

Conley, Patrick T. *Democracy in Decline: Rhode Island's Constitutional Development, 1776–1841*. Providence: Rhode Island Historical Society, 1977.

Connors, Richard J. *The Process of Constitutional Revision in New Jersey, 1940–1947*. New York: National Municipal League, 1970.

Cooper, John F. "The Citizen Initiative Petition to Amend State Constitutions: A Concept Whose Time Has Passed, or a Vigorous Component of Participatory Democracy at the State Level?" *New Mexico Law Review* 28 (Spring 1998): 227–269.

Cornelius, Janet. *Constitution Making in Illinois, 1818–1970*. Urbana: University of Illinois Press, 1972.

Cornwell, Elmer E., Jr., and Jay S. Goodman. *The Politics of the Rhode Island Constitutional Convention*. New York: National Municipal League, 1969.

Cornwell, Elmer E., Jr., Jay S. Goodman, and Wayne R. Swanson. *Constitutional Conventions: The Politics of Revision*. New York: National Municipal League, 1974.

———. *State Constitutional Conventions: The Politics of the Revision Process in Seven States*. New York: Praeger, 1975.

Coward, Joan Wells. *Kentucky in the New Republic: The Process of Constitution Making*. Lexington: University Press of Kentucky, 1979.

Croly, Herbert. *Progressive Democracy*. New York: Macmillan, 1914.

Crowley, Donald, and Florence Heffron. *The Idaho State Constitution: A Reference Guide*. Westport, Conn.: Greenwood Press, 1994.

D'Alemberte, Talbot. *The Florida State Constitution: A Reference Guide.* Westport, Conn.: Greenwood Press, 1991.

Dealey, James Q. *Growth of American State Constitutions from 1776 to the End of the Year 1914.* Boston: Ginn, 1915.

De Grazia, Alfred. *Public and Republic: Political Representation in America.* New York: Alfred A. Knopf, 1951.

De Witt, Benjamin Parke. *The Progressive Movement: A Non-Partisan, Comprehensive Discussion of Current Tendencies in American Politics.* New York: Macmillan, 1915.

Dinan, John J. *Keeping the People's Liberties: Legislators, Citizens, and Judges as Guardians of Rights.* Lawrence: University Press of Kansas, 1998.

———. "Framing a 'People's Government': State Constitution-Making in the Progressive Era." *Rutgers Law Journal* 30 (Summer 1999): 933–985.

———. "The Pardon Power and the American State Constitutional Tradition." *Polity* 35 (April 2003): 389–418.

Dishman, Robert B. *State Constitutions: The Shape of the Document.* New York: National Municipal League, 1960.

Dixon, Robert G., Jr. *Democratic Representation: Reapportionment in Law and Politics.* New York: Oxford University Press, 1968.

Dodd, Walter F. *The Revision and Amendment of State Constitutions.* Baltimore: Johns Hopkins Press, 1910.

Douglass, Elisha P. *Rebels and Democrats: The Struggle for Equal Political Rights and Majority Rule.* Chapel Hill: University of North Carolina Press, 1955.

Dullea, Henrik N. *Charter Revision in the Empire State: The Politics of New York's 1967 Constitutional Convention.* Albany, N.Y.: Rockefeller Institute Press, 1997.

Eastman, John C. "When Did Education Become a Civil Right? An Assessment of State Constitutional Provisions for Education, 1776–1900." *American Journal of Legal History* 42 (January 1998): 1–34.

Eaton, Amasa M. "Recent State Constitutions." *Harvard Law Review* 6 (25 May and 15 October 1892): 53–72, 109–124.

Elazar, Daniel J. *American Federalism: A View from the States.* 2nd ed. New York: Crowell, 1972.

———. "The Principles and Traditions Underlying State Constitutions." *Publius* 12 (Winter 1982): 11–25.

Elison, Larry M., and Fritz Snyder. *The Montana State Constitution: A Reference Guide.* Westport, Conn.: Greenwood Press, 2001.

Erdman, Charles, Jr. *The New Jersey Constitution of 1776.* Princeton, N.J.: Princeton University Press, 1929.

Ezell, John S. *Fortune's Merry Wheel: The Lottery in America.* Cambridge, Mass.: Harvard University Press, 1960.

Fairlie, John A. "The Veto Power of the State Governor." *American Political Science Review* 11 (August 1917): 473–493.

Faust, Martin L. *Constitution Making in Missouri: The Convention of 1943–1944.* New York: National Municipal League, 1971.

Fehrenbacher, Don E. *Constitutions and Constitutionalism in the Slaveholding South.* Athens: University of Georgia Press, 1989.

Finkelman, Paul, and Stephen E. Gottlieb, eds. *Toward a Usable Past: Liberty under State Constitutions.* Athens: University of Georgia Press, 1991.

Fino, Susan P. *The Michigan State Constitution: A Reference Guide*. Westport, Conn.: Greenwood Press, 1996.

Fischer, Victor. *Alaska's Constitutional Convention*. Fairbanks: University of Alaska Press, 1975.

Fordham, Jefferson B. *The State Legislative Institution*. Philadelphia: University of Pennsylvania Press, 1959.

Freund, Ernst. *The Police Power: Public Policy and Constitutional Rights*. Chicago: Callaghan, 1904.

Friedman, Lawrence M. "State Constitutions in Historical Perspective." *Annals of the American Academy of Political and Social Science* 496 (March 1988): 33–42.

Fritz, Christian G. "The American Constitutional Tradition Revisited: Preliminary Observations on State Constitution-Making in the Nineteenth-Century West." *Rutgers Law Journal* 25 (Summer 1994): 945–998.

———. "Rethinking the American Constitutional Tradition: National Dimensions in the Formation of State Constitutions." *Rutgers Law Journal* 26 (Summer 1995): 969–992.

———. "Alternative Visions of American Constitutionalism: Popular Sovereignty and the Early American Constitutional Debate." *Hastings Constitutional Law Quarterly* 24 (Winter 1997): 287–357.

———. "Fallacies of American Constitutionalism." *Rutgers Law Journal* 35 (Summer 2004): 1327–1369.

Gais, Thomas, and Gerald Benjamin. "Public Discontent and the Decline of Deliberation: A Dilemma in State Constitutional Reform." *Temple Law Review* 68 (Fall 1995): 1291–1315.

Galie, Peter J. *The New York State Constitution: A Reference Guide*. Westport, Conn.: Greenwood Press, 1991.

———. *Ordered Liberty: A Constitutional History of New York*. New York: Fordham University Press, 1996.

Galie, Peter J., and Christopher Bopst. "Changing State Constitutions: Dual Constitutionalism and the Amending Process." *Hofstra Law and Policy Symposium* 1 (1996): 27–52.

Gardner, James A. "The Failed Discourse of State Constitutionalism." *Michigan Law Review* 90 (February 1992): 761–837.

———. "What Is a State Constitution?" *Rutgers Law Journal* 24 (Summer 1993): 1025–1055.

Garner, James W. "Amendment of State Constitutions." *American Political Science Review* 1 (February 1907): 213–247.

Gertz, Elmer, and Joseph P. Pisciotte. *Charter for a New Age: An Inside View of the Sixth Illinois Constitutional Convention*. Urbana: University of Illinois Press, 1980.

Goebel, Thomas. *A Government by the People: Direct Democracy in America, 1890–1940*. Chapel Hill: University of North Carolina Press, 2002.

Goss, Kay Collett. *The Arkansas State Constitution: A Reference Guide*. Westport, Conn.: Greenwood Press, 1993.

Gove, Samuel K., and Thomas R. Kitsos. *Revision Success: The Sixth Illinois Constitutional Convention*. New York: National Municipal League, 1974.

Grad, Frank P. "The State Constitution: Its Function and Form for Our Time." *Virginia Law Review* 54 (June 1968): 928–973.

Graves, W. Brooke, ed. *Major Problems in State Constitutional Revision*. Chicago: Public Administration Service, 1960.

Green, Fletcher M. *Constitutional Development in the South Atlantic States, 1776–1860: A Study in the Evolution of Democracy.* Chapel Hill: University of North Carolina Press, 1930.

Griffin, Stephen M. *American Constitutionalism: From Theory to Politics.* Princeton, N.J.: Princeton University Press, 1996.

Grodin, Joseph R., Calvin R. Massey, and Richard B. Cunningham. *The California State Constitution: A Reference Guide.* Westport, Conn.: Greenwood Press, 1993.

Gunn, L. Ray. *The Decline of Authority: Public Economic Policy and Political Development in New York State, 1800–1860.* Ithaca, N.Y.: Cornell University Press, 1988.

Halevy, Balfour J., with the assistance of Libby H. Guth, comp. *A Selective Bibliography on State Constitutional Revision.* 2nd ed. New York: National Municipal League, 1967.

Hall, Kermit L. "The Judiciary on Trial: State Constitutional Reform and the Rise of an Elected Judiciary, 1846–1860." *Historian* 45 (May 1983): 337–354.

———. "Mostly Anchor and Little Sail: The Evolution of American State Constitutions." In *Toward a Useable Past: Liberty under State Constitutions,* edited by Paul Finkelman and Stephen E. Gottlieb. Athens: University of Georgia Press, 1991.

———. "The Irony of the Federal Constitution's Genius: State Constitutional Development." In *The Constitution and American Political Development: An Institutional Perspective,* edited by Peter F. Nardulli. Urbana: University of Illinois Press, 1992.

Hall, Kermit L., and James W. Ely Jr., eds. *An Uncertain Tradition: Constitutionalism and the History of the South.* Athens: University of Georgia Press, 1989.

Hall, Kermit L., Harold M. Hyman, and Leon V. Sigal, eds. *The Constitutional Convention as an Amending Device.* Washington, D.C.: American Historical Association and American Political Science Association, 1981.

Hammons, Christopher W. "Was James Madison Wrong? Rethinking the American Preference for Short, Framework-Oriented Constitutions." *American Political Science Review* 93 (December 1999): 837–850.

———. "State Constitutional Reform: Is It Necessary?" *Albany Law Review* 64 (2001): 1330–1353.

Hanson, Royce. *The Political Thicket: Reapportionment and Constitutional Democracy.* Englewood Cliffs, N.J.: Prentice-Hall, 1966.

Hardy, Leroy, Alan Heslop, and Stuart Anderson, eds. *Reapportionment Politics: The History of Redistricting in the 50 States.* Beverly Hills, Calif.: Sage Publications, 1981.

Hargrave, Lee. *The Louisiana State Constitution: A Reference Guide.* Westport, Conn.: Greenwood Press, 1991.

Heins, A. James. *Constitutional Restrictions against State Debt.* Madison: University of Wisconsin Press, 1963.

Heller, Francis H. *The Kansas State Constitution: A Reference Guide.* Westport, Conn.: Greenwood Press, 1992.

Henretta, James A. "Foreword: Rethinking the State Constitutional Tradition." *Rutgers Law Journal* 22 (Summer 1991): 819–839.

Henry, Sarah M. "Progressivism and Democracy: Electoral Reform in the United States, 1888–1919." Ph.D. diss., Columbia University, 1995.

Hershkoff, Helen. "Positive Rights and State Constitutions: The Limits of Federal Rationality Review." *Harvard Law Review* 112 (April 1999): 1131–1196.

———. "Positive Rights and the Evolution of State Constitutions." *Rutgers Law Journal* 33 (Summer 2002): 799–833.

Hicks, John D. *The Constitutions of the Northwest States*. Lincoln: University Studies of the University of Nebraska, 1924.

Hill, Melvin B., Jr. *The Georgia State Constitution: A Reference Guide*. Westport, Conn.: Greenwood Press, 1994.

Hill, William C. *The Vermont State Constitution: A Reference Guide*. Westport, Conn.: Greenwood Press, 1992.

Hitchcock, Henry. *American State Constitutions: A Study of Their Growth*. New York: G. P. Putnam's Sons, 1887.

Hoar, Roger S. *Constitutional Conventions: Their Nature, Powers, and Limitations*. Boston: Little, Brown, 1917.

Holcombe, Arthur N. *State Government in the United States*. 2nd ed. New York: Macmillan, 1926.

Holland, Randy J. *The Delaware State Constitution: A Reference Guide*. Westport, Conn.: Greenwood Press, 2002.

Horton, Wesley W. *The Connecticut State Constitution: A Reference Guide*. Westport, Conn.: Greenwood Press, 1993.

Hough, Franklin B., ed. *American Constitutions: Comprising the Constitution of Each State in the Union, and of the United States*. 2 vols. Albany, N.Y.: Weed, Parsons, 1872.

Howard, A. E. Dick. "State Constitutions and the Environment." *Virginia Law Review* 58 (February 1972): 193–229.

———. *Commentaries on the Constitution of Virginia*. 2 vols. Charlottesville: University Press of Virginia, 1974.

Hume, Richard L. "The 'Black and Tan' Constitutional Conventions of 1867–1869 in Ten Former Confederate States: A Study of Their Membership." Ph.D. diss., University of Washington, 1969.

Hurst, James Willard. *The Growth of American Law: The Law Makers*. Boston: Little, Brown, 1950.

Hyneman, Charles S., and Donald S. Lutz, eds. *American Political Writings during the Founding Era, 1760–1805*. 2 vols. Indianapolis, Ind.: Liberty Fund, 1983.

Ireland, Robert M. *The Kentucky State Constitution: A Reference Guide*. Westport, Conn.: Greenwood Press, 1999.

Jameson, John A. *A Treatise on Constitutional Conventions, Their History, Powers, and Modes of Proceeding*. 4th ed. 1887. Reprint, New York: Da Capo Press, 1972.

Johnson, Alvin W. *The Unicameral Legislature*. Minneapolis: University of Minnesota Press, 1938.

Johnson, David Alan. *Founding the Far West: California, Oregon, and Nevada, 1840–1890*. Berkeley: University of California Press, 1992.

Keiter, Robert B., and Tim Newcomb. *The Wyoming State Constitution: A Reference Guide*. Westport, Conn.: Greenwood Press, 1993.

Keller, Morton. *Affairs of State: Public Life in Late Nineteenth Century America*. Cambridge, Mass.: Belknap Press, 1977.

———. *Regulating a New Society: Public Policy and Social Change in America, 1900–1933*. Cambridge, Mass.: Harvard University Press, 1994.

Kenyon, Cecelia M. "Constitutionalism in Revolutionary America." In *Constitutionalism: Nomos XX*, edited by J. Roland Pennock and John W. Chapman. New York: New York University Press, 1979.

Kettleborough, Charles. *Constitution Making in Indiana*. 2 vols. Indianapolis: Indiana Historical Commission, 1916.

Keyssar, Alexander. *The Right to Vote: The Contested History of Democracy in the United States*. New York: Basic Books, 2000.

Kincaid, John. "State Constitutions in the Federal System." *Annals of the American Academy of Political and Social Science* 496 (March 1988): 12–22.

Kingsbury, Joseph B. "Unicameral Legislatures in Early American States." *Washington University Studies* 13 (October 1925): 95–119.

Kousser, J. Morgan. *The Shaping of Southern Politics: Suffrage Restriction and the Establishment of the One-Party South, 1880–1910*. New Haven, Conn.: Yale University Press, 1974.

Kruman, Marc W. *Between Authority and Liberty: State Constitution Making in Revolutionary America*. Chapel Hill: University of North Carolina Press, 1997.

Kurland, Philip B., and Ralph Lerner, eds. *The Founders' Constitution*. 5 vols. Chicago: University of Chicago Press, 1987.

Laska, Lewis L. *The Tennessee State Constitution: A Reference Guide*. Westport, Conn.: Greenwood Press, 1990.

Laughlin, Charles V. "A Study in Constitutional Rigidity. I." *University of Chicago Law Review* 10 (January 1943): 142–176.

Leahy, James E. *The North Dakota State Constitution: A Reference Guide*. Westport, Conn.: Praeger, 2003.

Lee, Anne Feder. *The Hawaii State Constitution: A Reference Guide*. Westport, Conn.: Greenwood Press, 1993.

Legislative Drafting Research Fund of Columbia University. *Constitutions of the United States: National and State*. 2 vols. Dobbs Ferry, N.Y.: Oceana Publications, 1962.

Leshy, John D. *The Arizona State Constitution: A Reference Guide*. Westport, Conn.: Greenwood Press, 1993.

Lincoln, Charles Z. *The Constitutional History of New York*. 5 vols. Rochester, N.Y.: Lawyers Co-operative Publishing, 1906.

Lobingier, Charles S. *The People's Law, or Popular Participation in Law-Making*. New York: Macmillan, 1909.

Luce, Robert. *Legislative Assemblies*. Boston: Houghton Mifflin, 1924.

Lutz, Donald S. *Popular Consent and Popular Control: Whig Political Theory in the Early State Constitutions*. Baton Rouge: Louisiana State University Press, 1980.

———. "The Purposes of American State Constitutions." *Publius* 12 (Winter 1982): 27–44.

———. *The Origins of American Constitutionalism*. Baton Rouge: Louisiana State University Press, 1988.

Maddex, Robert L. *State Constitutions of the United States*. Washington, D.C.: Congressional Quarterly, 1998.

Main, Jackson Turner. *The Upper House in Revolutionary America, 1763–1788*. Madison: University of Wisconsin Press, 1967.

Marshall, Susan E. *The New Hampshire State Constitution: A Reference Guide*. Westport, Conn.: Praeger, 2004.

Martineau, Robert J. "The Mandatory Referendum on Calling a State Constitutional Convention: Enforcing the People's Right to Reform Their Government." *Ohio State Law Journal* 31 (Spring 1970): 421–455.

Matzen, John Mathiason. *State Constitutional Provisions for Education: Fundamental Attitude of the American People Regarding Education as Revealed by State Constitutional Provisions, 1776–1929.* New York: Teachers College, Columbia University, 1931.

Mauer, John W. "Southern State Constitutions in the 1870s: A Case Study of Texas." Ph.D. diss., Rice University, 1983.

May, Janice C. *The Texas Constitutional Revision Experience in the '70s.* Austin, Tex.: Sterling Swift, 1975.

———. "Constitutional Amendment and Revision Revisited." *Publius* 17 (Winter 1987): 153–179.

———. "The Constitutional Initiative: A Threat to Rights?" In *Human Rights in the States: New Directions in Policymaking,* edited by Stanley H. Friedelbaum. Westport, Conn.: Greenwood Press, 1988.

———. *The Texas State Constitution: A Reference Guide.* Westport, Conn.: Greenwood Press, 1996.

McBain, Howard Lee. *The Law and the Practice of Municipal Home Rule.* New York: Columbia University Press, 1916.

McBeath, Gerald A. *The Alaska State Constitution: A Reference Guide.* Westport, Conn.: Greenwood Press, 1997.

McCarthy, Sister M. Barbara. *The Widening Scope of American Constitutions.* Washington, D.C.: Catholic University of America, 1928.

McClure, Wallace. *State Constitution-Making, with Especial Reference to Tennessee.* Nashville, Tenn.: Marshall and Bruce, 1916.

McDanel, Ralph C. *The Virginia Constitutional Convention of 1901–1902.* Baltimore: Johns Hopkins Press, 1928.

McHugh, James T. *Ex Uno Plura: State Constitutions and Their Political Cultures.* Albany: State University of New York Press, 2003.

McKay, Robert B. *Reapportionment: The Law and Politics of Equal Representation.* New York: Twentieth Century Fund, 1965.

McKay, Seth Shepard. *Making the Texas Constitution of 1876.* Philadelphia: University of Pennsylvania, 1924.

McLauchlan, William P. *The Indiana State Constitution: A Reference Guide.* Westport, Conn.: Greenwood Press, 1996.

McMillan, Malcolm C. *Constitutional Development in Alabama, 1789–1901: A Study in Politics, the Negro, and Sectionalism.* Chapel Hill: University of North Carolina Press, 1955.

Meller, Norman. *With an Understanding Heart: Constitution Making in Hawaii.* New York: National Municipal League, 1971.

Merriam, Charles E. *American Political Ideas: Studies in the Development of American Political Thought, 1865–1917.* New York: Macmillan, 1920.

Miewald, Robert D., and Peter J. Longo. *The Nebraska State Constitution: A Reference Guide.* Westport, Conn.: Greenwood Press, 1993.

Moe, Ronald C. *Prospects for the Item Veto at the Federal Level: Lessons from the States.* Washington, D.C.: National Academy of Public Administration, 1988.

Moran, Thomas F. *The Rise and Development of the Bicameral System in America.* Baltimore: Johns Hopkins Press, 1895.

Morey, William C. "The First State Constitutions." *Annals of the American Academy of Political and Social Science* 4 (September 1893): 201–232.

Morrison, Mary Jane. *The Minnesota State Constitution: A Reference Guide*. Westport, Conn.: Greenwood Press, 2002.

Munro, William Bennett, ed. *The Initiative, Referendum and Recall*. New York: D. Appleton, 1912.

National Municipal League. *Model State Constitution*. 6th rev. ed. New York: National Municipal League, 1968.

Nelson, Caleb. "A Re-Evaluation of Scholarly Explanations for the Rise of the Elective Judiciary in Antebellum America." *American Journal of Legal History* 37 (April 1993): 190–224.

Neuborne, Burt. "State Constitutions and the Evolution of Positive Rights." *Rutgers Law Journal* 20 (Summer 1989): 881–901.

Nevins, Allan. *The American States during and after the Revolution, 1775–1789*. New York: Macmillan, 1924.

New York State Constitutional Convention Committee. *Constitutions of the States and United States*. Albany, N.Y.: J. B. Lyon, 1938.

Novak, William J. *The People's Welfare: Law and Regulation in Nineteenth-Century America*. Chapel Hill: University of North Carolina Press, 1996.

Nunn, Walter H., and Kay G. Collett. *Political Paradox: Constitutional Revision in Arkansas*. New York: National Municipal League, 1973.

Oberholtzer, Ellis Paxson. *The Referendum in America, Together with Some Chapters on the Initiative and Recall*. New York: Charles Scribner's Sons, 1911.

Oesterle, Dale A., and Richard B. Collins. *The Colorado State Constitution: A Reference Guide*. Westport, Conn.: Greenwood Press, 2002.

O'Rourke, Vernon A., and Douglas W. Campbell. *Constitution-Making in a Democracy: Theory and Practice in New York State*. Baltimore: Johns Hopkins Press, 1943.

Orth, John V. *The North Carolina State Constitution: A Reference Guide*. Westport, Conn.: Greenwood Press, 1993.

Parkinson, George Philip, Jr. "Antebellum State Constitution-Making: Retention, Circumvention, Revision." Ph.D. diss., University of Wisconsin, 1972.

Perman, Michael. *The Road to Redemption: Southern Politics, 1869–1879*. Chapel Hill: University of North Carolina Press, 1984.

———. *Struggle for Mastery: Disfranchisement in the South, 1888–1908*. Chapel Hill: University of North Carolina Press, 2001.

Peters, Ronald M., Jr. *The Massachusetts Constitution of 1780: A Social Compact*. Amherst: University of Massachusetts Press, 1978.

Peterson, Merrill D., ed. *Democracy, Liberty, and Property: The State Constitutional Conventions of the 1820s*. Indianapolis, Ind.: Bobbs-Merrill, 1966.

Piott, Steven L. *Giving Voters a Voice: The Origins of the Initiative and Referendum in America*. Columbia: University of Missouri Press, 2003.

Pole, J. R. *Political Representation in England and the Origins of the American Republic*. New York: St. Martin's Press, 1966.

Poore, Benjamin Perley, comp. *The Federal and State Constitutions, Colonial Charters, and Other Organic Laws of the United States*. 2 vols. Washington, D.C.: Government Printing Office, 1877.

Porter, Kirk H. *A History of Suffrage in the United States*. Chicago: University of Chicago Press, 1918.

Ransom, William L. *Majority Rule and the Judiciary: An Examination of Current Propos-*

als for Constitutional Change Affecting the Relation of Courts to Legislation. New York: Scribner's Sons, 1912.

Reed, Alfred Zantziger. *The Territorial Basis of Government under the State Constitutions.* 1911. Reprint, New York: AMS Press, 1968.

Reock, Ernest C., Jr. *Unfinished Business: The New Jersey Constitutional Convention of 1966.* New Brunswick, N.J.: Center for Urban Policy Research Press, 2003.

Rodgers, Daniel T. *Contested Truths: Keywords in American Politics since Independence.* 1987. Reprint, Cambridge, Mass.: Harvard University Press, 1998.

Rohlfing, Charles C. "Amendment and Revision of State Constitutions." *Annals of the American Academy of Political and Social Science* 181 (September 1935): 180–187.

Ross, William G. *A Muted Fury: Populists, Progressives, and Labor Unions Confront the Courts, 1890–1937.* Princeton, N.J.: Princeton University Press, 1994.

Rubenstein, Harvey Bernard, ed. *The Delaware Constitution of 1897: The First One Hundred Years.* Wilmington: Delaware State Bar Association, 1997.

Saye, Albert B. *A Constitutional History of Georgia, 1732–1945.* Athens: University of Georgia Press, 1948.

Scalia, Laura J. "The Many Faces of Locke in America's Early Nineteenth-Century Democratic Philosophy." *Political Research Quarterly* 49 (December 1996): 807–835.

———. "Who Deserves Political Influence? How Liberal Ideals Helped Justify Mid Nineteenth-Century Exclusionary Policies." *American Journal of Political Science* 42 (April 1998): 349–376.

———. *America's Jeffersonian Experiment: Remaking State Constitutions, 1820–1850.* DeKalb: Northern Illinois University Press, 1999.

Schick, Thomas. *The New York State Constitutional Convention of 1915 and the Modern State Governor.* New York: National Municipal League, 1978.

Schlam, Lawrence. "State Constitutional Amending, Independent Interpretation, and Political Culture: A Case Study in Constitutional Stagnation." *DePaul Law Review* 43 (Winter 1994): 269–378.

Schmidt, Gregory Glen. "Republican Visions: Constitutional Thought and Constitutional Revision in the Eastern United States, 1815–1830." Ph.D. diss., University of Illinois, 1981.

Schouler, James. *Constitutional Studies: State and Federal.* 1897. Reprint, New York: Da Capo Press, 1971.

Sears, Kenneth C., and Charles V. Laughlin. "A Study in Constitutional Rigidity. II." *University of Chicago Law Review* 11 (June 1944): 374–442.

Selsam, J. Paul. *The Pennsylvania Constitution of 1776: A Study in Revolutionary Democracy.* Philadelphia: University of Pennsylvania Press, 1936.

Senning, John P. *The One-House Legislature.* New York: McGraw-Hill, 1937.

Shaeffer, John Nees. "Constitutional Change in the Unicameral States, 1776–1793." Ph.D. diss., University of Wisconsin, 1968.

Shalala, Donna E. *The City and the Constitution: The 1967 New York Convention's Response to the Urban Crisis.* New York: National Municipal League, 1972.

Shambaugh, Benjamin F. *The Constitutions of Iowa.* Iowa City: State Historical Society of Iowa, 1934.

Smith, Chuck. *The New Mexico State Constitution: A Reference Guide.* Westport, Conn.: Greenwood Press, 1996.

Stark, Jack. *The Wisconsin State Constitution: A Reference Guide.* Westport, Conn.: Greenwood Press, 1997.

———. *The Iowa State Constitution: A Reference Guide.* Westport, Conn.: Greenwood Press, 1998.

State Constitutional Conventions, Commissions, and Amendments, 1959–1978: An Annotated Bibliography. 2 vols. Washington, D.C.: Congressional Information Service, 1981.

State Constitutional Conventions, Commissions, and Amendments, 1979–1988: An Annotated Bibliography. Washington, D.C.: Congressional Information Service, 1989.

Steinfeld, Robert J. "Property and Suffrage in the Early American Republic." *Stanford Law Review* 41 (January 1989): 335–376.

Steinglass, Steven H., and Gino J. Scarselli. *The Ohio State Constitution: A Reference Guide.* Westport, Conn.: Praeger, 2004.

Stewart, William H. *The Alabama State Constitution: A Reference Guide.* Westport, Conn. Greenwood Press, 1994.

Stimson, Frederic J. *The Law of the Federal and State Constitutions of the United States.* Boston: Boston Book Company, 1908.

Stokes, Anson Phelps. *Church and State in the United States,* 3 vols. New York: Harper and Brothers, 1950.

Sturm, Albert L. *Constitution-Making in Michigan, 1961–1962.* Ann Arbor: Institute of Public Administration, University of Michigan, 1963.

———. *Thirty Years of State Constitution-Making, 1938–1968.* New York: National Municipal League, 1970.

———. "The Development of American State Constitutions." *Publius* 12 (Winter 1982): 57–98.

Suber, Peter. *The Paradox of Self-Amendment: A Study of Logic, Law, Omnipotence, and Change.* New York: Peter Lang, 1990.

Swindler, William F., ed. *Sources and Documents of the United States Constitutions.* 10 vols. Dobbs Ferry, N.Y.: Oceana Publications, 1973–1979.

Swisher, Carl Brent. *Motivation and Technique in the California Constitutional Convention, 1878–1879.* 1930. Reprint, New York: Da Capo Press, 1969.

Tarr, G. Alan. *Understanding State Constitutions.* Princeton, N.J.: Princeton University Press, 1998.

———, ed. *Constitutional Politics in the States: Contemporary Controversies and Historical Patterns.* Westport, Conn.: Greenwood Press, 1996.

Thompson, Barton H., Jr. "Environmental Policy and State Constitutions: The Potential Role of Substantive Guidance." *Rutgers Law Journal* 27 (Summer 1996): 863–925.

———. "Constitutionalizing the Environment: The History and Future of Montana's Environmental Provisions." *Montana Law Review* 64 (Winter 2003): 157–198.

Thomson, Bailey, ed. *A Century of Controversy: Constitutional Reform in Alabama.* Tuscaloosa: University of Alabama Press, 2002.

Thorpe, Francis N. "Recent Constitution Making in the United States." *Annals of the American Academy of Political and Social Science* 2 (September 1891): 145–201.

———. *A Constitutional History of the American People, 1776–1850.* 2 vols. New York: Harper & Brothers, 1898.

———, comp. and ed. *The Federal and State Constitutions, Colonial Charters, and Other Organic Laws of the States, Territories, and Colonies Now or Heretofore Forming the United States of America.* 7 vols. Washington, D.C.: Government Printing Office, 1909.

Tinkle, Marshall J. *The Maine State Constitution: A Reference Guide.* Westport, Conn.: Greenwood Press, 1992.

Tyack, David, Thomas James, and Aaron Benavot. *Law and the Shaping of Public Education, 1785–1954*. Madison: University of Wisconsin Press, 1987.

Utter, Robert F., and Hugh D. Spitzer. *The Washington State Constitution: A Reference Guide*. Westport, Conn.: Greenwood Press, 2002.

Wallis, John Joseph. "Constitutions, Corporations, and Corruption: American States and Constitutional Change, 1842 to 1852." *Journal of Economic History* 65 (March 2005): 211–256.

Ware, Ethel K. *A Constitutional History of Georgia*. New York: Columbia University Press, 1947.

Webster, William C. "Comparative Study of the State Constitutions of the American Revolution." *Annals of the American Academy of Political and Social Science* 9 (May 1897): 380–420.

Wells, Roger H. "The Item Veto and State Budget Reform." *American Political Science Review* 18 (November 1924).

Wheeler, John P., ed. *Salient Issues of Constitutional Revision*. New York: National Municipal League, 1961.

Wheeler, John P., Jr., and Melissa Kinsey. *Magnificent Failure: The Maryland Constitutional Convention of 1967–1968*. New York: National Municipal League, 1970.

White, J. Patrick. "Progressivism and the Judiciary: A Study of the Movement for Judicial Reform, 1901–1917." Ph.D. diss., University of Michigan, 1957.

White, Jean Bickmore. *Charter for Statehood: The Story of Utah's State Constitution*. Salt Lake City: University of Utah Press, 1996.

———. *The Utah State Constitution: A Reference Guide*. Westport, Conn.: Greenwood Press, 1998.

White, Thomas R. "Amendment and Revision of State Constitutions." *University of Pennsylvania Law Review* 100 (June 1952): 1132–1152.

Wilcox, Delos F. *Government by All the People, or The Initiative, the Referendum, and the Recall as Instruments of Democracy*. 1912. Reprint, New York: Da Capo Press, 1972.

Williams, Robert F. "The State Constitutions of the Founding Decade: Pennsylvania's Radical 1776 Constitution and Its Influences on American Constitutionalism." *Temple Law Review* 62 (Summer 1989): 541–585.

———. *The New Jersey State Constitution: A Reference Guide*. Westport, Conn.: Greenwood Press, 1990.

———. "Are State Constitutional Conventions Things of the Past? The Increasing Role of the Constitutional Commission in State Constitutional Change." *Hofstra Law and Policy Symposium* 1 (1996): 1–26.

———. *State Constitutional Law: Cases and Materials*. 3rd ed. Charlottesville, Va.: Lexis Law Publishing, 1999.

Williamson, Chilton. *American Suffrage: From Property to Democracy, 1760–1860*. Princeton, N.J.: Princeton University Press, 1960.

Wilson, John K. "Religion under the State Constitutions, 1776–1800." *Journal of Church and State* 32 (Autumn 1990): 753–767.

Winkle, John W., III. *The Mississippi State Constitution: A Reference Guide*. Westport, Conn.: Greenwood Press, 1993.

Wolf, George D. *Constitutional Revision in Pennsylvania: The Dual Tactic of Amendment and Limited Convention*. New York: National Municipal League, 1969.

Wood, Gordon S. *The Creation of the American Republic, 1776–1787*. Chapel Hill: University of North Carolina Press, 1969.

———. "Foreword: State Constitution-Making in the American Revolution." *Rutgers Law Journal* 24 (Summer 1993): 911–926.

Wooster, Ralph A. *The Secession Conventions of the South*. Princeton, N.J.: Princeton University Press, 1962.

Yarger, Susan Rice, comp. *State Constitutional Conventions, 1959–1975: A Bibliography*. Westport, Conn.: Greenwood Press, 1976.

Zagarri, Rosemarie. *The Politics of Size: Representation in the United States, 1776–1850*. Ithaca, N.Y.: Cornell University Press, 1987.

Zimmerman, Joseph F. *Participatory Democracy: Populism Revived*. Westport, Conn.: Praeger, 1986.

———. *The Recall: Tribunal of the People*. Westport, Conn.: Praeger, 1997.

Index

Barnard, Henry, 238
Barnes, William, 24
Bartlett, Richard, 206
Bartley, Ernest, 17
Bartow, John, 43, 74, 157
Bates, Martin, 249
Bates, William, 266
Baxter, George, 171
Baylor, Robert E. B., 39
Bayne, James, 105
Beard, Charles, 70
Beckner, William, 107
Beecher, Lyman, 257
Beeler, Joseph, 128
Bennett, James, 200
Berger, Victor, 344n3
Bicameralism, 137–183, 273, 275
    aristocratic virtues and, 142–144
    conference committees and, 175–176, 180
    debated in founding era, 140–144
    debated in Jacksonian Era, 144–160
    debated in Progressive Era, 160–171
    debated in Reapportionment Revolution,
        172–182
    defended on basis of tradition, 181–182
    defended as providing a deliberative check,
        141, 151–154, 164–166, 180–181
    defended as providing distinct perspectives,
        141–144, 145–149, 154–159, 177–180
    distinctions, electorates of chambers, 144,
        156–157, 163, 177–178
    distinctions, powers of chambers, 143, 154,
        158–159
    distinctions, property, 142–144, 145–149
    distinctions, qualifications of officeholders,
        143–144, 153–154, 158
    distinctions, representation of local
        government units, 166–171, 172–175
    distinctions, size of chambers, 143, 153,
        155–156, 163, 177
    distinctions, terms of office, 143, 153,
        157–158, 163–164, 178–179
    "federal principle" and, 166–171, 173–175
    opposed by supporters of unicameralism,
        149–151, 161–164, 173–176
    in U.S. Constitution, 137–138, 344n3
Biddle, Horace, 103, 106
Bird, Francis, 233
Birney, James, 265
Bishop, Richard, 80
Blacklists, 203
Blaine, James, 235, 385n6

Blaine Amendments, 235, 385n6
Blake, George, 229
Blocker, Jack, 268
Blood, James, 72
Bodfish, John, 193
Borah, William, 332n10
Borden, James, 42
Bothe, Elsbeth, 199
Bowdle, John, 79
Bowdle, Stanley, 20, 264
Bowman, Charles, 240
Boyer, Elroy, 59
Brackett, John, 94
Bradford, Edward, 77, 101, 107
Brazier, Geoffrey, 215
Brennan, James, 87, 90
Brennan, William J., 185
Brent, Robert, 34
Bristow, Joseph, 333n10
Broderick, Patrick, 128
Brown, George, 103
Brown, Gerry, 126
Brown, James, 157
Brown, Melville, 168
Browning, Abraham, 39
Bryan, Silas, 158
Bryan, William Jennings, 16, 56, 60, 129
Bryant, Wilbur, 128, 363n130
Bryce, James, 52
Burbridge, Arden, 202
Burrows, Julius Caesar, 384n6
Burt, Wellington, 53, 54, 265
Burtch, Milton, 241

California, 17, 367n177, 371n226
    Constitution, 15, 194
    Convention of 1849, 14, 44, 158, 249,
        250, 252
    Convention of 1878–1879, 19, 24, 235,
        236, 265
Campbell, Henry, 93
Campbell, J. C., 246
Campbell, John, 245, 264
Campbell, Thompson, 22
Canfield, Robert, 174
Caples, James, 265
Carbery, Joseph, 231
Carey, Robert, 196
Carland, John, 165, 166
Carlino, Joseph, 178
Carpenter, Benjamin Platt, 14, 153
Carr, Edward, 193

Ceaser, James W., 383n2
Chambers, George, 44
Chandler, Amariah, 234
Chandler, John (Maine), 229
Chandler, John (Pennsylvania), 158
Chandler, Walter, 300n6
Chapman, William, 73
Character of the citizenry, 222–270, 274,
    275–276
  education and, 237–247
  liquor and, 256–268
  lotteries and, 248–256
  provisions defended as a proper concern
    of government, 225–229, 231–233, 235–
    236, 239–242, 249–250, 254, 258–262
  provisions defended as proper for a
    constitution, 242–243, 250–251, 254,
    262–263
  provisions opposed as not a proper concern
    of government, 229–231, 233–234,
    236–237, 243–246, 251–252, 254–255,
    263–265
  provisions opposed as not proper for a
    constitution, 246–247, 252–253, 255–256,
    266
  religion and, 224–237
  U.S. Constitution and, 222–223, 384n6
Child-labor restrictions, 125, 188, 190, 194
Childs, Henry, 230
Ching, Huanani, 181
Chipman, Daniel, 14
Choate, Charles, 55, 92
Civil War, 9–10, 11, 25–26, 30
Claggett, William, 171
Clark, David, 259–260, 262
Clark, John, 46
Clark, Milton, 25
Clarke, Beverly, 68
Clayton, John, 40, 149
Cleveland, Frederick, 67
Clyde, George, 89
Coats, John, 262
Cogswell, Nathaniel, 234
Coleman, George, 234
Collective-bargaining rights, 196–201, 203
Colorado, 28, 135
  Constitution, 194, 195, 268
  Supreme Court, 135
Compulsory education
  adopted in northern states, 247
  adopted in southern states, 247
  in Massachusetts, 245–246

opposed, 243–247
  in Prussia, 245–246
  supported, 239–243
Comstock, George, 340n113
Conaway, Asbury, 170
Confederate States of America, 9, 11, 113–114
Connecticut, 9, 140, 141, 182, 231, 305n15
  Constitution, 43
  Convention of 1818, 225, 229, 299n78
  Convention of 1965, 174, 177, 178,
    370n224
Constitutional amendments
  as alternatives to conventions, 7, 10
  as avenue for overturning judicial decisions,
    49–50, 131–132
  consecutive-legislatures requirement,
    43–44, 56
  majority-in-the-election requirement, 11,
    56–58
  origin of amendment procedures, 4–42
  supermajority legislative-vote requirement,
    44–45, 56
Constitutional convention, federal, 6, 29,
    64, 99–100, 123, 124, 137, 184, 384n6,
    394n77
Constitutional conventions, state
  automatic convention provision, 58–59
  in Civil War era, 9–10, 11, 25–26
  critical scholarly assessment of, 2
  delegates to, 12–14
  in founding era, 9, 11, 140–144
  influence on constitution-making in other
    countries, 5, 276–277, 292n13
  interstate borrowing in, 14–17
  in Jacksonian era, 9, 144–160
  limited, 10
  number of, 7–9
  periodic convention question, 11, 45–47, 58–59
  popular rejection of the work of, 18
  procedures of, 12–18
  in Progressive Era, 10, 48–55, 59–60, 84–
    95, 160–171
  ratification of the work of, 17–18
  in Reapportionment Revolution, 10, 172–182
  recorded debates of, 18–28
Constitutional initiative
  origin of, 59–62
  prevalence of in late twentieth century, 7
Constitutional revision commissions
  as alternative to conventions, 7, 10
  empowered to submit amendments to
    people, 300n7

McClelland, Robert, 13, 70, 72, 157
McClinton, J. G., 243
McCormick, Joseph, 151
McCracken, Thomas, 218
McDonald, Nathan, 92, 93
McEwen, William, 236
McKay, Robert B., 364n147
McKiernan, Donald, 254
McNally, James, 209
Medill, Joseph, 191
Mercer, Charles, 295n18
Mercer, John, 339n107
Meredith, Charles, 116, 190
Meredith, William, 40
Merriam, Charles, 17
Merriam, John, 133
Merrick, William, 154
Michelman, Frank, 185
Michener, James, 13
Michigan, 11, 28, 182, 194
    Constitution, 266, 268
    Convention of 1835, 14, 232, 234, 299n78
    Convention of 1850, 14, 15, 43, 47, 70, 72, 73, 74, 157, 260, 266, 267
    Convention of 1867, 14, 107, 241, 245, 258, 263, 265, 297n44
    Convention of 1907–1908, 48, 52, 53, 54, 55, 60, 61, 85, 86, 88, 89, 92, 93, 117, 120, 259, 265
    Convention of 1961–1962, 13, 16, 118, 203, 210, 218, 219, 254, 370n224
Middleton, C. R., 169
Mill, John Stuart, 137, 241, 264
Millard, Frank, 218, 254
Miller, Amos, 237
Miller, George, 259
Miners' safety provisions, 189, 190, 191, 192, 194
Minimum-wage guarantees, 48, 85, 189, 194
Minnesota, 342n168, 370n218, 371n226
    Convention of 1857, 12, 79
Minshall, William, 108
Mississippi, 11
    Constitution, 357n64
    Convention of 1817, 358n65
    Convention of 1865, 25
    Convention of 1890, 297n39
Missouri, 11, 253
    Convention of 1875, 13, 35, 47, 115, 244, 298n71
    Convention of 1922–1923, 297n44
    Convention of 1943–1944, 366n172
Model State Constitution, 172

Monroe, James, 13
Monroe, Lyle, 208, 210
Montana, 182
    Convention of 1889, 14, 22, 169, 171
    Convention of 1971–1972, 175, 176, 208, 210, 213, 215, 217, 254, 297n42, 298n69, 370n225
Moore, L. W., 25
Morrill, Charles, 127, 162, 163, 164
Morrison, John, 69
Morton, Edward, 263
Moses, Robert, 13
Mudge, Enoch, 229, 230
Mueller, Jacob, 263
Municipal home rule, 6, 17
Mynatt, P. L., 152

Nasaw, David, 238
Nash, Simeon, 78, 83, 262
National Labor Relations Act, 197, 200
National Municipal League, 172
Nave, Christian, 150
Nebraska, 17, 134, 138, 172, 173, 176, 368n195
    Constitution, 268
    Convention of 1871, 240, 241, 242, 243, 244, 246, 297n44, 298n70
    Convention of 1919–1920, 57, 85, 90, 92, 93, 127, 128, 129, 131, 133, 162, 164, 166, 247, 363n130
Nelson, Ebenezer, 230
Nelson, Gaylord, 186
Nevada, 297n43, 367n176
    Convention of 1864, 15, 43, 72, 243
New Deal, 30
New Hampshire, 11–12, 28, 42, 140, 144, 231, 256, 300n7
    Constitution, 45, 305n15, 355n38, 356n41, 356n43, 358n65
    Convention of 1850–1851, 13, 299n77
    Convention of 1889, 263, 266
    Convention of 1902, 87, 89, 168
    Convention of 1912, 88, 90, 91
    Convention of 1918–1923, 87, 90
    Convention of 1948, 118
    Convention of 1974, 119, 213–214
    Convention of 1984, 116, 120, 218
New Jersey, 34, 140, 144
    Constitution, 305n15, 355n38, 356n41, 366n168
    Convention of 1844, 20, 23, 34, 36, 39, 101, 102, 106, 109, 147, 299n78, 358n65